7A37 1

D0624944

Resource Management for Individuals and Families

Third Edition

ELIZABETH B. GOLDSMITH
Florida State University

THOMSON ™

WADSWORTH

Australia • Canada • Mexico • Singapore • Spain
United Kingdom • United States

THOMSON

WADSWORTH

Sociology Editor: Robert Jucha
Assistant Editor: Stephanie Monzon
Editorial Assistant: Melissa Walter
Technology Project Manager: Dee Dee Zobian
Marketing Manager: Matthew Wright
Marketing Assistant: Tara Pierson
Advertising Manager: Linda Yip
Project Manager, Editorial Production: Cheri Palmer
Print/Media Buyer: Rebecca Cross
Permissions Editor: Joohee Lee

Production Service: Robin Lockwood Productions
Text Designer: From a design by Delgado Design, Inc.,
    with modifications by John Walker
Photo Researchers: Roberta Broyer and Billie Porter
Cover Designer: Bill Reuter
Cover Image: © PhotoDisc
Cover Printer: Coral Graphic Services
Compositor: Parkwood Composition Service
Printer: Courier

COPYRIGHT © 2005 Wadsworth, a division of Thomson Learning, Inc. Thomson Learning™ is a trademark used herein under license.

ALL RIGHTS RESERVED. No part of this work covered by the copyright hereon may be reproduced or used in any form or by any means—graphic, electronic, or mechanical, including but not limited to photocopying, recording, taping, Web distribution, information networks, or information storage and retrieval systems—without the written permission of the publisher.

Printed in the United States of America
1 2 3 4 5 6 7 08 07 06 05 04

For more information about our products, contact us at:
Thomson Learning Academic Resource Center
1-800-423-0563
For permission to use material from this text or product, submit a request online at **http://www.thomsonrights.com**.
Any additional questions about permissions can be submitted by email to **thomsonrights@thomson.com**.

Library of Congress Control Number: 2004106159

ISBN 0-534-62856-7

Thomson Wadsworth
10 Davis Drive
Belmont, CA 94002-3098
USA

Asia
Thomson Learning
5 Shenton Way #01-01
UIC Building
Singapore 068808

Australia/New Zealand
Thomson Learning
102 Dodds Street
Southbank, Victoria 3006
Australia

Canada
Nelson
1120 Birchmount Road
Toronto, Ontario M1K 5G4
Canada

Europe/Middle East/Africa
Thomson Learning
High Holborn House
50/51 Bedford Row
London WC1R 4LR
United Kingdom

Latin America
Thomson Learning
Seneca, 53
Colonia Polanco
11560 Mexico D.F.
Mexico

Spain/Portugal
Paraninfo
Calle Magallanes, 25
28015 Madrid, Spain

CONTENTS

PREFACE

Welcome to the third edition of *Resource Management for Individuals and Families*! The 21st century holds much promise and is cause for celebration. Unlike ever before, people are interested in the workings of their lives, how to make them better within the context of an increasingly complex and exciting world. I wrote this edition of *Resource Management for Individuals and Families* to capture both the excitement and the challenge of managing today. The study of resource management is relevant to everyday life and provides insight into how others behave. The content is both personally and professionally rewarding. Creating successful futures is the goal.

Visiting with instructors and students in Europe, Australia, Asia, Africa, the United States, the Caribbean, and Canada, I have found that learning how to make better choices is a universal concern. Stress, fatigue, and time management have no national boundaries. Making choices—those made yesterday and those to be made today and tomorrow—and how those choices affect people's lives is a central theme in the book. Sound decision making has never been easy, and it is increasingly difficult given the number of options and the amount of information out there. Since the last edition, the Internet has become more pervasive; and one of the great aspects has been that many instructors from around the world have contacted me by e-mail to tell me what they liked about the second edition and what they would like to see in the third. Thanks are extended to all who took the time to tell me how they are using the book in Botswana, Trinidad, and Finland, as only a few examples—believe me, as an author it is a thrill!

The latest census data and world population statistics are in this edition along with the newest technological advances impacting households. More definitions of families are explored. Individuals continue to search for the best ways to balance work and family life. In recognition of this, more coverage is devoted to how everyone is responding to and coping with change in the world of work and on the home front.

New theories and models such as the Resource Advantage theory and the GO model by Holly Hunts and Ramona Marotz-Baden of Montana State University have been added to keep the theoretical aspects of the study of management fresh. The book is a careful mix of research and practical applications, history, present, and future.

In response to requests by instructors, the chapter on managing finances has been expanded considerably to include the money and credit problems on everyone's minds. The stress and fatigue chapter has been expanded to include more on the importance of sleep and how to improve its quality. Researchers are finding new evidence of how much sleep impacts our ability to reason and function effectively. As alluded to previously, the third edition benefits from the feedback given by the students and instructors around the world who used the second edition. Closer to home, my students at Florida State University seem to especially appreciate the goal-setting material as they figure out what they want to do career-wise and, more importantly, where and how they want to live. They will say things like "I just want to be happy." And we use that as a basis to discuss what happiness is—a subject covered in the text. This edition follows their reactions as well as those of reviewers. Instructors, reviewers, and students alike emphasized that they did not want the basic structure of the book (i.e., the chapter flow from theory to application to future challenges) changed, but that they did want expanded coverage on certain topics. The most popular chapters with students are those on time, stress, and fatigue management. Often this book is referred to as the time management book, and the new cover reflects that. In addition, students find the applied chapters on work and family, human resources management, the environment, and finances to be especially useful.

Inclusion is a hallmark of *Resource Management for Individuals and Families*. The first edition of this book set itself apart from others in its emphasis on the management problems faced by singles and single parents as well as those faced by two-parent families. This approach is even more relevant today, as the number of singles and single parents is increasing and the number of people per household continues to decrease. However, the importance of families is not neglected, and the addition of the more expansive definition of family used by the American Red Cross is at the request of instructors who said that the Census Bureau's definition of family is too limited to stand alone. Every effort is made to speak to a wide variety of students, capturing their interests and taking into account their concerns and perspectives. More has been added on positive psychology, leadership, and the challenges involved in managing the second half of life and the retirement years.

ORGANIZATION OF THIS TEXT

Resource Management for Individuals and Families contains 14 carefully written, well-organized chapters to introduce students to the best of management thinking and practice. **Part I** begins with an explanation of management as a process of using resources to achieve goals. It establishes the foundation and introduces the management process model used throughout the book. **Chapter 1** addresses three questions:

- ◆ What is management?
- ◆ Why manage?
- ◆ Who manages?

Chapter 2 covers the interdisciplinary, historical, and theoretical foundations of the field. The history of the home continues to fascinate, and the public is increasingly interested in improving the home environment. This emphasis on home and environment as a context within which individuals and families manage sets it apart from other areas in the social sciences.

Part II examines the basic concepts underlying the field of management. These concepts such as values, resources, and plans are timeless and provide the foundation for the more applied chapters that follow. **Chapter 3** focuses on values, attitudes, and goals with a special section on college students' values and goals. **Chapter 4** goes right to the heart of the subject by exploring resources and resource strategy. **Chapter 5** provides the steps in decision making and explains how to solve problems. **Chapter 6** analyzes planning, implementing, and evaluating. Communication and the feedback part of the Management Process Model are explored in **Chapter 7.** Plans often fail because they were not properly communicated.

The chapters in **Part III** begin with the verb *managing.* The specific applications are to human resources, time, work and family, stress and fatigue, environmental resources, and finances. This is a "how-to" section with many helpful suggestions; one section, for example, discusses how to make homes more environmentally friendly and safer. The text goes beyond merely stating the problems and suggests possible solutions. **Chapter 8** explores population shifts and how they impact management and resource use. **Chapter 9** shows ways to use time more effectively. **Chapter 10** discusses workaholism and the problems associated with balancing work and family. Everyone feels stress and fatigue, and how to deal with them is the subject of **Chapter 11.** Sleep and the vagaries of human energy are also explored. **Chapter 12** brings up environmental problems and suggests solutions. Water, energy, noise, waste and recycling, and air quality are all discussed. The final chapter in Part III, **Chapter 13,** on managing finances, is one of the most important. Students are dealing with credit problems and loans and setting up new households and ways of living. The chapter explores how to make money stretch further in a changing economy.

Thinking about the future is the subject of **Part IV. Chapter 14** concludes the text with an innovative analysis of technology, quality of life, and family and global change, even a discussion of life in space. This section brings the book full circle—from the introductory discussions of the history of the study of management and the problems of contemporary families to the management issues on the horizon.

DISTINCTIVE FEATURES

Resource Management for Individuals and Families offers a new, interactive approach to teaching resource management through special features that are specifically designed to reflect the themes of choice and decision making, supporting students' interest and learning.

◆ **Management as a Process Approach** Throughout the book, a five-step model is used to illustrate the thinking and action parts of the management process. Beginning with identifying problems, needs, wants, or goals, the model progresses to clarifying values and identifying resources. Then it moves on to deciding, planning, and implementing, and finally ends with accomplishing goals and evaluating. The model takes place within an environmental context and is held together by feedback.

◆ **An Emphasis on Systems and Economic Theories** Rather than relying on only one theory, this text applies many theories to the decision-making behavior of individuals and families. No particular area of the field is overemphasized at the expense of others. This text is meant to be introductory and inclusive.

◆ **Pedagogy** Current research and managerial implications are presented in a readable and interesting style. Examples, advertisements, and photos are included to stimulate student interest.

- Each chapter begins with a quotation and two *Did You Know?* statements.

- Many chapters contain a new feature, **Suggested Activities,** with ideas for class or group discussion or for individual application such as recording sleeping patterns for three days and comparing one's sleeping pattern to the content in the text. The Suggested Activities are provided in response to instructors who wanted more ideas about how to apply the text to their students' lives.

- Chapters conclude with a **Web-Based Resources** section, which contains relevant Web sites. With each new edition of *Resource Management for Individuals and Families,* I have integrated the Internet into the text as a tool to use. In the current edition, all Web sites have been checked and updated. Each chapter ending has the following study aids:

- *Summary.* A brief review of the major topics discussed.

- *Key Terms.* A list of important concepts discussed in each chapter. To help the reader locate them, the key terms appear in boldface type within the chapter text.

- *Review Questions.* A list of questions meant to provide the basis for a review of textual material and to encourage thought and discussion on the chapter's content.

- *References.* Full citations of references noted in the chapter. An additional list of relevant historic and classic books appears at the end of Chapter 2.

- The book concludes with a *Glossary* of the key terms defined in the chapters and an *Index.*

ACKNOWLEDGMENTS

Resource Management for Individuals and Families would not have been possible without the inspiration from colleagues, instructors, students, and my own graduate experience at Michigan State University. I am extremely grateful to my major professors at MSU, most notably, Jane Oyer and Margaret Bubolz, and my dissertation director, the late Bea Paolucci. Numerous seminars held in Dr. Paolucci's honor over the years (most recently in 2002) have kept her spirit and influence alive. I am grateful to the faculty and administrators at Michigan State University who have upheld this tradition and provided an opportunity for those of us in resource management from around the world to gather in her name. Sue McGregor of Mount Saint Vincent University in Halifax, Canada, provided insight into the evolution of the management process model. Anita Subramaniam (originally from India) now teaching at Montclair State University in New Jersey discussed her students' views on management with me at conferences in Atlanta and in Wales. Shelby Hunt of Texas Tech University, whom I also met at a conference, corresponded with me about his Resource Advantage theory and the ways it is compatible with family resource theory. Sherman Hanna of Ohio State University provided comments and updates on his cited works on economic theory and risk.

Much of the historical content of the book was influenced by my sabbaticals in Washington, DC, and subsequent visits. I am indebted to Betty

Monkman, now curator emeritus of the White House, for her guidance regarding technology and the White House discussed in Chapter 1, and curators Bernard Finn, Anne Golovin, Steve Lubar, Edith Mayo, and Terry Sharrer of the National Museum of American History at the Smithsonian Institution for their critique of the three systems of household production/consumption given in Chapter 2. Anne Golovin and Edith Mayo are now retired but remain active in their field and serve as a continuing resource. Steve Lubar is back at the Smithsonian after a year's leave teaching at the University of Pennsylvania. Special thanks are extended to the Smithsonian Institution Office of Fellowships and Grants, Duke University, and the Herbert Hoover Presidential Library for their support.

The members of Wadsworth's staff should be recognized for their work, and especially for their enthusiasm. Special appreciation is given to Bob Jucha, editor, who saw the project from beginning to completion. Also to be thanked are Eve Howard, editor in chief, Stephanie Monzon, assistant editor, Melissa Walter, editorial assistant, Dee Dee Zobian, technology project manager, Matt Wright, marketing manager, and Cheri Palmer, production project manager. As you can see, a great deal of human effort goes into these books; they are truly a team effort. Most importantly, the reviewers of all the editions are to be congratulated for their patience, input, and inspiration.

The reviewers of the first edition of the text were the ground-breakers. My thanks are extended to the following pioneers: Maria Canabal, *Illinois State University;* Elizabeth Carroll, *East Carolina University;* Lillian Chenowith, *Texas Woman's University;* Janice Hogan, *University of Minnesota;* Ruth H. Lytton, *Virginia Polytechnic Institute and State University;* Teresa Mauldin, *University of Georgia;* Mary Ann Paynter, *Delaware State University at Dover;* and Alice Pecoraro, *Nicholls State University.*

For keeping the momentum going in the second edition, special thanks are extended to Celia Ray Hayhoe, *University of Kentucky (now at Virginia Polytechnic University);* Janice L. Heckroth, *Indiana State University of Pennsylvania;* Ellen Lacey, *Ball State University;* and Terri Walters, *Syracuse University.*

For the fresh ideas evidenced in this third edition, the following repeat and new reviewers are warmly thanked: Pat McCallister (first edition and this edition), *Eastern Illinois University;* Jeanne Hilton (second and this edition), *University of Nevada, Reno;* Linda Simpson, *Eastern Illinois University;* Michelle Meadows, *Eastern Illinois University;* Edward Mel Markowski, *East Carolina University;* Deana Weibel, *California State University, Long Beach;* and Wendy Reibolt, *California State University, Long Beach.*

Most importantly, my deep appreciation goes to my family: my parents Irving and Betty Beard, both big believers in higher education and supportive throughout my education and career; my husband, Ronald, the Richard M. Baker Professor of Marketing at Florida State University; and my sons, David and Andrew, who have grown from children to young men in the course of these editions.

Thank you for your kind attention and I invite you to send your comments and suggestions about this book to me in care of Wadsworth Publishing Company, 10 Davis Drive, Belmont, CA 94002.

Elizabeth B. Goldsmith is an advisor/consultant to the Florida Commission on the Status of Women, the White House, the National Park Service, *The Wall Street Journal* Classroom Edition, the U.S. Department of Justice, the University of the West Indies, and the United Nations. Her presentations and research focus on women and money, consumer education, and the history and functioning of homes. She serves on the Board of Trustees of the National Association of Insurance Commissioners, the Florida Motor Vehicle Repair Advisory Council, and the editorial boards of the *International Journal of Consumer Studies* and the *Journal of Family and Economic Issues*.

She has given papers in Australia, Finland, Germany, England, Japan, Malta, Mexico, Northern Ireland, Sweden, and Wales. Dr. Goldsmith is Professor of Family Resource Management and Consumer Economics at Florida State University where she has won teaching awards and was featured as a Distinguished Faculty Member in the FSU Bulletin. Her Ph.D.-granting alma mater, Michigan State University, named her an Outstanding Alumna. She is the author of numerous encyclopedia chapters, over forty journal articles, and other books including *Personal Finance* (also published by Wadsworth).

part 1

Introduction

chapter *1*

Management Today

MAIN TOPICS

Did you know that . . . ?

. . . The median age of first marriage in the United States is 25.1 years for women and 26.8 years for men.

. . . Among Americans between 25 and 34 years old, 29 percent of men and 33 percent of women have college degrees.

Give curiosity freedom.

—*Eudora Welty*

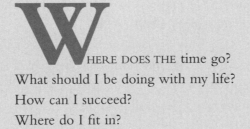

WHERE DOES THE time go?
What should I be doing with my life?
How can I succeed?
Where do I fit in?

Our life plans revolve around such questions. Asking questions and taking charge of one's life are important. This book is about the sorting-out process, the everyday things you do to take charge of your life, whether simply removing spam from your e-mail or making more complicated life decisions such as choosing where to live, whom to marry, and if and when to have children. When you choose, you are accountable for the resources used and the paths selected. **Choice** is the act of selecting among alternatives.

When we choose, we rely on what we have or what we can most easily access. For example, there is no sense searching for a $300-a-month apartment or an entry-level job that pays $100,000 a year if they don't exist. Risk is a factor in choice as well. Let's say a new housing development is being built in your town. The roads haven't even been put in yet, but people buy lots at a certain price based strictly on maps they are shown and their knowledge of the area, developer, and potential services. They are taking a huge risk. The purchase contract may include a time factor: Perhaps the lots will have to be built on within three years or sold back to the developer at the original purchase price, thus limiting the time in which the purchaser's investment can increase. The development may or may not grow in three years. The investment may decrease by half, but buyers are banking on the odds that the price of the lots will go up and they will build or sell.

In another example, beverage makers trying to keep pace with Japan's fad-driven culture launch more than a thousand new drinks each year, many claiming to boost energy or provide other health benefits (Terhune and Kahn, 2003). Vending machines provide easy access to the many beverages, but does anyone really need a thousand more beverage choices a year? How are decisions made in this frenzied atmosphere? One explanation is as follows:

> Riho Yamanaka, a 29-year-old Tokyo hotel manager, consumes up to four drinks a day and says she switches brands all the time. "When the new drinks come out, I probably try them at least once or so," says Ms. Yamanaka. "But I don't go for one particular brand." (Terhune and Kahn, 2003, p. B4)

Through our choices, we define our lives and influence other people's lives and the world in which we live. No decision is made in total isolation; we are constantly being influenced and influencing others. According to Stephen Covey, author of *The Seven Habits of Highly Effective People,* "Our basic nature is to act, and not be acted upon. As well as enabling us to choose our response to particular circumstances, this empowers us to create circumstances" (1989, p. 75).

The study of management explores how human beings react to change and how they cause change to happen. It has been said that the only thing humans can rely on is that things will change. Family life and household functioning, for example, have undergone enormous changes in the last 50 years. More women are working outside the home than ever before. Today, fewer than 25 percent of households have a mother, a father, and children living at home, yet our nation's housing stock is geared to this family constellation. There are now 105 million households, 14 million more than a decade ago. This means that there are fewer people per household.

Perhaps more important than the percentages and the numbers is the change in the way people are living. Furthermore, significant changes in families and households are occurring throughout the world and, in many cases, more rapidly than in North America. Given the changes already made in—and still to come to—the Internet, biology, medicine, social values, demographics, the environment, and international relations, what kind of world is emerging? Will people be happier and healthier in the future? "No one can say for sure, but one thing is certain: Continuing challenges will tax our collective abilities to deal with them" (Senge et al., 1999, p. 3).

This book explores past and future trends in a rapidly changing world, one that is becoming increasingly urban and mobile. Today, about half of the people on Earth (3 billion out of more than 6 billion) live in or around cities. By 2050, an estimated 75 percent of the world's population will be urban dwellers. This switch will have enormous implications for the environment, employment, transportation, and other factors affecting the quality of daily life. World populations are aging too. By 2025, according to estimates made by the U.S. Census Bureau's International Database on Aging, more than half of Japan's population will be over the age of 50 (Terhune and Kahn, 2003).

This first chapter introduces the fundamentals of management as they relate to individuals, families, and households. It begins by asking "What is management?" Some answers will emerge as we examine the management process and see how management can be put into action. Other important questions to be explored include "Why manage?" and "Who manages?" Management styles are influenced by several factors, and the study of management draws upon a number of other disciplines. Of necessity, life management must be both versatile and dynamic, for it applies to single adults as well as to families and must adapt to the changing composition of families. This chapter will examine some of these changes and show how the study of life management has adapted to them. The chapter concludes with a description of future chapters, relevant Web-based resources, and a summary.

WHAT IS MANAGEMENT?

Management is the process of using resources to achieve goals. In other words, management is the process of using what one has to get what one wants. The process includes the functioning, actions, thinking, and events that occur over time. Although situations change, the basic principles integral to management remain the same.

Management includes both thought and action. The importance of knowledge management, the "thought" part, cannot be underestimated. We all struggle to learn from past experiences, especially mistakes, and we struggle even more to apply the knowledge gained to new situations. Thus, we face several challenges when trying to initiate knowledge management; among them are

  ◆ Arrogance (the feeling there is nothing new to learn)
  ◆ Previous failed attempts (why try again?)
  ◆ Lack of commitment, drive, and awareness
  ◆ Lack of support, energy, or enthusiasm

These and other challenges, concepts, and themes recur throughout the book. They are reflected in the first seven chapter titles: values, attitudes, goals, resources, decision making, problem solving, planning, implementing, evaluating,

Management takes place at home, in the community, and at work. Everyday life is defined by where we are, what we are doing, who we are with, and how we react and plan.

and communication. Chapters 8–14 then apply these concepts to the specifics of managing human resources, time, work and family, stress, fatigue, environmental resources, and finances. Central to the discussion in each chapter is the way different personalities and situations affect how choices are made and acted upon.

Thus, the study of management is about how individuals and families decide, plan, and act in order to fulfill needs and accomplish goals in an increasingly complex society. According to Peter Drucker, the task of management is "to make people capable of joint performance, to make their strengths effective and their weaknesses irrelevant" (1989, p. 229). In a family, management fulfills this task by enabling the family to engage in collective decision making and by providing a framework that supports and maximizes the benefits to family members.

The Management Process

The **management process** involves thinking, action, and results. Because it is results-oriented, management is considered an applied social science. Management specialists evaluate the knowledge obtained through the study of management in terms of its ability to make an individual's or family's management practice more effective. People need results. It is inherently satisfying to commit to and work toward a goal.

Although management is practical, it is not necessarily simplistic. It becomes complex because individuals' and families' choices are constrained by limited resources. How people handle these constraints is what makes the study of management so interesting. If everyone had equal resources and abilities, the same dreams and wishes, and the same drive and ambition, then there would not be much to discuss. Everyone would lead identical lives. How boring would that be? In actuality, each individual has his or her own resource

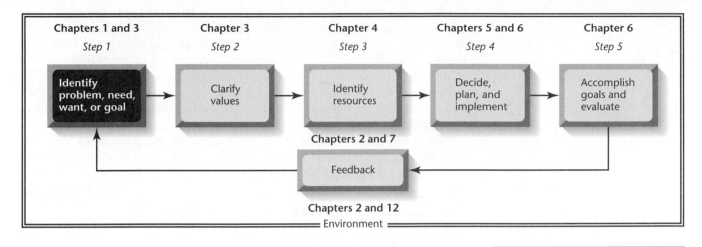

FIGURE 1.1
The Management Process

mix—attitudes, talents, and skills that are brought to bear on situations. Additionally, individuals vary in the way they respond to external and internal forces. Internal forces are the personal drives behind our actions. External forces include the ups and downs of the economy, the condition of the environment, and the rules and laws of society. Consequently, we must view management within the context of the greater environment, which changes constantly, as does the individual or group attempting to manage life within that environment.

The purpose of this chapter is to provide an overview of the management process; each aspect of the process will be examined in depth later in the book. Figure 1.1 provides a model of the management process and indicates the chapters in which each step is discussed. Each part of the model plays a critical role in the reinforcing circle, or loop, of the management process.

The process begins with a problem, need, want, or goal. The person initiating the management process identifies a problem or something that he or she desires. **Problems** are questions, dilemmas, or situations that require solving, such as "Should I buy or rent a home?" **Needs** are what we need to survive or sustain life, such as food and shelter. **Wants** are things that we desire, such as an expensive sports car, but that are not necessary for us to survive. In general conversation, the words *needs* and *wants* are sometimes used interchangeably, but in management they are viewed as distinct. Dennis Bristow and John Mowen identify four types of needs (personal communication, April 4, 1994):

1. *Physical needs:* A person's need to sustain life, obtain sensory pleasures, and maintain or enhance physical characteristics (e.g., muscle tone and physical beauty)

2. *Social needs:* An individual's need for relations and interactions with other people; the desire to be included in a group

3. *Wealth needs:* An individual's need to obtain money, goods, property, and other assets with monetary value that are transmittable between two or more people

4. *Information needs:* A person's need to gain knowledge and investigate, explore, study, and/or understand phenomena; the need to satisfy intellectual curiosity and engage in cognitive activity

For example, people need food, air, and shelter to survive. Wants are more specific; they are things or activities that make people feel comfortable and satisfied. Thus, a person may be hungry (a need) but may want to satisfy that hunger with a specific food, such as an apple or a slice of pizza. **Goals** are end results that require action. A college diploma is a goal of most college students. Passing courses and applying for graduation are the actions required to reach that goal. In the greater scheme of life, goals are arranged in a hierarchy from fairly ordinary to extraordinary.

Once individuals or families have identified the problem, need, want, or goal, they move to the next step, which is the clarification of values. What do they really want, and does it fit into their value system? **Values** are principles that guide behavior, such as honesty or loyalty. **Clarification** means to make clear, to make easier to understand, or to elaborate. As they move through the management process, people need to clearly identify what they want to achieve and to ensure that their goal-seeking behavior is compatible with their values. For example, an individual may desire more money, but robbing a bank probably doesn't fit the person's or society's value system. Management is based on values and goal-seeking behavior; without these, the process would be aimless and misdirected. Behavior has consequences.

The next step in Figure 1.1 involves identifying resources, finding out what one has to work with. **Resources** are whatever is available to be used, such as information, time, skills, human and mechanical energy, Internet access, and money.

The quantitative and/or qualitative criteria that reconcile resources with demands are known as **standards;** standards also provide measures of values and goals (DeMerchant, 1993). Standards are set by individuals and families for themselves, and they are also set by friends, employers, schools, and governments. For example, governments establish speed limits (a standard) as part of their traffic management in order to preserve life and property, and schools and businesses establish appearance or dress codes for their students and employees. During the management process, standards may have to be adjusted. Thus, standard setting is dynamic, meaning that it is subject to change. What is acceptable one year may not be acceptable the next. For example, a school may set school uniforms as the standard one year and do away with the practice the next.

The next step in the process has three aspects: deciding, planning, and implementing. **Decision making** refers to choosing between two or more alternatives. **Planning** requires making a series of decisions that lead to action, and **implementing** means putting plans into action. Plans give focus and direction to the pursuit of wants, needs, and goals. In working through this step, a manager evaluates and adjusts decisions and plans as needed. For example, an individual planning a trip may select a new route or time of arrival as circumstances change.

The last step of the management process sees goals accomplished or fulfilled and the process as a whole evaluated. Individuals are pleased when they achieve their hard-sought goals, but they often overlook evaluation, which in many ways is the most important step in the process. Was the problem solved? What was learned? Which decisions or plans worked and which failed? What adjustments should have been made? The answers to these questions are part of the **feedback** (information that returns to the system) that enables the individual's overall management knowledge and ability to grow.

The management process is never stagnant. "It deals with action and application; and its test are results," says Peter Drucker (1989, p. 231). One learns and grows from each decision. New situations provide opportunities for advancement and self-learning. By evaluating past experiences, people learn how to approach the world and discover where their skills and talents lie. In many ways, the study of management is a discovery of self and of how others deal with the world.

So far we've looked at the management process primarily as an internally driven system (people's problems, wants, needs, and goals motivate them to act), but in fact the process takes place in the larger context of the external environment. For example, a person at a busy fitness center may want to use the treadmill but will have to wait if someone else is using it. The environment, therefore, can present limitations or barriers to an individual's or family's course of action. As previously noted, the rules and laws of society also affect how wants and needs are fulfilled and what goals are feasible. Thus, the management process must be viewed within an environmental context as Figure 1.1 indicates. Environment refers to everything outside the individual.

Let's note two other features of the management process. First, in certain situations and decisions (especially hurried ones), the steps may not progress in exactly the order shown in Figure 1.1; sometimes several steps may occur simultaneously. Second, although understanding the individual components of the process is important, the management process is far more than a set of concepts. The essence of the process is that the concepts are interrelated. The process may start with a problem or a need and end with a solution, but the critical element is what happens in between. From the first step to the last, management knowledge, skills, and tools are used. **Management tools** are measuring devices, techniques, or instruments that are used to arrive at decisions and plans of action; examples include clocks, lists, forms, calendars, budgets, and timetables. Are you a list maker? Are you very conscious of what time it is? Did you know that the mechanical clock was invented 500 years ago in the fourteenth century? Before that, people did not think of time in fixed units, but more as a progression, a cycle based on nature. Of course, nature is not linear; it ebbs and flows in an inexact way. For example, depending on where you live, the first day of spring (March 21) may find the ground covered with snow. The calendar says it is spring; nature says it is not. In this case, using weather as a time measure may be more appropriate than using a calendar.

Successful Plans: Putting Management into Action

Planning is the operationalization of choices; often, it means making a list of steps to be taken. This is the stage when people say, "Okay, we know what we want; now how are we going to get there?" So a particularly critical management skill is the ability to create and execute an effective plan. Planning helps individuals to

- ◆ Highlight important problems and opportunities
- ◆ Invest resources in the right tasks
- ◆ Encourage the development of goals
- ◆ Make decision making more efficient and effective
- ◆ Motivate and coordinates efforts
- ◆ Provide a feeling of growth and accomplishment
- ◆ Involve others

How much planning is necessary? The answer depends on the situation and individual's goals, resources, levels of motivation, and abilities. One fundamental management principle is that planning skill increases with knowledge, practice, and effort. The more individuals plan, listen to feedback, and evaluate their decisions, the stronger their management skills become.

To be successful, a plan needs to be realistic, clear, flexible, and well thought out and executed. The experience of job hunting provides a good example of how planning works and how feedback can help individuals make adjustments to their plans. Most college students want to graduate and get a good job that uses their skills, education, and training. Beyond this generalization, an individual student's career goals become more specific.

For example, Jennifer's goal is to be employed in a state government job in human services when she graduates. Her bachelor of science degree and senior-year internship provide her with knowledge, skills, contacts, and a tools base. She is computer-savvy and knows how to analyze data and reports. In terms of values, she wants to serve people in a meaningful and caring way, and she especially likes working with children. As part of her career plan, she wants a job that will start soon after her May graduation. In January she begins filling out applications, sending out résumés, including an online portfolio, and interviewing. But many of her letters and applications go unnoticed, and she receives very few responses. By April she begins adjusting her plan to include more than government jobs. She applies for jobs in nearby states, in the human resources departments at various companies, and at other venues through the career services center on campus. At Jennifer's first interview, the interviewer tells her (provides feedback) that she should rewrite her résumé so that it highlights her past work experiences more clearly. So Jennifer rewrites it and has three more interviews. In June she is hired and begins work in July; her job is not what she had envisioned, but it does use her skills and provides potential for growth. She is pleased to be working with families and children, and in hindsight she is glad she has had two months off between graduation and the start of her new job. Jennifer feels that managing this first professional job search has taught her skills, such as the need to be flexible and listen to interviewers' feedback, that will help her the next time she looks for a job.

Why Manage?

The answer to the question "Why manage?" is that people have no other choice. Certainly, life involves nonmanaged actions, such as everyday activities that do not require a lot of thought or planning (getting up in the morning and brushing one's teeth), but the bigger things that most people want, such as a job and a family life require management skills. Essentially, management takes people from where they are to where they want to go. Having a future to work toward is integral to people's sense of well-being. Humans need to feel in control of their lives. But being in control is only one of the many benefits management offers. Management also provides new ways of critiquing life situations and offers new perspectives on the nature of change. When people are frustrated or confused, management supplies constructive order, reduces chaos, and suggests steps to follow. For example, familiarity with the management process helped Jennifer plan, make adjustments, and overcome discouragement in her job search.

As a field of study, management is exciting and challenging because it is

◆ Change-oriented

◆ Economically, culturally, and socially significant

◆ Dynamic, intriguing, and complex

◆ Personally and professionally rewarding

◆ Integral to developing leadership and teamwork skills and receptive to community involvement

Furthermore, the study of management provides a great deal of insight into a major area of human behavior—the decisions people make and the actions taken based on those decisions. Knowledge of management will help students of human behavior to better understand themselves and the actions of those around them.

Few subjects are more positive and more encouraging than management or more appropriate for college students who are about to embark on new life paths. According to Peter Drucker, "practically all people with schooling beyond high school, in all developed countries—in the United States the figure is 90 percent—will spend all their working lives as employees of managed organizations and could not make their living without them" (1986, p. 352). As this quotation suggests, management is applicable to all life stages. The ever changing environment, coupled with their own changing needs, impels individuals to constantly search for new courses of action, goals, and solutions to problems. It is important to realize that despite difficulties, new ideas do spread and new options open up all the time.

Who Manages?

The answer to the question "Who manages?" should be obvious by now. Everyone does. Management is such a natural and normal part of life that few people stop to think about how they do it. The management process should be employed every time someone makes a decision involving school, career, or personal life. Using this process, individuals consider their needs and wants, their resources, their preferences, the situation, the other people involved, and so on. Then they create a plan of action and implement it.

The individual making decisions lies at the heart of the management experience. As Figure 1.1 illustrates, however, management is much more than decision making; it is a multifaceted process involving many concepts, actions, and reactions. Besides those already mentioned, management includes organizing, scheduling, synthesizing, analyzing, resolving tension, negotiating, reaching agreement, mediating, problem solving, and communicating. In other words, although management is fundamental to human life, it is often a difficult process. Consider the decision Jason has to face at age 24. Should he stay at home and live with his parents while he works and builds up his savings, or should he rent an apartment and try to make it on his own even though the rent will take nearly all of his earnings? If he decides to live with his parents, should he stay for six months? A year? What factors should Jason consider besides money in making his decision?

Throughout this book most examples will involve individuals, households, and families, but the basic principles are applicable to all walks of life. As we've seen, however, management is particularly applicable to career situations.

Being on time, organizing and finishing work, and scheduling appointments are behaviors that take place in the office as well as in the home.

Influences on Management Styles

Whether at home or at work, people are constantly searching for ways to do things more efficiently and effectively. Commuters try to find routes that will cut 10 minutes off their travel time, and retirees try to find ways to stretch their dollars further. Although everyone manages, each person has his or her own **management style,** or characteristic way of making decisions and acting. Five factors influence management styles:

1. History influences the way a person makes decisions and the options he or she considers. "History" can apply to individuals, families, and societies.
2. Biology dictates basic physiological needs such as food, shelter, air, and water.
3. Culture provides a systematic way to fulfill needs. As social beings, people care about each other.
4. Personality is the sum total of individual characteristics, enduring traits, and ways of interacting. For example, personality affects how a person interacts with the environment.
5. Technology applies method and materials to the achievement of objectives. Technology includes laws, techniques, tools, material objects, and processes that help people get what they want.

Maslow's Hierarchy of Needs

Of these influences, the most fundamental is biology. According to psychologist Abraham Maslow (1908–1970), physiological needs (such as those defined by Bristow and Mowen earlier in the chapter) must be met before higher-order needs are undertaken. He hypothesized that each individual has a series of needs ranging from low-order needs to higher-order needs (see Figure 1.2). In Maslow's hierarchy of needs, physiological needs (e.g., thirst, hunger) must be at least partially met before higher-order needs such as safety,

FIGURE 1.2
Maslow's Hierarchy of Needs

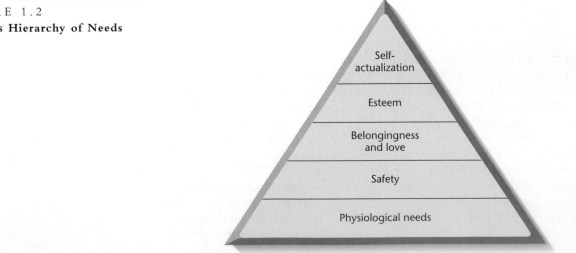

a sense of belonging and love, self-esteem, and self-actualization can be fulfilled (Maslow, 1954). The highest level of need, self-actualization, is fulfillment of one's highest potential. Self-actualizers fully integrate the components of their personality, or self. In other words, they attain self-realization, the process by which individuals have the opportunity to invest their talents in activities that they find meaningful.

Of the other factors influencing management style, history, culture, and personality help define human needs and aspirations. Technology provides the means by which humanity progresses.

Technology

Although we'll look at technology in more detail later in the book, it's important to consider it briefly here because it plays a significant role in management and will play a larger one in the future. It's important to study technology because "if we are to have a fuller understanding of the social and economic context of the family, it is necessary to explore its technological environment" (Burton, 1992, p. 383). Technology differs from the other influences on management style (i.e., history, culture, and personality) because it is usually visible; technological advances are easily observed and measured. For example, one television set per household used to be the norm. Now, American households average 2.8 televisions; 65 percent of all households subscribe to cable television services, and 95 percent have access to cable.

Today, most Americans have cell phones, one of the fastest-growing technologies in recent history. "The past two years have seen cellular subscribers soar by more than 40 percent. . . . And Americans' cell phone use has risen sharply, from 89 billion minutes in 1998 to nearly 200 billion in just the first six months of [2001]" (The Complete Cell-Phone Guide, 2002, p. 14). On typical days cellular technology carries about 30 percent of 911 calls. On September 11, 2001, in the hours immediately following the terrorist attacks in the United States, total cellular traffic nearly doubled. According to Danielle Perry, a spokeswoman for AT&T Wireless, "We had the highest calling volume we've ever had" (The Complete Cell-Phone Guide, 2002, p. 14). Cell phone use varies by age group. "American cell phone users age 25 to 34 are more than four times as likely to use their mobile phones as their primary telephone than those over age 35" (Phone Home, 2001, p. 18). And this is not an American phenomenon: Finland and Japan are well ahead of the United States in cell phone use. Telephones are both time-savers and time-users. Before the invention of the cell phone, how did people reach each other, and how did they spend that time? In addition, e-mail, instant messaging, and the Internet have added new dimensions to communication. More than 50 percent of American households have personal computers, 23 million have more than one personal computer, and about two-thirds of Americans are online regularly.

Technology by itself is neither good nor bad, nor is it neutral (Wilson, 1994). The use of technology determines its worth. The most documented house in the United States, the White House, provides some examples of this phenomenon. In 1879, President Rutherford B. Hayes had the first telephone installed in the White House, but it was rarely used because hardly anyone else in Washington had a telephone, so there was no one to call or to call in (Seale, 1986). When the typewriter was introduced to the White House in 1880, it was put to more immediate use. Previously, all presidential correspondence had to be handwritten by a clerk, so the typewriter was clearly a useful innovation. In 1891, during Benjamin Harrison's administration, electric lights were installed in the White House (Seale, 1986). The president was afraid of being shocked, however, so he refused to operate the electric lights and summoned servants to turn them off and on. To show the progression of technology, over a hundred years later during the Clinton administration, the White House was rewired so that computers could be used more readily and television interviews could take place in a greater variety of locations without the necessity of dragging long, heavy cables about.

When microwave ovens were introduced in the 20th century, many people were not sure that they were really safe and useful. Today, microwave ovens are pervasive. Technology is more than a system of machines: "Each technology is an extension of human lives; someone makes it, someone owns it, some oppose it, many use it, and all interpret it" (Nye, 1990, p. ix). Further, today's technologies constantly crisscross, so that a discovery in one industry may revolutionize another industry and its technology (Drucker, 1999). It is becoming increasingly important, then, to be knowledgeable in a variety of fields and to keep up with developments in other disciplines.

Interdisciplinary Foundation

As the previous section explained, various factors (e.g., history, biology, culture, personality, and technology) influence individuals' management style. But the field of resource management is even broader than these influences suggest. Although the discussion here will be limited to the connections between management and some of the social sciences—anthropology, psychology, sociology, and economics—other disciplines have also contributed to the development of the field. These include geography, political science, agriculture, philosophy, organizational behavior, marketing, biology, chemistry, engineering, and physics. For example, philosophy contributes to our understanding of values, marketing to the consumption decisions made by individuals and families, and engineering to the mechanics and functioning of the home. Geography tracks regions, landscapes, and other spatial units. The distribution of people, resources, and culture is a driving force in geography. Connections to political science may seem obscure, but public policy affects individual and family life through services offered, taxes, and the ultimate control of resources.

Anthropology

The word *anthropology* comes from the Greek *anthropo* (man) and *logy* (science). Simply defined, anthropology is the science of human beings. Anthropologists seek to study and interpret the characteristics of a particular population or activity in its place in time. This includes communities, subcultures, and entire societies. Of anthropology's many subfields, cultural anthropology is the most relevant to management.

Culture affects what people learn and how they behave. Culture applies to management on two distinct levels: as a set of general attributes of people in a society or group and as material culture, or the objects and tools individuals and families use. (Because the family is the social group of interest in this book, discussions of material culture will focus on objects associated with the family and home use.) Culture also refers to patterns. Those who study management are interested in repetitive patterns of living. The characteristic way, or pattern, in which an individual conducts her or his life is called a **lifestyle.** Needs, wants, tastes, styles, and preferences all contribute to lifestyles.

Psychology

The word *psychology* is formed by combining *psyche* (the mind) and *logy* (science). Psychology focuses on how the individual thinks and behaves. Communication of meaning is a driving force in psychology.

Social psychology and cognitive psychology are particularly relevant to the study of management. Social psychology is the study of individual behavior within a group; it examines attitudes, problem solving, social influences, leaders and followers, and communication. These topics will be discussed in depth in future chapters. Cognitive psychology explains the nature of human intelligence and how people think. It is dominated by the information-processing approach, which analyzes thinking processes as a sequence of ordered stages. Values, attitudes, and decision making are integral to cognitive psychology as well as to management.

Sociology

Whereas psychology focuses on the individual or the individual operating in groups, sociology emphasizes the collective behavior of social groups, including organizations and communities. *Sociology* comes from the Latin *socius* (companion or associate) and *logy* (science).

Sociology applies the scientific method to the study of human society. It explores why some groups function the way they do. For example, sociological studies investigate the norms and roles of retired workers, schoolchildren, and employed women. Because the family is a societal group, sociology coupled with family relations contributes much to our understanding of family managerial behavior. Families usually share common goals or purposes and interact in pursuit of these objectives. Each member of the family is perceived by others as a member, and all members are bound together by traditions and networks. Sociologists study customs, structures, and institutions, as well as how individuals function in groups and organizations. Sociologists research the connections between work and family. They are particularly interested in conflict (social disorder) and cohesion (social order) as driving forces.

Economics

Economics is the social science concerned with the production, development, and management of material wealth at different levels: households, businesses, or nations. It tracks markets, industries, and economies as key units of study. The driving force of change is economic value, worth, and scarcity (constraints). Economists study human behavior within the context of the relationship between desired end results and scarcity. Specifically, it covers human resource planning, labor market changes, cost-benefit analyses, and the resources of land, natural resources, and capital (human-made resources). For the purposes of resource management, the most relevant topics are those related to human resource planning, financial management, households, and specifically microeconomics, which focuses on the behavior of individual consumers. The most basic economic problem is how individuals decide how to allocate scarce resources to achieve the results they desire.

In conclusion, management works in tandem with other disciplines—the interdisciplinary influences are noted in Table 1.1. It deals with people, their values, and their growth and development; and in so doing, it concerns itself with the social structure and the community.

TABLE 1.1
The Interdisciplinary Influences on the Study of Resource Management

Discipline	Unit of Analysis	Focus/Drive*
Anthropology	Communities Dominant culture & subcultures Societies	Culture
Psychology	Individuals	Communication & self-knowledge
Sociology	Social groups Organizations Communities Families	Conflict & cohesion
Economics	Households Markets Industries Economies	Value, worth, scarcity

*All these disciplines share an interest in understanding human behavior.

Concepts and skills integral to management, such as attitudes, decision making, and planning, are also integral to other disciplines. Knowledge from anthropology, psychology, sociology, economics, and other disciplines provides direction and strength to management research and theory. The next section shows how these theoretical aspects of management can be applied to contemporary problems.

LIFE MANAGEMENT FOR INDIVIDUALS AND FAMILIES

Although management principles can be applied to individuals, families, groups, organizations, governments, and businesses, this book focuses on individual, family, and household management—on what can be called life management. This section discusses life management and provides definitions of several key family and household terms.

Life management encompasses all the decisions a person or family will make and the way values, goals, and resource use affect decision making. It refers to more than just specific goal achievement. In life management, "people are seen as possessing a 'self' which helps regulate their actions":

> Another basic premise is that humans assess situations, speculate about the implications of self and others, take the role of others in order to conduct concerted action, and engage in a process of asking and answering "what if . . . ?" questions before engaging in social actions. (Kaplan & Hennon, 1992, p. 127)

Thus, life management includes all the events, situations, and decisions that make up a lifestyle. Life management is a holistic approach that looks at management as a process that evolves over a life span. The process takes place in a social context as part of the environment that surrounds individuals and families.

Managing the Second Half of Life

The second half of life presents its own unique challenges. Patterns (personal, family, work, leisure) established in the first half of life may no longer suffice. Children grow up and leave; some grown children return home after a failed marriage or a financial loss; jobs may prove less challenging, an expected promotion does not come through, or an early retirement buyout package is offered. In one case, a man in his 50s took advantage of a generous buyout package from a car company and started his own scrap metal business with two friends from the same industry. They knew there was a market, they knew where the sources of scrap metal were, and they put their expertise together. Although they are no longer in the car industry per se, they are in a related industry in which they travel the world buying up the metal and transporting it to car factories. As owners of a new, smaller company, they are enjoying the freedom of working closely together. Often the most successful career transitions are made this way, in finding a new way to use old skills, knowledge, and relationships. As another example, four friends formed a partnership and bought land on the side of a mountain where they are selling off property and building retirement homes for themselves and their families.

Individuals may find themselves having spent their first 25 years getting educated and the next 25–30 years on the job, and then facing the prospect of 30–40 years of retirement. How they react to this scenario has a great deal to do with their personality and the details of the actual situation, such as finances and health. Even if they remain employed, work may be redefined by the workers themselves or by the demands of the workplace. Many people question the nature of their work at midlife; most do not want to stay in the same job for 30 years. Unless they manage options or find new opportunities, they may deteriorate, become bored, "retire on the job," lose all joy in work and in life, and become a burden to themselves and those around them (Drucker, 1999, pp. 188–189).

Some, of course, refuse to retire or to accept society's definition of aging. When Federal Judge Milton Pollack—at 96 years old the third oldest federal judge in the United States—was asked about retirement, he said, "Having a daily occupation keeps me active and I have no plans to leave the bench" (Davis and Smith, 2003, p. C1). Guitarist Joe Perry of Aerosmith, a 1970s rock 'n' roll band that still performs, says "Society programs you to be a couch potato, and you don't have to be. . . . This isn't about rock 'n' roll: it's about getting out there and living life instead of just watching it go by. . . . I don't think of myself as being 52; I just think of myself as being (Umminger, 2003, p. 4D). Another member of the band, bassist Tom Hamilton, says "You have to make sacrifices. You can't open a bag of potato chips whenever you want." Joe responds, "You can but you can't eat it" (Umminger, 2003, p. 4D). The band members said they have to watch what they eat and work out in gyms because fans don't want to see a fat rocker. With aging and growth come compromises; staying active is not easy.

For those of us in less public professions than rock stars, possible solutions to workplace ennui include

◆ Enriching the present job by taking advantage of training opportunities or travel; teaming up with colleagues on projects.

◆ Starting a second or different career or moving to another organization or locale. As an example of the twists and turns this can take, a woman sold her large urban interior design firm after 20 years and downscaled to a corner of a fabric store in a small city. In a few years that store moved and joined forces with a leading furniture store, which led to more work (and money) for the interior designer than ever before, but in an environment shared with more people, a situation she enjoyed. Her overhead was low because her rent was low, and the only person she had to pay was herself. She set her own hours, decided how many clients to take, and used the furniture store to display her skills.

◆ Developing a parallel career: keeping the basic job but adding another track such as a part-time job, possibly an outgrowth of a hobby or interest area.

◆ Joining in a nonprofit activity such as community service, politics, school boards, neighborhood associations, and so on.

In addition to the obvious changes that may occur during the second half of life in families, health, or jobs, more subtle changes may take place, such as redefining success or determining what is important.

People of all ages need to feel that they are making a contribution at home, at the workplace, or in the community. Indeed, as more workers become knowledge workers, the need to retire has become less evident than it was when most people were manual laborers and the physical limitations of age prevented continued employment. Now that work is less physically defined and people are living longer, and as more people work in their homes (using computers and broadband connections), a societal redefinition of retirement is under way.

Singles, Households, Nonfamily Households, and Families

Management can be an individual or a group activity. Traditionally, the study of management has focused primarily on the family, but the growing number of single adults means that the field must pay equal attention to their lifestyles and needs. The number of single adults is increasing for several reasons. For one thing, the population is aging, resulting in more elderly singles. In addition, because the age at first marriage is rising, there are many more young adult singles.

In 1900, the average life expectancy in the United States was 47, and only 3 percent of the population lived past 65. Now, the average life expectancy is over 70. A boy born in 2000 will reach 73 on average; his sister will live into her 80s. Of course, many will live well into their 90s and some into their 100s. According to the Census Bureau, the median age at first marriage for females rose from 20.3 in 1960 to 25.1 in 2000. The corresponding figures for males are 22.8 and 26.8. This delay of marriage until a later age for both males and females is a significant demographic change. In 2000, an American woman, on average, will have her first child at age 26. This is later than the age at which her mother had her first child. Between the ages of 25 and 34, 29 percent of men have college degrees as do 33 percent of women.

A single lifestyle has both pluses and minuses. For example, on the positive side, single adults enjoy increased freedom of action, privacy, and solitude, whereas on the negative side they may experience more loneliness. *Solitude* connotes a sense of enjoyment in being alone. Most of us enjoy periods of peaceful, uninterrupted reading. Solitude has the advantage of being restful and life-restoring.

Singles may feel burdened by their inability to share responsibilities. Single people have to take care of everything by themselves. Generalizing about singles is difficult, however, because many singles live with friends or family members, have pets, and enjoy the support of coworkers and neighbors.

Cohabitation has increased in this country. About 10 million unmarried heterosexual American adults live with partners—seven times as many as in 1970—but cohabitation hasn't replaced marriage (Mithers, 2003). There are about 55 million married couples in the United States. Cohabiting couples stay together about two years on average; after five years, 55 percent of couples marry. By the age of 30, three-quarters of women have married and about half of them lived with their mates first.

Many popular images of singles are incorrect or confused. Consider the common belief that elderly singles choose to retire primarily in the Sunbelt states, especially Florida. Actually Nevada's elderly population grew by more than 70 percent during the 1990s, whereas Florida's grew only 18.5 percent. Elders are flocking to North Carolina, South Carolina, Georgia, Alaska, Arizona, New Mexico, Hawaii, Utah, and Colorado. The greatest rise in elderly growth is taking place in the suburbs (Frey, 2001). They are also attracted to the university towns of State College, Pennsylvania; Iowa City, Iowa; Bloomington, Indiana; Madison, Wisconsin; Austin, Texas; and Raleigh-Durham, North Carolina. In addition, large numbers of elderly live in the rural Midwest. The phrase "aging in place" refers to the phenomenon of people staying where they were brought up or spent their working years—for example, in the Midwest or in the suburbs. Census data reveal that working-age singles tend to cluster in cities such as New York, Washington, Austin, Denver, Seattle, and San Francisco. If trends hold true, more elders, along with the rest of the population, will migrate West and South in the future. It is also not an unusual pattern to see active elders retire to warm-weather states and then when they become older and frailer move back to the areas from which they migrated or move closer to grown children. As the baby boomers become absorbed into the ranks of the elderly over the next 30 years, the movements of vast numbers of elderly will have obvious impacts on communities.

People's lifestyles can be categorized by housing units rather than by marital status. According to the Census Bureau, a **household** comprises all persons who occupy a "housing unit"—that is, a house, an apartment or other group of rooms, or a single room that constitutes "separate living quarters." A household includes the related family members and all the unrelated persons, if any, such as lodgers, foster children, wards, or employees who share the housing unit. A person living alone or a group of unrelated persons sharing the same housing unit is also counted as a household. Household change generally parallels population change. Household growth in the 1990s was fastest in Nevada, according to the Census Bureau. The smallest gains in new households were in slow-growing states, mainly in the Northeast. A nonfamily household is defined as those who live alone or with nonrelatives. These have risen to 32 percent in 2000 from 30 percent in 1990 (see Table 1.2).

Cohabitation, discussed earlier, contributes to the rising number of nonfamily households. It is estimated that a quarter of the time, one cohabitating partner wants to marry, while the other doesn't. Although most people think of cohabitants as young adults, they may be older. The majority of people who have experienced a divorce will try cohabitation before remarrying, but the trial run may be quite short. Here is a case in point:

TABLE 1.2
Household Changes

This table shows changes in households between 1990 and 2000.*

	Family Households	Nonfamily Households	Total Number
1990	64.5 million	27.4 million	91.9 million
2000	71.8 million	33.7 million	105.5 million
% Growth	11	23	15

Source: U.S. Census Bureau

Leah, a bank sales manager in Los Angeles, was 20 and deeply in love, but she and her 22-year-old boyfriend never even considered living together. "Our parents couldn't have taken it," she says. "So we got married." Today, 49, divorced and the mother of two children, 15 and 13, Leah is in love with a man she's been dating for two years and choosing a different road. "Eventually we'll marry," she says. "He's ready now. But I want to live together first. . . . Living together doesn't feel like as big a commitment." (Mithers, 2003, p. 93)

No universal definitions of the family exist; however, a number of definitions are considered appropriate (Munro & Munro, 2003). According to the Census Bureau, the word **family** refers to a group of two or more persons related by birth, marriage, or adoption and residing together in a household. Some feel that this definition is too narrow. A free-form definition would indi-

Television sit-coms have changed from I Love Lucy *and* The Cosby Show, *conventional depictions of families with husbands, wives, and children, to those portraying other types of living arrangements and relationships such as the ones depicted on* Friends, Seinfeld, *and* Will & Grace. *Nighttime television reflects trends in the general population by including households with single parents, singles, and nonrelatives living together.*

© Photofest

cate that the family is whatever an individual says it is. The definition of immediate family used by the American Red Cross Disaster Services Program includes mother, father, spouse, dependent children, dependent grandchild/grandchildren, dependent stepchild/children, regularly financially supported significant others, fiancés, housemates, and/or other family members. They use this definition to determine who qualifies for aid in a disaster. Setting parameters is important because when money is involved, someone may claim to be a fiancé or a long-lost relative: What happens, for instance, when three women say they were fiancés of the same man? The American Red Cross asks for verification before aid is disbursed. Examples of acceptable forms of verification include

- ◆ Joint current ownership of a home
- ◆ Joint current rental agreement/lease
- ◆ Joint current bank account or credit cards
- ◆ Joint current ownership or holding of investments
- ◆ Current utility bill with both names
- ◆ Joint obligation on a current loan
- ◆ Current joint renter's or homeowner's insurance policy
- ◆ Registration with a state or a local domestic partnership registry or certification of a union celebrated overseas.

Immediately following the September 11, 2001, disasters, the American Red Cross assisted families of the 3,333 deceased or seriously injured, opened 55,370 cases, made 131,185 disaster health contacts, and made 236,498 disaster mental health contacts. As of May 24, 2002, $979.1 million was donated for services to those directly affected, and $570.4 million was spent nationally. "The outpouring of financial support from the American people for the victims and their families was astounding" (Goodman, 2002, p. 1). The American Red Cross is allied with the International Red Cross and other groups who share a common goal of relieving suffering. The organization's definition of family is considered more inclusive than the U.S. Census Bureau's definition. From the Census Bureau's point of view and for those who rely on census data, consistent definitions of families and households are important so that comparisons can be made from decade to decade.

A family includes among its members the householder. According to the Census Bureau, the **householder** is the person (or one of the persons) in whose name the home is owned or rented. If a home is owned or rented jointly by a married couple, either the husband or the wife may be listed first. Prior to 1980, the husband was always considered the household head (householder) in married-couple households. The American Red Cross has another definition of household. It says that a household is defined as

> A family or other group of individuals who live together and act jointly in conducting most or all domestic activities, or an individual who lives alone or lives with others but acts alone in conducting most or all domestic activities. Examples of domestic activities are having meals together and sharing responsibility for maintaining a home (for example, jointly paying for utilities). (Goodman, 2002, p. 2)

According to the Census Bureau, since 1980 the percentage of family households has declined, and the percentage of people living alone has risen. The average number of people per household in the United States has dropped from 5 persons in 1900 to 2.75 persons in 1980 to 2.63 persons in 1990 to

2.5 persons in 2000. The most dramatic growth in single-person householders is occurring among those aged 45 to 64. More than one in every nine adults aged 15 and over lived alone in 1990, representing a substantial increase since 1970; the number of women living alone increased by 91 percent, whereas the number of men living alone rose by 156 percent (Saluter, 1990). About 2 million Americans are in prisons.

Changes in Family and Household Composition

To summarize, the term *family* refers to relationships, usually by marriage or through children, shared commitment, or shared resources over time, or to genetic relationships; and the term *household* refers to housing units and the occupants who share the residence. The number of single adults in the United States is growing, and households and families have fewer people on average. However, these changes do not indicate that the number of families is declining. These statistics do indicate significant changes in the composition and size of families. According to the last census, in the United States, there are

◆ 54.5 million married-couple families

◆ 24.8 million families with children under age 8

◆ 60 million households without children

◆ 12.9 million female householders, with no husband present

◆ 4.4 million male householders, with no wife present

◆ 4.9 million male-female unmarried-couple households, 293,365 female-only unmarried-couple households, and 301,026 male-only unmarried-couple households

To provide perspective, "This image of the old-fashioned family is sort of put up as a goal (by) people who think the past is always better than the present," says Arizona State University demographer Paul Glick. "But people have options now they didn't have before. . . . Times have changed" (Usdansky, 1992). In 1950, families averaged three children compared to one or two children per couple in 2000. Ray Marshall, a former U.S. secretary of labor, has identified another change in family life: "In 1950, 70 percent of American families were headed by men whose wages were the sole source of income. Today only about 10 percent fit that description and fewer than one in eight families consists of a married couple with children in which the mother does not work outside the home" (1991, p. 15). Just as the family has changed, so have social and economic conditions. Marshall suggests that the following have been particularly significant: (1) technological innovations, especially in information, communications, and transportation; (2) the internationalization of the economy; and (3) changes in prevailing attitudes. He also points out that neither the family nor economic conditions were ever as stable as they seem to be in Americans' idealized memories of life in the 1950s. Actually, he says, both have always been in a state of flux.

In another trend, individuals are increasingly putting off marriage and childbirth to later years and are living long enough to experience single living several times during their life. For example, a woman may be single during her twenties, marry for a few years, divorce, remarry, and then be widowed. When high school classes convene for their twentieth reunion, it is not unusual to find several people who have been married three or four times.

Although the statistics given so far describe conditions in the United States, changes in the composition of families are a global trend. Timeworn traditions concerning the proper age for marriage and the propriety of divorce are being questioned. One study of 62 societies found that most young people who divorce do so after four years of marriage and that most of them eventually remarry (Fisher, 1992). In the United States, a Gallup poll (based on figures from the National Center for Health Statistics) revealed that the average age at second marriage is 39.2 for men and 34.8 for women (Beck, 1992).

Regardless of family stage or type, the main difference between individual and family decision making is that decisions are more complex when made by two or more persons. The bigger the family, the more complicated the decision-making process, because more people's needs have to be considered, and resources have to stretch further. Family decision making is an important area of study because "the family provides the setting in which essential resources are created, transformed, allocated, and exchanged to meet physical, safety, and higher level needs of individuals" (Rettig & Bubolz, 1983, p. 418).

In conclusion, managing a life, whether as an individual or as a member of family, within the context of the mounting pressures and stresses of everyday existence is not an easy task. As we have seen, not only families but also the society and economy in which they live are undergoing dramatic changes. People try to adapt and to influence these changing situations through the choices they make. Management provides the opportunities to shape future outcomes for the benefit of individuals, families, and communities.

WHAT LIES AHEAD?

This book is divided into four parts. Part 1 includes the present chapter and the next one on management history and theories. These two introductory chapters provide a framework for interpreting the management concepts and applications to come. Part 2 covers management concepts and principles; values, attitudes, and goals; resources; decision making; planning, implementing, and evaluating; and communication. Each chapter in Part 2 will elucidate the steps in the management process model presented in Figure 1.1. Part 3 on management applications has chapters on managing human resources, time, work and family, stress and fatigue, environmental resources, and finances. The book concludes in Part 4 with a chapter on future challenges. Each chapter begins with a quotation, a chapter outline, and a "Did You Know?" section and concludes with Web-based resources, a summary, key terms, review questions, and references. At the end of the book is a glossary and an index.

Web-Based Resources

Innumerable Web sites touch on management. World and U.S. population figures, along with social and economic information, can be obtained from **www.census.gov.** There are enough charts and statistics to answer nearly any question about demographic changes. An interesting feature of this site is a U.S. and world population update that occurs every five minutes so that you can watch the population grow.

Gallup polls on many topics relevant to life management for individuals and groups are available at **www.gallup.com**. Similarly, results of Roper polls are available at **www.roper.com**.

For news on the job market, specifically for job openings by area of the country or field of specialization, check **www.monster.com**. When one types in the word "family" or "consumer," over 5,000 job openings are shown, with new listings each week. Further updates on employment and the economy can be obtained from Dow Jones Business Information services at **www.dowjones.com**, and business news can be found at **www.cnbc.com**. National and international news services abound, providing articles on trends among singles, households, and families. Two examples are **www.c-span.org** and **www.cnn.com**.

Summary

Management is a way of thinking and acting. The study of management is motivated by curiosity and the desire to understand human behavior and, in particular, changes in family and household behavior. This chapter addressed the following questions:

- ◆ What is management?
- ◆ Why manage?
- ◆ Who manages?

Management is the process of using resources to achieve goals. Besides resources and goals, management involves many interacting elements, including problems, needs, wants, values, decision making, planning, implementing, communication, and feedback, all operating within an environmental context.

The unique contribution of management is the insight it provides into decision making and decision implementing. Management is necessary because it provides a sense of direction and purpose. Everyone manages, some with more skill than others. Many of the principles of management are timeless, but the application of management to everyday life is constantly changing. Examples of change include the dramatic increase in the number of single adults and the trend toward marrying at a later age. Different definitions of family and household were presented.

The evolving nature of society and technology has made management an increasingly necessary and far more complex subject. Given the environmental, economic, and social problems in the world today, the need for skilled managers at all levels has never been greater. Many challenges lie ahead for the thinker and the planner in all of us.

Key Terms

choice	implementing	needs
clarification	life management	planning
decision making	lifestyle	problems
family	management	resources
feedback	management process	standards
goals	management style	values
household(er)	management tools	wants

Review Questions

1. Why are there fewer people per household today?

2. Why does the management process involve more than decision making? What other factors or elements are involved? Why is the last step, evaluation, often ignored?

3. What fields of study have affected the study of management? Select one and explain its relevance to the field of resource management.

4. How does technology influence management style? Give an example of a technological change in the 20th or 21st centuries.

5. Given the American Red Cross definition of family and the U.S. Census definition of family, would college students sharing an apartment be considered a family? Would cohabitating homosexual or heterosexual couples sharing a house be considered a family? Explain your answers. If you are from a country other than the United States, what is the usual definition of family in your country?

References

Beck, M. (1992, December 7). The new middle age. *Newsweek,* 51.

Burton, J. (1992). Household technology: Implications for research and policy. *Journal of Family and Economic Issues,* 13(4), 383–394.

Covey, S. R. (1989). *The seven habits of highly effective people.* New York: Simon & Schuster.

Davis, A., & Smith, R. (2003, July 3). Judge Pollack's investor lectures. *The Wall Street Journal,* C1.

DeMerchant, E. (1993, February). Standards: An analysis of definitions, frameworks and implications. *Proceedings of the Eastern Regional Home Management-Family Economics Conference,* Blacksburg, VA.

Drucker, P. F. (1986). *The frontiers of management.* New York: Dutton.

Drucker, P. F. (1989). *The new realities.* New York: Harper & Row.

Drucker, P. F. (1999). *Management challenges for the 21st century.* New York: HarperCollins.

Fisher, H. S. (1992). *Anatomy of love: The natural history of monogamy, adultery, and divorce.* New York: Norton.

Frey, W. (2001, November). Seniors in suburbia. *American Demographics,* 18–20.

Goodman, A. (2002, May 29). Testimony before the select committee on lower Manhattan redevelopment, New York City Council, New York City.

Kaplan, L., & Hennon, C. (1992). Remarriage education: The personal reflections program. *Family Relations,* 41, 127–134.

Marshall, R. (1991). *The state of families, 3: Losing direction, families, human resource development, and economic performance.* Milwaukee, WI: Family Service America.

Maslow, A. (1954). *Motivation and personality.* New York: Harper & Row.

Mithers, C. (2003, July). What have we learned from living together? *Ladies' Home Journal,* 93.

Munro, B., & Munro, G. (2003). Definition of family. In J. J. Ponzetti, Jr. (Ed.), *International Encyclopedia of Marriage and Family.* New York: Macmillan Reference USA.

Nye, D. (1990). *Electrifying America: Social meanings of a new technology, 1880–1942.* Cambridge, MA: MIT Press.

Phone home. (2001, December). *American Demographics,* 18.

Rettig, K., & Bubolz, M. (1983). Perceptual indicators of family well-being. *Social Indicators Research,* 12, 417–438.

Saluter, A. F. (1990). Marital status and living arrangements: March 1990. *Current population reports,* Series P-20, No. 450. Washington, DC: Department of Commerce, Bureau of the Census, 1–13.

Seale, W. (1986). *The president's house.* Washington, DC: White House Historical Association.

Senge, P., Kleimer, A., Roberts, C., Ross, R., Roth, G., & Smith, B. (1999). *The dance of change.* New York: Doubleday.

Terhune, C., & Kahn, G. (2003, September 8). Coke lures Japanese customers with cellphone come-ons. *The Wall Street Journal,* B4.

The complete cell-phone guide. (2002, February). *Consumer Reports,* 14.

Umminger, A. (2003, August 18). They walk their way. *USA Today,* 4D.

Usdansky, M. (1992, May 30). Diverse fits nation better than normal. *USA Today.*

Wilson, B. (1994). Final thoughts. *Educom Review,* 29(1), 15.

Management History and Theories

MAIN TOPICS

Did you know that . . . ?

. . . 43 percent of Americans say cooking is their favorite pastime—second only to watching television.

. . . In 1987 the average household had 7 battery-operated appliances; today that number is 27.

Other things may change us, but we start and end with family.

—*Anthony Brandt*

Management provides a road map or guide. Various theories have been formulated to explain managerial behavior and to help us understand how and why people plan, decide, and act the way they do. This chapter explores the nature of theory and its application to management. It also covers the history of the study of resource management as it relates to individuals, households, and families, along with changes in homes. Across North America and Europe there has been a revival of interest in the old ways of doing things and of collecting household goods such as furnishings and appliances from the past or reproductions of such. Here is an example regarding vacuum cleaners:

> Store owners from Virginia to Oregon say they can barely keep them in stock. "As soon as I get one, it just flies out the door," says Istikar Ahmed, who runs a vacuum store in the Washington suburbs. . . . Joe De Maria, for instance, has shelled out more than $900 for vacuums during the past four years—he's got four—and each one has fallen short. Not only do they break down but he says they don't pick up the dirt left by his children and two hairy dogs. "The attachments are so short, you can't get under the couch," the Miami homeowner complains. What's his dream machine now? "My mother's old metal Kirby, which you could bang into the furniture, or throw down the stairs," he says. (Fletcher, 2002, p. W9)

Common household objects such as vacuum cleaners are part of the larger picture of how people live; although keeping a clean house may not be everyone's number one concern, it is something everyone has to deal with to some degree. A knowledge of the evolution of management theory (the ways and whys of doing things) provides a useful background for understanding the management process diagrammed in Figure 1.1, which is repeated here as Figure 2.1. This chapter specifically addresses the feedback and environmental components of the model.

HISTORY OF MANAGEMENT

The Early Years of Management

Although managers and management have existed since the beginning of organized civilization, the earliest records of management are found on the walls of cave dwellings in western Europe. These cave drawings indicate which members of the societal unit hunted, gathered food, and reared children. Over time around the globe, village centers sprang up as people went from subsisting on wild resources to farming. This more settled approach led to larger towns. Populations grew and with them the need for more advanced systems of food storage and fresh water access. Homes lasted longer and attention was paid to pottery and other forms of food display and storage and to stone carving and other forms of decoration. Much of what we know about these human ancestors and their households comes from archaeological digs that reveal the kinds of settlements people lived in, the cooking pots used, foods eaten, and ornamentation.

Much later, in ancient Greece and Rome, home management became the subject of philosophical discussions. Several Bible verses refer to the importance of keeping an orderly home. Since the Middle Ages, numerous books about household management have been published. A contemporary book

FIGURE 2.1
The Management Process Model

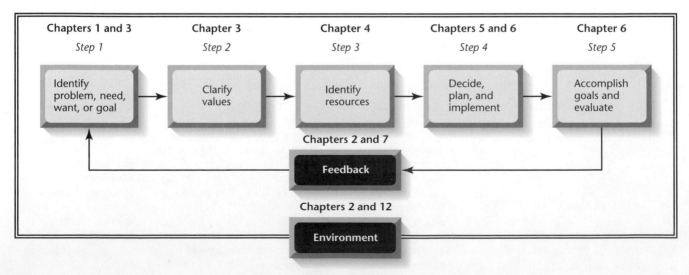

summarizes the household accounts of an estate in medieval England (Woolgar, 1993). Diaries and memoirs explain what it was like to live in previous eras. By the 18th century, for instance, standards of hygiene were undergoing a transformation. After trying out her new shower in 1799, a Philadelphia woman named Elizabeth Drinker noted in her diary that she tolerated the new experience "better than expected, not having been wet for 28 years" (Crossen, 2002).

Ben Franklin (1706–1790), inventor of the Franklin stove, bifocals, and the lightning rod, popularized the adage "time is money." He was also deputy postmaster in charge of the mails in the northern colonies. By 1792, the U.S. post office had a regular mail delivery schedule. In the 19th century, middle-class households commonly owned clocks, whereas in the previous century only the wealthy had clocks. The stopwatch, a timepiece that can be instantly started and stopped by the press of a button, was invented in the 1880s. New inventions were altering the way homes functioned and looked. The first vacuum cleaners were hand-pumped models of wood and canvas almost as big as coffee tables. One of the most welcome additions to homes was running water usually in the form of a kitchen sink with cold water.

Home management, or domestic management, emerged as a formal subject of study in the United States in the 19th century. High school and college courses covered a wide range of management topics. The courses and the home care books written for the general public offered advice for healthful living; among other things, they extolled the virtues of early rising, cleanliness, sunshine, and fresh air. The first textbook to mention household management in the title was Maria Parloa's *First Principles of Household Management and Cookery,* published in 1879. Parloa advised that "a bed that has been made up a week or more is not fit to sleep in; as moisture gathers, which often proves fatal to persons sleeping in one" (Parloa, 1879, p. 7). Ellen H. Richards, an American chemist and founder of the home economics movement, is credited with forming the bridge between scientific analysis and household management through guiding the discussions at the Lake Placid Conferences, held in New York from 1899 to 1908. During these years, the economy was growing, and the nation was prosperous; yet many Americans lived on farms, and life was hard. The labor force participation rate for men age 65 and over was 80 percent. "People literally worked until they died or until they couldn't work any more, retirement was a privilege of the well to do" (Willis & Young, 2003, p. 84).

Authors Lillian Gilbreth and Christine Frederick toured the United States and Europe on the lecture circuit spreading the word about the new scientific methods of efficient home management and household production (Gilbreth, 1927; Frederick, 1918). Frederick, based in New York and married to an advertising executive, designed a model kitchen in her home that is now on display at the Smithsonian's National Museum of American History and testified before Congress about the important role that women play as consumers. Gilbreth saw the home as a workplace and the homemaker as both worker and manager. She and her husband, Frank, a factory efficiency expert, had twelve children. Their lives were portrayed in his book, *Cheaper by the Dozen,* which formed the basis of two movies. When Frank died in 1924, Lillian took up his cause and applied work-saving methods to the home. She designed the Gilbreth management desk that was displayed at the 1933 World's Fair. Her goal was to increase productivity, reduce drudgery, and accumulate "happiness minutes," which she thought of as time spent in leisure or creative pursuits (Smithsonian, 2000). She redesigned kitchens based on photographs of operations in the room and, in later life, applied her knowledge to bettering living conditions for the disabled.

Nationwide, government- and industry-sponsored experimental kitchens and college residential laboratories (more commonly known as home management houses) were set up to record the time required and the human and mechanical energy used to perform household tasks. Two of the earliest colleges with residence courses were Stout Institute in Wisconsin (now the University of Wisconsin, Stout) and the University of Illinois. Florida State University was unique in being the first college to build a house specifically for home management. The usual way it worked was that during students' senior year they moved into the home management house or residence for a semester; where they experienced living on a budget, record keeping, time and meal management, and other forms of efficiency. They shared rooms and simulated family and household conditions. Some campuses offered multiple houses or apartments and different levels of living conditions and budgets. With changes in college life and professional training, the need for this type of experience lessened and by the 1970s and 1980s most campuses transformed the houses into another use such as child-care centers or faculty offices or removed them to make way for parking lots or classroom buildings.

When management practitioners such as Frederick and Gilbreth applied techniques that were being used in the workplace to the home, they were emulating the work of Frederick Taylor (1856–1915), among others. Known as the father of scientific management, Taylor was famous for his time and motion studies. He proposed scientific management principles designed to maximize production efficiency. By carefully studying the most efficient ways assembly-line jobs could be performed and implementing changes to increase efficiency, he was able to achieve significant productivity improvements (Taylor, 1911). Taylor revolutionized assembly lines. He was not afraid of work. He was so willing to pitch in that when confronted with a blocked drain in a factory, he put on overalls, tied shoes to his elbows and knees, and crawled through the muck to remove the obstruction (Wooldridge, 2000). He believed in the carrot (reward) and stick (punishment) approach. Taylor promoted time clocks, synchronization, and anything that would speed up work. Some workers thought he went too far and criticized him for depersonalizing the workplace. His influence went beyond business: His scientific management principles were applied to nonprofit organizations and government agencies and facilities, including the Watertown Arsenal of the U.S. Army. Others observing his work applied the same principles to the home by redesigning floor plans, standardizing and updating equipment, and suggesting better work methods (e.g., saving steps and using less time and human energy in such tasks as keeping household accounts, making beds, washing dishes, and cooking). These improved work methods in the home, known as **work simplification,** became an integral part of the study of management.

American homes were changing rapidly. Of course, regional and individual variations existed, but in general the time period between 1900 and the present can be divided into three eras—premodern, modern, and postmodern. Tables 2.1, 2.2, and 2.3 summarize the main characteristics of household production and consumption patterns in representative decades. Notice that in 1900 most houses did not have indoor plumbing. Although Thomas Edison had invented the incandescent lightbulb in 1879, only 8 percent of U.S. homes had electricity by 1907 (Cowan, 1983). In 1909, even the houses that had electricity did not have the number of wall outlets we are used to today, so wires and cords for appliances had to be screwed into the central light fixture or

© Bettmann/CORBIS

Philadelphia-born Frederick Winslow Taylor, the well-educated son of a lawyer, became a machinist whose factory-floor observations prompted him to decry workers who "soldiered"—the slackers of his day. His Principles of Scientific Management, *published in 1911, offered solutions for improving industrial efficiency, from piecework incentives to time cards and worksheets.*

TABLE 2.1
**Household Production/
Consumption System I:
Premodern (early 1900s)**

Typical families in the early 1900s made most of their own clothes, food, and household cleaning products. They were likely to buy such basics as soap, flour, and baking powder.

◆ *Household work:* Hands-on, arduous, specific, repetitive.

◆ *Kitchen/laundry equipment:* Inside sink (probably only cold water), stove, washtub or wringer washer, possibly an icebox.

◆ *Bathroom equipment:* Outdoor privy, indoor slop buckets, bathtubs or buckets for washing filled with water heated on the stove; the rich and/or city dwellers might have indoor plumbing.

◆ *Servants:* One servant for every 15 households.*

◆ *Shopping:* Home delivery is common—doctors, peddlers, and tailors come to the home; groceries, ice, baked goods, and dairy products are all delivered. At stores, shop owners take products off the shelf and hand them to the customer. Catalog shopping becomes popular; catalogs offer everything from medicines to whole houses. Beginning of exposure to media advertising and brands.

◆ *Electricity:* Newly introduced, rare in homes except those of the rich, particularly those who live in cities. Mostly used for lighting.

◆ *Lighting:* Kerosene (mostly lower and working class, rural), gas (upper, middle class, urban), candles, and some electricity.

*R. S. Cowan, *More Work for Mother* (New York: Basic Books, 1983), pp. 99 and 240.

lightbulb socket. Many people had been brought up in tall Victorian houses with parlors in the front and kitchens in the back or in the basement. Upper-class homes would have been filled with bric-a-brac and art brought back from trips abroad. President Theodore Roosevelt, as well as other wealthy people of the time, went on safaris and decorated their homes with stuffed animal heads and bear and tiger rugs—souvenirs of their visits and their shooting prowess.

People were collectors more than decorators. Kitchen and laundry equipment were primitive in the premodern era, and housework was backbreaking labor. Furthermore, it increasingly had to be done by the sole adult woman in the household because by the late 19th century, servants were disappearing: They could find more lucrative employment in the growing number of factories and shops. American families were also experiencing a radical change in the way things were bought and made. According to historian Susan Strasser, the period from 1885 to 1915 was a time of "massive transformation": "During this period there was a transformation in the factory and in the distribution process. All the really major innovations came in during this time" (Goldsmith, 1993, p. 47). Introduction of the automobile created a veritable revolution in transportation, which led to great changes in the marketplace

Courtesy of the Hoover Company, North Canton, Ohio

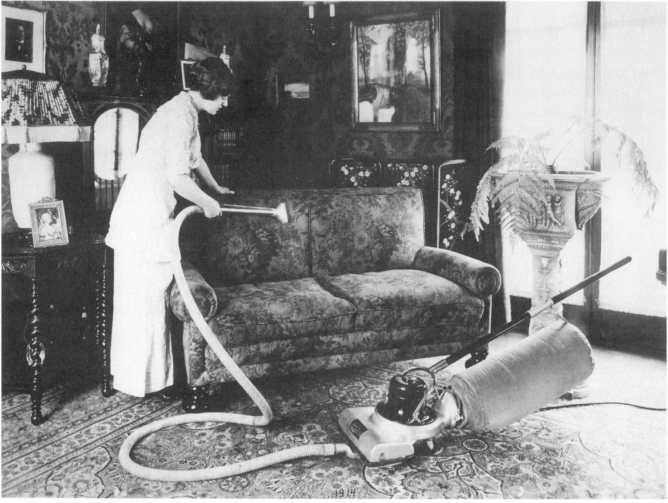

Many of the early household technologies such as this vacuum were heavy and cumbersome. (Courtesy of the Hoover Company, North Canton, Ohio.)

and consumer demand. There were about 8,000 cars (horseless carriages) in 1900 and less than 10 miles of concrete road in the United States. By 1910 the automobile had changed everything, including what was inside homes as well as the actual location of homes: Living in the suburbs now made more sense. The gap between rural and urban life began to narrow, and this trend would continue through the 1920s and 1930s.

One of the primary changes affecting the home was the switch from making most goods at home to purchasing mass-produced items at the store. Things that used to take all day to make (e.g., soap and bread) could now be bought in minutes. A time revolution, as well as an economic, social, and technological one, was taking place. The value of light, air, and sunshine was revisited. Heavy draperies were replaced with pulled-back, lighter curtains. Homes were redesigned. A popular style introduced in the Midwest, especially around the Chicago area, and throughout the South was the bungalow, with its more horizontal lines and one or one and a half stories:

It incorporated a number of progressive ideals of the early 1900s—the straightforward use of materials, an informal way of living, and accessibility to outdoors.

Typical families in the mid-20th century bought most of their clothing, food, and household cleaning products from stores.

- ◆ *Household work:* Hands-on and machine-aided, somewhat arduous, specific, repetitive.
- ◆ *Kitchen/laundry equipment:* Sink (with hot and cold water), stove, refrigerator, washing machine, perhaps a dryer and a dishwasher.
- ◆ *Bathroom equipment:* Sink, toilet, bathtub/shower (one or two bathrooms in the average new home).
- ◆ *Servants:* One to every 42 households.*
- ◆ *Shopping:* Home delivery less common than in the early 1900s. Customers serve themselves at stores. Moderate exposure to media advertising and brands. Shopping centers begin.
- ◆ *Electricity:* In over 80 percent of homes.†
- ◆ *Lighting:* Electric most common, kerosene still used in some rural areas.

*R. S. Cowan, *More Work for Mother* (New York: Basic Books, 1983), pp. 99 and 240.
†*Historical Statistics of the United States* (Washington, D.C.: U.S. Government Printing Office, 1975).

TABLE 2.2
Household Production/ Consumption System II: Modern (1950s)

The first Bungalow owners were interested in affordable homes that would both simplify their lives and allow them to enjoy the outdoors as part of their daily routines. Most were middle-class families who felt secure enough about their social standing that they didn't need to use shelter as an outward display of their worth. (Connolly & Wasserman, 2002, p. 8)

In 1900, the economy was strong and prices were low. It was a good time to be a consumer. Sanitation and health improved. Books and collectibles were kept clean behind glass doors. By the 1920s chrome, metal, and glass infiltrated homes—what was sleek, modern, and curved was preferred. Pianos provided entertainment in the home, as did record players and radios in later years. Outside the home, movie theaters sprang up. Hollywood lifestyles portrayed on the screen and in the press brought a new level of glamour and sophistication to rural areas. By the 1930s central air conditioning added comfort to high-rise buildings.

From 1910 to 1940, the United States and other industrialized nations saw a great expansion of high school education. Students were encouraged to graduate from high school. After graduation they went to work in towns and in factories.

In the 1930s and 1940s, daily chores in middle-class homes included shoveling coal into furnaces, washing and drying dishes, carrying laundry out to be hung on clotheslines, canning fruits and vegetables, and mending clothes. Books of the time still carried very specific instructions on the "right way to live." For example, *The Settlement Cook Book* (1948 edition) begins with the proper way to run a household, including how to air out a room by lowering the upper sash of one window and raising the lower sash of the opposite window. There were even sections on the proper feeding of infants and invalids, including this piece of advice: "Use the daintiest dishes in the house. Place a clean napkin on the tray and, if possible, a fresh flower." Small children were to have cooked cereal at seven o'clock and diluted orange juice at nine o'clock. In looking back, some people cringe at the idea of this much routine, while others revel in it. "The notion of a domestic life that purrs along, with routines and order and carefully delineated standards, is endlessly appealing to me. It is also quite foreign, because I am not a housewife. I am an 'at-home mother,' and the difference between the two is vast," says contemporary writer, Caitlin Flanagan (2003, p. 141). Flanagan says that being an at-home mother today has little to do with the house itself and much more to do with the fact that the home is where the children happen to be.

The end of World War II brought an all time high in housing demand. Color, frills, and the latest appliances became important after the austere war years. By the 1950s, most houses had indoor plumbing, electricity, a modern kitchen, and laundry equipment. New homes sported large picture windows in the front. The sole television in the home drew the family from the kitchen into the living room. As shopping centers began to spring up, home delivery became less common, and families drove to the store to shop.

In the 1960s, the casual lifestyle came into vogue in the form of fondue pots, shag rugs, conversation pits in living rooms, and barbecue pits outside. Gold and avocado green invaded kitchens and the rest of the house. By the end of the decade, psychedelic colors and lively prints came into vogue. Color televisions replaced the old black and whites. The 1970s and 1980s saw a return of interest in country style décor, quilts, and collectibles, leading to an eclecticism or mix of styles popular through the 1990s. Great rooms replaced separate living and family rooms. Master bedrooms and bathrooms became master suites; and kitchens increased in size. Microwave ovens were added to the usual appliance package of stoves, refrigerators, and dishwashers.

The bungalow, with its low-slung style and more casual appearance, was a departure from the tall Victorians it replaced.

© Photodisc Red/Getty Images

The postmodern era, dating from the 1990s to the present, has seen vast changes in household functioning and design. By 2003, the average new American home was 2300 square feet, and four bedrooms and three bathrooms became the norm in new construction. Homes were considerably larger than the 1950s house. The average U.S. household now has 2.6 televisions. Computers, cell phones, and the Internet have changed how families live and communicate. Household equipment has become more sophisticated, and shopping easier, but individuals and families still devote many hours each week to household tasks and food preparation.

These household and consumption changes have been accompanied by changes in the field of management, which has expanded beyond its initial emphasis on efficiency and economy in the home to include much more. No longer is management primarily concerned with household tasks and the streamlining of work methods in the home, although it should be noted that the home continues to be central to people's lives. As a basic human need in Maslow's hierarchy (see Chapter 1), shelter will always be at the forefront of human endeavor. When asked which one or two of a dozen items says the most about you, Americans rank home number one, ahead of their jobs, hobbies, and the like. As people age, they place more value on their home ("There's No Place Like Home," 1997). However, the point is that management has progressed to encompass a greater life view including a myriad of individual, family, and societal concerns from teenage pregnancy to elder care. In other words, today, the discipline is defined more as life management than

Typical families in the early 21st century rely heavily on stores for food, clothing, and household cleaning products and on restaurants for meals. Purchase of prepared and frozen food is common.

◆ *Household work:* Hands-on and machine-aided, somewhat arduous, specific, repetitive.

◆ *Kitchen/laundry equipment:* Sink, stove, dishwasher, microwave oven, refrigerator, washing machine, dryer.

◆ *Bathroom equipment:* Sink, toilet, bathtub/shower (multiple bathrooms and sinks common in average new home; also whirlpool baths widely available).

◆ *Servants:* Rare, partially replaced by child-care centers and cleaning services.

◆ *Shopping:* Home delivery expands with toll-free catalog shopping by phone and the use of Internet shopping using computers. Stores with customer self-service usual. Malls, multipurpose superstores common. Pervasive exposure to media advertising and brands.

◆ *Electricity:* In nearly all homes.*

◆ *Lighting:* Electricity most common.

*98 percent of all Americans have telephones, electricity, and a flush toilet.

TABLE 2.3
Household Production/ Consumption System III: Postmodern (early 21st century)

as home management. Accordingly, it is referred to as resource management or, simply, as management.

As a way to provide a prospective on how times have changed, the Cato Institute in Washington, DC, lists the following comparisons between American life now and a century ago:

◆ Four times as many adults are getting their high school diplomas.

◆ Six times as many women now have bachelor's degrees.

◆ More than 70 percent of Americans have at least one automobile, a VCR, a microwave oven, air conditioning, and a washer and dryer.

◆ Accidental deaths have dropped by 61 percent, despite all the additional cars and airplanes and the millions of people using them.

Although not every social, educational, and housing change can be documented here, there can be no doubt that life in the United States has changed in a way that most people would define as progress. In the last few years a resurgence of interest in the home has been evidenced by television channels and programs devoted entirely to home remodeling and repair, interior design, and cooking; by the growth in real estate and the remodeling market; by the proliferation of giant home supply stores; and by the increase in the number of online and print sources on housing and home design. The garage is the next frontier. The percentage of two-car garages in U.S. households went from 48 percent in 1973 to 64 percent in 2001; and 18 percent of 2001 households had three-car garages.

> In a national survey of homeowners, Whirlpool found that the garage basically functions as America's junkroom, holding all the items the house won't—or can't. . . . Whirlpool sees the garage as the next master bath—a room just waiting to be "accessorized": But don't use that term around men, its target market. Whirlpool calls the new line "Gladiator," and nearly every item features a rugged design made of steel. The devices range from a small, portable fridge that basically functions as a beer box to an interlocking "gear wall" designed to replace Pegboard. (Hallinan, 2002, p. B1)

It's clear that changes in the interplay between homes and the people who live in them are not lost on designers, retailers, and researchers. Ted Selker, an associate professor at the Massachusetts Institute of Technology, says, "The kitchen of the future for me is about creating a value and having relationships mesh with how we work in the home . . . to make cooking for four at home more fun than having takeout or more fun than going to a fancy restaurant" (Sessa, 2000, p. D4). He adds that the kitchen table "has always been a place where people gather," but today, "people have been leaving the kitchen and going to the bedroom or wherever the computer is" (Sessa, 2000, p. R20). One idea being explored in the MIT project is to turn the kitchen table into the computer center, thus making the kitchen once again the family center. Another design idea underway is combining the dining room with the study, family room, or sunroom and making that the place for the computers, homework, and other activities. Harnessing technology and creating multipurpose rooms are not new endeavors; what is new is the number and types of combinations being explored.

For a list of landmark books and other references, consult the end of this chapter. The list is provided as an aid to further study and as a way for you to appreciate the research and theoretical work that forms the basis for your studies in this field.

Four Eras of Management

To help describe management's development in the 20th century, several theorists have organized its history into chronological categories. For example, Gross, Crandall, and Knoll (1980) conceptualized home management as having six stages of development, and Berger (1984) used these stages as a framework for reviewing management research between 1909 and 1984. Carole Vickers introduced a simpler version that divided family/home management history into four principal eras:

1. *Era one (c. 1900–1930s):* Health, sanitation, hygiene, and the importance of household production as a legitimate form of economic production

2. *Era two (c. 1940s–early 1950s):* Household equipment, efficiency, step saving, task simplification, and standardized work units

3. *Era three (c. 1950s–1960s):* Family values, goals, standards, resources, decision making, organization and process, optimization of families, gradual swing away from work performance in the home

4. *Era four (c. 1970s–1980s):* Development of a systems framework emphasizing the interconnections among family, home, and the greater society. Leading theorists Ruth Deacon and Francille Firebaugh (1988) showed how systems theory could be applied to individual and family management problems.

To extend the eras delineated by Vickers to today: A systems framework still dominates the study of management. In addition, theorists have become increasingly aware of the role economics plays in the management behavior and choices of individuals and families. Later sections of this chapter will examine the contributions of systems and economic theory to management in more detail.

Legislation Policy and Research

The evolution of management in the 20th and 21st centuries has been affected by legislation, policy, and research as well as by technological, economic, and societal changes. In 1914, Congress passed the Smith-Lever Act to improve life in rural America by providing funds for extension programs through the Department of Agriculture. The Smith-Hughes Act, passed in 1917, provided funding for the training of teachers in primary and secondary schools in what was then called home economics. In 1925, the Purnell Act extended the Smith-Lever Act and provided funds for economic and sociological investigations to develop and improve rural home life. The grants were administered by the U.S. Bureau of Home Economics, then part of the U.S. Department of Agriculture (USDA). Currently, the USDA, as well as many other government agencies in the United States and in other countries, associations, and private foundations fund management research for both urban and rural populations. Employment opportunities in resource management exist in government at the county, state, and federal level through the Cooperative Extension Service administered through the USDA.

The 1920s saw a great deal of discussion about the nature of management from a variety of sources, including business, government, and education. For example, attendees of the first worldwide Management Congress held in Prague in 1922 concluded that management principles were universal and could be applied to a variety of business and nonbusiness situations (Drucker, 1999). Since then, numerous other conferences, acts, and policies have had an impact on individuals and families, and many of these will be discussed throughout the book. Interest in improving human rights surged worldwide from the 1970s to the 1990s. And, certainly, consumer protection legislation improved greatly over the last century.

During the 20th century, the field of resource management emphasized raising living standards, quality of life, and well-being through a variety of means, including improvements in health and nutrition, welfare, child labor laws, education, and work leave policies. A topic such as welfare reform comprises many factors critical to its success, such as prevention of child abuse and neglect, financial support for children, child care, availability of transportation, education and employment, use of social indicators for evaluation and policy analysis, and community-based planning. Each of these requires research to determine human needs and the best ways of addressing them.

Research is the collection, processing, and analysis of information. Because management falls within the realm of applied social science, the results of research studies should be useful and made available to citizens and policy makers. Collection methods include survey, observation, mechanical measurement, focus groups, archival research, physiological measures, diaries or records, and laboratory and field experiments. A combination of methods is often used to cross-check results.

What topics are covered in management research? According to Israelsen, most management research falls into one of two categories: (1) financial/economic resources and (2) human/household resources:

> Specific financial resources research topics have included income and expenditure, impact of women's employment upon family income, financial management, budgeting, debt, saving, financial security and retirement, financial satisfaction, financial support from kin, adolescents and money, determination of living standards, marriage and money issues (resource exchange, conflict over money, marital adjustment and money), economic impact of divorce upon women, and financial decision-making.
>
> The study of human and household resources has historically dealt with topics such as the effect of women's employment upon family life, division of household work between family members, time use/management, household production, household tasks, household satisfaction, household management styles, adolescents and work, and decision-making. (1990, p. 4)

One of the most-studied topics has been time use. Researchers have explored time spent on housework, home-based paid work, and child care; who does what and when; and how factors such as employment, income, and size of family affect time use, demands, and household production and consumption (see, for example, Bryant, 1992; Davey, 1971; Goebel & Hennon, 1982; Goldsmith, 1977; Hafstrom & Paynter, 1991; Hafstrom & Schram, 1983; McCullough & Zick, 1992; Owen, 1991; Sanik, 1981; Schnittgrund, 1980; Stafford, 1983; Walker & Woods, 1976; Warren, 1940; Wilson, 1929; Winter, Puspitawati, Heck, & Stafford, 1993). A recent study revealed that for 21-year-olds,

> Telecommunications, television, and the Internet are so ubiquitous in their lives that they bounce seamlessly from one to another, sometimes consuming several media simultaneously. MTV found evidence of this when it recently asked 18- to 24-year-olds how many hours a day they spend surfing the Web, downloading music and e-mailing friends. The company's researchers were shocked when they added up the hours and found that the average time totaled more than 24 hours a day. "Young people manage to squeeze 31 hours into a 24-hour period," says Betsy Franck, executive vice president of research and planning for MTV Networks, in New York. "They'll read a magazine while watching TV while going online. They're the masters of multitasking." (Weiss, 2003, pp. 31–32)

Researchers also commonly investigate issues of safety, health, and economic well-being. They have turned their attention to the interchange between work and family, including the effects of home-based business on the family.

THEORY OVERVIEW

The study of management is a combination of theory, concepts, technique, research, and practice. There is not one management theory or framework, but several. Management is an interdisciplinary field that borrows concepts and theories from related disciplines (see Chapter 1). **Theory** is an organized system of ideas or beliefs that can be measured; it is a system of assumptions or principles. The word *theory* comes from the Greek verb *theorein* (to behold or contemplate). We form theories, for example, when we wonder why a couple has decided to marry or divorce. We look for clues to the outcome—why is the couple compatible or not compatible? A theory summarizes what is known about a phenomenon and permits the formation of **hypotheses,** or predictions about future occurrences. For example, a mother may hypothesize that buying back-to-school clothes for her 13-year-old daughter is a waste of time unless they shop together, because she has observed that whatever she buys on her own will not fit her daughter or suit her taste. The mother's prediction of her daughter's response is based on past purchasing mistakes. Likewise, other theories and hypotheses about human behavior are based on observations, past experience, and research.

Theories are useful because they reduce wasted time and effort and provide ways of structuring one's thoughts and knowledge about behaviors. Manual Castells, author of *The Information Age* and a professor at the University of California at Berkeley, says that all major trends of change are related and that we can make sense of their interrelationship. Further, he says, "I believe, in spite of a long tradition of sometimes tragic intellectual errors, that observing, analyzing and theorizing is a way of helping to build a different, better world. Not by providing the answers that will be specific to each society . . . but by raising some relevant questions" (1996).

Functions of Theory

The primary function of theory is to organize observations and other information so that individuals can make sense of the events that occur around them. For example, researchers can observe the way people behave in situations requiring the allocation of resources, planning, and the implementation and evaluation of decisions. A theory of management not only attempts to explain the observed behavior of people in general but also seeks to provide an understanding of a single individual's or family's behavior. Comprehension of behavior provides the basis for two other functions of theory: (1) to predict future behavior (as in the mother/daughter clothes-buying example) and (2) to control or alter behavior (Arndt, 1984). People are constantly making predictions about their own and others' behavior. For example, perhaps we assume we will like or dislike oysters based on a past experience of eating them. Most predictions are so automatic that we don't even think about them. When we look at a restaurant menu, we unconsciously skip over the salad section if we never eat salads. However, when an unconscious prediction turns out differently than expected (e.g., a friend who is always late shows up ahead of time), we realize that we have made a prediction and that the prediction was wrong. In the case of the early arriving friend, we are pleasantly surprised.

Theory of behavior has many aspects. Predicting behavior is one aspect; controlling behavior is another. Although the word *control* sometimes has a negative connotation, as in brainwashing or mind control, in management it has a more prosaic meaning. **Controlling** refers to the things people do to check their course of action. For example, you may be concerned over whether you have enough money in your bank account to cover your credit cards or whether you can get a better grade on the next test. These concerns involve both predictions and possible alterations of behavior.

As a final comment on the function of theory, consider Kurt Lewin's statement that "There is nothing so practical as a good theory." Theories provide a useful way to organize information. Without theories the prediction of future events would be nearly impossible.

Theories Ahead

Before a new theory can be promoted, the theorist must first develop definitions of key terms, formulate statements or assumptions, and then test the theory. One of the problems in developing and explaining theories is that they are abstract, but once a theory is put into action and the subsequent behavior can be observed, the thought processes behind the behavior become more understandable. Because so many studies and books have used systems theory, most of this chapter will now focus on its components and applications. The remainder of the chapter will examine the application of economic theory—specifically, optimization, satisficing, and risk aversion—to the study of management. Other theories specific to resource exchange, time, stress, and fatigue will be covered in future chapters.

SYSTEMS THEORY

The dynamic and ongoing nature of systems theory makes it particularly applicable to managerial thought and behavior. One of the reasons systems theory has endured is its versatility—it fits nearly every situation. The principle underlying systems theory is that the whole is greater than the sum of its parts. This emphasis on the whole and the interconnectedness of its different parts is appropriate for the eclectic, interdisciplinary field of management. Also, since individuals and families are part of larger behavioral and environmental systems, it makes sense to view them as part of a whole rather than as isolated units. **Systems theory** emphasizes not only interconnectedness but also the interactions among different systems. It focuses on the behavior of feedback and its complexity. The circle in the drawing above represents the circular nature of systems.

A **system** is an integrated set of parts that function together for some end purpose or result. Systems may be composed of living or nonliving things. Because management focuses on human behavior, the emphasis in this book is on living systems in the context of environments—in particular, the home, work, and community environments. A system as a whole has characteristics that set it apart from other systems. For example, a family is a system. Families have things in common with other families, such as streets, neighborhoods, or schools, but at the same time they have distinct traditions, ways of living, and consumption patterns. The place or point where independent systems or diverse groups interact is called the **interface.** A doctor's office may serve as the interface between a patient's home and medical services.

Boundaries are the limits or borders between systems. They separate one domain from another. Everyone has personal and family boundaries. Boundaries may be visible, as in fences and doors, or invisible, as in rules of behavior or unmarked borderlines between properties. For example, young children learn early in life where their yard stops and their neighbor's begins. They carry this lesson about boundaries into adulthood. Thus, boundaries maintain functions and influence human behavior.

Homes and workplaces are filled with visible and invisible boundaries. One of the survival skills necessary for any new employee is to learn where the boundaries are—who talks to whom, how flexible lunch breaks are, and which doors are kept open and which remain closed. In a home situation, consider how quickly visiting relatives learn house rules and behavior, such as when breakfast is ready, who gets the bathroom first, and how loud and how long the television can be played. The boundaries of a system determine what is allowed and what is not.

Open and Closed Families

Some families are more open to the outside environment than other families; in other words, they more freely exchange information and materials with outside influences. To use systems terminology, families can be categorized as mostly morphogenic or morphostatic. **Morphogenic system**s are adaptive to change and are relatively open. In an open system, matter and energy are freely exchanged between the system and its environment. Its boundaries are permeable. In contrast, **morphostatic systems** are resistant to change. They are stable and relatively closed.

A relatively open family may have neighborhood children in and out of the house much of the day, chat with neighbors often, spend a lot of time on the telephone, entertain often, and leave the blinds open. A relatively closed family may not know neighbors' names, while keeping the blinds shut and staying to themselves. Even without meeting the new family on the block, neighbors may be able to surmise something about their relative openness by the changes they make to the yard or the exterior appearance of the house. At the same time, a quick prediction based only on appearances may turn out to be wrong. A seven-foot-high fence may be a sign that a family is closed or may simply indicate the presence of a large dog.

Although a family's overall style will be open or closed, variations exist within families, and boundaries can exist between family members. For example, one member of a family may not speak to another. Some family members may be very open and gregarious, whereas others are more private and take a more contemplative approach to life. Within families, each member sets her or his own boundaries of space and privacy. Conflict can occur when boundaries are not respected. Think how often the plots of television soap operas revolve around a violation of privacy, such as parents reading a teenager's diary or mail or one family member's overhearing another's supposedly private conversation.

In addition, situations can alter the way a family interacts with others and their environment. For example, a family crisis can turn a relatively open family into a closed family, at least temporarily. Closure may be a protective mechanism until an adjustment period has passed. Systems theory emphasizes the adaptive nature of families.

Subsystems and System Elements

A **subsystem** is a part of a larger system. Individuals and families are subsystems of communities. Communities are subsystems of counties, which are subsystems of states, and so on. Each system at each level has a reason for existing. This interconnectedness of systems is the reason management is no longer limited to the infrastructure of the home; theorists realize that decisions made in the home ultimately affect the community, the country, and the world and vice versa. For example, families and economic institutions have always been closely related. Families supply work and society supplies wages that families use to buy goods and services and pay taxes. Thus, each subsystem affects other systems. This emphasis on how the interaction of parts affects the whole is the essence of systems theory.

Inputs, Throughputs, and Outputs

Management has borrowed several systems terms from computer terminology and applied them to the individual and the family. Three of these terms—inputs, throughputs, and outputs—form the basic elements in systems theory as it is applied to management. **Inputs** are whatever is brought into the system (i.e., things, ideas, information). The processing of inputs is called **throughput,** or transformation. Any system is subject to a succession of different states, and the transitions from one state to another are called **transformations** (Sieburg, 1985). The term **outputs** refers to the end results, or products, leftovers, and waste. Figure 2.2 presents a managerial action model showing the interaction of inputs, throughputs, and outputs. In the model, inputs such as resources and demands are transformed through planning, decision making, facilitating, and other throughputs into the outputs of met demands, altered resources, and satisfaction/dissatisfaction. **Demands** are

FIGURE 2.2
Managerial Action Using the Systems Approach

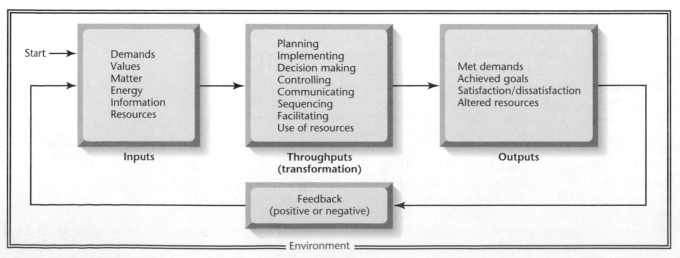

events or goals that require action. For example, if a landlord demands that rent be paid on time, tenants need to respond to this demand. *Facilitating* means to make something easier. Facilitation helps move the managerial process along.

Sequencing occurs when one thing follows another, as in a series of events. For example, scenes in a play follow in sequence. In resource management, events occur in sequence to ensure a successful outcome. Before writing a check to the landlord, tenants determine that they have enough money in their checking accounts to cover the rent. This process is facilitated if the tenants have kept their accounts balanced and their records up-to-date. Calculating whether they have enough money in the account after they have written checks for the rent would be placing events out of sequence.

Sharpe and Winter (1991) applied inputs, throughputs (transformations), and outputs to the concept of managerial effectiveness. They hypothesize that effective management leads to satisfactory outcomes but that there are many potential ways to be a more effective manager. For example, they hypothesize that managerial effectiveness increases when the manager has goals (inputs) that are clear, actionable, and verifiable and when the manager generates workable alternatives (transformations). Increased efficiency in the use of time and evaluation are two output hypotheses. These hypotheses illustrate how input, throughput, and output can be applied to management.

Feedback

Feedback occurs when part of the output is returned to the input in the form of information. The term *feedback* was introduced in Chapter 1 as part of the management process diagrammed in Figure 1.1. It also appeared earlier in this chapter in Figure 2.1. Figure 2.3 is a model that focuses specifically on the feedback loop. This model begins with a current assessment of the performance or situation and then proceeds to the establishment of objectives and goals. As in most management models, an evaluation component leads to further feedback. The feedback loop is important because it reinforces the concept that feedback affects future decisions and the allocation of resources. The model in Figure 2.3 also demonstrates that feedback is not an end in itself, but a process or operation.

Feedback can be positive or negative. In general conversation, the words *positive* and *negative* connote good and bad, but in systems terminology the words are used differently. **Positive feedback** is information put into the system that anticipates and promotes change; thus, it indicates that a new

FIGURE 2.3
Model of the Feedback Loop in Management

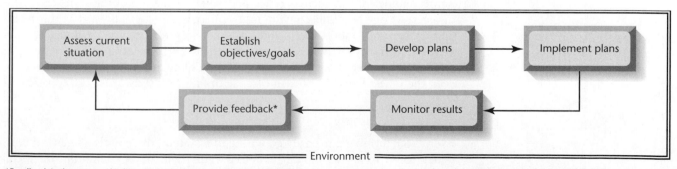

*Feedback is the return of information about the result of managerial action.

course of action is needed. **Negative feedback** is information put into the system that indicates that the system is deviating from its normal course and that corrective measures may be necessary if the desired steady state is to be maintained. Individuals and families use feedback to make future decisions. For example, negative feedback may reinforce a previous decision as being correct and emphasize that no further change is needed.

To illustrate positive feedback, consider the situation of John, a college student who receives a B+ on a midterm exam in a course where the grade is based on the midterm and the final exam. Since John wants to get an A in the course, his midterm grade indicates that he will have to study harder for the final to earn an A in the course. Therefore, the B+ grade (although it is a disappointment) gives John positive feedback. Since he enjoys the class and thinks he is capable of getting an A, he plans to study harder to improve his grade. Kevin, sitting next to John, also gets a B+ on the midterm, but he decides to put his energies elsewhere and is prepared to settle for a B in the course. Thus, the test grade gives Kevin negative feedback; he chooses to maintain the system by studying at his current pace rather than by intensifying his work. Feedback serves an important function. People use feedback to learn whether they are doing and saying the right things. Their future decisions hinge on the type of feedback they receive and how they act on that feedback. The concept of feedback will be covered more extensively in the chapter on communication.

Entropy

According to systems theory, each system has a tendency to run down and possibly misfunction as its energy flow ebbs and becomes less structured. This tendency toward disorder or randomness is called **entropy.** It is more likely to occur in a closed system than in an open system because a closed system receives few inputs from outside and thus has no source for renewed energy (Sieburg, 1985). For example, an executive who works 60-hour weeks and eventually wears down and needs a vacation is experiencing entropy. The vacation revitalizes the executive, and she returns with renewed energy and vigor. In a system, entropy can refer to a lack of energy as well as a lack of information. Entropy unchecked leads to disorganization and disruption; order is destroyed.

Murphy's Law and Systems Theory

Plenty of attention is paid to various rules and laws that influence our lives. Murphy's Law is named after an Air Force captain who noticed during rocket-sled deceleration tests that a crucial gauge had been wired wrong and summarized: "If there's more than one way to do a job and one of those will end in disaster, then somebody will do it that way" (Edwards, 2002, p. 72). Even a nontechnological toy, such as roller skates, left at the top of the stairs can spell disaster. As our homes become more complex technologically and as this technology becomes more interlocking, the chances for something going wrong increase. Murphy's Law most simply stated is "if something can go wrong, it will." A more specific explanation of Murphy's Law is that "in complex systems even the tiniest flaw can cause a cascade of failures" (Edwards, 2002, p. 72).

Homeostasis

Even though things can easily go wrong in a system, there is also a general tendency for it to try to remain balanced. This tendency to maintain balance, called **homeostasis,** works as a control device. When something gets out of control, tension is created, and the system becomes unbalanced, triggering the homeostasis mechanism. For example, people who have a Monday through Friday workweek use the weekend to renew their sense of balance and get their home and family life back in order. They run errands, answer mail, wash clothes, mow their lawns, and spend time with their families and friends. By Sunday night, they hope they will have achieved a feeling of homeostasis—a sense that things are back under control and in order for the week ahead.

Equifinality and Multifinality

The concepts of equifinality and multifinality are also important in systems theory. **Equifinality** refers to the phenomenon in which different circumstances and opportunities may lead to similar outcomes. **Multifinality** refers to the phenomenon in which the same initial circumstances or conditions may lead to different conclusions or outcomes. For example, consider the situation of two friends, Brett and Nick, who are high school seniors deciding which college to attend. Although they have been accepted by the same colleges and have the same backgrounds and career goals, Brett chooses to stay at home and attend a community college, and Nick chooses to go away to a four-year college. This different outcome given the same initial conditions is an example of multifinality. Now consider the situation of Megan and Tia, two students who have never met. Even though they have totally different backgrounds and ambitions, they end up choosing the same college—an example of equifinality, a similar outcome given different initial conditions.

Equifinality and multifinality are useful concepts because they illustrate the complex nature of management. Different outcomes, given the same initial surface factors, may indicate that other factors are at work—not apparent to the outside observer. For example, individual tastes, preferences, and attitudes play a large part in decisions and outcomes. Nick might be ready for a four-year college away from home, but Brett may not. Expense might be another consideration in their decisions. Megan and Tia may have more in common than is readily apparent, or both may be attracted to the same feature of a particular college.

The Personal System

The goal of personal systems management is to recognize and to make productive the specific strengths and abilities of each individual. Respect for the uniqueness of the qualities of each individual is a critical part of management. Each person is a system composed of many subsystems, including the (1) biological/physiological, (2) behavioral, (3) psychological, and (4) social. Each subsystem in turn has many components. For example, values and ethics are part of the psychological subsystem; they provide integrity and direction to decisions, guiding individuals through the many moral dilemmas they encounter each day. After a day of shopping, for instance, Kayla examines her receipts and discovers that the salesperson at the music store neglected to charge her for one of the compact discs she purchased. Will Kayla go back and pay for the extra disc? Her decision will be guided by the values and ethics of her psychological subsystem.

Each individual's personal system exists within a greater system of relationships, friendships, and family. Inputs to the personal system include other people, the environment, heredity, and past experiences, all of which help shape the individual's personal management style. Due to the dynamic nature of systems, the individual is always changing and always interpreting feedback.

Industry and government are interested in how people's attitudes change. The Gallup organization regularly monitors people's attitudes on a variety of subjects, including conditions in the United States and in their personal lives. In one survey, respondents reported that they were more satisfied with their personal lives than with the way things were going overall in the United States. One study indicates that since the beginning of the 1980s, Gallup polls have consistently indicated that about 80 percent of Americans are satisfied with the way things are going in their lives (Newport & Hueber, 1990). The researchers conclude from this that Americans have a remarkable ability to think positively about their own personal life situations, even while seeing things about them in a more negative light. In another survey, the Roper organization found that as people age, their home becomes more important to them, and clothes and jewelry become less important as a means of defining self.

Family Systems Theory and Management

The goal of family systems management is to recognize and to make productive the specific strengths and abilities of each family. In family systems, boundaries change over time as families change. The permeability of boundaries alters as family members age and move on to other life stages. Interactions within families are qualitatively and quantitatively different from interactions among other groups. Family systems theory has come to be one of the leading theories in clinical and programmatic work with families. It is useful, for example, in helping a family who has undergone a traumatic event. Anyone studying to be a marriage and family therapist would learn about family systems theory. In practice, the focus may be on a particular subsystem such as the marital (or couple), parental, or sibling subsystem. Family systems theory also assumes that families share goals and work together to achieve them. An example of a family goal would be that each of the children go to college. To reach this goal all family members may work extra jobs or put in overtime or make financial investments to accumulate enough money; in addition, the children may study extra hard in school to get good grades and/or to excel in athletics or music or other activities leading to better scholarships and financial aid.

In short, "Family systems theory allows one to understand the organizational complexity of families, as well as the interactive patterns that guide family interactions. One of the central premises of family systems theory is that family systems organize themselves to carry out the daily challenges and tasks of life, as well as adjusting to the developmental needs of its members" (Fleming, 2003, p. 643).

Another important aspect of family systems theory is that families are dynamic in nature and have patterns of rules and strategies that affect the interactions that take place. Rules would include such things as mealtimes and bedtimes. According to an Impulse Research poll, 67 percent of American families have assigned or "usual" seats at the table. What happens when someone upsets this rule and sits in someone else's chair?

According to McCubbin and his colleagues (1997), families are especially resilient because (1) they establish patterns of functioning after being challenged and confronted by risk factors, a characteristic referred to as elasticity, and (2) they have the ability to recover quickly from a misfortune, trauma, or transitional event, an ability referred to as buoyancy. The discovery of factors that enhance a family's resiliency is a subject of interest to researchers. McCubbin and his colleagues predict that the 21st century will be characterized as the era of family transformation and stress. They have identified ten general resiliency factors that will help families survive and prosper:

1. Family problem-solving communication
2. Equality
3. Spirituality
4. Flexibility
5. Truthfulness
6. Hope
7. Family hardiness
8. Family time and routines
9. Social support
10. Health

Family systems theory also emphasizes the importance of family history, a psychological perspective introduced by Murray Bowen in the 1970s and set forth more recently by Monica McGoldrick in *You Can Go Home Again*. McGoldrick emphasizes that people and their problems do not exist in a vacuum but are part of a broad family system. Thus, family patterns of working, relating, and dealing with stress can reverberate through generations (Shellenbarger, 1998). She says that

> The "family" comprises the entire emotional system of at least three and increasingly four generations, who move through life together, even though they often live in different places. As a family we share a common past and an anticipated future. The patterns of family life cycle are changing dramatically, so that there is less continuity than ever before between the demands on current families and the patterns of past generations. Thus it is easy to lose all sense of connection with what has come before in your family, and this can be a serious loss. (McGoldrick, 1995, p. 30)

Further, McGoldrick says,

> While each family is unique in its particular history, all families are alike in their underlying patterns. Famous families may, because they are in the spotlight, have certain responses to their notoriety, but all families have basic ways they deal with love, pain, and conflict; make sense of life and death; cross time, class, and cultural barriers. All families must find ways of dealing with loss and of integrating new members. (p. 30)

Application of Systems Theory to Households

In the previous two sections, we have focused on the management of personal and family lives. Systems theory and terminology can also apply to homes. For example, the concepts of inputs, throughputs, outputs, and feedback can be applied to both simple and complex household operations.

An example of a simple household operation is doing the laundry. Water, detergent, and clothes are inputs for the washing machine. The throughput is the cleansing, rinsing, and spinning action, and the outputs are dirty wastewater and clean clothes. If the clothes are not clean, this signals (provides feedback) that something is wrong with the system, and a change is needed.

More complex household operations include preparing meals, establishing schedules, and caring for children. For example, meal preparation involves deciding what to eat, shopping (the average grocery store offers more than 30,000 different products), preparing food, serving, eating, and cleaning up. Setting schedules requires communication and the coordination of activities, people, and time. Child care involves innumerable decisions, tasks, and responsibilities in addition to emotional factors. Family economists have tried to put a dollar value on household work, which has been used in determining life insurance and other financial needs and in resolving court cases involving divorce or the injury or death of a stay-at-home spouse or parent. Estimates run anywhere from $30,000 to $500,000 a year to replace typical in-home services (Weston, 2003). Whatever the figure, household work and in-home child care have value. The figures are often constructed from the U.S. Bureau of Labor Statistics averages for a variety of occupations, such as

- ◆ Bookkeeper, $11.94 an hour
- ◆ Chauffeur, $8.67 an hour
- ◆ Child-care worker, $8.91 an hour
- ◆ Food-preparation supervisor, $11.70 an hour
- ◆ Maid, $8.02 an hour

To calculate, the number of hours the service typically takes is determined; other factors, such as the ages of the children, are also taken into account. Critics of this approach say that, realistically, if a wife and mother, for example, is the victim of a car accident, her family will not replace her with a team of bookkeepers, chauffeurs, and so on. Furthermore, emotional loss is not added into these types of calculations. According to the Bureau of Labor Statistics, 40 percent of mothers with children under age 6 stay home, and 13 percent of all U.S. households include a stay-at-home spouse.

Much more goes into household systems than the work input of an at-home spouse. All members contribute to household production and consumption. Inputs may be rented, leased, provided by the community, or owned. Raw materials, market goods and services, durables, labor, knowledge, and management skills are inputs to the household system. These various inputs lead to the production of goods and services that may be consumed or given as gifts, sold, or bartered (Magrabi, Chung, Cha, & Young, 1991). An example of household production would be preparation of a meal. This activity contributes to household well-being and the desired end result (output, goal) of improved human resources. Household production/consumption does more than satisfy immediate needs—it provides for an increased human capability, a provision for the future.

Human Ecology and Ecosystems

Conditions in the greater environment have an important influence on how households and families function. The study of how living things relate to their natural environment is called **ecology.** Adding the word *human* produces the term **human ecology,** which simply means humans interacting with their environment. A more comprehensive definition of human ecology says that it is the study of how humans—as social, physical, and biological beings—interact with each other and with their physical, sociocultural, aesthetic, and biological environments as well as with the material and human resources of these environments (Bubolz & Sontag, 1988).

Human ecology views humans and their near environments as integrated wholes, mutually influencing each other (Bubolz & Sontag, 1988). The **environment** is the sum of the external conditions influencing the life of an organism or population (Naar, 1990). In this book, the emphasis in considering environment is on the quality-of-life conditions for individuals and families.

The *environment* is essentially everything that surrounds humans; but because this concept is so broad, theorists have divided the environment into the microenvironment and the macroenvironment. The **microenvironment** (also called the microhabitat or near environment) is the environment that closely surrounds individuals and families. Apartments, sorority and fraternity houses, classrooms, libraries, and dormitory rooms are part of a college student's microenvironment. The **macroenvironment** (also called the macrohabitat or far environment) surrounds and encompasses the microenvironment. Sky, trees, and oceans are part of the macroenvironment.

Family Ecosystem

The **family ecosystem** is the subsystem of human ecology that emphasizes the interactions between families and environments. According to Paolucci, Hall, and Axinn (1977), the family ecosystem has three basic elements:

1. *Organisms:* These are the family members.
2. *Environments:* Both the natural and human-built environments are included.
3. *Family organization:* This functions to transform energy in the form of information into family decisions and actions.

The ecosystem approach is useful because it emphasizes the interaction between families and the conditions that surround them. A change in a single component of the family ecosystem has an impact on the other parts. For example, if one family member has an alcohol or drug abuse problem, it will affect everyone else in the family. Figure 2.4 illustrates the many ways family organisms (O) and environments (E) relate to one another. The example of alcohol or drug abuse internal to the family is depicted as O ↔ O, family organism affecting family organism. Examples of E → O are fires or hurricanes destroying homes and communities. A family's decision to cut down a tree in the yard is an example of O → E. A tropical storm hitting a deserted island is an example of E ↔ E. The study of management emphasizes human interactions with environments, which are diagrammed as O ↔ E. Most management situations involve individuals or families interacting with each other and with factors in their environment.

Global Ecosystems

Global ecosystems encompass all the family ecosystems and are regulated by interactive physical, social, political, economic, chemical, and biological

E ⟶ O	Environment affecting family organisms (members)
O ⟶ E	Family organisms affecting environment
O ⟷ O	Family organisms affecting family organisms
E ⟷ E	Environment affecting environment
O ⟷ E	Reciprocal effect of family organisms and environments

FIGURE 2.4

Interdependence of the Components of a Family Ecosystem

Source: B. Paolucci, O. Hall, and N. Axinn, *Family Decision Making: An Ecosystem Approach* (New York: Macmillan College Publishing Company, 1977), p. 16.

processes. To begin to understand the global ecosystem, one must understand the dynamics of family ecosystems. For instance, each family contributes to the greater society and is a microcosm of the larger social system in which it exists. Jesse Jackson's quilt metaphor is an excellent illustration of those concepts: "America is not like a blanket—one piece of unbroken cloth, the same color, the same texture, the same size. America is more like a quilt—many pieces, many colors, many sizes, all woven and held together by a common thread" (Jackson, 1988). Each patch in the quilt adds a special nuance of color, pattern, strength, utility, and texture to the finished product. Collectively, the sum of all the parts is infinitely more interesting than the individual pieces. Each extended family and each nation benefits from the combined strength of their various people and cultures.

Millions of family ecosystems combine to form national ecosystems that in turn make up the global ecosystem. Human ecology emphasizes the global interdependence of individuals, families, and communities, with the resources of natural, constructed, and behavioral environments, for the purpose of wise decision making and use of resources essential to human development and the quality of life and the environment (Bubolz & Sontag, 1988).

In homes, family ecosystems interact with the systems that supply food, heat, health care, information, water, gas, electricity, clothing, and transportation. These same systems operate in the global ecosystem on a much larger scale. The welfare of nations depends on these life-support systems. For example, maintaining an adequate food supply is a concern at the household level, the national level, and the global level.

International environmental issues will continue to dominate the global policy agenda of the 21st century. Long-range solutions to environmental problems will require planning and cooperation among nations. Since planning is a fundamental part of management, this field will play an increasingly vital role in encouraging the conservation of resources and the promotion of informed and sound health and environmental attitudes and practices at the individual, family, and household levels.

ECONOMIC THEORY

Although systems theory has been the dominant influence on management over the last few decades, the application of economic theory to management has attracted renewed attention.

Economic thinking is based on eight guideposts (Gwartney, Stroup, Sobel, & Macpherson, 2003):

1. The use of scarce resources is costly; trade-offs must always be made.
2. Individuals choose purposefully, trying to get the most from their limited resources.
3. Incentives matter.
4. Individuals focus on the difference in the costs and benefits between alternatives.
5. Information can be scarce and is costly to acquire.
6. Actions may generate second effects; in other words, decisions have both immediate effects and spin-off, or later, effects.

7. Preferences vary between individuals. A ticket to the ballet may be worth $100 to one person and absolutely nothing to another. Value is subjective.

8. Theory is useful in making predictions. The focus in economics is on the behavior of a large number of individuals.

According to Sherman Hanna (1989, 1997), "The most obvious application of economic theory to family resource management is in terms of the maximization of satisfaction or utility subject to resource constraints. The potential application of the economic framework is very wide, extending to all consumer purchases of products and services, and also including labor force, fertility, and even marriage decisions." Thus, the second point in the list of guideposts is often cited in family resource management.

Economic theory assumes that individuals seek to maximize satisfaction from the decisions they make. It also assumes that individuals are rational (use reason in making decisions) and will act in their own self-interest. Economic theory focuses on the interaction between buyers and sellers. Economists are basically concerned with the nature of exchange—for example, what things cost and what is gained in return.

Optimization and Satisficing

Economic theory includes many subtheories. One of these is **optimization,** which means obtaining the best result, such as maximizing profit for a business or maximizing satisfaction for a household (Hanna, 1989, 1997). Optimization refers to the effective use of resources to gain the most satisfaction. Holly Hunts and Ramona Marotz-Baden of Montana State University write that

> Optimizing means that all assessment tools are considered in the search for the best choice. An optimizing search is thorough, and the choice that meets the assessment tool standards of high quality while considering cost is the choice made. An example might be choosing a wedding dress. A young woman may search tirelessly for months for the perfect dress—looking at patterns, looking at magazines, attending bridal shows, and searching the Internet. Optimizing is possible when time is not limited and when true quality can be measured. (2003, p. 5)

Although in theory individuals and families will seek to optimize their resources, in reality they often do not behave in optimizing ways. For example, they may not buy the low-cost generic product in a grocery store even though it has the same quality as a more expensive brand-name product. Or they may not buy the lowest-cost airplane ticket because they do not want to fly at an inconvenient time or do not plan far enough ahead to get the lowest price. Comparison shopping can save money, but some people may feel it is not worth the aggravation, time, energy, and patience required. An optimization approach to consumption-related problem solving may include

1. An examination of utility or objective

2. A consideration of the desired consumption levels of different goods and services

3. An analysis of constraints or limitations

Much of what is consumed today has evolved, sometimes rapidly, as a result of cultural and technological changes that occurred in the late 19th and 20th centuries. In addition, the massive migration from rural to urban areas as well as massive immigration into the country have had enormous impact on the overall economy as well as on economic theory and application. Similar conclusions can be drawn worldwide (the trend from rural to urban is global, for example), although each nation has its own timetable.

Intensive information seeking is an important aspect of optimization theory. Since economic theory emphasizes the measurable and the rational, information seeking is heralded as a logical course of action. Theorists reason that the more people know, the more informed (better) their decisions will be. This makes intuitive sense, but not everyone does what is reasonable and logical all the time. Besides even the best-informed decisions can go wrong. For example, Randall and Elaine spent months researching which car to buy. They read articles about new cars, checked the recommendations of *Consumer Reports* magazine, and then went out and bought the worst car of their married life. Apparently, the marketplace is less than perfect (i.e., an individual car can be poorly manufactured even though the model is highly recommended).

Furthermore, people must consider the possible outcomes in deciding how much planning and implementing effort is optimal. Expending considerable effort to obtain information about a choice that will have little long-term effect on the family may not be a wise use of time and other resources. Decisions may fail because of lack of access to information, inability to process information, or the lack of time to gather or process information. Not everyone has equal access to the Internet, for example, although schools and communities are working to make the distribution of this technology more equitable.

Attempts have been made to integrate economic and social systems theories. For example, mate selection is an intriguing example of a decision that is not based entirely on reason. Gary S. Becker, professor of economics at the University of Chicago and winner of the Nobel Prize in economics, posits that the economic forces that influence people to get married and have children are as powerful as the forces that govern decisions to buy a new car or change jobs ("Family Values," 1992–1993). Others disagree. They argue that selecting a mate, having children, and other highly personal choices are more emotional than rational. Less controversial is the use of optimization theory by household and business managers. Decisions that are largely objective, such as which refrigerator or laser printer to purchase, may be well suited to a short information search and a rational decision. Thus, optimization may be most useful in simple, straightforward situations involving a short information search and little emotion. Whether it is applicable in decision situations such as mate selection, as suggested by Becker, is open to debate. But since the basic point of optimization is the maximization of satisfaction through obtaining the best result, the theory should be applicable to a variety of situations.

Satisficing refers to picking the first good alternative that presents itself (Simon, 1959). The individual stops searching once it appears that an initial choice will suffice. This strategy makes sense when time and choices are limited. Someone with a flat tire who is late to work may not want to take the time to comparison shop for tires. She will probably buy a tire as quickly as possible so she can proceed on her way. Hunts and Marotz-Baden describe satisficing:

> For example, if a husband is searching for a car and the minimum assessment standards include that it started when the key was turned and that it cost less than $10,000, then the first car that met those minimum standards would be chosen. In goods and services where it is difficult to determine true quality until the good or service is consumed, consumers often satisfice. Childcare is an example. The first

child care center that is a reasonable distance from work and home, is within the family budget, and looks inviting might be the one chosen, simply because it met minimum assessment tool standards. (2003, p. 5)

Applying economic theory to personal consumption is complicated because "values other than efficiency are important for many people, including satisfaction derived from the process rather than the end-product, and creation of unique products not available from the market" (Hanna, 1989, 1997). Thus, shopping in and of itself is an enjoyable activity for many individuals, and this should be considered in discussions of rational economic behavior. The fastest choice may not be the best choice if shopping itself creates satisfaction. Furthermore, according to Hanna (1989, 1997), "in the business world, firms that do not adopt more efficient ways of doing things will not survive in the long run, but households can just muddle along using inefficient techniques." This statement makes one wonder: How efficient do households have to be to exist and function? Are they really "small factories" as Gary Becker says? How much of economic theory, with its emphasis on rationality and logic, can be applied to households and families? Questions such as these fuel management research.

Risk Aversion

The possibility of experiencing harm, suffering, danger, or loss is known as **risk.** Although we tend to associate risk with physical danger, it can also involve such things as losing money, energy, time, or reputation. In the last section, car buyers Randall and Elaine experienced consumer risk, but risk can also take other forms, including health and safety risk, educational risk, relationship risk, occupational risk, and financial risk. Foxall, Goldsmith, and Brown (1998) have identified several types of perceived risk that affect decision making:

- ◆ *Functional or performance risk:* The possibility that a choice may not turn out as desired or have the expected benefits
- ◆ *Financial risk:* The possibility that substantial amounts of money may be lost. An example of this is investing in stocks versus investing in bonds. The risk involved could be explained as
  - ◆ If held for only a short time—1 to 3 years, for example—stocks are more risky. However, when held over lengthy periods, like 20 or 30 years, historically, the rate of return on stocks has been both higher and less variable than that of bonds. What does this imply about where persons saving for their retirement while in their twenties and thirties should place their funds? (Gwartney et al., 2003, p. 686)
- ◆ *Physical risk:* The possibility that harm may come from a choice
- ◆ *Psychological risk:* The possibility that a choice may damage a person's image of self or self-esteem
- ◆ *Social risk:* The possibility that a choice will not be approved by others or may cause social embarrassment or rejection
- ◆ *Time risk:* The possibility that the ability to satisfy wants will decline over time. In economics, it is assumed that a consumer would nearly always prefer to receive a good or service now rather than later.

To summarize, not all risk is bad and it carries with it many characteristics. A person may be risk-averse or risk-loving or risk-neutral. Changing jobs or spouses involves risk. Traveling or moving involves risk. Indeed, *people like a certain amount of risk; otherwise, games, gambling, quiz shows, and competition would not exist.* Risk provides a little excitement and a release from tedium. One person may dream of winning the lottery and quitting his boring job. Another may take up skydiving to spice up her life. As these examples suggest, risk is not an absolute. The perception of risk varies from person to person. One individual may think riding down the Grand Canyon on the back of a mule is an exciting adventure, whereas another may view it as foolhardy.

Trying to avoid the dire outcomes associated with risk is a rational course of behavior. In economic theory, the avoidance of risk is called **risk aversion.** Risk-averse individuals and families seek to minimize problems and maximize satisfaction by avoiding risk. For example, a risk-averse individual who dislikes heights and enclosed spaces would avoid riding elevators to the top of tall buildings. Just as different people perceive risk differently, the amount of risk aversion varies from person to person, family to family, and situation to situation.

Although some people feel comfortable betting on horse races or playing slot machines, others would never dream of spending money on gambling. The amount of risk a person is likely to take also varies by stage in the life cycle. A person who is 18 years old is likely to take more risks than someone who is 84. People's resources also affect the amount of risk they are likely to assume. *What constitutes a risk depends on the individual.* The greater the resources, the more confident an individual will feel about taking a risk. If the decision fails, the individual will not feel the loss as keenly as someone with fewer remaining resources.

Yet even people with substantial resources may be wary of risk or feel uncertain in new situations. Ultimately, an individual's management skills may affect both his or her perception of the uncertain situation and the decision that he or she makes (Jensen, 1987). The decision maker estimates how much risk the situation involves and tries to turn an uncertain outcome to his or her advantage. Ideally, "the process of problem definition, setting goals, developing alternative courses of action, deciding among alternatives, carrying out the activity and evaluating the results will bring about increased satisfaction even under conditions of uncertainty" (Jensen, 1987). Understanding the principles of perceived risk and being sensitive to the presence of risk can help the decision maker use risk-reduction strategies (e.g., gathering more information or following safe procedures) more effectively (Foxall, Goldsmith, & Brown, 1998). Chapter 5 discusses the relationship of risk and uncertainty to decision making in more detail.

A tenet of economics is that humans try to get maximum benefit for the least amount of effort, including the use of resources that will given them an acceptable level of the benefit desired (Hunt and Marotz-Baden, 2003; Gwartney et al., 2003). Risk aversion is part of the equation. It provides insight into the study of management. The fundamental principle of the maximization of satisfaction through the avoidance of risk provides plausible explanations for many types of decisions.

Web-Based Resources

For information on historic homes, go to **www.nr.nps.gov,** the Web site of the National Register of Historic Places, or go to **www.nps.gov,** for the National Park Service, and click on Links to the Past. If you are interested in researching your **genealogy** (an account of the descent of a person or family from an ancestor or ancestors), begin by writing down what you know about your parents, grandparents, or other relatives, including their full names, birthdates, birthplaces, wedding dates, and dates of death. Search your house for information in old books, photograph albums, clothes, trunks, attics, and so forth. Talk to older relatives about their older relatives and explore outside resources. To involve relatives who live at a distance, send them photocopies of photographs or other evidence you want them to identify or verify.

When you have gathered as much information as possible, turn to the Internet. To illustrate the popularity of genealogy searches, nearly 13 million people visit genealogy sites to connect, share photos, and trace ancestral roots each month (Schatz, 2003). An Internet search is so much easier than the old-fashioned method of going to libraries and museums and digging through dusty records by hand. Most sites will ask that you type in a name and then click Search. Be forewarned that many sites charge a fee to conduct a search and that the list that follows (as with all the Web sites listed in this book) is not endorsed by the author. That said, a search can be an enlightening experience. The more details you know about your ancestors, such as full names, birthdates, and birthplaces, the more likely you are to have a successful search. Genealogy Web sites include

www.genealogytoday.com
www.familytree.com
www.myfamily.com
www.rootsweb.com
www.genealogy.com
www.familysearch.org
www.cyndislist.com
www.ancestry.com
www.afrigeneas.com
www.ccharity.com
www.onegreatfamily.com

In the United States, all states have a Vital Statistics Division of the State Department of Health, which may provide useful information, usually for a fee. Other resources include immigration, marriage, church, and military service records. Visit libraries and archives, religious organizations that keep records, and genealogical societies—or go to the Web sites for these groups.

For information about human population changes, the best resource in the United States is **www.census.gov.** This site also notes changes in world populations and provides links to census data in other countries.

Summary

The study of management as taught and practiced today has its roots in the 19th century. As it has adjusted to technological, social, and economic changes in the 20th and 21st centuries, the field has necessarily become far more complex than it was originally. One particularly significant change in the 20th century was the transformation of the home from being primarily a producer to primarily a consumer of goods and services. Not only has the amount of household production declined, but the types of products it does produce and consume have also changed significantly. Who stays at home has changed as well. In the first half of the 20th century most adult women stayed at home, but by 2003 only about 13 percent of U.S. households included a stay-at-home spouse.

The study of management relies heavily on systems theory. In general systems theory, each part contributes to the behavior of the whole, and the whole is greater than the sum of its parts. Feedback can be positive or negative; it is modeled as a loop (Figure 2.3). Family systems theory emphasizes the ways families organize themselves to carry out daily challenges and tasks. Because the parts of a system are interrelated, systems are especially vulnerable to Murphy's Law (if something can go wrong, it will go wrong), and the tiniest flaw can cause damage. But, for the most part, systems try to balance themselves.

Polls show that Americans tend to be more satisfied with their personal affairs than with overall conditions in the United States, which is part of the greater environment. Families and environments are interdependent within the global ecosystem. Environments, near and far, provide the setting for human interactions, although individuals and families vary in the degree to which they are open or closed to the environment.

Economic theories play a role in management. According to optimization theory, the individual increases her or his chance for satisfaction and minimizes problems in a rational way by searching for information. Satisficing means that individuals choose the first good option that presents itself. Risk aversion holds that the goal is to maximize satisfaction by avoiding risks, although some people are risk-lovers or neutral about risk.

Underlying both systems theory and economic theory is the belief that behavior is not random and occurs for some reason or reasons. One of the few absolutely undisputable principles in resource management is that most behavior is rational and that individual preferences and situations play a great part in behavior. Theories provide useful ways to organize information, allowing for predicting future behavior. They do not explain everything, but they provide valuable starting points and frameworks. The next chapter goes beyond the realm of the theoretical to explore how values affect decision making and how goals drive managerial behavior.

Key Terms

boundaries	inputs	risk aversion
controlling	interface	satisficing
demands	macroenvironment	sequencing
ecology	microenvironment	subsystem
entropy	morphogenic systems	system
environment	morphostatic systems	systems theory
equifinality	multifinality	theory
family ecosystem	negative feedback	throughputs
genealogy	optimization	transformation
homeostasis	outputs	work simplification
human ecology	positive feedback	
hypotheses	risk	

Review Questions

1. Compare and contrast typical homes and household tasks in 1900, in 1950, and today according to the information given in the chapter.

2. "There is nothing so practical as a good theory," says Kurt Lewin. Explain why theory is useful.

3. What is the difference between positive and negative feedback?

4. How is a family a system? According to McCubbin and his coauthors, why are families especially resilient?

5. Economist Gary Becker says a household can be regarded as a "small factory." What does he mean by that? What is produced in households?

References

Arndt, W. (1974). *Theories of personality.* New York: Macmillan.

Berger, P. S. (1984). Home management research: State of the art 1909–1984. *Home Economics Research Journal,* 12(3), 252–264.

Bryant, K. (1992). Human capital, time use, and other family behavior. *Journal of Family and Economic Issues,* 13(4), 395–406.

Bubolz, M. M., & Sontag, S. (1988). Integration in home economics and human ecology. *Journal of Consumer Studies and Home Economics,* 12, 1–14.

Castells, M. (1996). *The information age* (Vol. 1). Cambridge, MA: Blackwell.

Connolly, M., & Wasserman, L. (2002). *Updating classic American bungalows.* Newtown, CT: Taunton Press.

Cowan, R. (1983). *More work for mother.* New York: Basic Books.

Crossen, C. (2002, December 11). Buying home spigots, water was never taken for granted. *The Wall Street Journal.*

Davey, A. (1971). Relationship of family interaction to family environment. Unpublished Ph.D. thesis, Michigan State University, East Lansing.

Deacon, R. E., & Firebaugh, F. M. (1988). *Family resource management: Principles and applications* (2nd ed.). Boston: Allyn & Bacon.

Drucker, P. (1999). *Management challenges for the 21st century.* New York: Harper Business.

Edwards, O. (2002, October 7). Mores. *Forbes.*

Family values. (December 26, 1992–January 8, 1993). *Economist,* 325(7791), 37–40.

Flanagan, C. (2003, September). Housewife confidential. *Atlantic Monthly,* 141–142.

Fleming, W. (2003). Family systems theory. In J. J. Ponzetti, Jr. (Ed.), *International Encyclopedia of Marriage and Family* (2nd ed., Vol. 2). New York: Macmillan Reference USA.

Fletcher, J. (2002, August 10). Out with the new, in with the old. *The Wall Street Journal,* W9.

Foxall, G., Goldsmith, R., & Brown, S. (1998). *Consumer psychology for marketing.* London: Routledge.

Frederick, C. (1918). *The new housekeeping.* New York: Doubleday.

Gilbreth, L. (1927). *The homemaker and her job.* New York: Appleton.

Goebel, K. P., & Hennon, D. B. (1982). An empirical investigation of the relationship among wife's employment status, stage in the family life cycle, meal preparation time, and expenditures for meals away from home. *Journal of Consumer Studies and Home Economics,* 6, 63–78.

Goldsmith, E. (1977). Time use of beginning families with employed and unemployed wives. Unpublished Ph.D. thesis, Michigan State University, East Lansing.

Goldsmith, E. (1993). Home economics: The discovered discipline. *Journal of Home Economics,* 85(4), 45–48.

Gross, I. H., Crandall, E. W., & Knoll, M. M. (1980). *Management for modern families* (4th ed.). Englewood Cliffs, NJ: Prentice-Hall.

Gwartney, J., Stroup, R., Sobel, R., and Macpherson, D. (2003). *Economics: Private & public choice* (10th ed.). Cincinnati, OH: South-Western.

Hafstrom, J,. & Paynter, M. (1991). Time use satisfaction: Home, farm, and labor force workload. *Lifestyles: Family and Economic Issues,* 12(2), 131–143.

Hafstrom, J. L., & Schram, V. R. (1983). Housework time of wives: Pressures, facilitators, constraints. *Home Economics Research Journal,* 11, 245–254.

Hallinan, J. (2002, August 12). Help for hopeless garages. *The Wall Street Journal,* B1.

Hanna, S. (1989, 1997 renewed copyright). Optimization for family resource management. *Proceedings, Southeastern Regional Family Economics/ Home Management Association.*

Hunts, H., & Marotz-Baden, R. (2003). Family systems theory, a new look at an old friend. *Consumer Interests Annual,* 49, 1–13.

Israelsen, C. (1990). Family resource management research 1930–1990. *Financial Counseling and Planning,* 1, 3–39.

Jackson, J. (1988, July 23). Address to 1984 Democratic National Convention. *Congressional Quarterly Weekly Report,* 46(30), 2057.

Jensen, H. (1987). Household risk management and human resources. In R. E. Deacon & W. E. Huffman (Eds.), *Human Resources Research, 1887–1987: Proceedings* (pp. 161–171). Ames, IA: College of Home Economics, Iowa State University.

Magrabi, F. M., Chung, Y., Cha, S., and Young, S. (1991). *The economics of the household.* New York: Praeger.

McCubbin, H., McCubbin, M., Thompson, A., Hans, S., & Allen, C. (1997, Fall). Families under stress: What makes them resilient? *Journal of Family and Consumer Sciences,* 2–11.

McCullough, J., & Zick, C. (1992). The roles of role strain, economic resources and time demands in explaining mother's life satisfaction. *Journal of Family and Economic Issues,* 13(1), 23–44.

McGoldrick, M. (1995). *You can go home again.* New York: Norton.

Naar, J. (1990). *Design for a livable planet.* New York: Harper & Row.

Newport, F., & Hueber, G. (1990). Satisfaction levels and approval of President Bush. *Gallup Poll Monthly.*

Owen, A. (1991). Time and time again: Implications of time perception theory. *Lifestyles: Family and Economic Issues,* 12(4), 345–349.

Paolucci, B., Hall, O., & Axinn, N. (1977). *Family decision making: An ecosystem approach.* New York: Wiley.

Parloa, M. (1879). *First principles of household management and cookery.* Boston: Houghton, Osgood.

Richards, E. (1904). *The art of living right.* Boston: Whitcomb and Barrows.

Sanik, M. M. (1981). A division of household work: A decade comparison, 1967–1977. *Home Economics Research Journal,* 10, 175–180.

Schatz, E. (2003, April 29). Digging for your family roots in cyberspace. *The Wall Street Journal,* D2.

Schnittgrund, K. (1980). Productive time of household heads. *Journal of Consumer Studies and Home Economics,* 4, 239–248.

Sessa, D. (2000, November 13). Have dinner. *The Wall Street Journal,* R20.

Sharpe, D. L., & Winter, M. (1991). Toward working hypotheses of effective management: Conditions, thought processes and behaviors. *Lifestyles: Family and Economics Issues,* 12(4), 303–323.

Shellenbarger, S. (1998, April 28). Work and family. *The Wall Street Journal,* B1.

Sieburg, E. (1985). *Family communication.* New York: Gardner Press.

Simon, H. (1959). Theories of decision-making in economics and behavioral sciences. *American Economic Review, 49,* 253–283.

Smithsonian (2000). National Museum of American History, On Time exhibit, Washington, DC.

Stafford, K. (1983). The effects of wife's employment time on household work time. *Home Economics Research Journal, 11,* 257–266.

Taylor, F. W. (1911). *Principles of scientific management.* New York: Harper & Brothers.

There's no place like home. (1997, January). *American Demographics,* 26.

Vickers, C. (1984). Themes in home management. In M. East and J. Thomson (Eds.), *Definitive Themes in Home Economics and Their Impact on Families, 1909–1984.* Washington, DC: American Home Economics Association.

Walker, K. E., & Woods, M. E. (1976). *Time use: A measure of household production of family goods and services.* Washington, DC: American Home Economics Association.

Warren, J. (1940). Use of time in its relation to home management. Cornell University Agricultural Experiment Station Bulletin 734.

Weiss, M. (2003, September). To be about to be. *American Demographics,* 29–36.

Weston, L. P. (2003, June 14). What's a homemaker worth? The shocking truth. Retrieved March 2, 2004, from **http://moneycentral.msn.com/content/CollegeandFamily/P46800.asp**

Willis, G., & Young, L. (2003, April). Retire happy. *Smart Money,* 84.

Wilson, M. (1929). *Use of time by Oregon farm homemakers.* Oregon Agricultural Experiment Station 256.

Winter, M., Puspitawati, H., Heck, R., & Stafford, K. (1993). Time-management strategies used by households with home-based work. *Journal of Family and Economic Issues,* 14(1), 69–92.

Wooldridge, A. (2000, April 28–29). Where business profs walk tall. *The Wall Street Journal Europe.*

Woolgar, C. (1993). *Household accounts from medieval England.* Oxford: Oxford University Press.

For Further Reading*

Andrews, B. R. (1935). *Economics of the household*. New York: Macmillan.

Becker, G. S. (1981). *A treatise on the family*. Cambridge, MA: Harvard University Press.

Beecher, C. (1841). *Treatise on domestic economy*. Boston: Marsh, Capen, Lyon, & Webb.

Bonde, R. L. (1944). *Management in daily living*. New York: Macmillan.

Bratton, E. C. (1971). *Home management is*. Boston: Ginn.

Cushman, E. M. (1945). *Management in homes*. New York: Macmillan.

Fitzsimmons, C., & Williams, F. (1973). *The family economy, nature and management of resources*. Ann Arbor, MI: Edwards Brothers.

Gilbreth, L., Thomas, O. M., & Clymer, E. (1955). *Management in the home*. New York: Dodd, Mead.

Goodyear, M. R., & Klohr, M. C. (1965). *Managing for effective living* (2nd ed.). New York: Wiley.

Kyrk, H. (1933). *Economic problems of the family*. New York: Harper & Row.

Kyrk, H. (1953). *The family in the American economy*. Chicago: University of Chicago Press.

Liston, M. (1993). *History of family economics research: 1862–1962*. Ames, IA: University Publications, Iowa State University.

Magrabi, F. M., Chung, Y. S., Cha, S. S., & Yang, S. (1991). *The economics of household consumption*. New York: Praeger.

May, E. E., Waggoner, N. R., & Boethke, E. M. (1974). *Independent living for the handicapped and the elderly*. Boston: Houghton Mifflin.

Oppenheim, I. (1976). *Management of the modern home* (2nd ed.). New York: Macmillan.

Paolucci, B., Hall, O. A., & Axinn, N. (1977). *Family decision making: An ecological approach*. New York: Wiley.

Reid, M. G. (1934). *Economics of household production*. New York: Wiley.

Rice, A. S., & Tucker, S. M. (1986). *Family life management* (6th ed.). New York: Macmillan.

Richards, E. H. (1900). *The cost of living as modified by sanitary science*. New York: Wiley.

Stage, S., & Vincent, V. (1997). *Rethinking home economics*. Ithaca, NY: Cornell University.

Starr, M. C. (1968). *Management for better living*. Lexington, MA: Heath.

Steidl, R. E., & Bratton, E. C. (1968). *Work in the home*. New York: Wiley.

Swanson, B. B. (1981). Introduction to home management. New York: Macmillan.

Talbot, M., & Breckinridge, S. (1919). *The modern household*. Boston: Whitcomb & Barrows.

*When a book has appeared in several editions, the newest is cited. This list of seminal works (textbooks, popular books, and reference books) is intended to supplement those already cited in the reference list; it is not meant to be comprehensive. In addition, management articles can be found in the *International Journal of Consumer Studies, Journal of Family and Consumer Sciences* (formerly the *Journal of Home Economics*), *Family and Consumer Sciences Research Journal* (formerly the *Home Economics Research Journal*), *Journal of Marriage and Family, Journal of Consumer Affairs, Journal of Family and Economic Issues, Journal of Consumer Education, Kappa Omicron Nu Forum, Canadian Home Economics Journal,* and in the journals of allied fields. Other sources for management theory, research, and applications are theses and dissertations, Agricultural Experiment Station Bulletins, the *Family Economics Review* and other government publications, and conference proceedings.

part 2

Management Concepts and Principles

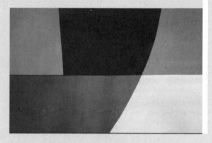

chapter 3

Values, Attitudes, Goals, and Motivation

MAIN TOPICS

Did you know that . . . ?

. . . About 23 percent of New Year's resolutions are broken the first week, 45 percent by the end of January.

. . . On average, nearly one-third of college freshmen do not return for their sophomore year.

Don't bunt. Aim out of the ballpark.

—*David Ogilvy*

WHAT IS IMPORTANT to you? Fame? Family? Friends? Happiness? Values, attitudes, and goals underlie our interpersonal relationships and lifestyle choices, such as whom we live with, what we consume, and what work we do. People who report being happy when they are 20 years old report being equally happy when they are 70. Conversely, 20-year-olds who report being unhappy at 20 are still unhappy at age 70 (McIntosh, Martin, & Jones, 1997). Fulfilling goals can bring happiness (Csikszentmihalyi, 1997). Happiness falls into three categories:

> There's the pleasant life with lots of richly positive emotions in the past, present, and future. . . . A second type of happy life is one in which you are totally absorbed and immersed in what you do. It is feeling positive about knowing you are using your highest strengths and virtues in love, work and play. The third type of meaningful, happy life is using your highest strengths in service to others, for something larger. (Condor, 2002, p. 4D)

This chapter explores these and related concepts. Why does happiness matter? How often have you heard someone say, "I just want you to be happy" or express that sentiment regarding someone else? For example, on the occasion

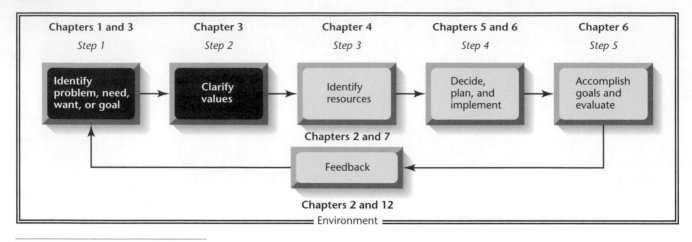

Chapters 1 and 3	Chapter 3	Chapter 4	Chapters 5 and 6	Chapter 6
Step 1	Step 2	Step 3	Step 4	Step 5
Identify problem, need, want, or goal	Clarify values	Identify resources	Decide, plan, and implement	Accomplish goals and evaluate

Chapters 2 and 7

Feedback

Chapters 2 and 12

Environment

FIGURE 3.1
The Management Process Model

of the second marriage of Nikki, her closest friend, Lisa said to acquaintances, "I just want her to be happy this time."

As noted in Chapter 1, management is the process of using resources to achieve goals. The goals people seek and the way they perceive and use resources are affected by their values and attitudes. Setting goals is a necessary first step because, after all, you can't get what you want until you have a clear idea what it is that you want. This chapter focuses on step 1 (identifying problem, need, want, or goal) and step 2 (clarifying values) in the management process model (see Figure 3.1).

The chapter begins with a discussion of values and attitudes and then proceeds to goals. The values and goals of college students in particular are examined. Since the successful achievement of goals is closely linked to motivation, it plays an important part in this chapter. Consider the motivation and achievement of Charles Lindbergh, the first aviator to fly nonstop across the Atlantic Ocean from the United States to Europe. Discussing his flight in an article in the *New York Times* on May 13, 1927, he said:

> We (that's my ship and I) took off rather suddenly. We had a report somewhere around 4 o'clock in the afternoon before the weather would be fine, so we thought we would try it.

In the same article, F. Scott Fitzgerald, the renowned novelist, described the flight of the *Spirit of Saint Louis* more eloquently:

> In the spring of '27 something bright and alien flashed across the sky.
> A young Minnesotan [Lindbergh] who seemed to have had nothing to do with his generation did a heroic thing, and for a moment people set down their glasses in country clubs and speakeasies and thought of their old best dreams.

Articles in *Business Week, Science,* and *Time* questioned whether the spirit of invention, technological advance, and adventure epitomized by Lindbergh's solo flight was declining (Mansfield et al., 1988). But in the 1990s, widespread innovations in computers and telecommunications spurred new hope that technology and the spirit of adventure were still very

Charles Lindbergh with his plane, the Spirit of St. Louis, *ready to start on his attempt to cross the Atlantic.*

© Bettmann/CORBIS

much alive. There's no denying that the 20th century brought an incredible amount of innovation and progress to our world and that the 21st century holds even greater promise.

Business will change more in the next 10 years than it has in the past 50, driven by the Internet, personal computers, innovative software, and new generations of digital devices. The industrial revolution of the 19th century was about enhancing muscle power. The current revolution—the digital revolution—is about enhancing the power of the mind (*Business Week,* 1999, p. 1).

Encouraging the reader to think about the issues surrounding goals and personal and societal values, to set priorities, to seize opportunities, and to move forward are the behavioral goals of this chapter.

VALUES AND ATTITUDES

Values are principles that guide behavior. For example, a person who values honesty will try to act in honest ways. Values are deep-seated psychological constructs that direct individual preferences and strategies for goal achievement. They form the foundation for behavior, including goal-seeking behavior. Each person has an internally integrated value system called a **value orientation,** which is expressed in part in the way he or she makes judgments. A person's judgments are based on the value meanings derived from his or her feelings (the **affective domain**) and thinking (the **cognitive domain**) about events, situations, groups of people, and things. Both the affective and the cognitive domains are based on previous experience. Thus, valuing is an ongoing, never-ending process that forms an integral part of an individual's personality and behavioral systems. Different generations may hold slightly different values (see Table 3.1).

Behavior is what people actually do. The word *behavior* implies action. Often a gap exists between values (the ideal) and behavior (the actual). For example, a man may say that he is on a strict weight-reducing diet, yet stuff his grocery cart with candy bars. Another person may say that she thinks a speed limit of 55 mph is a good idea, yet habitually drive much faster. Knowing of the gap between values and behavior, researchers are careful to ask survey questions not only about values and attitudes but also about actual behavior.

Consider shopping online while at work and its intersection with values. "Once the haven of closet solitaire players, the office computer is now the place to buy that anniversary present, order that Mother's Day bouquet or bargain-hunt for the lowest prices on DVD players" (de Lisser, 2003, p. A1). Research shows that online shopping surges in the middle of the workday and falls off in the evening and on weekends. Some workers say this beats going to the mall at lunchtime and in the long run saves their company time. Rick Dalmazzi, president of Certicom, an encryption company based in Hayward, California, doesn't get upset about his employees shopping online with company computers "within reason" because they all work more than 40 hours a week: "We have a philosophy around here that people should be comfortable at work and if they're comfortable at work, they'll work harder,"

TABLE 3.1
Values of Three Generations

Percent of U.S. adults who say selected things are very much a part of the American Dream, by generation.

	Matures*	Boomers†	Xers‡
Having a happy marriage	77%	74%	70%
Living in a decent, secure community	75	81	71
Owning your own home	74	79	81
Having children	64	59	51
Unlimited opportunity to pursue dreams	63	71	70
College education for self	50	56	63
Being a winner	45	40	50
Living where everyone shares my values	41	38	28
Becoming wealthy	33	37	46

*Matures (everyone born before 1945)
†Boomers (born between 1946 and 1964)
‡Xers (born between 1965 and 1976)
Source: Yankelovich Partners. Copyright © 1998 Primedia Intertec. Used with permission.

Mr. Dalmazzi says. "I'm totally fine with these areas where business life and personal life mix" (de Lisser, 2003, p. A8). Less employee-friendly companies have considered using software to filter retail sites, but they are reluctant to do so because employees could have a business-related reason to view them. For the most part, the decision is up to the employee about what is an appropriate amount of Internet shopping during office hours.

Environment plays a role in behavior. For example, maybe it is more difficult to maintain an average weight today because of the plenitude and easy availability of food. Twenty years ago the typical restaurant plate was 10 inches in diameter; now it is 12 inches. Currently, the United States has 227,208 fast-food outlets—one for every 1,000 people. That is up from one for every 1,400 people in 1990 and one for every 2,000 people in 1980. The fastest-growing food chains sell themselves as upscale or nutritious as well as convenient. In 2003, Subway Restaurants opened a new store in the United States every 3 hours on average and Starbucks Corporation a new store every 11 hours (Leung, 2003, October).

Attitudes are outlooks that may express values, serve as a means of evaluation, or demonstrate feeling in regard to some idea, person, object, event, situation, or relationship. They are states of mind or feelings, likes, and dislikes about some matter such as liking or disliking Subway sandwiches or Starbucks coffee. Everyone has her or his own unique set of attitudes, but the number of attitudes varies from person to person. One person may have attitudes on everything and everybody, whereas someone else may have few attitudes. Think how dull television talk shows would be if the guests and the audience had no attitudes or opinions to express. Attitudes can range from the significant to the petty.

Sometimes values and attitudes are confused. They do share the characteristic that both are abstract. In addition, both can be either explicit, meaning that they are held at the conscious level and are readily verbalized, or implicit, meaning that they are held subconsciously and can only be identified by behavior. But values and attitudes also differ in several respects. Whereas values are fairly constant (as deep-seated psychological constructs), attitudes are more transitory and subject to change. Values represent broad tendencies and highly prized beliefs (e.g., helpfulness, courage, and ambition), whereas attitudes are narrower predispositions (e.g., having a particular attitude about a clothing style, rap music, or modern art). Advertising plays on both values and attitudes by appealing to people's feelings about cleanliness, youthfulness, power, and prestige.

Goals are end results, the purpose toward which much behavior is directed. Goals are linked to deadlines, accomplishments, completion, or achievement. They are most likely to be attained if they are specific and stated in measurable terms. For example, rather than merely hoping to finish a race, an experienced runner is likely to set a goal of cutting X number of seconds off his or her best recorded time. Goals give shape, meaning, and direction to people's lives. A life without goals would be aimless. A survey of 1,000 people conducted by Market Facts TeleNation found the top priorities to be

1. Physical and spiritual well-being
2. Financial stability
3. Relationships
4. Personal or professional development
5. Work and career happiness
6. Service to others

Every day people make complex decisions that reflect their attitudes, values, and goals. If students value good grades, they decide to spend time studying. Attitudes often occupy a middle ground between values and goals. Students who hate studying (an attitude) are going to have difficulty working out the relationship between their value of intellect and their goal of attaining good grades.

Types of Values

Because the world is filled with an almost infinite array of different stimuli, one of the most basic human functions is to classify concepts, objects, and events into clusters or groups. In so doing, people simplify their world and lay the groundwork for interpretation and action. For example, values can be classified in four different ways:

1. Absolute and relative
2. Intrinsic and extrinsic
3. Traditional, personal, and professional
4. Instrumental and terminal

Each of these will be discussed in the following sections.

Absolute and Relative Values

Absolute values are extreme and definitive; such values can be described in terms of black and white, as in the phrase "honesty is the best policy." People who hold honesty as an absolute value would say that honesty is right in all situations. **Relative values** are interpreted based on the context. They can be visualized as shades of gray that depend on the situation for definition. A person who holds honesty as a relative value will usually be honest, but in certain situations will put friendship, politeness, or consideration first. For example, if a friend gets a terrible haircut and asks how it looks, Person X, who has absolute values, will respond that the haircut is awful. Person Y, who has relative values, will simply say that her friend's hair might be a little short. In this situation, Person Y is placing the values of friendship and sensitivity over the value of total honesty.

People with more relative values tend to seek additional information about an event or situation. They want more details or knowledge before expressing an opinion or taking action.

Intrinsic and Extrinsic Values

Values can also be classified as **intrinsic values,** which are ends in themselves (internally driven), or **extrinsic values,** which derive their worth or meaning from someone or something else. A couple finding their own way around a foreign city might find that experience intrinsically rewarding. They are demonstrating the values of independence and self-reliance. On the other hand, winning an Academy Award has extrinsic value because in this case a group of people have rewarded an individual for professional excellence.

The concepts of intrinsic and extrinsic can be applied to leadership. "Internal leadership skills reflect intrinsic values such as honesty, integrity, respecting others, professional ethics, and developing vision. . . . External leadership is demonstrated with actions such as taking risks, sharing a vision, fostering collaboration, giving power away, being a role model, communicating well, and celebrating success" (Buck, 2003, pp. 8, 9).

Traditional, Personal, and Professional Values

Traditional values are those commonly held by the predominant society in which one lives. A traditional value or societal standard widely held in the United States and Canada is that children should begin going to school around the age of five or six. Another value of these two nations is that education is important and a key to future success.

Weddings are value-laden traditional events. The wedding veil has evolved over the centuries: It symbolizes youth, innocence, modesty, and mystery. In the United States the color is white. In Japan many brides still wear the traditional tsuno-kakushi—a white hood that symbolizes hiding the horns of jealousy. A Finnish bride may wear a gold crown, which she places on the head of a bridesmaid during the reception dance to signal that the bridesmaid may be the next to marry. The American tradition is for brides to toss the bouquet to a group of unmarried women. The tradition of wearing something old stands for continuity and the wearing of something new for the future. A borrowed object refers to happiness, and blue stands for fidelity, purity, good fortune, and love. In the past in the United States another tradition was for the bride to wear a penny in her shoe (or in England a sixpence) symbolizing good fortune or luck. The significance of the train on the wedding dress originated in the Middle Ages, when train length indicated rank in court: The longer the train, the higher the prestige. If you've seen images of Princess Diana's wedding gown, you'll remember the extreme length of the train.

Values can be a focal point for discussion and policy. For example, government campaigns encourage families to eat together more often. These campaigns exist in part because of evidence showing that when families eat together, there is less likelihood of criminal or juvenile problems, as well as higher degrees of interaction, higher grades, and better nutrition. The traditional family meal is under threat as more people eat alone. According to a report compiled by FFP Complete, a market research department of Taylor Nelson Sofres, nearly one in two meals consumed in Britain are eaten by solitary diners, and convenience food is becoming more popular. This British report also indicated that many people appear to be eating separately at different times even though they live together. In the United States, Sara and Jack, a married couple in their early 50s with grown children, told the author of this book that that they eat their dinners on trays in front of the television every night. He is exhausted from his day as a golf pro dealing with the public, and she from her job in real estate, likewise dealing with the public. She says this is a second marriage for both of them, and they fell into this pattern quickly and are both happy with it. Their situation raises the interesting question: Should government be involved in trying to change people's eating patterns?

Each person has to separate out societal values or messages from what she or he truly wants. When someone finds himself or herself thinking, *I should be a better friend,* or *I should be thinner,* or *I should have a house that reflects my stature in the community,* he or she should stop and ask *Says who?* These thoughts often reflect extrinsic messages that you have internalized, but are they really you? Personal values are those that individuals hold for themselves, such as courage (standing up for one's beliefs), forgiveness (the ability to pardon others), and the right to pursue happiness. Perhaps you value solitude, health, and frugality more than others in your community do. People pride themselves on their personal values.

Personal values affect consumption patterns. The under-25 group is spending less on clothes, cars, and entertainment and more on home furnishings and homes, according to the Bureau of Labor Statistics:

> Justin Townsend, a computer consultant in Allen, Texas, lives in a house on a cul de sac with a big backyard and a swimming pool. When friends visit and give the place the once-over, they often ask where his parents are. "There are no parents," says Mr. Townsend, all of 22 years old. "It's my house." Tired of renting, he got a 100% loan last year and bought the $152,500 suburban house. He wanted a living room large enough for his pool table. "I couldn't really do that with a condo," he says. (Leung, 2003, July 16, p. B1)

Justin is part of a national trend toward home ownership at an earlier age. The number of homeowners who are under 25 doubled to 1.5 million in 2002, up from 792,000 in 1993 according to U.S. Census data. Successful, young Generation-Xers are not waiting until they are 30 and married to buy a house. According to David Tufts, executive vice president at Coldwell Banker, "These people are much more focused on success and lifestyle" (Leung, 2003, July 16, p. B1). Other examples of personal values include

- ◆ Giving the gift of time
- ◆ Putting someone else's feelings first
- ◆ Forgiving a wrong
- ◆ Expressing gratitude
- ◆ Mentoring another student or a fellow employee
- ◆ Serving the community

Professional values are related to jobs and careers; examples include being ambitious, capable, or logical. The same value can fall into all three categories. For example, a society, an individual, and a profession may all hold politeness as a value. Conversely, societal, personal, and professional values may be in

SUGGESTED ACTIVITY

List the parts of your life that are most important to you, ways you look after yourself, personal characteristics you value in yourself and in others. Do your relationships nurture these types of values? Does your current lifestyle match your values? Where is there a disconnect? Perhaps cleanliness and orderliness are important to you, but your apartment, house, or dorm room is a mess—is that a temporary or permanent state?

conflict. Employees who place a high value on honesty and integrity might expose the wrongdoing of the company or government agency. Their values are in conflict with the values of their employer.

One of the goals of a job interview is to determine whether there is an appropriate fit between the prospective employee's values and those of the organization. To help determine this, some organizations give psychological tests to applicants.

Instrumental and Terminal Values

SUGGESTED ACTIVITY

Review Table 3.2 and circle your top 3 terminal values and your top 3 instrumental values. Discuss in class why these are important to you.

Milton Rokeach, one of the most respected authorities on values, divided values into two types: terminal values and instrumental values (see Table 3.2). Terminal values are preferences for end states of existence, such as equality, freedom, or a comfortable life. Instrumental values are preferences for general modes of conduct, such as being helpful, loving, or intellectual. An individual taking the Rokeach Value Survey is asked to rank the values in each list from 1 (most important) to 18 (least important). Of particular significance are the top three values—these tend to be consistent over time.

Rokeach defined values as global beliefs that guide actions and judgments across a variety of situations. He concluded that values are individual attributes that affect attitudes, motivation, needs, and perceptions (Rokeach, 1973).

Values, Lifestyles, and Consumption

Henry David Thoreau said, "My life is like a stroll upon the beach, as near the ocean's edge as I can go." Values, lifestyles, and goals are shaped by experiences and are influenced by many sources, including parents, siblings, friends, teachers, religions, organizations, the media, and others.

Shopping behaviors provide an example of values in action. A person who comparison shops has different values (and perhaps resources) than a person who buys the first thing she or he sees. Choosing what to buy and where to shop are examples of consumption decisions based on values and lifestyle. Consider the differences between the consumption styles of college students Chelsea and Anthea. Chelsea usually shops at The Gap, but if she does not have much money to spend, she goes to Old Navy or another less expensive store. She goes clothes shopping every week. Anthea prefers department stores and tries to find what she needs as quickly as possible so she can leave. She sees shopping as a chore, so she goes only a few times a year and has turned to shopping over the Internet.

VALS: A Self-Test of Consumer Values

At SRI Business Consulting's Web site (**www.sric-bi.com**), you can answer a series of questions (by clicking on VALS and then VALS Survey), and your answers will be evaluated online. Your answers are value indicators, and at the end of the survey, you will be told which of the following eight categories you fall into (see Figure 3.2):

- ◆ Innovators (with the highest resources and innovation)
- ◆ Thinkers
- ◆ Achievers
- ◆ Experiencers
- ◆ Believers

TABLE 3.2
Terminal and Instrumental Values

Terminal Values (end states of existence)	Instrumental Values (modes of conduct)
A comfortable life (a prosperous life)	Ambitious (hard-working, aspiring)
An exciting life (a stimulating, active life)	Broadminded (open-minded)
A sense of accomplishment (lasting contribution)	Capable (competent, effective)
A world at peace (free of war and conflict)	Cheerful (lighthearted, joyful)
A world of beauty (nature and the arts)	Clean (neat, tidy)
Equality (brotherhood, equal opportunity)	Courageous (standing up for your beliefs)
Family security (taking care of loved ones)	Forgiving (willing to pardon others)
Freedom (independence, free choice)	Helpful (working for others' welfare)
Happiness (contentedness)	Honest (sincere, truthful)
Inner harmony (freedom from inner conflict)	Imaginative (daring, creative)
Mature love (sexual and spiritual intimacy)	Independent (self-reliant, self-sufficient)
National security (protection from attack)	Intellectual (intelligent, reflective)
Pleasure (an enjoyable, leisurely life)	Logical (consistent, rational)
Salvation (saved, eternal life)	Loving (affectionate, tender)
Self-respect (self-esteem)	Obedient (dutiful, respectful)
Social recognition (respect, admiration)	Polite (courteous, well-mannered)
True friendship (close companionship)	Responsible (dependable, reliable)
Wisdom (a mature understanding of life)	Self-controlled (restrained, self-disciplined)

Source: From "The Role of Values in Public Opinion Research," by Milton Rokeach, *Public Opinion Quarterly*, 32:554, Winter 1968–1969. Reprinted by permission of University of Chicago Press.

◆ Strivers

◆ Makers

◆ Survivors (with the lowest resources and innovation)

The VALS research was developed in the 1970s and 1980s by SRI International and Arnold Mitchell (Mitchell, 1983) and has since been modified. The VALS questionnaire on the Web site identifies an adult's VALS type.

FIGURE 3.2

The VALS™ Segments

*VALS places U.S. adult consumers into one of eight segments based on their responses to the **VALS questionnaire**. The main dimensions of the segmentation framework are **primary motivation** (the horizontal dimension) and **resources** (the vertical dimension).*

Source: Reprinted by permission of SRI Consulting Business Intelligence. All rights reserved.

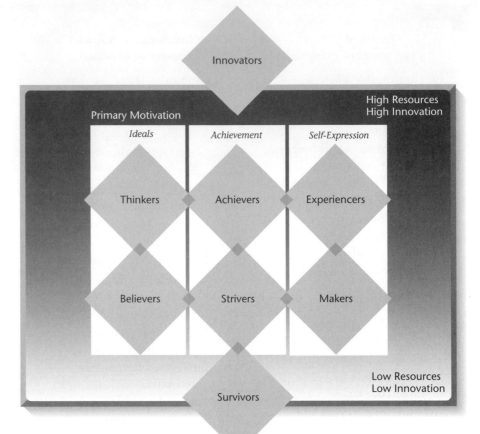

Primary Motivation

Consumers buy products and services and seek experiences that fulfill their characteristic preferences and give shape, substance, and satisfaction to their lives. An individual's primary motivation determines what in particular about the self or the world is the meaningful core that governs his or her activities. Consumers are inspired by one of three primary motivations: ideals, achievement, and self-expression. Consumers who are primarily motivated by ideals are guided by knowledge and principles. Consumers who are primarily motivated by achievement look for products and services that demonstrate success to their peers. Consumers who are primarily motivated by self-expression desire social or physical activity, variety, and risk.

Resources

A person's tendency to consume goods and services extends beyond age, income, and education. Energy, self-confidence, intellectualism, novelty seeking, innovativeness, impulsiveness, leadership, and vanity play a critical role. These personality traits in conjunction with key demographics determine an individual's resources. Different levels of resources enhance or constrain a person's expression of his or her primary motivation.

The company gathers this data and integrates the information into other questionnaires. Individual responses are strictly confidential. Any information you provide will not be sold or revealed in any way. If you take the survey, you will note that several questions are similar—the researchers are cross-checking answers and looking for consistency. If you answer a certain question one way one time that may be a mistake or random but if you answer it the same way four times that is a more reliable value indicator.

Nonprofit organizations and businesses like banks and medical centers use the results to understand preferences, attitudes, needs, and interests. Nonprofit organizations can use the data to analyze consumer attitudes toward such things as energy conservation or pension plans. Because it relies on words, a weakness of VALS is that it measures only a small portion of human experience. Future developments may include more sensory interactive experiences such as a multimedia game. Note the use of the word resources in the typologies and Figure 3.2. According to SRIC,

> A person's tendency to consume goods and services extends beyond age, income, and education. Energy, self-confidence, intellectualism, novelty seeking, innovativeness, impulsiveness, leadership, and vanity play a critical role. These personality traits in conjunction with key demographics determine an individual's resources. Different levels of resources enhance or constrain a person's expression of his or her primary motivation. ("The VALS Segments," 2003)

By collecting data over time, the company running VALS tracks shifts in consumer values and lifestyles. In the VALS system, values refer to a wide array of an individual's beliefs, hopes, desires, aspirations, and prejudices.

> Consumers buy products and services and seek experiences that fulfill their characteristic preferences and give shape, substance, and satisfaction to their lives. An individual's primary motivation determines what in particular about the self or the world is the meaningful core that governs his or her activities. Consumers are inspired by one of three primary motivations: ideals, achievement, and self-expression. Consumers who are primarily motivated by ideals are guided by knowledge and principles. Consumers who are primarily motivated by achievement look for products and services that demonstrate success to their peers. Consumers who are primarily motivated by self-expression desire social or physical activity, variety, and risk. ("The VALS Segments," 2003)

Marketers, retailers, and advertisers use the VALS research to help them design advertisements, displays, and products that attract the type of consumer they want to reach. The information derived from VALS has been linked with numerous major databases used by population analysts and consumer product companies. Here is an example of how VALS was used by one company: "A Japanese auto manufacturer repositioned its product line in the United States by using VALS to understand target consumer perceptions of its product mix better. The resulting advertising campaign based on VALS, increased sales 60% in six months" ("Consumer Demand," 2003). Although VALS is one of the best measures of values, it emphasizes individual attitudes and values, however, many consumption decisions are made by the household or are heavily influenced by several people. For example, two people would probably make the decision to purchase a king-size bed.

Societal and Cultural Values

Although values are enduring and measurable, they are not static. An individual's and society's values can change through an evolutionary process. They may be influenced by all of the following:

- ◆ Family or societal upset
- ◆ Technological, economic, and cultural changes
- ◆ Dramatic events, such as war, famine, or disease
- ◆ Environmental threats

The Great Depression, which began in October 1929 and lasted through the 1930s, influenced an entire generation to be cautious spenders. Thrift and security remained very important values to these people well after the Depression was over. More recently, fear of AIDS and the desire to practice safe sex have prompted more people to use condoms. Personal health and safety are the values that prompt the use (a behavior) of condoms. In regard to environmental safety (a value), people are more aware than ever before of the dangers of environmental threats, such as unclaimed floating barges laden with garbage, oil spills, and polluted air. Corresponding behaviors range from personal accountability (e.g., recycling or joining clean-up crews) to national accountability (e.g., the promotion of environmental legislation and more government enforcement of environmental regulations).

Values are the cornerstones of a society's culture. They stand for what is worthwhile, preferred, and consistent. **Cultural values** are generally held conceptualizations of what is right or wrong in a culture or what is preferred. Customs, manners, and gestures are indicators of cultural values. For example, bowing in deference to one's superiors or elders is customary in South Korea but would be unusual in the United States. Bowing is the outward behavior that reflects the underlying value of deference or respect. The deeper the bow, the more respect is shown. In the United States, respect for the elderly would more likely be displayed by use of formal names ("Mr. Smith," not "Joe") and by giving up seats on trains and buses as well as by offering other forms of aid.

People in Western cultures such as Canada, the United States, Australia, and most countries in Western Europe customarily eat three meals a day, whereas eating five meals a day is customary in East and Southeast Asian cultures. Even the meaning of gestures (a behavior) varies by culture. For example, the hand sign for "okay" in the United States is considered an obscene gesture in some Latin American countries.

Understanding cultural differences can be helpful in a variety of contexts, including management and planning of workplaces, transportation systems, and homes. For instance, supervisors who keep a close watch on their workers may be viewed as caring in some cultures, but overbearing and belittling in others. Cultures also vary in the types of mass transit they prefer and the amount of crowding people will accept in subways and trains. Typical cultural values and standards of comfort, function, and beauty influence floor plans of homes and interior designs.

For example, consider the differences between values in the United States and Japan. The Japanese tend to be more concerned with consensus and are group-oriented. Consequently, Japanese businesses offer their employees more security and longer-term employment than most American businesses. A study comparing the work values of American and Japanese men found significant differences (Engel, 1988). Japanese men placed a higher value on group involvement and loyalty to their employer and country. American men placed more emphasis on individualism, independence, and self-sufficiency and tended to believe that education and hard work led to success. These cultural differences in values start in the home. A study comparing Japanese American parenting styles with the practices of Americans of European ancestry found that ethnicity does affect how parents interact with and rear their children; child-rearing techniques varied considerably between the two groups (O'Reilly, Tokuno, & Ebata, 1986).

Cultural differences exist between Japan and the United States, despite their common bond of a strong industrial base. As contacts between the countries increase through mass media, travel, and business exchange, the values gap appears to be narrowing (O'Reilly et al., 1986). This trend provokes criticism from some observers, including Willis Harman, author of *Global Mind Change:*

> The industrialized world, having lost any consensus on ultimate meanings and values, steers itself mainly by economic and financial signals serving as pseudo-values. Part of the developing world is scrambling to catch up with the West; other parts are seeking some attractive alternative to scrapping their own cultural roots and adopting the alien culture of the West. (1998, p. 126)

One does not have to cross national borders to find cultural differences in values, attitudes, and behavior. They exist everywhere within countries. Regional food preferences are a good example. The food in northern Italy is quite different from the food in southern Italy. In the United States, grits are a favorite food in the South, but are rarely eaten elsewhere. People from different regions of the United States perceive and use time differently. A study conducted by Hilton Hotels Corporation found that 48 percent of the people living on the West Coast of the United States make time for their ideal weekend, compared with 38 percent of those on the East Coast (Rigdon, 1991). When asked about their goals, 72 percent of westerners said personal goals, such as vacations and hobbies, were among their top priorities for the 1990s compared with 55 percent of easterners. The study concluded that easterners appear to be always working, whereas westerners work hard but also play hard.

Families, Values, Standards, and Households

All families have values and value orientations, and the way they maintain their homes is an expression of those values. As Chapter 1 explained, standards are the quantitative and/or qualitative criteria used to measure values and goals and reconcile resources with demands. Different family members may have different time and household work standards. What is "on time" to one family member may not be "on time" to another. And a teenager's standard of a clean bedroom may not be the same as his parents'. Standards also vary greatly between households. Dennis, a 13-year-old, told his parents about the variations he had observed in the household cleaning standards of his three friends:

> We don't like going to Daryl's house because it is sterile. It is so clean it is spooky, like nobody lives there and we are afraid to touch anything. They even clean the driveway. The only things in Daryl's room are a bed, a dresser, and a desk. Steve's house is a mess because they have that awful dog tearing up everything. Brent's house is about like ours, somewhere in the middle. So we usually end up at our house, sometimes at Brent's.

The physical and emotional quality of home and family life has been a subject of debate across time and across cultures. Two national surveys about family values and patterns of behavior indicated that people in the United States think the family is falling apart everywhere but in their own home. This paradox is called the "I'm OK, but you're not" syndrome. According to one survey, "four out of five Americans claim they wouldn't give up Thanksgiving dinner with their family for $1,000." Nevertheless, two out of three Americans say that family values have grown weaker. The researchers summed up this paradox as follows: "Some of this is real change. . . . But some is the same pattern you find when you ask people about schools or crime or members of Congress. Everyone else's is terrible, but theirs is OK."

SUGGESTED ACTIVITY

Make a list of your family's values and give an example of each. This could be an action, a memory, an activity, or a saying that demonstrates the value.

Couples may or may not have compatible values:

> Daniel Caine, president of Split-Up.com, a financial-planning firm for divorcing couples, says divorce is rooted in five areas: insecurity, money, communication, clash of values, and insufficient separation from family. He recommends asking: Are you comfortable with my religious observance? My family? My urge for wealth? "Opposites attract," he warns, "but that doesn't mean they stay together." (Zaslow, 2003, p. D1)

In a 1988 poll of 200 new brides by Diamond Cutters International, 46 percent said yes and 54 percent said no to the question "Would you ever consider trading in your engagement ring for a bigger, better diamond?" When these women were polled fifteen years later, of the 46 percent who said yes, 81 percent were divorced. Of the more sentimental types who said no, 78 percent were still married. The psychiatrist who monitored the study, Francisco Montalvo, said the results suggest that people who are "hard-wired" to upgrade rings may also be driven to upgrade houses, cars, and even spouses (Zaslow, 2003).

Value Formation and Socialization

Values are shared by most members of a society and are passed on to younger members by senior members. Families, especially parents, play a fundamental role in forming children's values. The ability to cope with and adjust to life problems and demands is based on the psychological foundations of early family experience. One study of college students found that the more positive the family experience, the more likely the students were to have a positive attitude and believe they were in control of their lives (Parish & Nunn, 1988). Parents perceive that within their society certain competencies and values are important for their child's growth and development. For example, parents influence their children's dress and grooming standards, manners and speech, and educational motivation. Thus, the culture's child-rearing patterns reflect the parents' and the greater society's values and the environmental context in which the parents live. As the society changes, so do the values parents impart to their children. A study examined changes in values in children in the United States from 1964 to 1984 and found that parents in more recent years desired their children to have more autonomy or self-direction (to have good sense, sound judgment and be honest, responsible, and considerate) and were less concerned with conformity or obedience (obeying parents, having good manners, and being neat and clean (Alwin, 1989).

The process by which children learn the rules and values of a society is called **socialization.** Although the family is the primary socializer of children, parents are not the only influence. Values are affected by a host of variables, conditions, and sources, such as the media, friends, and extended family. Furthermore, to imply that socialization is only a childhood experience would be misleading. Although socialization starts in infancy, it is a lifelong process influenced by many sources.

A subsystem of socialization is called consumer socialization; through this process, people acquire the skills, attitudes, and information necessary to function in the marketplace. Children initially learn much of their consumption behavior from accompanying their parents on shopping trips. By adolescence, children are likely to shop with friends. In fact, going shopping with friends has become such a popular teen activity that some malls in the United States have limited teen shopping hours. This practice raises an interesting question of societal values: Should stores be able to restrict who shops in them?

The New Traditionalism

Dominant social and cultural trends are often counterbalanced by other trends. For example, the value of traditionalism (going back to basics) appears to recur in cycles. It is estimated that 29 percent of Americans can be called "heartlanders," or *traditionalists*. They hold traditional views, specifically believing in the value of small town and country life (Ray, 1997). Traditionalists are a smaller group within the U.S. population than *modernists* (47 percent), who place a high value on personal success, consumerism, materialism, and technological rationality. The other main group consists of the *cultural creatures* (24 percent), who put a strong emphasis on having new and unique experiences and are attuned to global issues and social causes.

Figure 3.3 shows an advertisement for *Good Housekeeping* magazine that suggests that many families adopt a lifestyle called the "New Traditionalism."

FIGURE 3.3

The New Traditionalists

Source: Reprinted by permission. Copyright 1989 The Hearst Corporation. All rights reserved.

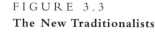

THE NEW TRADITIONALISTS.

THEY'RE THE CUSTODIANS OF THE GREAT AMERICAN BRANDS.

Diane and Ian Ingersoll are today's pioneers. They design and build Shaker furniture. They live a simple, solid family life. And suddenly their furniture, and their lifestyle, has a whole new following.

The Ingersolls embody the most powerful social force in America today – the New Traditionalist movement. For marketers – it signals the end of "conspicuous consumption" and the trend to "conscientious consumption."

New Traditionalists shop more strategically, more conscientiously than most people – they read labels, they take environmental concerns seriously, they stay more loyal to the products they know and trust. And at a time of diminishing brand loyalty, they are the true custodians of America's brands.

They put their trust in Good Housekeeping, because we have always stood for the values they are seeking. No one speaks to the New Traditionalist with the authority of Good Housekeeping – the Magazine, the Institute, and the Seal.

AMERICA BELIEVES IN GOOD HOUSEKEEPING

According to the advertisement, the new traditionalist family is made up of conscientious consumers who read labels, are brand-conscious, and take environmental concerns seriously. Further, according to the advertisement, the new traditionalists put their trust in *Good Housekeeping* because they share the magazine's value orientation—illustrating that a media entity, such as a magazine, can have a value orientation just as individuals and families have. Newspapers, books, and television and radio shows also take value stances. For example, many magazines and newspapers will not publish cigarette advertisements.

The renewed interest in traditionalism is not the exclusive domain of one magazine. Clothing and home furnishings retailers have noticed a renewed interest in traditional patterns, styles, and fabrics. The new traditionalists put the well-being of families and children ahead of ostentatious consumption. A car advertisement directed to the new traditionalists would emphasize the car's safety (e.g., airbags, low accident rate) over its speed. According to Levin (1989), middle-class traditionalists also tend to make prudent provisions for the future in the form of savings and investments and believe that individuals and governments alike should pay their bills.

Another survey identified six types of families, including one called "traditionalists." According to this survey, the largest group, representing 24 percent of all families, consists of the "family enthusiasts," who embody nearly all of the traditional values and some other characteristics as well. Family enthusiasts like to stay within the proper bounds of society. As a group, they are young and optimistic. Overall, the survey's respondents said that values are best taught by parents in the home.

Attitudes

As noted earlier in this chapter, *attitudes* are favorable or unfavorable feelings or ideas about some matter. They are expressions of likes and dislikes. People have attitudes about other people, objects, and issues. Examples of attitudes are prejudice about racial or cultural issues, notions about the characteristics of rich people versus poor people, and ideas about war, space exploration, or politics. Letters to the editor in newspapers and magazines and Internet chat rooms are filled with attitudes and opinions.

Attitudes are learned. Just as with values, children learn their attitudes primarily from their families, but in time those attitudes are also shaped by other environmental influences. As they develop into adults, "men and women accumulate information that shapes their perceptions of their roles as men and women, their roles as parents, their behaviors, their attitudes and their belief systems" (Palkovitz & Copes, 1988, pp. 191–192). For example, household management practices (ways of planning and doing work in the home, standards of cleanliness, and assigning tasks) are learned first in childhood. Adults choose to accept, reject, or modify the household management practices they learned in their youth.

Once learned, attitudes influence behavior. Two experts on the effects of attitudes on behavior, Icek Ajzen and Martin Fishbein (1980), developed a theory of reasoned action that assumes that human beings are usually quite rational and make systematic use of the information available to them. Ajzen and Fishbein posit that individuals consider the implications of their actions before they decide to engage in a given behavior or not. In their theory, a person's intention to perform (or not to perform) a behavior is the immediate determinant of the action. The individual's positive or negative evaluation of performing a behavior is her or his attitude toward the behavior. The second factor in the intention to act is called the subjective norm. This refers to the person's perception of the social pressures put on him or her to perform or not perform the behavior in question. Ease or difficulty of behavior is also a factor. Thus, intention to behave a certain way will be affected by whether the person evaluates the behavior as positive, by what other people think, and by whether the action is perceived as easy or difficult. Beliefs shape attitudes and subjective norms, which in turn lead to intention and then actual behavior.

Because attitudes are not directly observable, they must be determined by research or by observation of behavior, although care should be taken in inferring attitudes and values based solely on behavior. For example, the distance between two people who are talking with each other may be indicative of their attitudes (likes and dislikes) toward each other, but it may also reflect cultural standards of behavior (see Chapter 7). As another example, work behavior is often easy to observe. Is the person a loner? Or a team player? Is a person always late? Or early? Reliable? Or unreliable? Is the person's work neat? Or sloppy? Attitudes about time, independence, control, obedience to authority, and conformity to rules all affect work behavior.

GOALS AND MOTIVATION

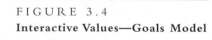

Some attitudes and values are held more strongly than others. Likewise, some goals are pursued more strongly than others. If goals are to be achieved, they must be specific and realistic.

Figure 3.4 shows the relationship between values and goals. Once a goal has been identified, values provide the impetus—the start—toward goal attainment. A person fulfills a desire or a need by engaging in goal-seeking behavior—leading, one hopes, to goal achievement. The seeking of goals requires energy, commitment, and motivation. As the figure shows, not all goals are reached; some have to be reformulated or dropped. Accordingly, flexibility is one of the most important characteristics of goal setting. Knowing when to let go of unrealistic or unattainable goals is an important step in the management process. Goals should be constantly reevaluated and updated. If goals are not fully committed to (and are not exciting and compelling), they have little chance of succeeding. Here are some pointers to remember when you set goals:

- ◆ What benefits will attaining this goal bring to my life?
- ◆ What will I be able to do once this goal is achieved?
- ◆ How will this goal benefit others?
- ◆ How will I feel when I have achieved this goal?

Goals versus Habits

Goals are things people are trying to accomplish. Not all behavior is goal-directed or goal-activated; some is simply basic survival behavior or habit,

FIGURE 3.4
Interactive Values—Goals Model

| Identify goal desired | → | Values | → | Goal formation and commitment | → | Goal-seeking behaviors | → | Goal attainment, rejection, or reformulation |

such as watching television. **Habits** are repetitive, often unconscious patterns of behavior. Confucius said that "the nature of men is always the same; it is their habits that separate them." In other words, habits are unique to the individual. They can be either good or bad. Whining and overeating are bad habits. Treating others with respect and courtesy are good habits.

Goals encompass more than just the fulfillment of immediate wants and needs. For example, graduating from law school is a goal, but eating a hamburger is not—it is the fulfillment of a need, hunger. Mihaly Csikszentmihalyi, author of *Flow: The Psychology of Optimal Experience,* says that

> The earliest explanations of human behavior, starting with Aristotle, assumed that actions were motivated by goals. Modern psychology, however, has shown that much of what people do can be explained more parsimoniously by simpler, often unconscious causes. . . . I do not claim that most people most of the time act the way they do because they are trying to achieve goals; but only that when they do so, they experience a sense of control which is absent when behavior is not motivated by consciously chosen goals. (1990, p. 242)

Goal Attributes

Not all goals are created equal; each has certain characteristics or attributes. For example, goals vary in

- ◆ *Intensity:* Commitment, how much the goal is desired
- ◆ *Complexity:* The number of the goal's interrelationships
- ◆ *Priority:* How important the goal is
- ◆ *Resource Use:* How much the goal is going to cost (energy, money) and how many resources will be put into this goal versus other pursuits
- ◆ *Timing:* How long it will take to attain the goal

These goal attributes are demonstrated by the behaviors of Roger and Stephanie. Roger, a 20-year-old, worked for eight years on a paper route and after-school jobs and saved every penny to buy a Corvette. Stephanie, a 22-year-old, made finding the best job her top priority her senior year in college and put that goal before everything else.

Goals influence action in four ways (Locke, 1968):

1. By directing attention
2. By fostering strategy development
3. By mobilizing effort
4. By increasing persistence

In the preceding examples, Roger and Stephanie directed their attention, developed strategies, mobilized effort, and persisted until they reached their goals. Both were highly goal-driven. Goals provide a sense of purpose and direct behavior toward a positive end result (e.g., a Corvette, a job).

Although goals are generally regarded as positive, problems can surface when goal conflict occurs in families or other groups. Conflict develops when goals compete or subvert each other. If a family's goal is to eat a leisurely Sunday dinner together, conflict may arise if the teenage children would rather skip dinner and spend the afternoon with their friends.

Types of Goals

For purposes of discussion, it is useful to assign goals to categories. Among the ways goals can be categorized are the following:

Striving for goals has often been compared to climbing a mountain.

- *By time:* short term, intermediate, or long term
- *By role:* personal, professional, societal, or familial
- *By type:* primary or secondary

Each category will be discussed in the following sections.

Goals and Time

In terms of time, goals can be separated into short-term, intermediate, and long-term goals.

- Short-term goals usually take less than three months to accomplish.
- Intermediate goals can usually be achieved in three months to one year.
- Long-range goals usually take more than one year to achieve.

A fall-semester college junior may have a short-term goal of finishing current coursework, an intermediate goal of finishing the year, and a long-term goal of graduating. College students are assumed to be long-term planners. For example, job recruiters typically ask college interviewees, "What do you plan to be doing five years from now?" With this question, the recruiter finds out whether the student has thought ahead, is a realistic planner, and is ambitious.

Sometimes people think of goals as a luxury reserved for the wealthy and better educated. Certainly, setting long-term goals implies a secure future or at least one partially under control. Low-income families do not always have the resource base to think beyond short-term goals. In the VALS typology discussed earlier, they may be survivors; their attention is focused on immediate survival. In terms of Maslow's hierarchy of needs, they are concerned with the physiological and safety levels of the hierarchy. For them, planning a year in the future would be a luxury. At the other extreme are celebrities who may have managers or agents who plan their schedules five years or more in advance.

Goals and Roles

Another way to categorize goals is by role. In this typology, goals can be personal, professional, societal, or familial. Personal goals include such things as learning how to swing dance, ski, skydive, or ride a horse. Professional goals are related to one's job or career; they might include improving computer skills, writing a contract, or conducting an interview. You achieve career success when you reach the goals you have set for yourself; because the goals are individually defined, they vary among individuals. For some, success is defined by titles, awards, frequent promotions, or salary increases; for others, these are less important, and success is defined by completion of difficult projects, for example. One way to envision success is to pay attention to the winners in a field—who they are and what they do, with special focus on those with continued success rather than a singular moment of glory.

Societal goals are commonly held by the greater society; they include such goals as having a full-time job by a certain age, marrying, having children, and retiring. Familial goals are related to being a son, daughter, parent, or other family member. At any one time, a person might be achieving personal and professional goals while considering or reacting to societal or familial goals.

An individual can have one or two goals or dozens. People who are professionally oriented may have many career goals and ignore personal goals. Other people may have no professional or career goals (their job is simply something they do to earn money, so they go home at five o'clock and forget about it) and are interested only in personal or family goals. Management comes into play because goals must be prioritized and strategies developed. What is most important? How do people go about getting what they want?

Goals by Type: Primary and Secondary Goals

Goals can also be categorized as primary and secondary (Dillard, Segrin, & Hardin, 1989):

- ◆ Primary goals are formed to influence process and progress.
- ◆ Secondary goals motivate the individual and ultimately lead to and complement the primary goal.

For example, if a person's primary goal is to attain a college degree, then his or her secondary goals would include being accepted into a college, passing courses, and completing graduation requirements. Secondary goals are smaller; they motivate and collectively add up to the primary goals.

Setting Goals

The beneficial effect of goal setting on task performance is one of the most validated concepts in psychology. Ninety percent of the reported studies have found that goal setting has positive or partially positive effects on task performance (Locke, Shaw, Saari, & Latham, 1981). Simply stated, people accomplish more when they set goals. A study of survivors of concentration camps found that those who had a purpose for living and well-defined goals were able to withstand greater deprivation, including starvation and torture, than those without goals (Powell & Enright, 1990). Many of the survivors said that their main goal was to see their families again.

To be helpful, goals should have certain characteristics. First, goals must be reasonable, affordable, and within the resources of the goal setter. For example, a person who wants to buy a house must have the resources to make a down payment and meet the monthly payments. Saying that goals should be realistic and attainable does not mean that they should be easy to accomplish. Indeed, goals should present some challenge for the goal setter.

Goals should also be clearly formed and simply stated. When asked about his formula for success, J. Paul Getty, one of the richest men in the world, said "Rise early. Work late. Strike oil." The importance of having clear, specific goals cannot be overemphasized. The goal of buying a new car is too vague because it cannot be visualized. The goal of buying a certain type of car in one year is effective, however, because it allows the mind to form a specific picture of the car and focuses attention on actions and a time frame for achieving the goal. When the person sees advertisements for that particular car or passes one in a parking lot, her decision to try to buy that car will be reinforced. Of course, during the year, she may decide on another model, but at least initially visualizing a specific car can be helpful.

Goals provide an avenue for freedom, a sense of control, and, as noted before, a sense of direction and purpose. A lack of initiative and direction can lead to unstable goals, however (Robbins, Payne, & Chartrand, 1990). In that case, the person will vacillate and change goals frequently without reason, thereby losing the sense of purpose goals can provide.

Optimism, Goals, and Well-Being

In *Learned Optimism*, Martin Seligman, a past president of the American Psychological Association and professor of psychology at the University of

Pennsylvania, writes that optimism is essential for a good and successful life. Optimism is necessary for achieving goals because it allows an individual to use the wisdom won by a lifetime of trial and error to better effect (Seligman, 1991, 2002). **Optimism** is a tendency or a disposition to expect the best outcome or to think hopefully about a situation. According to Seligman, flexible optimism—optimism with its eyes open—provides limitless benefits. He adds that habits of thinking and living need not go on forever; in other words, people are not stuck with their pasts, but can learn from them. Seligman points out that "the most significant finding in psychology in the last twenty years is that individuals choose the way they think" (1991, p. 8). The kinds of phrases associated with optimism include a person saying or thinking

- "I'm usually lucky."
- "I'm talented."
- "My rival is no good."
- "I'm smart."
- "I'm good at lots of things."
- "I give everything my best shot."
- "I have a lot to look forward to."

In pursuit of understanding the linkages between health and illness, other researchers have explored the relationship between optimism and general well-being. For example, a study of attorneys revealed a significant relationship between optimism and general well-being. Optimism was defined in this study as the degree to which one has a favorable approach to the world (Sweetman, Munz, & Wheeler, 1993). *An optimist is more likely to think that goals are reachable.* A study by scientists at the Mayo Clinic in Rochester, Minnesota, revealed that optimists had 19 percent greater longevity, in terms of their expected life span, than did pessimists (Danner, Snowdon, & Friesen, 2001).

A Harris poll revealed that Americans are happier and more optimistic about their future than are most Europeans. Within Europe the percentage of people who were very satisfied with their lives varied from 64 percent in Denmark to 26 percent in Finland. Those in between included the Netherlands, Luxembourg, Sweden, United Kingdom, Ireland, and Austria. Irish and Swedish respondents to the telephone poll said their lives had improved more in the last five years than did Americans. The most optimistic European country was Spain. Germany and the Mediterranean countries indicated they were less happy and optimistic than Northern Europeans (Taylor, 2003). Not all evidence comes from surveys. In anecdotal evidence, curators at a New York retrospective exhibit of works by Matisse and Picasso noted that the colorful, cheerful works of Matisse drew far more visitors than did Picasso's (Goodale, 2003).

Importance of Challenge

How does a person choose which goals to pursue? The study of management assumes that if someone devotes the required resources, plans well, and makes the sacrifices necessary, almost anything is achievable. Consequently, people should aim high and set goals that force them to do their best. Setting specific and challenging goals leads to higher performance than setting easy goals (Locke et al., 1981). By creating a challenge, goals affect performance by directing attention, mobilizing effort, increasing persistence, and motivating strategy development.

Anthony, who is single and 25, listed his goals for the next five years as follows:

- ◆ *Career/work:* Own a fitness center
- ◆ *Home:* Have a nice apartment
- ◆ *Personal:* Date someone seriously, have lots of friends
- ◆ *Leisure:* Work out every day

Do Anthony's goals seem realistic for someone who works full-time in a gym and has a college degree in nutrition and fitness? How much does it cost to open a fitness center? To rent an apartment? What secondary goals does he need to accomplish in order to reach his primary goal of owning a center?

Anthony's goal of owning a fitness center has created a very real challenge for him and forced him to develop strategies to achieve it. Anthony's strategies include learning all he can from the gym where he now works before opening his own fitness center and fulfilling his secondary goals of paying off his college loans and credit cards and saving money. According to Csikszentmihalyi, "of all the virtues we can learn no trait is more useful, more essential for survival, and more likely to improve the quality of life than the ability to transform adversity into an enjoyable challenge" (1990, p. 200).

Plans for Attaining Goals

Once goals are set, a plan for achieving them must be developed. Planning includes all managerial activities that determine results and the appropriate means to achieve those results. It involves the following four steps:

1. Set specific goals and prioritize them.
2. State the goals clearly and positively. For example, "I will be a nonsmoker by January 1"—not "I will stop smoking." "I will lose five pounds"—not "I will lose weight."
3. Forecast possible future events and the resources that will be needed to deal with them. This entails determining both the level of material resources that will be needed and the amount of effort that will be required.
4. Implement the plan by following through with goal-directed activity

Note that the planning process begins with prioritizing goals. Prioritizing involves ranking goals by the degree of commitment to them. Commitment is the sense of obligation one feels toward the goal. If a goal is not enticing or inspiring, something is wrong, and the goal will not serve its function of motivating the person to greater effort. Prioritizing forces people to decide what they really want and how they are going to get it.

A New Year's Eve tradition in many countries is to make resolutions, which are types of goals. About 23 percent of New Year's resolutions are broken in the first week, 45 percent by the end of January (Norcross & Prochaska, 1998). People fail to keep their resolutions because their willpower is not enough, they haven't chosen realistic resolutions, and fail to devise a plan to work on them every day. Even the smallest step makes a difference in the long run.

Obstacles to Goal Achievement

Crises happen. All the goal setting in the world cannot stop unplanned events from altering the course of resource use. Obstacles to achieving goals include, but are not limited to, the following: time, parents, family, rules, peers, social

SUGGESTED ACTIVITY

Keep a journal. Each week write down your goals (short, intermediate, and/or long-term). For one month do not look back at the previous entries; then read all of them at once. Do you see a pattern? Were any of the goals accomplished? Or was significant progress made on any of them? If yes, keep on; if not, perhaps goals need to be reevaluated.

customs, demands, imagination, money, health, and natural disasters (e.g., hurricanes, tornadoes, floods).

Obstacles alone do not determine the fate of human goal-seeking behavior. Instead, the way people perceive and react to obstacles will determine whether they will reach their goals. One way to overcome obstacles is to divide larger goals into smaller ones, which allow a person to make progress a little at a time. It also helps to find a trusted, nonjudgmental friend who is willing to talk about one's goals and periodically check on how projects are going. Monitoring one's progress by marking deadlines on a calendar is useful as well. Everyone should also become aware of when roadblocks are likely to occur. Is it at the start of projects? In the middle? At the end?

Resilience is defined as the ability to overcome obstacles and to achieve positive outcomes after experiencing extreme difficulties. Individual traits associated with resilience include intelligence, competence, a good-natured temperament, internal locus of control, and self-esteem. Researchers also note that relationships can help protect a person from stress and promote positive growth. In other words, resilience—although an inner ability (involving courage and fortitude)—is helped and accentuated by strong encouraging relationships. Renee Spencer (2000) found a number of studies indicating that one supportive adult can provide good outcomes for children coping with poverty, malnutrition, separation from a parent, marital discord in the home, divorcing parents, and parental mental illness.

Finally, goals need to be reevaluated. Resistance to goals may mean it is time to change them or to take a break. Pursuing goals requires energy.

Needs for Achievement: the n Ach Factor

People can make themselves miserable trying to set impossible goals such as earning a million dollars in a year or insisting that everyone be happy every minute of a family vacation. Healthy goals are a little out of reach, but they are not impossible dreams. Compromise and flexibility rule the day.

In a classic study, David McClelland, a Harvard psychologist, stressed that individuals vary in their need for achievement, which he called "n Ach" (McClelland, 1961). He found that each individual has a different level of motivation for overcoming obstacles, desiring success, and expending effort to seek out difficult tasks and do them well as quickly as possible. He emphasized that the achievement motive can be expressed as a desire to perform in terms of a standard of excellence or to be successful in competitive situations. *You can choose to act in ways that help you achieve goals.*

A person possessing high n Ach takes moderate risks, not high risks as one might assume. This phenomenon can be demonstrated by the ring-toss game. Low achievers will stand very near the peg and drop the rings over it or stand far away and wildly throw the ring. High achievers will carefully calculate the exact distance from the peg that will challenge their abilities, yet still give them a chance for success. Thus, low achievers take a low or high risk, and high achievers take a moderate risk. Research indicates that this pattern holds true in most walks of life and for children as well as for adults.

Lifestyles, Goals, and Feedback

Each person has a basic notion of what he or she wants in the way of food, shelter, and companionship; these basic needs evolve into a more complicated set of needs that combine to form a lifestyle. Likewise, goals often start simple and evolve into more complicated notions. A recent college graduate might want a job, any job, to get started and then, as time goes by, develop a more specific definition of what a good job is.

Forming short-term goals is a way to conserve the time and energy needed to reach long-term goals. Short-term goals have the advantage that they can be completed fairly rapidly, giving a sense of accomplishment. An author, for example, might write newspaper and magazine articles during the same time period she is writing a novel so that she always has something in process, in the mail, or in print.

Individuals and families need feedback to determine whether their goals are viable or need to be changed. Goals are generally thought of as positives in life, but they can be self-defeating if they are too difficult. Goals can also have a negative effect if they cause people to be so single-minded that they do not see other possible goals or courses of action that might be better. Both depression over failure to be an overnight success and a single-minded focus on today without a thought of the future can be self-defeating. Listening to feedback helps keep goals realistic and on track.

College Students' Values, Goals, and Life Outcomes

Psychologists conducted a fascinating study of college yearbook photos. They compared the actual life outcomes of women students whose photos showed a genuine smile, called the Duchenne smile (named after its discoverer Guillaume Duchenne), with those of women whose photos showed an inauthentic smile, called the Pan American smile. In the Duchenne smile the corners of the mouth turn up, and the skin around the corners of the eyes crinkles (like crow's feet). The muscles that control these functions are connected, and it is difficult to voluntarily control them. The Pan Am smile is a fake smile named after flight attendants posing in advertisements for a now defunct airline. Dacher Kelter and LeeAnne Harker (2001) of the University of California at Berkeley found that the women with a Duchenne smile were more likely to be married, to stay married, and to experience more personal well-being over a 30-year period. Others questioned whether the results had more to do with good looks than the smile itself, so the investigators went back and rated how pretty each of the women seemed. They found that looks had nothing to do with good marriages or life satisfaction. It turns out that a genuinely smiling woman was simply more likely to be well-wed and happy (Seligman, 2002).

College students' values, goals, and life outcomes have been the subject of many studies. In the last two decades, researchers have found that, overall, college men and women have similar goal and value orientations. For example, Hammersla and McMahan (1990) studied 303 college students and found that women were about as goal-oriented as men. They found that college students placed a high value on relationships with members of the opposite sex and said they were willing to sacrifice most other goals for the relationships, should that be necessary. Two other researchers found that college women rated personal development and social skills higher than college men did (Kaufman & Creamer, 1991). The study showed that among these students, women were more likely than men to invest significant effort in relations with peers.

In a study of work attitudes, over two-thirds of college men and women endorsed "equal emphasis on family and career," and 90 percent expected husband and wife to participate equally in the care and discipline of children (Phillips & Johnston, 1985). Sometimes it is difficult to coordinate family life with other drives and goals, however. For example, Raina and Vats (1990) observed that achievement and prestige are top priorities for men. More research is needed on the choices and sacrifices men and women make, as well as the tensions between goal achievement and interpersonal relationships among both men and women (Hammersla & McMahan, 1990).

For many students, the college years serve as a transition stage between living at home with parents and living on their own—a physical and emotional bridge between childhood and adulthood. In reflecting back on their relationship with their parents, women undergraduates in one study reported spending more time with their mothers than with their fathers (Miller & Lane, 1991). Both male and female students said they received more positive treatment from their mothers and experienced more positive emotions and closeness with their mothers than with their fathers. Further, Miller and Lane's study found that individuation and well-being were facilitated when students had close, personal relationships with parents rather than distancing relationships. Thus, a close family relationship led to a more successful adjustment to college life for students.

Miller and Lane's findings seem to indicate that fathers have contributed less than mothers to their children's sense of well-being, but to cite the results of only one study on such an important topic would be misleading. Study after study documents the importance of both the mother and the father to a child's development. One series of studies on college students' career expectations found that fathers had an important influence on their sons' and daughters' career expectations—specifically, their salary and work hour expectations (Goldsmith, Hoffman, & Hofacker, 1993; Hoffman, Goldsmith, & Hofacker, 1992; Hoffman, Hofacker, & Goldsmith, 1992).

© Royalty Free/CORBIS

The happiest college students surround themselves with family and friends.

Another study by Flanagan (1990) revealed the association between parents' current career status and children's goals. She found that mothers and fathers who received promotions (those moving up in their careers) were the most likely to expect their children to go to college. Parents who were temporarily laid off were least likely to encourage their sons and daughters to go to college. Adolescents whose parents received promotions had clear, consistent goals, whereas adolescents whose parents were laid off had a limited view of future options.

Because college is a transitory stage, goal instability is not unusual during the college years. For example, students may change their majors and career choices many times. One study found that the degree of goal instability was associated with the prediction of adjustment during entry to college. For example, goal instability was related to personal control and esteem, but was also related to depression and anxiety (Robbins, Payne, & Chartrand, 1990). In other words, goal instability is not unusual for college students and can even be helpful, but it can also be uncomfortable for the individual experiencing it.

Another study found that nearly one-third of college freshman do not return for their sophomore year. The main reasons they do not return are job opportunities, financial circumstances, and personal situations (Cravatta, 1997). The no-return rate was much higher for community colleges than for four-year universities.

Although college students have the same array of values as the general population, the media and social scientists over the years have attempted to categorize the general typology of college students by decade or generation. For example, students of the 1950s have been described as conservative and conforming, as holders of traditional values who had only slight concern for societal problems. After graduation, supposedly, a typical student from these years went on to become the "organization man" who obeyed the law, fulfilled obligations, and strove to get ahead (Whyte, 1957). Some commentators disagree with this characterization. David Halberstam, author of *The Fifties* (1993), writes that the 1950s were a decade of enormous change, some good, some bad, but certainly the 1950s were not boring or rule-driven. As examples of change, he notes that 1950s America experienced the Korean War, the development of the hydrogen bomb, and significant advances in civil rights.

The late 1960s and early 1970s are considered years of unrest and change, characterized by the advent of the peace movement, the women's liberation movement, and other societal causes. College students challenged traditional ways of doing things, questioned material gain, and extolled the virtues of individual rights and freedom. Values changed on campuses, exemplified by the widespread introduction of coeducational dormitories and the end of dress codes and curfews.

In the 1980s, the college culture moved back to material goals; students flooded business schools and became more egocentric and less committed to broad sociopolitical change. The students of the 1980s grew up during the downsizing of certain businesses; they saw or experienced social and personal insecurities. As a result, they became more savvy and more skeptical (Stoneman, 1998).

Students of the 1990s enjoyed the benefits of a strong economy and a good labor market. They had more money than their predecessors. Colleges realized that standard dormitory-style living was becoming less attractive to students. Most built or renovated dormitories; others allowed privatized on-campus apartments.

How will current students compare with those of previous generations? One trend is the growing concern over crime in society and substance abuse on campuses and the subsequent increase in more secure and substance-free dormitories on campuses (Seligmann, 1991). Another trend is increasing acceptance of fragmentation and extreme individuality. In the 1990s a common theme was "I want to decide something for myself and on my own, and not try to be part of the crowd" (Stoneman, 1998). Note that this last study is from 1998; newer studies indicate a return to social engagement and involvement by college students. Perhaps this is in reaction to the types of disengagement experienced in many areas of life: political apathy, retreat from church attendance, eroding union membership, and the decline of bridge clubs, dinner parties, Rotary Clubs, volunteering, and blood donation (Putnam, 2000). College students are often at the forefront of new thought and action. Through intensive orientation programs, parents' weekends, and other such activities, campuses are trying to build a sense of community and purpose that meets students' needs. *It appears that the happiest people (college students or anyone else) "surround themselves with family and friends, don't care about keeping up with the Joneses next door, lose themselves in daily activities, and most important, forgive easily"* (Elias, 2002, p. A1).

Motivation

"The biggest human temptation is . . . to settle for too little" says Thomas Merton, an American monk and spiritual writer. Thomas Edison and his staff tried 3,000 ways to perfect a lightbulb before they found one that worked. A motivated person has to take risks and overcome obstacles in order to achieve goals. The word *motivation* comes from the Latin word *movere* (to move). In management, **motivation** refers to movement toward goals or other desired outcomes and also to vigor, drive, persistence, creativity, direction, and sustained energy. One of the goals of nurturing children is to build each child's strengths and virtues as well as to help them find a niche where their positive traits can develop to the fullest.

Motivated individuals work hard. However, motivation is not just a personal construct; it is the driving force behind companies and organizations. Car salespeople try to sell a certain number of cars per month to reach a quota. Real estate salespeople try to sell enough houses in a year to be on the "million dollar seller list." Girl Scouts try to sell enough boxes of cookies to go to camp. Goal setting's potential for improving productivity is so well established that it is rarely questioned as a management technique.

Motivation is a process rather than an end state. The process begins with an unsatisfied need that creates tension. This tension drives a person to undertake a search (for resources or information), which leads to the need being satisfied and the tension reduced (Robbins, 1991). Hence, the person does not feel satisfied until her or his need is fulfilled or the goal attained.

Internal and external factors contribute to the motivation to achieve goals. **Intrinsic motivation** involves the underlying causes and the internal need for competence and self-determination. It refers to the pleasure or value a person derives from the content of work or activity. If a student works hard in school, the satisfaction he or she derives from learning and mastering a subject provides the intrinsic motivation to keep learning. **Extrinsic motivation** involves forces external to the individual—environmental factors such as titles, raises, preferred offices, promotions, and other forms of rewards. For a student, extrinsic motivators include "A" grades, the honor roll, the dean's list, the honor society, scholarships, and other forms of recognition for academic performance.

Both intrinsic and extrinsic motivation are important for goal achievement. Children need to experience both types. They should feel good about learning (intrinsic), and they should also feel that their efforts are recognized by others (extrinsic). In the home, the family members who do housework should feel good about living in a clean house and about having their cleaning efforts noticed and appreciated by other family members.

One of the unsolved mysteries of life is why some people have more intrinsic motivation than others. These people work hard regardless of the number and quality of external rewards. Are the answers in genetics? In early childhood or work experiences? In temperament? Psychologists and others are searching for the answers to these questions. Martin Seligman says that

> A composer can have all the talent of a Mozart and a passionate desire to succeed, but if he believes he cannot compose music, he will come to nothing. He will not try hard enough. He will give up too soon when the elusive right melody takes too long to materialize. Success requires persistence, the ability to not give up in the face of failure. (1991, p. 101)

Far more is known about the workings of extrinsic motivation than about intrinsic motivation. For example, extrinsic rewards are most effective if

- ◆ They are specific.
- ◆ They are given immediately after a good work performance.
- ◆ They are valued by the receiver.
- ◆ They are equitable.

What one person perceives as a reward may not be perceived as desirable by another. For example, a trip at the company's expense to a convention might be valued by one employee, but considered a burden by another. As another example, a child who does not like candy will not view a candy bar as a reward. Rewards should be appropriate to the individual and at the same time be perceived as equitable by the family or organization.

Web-Based Resources

Many Web sites, some interactive, discuss values and attitudes. The main polling organizations, such as Gallup (**www.gallup.com**) and Roper (**www.roper.com**) report regularly on the state of values and attitudes in the United States and in other countries. As more companies (the primary financial supporters of the polling organizations) sell globally, the polling organizations have found that they need to collect more values and attitude data internationally. Government agencies and politicians also use data from polling organizations.

To join an online discussion of the changing nature of the American character, go to the *Wall Street Journal* Interactive Edition at **http://wsj.com**. Other newspapers and magazines run similar discussion groups.

For information on population trends and changes in values by age groups, location, gender, and so forth, go to the American Demographics Web site at **www.demographics.com**. This site does not give predictions about values, but rather reports the present state of values held by various groups.

For a detailed questionnaire on positive psychology, signature strengths, and various aspects of that movement, including happiness, go to **www.authentichappiness.org**. Examples of signature strengths are kindness, leadership, love of learning, critical thinking, self-control, playfulness and zest, and appreciation of beauty. Students interested in learning more about the VALS survey described in this chapter can find it at **www.sric-bi.com**.

Summary

Values, attitudes, and goals, are three of the most important concepts in the management process. Values are principles that guide behavior. They stand for what is worthwhile, preferred, and consistent. Sometimes there is a gap between values and actual behavior. Environmental conditions affect behavior. Families play a fundamental role in the formation and transmission of values. Parents, as the primary socializer of children, greatly influence their children's values. Goals are end results, the things people are working toward. Motivation and optimism are important elements in achieving goals. Attitudes are states of mind or feelings, likes and dislikes, about some matter. They often occupy a middle ground between values and goals.

A value or goal change recently evidenced is the growing number of people in their 20s, married or not, buying houses, a sign of settling down and establishing roots. This trend may be a symbol of optimism, an area studied by many psychologists including Martin Seligman. A Harris poll revealed that Americans are generally happier with their lives and more optimistic about their futures than Europeans, although results vary depending on the individual nation within Europe.

When two people date or become close friends, they try to find out about each other's values, attitudes, and goals, especially which they have in common. Do they enjoy the same activities? Do they have similar or compatible views about leisure, work, religion, and politics? Do they have similar reactions to situations and people?

Selecting one's life goals is a complex task that is easier for people who have been raised in a supportive environment. Whether an individual family is supportive depends to a great extent on how much energy and enthusiasm family members invest in each other, especially in each other's goals. The family that encourages their children's development by attending school plays and sporting events, music recitals, award ceremonies, and science and history fairs is a family that recognizes and rewards hard work, performance, and achievement. To be achievable, goals should be clear, realistic, and challenging, but not overwhelming. Most importantly, goals should be flexible. McMinn (1988) warns, "Don't have such a tenacious grip on the boat that if it begins to sink, you go down with it." Goals are influenced by outside forces (extrinsic motivation) and forces within the individual (intrinsic motivation). The motivation process starts with an unsatisfied need or unmet demand that creates tension and is resolved with a satisfied need and reduced tension. Goals give direction to life and values serve as a guide. However, goals cannot be set without consideration of resource availability. Resources are the subject of the next chapter.

Key Terms

absolute values	extrinsic motivation	optimism
affective domain	extrinsic values	relative values
attitudes	habits	resilience
behavior	intrinsic motivation	socialization
cognitive domain	intrinsic values	value orientation
cultural values	motivation	

Review Questions

1. What does Henry David Thoreau mean when he says, "My life is like a stroll upon the beach, As near the ocean's edge as I can go." How does this statement relate to the ideas in the chapter?

2. It has been said that optimism is back in style after a wave of cynicism in the late 1990s and early 2000s. Why would people have renewed optimism? What do we know from Chapter 2 about systems theory that would support a return to optimism after a period of cynicism? How is a trend of house buying at an early age a symbol of optimism?

3. Why does Martin Seligman say in *Learned Optimism* that optimism is essential for achieving goals?

4. What is the difference between intrinsic and extrinsic motivation? Which one do researchers know more about? Why?

5. Bob Greene, author of *Make the Connection,* says "Each morning when you wake up, take a few moments to state what is important to you, what you wish to accomplish, and the steps you will take that day to work toward your goals. These can be goals that relate to your body and health, or anything else you want to accomplish. The beauty of this daily renewal is that no matter how yesterday went, you have the opportunity to improve on it and better yourself today." What are your goals for today? What steps are you taking? What do you think about Greene's statement regarding the daily renewal of goal setting?

References

Ajzen, I., & Fishbein, M. (1980). *Understanding attitudes and predicting social behavior.* Englewood Cliffs, NJ: Prentice-Hall.

Alwin, D. F. (1989). Changes in qualities in children in the United States, 1964–1984. *Social Science Research, 8,* 195–236.

Buck, S. (2003). Building capacity through leadership development programs. *Journal of Family and Consumer Sciences, 95*(3), 8–11.

Business Week (1999, Summer).

Condor, B. (2002, September 3). Find your strengths, then your happiness. *Tallahassee Democrat,* 4D.

Consumer demand. (2003). Retrieved September 3, 2003, from **http://www.sric-bi.com/consulting/ConsumerDmd.shtml**

Cravatta, M. (1997, November). Hanging on to students. *American Demographics,* 41.

Csikszentmihalyi, M. (1990). *Flow: The psychology of optimal experience.* New York: Harper & Row.

Csikszentmihalyi, M. (1997). *Finding flow.* New York: Basic Books.

Danner, D., Snowdon, D., & Friesen, W. (2001). Positive emotions in early life and longevity: Findings from the nun study. *Journal of Personality and Social Psychology, 80,* 804–813.

de Lisser, E. (2002, September 24). One-click commerce: What people do now to goof off at work. *The Wall Street Journal,* A1 and A8.

Dillard, J. P., Segrin, C., & Hardin, J. (1989). Primary and secondary goals in the production of interpersonal influence messages. *Communication Monographs, 56*, 19–36.

Elias, M. (2002, December 9). What makes people happy. *USA Today*, A1.

Engel, J. (1988). Work values of American and Japanese men. *Journal of Social Behavior and Personality, 3*(3), 191–200.

Flanagan, C. A. (1990). Families and schools in hard times. *New Directions for Child Development, 46*, 7–26.

Goldsmith, E., Hoffman, J., & Hofacker, C. (1993). Insights into the long-term effects of parents' careers on reported parent offspring closeness. *Journal of Employment Counseling, 30*(2), 50–54.

Goodale, G. (2003, July 3). Sunny side up. *Christian Science Monitor*. Retrieved from **www.csmonitor.com**.

Halberstam, D. (1993). *The fifties*. New York: Villard.

Hammersla, J. F., & McMahan, L. (1990). University students' priorities and life goals vs. relationships. *Sex Roles, 23*(112), 1–14.

Harman, W. (1998). *Global mind change* (2nd ed.). San Francisco: Berrett-Koehler.

Hoffman, J., Goldsmith, E., & Hofacker, C. (1992). The influence of parents on female business students' salary and work hour expectations. *Journal of Employment Counseling, 29*, 79–83.

Hoffman, J., Hofacker, C., & Goldsmith, E. (1992). How closeness affects parental influence on business college students' career choices. *Journal of Career Development, 19*(1), 65–73.

Kaufman, M., & Creamer, D. (1991). Influences of student goals for college on freshman-year quality of effort and growth. *Journal of College Student Development, 32*(2), 197–206.

Kelter, D., & Harker, L. (2001). Expressions of positive emotion in women's college yearbook pictures and their relationship to personality and life outcomes across adulthood. *Journal of Personality and Social Psychology, 80*, 112–124.

Leung, S. (2003, July 16). New kids on the block. *The Wall Street Journal*, B1.

Leung, S., (2003, October 1). A glutted market leaves food chains hungry for sites. *The Wall Street Journal*, A1.

Levin, D. P. (1989, February 27). Luxury cars lose some status. *New York Times*, B1.

Locke, E. A. (1968). Toward a theory of task motivation and incentives. *Organizational Behavior and Human Performance, 3*, 157–189.

Locke, E., Shaw, K., Saari, L., & Latham, G. (1981). Goal setting and task performance: 1969–1980. *Psychological Bulletin, 90*, 125–152.

Mansfield, E., Romeo, A., Schwartz, M., Teece, D., Wagner, S., & Brach, P. (1988). *Technology transfer, productivity and economic policy*. New York: Norton.

McClelland, D. (1961). *The achieving society*. New York: Van Nostrand Reinhold.

McIntosh, W., Martin, L., & Jones, J. (1997). Goal beliefs, life events, and the malleability of people's judgments of their happiness. *Journal of Social Behavior and Personality 12*(2), 567–575.

McMinn, D. J. (1988). *Strategic living*. New York: Baker House.

Miller, J. B., & Lane, M. (1991). Relations between young adults and their parents. *Journal of Adolescence, 14*, 179–194.

Mitchell, A. (1983). *The nine American lifestyles: Who we are and where we're going*. New York: Macmillan.

Norcross, J., & Prochaska, J. (1998). *Changing for good*. New York: Avon.

O'Reilly, J. P., Tokuno, K., & Ebata, A. (1986). Cultural differences between Americans of Japanese and European ancestry in parental valuing of social competence. *Journal of Comparative Family Studies, 17*(1), 87–95.

Palkovitz, R., & Copes, M. (1988). Changes in attitudes, beliefs, and expectations associated with the transition to parenthood. *Marriage and Family Review, 12*(3/4), 183–197.

Parish, T. A., & Nunn, G. D. (1988). The importance of the family in forming life values and personal values. *Journal of Psychology, 122*(5), 519–521.

Phillips, S. D., & Johnston, S. L. (1985). Attitudes toward work roles for women. *Journal of College Student Personnel, 26*, 334–338.

Powell, T. J., & Enright, S. J. (1990). *Anxiety and stress management*. London: Routledge.

Putnam, R. (2000). *Bowling alone*. New York: Simon & Schuster.

Raina, M. K., & Vats, A. (1990). Life goals of Indian and American college students. *International Journal of Intercultural Relations, 14*, 57–71.

Ray, P. (1997). The emerging culture. *American Demographics*, 29–34, 56.

Rigdon, J. (1991, August 14). Managers who switch coasts must adapt to different approaches to use of time. *The Wall Street Journal*, B1.

Robbins, S. B. (1991). *Organizational behavior* (4th ed.). Englewood Cliffs, NJ: Prentice-Hall.

Robbins, S. B., Payne, E. C., & Chartrand, J. M. (1990). Goal instability and later life adjustment. *Psychology and Aging, 5*(3), 447–450.

Rokeach, M. J. (1973). *The nature of human values*. New York: Free Press.

Seligman, M. (1991). *Learned optimism*. New York: Knopf.

Seligman, M. (2002). *Authentic happiness*. New York: Free Press.

Seligmann, J. (1991, December 16). College without chemicals, *Newsweek*, 59.

Spencer, R. (2000). *A comparison of national psychologies.* Project Report, No. 5, Wellesley, MA: Stone Center Working Paper Series.

Stoneman, B. (1998, December 4). Beyond rocking the ages: An interview with J. Walter Smith. *American Demographics,* 1–7.

Sweetman, M., Munz, D., & Wheeler, R. (1993). Optimism, hardiness, and exploratory style as predictors of general well-being among attorneys. *Social Indicators Research, 29,* 153–161.

Taylor, H. (2003, May 21). *Americans are far more optimistic and have much higher life satisfactions than Europeans.* Retrieved March 22, 2004 from **http://www. harrisinteractive.com/harris_poll/index.asp?PID=378.**

The VALS segments. (2003). Retrieved September 3, 2003, from **http://www.sric-bi.com/VALS/types.shtml**

Whyte, W. H. (1957). *The organization man.* Garden City, New York: Doubleday.

Zaslow, J. (2003, February 6). Ready to pop the question? Hold off until you've done the interrogation. *The Wall Street Journal,* D1.

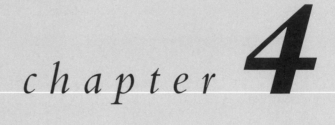

chapter 4

Resources

MAIN TOPICS

Did you know that . . . ?

. . . Dishwashers assembled in the United States may have Chinese
motors and Mexican wiring.

. . . There are more than 15 million college students in the United
States.

It often happens that I wake at night, begin to think about a serious problem and decide I must tell the pope about it. Then I wake up completely and remember I am the pope.

—*Pope John XXIII*

RESOURCE RECOGNITION, CREATION, and exchange are the subjects covered in this chapter. Exchanging resources facilitates the pursuit of human satisfaction or happiness. Learning new skills and getting an education are examples of resource creation. Individuals, families, and communities are constantly moving in new directions, seeking new ways to trade and network. From the individual standpoint, effectively using what you have (resources) to get what you want is a lifelong challenge.

Resources are mobile, complex, and interconnected. Examples of resources are: expertise, time, people, space, money, materials, objects, food, intelligence, and energy. They may be internally exchanged within the family or externally exchanged between the family and the greater environment, such as a shopping or real estate environment. One proposition is that entities with a relatively high level of **resource capacity** (meaning the amount that can be contained) "are more likely to engage in internal exchange, while entities that are lacking in resources are more likely to utilize external exchange" (Lusch, Brown, & Brunswick, 1992). According to a classic study by Alderson (1958),

> The household as an organized behavior system must be given special attention . . . in marketing. The household is an operating entity with an assortment of goods and assets and with economic functions to perform. (p. 25)

Thus, one model of resource exchange in a household would suggest that households would select internal exchange when they have the expertise, time, and resource capacity to indulge in an internal exchange; but when these are lacking, a search for an outside or external exchange will ensue. An example would be homeowners deciding to paint a bedroom themselves rather than hire a painter. Another example would be 45-year-old newly-weds deciding to host a reception at their house rather than reserving a reception hall at a hotel, church, or club. External exchange is usually necessary for auto repair or other tasks requiring expertise beyond the typical individual's capacity. Wise competitors and service providers use advertising to show what they can provide and how they can make life easier.

The worth of internal exchanges tends to be undervalued in our society, and one of the goals of this book is to extol the virtues of building one's human capacity. Companies that combine do-it-yourself products or customization along with free instruction are providing both internal and external exchange—these types of products/activities will be increasingly popular in the future because they provide satisfying experiences—an end product with a personal touch. According to Zuboff and Maxmin (2002),

> The new individuals seek meaning, not just material security and comfort. They enjoy their things but place an even higher value on the quality of the lives they lead, in which those possessions play a part. They insist on self-expression, participation, and influence because they share the certain knowledge that the singularity of their own lives cannot be deduced from the general case. No longer born to a biography, their identities must be invented as they go—cobbled together from personal initiative and private judgment. (p. 93)

Another fundamental principle is that resource use changes over time. We no longer go down to the stream and rinse clothes out. We use washers and dryers, detergent and softeners, electricity, and piped-in water to get clothes clean. Or we may choose to drop clothes at a laundry or dry cleaner and exchange money for human time and energy. Many management activities have been transformed from simple but labor-intensive actions to complex processes requiring investments of time, human and mechanical energy, and money. As another example, the resource use of college students over the past few decades has changed considerably. Middle-aged parents remember themselves as cash-strapped, existing for weeks on peanut-butter sandwiches, living in run-down dormitories and apartments, but today's college students have more cash, credit, and possessions. For example, one study (Speer, 1998) reports that

◆ Nearly all college students have computers.
◆ At least three-quarters have credit cards.

◆ Seventy percent have cable TV.

◆ Seventy-five percent ate at a fast-food restaurant in the past week.

◆ Fifty percent bought dishwashing detergent in the past month (compelling anthropological evidence that students also buy and cook food).

◆ Forty-seven percent shopped at a mall in the past week.

The college market is growing. In 2000, 15,312,289 students were enrolled in U.S. institutions of higher education, according to the *Digest of National Statistics 2002*. That number is expected to grow by 2007 to over 16 million. College graduates have higher-than-average lifetime earnings (compared to the general population), and they spend more money on virtually everything. Money is just one of the resources used by college students; time, energy, and space are others.

This chapter explores the subject of resources from a variety of theoretical and applied viewpoints. Resource theory analyzes, predicts, and explains the nature of resources as well as their perception, exchange, and use. During economic hard times such as those the United States experienced in the early 2000s, stretching resources to meet individual and family needs was a practical concern.

Identifying resources (and then deciding how to allocate them) is an integral part of the management process, as Figure 4.1 shows.

RESOURCES DEFINED

Resources are what is available to be used. They are assets—anything with a real or perceived value used to attain or satisfy something. *A resource is any entity, tangible or intangible, that contributes to the ability of an individual or family to produce valued outputs. Some of the valued outputs may have value only for the individual or the family; other outputs may have market value.*

FIGURE 4.1
The Management Process Model

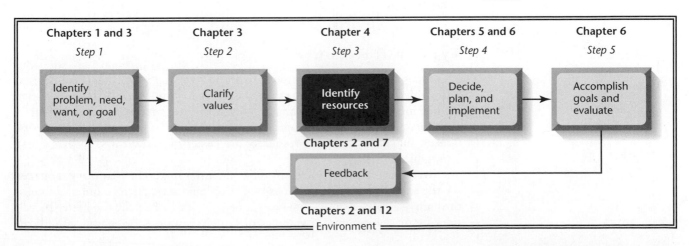

Chapters 1 and 3	Chapter 3	Chapter 4	Chapters 5 and 6	Chapter 6
Step 1	*Step 2*	*Step 3*	*Step 4*	*Step 5*
Identify problem, need, want, or goal	Clarify values	Identify resources	Decide, plan, and implement	Accomplish goals and evaluate

Chapters 2 and 7

Feedback

Chapters 2 and 12

Environment

Not all resource use is directed toward long-term goals; some resources are used to provide for more immediate wants and needs. For example, a librarian spending ten dollars on lunch is satisfying hunger, an immediate need. The cost of buying lunch is weighed against the time and expense involved in making and bringing a lunch to the library.

In management, time, energy, and money usually receive the most attention, and these resources will be referred to throughout this chapter and the book as a whole. But resources can take other forms. A sense of humor or a pleasant personality is a resource. Knowledge is a resource. A high school diploma is a resource. Everyone has a unique set of resources and uses those resources differently. Our homes are resources as well. Author David McCullough says:

> We're shaped by the buildings we live in and work in. The rooms in which things happen shape what happens in those rooms—the size of the room, the way the light falls through the windows, the prospect outside the windows. All of that bears on how people feel and how they act. (Kovach, 2003, p. 226)

Resourcefulness is the ability to recognize and use resources effectively. A resourceful person skillfully uses resources to cope with daily challenges. When resourceful people encounter a problem, they solve it or find a way around it, rather than being defeated by it. Resourcefulness is learned in families, schools, work situations, and social organizations. For example, if the electrical power goes out at home, children observe how their parents cope and substitute alternative sources of energy and light. In an office, if the copy machine breaks down, the employees substitute temporary alternative resources (e.g., using the machine in another office or going to a copy center). Along with families, schools and community youth organizations, such as Boy Scouts, Girl Scouts, 4-H, and the YMCA and YWCA, encourage the development of resourcefulness in children. An individual may also be a resource creator; learning new skills and furthering one's education are examples of resource creation, according to Resource-Advantage theory, which will be discussed later in this chapter.

One of the most basic concepts in management is that material resources are limited, so decisions have to be made about their allocation. By helping individuals learn to be more resourceful, resource management can contribute significantly to their quality of life. It is not enough to win millions of dollars, as lottery winners who have lost all their money will attest; more important to one's lifestyle in the long run is what one does with the money to retain it and make it grow.

Types of Resources

Resources can be classified in several ways. One way is to categorize them as intangible or tangible. **Intangible resources** cannot be touched; examples include integrity, confidence, and literacy. **Tangible resources** are real, touchable, or capable of being appraised; some examples are jewelry, land, and houses. Obviously, tangible resources are easier to observe and measure than intangibles.

Resources can also be classified as human or material. **Human resources** are the skills, talents, and abilities that people possess. Such resources increase through use. For example, the more a person rides a bicycle, the better bicycle rider he or she becomes. Examples of human resources are emotion and caring. Friendships are interesting human resources that change over time, some more lasting than others. Consider the story of nine sorority friends who graduated from the University of Illinois, determined to remain friends forever. Two years after they graduated, "They were idealistic young working women, talking excitedly about love, men and each other. They reminisced about sorority days, and vowed to remain central to each other's lives because, as one of them insisted, 'You can have the career, the family—and keep your old girlfriends, too.'" (Zaslow, 2003, June 24, p. D1). What happened to them? As they turned 40, eight were still friends. All were in their first marriage. Altogether, the friends had 19 children (three sets of twins). Five worked part-time, and six lived in the suburbs of Chicago; in fact, two lived across the street from each other.

Karen Roberto, director of the Center for Gerontology at Virginia Polytechnic Institute and State University, says, "If women are friends at 40, there's a strong likelihood they'll be life-long friends" (Zaslow, 2003, June 24, p. D1). The most likely time for women's friendships to fall off is between the ages of 25 and 40 because women are busy marrying, raising children, and establishing careers during those years. The way the former sorority sisters kept up was by scheduling play dates with their children, going on family vacations together, sending e-mail, calling, and celebrating one another's birthdays. What about males and friendship patterns?

> Men tend to build friendships until about age 30, but there's often a steady fall-off after that. . . . Male friendships are more likely to be hurt by geographical moves, lifestyle changes, or differences in career trajectories. And many men turn to wives, girlfriends, sisters or platonic female friends to share emotional issues, assuming male friends will be of little help. (Zaslow, 2003, June 24, p. D1)

Men and women often reestablish friendships or make new friendships near the retirement years because as one gets older, having other people around makes a person feel more connected. Older people may travel or do volunteer

© Richard Smith/CORBIS

If women are friends at 40, they will probably remain friends. What do you suppose these women are talking about?

work or join clubs such as garden clubs, investment clubs, golf groups, or bowling leagues. There is more time for others, for leisure, and for learning when child raising and career responsibilities diminish.

Considering that time is short, how does one disentangle oneself from friendships that are no longer desirable? asks journalist Jeffrey Zaslow. Studies show that only 15 percent of people say they can end a friendship, and women have a harder time with ailing relationships than men. Moving helps as does changing jobs and other tactics:

> Ms. Blieszner, a Virginia Tech professor, employed what researchers call "the fade out." She limited contact with her glum friend. "I drifted away, and it worked," she says. . . . If possible, winding down a friendship by feigning a busy calendar is preferable to a dramatic confrontation, says sociologist Jan Yager. (It lessens the likelihood of a vendetta.) If the person doesn't get the message, step up the frankness of your hints. (Zaslow, 2003, March 6, p. D1)

The sum total of human resources, all the capabilities and traits that people use to achieve goals and other resources, is called **human capital**. Investing in human capital is a lifelong personal goal for many people and a professional goal for those employed in the helping professions (e.g., counseling, education, and social work). Government also invests in human capital through such programs as free school lunches and Head Start. As another example, employers and employees create value, based not only on some unit of labor in the current moment, but also on their entire store of knowledge and experience—their human capital.

> It's said that a tourist once spotted Pablo Picasso sketching in a Paris cafe and asked if he would sketch her, offering to pay him fair value. In a matter of minutes, Picasso was finished. When she asked what she owed him, Picasso told her 5,000 francs.
> "But it only took you a few minutes," the tourist said.
> "No," said Picasso, "it took me all my life." (Kay, 1999)

Our knowledge-based economy is full of Picassos. What goes into a personal or professional decision is not just the time immediately absorbed. The years of experience and education a person has accrued is applied to the situation at hand.

One of the goals of education is to increase human capital. By going to college, students invest in their human capital development. When parents pay tuition fees and alumni provide scholarships, they are also investing in students' human capital.

Although everyone has human capital and the potential for growth and development, only 4 to 10 percent of human potential is used, according to one estimate (Peters & Waterman, 1982). How accurate is this estimate? What happens to the remainder? How can the remaining 90+ percent be tapped? Scientists have a long way to go before they will completely understand the boundaries and potentials of human capital.

Material resources include natural phenomena, such as fertile soil, petroleum, and rivers, and human-made items, such as buildings, money, and computers. Material resources decrease through use; that is, buildings deteriorate, money is spent, and computers break down or become outdated.

Lifestyles are based on a combination of human and material resources. **Resource stock** is the sum of readily available resources an individual possesses. Each individual has a resource stock that she or he draws on to make and implement decisions.

SUGGESTED ACTIVITY

TV psychologist and author Dr. Phillip C. McGraw (Dr. Phil) recommends doing a 10-7-5 exercise in which you write down 10 defining moments of your life (these are experiences that helped mold you into who you are today), the 7 critical choices you have made, and the 5 pivotal people who have influenced you. Try it. See if any patterns emerge about your resource stock.

Resources and Economics

Regardless of type, resources have the power to satisfy wants and enhance lives. Individuals use resources differently at different times in their life span. For example, parents have a difficult time understanding why their children "waste money" on candy and poor-quality toys, because the parents would make different choices. In childhood, much resource use is directed to the satisfaction of immediate personal wants and needs; hence, candy is a good purchase in the mind of a 5-year-old.

This book is primarily about management, not economics. Nevertheless, most decisions are affected by economic realities. For example, many people would like to go on a trip abroad, but how many can afford to go on the spur of the moment? Everyone is a consumer, if not of trips, then of food and shelter. Patterns in food consumption are an intriguing case in point. Over the last decade, the levels of eating out and bringing prepared foods into the home have risen sharply. According to the National Restaurant Association, in the United States, almost half of all adults (46 percent) are restaurant patrons during a typical day. In an average month, 78 percent of U.S. households used some form of carryout or delivery. Young consumers are most likely to patronize restaurants: About 6 out of 10 people between 18 and 24 years old are restaurant patrons on a typical day, compared to 3 out of 10 adults over 65.

The most likely meal to be eaten out is dinner (see Figure 4.2). The number of eating and drinking establishments owned by African Americans and women increased at double-digit rates over the past decade, with sales also rising dramatically. Saturday is the most popular day to eat out. Monday is the least popular. August is the most popular month to eat out. One out of five takeout-food consumers is a daily user.

As Chapter 1 explained, economics refers to the production, development, and management of material wealth. It is also concerned with distribution and consumption. Any economic system must address four questions:

1. What goods and services are going to be produced?
2. How are the goods and services produced?
3. Where are goods and services produced?
4. Who will get these goods and services?

Where things are produced is getting more complicated. Maytag dishwashers, for example, have Chinese motors and Mexican wiring, but are put together in U.S. factories (Aeppel, 2003). This three-tiered, or triad, approach is increasingly used in manufacturing to keep costs down. It used to be that bulky appliances for the U.S. market were all made in the United States because they were so expensive to transport; but as sharply lower labor and production costs became available in other countries, this offset the expenses involved in moving parts. In addition, totally produced and assembled appliances are being sold worldwide from China, South Korea, and New Zealand.

In economics, a central concept is **scarcity,** which means a shortage or an insufficient amount or supply. In the 1980s, toy stores experienced a run on Cabbage Patch dolls for Christmas. Evening news programs showed parents fighting over dolls and told of the disappointment of children who did not receive one. In this instance, the demand far outweighed the supply, creating a shortage. A year later, stores had an oversupply of the same dolls, which were no longer in great demand. In the 1990s, a similar run on another set of toys,

Beanie Babies, happened with the same problems of overdemand and undersupply.

Scarce goods are economic goods. Food, clothing, and shelter are examples of economic goods. So are parks, trees, and clean air. Leisure is also an economic good because most people feel they do not have enough leisure time. Juliet Schor, author of *The Overworked American,* writes:

> When surveyed, Americans report that they have only sixteen and a half hours of leisure a week, after the obligations of job and household are taken care of. Working hours are already longer than they were forty years ago. If present trends continue, by the end of the century Americans will be spending as much time at their jobs as they did back in the nineteen twenties. . . . U.S. manufacturing employees currently work 320 more hours—the equivalent of over two months—than their counterparts in West Germany or France. (1991, pp. 1–2)

Economic thinking recognizes that obtaining any scarce good involves a cost, which leads individuals and families to economizing behavior and goal setting. People use their skills, energy, and ingenuity to produce economic goods. They struggle constantly to reduce scarcity and better provide for their needs.

No society has enough economic goods or resources to satisfy everyone's wants and desires, nor does any individual have enough income or wealth to satisfy her or his every want or desire. Scarcity exists as long as people cannot purchase everything at zero price. Theoretically, the richest person and the poorest person in the world experience scarcity. Each person defines for himself or herself what constitutes scarcity. A related concept is availability. Resources are described as being available or not depending on how scarce or abundant they are.

Choice and Opportunity Costs

Scarcity forces people to make choices and decisions about the allocation of resources. Should a person buy a new car or keep an old one and invest in a prepaid tuition plan? Each decision involves a cost; for example, saving for a car means that money cannot be spent for something else. Economics assumes that people will make choices that improve their lives. Management offers a guide for making the best choices about how to use and allocate resources such as time and money. The end goal of these choices is maximizing satisfaction.

The highest-valued alternative that must be sacrificed to satisfy a want or attain something is called **opportunity cost.** When someone quits a paid job

FIGURE 4.2

Distribution of Restaurant Customer Traffic

August is the most popular month to eat out, and Saturday is the most popular day of the week for dining out. The most popular occasions are (1) birthdays, (2) Mother's Day, and (3) Valentine's Day.

*Commercial establishments only

Source: National Restaurant Association, www.restaurant.org

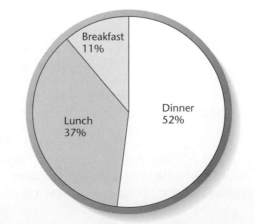

to stay home with children, he or she is experiencing opportunity costs. One way to conceptualize opportunity costs is to think of them as trade-offs. Life is full of trade-offs. Choosing one activity over another involves a trade-off. For example, choosing to buy one product over another may involve a trade-off between quality and cost. To get a desired good or outcome, it is necessary to trade off some other desired good or outcome—for example, time with friends versus time with family. Trade-offs, then, require sacrifice—something must be given up to gain something else. In short, there is no free lunch.

Household Activities: Trade-offs and Time

The basic activities of any household include many examples of resource trade-offs. In each household, the manager (or managers) must decide how the family resources of time, labor, and money will be allocated. Among other things, the manager must decide which aspects of household production should be carried out by the unpaid work of household members or obtained through market goods and services. A restaurant meal could replace a home-cooked dinner, for example, or a gardener could be hired to care for the lawn and a housekeeper to care for the house. Often a household's trade-offs are between time and money. Obtaining goods or services from outside is more costly than producing them within the household. Buying frozen pre-prepared meals at the store costs more than cooking at home, and sending clothes to the laundry costs more than washing them at home. But as time becomes an increasingly scarce commodity, more families are choosing time-saving options and relying on time-saving equipment such as microwave ovens and dishwashers.

In a nationwide survey, women 18 years and older were polled about how they felt about cooking at home. Almost 44 percent said they "enjoy it very much," and another 35 percent said they "liked it somewhat"—that amounts to four out of five women who like to cook for themselves or their families. How much do they cook at home? A third said every day, and almost half said four to six days a week (Weber, 2000). In 2000, 44 percent of weekday meals were prepared in 30 minutes or less compared to 40 percent in 1993 (Bernstein, 2001). Frozen-food sales have jumped since then too.

In small towns and suburbs, the kitchens in homes with families are growing in size, whereas in cities, kitchens—especially those in apartments with singles—are growing smaller as a reflection of the need for less cooking:

> Like many food-obsessed New Yorkers, Tom Piscitello has grand plans for his kitchen. No, he's not installing zillions of dollars of commercial equipment. He's putting in a guest bedroom. "The room is just the perfect size for a double bed," says Mr. Piscitello, a 42-year-old bachelor who hasn't cooked on his stove in six years. A kitchen, he says, is a waste of space and money: "It's just cheaper to eat out." (Bernstein, 2001, p. D1)

Doing laundry is another example of the trade-offs between time and human energy:

> The suburban home shared by Beth Sunderman, her husband, three sons, two dogs and two school-science-fair rats runs on a tight schedule. The boys are home from school at 3, in the car by 5 for baseball practice, and back home at 8:30 for showers, snacks, schoolwork and bedtime. In the background, "there is always a hum," says Ms. Sunderman. "You get sick of listening to it." It's her washer and dryer. Ms. Sunderman has figured out how to do nearly every household chore more efficiently—by microwaving dinner, for example, or having the boys unload the dishwasher. But she can't escape the 15 hours of laundry she does each week. (Nelson, 2002, p. A1)

Procter & Gamble provides the following information:

◆ 35 billion loads of laundry are done in the United States each year.

◆ 1,100 loads of laundry are started every second in the United States.

◆ In the United States each person generates one-fourth ton of dirty clothes per year.

◆ *The average American woman spends 7 to 9 hours a week on laundry.*

Despite talk of household work equality, laundry is still primarily a female chore. Newer washers use fewer gallons of water, but since washers can last 25 years, the overall change in water use will occur gradually. Tougher energy-use standards were instigated in 2004 to meet U.S. federal rules. Regarding technique, L. D. Metcalfe, director of strategic global alliances at Whirlpool Corporation says, "Their mother taught them. It's handed down like folklore from generation to generation" (Nelson, 2002, p. A1).

Laws of Supply and Demand

Scarcity affects the price or worth of a resource. According to the law of demand, as the price of a good or service rises, the quantity demanded of that good or service falls. Conversely, as the price falls, the quantity demanded will rise. The supply and demand curve is shown in Figure 4.3.

FIGURE 4.3
Supply and Demand Curve
When buyers and sellers interact in the market, the equilibrium price is at the point of intersection of the supply and demand curves.

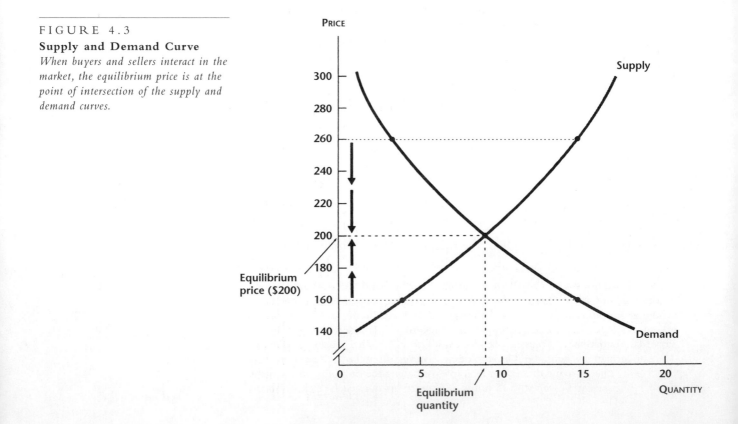

The law of supply is the law of demand in reverse. According to the law of supply, as the supply of a good or service goes up, the price goes down. Conversely, as the supply goes down, the price goes up.

Aren't more people likely to apply for a job that pays $50 an hour than for one that pays $5.15 an hour? Isn't a one-of-a-kind Louis XV desk more valuable than a mass-produced desk from a discount store? Thus, the price paid for goods and services is influenced by supply and demand. In economic theory, the right price is reached when supply and demand are equal.

When prices change radically, they are probably reacting to real or perceived changes in supply or demand. For example, if the weather is too wet and the peanut crop is destroyed, the price of peanut butter will skyrocket. Grocery shoppers will watch for sales on peanut butter and stock up or substitute another sandwich ingredient for the high-priced peanut butter.

Economic Well-Being

Economic well-being is the degree to which individuals and families have economic adequacy and security. It refers to the desire or extent of protection against economic risks, such as loss of employment, illness, bankruptcy, bank failures, poverty, and destitution in old age (McGregor & Goldsmith, 1998). It is a function of many variables in combination, including money income, financial assets, human capital, durable goods and services, time, ability to manage, control over financial affairs and resources, values, job security, retirement plans, ability to adjust to changes, and lifestyle decisions. Economic well-being is often used as a measure of quality of life. Each person and each family defines what constitutes economic well-being for them. Based on the results of a study of the financial well-being of adults in an eight-state region, researchers came to the following conclusion:

> When working with families and individuals in matters of financial concern, it is critical to recognize that although income is important in predicting perceived economic well-being, other factors contribute to this perception. These perceptions, attitudes, and skills affect the use of resources and how environmental factors are perceived. Each family has a distinctive composition and is predisposed to characteristic modes of thought reflecting the circumstances unique to it. (Kratzer & Keefe, 1993, p. 43)

Allocation and Recognition of Resources

Management is the process of using resources to attain goals through planning and of taking the steps necessary to meet goals. A crucial part of the management process is the allocation of resources to appropriate goals. As explained in the previous chapter, goals can be prioritized and divided into short-term, intermediate, and long-term goals. In theory, resources should be allocated to meet the most important goals first, but in practice, resources are often diverted to more immediate needs or demands.

Everyone has different types and amounts of resources and different life demands. As explained in the previous chapter, many people who live from day to day do not have the luxury of allocating resources toward long-term goals. Their resources have to go to basic survival needs.

Resource recognition is the realization of the skills, talents, and materials one possesses. Lack of resource recognition is often a problem for teenagers. As they develop their adult identity, they become more aware and more confident about their resources and how to allocate them. One of the goals of education is to help students become aware of their strengths and how to capitalize on them.

Regulation of Resources

Who should control resources? Many conflicts, from family feuds to full-scale wars, have been fought over this question. How should resources be divided? Which resources should be publicly held? Which should be privately held? **Private resources** are owned and/or controlled by an individual, family, or group. **Public resources** are owned and used by all the people in a locality or country; a national park and a county-owned swimming pool are examples.

In 1776, Adam Smith published *An Inquiry into the Nature and Causes of the Wealth of Nations,* which advanced a theory justifying capitalism. He argued that with economic freedom individuals will follow their own self-interest to fulfill themselves and their families, thereby benefiting society as a whole. Smith used the term *laissez-faire* to suggest that government should leave business alone. According to him, the "invisible hand" of competition would guide the marketplace. To a certain extent, society still adheres to much of Smith's laissez-faire theory, but societal and economic developments in the 20th century led many people to believe that government needs to serve as a regulator of the economy, at least to a certain degree. How much governmental regulation is desirable in such areas as health care and welfare reform is a public debate that continues in the 21st century.

Economic Resources and Employee Benefits

Economic resources refer to wealth in any form, including credit, money, benefits, and stocks and bonds. Household equipment, cars, savings, property, and investments are forms of wealth, whereas commissions, wages, interest, dividends, bonuses, pensions, and royalties are forms of money income. Wealth is a measure of what has been accumulated, whereas income is earned or given to the recipient (e.g., child support, alimony, and government transfer payments such as welfare payments).

Employee benefits are goods and services that are part of an individual's or family's resource base. When determining personal and family assets, the value of benefits should be estimated along with income and wealth. Typical employee benefits are health insurance, life insurance, paid vacations and sick leave, and retirement programs. Many employers offer cafeteria plans, which allow employees to choose the benefits they want. For example, employees may add a dental plan or a child-care assistance plan to their basic benefit package.

Resource Attributes and a Model

In a household, someone has to decide what will be done; by whom it will be done; when, where, and how it will be done; and which resources will be required. The person (or persons) who does this is the manager. He or she makes decisions about how money is spent, initiates goals, sets objectives, makes plans, keeps records and timetables, makes doctor and dentist appointments, and performs a host of other tasks. The manager may be one person, or management responsibilities may be split among several people. As children grow older and more independent, they take on more responsibility for scheduling their own time, money, and work. According to Bryant (1990), performance of household management activities leads to direct satisfaction (leisure, comfort) or indirect satisfaction (work completed).

The characteristic way an individual or family manages resources is shaped by five forces:

1. Psychological/personality forces (including value orientations) that shape individual choices and preferences
2. Economic forces that regulate the exchange of money, energy, materials, services, and information
3. Technological forces that generate problem-solving inventions, tools, and methods
4. Sociocultural forces that regulate mores, norms, and customs
5. Political-legal forces that allocate power and provide constraining and protecting laws and regulations

These forces constantly interact with each other; any decision about resource allocation will be affected by several or all of these forces.

Attributes

Household resources can be classified as human (time, skills, energy of members) or physical. Resources also have certain other characteristics or attributes (this list is adapted and expanded from Paolucci, Hall, & Axinn, 1977):

- ◆ Resources are interdependent.
- ◆ Sometimes resources are exchangeable.
- ◆ Material resources are limited.
- ◆ Resource use relies on the person's ability to process information and make decisions.
- ◆ Sometimes resources can be stored. Examples include fuel, books, furniture, and clothes.

Resources can also be characterized by their affective, cognitive, and psychomotor attributes. Affective attributes refer to feelings about or expressions of resource use. Expressions of love, gratitude, and caring are examples of affective attributes. Which resources are shared and with whom are affected by feelings. Someone is more likely to share private information with a friend, for example, than with a stranger.

Cognitive attributes refer to the knowledge aspects of resource use. Existing knowledge based on past learning and experiences is applied to new situations. The ability to synthesize (bring together information and knowledge), analyze, and evaluate new situations is a crucial part of the cognitive attribute. A resourceful person has a high degree of cognitive ability.

Psychomotor attributes refer to physical reactions to mental stimuli, such as the capacity to respond to threats or to perform work. Being able to respond quickly and appropriately to physical and mental demands is also a part of being resourceful.

Activities such as learning and teaching require all three attributes. For example, teaching others to use computers requires good hand-eye coordination (psychomotor ability), knowledge (cognitive ability), and the ability to communicate in an interesting way (affective ability). Most jobs require all three attributes (e.g., surgeon, nurse, and child-care worker).

Foa & Foa Resource Model

Anything that can be used is a resource, but to think of resources in this way makes the concept too expansive to be very helpful. Resources can be examined in a meaningful and systematic way if they are arranged in an interactive model. *One such model is the Foa & Foa Resource Model, which illustrates the interdependence of resources* (Figure 4.4). Resource theory was first promulgated by Uriel Foa in 1971 and explained further in 1974 in *Social Structures of the Mind,* which he published with Edna Foa. The theory provides a framework for understanding social interactions and the relationships that form between individuals in everyday life (Converse, 1993). These relationships provide the means by which individuals can obtain needed resources—love, services, goods, money, information, and status—from others. In the model, the resources at the top of the circle (love, status, and services) are more particularistic than the ones at the bottom (information, money, and goods). In other words, people are more selective when exchanging love (only with family and friends) than when exchanging money (with nearly anyone, including store clerks and bank tellers). In the model, resources close to each other on the circle are more likely to be exchanged than those opposite each other. For example, a mother who loves her baby provides care by feeding or diapering the baby (a service). Note that love and money are directly opposite each other.

Several researchers have attempted to apply the Foa & Foa model to different populations and situations to see how well it works in reality. For example, Kathryn Rettig, Sharon Danes, and Jean Bauer used the model in a study of the problems of economically stressed farm families. They found that "family life quality is negatively affected by economic hardship, particularly for women" (1993, p. 149). Further, the study revealed that "the exchanges of services in the family setting were perceived by women to be less satisfying, compared to men, at the time of most severe stress" (p. 149). The researchers concluded that resource theory is useful in exploring questions of quality of life and economic hardship. In an earlier article on the Foa & Foa model, they stated:

> Each person has a unique motivational state for engaging in resource exchanges which results from a combination of past and present experiences. The larger the amount of a resource possessed by a person, the more power one has with this resource and the more likely it is to be given to others. (1991, p. 274)

FIGURE 4.4
Foa & Foa Model
of Resource Exchange

Source: Foa, U., Converse, J., Tornblom, K., and Foa, E. (Eds.) (1993). *Resource Theory: Explorations and Applications.* Reprinted with permission of Elsevier.

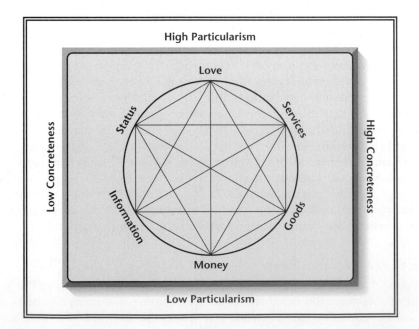

Using the Foa & Foa Resource Model in a study of older women, Rosemary Blieszner (1993) found a distinction between how the women interacted with close versus casual friends. Specifically, the means for giving and receiving love and status were higher for close friends than for casual friends; thus, Blieszner's results lend support to the proposition that people reserve exchanges of particularistic resources for special relationships.

Resource Advantage Theory

As mentioned earlier in the book, a number of disciplines have affected the study of resource management as it relates to individuals and families. When it comes to resource use, many insights can be gained from developments in marketing. This section will describe Resource Advantage theory, which applies entrepreneurship and leveraging to resource management. **Entrepreneurship** is defined as the process of creating value by bringing together a unique package of resources to exploit an opportunity (Stevenson, Roberts, & Grousbeck, 1989). This is such a broad definition that it applies to human services or human sciences as well as to marketing. Indeed, many family and consumer scientists (or human scientists or human ecologists) are entrepreneurs. The field is being asked to be more enterprising, to reach more people, to be more entrepreneurial in the way family and community needs are met. Also many people trained in human sciences are themselves business owners (of bed-and-breakfasts or stores, for instance), estate managers, realtors or investors in real estate, and public speakers or writers—or they engage in some other form of commerce. An estate manager, for example, "can earn between $80,000 and $150,000 a year supervising household staff and financial matters for mansions of 20,000 square feet or more" or for managing multiple homes, according to Mary Starkey, president and founder of Starkey International Institute, a Denver-based training and placement firm (Maher, 2002, p. B8). She says her business "fields between 30 and 40 calls per week from individuals or families interested in hiring estate managers." When it comes to positions such as estate manager, many people have started in another job and had a hobby or interest that developed into a business or vocation. They are opening themselves up to more creative ways to apply the basic principles learned in management. Being more enterprising, more open to resource potential, is a way to not only survive but also to thrive, especially in slow economic times. Enterprising students find out about job opportunities and internships, contact companies directly, use the Career Services Center on campus, go on the Internet, and approach speakers at trade fairs or other industry or campus events.

 Leveraging means most simply doing more with less. It has to do with being more effective in the use of resources. In order to succeed, businesses exploit underutilized resources and skills and use creative means to contract, barter, borrow, share, rent, buy, sell, and outsource. Leveraging means to go beyond mere efficient use of resources into more creative realms where managers are not constrained by their current resource base. Through leveraging, managers are able to do the following (Morris, Schindehutte, & LaForge, 2002, adapted from page 8):

◆ Stretch resources

◆ Use resources in novel ways

◆ Use other's people or other firm's resources

◆ Complement one resource with another—bringing a higher value

◆ Use certain resources to obtain other resources

The leader in Resource-Advantage (R-A) theory is Shelby Hunt, the professor of marketing at Texas Tech University. He and others developed the R-A theory as a knowledge discovery process (Hunt, 2000, 2003; Hunt & Morgan, 1996, 1997). Hunt says that R-A theory is significantly broader than, but not inconsistent with, the way we view family resource management (personal communication, April 9, 2003). He says one idea would be to consider the resource of "family competence" or "household competence"—that is, some households are superior to other households in doing things that produce valued outputs. Bringing it back to the business context, R-A has been described as "an evolutionary, process theory of competition in which each firm in an industry is a unique entity in time and space as a result of its history" (Hunt & Morgan, 1996, p. 78). In R-A theory,

> Competition is in an ongoing struggle among firms to achieve a comparative advantage in the marketplace. The source of advantage derives from innovation, which is viewed as endogenous to competition. Specifically, superior financial returns flow to those firms that are able either to create value more efficiently or to efficiently create more value for customers; this represents the link to entrepreneurial behavior. Entrepreneurship is the means by which firms discover, create or assemble resource assortments that allow them to produce valued market offerings. . . . R-A theory defines resources broadly to include such phenomena as organizational culture, knowledge, competencies, and argues that many of these non-economic resources are replicable rather than scarce. (Morris et al., 2002, p. 9)

There is no denying that the word *competition* has some negative connotations. Margaret Wheatley in *Leadership and the New Science* says:

> I crave companions, not competitors. I want people to sail with me through this puzzling and frightening world. I expect to fail at moments on this journey, to get lost—how could I not? And I expect that you too will fail. Even our voyage is cyclical—we can't help but move from old to new to old. . . . To stay the course, we need patience, compassion, and forgiveness (1999, p. 174).

Resource-Advantage theory has been widely used by organizations around the world, specifically in companies in Japan and Europe (including Germany) as well as the United States. Hunt (2003) notes that the factors affecting competition to the firm include

◆ Reinvestment

◆ Knowing self

◆ Adaptation

◆ Proactivity (moving ahead positively)

and the factors external to the firm are

◆ Consumers (who constantly change, may not like a firm's products)

◆ Government actions (fair or not, more visibly successful firms are often a target)

◆ Competitor actions (including acquisitions, imitation of resources, substitution of resources, and major innovations in resources)

What can applied social scientists, such as students of family resource management, glean from this? For one thing, we can gain awareness, especially as a means to stimulate thinking: Do families and households compete with each other for scarce resources? Is an example of this the idea of "keeping up with the Joneses"? Is another the way neighbors often are at odds with each other over property lines? Perhaps a more positive way is to ask, Are families and households proactive in their approach to resource use? Are they as effective in their resource use as they can be? To take it a step further, *Are some households superior to other households in doing things that produce valued outputs,* as Hunt suggests? Much of the study of resource management from the social side is about knowing self, knowing how to organize, strategize, and plan successfully—all advantages. Some people may find the competitive aspects of R-A theory objectionable, but it is presented here as a new way of looking at resource management—the idea of resource creation is important as we explore the many ways individuals and families cope.

Other Resource Allocation Factors: Utility and Accessibility

A basic concept in management is that resources are not useful unless they are perceived as useful. **Utility** is the value, worth, applicability, productiveness, or, simply, usefulness of a resource. Utility is in the eye of the beholder. For example, a papier-mâché castle made by a 10-year-old boy may not have any market value, but to him it has great value and is useful in play.

Newspaper surveys have found that their readers look for news they can trust and that has utility (Ridder, 2003). If they read the local newspaper and don't find anything they can use, they will turn to other news sources.

Economists and anthropologists recognize different kinds of utility, such as time, place, form, and diminishing utility, and also observe that various cultures view resources and utility differently. The concept of utility is learned and subjective. Time utility refers to the availability of a resource when it is needed. Arriving at a closed store with a fistful of dollars is a frustrating and useless activity. Place utility refers to location. Form utility means that the resource is in an accessible and usable form. Diminishing utility refers to the concept that the first use is more desirable than a later use. Drinking beer is a classic example. The first sip is more tasty and satisfying than subsequent sips, and if too much is drunk, there is an undesirable negative effect.

To be useful, a resource has to be accessible. Cell phones make messages more accessible. As another example, money locked up in a bank vault overnight is not useful; with the invention of the automatic teller machine, however, money is accessible day or night. The 24-hour grocery store, 24-hour catalog shopping services, and Internet shopping have also expanded accessibility. The general trend is toward greater accessibility of resources.

Decision Making and Resources

In making any decision, an individual considers accessibility and other resource attributes. By finding out all the information possible about a person, place, or situation before making a decision, some potential problems can be avoided. In deciding which college to attend, for example, a student considers location, tuition costs, housing options, and availability of courses.

Decision making uses up a vital resource, however—time. A basic economic principle is that the total cost of an item is equal to its monetary cost plus its time cost.

SUGGESTED ACTIVITY

Identify a shopping situation where you want to respond in a more resourceful way, where you want to change from your usual way of shopping. Create a vision of yourself in the situation. How are you responding to the products offered? What do you see? How do you feel as you make choices?

To save time, consumers rely on established shopping behaviors (e.g., going to the same stores, buying the same brands, going to the same barber). They are open to change when they have the time, when they perceive a need for a change, and when they realize there is a disparity between what they want and what they are getting. When the motivation for change is present, new alternatives are considered. From an economic standpoint, the best alternative is the one providing the most benefit for the least cost in time and money.

Knowledge, Education, and Health: Vital Resources

Have you ever heard the phrase "without your health you have nothing"? For centuries, scholars have debated the question of what our greatest resource is. Is it money, possessions, land, health, capacity to love, or something else? Peter Drucker (1999) says that our primary resource is knowledge, and the leading social groups will be knowledge workers. Knowledge is gained through experience or study. E. F. Schumacher, author of *Small Is Beautiful,* says that education is the most vital of all resources. He states that "all history as well as all current experience—points to the fact that it is man, not nature, who provides the primary resource: that the key factor of all economic development comes out of the mind of man" (1973, p. 79). Schumacher suggests that the development of nations should not start with goods, but with people and their education, organization, and discipline. An educated population leads to economic development through expanded work opportunities and better planning skills. Schumacher says, therefore, that investing in human capital should come before other types of investment.

Cultural Perceptions of Resources

Culture is the sum of all socially transmitted behavior patterns, beliefs, arts, expectations, institutions, and all other products of human work and thought characteristic of a group, community, or population. Language, ideas, customs, taboos, codes, tools, techniques, music, rituals, and ceremonies are all part of culture. In families, culture is transmitted from one generation to another. Members of cultural groups share common interests and goals. Margaret Mead, anthropologist and author of *Coming of Age in Samoa,* said:

> Each primitive people has selected one set of human gifts, one set of human values, and fashioned for themselves an art, a social organization, a religion, which is their unique contribution to the history of the human spirit. Samoa is only one of these diverse and gracious patterns, but as the traveler who has been once from home is wiser than he who has never left his own door step, so a knowledge of one culture should sharpen our ability to scrutinize more steadily, to appreciate more lovingly, our own. (1928, p. 131)

As explained in the previous chapter, cultural values are generally held concepts of right or wrong that are shared by members of cultural groups. Cultures have the following six attributes:

1. They develop over time.

2. They supply boundaries or limits of acceptable behavior

3. They provide a sense of belonging, identity, and security. Saying "I am an African American," or "I am Catholic," or "I am a member of the Smith family" implies an identification with a cultural group.

4. They are so pervasive that they are often taken for granted. Familiar traditions, such as turkey at Thanksgiving or a decorated tree at Christmas, are expressions of culture and provide a sense of continuity and identity to individual and family life.

5. They can be constrictive. In a teenage clique, members may feel forced to act, dress, and think alike. Conformity to the group may take precedence over the identity of the individual.

6. They can be enriching or expressive. Culture can provide a style or a format for intellectual, social, or artistic expression.

Attributes 5 and 6 may seem contradictory, but they demonstrate that culture can be many things. Culture can mold people and at the same time provide a means for individual expression. The boundaries cultures set are called **norms.** Norms, which are based on cultural values, are rules that specify, delineate, encourage, and prohibit certain behaviors in certain situations. One norm of the classroom is for students to sit in chairs at desks. Standing on the desks would go against the norm. Norms are useful because they guide behavior, letting people know how to act in given situations. Manners and etiquette are other types of norms.

A number of studies indicate that human **cognition** (the mental process or faculty by which knowledge is acquired) is not the same everywhere. Humans come to know things through perception, reasoning, and intuition. No one is sure why differences exist, although clues may be found in child rearing and social practices. Richard Nisbett, in *The Geography of Thought: How Asians and Westerners Think Differently . . . and Why,* says the characteristic thought processes of Asians and Westerners differ greatly (Begley,

These high school students are on a field trip. Do you see evidence of conformity in their appearance?

© Peter Hvizdak/The Image Works

2003). For example, if you ask which of the following two go together—a panda, a monkey, and a banana—a Japanese man is more likely to select the monkey and the banana and a British man, the panda and the monkey. Westerners are more likely to see categories (animals), whereas Asians are more likely to see relationships (monkeys eat bananas). Why is this important to know? Understanding such differences is important for cultural exchange, education, global business, and political relations. For example, Westerners may believe a deal is a deal, and Easterners may be more inclined to change agreements as conditions change: They see relationships between things. Americans are more likely to predict a rise in life quality (an optimism), whereas the Easterners realize that upward trends could very well reverse (Begley, 2003).

None of this is set in stone, and many more studies are under way, but there is enough evidence regarding differences in thinking styles to indicate that cultures may have a difficult time understanding one other. For example, one researcher on hearing the panda, monkey, and banana question said that the way they are arranged (the order) may affect the choices made and that a great deal of research would have to be done to rule out order effect. Ruling out that possibility and going back to the original idea, of particular interest to researchers are the areas of the world that mix Eastern and Western cultures such as Hong Kong. What happens when parents come from significantly different cultures? Which culture becomes dominant, and how are the children raised? And what happens when workplaces mix two distinct cultures as in the case of an international merger such as Daimler-Chrysler?

Cultures and Subcultures

Usually, a single dominant culture provides the major influence on behavior. Citizens of a certain nation share a common language, customs, and history. Subcultures, or subsystems of the dominant culture, may have a strong influence also. These subcultures may have a religious, ethnic, political, racial, social, or economic base. Individuals can belong to a dominant culture and several subcultures at the same time.

Culture is transmitted through a variety of channels, including parents, schools, community organizations, churches, employers, and government. An individual may live and travel in many different cultures. Individuals may change their language, form of dress, or way of acting as they move between different cultural systems. They may dress and act a certain way at work and dress and act quite differently at home.

RESOURCES, FAMILIES, AND HOUSEHOLDS

Cultural expectations of families and households may have changed more rapidly than actual behaviors. In other words, there may be a disconnect between what people are thinking is happening and what is really happening. When sociologists and family specialists study families, they find discrepancies between ideals and behaviors when it comes to household work and child rearing.

Many women and men in 21st-century America feel conflicts related to the "stalled revolution"—the uneven changes that have occurred in gender ideologies and the structures of work and family institutions (Gerson, 2002;

Hochschild, 1989; LaRossa, 1988). Ideals about men's and women's proper roles in paid work and family life have shifted over the past half century toward more gender-neutral, egalitarian views alongside the massive movement of women, especially mothers, into the paid labor force (Brewster & Padavic, 2000; Spain & Bianchi, 1996; Thornton, 1989; Thornton, Alwin, & Camburn, 1983). In contrast to mothers' greater investments in market work, fathers' complementary behavior in family caregiving has not changed as quickly. Although fathers' involvement in housework and child rearing has increased it remains limited (Hochschild, 1989; Robinson & Godbey, 1999).

To summarize, most people think things are more egalitarian, but studies show that women still do about two-thirds of the housework. Child rearing is more difficult to study because it involves many aspects that are hard to measure, such as nurturing and disciplining activities. The amount of interaction time is often used as a measure.

There is no doubt that during the past 30 years, families and households have undergone vast changes. The principal developments include increased labor force participation by women, smaller households but more of them, more single-parent families, an aging population, internationalization of the economy, changes in prevailing values and attitudes, and technological innovations, especially in communications, information, and transportation. Nearly every social and economic institution has been altered. In the United States, according to Ray Marshall, a former secretary of labor:

> We have moved from an economy in which economic success depended heavily on natural resources and economies of scale to one that is more competitive and knowledge intensive. In the economy of the 1990s and beyond, success depends mainly on the quality of human resources, and the quality of human resources depends heavily on what happens to families. (1991, pp. 103–104)

Marshall identified several economic and labor market changes associated with the dramatic changes in families and households:

◆ There has been a decline in the proportion of family households, especially those classified as "traditional" (i.e., married families with children). These families have also become smaller. Simultaneously, nonfamily and single-person households have proliferated.

◆ Fertility rates have declined because women are having fewer children and at older ages.

◆ Despite their decline, a substantial majority of Americans live in family households.

Although child rearing may not be egalitarian, there is evidence that men are spending more time with their children. The Changing Workforce survey of 2,877 workers showed that fathers were spending a half-hour more each workday, and one more hour each day off, caring for and doing things with their children than in 1977 (Shellenbarger, 1998).

As families become more mobile and both parents increasingly work outside the home, raising children is becoming more difficult, and the family must rely more on outside resources. As social historian Barbara Whitehead says, "Raising children isn't an individual act. It is a social and communal enterprise, involving kin, neighbors, other parents, friends, and many other unrelated adults. Typically, hermits don't raise kids; villagers do" (1990, p. 5). Senator and former First Lady Hillary Rodham Clinton's book *It Takes a Village* expressed a similar point of view.

Some solutions to family problems lie in changes in family and work policies in the private and public sectors. The Family and Medical Leave Act, enacted in 1993, is one example of a public policy designed to strengthen families. Through this act, companies with more than 50 employees must allow them (male or female) to take up to three months unpaid leave for the birth or adoption of a child or the care of a critically ill family member. Essentially, workers will not have to choose between their job security and their family's well-being during times of family crises, emergencies, or upheaval. Besides public policies, employers, schools, friends, extended family, and community and religious organizations can also help support families. Chapter 8 discusses specific human resource problems of families, and Chapter 10 has more details about the Family and Medical Leave Act.

Consumption and Resources

The United States has been called a throwaway society and a consumer society. In the 19th century, both Canada and the United States practiced "cut and get out" forestry (Aley, Burch, Conover, & Field, 1999). The 20th century saw more sensitivity to the environment, but new building booms brought construction too close to shorelines, which affected barrier dunes and floodplains. Cities in desert areas in the United States grew beyond the capacity of the environment to sustain them. Dust bowls and soil loss resulted, as did more strain on water sources. To **consume** means to destroy, use, or expend. In the 21st century, the sustainability of our natural resources is an important issue requiring a renewed look at (1) policy, (2) conditions, (3) planning, (4) household impact, and the (5) management of ecosystems. The enormous productive capacities and market forces of the United States have been committed to satisfying human needs and desires, often with little overall regard to future effects. Figure 4.5 illustrates how much more land, water, fossil fuels, and forest products a person in the United States consumes compared to a person in China.

FIGURE 4.5
Resource Use in the United States and China Compared

Source: As adapted by Francis Sizer and Eleanor Whitney, *Nutrition: Concepts and Controversies,* Eighth ed. (Belmont, CA: Wadsworth, 2000).

In the United States, one person depends on these amounts of resources each year:

In China, one person depends on:

	Land for crops, pasture, forests	Water	Fossil fuel (oil equivalents)	Forest products
	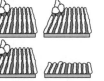 3.2 hectares	2.5 million liters	8,000 liters	14 tons
	0.5 hectares	460,000 liters	413 liters	0.03 tons

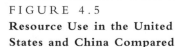

If this course of consumerism continues, waste will become an increasingly difficult problem. Although some waste cannot be helped, much packaging and many products themselves are unnecessary. For a time, a U.S. appliance manufacturer sold $25 lamps that were designed to be discarded when the bulbs burned out. Lighters, razors, and disposable cameras are made for a single use and then thrown away. Convenience has come to be valued over cost per use and sensitivity to the environment.

From the perspective of resource conservation, is the use of disposables a good thing? Obviously, no. The customs and values of U.S. culture traditionally supported thrift and conservation. Planned obsolescence and unnecessary waste are at odds with these values. Many people are beginning to question or reject the notion of the throwaway society as evidenced by a widespread acceptance of recycling and the increased purchasing of products made from recycled materials. Americans have shown an interest in ecotourism, more natural golf courses, and local environment-friendly residential and commercial landscaping.

Resource Strategy

Underlying much of management is the concept of strategy. A **strategy** is a plan of action, a way of conducting and following through on operations. Strategy implies the careful thinking out of details and the consideration of outcomes. Usually, the word *strategy* is associated with military or business management operations, yet it has many applications for individual, household, and family management as well. Strategy revolves around the following questions:

◆ What do I want to accomplish? Or, what do I want to create?

◆ What is important?

◆ How will a plan contribute to goal achievement?

A successful resource strategy incorporates planning what is owned versus what is desired. If a couple wants to buy a new house, they have to form a strategy to save for the down payment. A person who wants to lose weight should reevaluate eating and exercise habits to form a weight-loss strategy and then set a timetable and a goal for weight reduction. Similar plans of action or strategy could be set up to reduce household waste or unnecessary spending. Finding a job also involves strategy.

Web-Based Resources

Resource use affects all aspects of life; hence, the number of potential Web sites is almost limitless. A growing area of interest in resource management is the field of health care management. For example, information on women's health can be obtained from **www.acog.org** (American Academy of Obstetricians and Gynecologists) and **www.nof.org** (National Osteoporosis Foundation). Information on maintaining healthy weight for men and women is available at **www.navigator.tufts.edu** (Tufts University Nutrition Navigator), **www.eatright.org** (American Dietetic Association), **www.nhlbi. nih.gov** (National Heart, Lung, and Blood Institute), and **www.acefitness.org** (American Council on Exercise). The Department of Health and Human Services' health resource guide can be found at **www.healthfinder.gov**. For information about Healthy People 2010, an alliance of over 600 health organizations promoting health and disease prevention, visit the Web site at **www.health.gov/healthypeople.**

Summary

Resources are central to the management process and to the pursuit of human satisfaction. Without human and material resources, there would be nothing to manage. For individuals, families, and communities, resources are the essential means of exchange (internal and external). Resources are used to attain goals and meet demands. We vary in our resource capacity.

For families and households, resource use provides a life space and a lifestyle around which an individual's and family's needs are met. Knowledge, education, and health are vital resources, especially during times of turmoil, doubt, and fear.

The Foa & Foa Resource Model illustrates the interchangeability of resources. From the fields of marketing and organizational behavior, Resource Advantage theory explores the benefits of entrepreneurship and leveraging (doing more with less) and adds to our understanding of resource creation. Resources can be looked at from many points of view since resource use underlies all human endeavor. Because of scarcity, an individual tries to make choices that maximize benefits and minimize costs. The way a person goes about doing so is culturally defined. A number of studies indicate that human cognition is not the same everywhere: Cultural differences in thought processes or perceptions exist. An ongoing issue is the gendered division of labor in the home for both housework and child rearing. Women do about two-thirds of the housework and most of the child rearing, although studies suggest that men are spending more time with their children than in the past.

Management provides a way of looking at problems in an organized, rational, and still compassionate manner. Material goods and wealth are not the sole determinants of happiness. Wealth and goods can help assure an easier life, but not necessarily a happy one. The elusive nature of happiness and the search to find the right life balance underlie the study of management. Individuals make decisions purposefully, always seeking to better their circumstances. This constant striving drives people to seek better solutions and explains the "why" behind much of human behavior.

The next chapter takes the information presented so far and puts it together in the decision making process. Later in the book, the resource concepts covered in the present chapter will be applied to specific environmental and human problems.

Key Terms

cognition	intangible resources	resource capacity
consume	leveraging	resourcefulness
culture	material resources	resource stock
economic well-being	norms	scarcity
entrepreneurship	opportunity cost	strategy
human capital	private resources	tangible resources
human resources	public resources	utility

Review Questions

1. Regarding friendships as a human resource, how many friends do you have? How long have you had them? Do you think certain friendships will continue over the next five years? Which ones and why?

2. What does the story about Picasso and the tourist illustrate about the nature of human capital? Name one skill, talent, or ability that you have built up over the years.

3. What does the Foa & Foa Resource Model illustrate?

4. Why is the United States called a throwaway society? How does U.S. per capita consumption compare to that of China?

5. What role does strategy play in resource management? A college senior, Alison, figures that she will need a minimum starting salary of $28,000 to live in Charleston, South Carolina, based on a budget she developed. She wants to live in Charleston because she has friends there, but she is having trouble finding a job because she goes to school 500 miles away. Alison's main expense will be at least $600 a month for rent. If you were Alison what would you do next? In other words, what would your strategy be?

References

Aeppel. T. (2003, October 6). Three countries, one dishwasher. *The Wall Street Journal*, B1.

Alderson, W. (1958). The analytical framework of marketing. In Delbert J. Duncan (Ed.), *Proceedings: Conference of Marketing Teachers from Far Western States* (pp. 15–28). Berkeley, CA: University of California, School of Business Administration.

Aley, J., Burch, W., Conover, B., & Field, D. (1999). *Ecosystem management*. Philadelphia: Taylor & Francis.

Begley, S. (2003, March 28). East vs. West: One sees the big picture, the other is focused. *The Wall Street Journal*, D1.

Bernstein, E. (2001, January 12). The disappearing kitchen. *The Wall Street Journal*, D1.

Blieszner, R. (1993). Resource exchange in the social networks of elderly women. In U. Foa, J. Converse, K. Tornblom, & E. Foa (Eds.), *Resource theory: Explorations and applications*. San Diego: Academic Press.

Brewster, K., & Padavic, I. (2000). Change in gender ideology, 1977–1996: The contributions of intracohort change and population turnover. *Journal of Marriage and the Family, 62*, 477–487.

Bryant, W. K. (1990). *The economic organization of the household*. Cambridge: Cambridge University Press.

Converse, J. (1993). Preface. In U. Foa, J. Converse, K. Tornblom, & E. Foa (Eds.), *Resource theory: Explorations and applications*. San Diego: Academic Press.

Drucker, P. (1999). *Management challenges for the 21st century*. New York: Harper.

Foa, U. (1971). Interpersonal and economic resources. *Science 171*, 347.

Foa, U., Converse, J., Tornblom, K., & Foa, E. (Eds.) (1993). *Resource theory: Explorations and applications*. San Diego: Academic Press.

Foa, U., & Foa, E. (1974). *Societal structures of the mind*. Springfield, IL: Charles C. Thomas.

Gerson, K. (2002). Moral dilemmas, moral strategies, and the transformation of gender: Lessons from two generations of work and family change. *Gender & Society, 16*, 8–28.

Hochschild, A. (1989). *The second shift*. New York: Avon.

Hunt, S. D. (2000). *A general theory of competition*. Thousand Oaks, CA: Sage.

Hunt, S. D. (2003). Resource-advantage theory: Toward a general theory of marketing. Presentation at *Association of Marketing Theory and Practice Annual Meeting*, Hilton Head, SC.

Hunt, S., & Morgan, R. (1996). The resource-advantage theory of competition: Dynamics, path dependencies and evolutionary dimensions, *Journal of Marketing, 60*(4), 107–113.

Hunt, S. D., & Morgan, R. (1997). Resource-advantage theory: A snake swallowing its tail or a general theory of competition, *Journal of Marketing, 61*(4), 74–82.

Kay, I. (1999, January 18). Don't devalue human capital. *The Wall Street Journal*.

Kovach, R. (2003). Conversation with David McCullough. In Elfreida Abbe (Ed.), *The Writer's Handbook*. Boston: Writer.

Kratzer, C. Y., & Keefe, D. (1993). Towards development of an ecological model for predicting perceived economic well-being. In C. Y. Kratzer (Ed.), *Change and exchange: The Proceedings of the Southeastern Regional Association of Family Economics—Home management*, Roanoke, Virginia, 35–45.

LaRossa, R. (1988). Fatherhood and social change. *Family Relations, 37*, 579–589.

Lusch, R., Brown, S., & Brunswick, G. (1992). The general framework for explaining internal vs. external exchange. *Journal of the Academy of Marketing Science, 20*(2), 119–134.

Maher, K. (2002, August 27). The jungle: Focus on retirement, pay and getting ahead. *The Wall Street Journal*, B8.

Marshall, R. (1991). *The state of families, 3: Losing direction, families, human resource development, and economic performance*. Milwaukee, WI: Family Service America.

McGregor, S., & Goldsmith, E. (1998, Summer). Expanding our understanding of quality of life, standard of living, and well-being. *Journal of Family and Consumer Science, 22*, 2–6.

Mead, M. (1928). *Coming of age in Samoa*. New York: Blue Ribbon Books.

Morris, M., Schindehutte, M., & LaForge, R. (2002). Entrepreneurial marketing: A construct for integrating emerging entrepreneurship and marketing perspectives. *Journal of Marketing Theory and Practice, 10*(2), 1–19.

Nelson, E. (2002, May 16). In doing laundry, Americans cling to outmoded ways. *The Wall Street Journal*, A1, A10.

Paolucci, B., Hall, O., & Axinn, N. (1977). *Family decision making: An ecosystem approach*. New York: Wiley.

Peters, T., & Waterman, R. (1982). *In search of excellence*. New York: Harper & Row.

Rettig, K., Danes, S., & Bauer, J. (1991). Family life quality: Theory and assessment in economically stressed farm families. *Social Indicators Research, 24*, 269–299.

Rettig, K., Danes, S., & Bauer, J. (1993). Gender differences in perceived family life quality among economically stressed farm families. In U. Foa, J. Converse, K. Tornblom, & E. Foa (Eds.), *Resource theory: Explorations and applications* (pp. 123–155). San Diego: Academic Press.

Ridder, P. A. (2003, October 7). *Newspapers Today*. Speech at Florida State University, College of Business Speaker Series.

Robinson, J., & Godbey, G. (1999). *Time for life: The surprising ways Americans use their time*. University Park, PA: Pennsylvania State University Press.

Schor, J. B. (1991). *The overworked American: The unexpected decline of leisure*. New York: Basic Books.

Schumacher, E. F. (1973). *Small IS beautiful*. New York: Harper & Row.

Shellenbarger, S. (1998, April 15). Researchers are amazed: Men are helping more. *The Wall Street Journal*, B1.

Smith, A. (1973). *An inquiry into the nature and causes of the wealth of nations*. New York: Modern Library. (Original work published 1776)

Spain, D., & Bianchi, S. (1996). *Balancing act: Motherhood, marriage and employment among American women*. New York: Russell Sage Foundation.

Speer, T. (1998, March). College come-ons. *American Demographics*.

Stevenson, H., Roberts, M., & Grousbeck, H. (1989). *Business ventures and the entrepreneur*. Homewood, IL: Irwin.

Thornton, A. (1989). Changing attitudes toward family issues in the United States. *Journal of Marriage and the Family, 51*, 873–893.

Thornton, A., Alwin, D., & Camburn, D. (1983). Causes and consequences of sex-role attitudes and attitude change. *American Sociological Review, 48*, 211–227.

Weber, N. (2000, July 27). Who's in the kitchen? It's mom as always. *The Wall Street Journal*, A23.

Wheatley, M. (1999). *Leadership and the new science: Discovering order in a chaotic world* (2nd ed.). San Francisco: Berrett-Koehler.

Whitehead, B. D. (1990, Spring/Summer). The family in a friendly culture. *Family Affairs, 2*(1–2), 5.

Zaslow, J. (2003, June 24). Staying in touch: One more thing that women are better at than men. *The Wall Street Journal*, D1.

Zaslow, J. (2003, March 6). Making friends isn't so hard—it's getting rid of them that's tough. *The Wall Street Journal*, D1.

Zuboff, S., & Maxmin, J. (2002). *The support economy*. New York: Viking.

chapter 5

Decision Making and Problem Solving

MAIN TOPICS

Did you know that . . . ?

. . . The percentage of families with small children where the father works and the mother stays home has been steady or creeping slightly higher.

. . . American households today spend 30 percent less time doing housework per week than in 1965.

You can have any color you want as long as it's black.
—*Henry Ford, referring to his new automobile line in 1914*

IMAGINE VOLUNTEERING FOR a lifestyle that forces you to give up nearly half your household income, sell your toys, forgo vacations of the kind your friends enjoy, and work as if three or four lives depended on your next paycheck. That's the world of many solo-breadwinner dads. Bo Rogers, Mesa, Ariz., sold his motorcycle and gave up his gym membership, workouts and racquetball games after he and his wife Melanie had the first of their two children, so she could quit her job. Now, Bo, who is paid solely on commission as a heating and air-conditioning salesman, feels pressured and stressed. (Shellenbarger, 2003, p. D1)

These are the kinds of decisions that young families make. Reversing a trend of nearly a quarter of a century, more families are opting to have a stay-at-home mother. According to the Bureau of Labor Statistics, in 2002, the number of such families increased to 38.7 percent of all families with children under six, from 37.8 percent in 2001 and from a recent low of 35.2 percent in 1994. It is too early to declare a lasting trend, but the numbers seem to indicate a move in that direction. Such changes may indicate not only a social trend but also a technological change. Computers and the Internet have made it more difficult to determine who is employed for pay and who is not, because so much can be done from any location. So it is difficult to know whether the stay-at-home mothers are completely unemployed or whether they are working part-time from home. They also may be working in a family-owned business or supporting their husband's career or working seasonally.

Not everyone is choosing to stay at home and have children. Another trend to consider may seem to contradict the trend just described:

> Anne Hare and her husband made a momentous decision three years ago: They would not have children. It's not that they don't like kids, she says. They simply don't want to alter the lifestyle they enjoy. "With kids, especially young kids, infants and toddlers, you really can't do the active stuff we like to do," said Hare, 43, a fitness-program coordinator from Gainesville, Ga. Hare is among 26.7 million women ages 15 to 44 who are childless, according to new Census Bureau data. . . . The number of women forgoing or putting off motherhood—nearly 44 percent—has grown nearly 10 percent since 1990, when 24.3 million were in that class. (Armas, 2003, p. 8a)

Besides personal choice, some influences on this trend include more women going to college and entering the workforce, then delaying motherhood or deciding not to have children; more choosing adoption; changes in societal attitudes; more reliable forms of birth control; and economic factors. The women most likely to be childless are Asian (just over half), followed by non-Hispanic whites (46 percent), blacks (39 percent), and Hispanics (36 percent).

Good decisions meet several criteria. As the previous examples show, they have to be personally acceptable. Acceptance signifies that the key players in the decision acknowledge that it is reasonable and workable. Decisions also have to have quality, flexibility, and clarity. Quality means that the decision meets some standard, objective, or goal. If the decision does not do so, or if someone involved in the decision does not accept it, then the decision is likely to be ineffective. Therefore, family decisions are more likely to succeed if they have the support of family members and are linked to an agreed-upon standard, objective, or goal. In other words, in families, as in other groups, decisions that are co-created have a better chance of success than those that are individually created. Flexibility means that the decision not only should be appropriate to the situation but also should be adjustable if the situation changes. For example, becoming engaged to be married may seem like a good decision under certain circumstances, but when attitudes or circumstances change (e.g., compatibility wanes, expectations change, another love interest comes into the picture), the couple may choose to break the engagement or wait a while. Clarity refers to how clear the decision is. Vague decisions do not work because they lack definition and commitment. Regarding fathers working and mothers staying at home (or vice versa), David Stevenson, an art director for a New York publishing house, who works so that his wife Noreen, a former media buyer, can stay home with their two small children, says:

> You both commit not just to the marriage, but to this structure that you've set up—this notion that she will stay at home, I'll work, and we're in it together. . . .

You gain a certain strength from that—the stamina to press on when things get crazy. (Shellenbarger, 2003, p. D1)

He adds that they remind themselves that the rough spots are only temporary and try to laugh about the problems, knowing they will pass. Another employed dad says, "If they want me to work longer hours, I work longer hours. If they want me to travel, I travel" (Shellenbarger, 2003, p. D1).

DECISIONS DEFINED

Decisions are conclusions or judgments about some issue or matter. Management recognizes the influence of values on decisions and the role of goals in providing direction to decisions. The decision process begins when a change or a thing is desired. **Decision making,** the process of making a choice between two or more alternatives, is an integral part of the overall management process (see Figure 5.1). In systems terminology, decision making is part of the transformation process that incorporates various inputs and culminates in outputs. Sometimes the process involves negotiation or bargaining with others. The previous chapters on values, attitudes, goals, and resources have laid the groundwork for a full discussion of the decision-making process. This chapter begins by explaining the relationship between decision making and management and then describes the steps in decision making. Decision models and rules are examined, along with their application to individuals and families. The chapter explains the difference between decision making and problem solving and explores the concepts of risk and uncertainty.

Decision Making as Part of Management

Why do we spend so much of our time being active? Why don't we just lie in bed and watch the world go by? *Because when it comes to living, we are programmed as humans to be active, to accomplish things, to find out what is*

FIGURE 5.1
The Management Process Model

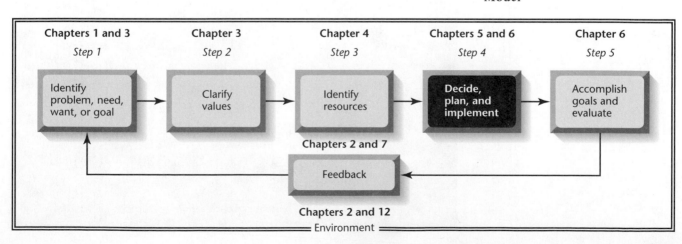

going on. We want to have an impact. An active life requires decisions and effort. People have to want something they do not have, and they have to make decisions and plans to bridge the gap between what is and what could be.

Decision making is essential to maintaining and improving life conditions, including home design. Values guide decisions. A decision maker values an issue or a life condition enough to spend time thinking about it. Values also influence decision makers because they realize that the choices they make will have positive or negative consequences. For example, "design decisions influence how comfortably we live and how much it costs us to attain the lifestyle we aspire to, and thus deserve extraordinary consideration" (Chiras, 2000, p. 2).

Decisions vary in intensity and importance. The purpose and content of decisions are related to other aspects of the management process, such as planning, implementing, and cost-benefit analysis. For example, each decision entails a cost in time and energy and sometimes money. Decision makers try to minimize the costs and maximize the benefits of a decision.

This desire to maximize positive outcomes and to minimize mistakes motivates individuals to make the best decisions that they can. Curiously, the plots of many movies, books, and television shows feature individuals who do just the opposite. These characters make decisions that minimize positive outcomes and maximize mistakes. Watching the characters disentangle themselves from their mistakes and put their lives back in order can be interesting and enlightening. Observing how others make decisions and solve problems on television, especially on dating, game, and reality shows like *Survivor,* can help sharpen an individual's own decision-making and problem-solving skills.

Decision situations present both problems and opportunities. In analyzing decision situations, individuals appraise alternatives and identify useful information and resources. An important resource is time. An individual or family can save time by eliminating alternatives that do not fit their values. Why waste time considering an alternative that is morally or ethically unacceptable? Ralph Keeney (1988), a values expert, suggests that if "we begin with values," then "we might not even think of situations as decision problems, but rather as decision opportunities": "Periodically, we might examine achievement on the basis of our values and ask, 'can we do better?'" (p. 466).

The main characters in the long-running TV show "Friends" experienced mistakes, trial and error, indecision, steps forward and steps back, problem solving, value dilemmas, misunderstandings, humor, and through it all friendship.

© Photofest

Since it is value-based, decision making is highly personalized. Each individual's personality and usual modes of thinking and acting influence the way he or she makes decisions. Each person's decision making also tends to follow a pattern, with successful decisions being repeated again and again. The characteristic way that a person makes decisions is called her or his **decision-making style.** Thus, decision-making styles are affected by individuals' values, knowledge, ability, and motivation. The types of decisions made, the speed at which decisions are made, and the amount of information gathered before making a decision are all part of a person's style. For example, some individuals are quick deciders; others are more deliberate. Differences in style are also evident in the evaluation phase at the end of the decision-making process. Some individuals look back and agonize over every thought and action, whereas others think about past decisions only for a few minutes and then go on.

Some decision styles are irritating. Suppose you go to a meeting, and the boss asks your opinion. You invest time and effort and present an opinion, then find out the decision had already been made. How would you feel? Similarly, in a family, how do children feel after being asked for their opinion, only to find out that their parents had already made the decision?

Steps in Decision Making

Decision making involves a series of steps that result in the choice of an alternative. The process can be long or short. Obviously, more time will be spent deciding where to build a new home than in choosing which movie to see. When the process is long and complicated and includes a sequence of intentions, it constitutes a **decision plan.** Decision plans can be specific or general. For example, Zak's plan to buy his favorite cereal and milk at the grocery store this afternoon is a specific decision plan. Jennifer's plan to buy a car next year is a general decision plan because she does not know what kind of car she wants or exactly when she will buy it. Because decision making is a transformation process, the inputs, such as how much money and time Zak and Jennifer have, will affect the decisions.

Decision makers use different strategies for different situations. The strategy selected will depend on (1) the decision involved, (2) the characteristics of the decision task, and (3) the decision-making style of the decider. In general, though, most people follow six steps in making decisions. The acronym DECIDE provides an easy way to remember these steps (adapted from Malhotra, 1991):

- ◆ Define the decision (distill and define the issue).
- ◆ Estimate resources.
- ◆ Consider alternatives.
- ◆ Imagine (visualize) the consequences of alternative courses of action.
- ◆ Develop an action plan and implement it.
- ◆ Evaluate the decision.

These steps are discussed in detail in the next paragraphs.

Step 1: Define the Decision

In defining the decision, the individual should take into account the purpose of the needed behavior, the relevant background information, what information is needed, and how it will be used in decision making. In so doing, the layers of a potential decision are peeled back to reveal the core of the situation. Once the decision has been defined, the decision maker can move on to the next step.

Step 2: Estimate the Resources Needed

The decision maker has to decide what resources will be needed. As discussed in the previous chapter, resources include time, energy, money, information, and anything else that is useful to the decision and subsequent planning and action. The number of possible alternatives is limited by the resources possessed or anticipated in the future. A ski vacation in Utah is out of the question if a person has only a hundred dollars to spend.

Step 3: Consider Alternatives

Given the limitations on their resources, individuals seldom consider all alternatives. For example, test-driving every car on the market before choosing one would be impractical. Instead, a prospective buyer would eliminate many models because of their cost, accessibility, features, and style or because they did not suit her tastes and preferences; then she would test-drive just a few cars. Narrowing down the possibilities to one or two acceptable alternatives is an important part of the decision process.

Step 4: Imagine the Consequences of Alternative Courses of Action

Imagining or thinking through the most likely alternatives is the next step. Envisioning what will happen if a certain decision is made is so enjoyable or distasteful that some people get stuck on this step. For example, in consumer decision making, this step involves **prepurchase expectations,** which are beliefs about the anticipated performance of a product or service. Before buying, people usually try to imagine how much pleasure or pain they will get from the purchase.

Step 5: Develop an Action Plan and Implement It

Once an alternative is selected, a course of action, a strategy, must be developed. Putting the decision into action is called *implementation*. During this step, the decision maker monitors the progress being made and evaluates how well implementation is proceeding. Are things going as planned? On schedule? Are adjustments to the plan necessary?

Step 6: Evaluate the Decision

After the process has been completed, the decision maker looks back to judge how successful the decision was. "Did I make the right decision?" "Should I have done something else?" In consumer decision making, this step involves **postpurchase dissonance.** After a major purchase, such as a car, the buyer is likely to seek some reinforcement for the decision by talking to other owners of the same model or reading advertisements or news stories about the car. Being assured that the right decision was made reduces doubt or anxiety. The right decision will also be reinforced if, for example, the bag boy or girl at the grocery store says, "hey, cool car" when loading groceries in the car's trunk. The chances of postpurchase dissonance, at least the suffering about whether one made the right decision or not, is reduced if there are no or few alternatives. Let's say someone moves to a town, and there is only one house for sale. The person will buy it and not look back, because there were no other choices at that time. However, if confronted with dozens of choices, that homebuyer is more likely to wonder if he or she made the best decision.

Models, Rules, and Utility

Although change is a necessary part of life, many individuals are reluctant to change and continue to follow existing patterns of behavior. Adhering to established goals and objectives and the plans, strategies, and tactics devised for attaining those goals is referred to as "maintaining the status quo." According to Silver and Mitchell (1990), when faced with uncertain alternatives, most people tend to stay with the status quo. But if a person, family, or organization wants to change or to understand the mechanisms of decision making, they may find decision-making models useful. These models assume that rational decision makers will evaluate alternatives and then make the best possible choice.

Because decision making is an abstract concept, decision-making models are useful because they provide a way to visualize how the elements of a decision interact. Figure 5.2 shows examples of the central-satellite and chain models. In the central-satellite model, a central decision is surrounded by decisions that are offshoots of the central decision. In the chain model, each decision builds on the previous one, forming a sequence of decisions, such as the steps involved in preparing a meal. The chain model is appropriate for smaller, systematic decisions, whereas the central-satellite model is suitable for larger, more complicated situations. Businesses such as catering services or conference and wedding planning services use both models to organize receptions, banquets, meetings, and events.

SUGGESTED ACTIVITY

Put one example of your own decisions in each of the central-satellite and chain models. Remember that the chain model is sequential, and the other has a large decision in the middle surrounded by smaller decisions or categories of decisions.

FIGURE 5.2
Examples of Decision Situations Using the Central-Satellite and Chain Models

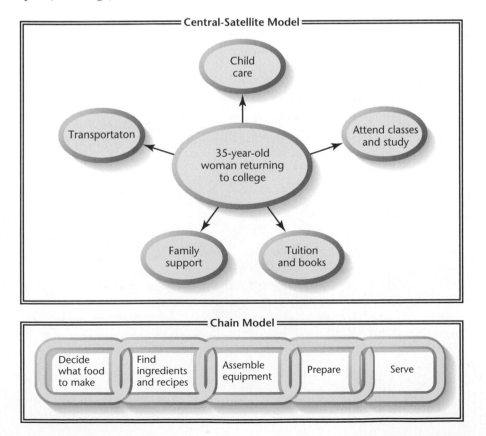

As illustrated in Figure 5.3, values lie at the base of decisions. Two other concepts in management, resources and goals, also play important roles. Decision trees are commonly used in business strategy sessions, but they can also be used by individuals in personal and professional decision making. The model shows that people select alternatives based on their goals and perception of available resources and that values underlie decisions. A more usual method used by many individuals in choosing between alternatives (e.g., whether to move to one locale over another, which job offer to select) is to make pro and con lists.

Decision Rules

Models operate on certain principles or rules of logic. **Decision rules** are principles that guide decision making. One decision rule is that decision makers will seek the best outcomes. Another decision rule is that individuals will try to use their time to best advantage, wasting as little as possible. However, this varies by situation and by culture. A study of Chinese students found that they were not very time-conscious, but they were quite price- and quality-conscious (Fan & Xiao, 1998).

Utility

One of the most important decision rules is the necessity to optimize utility, or the usefulness of decisions. The concept of utility underlies much of the study of economics and is strongly associated with the study of management. Rational decision makers are assumed to seek the maximum utility (satisfaction) from the decisions they make. Furthermore, the utility concept focuses on how choices are made and on how that process can be improved. A related decision rule is that consumers have limited information; they may not be aware of all the alternatives that exist. The next section on reference groups provides one explanation of why individuals may have only partial knowledge.

Reference Groups

Decisions have histories. For example, Allison orders pepperoni pizza because she knows from past experience that she likes it. Besides past experiences, past

FIGURE 5.3

A Decision Tree: Values Lie at the Root of All Decisions

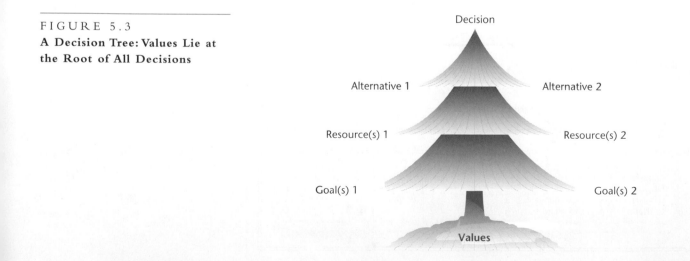

Decision

Alternative 1   Alternative 2

Resource(s) 1   Resource(s) 2

Goal(s) 1   Goal(s) 2

Values

and present relationships affect an individual's decision making. If Allison begins dating Trae, who is a vegetarian, and he prefers pizza with cheese, green peppers, olives, and onions, they have several options: They can order two pizzas, or they can order a pizza that is half pepperoni and half vegetarian, or Allison can learn to skip the pepperoni. This simple joint decision-making situation illustrates how many choices exist and how individual tastes and relationships affect those choices.

The people who influence an individual or provide guidance or advice are members of that person's **reference groups.** Trae and Allison are members of each other's reference groups. The diagram in Figure 5.4 illustrates a typical college student's reference groups. An individual does not have to be present in person or geographically close to be a member of a reference group. A person is considered part of a reference group if the memory of her or his values and attitudes affects someone's decision making. For example, Rob, a newspaper editor, has not seen his high school journalism teacher for many years, but she is still a member of Rob's reference group because he thinks of her often and remembers what she taught him when he makes decisions about his paper.

Reference groups can be divided into two types, primary and secondary, depending on the amount of contact the individual has with a person or group. An individual has regular contact with the people in primary reference groups. Family, coworkers, and close friends fall into this category. Secondary reference groups include those individuals and groups with whom contact is infrequent, such as distant relatives, organizations, and professional associations. The influence of reference groups on decision making and behavior cannot be overestimated. For example, one study showed that family members' smoking behavior influenced college students' smoking behavior. The study compared

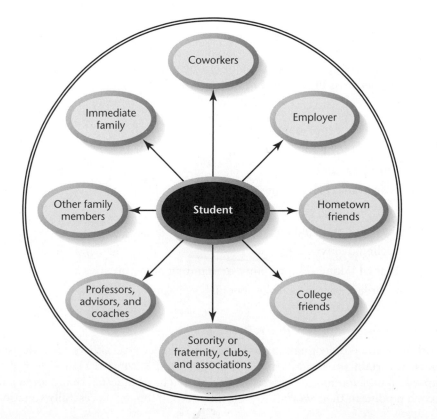

FIGURE 5.4
**A College Student's
Reference Groups**

Oregon college students in 1963–1964 with students in 1986–1987 (Gray & Donatelle, 1990). In 1963–1964, the student respondents said their smoking behavior was most influenced by whether their father, mother, or older sister smoked. In 1986–1987, students who smoked were most likely to say they had been influenced by an older brother or brothers who smoked. The authors concluded that factors that influence smokers appear to change over time. When students in 1986–1987 were asked why they smoked, the main reasons they gave were peer smoking and stress.

Personal Decision Making

Although all decisions—from which car to buy to whether to smoke—are influenced by others, *ultimately the individual is responsible for his or her own decisions*. Individuals begin learning how to make decisions at an early age. During the socialization process, children are given the opportunity to make choices and to learn from decision situations. By the time they become adults, most people assume they are competent decision makers. In reality, however, this assumption may fall short if there is a difference between the actual and perceived quality of decisions. The actual quality of decisions refers to what is truly happening. The perceived quality of decisions refers to what an individual thinks is happening in the decision process. Potentially, then, people can deceive themselves into thinking that a poor decision is a good one or at least an acceptable one. Experience and improved decision-making skills can narrow the gap between the perceived and the actual.

Decision-making style is affected not only by an individual's socialization, knowledge, ability, and motivation, but also by his or her personality traits, such as compulsiveness, open-mindedness, innovativeness, self-confidence, and courage. Another factor that can affect decision-making style is self-esteem.

Low self-esteem often results in indecisiveness. In other words, someone who is unsure of her or his ability to make sound decisions is likely to be indecisive. Indecisiveness can be a major problem for individuals, families, and organizations. Possible causes of indecisiveness are

- Stress
- Ill health, depression
- Fear of the unknown
- Procrastination
- Fear of making a wrong decision or mistake
- Fear of acting on one's own
- Lack of "good judgment"
- Feeling overwhelmed
- Fear of taking responsibility or standing alone on an issue
- Overdependency on other people's opinions

Indecisiveness and the Peter Principle

Although some individuals always seem to be indecisive, others are indecisive only in certain situations. Lawrence J. Peter and Raymond Hall (1969) proposed an explanation for indecisive behavior. They suggested that people may reach a point in their work in which they can no longer successfully function.

Specifically, they said that people tend to be promoted until they reach a level beyond their competence—a point at which they can no longer make and implement effective decisions. They called this phenomenon the **Peter Principle.** Even though the Peter Principle is pervasive, it can be avoided by fitting the right person to the right job and by making performance expectations clear from the outset. Examples of this principle can be found in a variety of organizations and settings, including the home and the community.

Avoiding Decisions

Being indecisive is linked to another decision-making phenomenon—avoidance. Passing the decision-making buck is one way individuals avoid decisions. According to Delaney (1982), avoidance typically results in statements such as the following:

- ◆ "I thought you were going to settle this."
- ◆ "That's not my job."
- ◆ "You're the boss. Don't ask me what I think, just tell me what to do."
- ◆ "Why is it up to me?"

Failure to assign clear responsibility for tasks in the home or the office may lead to some of these remarks. When chores are not assigned and the dishes are not done or the garbage is not taken out, family members may all say "That's not my job." Parents and children need to have a clear understanding of who will do what in the home. At the same time, tasks, chores, and duties are not static. Nonperformance may result because goals and priorities have changed; they are no longer commonly held beliefs about how to act. There is a fundamental difference between compliance and commitment. Complying means going along with some idea or action. Commitment signifies belief in an idea or action. High-commitment workplaces and households are more productive and more comfortable places to be.

Decidophobia

Not making decisions is also a decision. **Decidophobia** is the fear of making decisions, specifically the fear of failure. Sometimes the problem stems from being overwhelmed with choices. Sherwin Williams has over 1,400 different colors of paint—how could a decidiphobic choose given that array of choices? Here is another example of consumer overload—in one year U.S. manufacturers came up with 150 new deodorant and antiperspirant products, whereas a few years earlier the number was only 20 (Forelle, 2003).

A person with decidophobia is frozen and cannot choose an alternative or form a plan of action. Decidophobics see decisions as problems, not as opportunities. Here are a few ways decidophobics can break out of the nondecisive mode:

- ◆ Use the decision-making models and the DECIDE acronym, which divide decisions into parts. Often it is easier to break a big decision into smaller parts and make those decisions first.
- ◆ Moderate expectations.
- ◆ Start each day with the single most important task and complete it. If you are a list maker, do not have more than five items on the list; that way you are more likely to get everything done and feel a greater sense of accomplishment and control.

◆ Step back from the decision; sleep on it overnight; give it some time. You might even think about a vacation or a change of scene as a way to get perspective.

◆ Talk it over with caring friends or family members: Perhaps there is a fresh approach, an avenue you have not considered, or perhaps talking about it will at least offer the chance to clarify what you really want. Mark Twain said, "I can teach anybody how to get what they want out of life. The problem is that I can't find anybody who can tell me what they want."

Decidophobia is a learned behavior, a type of helplessness (dependency on others) or a form of perfectionism. So that they don't establish this pattern, young children should be given the opportunity to experience decision making (e.g., choosing the red shirt or the blue shirt, the apple or the orange) in order to develop decision-making skills. Setting up a variety of activity areas or learning centers in preschools or kindergartens is an excellent way to provide children with early decision-making experiences. During free time, the children can choose the activity they want to engage in, whom they want to be with, and what they want to accomplish—all useful life preparation skills.

Intuition

Intuition plays a role in decision making. One way to increase decision-making acumen is to trust feelings and instincts (Kaye, 1996). As mentioned earlier in the chapter, a multistep approach is not always necessary to select a course of action. Sometimes decisions are influenced by **intuition,** or the sense of knowing what to do without going through rational processes. For example, Brad accompanies Kirsten, his wife, to two out-of-state interviews. Brad likes one state but cannot stand the other, although he cannot give specific reasons for his feelings. Fortunately, Kirsten gets offers from both employers, and she and Brad choose the state they both feel good about. Since it is difficult to measure, intuition is one of the least scientific aspects of decision making, but it is still recognized as a factor.

As another example, when making an offer on a house, should you pay the suggested price of $250,000 or should you offer $240,000 or $245,000? What does your research of house prices in the area (price per square foot and so forth) tell you? What does your intuition tell you? Should you go lower and hope the homeowner takes the offer, but be ready to renegotiate if necessary? Or should you offer the suggested price? Sizing up situations involves rational decision making and information seeking as well as intuition.

FAMILY DECISION MAKING, INCLUDING DIVISION OF HOUSEHOLD WORK

The main difference between personal and family decision making is that the latter is more complex. The more people involved in making a decision or potentially affected by a decision, the more complex the decision process is likely to be. Consider, for example, how difficult it can be for five coworkers to decide where to go to lunch or for a group of friends to decide which movie to see. Similar difficulties can arise in a family setting, depending on how many family members are involved in each decision. In a simple situation, only one family member is involved in making a decision, and everyone else simply accepts whatever that person decides. For example, one person may suggest going to the school basketball game, and the entire family agrees and accepts the decision. In a more complex situation, each family member may suggest a different course of action. Instead of agreeing to go to the basketball game together, the family members go off in different directions: The teenage son goes to the basketball game, the mother to a PTA meeting, the daughter to a friend's house, and the father to a club meeting. If the family has only one car, this is going to be a difficult situation to manage. These examples illustrate two of the questions raised by family decision making: Will the manager alone make most of the decisions, or does each family member have a say? Are most decisions made smoothly, or is conflict more usual?

Homes and families can provide a base for cooperation, coordination, and negotiation. Family members bring to this base their own needs and wants, but sometimes one family member's needs and wants are in conflict with another's. When conflict rather than harmony is characteristic of the home or family, the decision-making process becomes more complicated.

A practical example of a family decision-making situation is who does what in the home. Women are more likely to do the laundry, prepare meals, shop for groceries, clean the house, care for children, buy gifts, make decisions about furniture and decoration, and wash dishes. Men are more likely to do yard work, make minor home repairs, and keep the car in good condition. Coltrane (1989) concluded: "Generally, mothers were more likely than fathers to act as managers for cooking, cleaning, and child care, but over half of the couples showed responsibility in all areas" (p. 480).

In regard to household work, the trends are toward

◆ Less time spent overall on housework *(American households spent 30 percent less time on household chores in 2000 than in 1965.)*

◆ More husband participation

◆ More shared responsibility in the home

To break this down further,

◆ In 1965, married women spent an average of 33.9 hours on housework; in 1995, the number was 19.4.

◆ Married men spent an average of 4.7 hours on housework in 1965, compared to 10.4 hours in 1995. For married men, the average weekly housework hours in 1965 were 4.7 compared to 10.4 in 1995 (Bianchi, Milkie, Sayer, & Robinson, 2000).

In more and more households, partners share activities such as child care and grocery shopping. For example, one study revealed that 14 percent of men and women share grocery shopping duties. In response to this and the research finding that men are more likely to buy whatever they see, Audrey Guskey, a marketing professor at Duquesne University, says that stores court men with end-of-aisle displays of chips, beer, and soft drinks—items men commonly buy on impulse (Meyer, 1997). Who shops and who does what in the home continue to be contested terrains. Household members need to have clean living quarters, food to eat, and clean clothes to wear; and if there are children, they need to be cared for. Homes that are clean and neat seem calmer, roomier, and healthier.

Individuals who live together have to decide on a standard of living, a comfort zone they can live with. Possible solutions to getting the housework done more efficiently and more pleasantly include

◆ Trying team work: picking a half hour or hour a week to clean together, perhaps Saturday morning, and concentrating on tasks like mopping floors and cleaning bathrooms.

◆ Keeping communication lines open, renegotiating tasks.

◆ Not wearing shoes in the house and having a place or box near each entry door where shoes are kept; or at least having outside mats to rub shoes on before entering the house.

◆ Having a chart or checklist; rewards for completion of tasks.

◆ Buying the latest equipment and products to make the tasks easier. For a two-story house, putting cleaning supplies and vacuum cleaners on each floor; in a multi-bathroom house, putting cleaning supplies in each bathroom.

◆ Multitasking by playing music or listening to a book on tape while cleaning; folding laundry while watching television.

◆ Using time fragments, cleaning for short periods of time and taking a break.

◆ Cleaning from the top down, since dust settles, starting at the top of a bookshelf or ceiling fan and working downward.

◆ Using space fragments, dividing a room into areas and cleaning one area at a time.

◆ Attacking the area that is most visually bothersome first.

◆ Reading labels, making sure the products are being used correctly. If the label says to leave the product on for 10 minutes for best results, do it.

◆ Hiring help, outsourcing. At what point does doing so make financial sense, figuring in satisfaction and pleasure?

Economists are looking at household production in a fresh way. In 2003, the Bureau of Labor Statistics launched its first ever study of household time use in an effort to collect reliable data on this subject. As this book went to press, final reports were not in, but they should shed light on who can afford a babysitter, a personal trainer, a lawn service, and/or a personal shopper. An initial finding, for example, indicated that if a person's income is more than $44,000 a year, it makes more financial sense to hire a lawn service than do it oneself (assuming the person dislikes this task). Tasks can be divided into two categories: consumption, which is enjoyable, and production, which feels more like work. Take gardening, for example. Is that work or leisure? If a person hates it, then hiring someone to do it makes sense.

Families, Environment, and the Elbing Model

According to Marshall (1991), "the future of American families is not predetermined, but depends heavily on the choices made by families, employers and especially public institutions" (p. 5). Consequently, family decision making is strongly influenced by families' awareness of what is feasible and acceptable in the environment in which they live. Alvar Elbing developed a model (see Figure 5.5) to illustrate how two individuals in a family make decisions given their reference groups, perceived and acceptable alternatives, and environmental constraints. The Elbing model demonstrates that decisions are influenced by many factors and considerations. The *XYZ* section in the center of the model represents the solution, because alternatives are perceived by both individuals and are acceptable in the environment.

Accommodation, Consensual, and de Facto Decision Making

There are three types or styles of family decision making: accommodation, consensual, and de facto. In **accommodation,** the family reaches an agree-

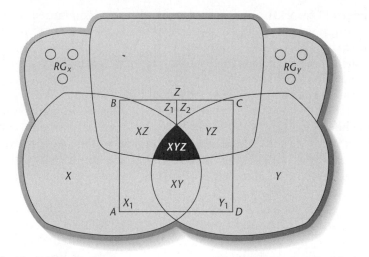

FIGURE 5.5
The Elbing Model for Viewing Alternatives in a Family Decision Situation

Source: Adapted from Alvar O. Elbing, Jr., "A Model for Viewing Decision Making in Interaction Situations from an Historical Perspective." In Alvar Elbing, *Behavioral Decisions in Organizations.* Copyright © 1970 by Scott, Foresman and Company.

ABCD: Family decision situation
   X: Family member
   Y: Family member
   Z: Environment
RG$_x$: Reference group for member *X*
RG$_y$: Reference group for member *Y*
XZ: Alternatives perceived by *X* and acceptable in existing environment.
YZ: Alternatives perceived by *Y* and acceptable in existing environment.

XY: Alternatives perceived by both *X* and *Y* but *not* acceptable in the environment.
X$_1$ and Y$_1$: Alternatives perceived by one member but not acceptable in the environment.
Z$_1$ and Z$_2$: Acceptable alternatives not perceived by family members.
   Solution
   XYZ: Alternatives perceived by both family members and acceptable in the environment.

ment by accepting the point of view of the dominant person. Power is a critical factor in accommodation. In **consensual decision making,** the family reaches a mutual agreement equally acceptable to all individuals involved. **De facto decision making** is characterized by a lack of dissent rather than by active assent. It usually occurs when no one really cares about the outcome of the decision. For instance, no one in a family may have strong feelings about which television show to watch.

Families in which the husband and wife share equally in making most of the decisions are **syncratic.** Families can also be **autonomic,** which means that an equal number of decisions are made by each spouse. Thus, in syncratic families the decisions are shared, whereas in autonomic families the spouses make an equal number of separate decisions. According to a classic study by Blood and Wolfe (1960), the partner who commands the greater amount of material resources will achieve greater power in spousal decision making. Newer studies suggest that decision-making power in couples is also related to their emotional interdependence and ability to control each other and influence the ultimate degree of consensus. Godwin and Scanzoni (1989) theorized that the more modern the gender role preference of the wife, the less control her husband had. Their study of 188 married couples revealed that socioemotional factors affected both coerciveness and control. Specifically, emotional bonding contributes to spouses' influence over each other and also to whether they reach a consensus. "Spouses who reached higher levels of consensus included husbands who had patterns of previous cooperativeness during conflict situations, more equitable economic resources of the spouses, wives whose communication styles were less coercive, and spouses who demonstrated greater control" (p. 943). Further, husbands who were committed to the marital relationship were more likely to respond positively to their wives' suggestions, ideas, and directives.

In conclusion, it appears that explaining decision-making power (who decides what and to what extent) in couples is more complicated than simply looking at who contributes the greater amount of resources. Other important factors include how close the husband and the wife are, the degree of cooperativeness and communication between them, and their levels of education. For example, a study in India revealed that literate women participated to a greater extent in decisions related to health and size of the family, their children's education, and the family's investments and savings than did illiterate women (Mohanty, 1996).

The types of decision making discussed so far have involved couple-centered families in which most decisions are made by the spouses. An alternative to this is child-centered families in which the children make or affect most of the decisions of the whole family, including the choice of foods, television shows, and activities. Actually, the difference between couple-centered and child-centered families is not absolute, for children affect decisions in every family. Nevertheless, children do have more influence in some families than in others. The next section will discuss family and couple consumer decision making and show how children influence parents' buying behaviors.

Consumer Decision Making in Families

"A prerequisite for consumers to make good decisions is to have all the relevant information about the decision at hand" (Lee & Hogarth, 2000, p. 277). Decision making in the marketplace provides an excellent illustration of family decision making. How one family spends money may not seem that important, but, collectively, family spending amounts to billions of dollars when multiplied across all families. For this reason, manufacturers and advertisers spend enormous amounts of money on consumer research to determine who decides what in a family and why. In short, consumer decision making is big business and the driving force behind the well-being of national economies.

Families must decide (1) what to buy, (2) where to shop, (3) how much to pay, (4) when to buy, and (5) who should buy. The first decision is the most important—families have to decide if they want to buy something. This decision leads to the other four. Deciding what to buy is more difficult when there are countless brands to consider. For example, 34 new food products are launched each day in the United States (Mogelonsky, 1998). Let's consider the "when to buy" decision. *There are life change points that radically affect consumption.* Examples are marriage, having children, moving, getting a job, getting a dog, buying a house, empty nesting, and retiring. Newlyweds are the ultimate consumer, buying more in the first six months of marriage than a settled household does in five years (Ellison & Tejada, 2003). The publisher of *Bride's* and *Modern Bride* magazines estimates that U.S. newlyweds spend $70 billion establishing their households. In many instances, life changes stimulate gift buying as well as buying for one's own consumption. Jason, a 24-year-old recent college graduate, explained it this way:

> All my friends are getting married. So my girlfriend and I are buying wedding gifts every couple of months and we've never done this before. We try to find something that fits what they like to do, like cooking, keeping in mind what their style is— contemporary or traditional.

Cueing into life changes has not escaped marketers:

> Corporate marketers say certain points in life make consumers especially vulnerable to sales pitches, with the soon-to-be-married often being the most susceptible. It's a time when they aren't just choosing a marriage partner, but also are making brand decisions about toothpaste, detergent, and appliances that could last even longer. Unless a couple has been living together for years, weddings represent a moment when two sets of habits and brand preferences meet and usually only one survives (Ellison & Tejada, 2003, p. B1).

The family decision-making process involves eight distinct roles (see Table 5.1). These roles provide a way of conceptualizing how family members make decisions—some family members are buyers, others users, others influencers, and so on. For example, a mother or father buys disposable diapers, the baby uses them, and the parent who changes the diaper disposes of it.

SUGGESTED ACTIVITY

Is there a life change point in your immediate future? If so, how will it affect your consumption patterns?

Family decision-making purchases can involve conflict. For example, a couple may differ about the amount of money to spend, the brand or type of good to buy, the stores to shop in, or who should make the purchase. Conflict will decrease if the couple agrees on which goals are desirable. Purchasing decisions may be influenced by a number of variables, including reference groups, work life, leisure pursuits, culture, subculture, social class, stage in the life cycle, mobility, geographical location, and children. For instance, young families with preschool children have different buying decisions to make than retired couples. Joint decision making is most common among the middle class, whereas autonomous decision making is most likely in the upper and lower classes (Loudon & Della Bitta, 1988).

Children have a significant influence on their parents' buying habits. A study by Infocus Environmental of Princeton, New Jersey, found that one-third of parents changed their shopping habits because of environmental information their children gave them. When questioned about their information source, the children said they learned about the environment in school. The study reported in *Marketing News* (Schlossberg, 1992) indicated that children affect their parents' buying and shopping habits by encouraging them to purchase items in recyclable packaging (24 percent) and to avoid products in containers that are not recyclable or biodegradable (17 percent). The study concluded that children are influencing far more than the particular foods their parents purchase and that they are having a significant impact on their parents' environmental consciousness.

Getting Out of the House

Much of the previous coverage has been on children, consumption, and household responsibilities, joint decision making, and so on. It is also important to note that a surprising number of Americans are less home-focused: They are getting out of the house—going to gyms, parties, restaurants, clubs, and bookstores. This trend is called **hatching,** a term that refers to local-area nesting, finding other places outside of the work or the home where one can spend time. Hatching has also been called "the third space" and is epitomized by television shows like *Cheers* and *Friends*.

People are looking for ways to reconnect through discussion groups, book clubs, investment clubs, ghost hunting clubs, morning walking groups. They may purposely move to planned urban developments (PUDs) with built-in activities and town centers with shops and restaurants, birdwatching groups,

There are eight distinct roles in the family decision-making process. A look at these provides further insight into how family members interact in their various consumption-related roles:

1. *Influencers:* Family member(s) who provide information to other members about a product or service

2. *Gatekeepers:* Family member(s) who control the flow of information about a product or service into the family

3. *Deciders:* Family member(s) with the power to determine unilaterally or jointly whether or not to purchase a specific product or service

4. *Buyers:* Family member(s) who make the actual purchase of a particular product or service

5. *Preparers:* Family member(s) who transform the product into a form suitable for consumption by other family members

6. *Users:* Family member(s) who use or consume a particular product or service

7. *Maintainers:* Family member(s) who service or repair the product so that it will provide continued satisfaction

8. *Disposers:* Family member(s) who initiate or carry out the disposal or discontinuation of a particular product or service
   The number and identity of the family members who fill these roles vary from family to family and product to product.

Source: Leon G. Schiffman and Leslie Lazar Kanuk, *Consumer Behavior,* 4th ed. © 1991 Pearson Education (Englewood Cliffs, N.J.: Prentice-Hall, 1991), p. 341. Adapted with permission of Pearson Education.

gardening, hiking, photography, running, and boating. Some of these activities are free and some are costly. For individuals returning to outdoor activities a whole range of gadgets, clothing, and accessories is necessary. Getting out there isn't cheap:

> "My husband would have a stroke if he knew the price," says Jackie Menefee, who put together a quick weekend getaway to get out for a change. The couple made a two-hour drive from their Chesapeake, Va., home to an ocean resort for two nights of pampering and a Champagne tasting. They had a good time, but she wasn't prepared for a $600 tab. "It was very upscale," she says. (Daspin, 2003, p. W9)

On a more modest scale, one homeowner drives to Home Depot or Lowe's, home supply stores, every Saturday morning, and looks around and drinks a cup of coffee. Others go to flea markets, garage sales, or antiquing with friends. Another says this:

> Carol Ann Band says she's just happy to get out. Between growing her own vegetables for home-made baby food to weekly Sunday dinner with relatives, all the time spent in the house is wearing thin. Now the 37-year-old in Fresno, Calif. has hit on a way to relieve the stress: she joined a women's tennis league and is playing a couple times a week. "I'm a better mom for the hours I take away," she says. (Daspin, 2003, p. W9)

As we know from systems theory, activities wax and wane. There is a cyclical, or wavelike, effect, and the nesting instinct is not immune from this effect. It goes in and out of fashion. In the early 1980s the term *cocooning* caught on big as people retreated from the dirt and crime of the streets into their safe and warm homes. Baby boomers were buying their first homes and filling them up with oversized furniture and children's equipment. The phrase "couch potato" emerged. September 11, 2001, brought another wave of nesting behavior as families drew closer in the wake of the terrorist attacks and uncertainty that followed. National, international, and business travel slowed. Huge sectional sofas began to sell as well as home theaters costing $100,000 and more. At the same time, sociologists noticed a countermovement of people looking for companionship and connectedness outside the home. Church attendance and library use went up for a while. Perhaps there is a limit to how much home and family time is possible. "You can only cocoon with your family for so long," says Erik Gordon, a professor who studies consumer trends at the University of Florida. "Even if they don't drive you nuts, they bore you" (Daspin, 2003, p. W1).

The search for the right balance of inside and outside the family/home continues, and much of it is driven by the person's life stage as well as by environmental and economic conditions. Much of what this book is about is that search and the factors that play into it.

PROBLEM SOLVING

Problems are questions or situations that present uncertainty, risk, perplexity, or difficulty. **Problem solving** involves making many decisions that lead to a resolution of the problem. In some disciplines the terms *decision making* and *problem solving* are used interchangeably, but in resource management they are used differently. Decision making encompasses all sorts of situations (many of them routine), needs, and wants, whereas problem solving implies that a certain degree of difficulty or risk is involved. As noted earlier, the more people involved in a decision, the more complex the decision process. Thus, family problem solving is usually more complex than individual problem solving. Because problems arise from difficulty, they put even more strain on families than routine decision making. If any family member has hidden agendas or demands, problem definition or analysis can be extremely difficult. Skilled family managers can often spot potential problem areas and try to resolve them before they become full-blown problems involving intense family conflict.

Definition, Analysis/Timing, and Plan of Action

Usually people do not spontaneously become aware of a problem and then suddenly decide to search for and analyze relevant information (Fay & Wallace, 1987). Instead, the person or family is motivated by dissatisfaction with the current state of things. As motivated processes, problem awareness and analysis are subject to five levels of motivation influences:

1. Needs, motives, and goals of the problem solver
2. Perceptions and beliefs of the problem solver
3. Values of the problem solver
4. Resources of the problem solver
5. Learning, background, and previous experience of the problem solver

These influences affect the way a person defines a problem and makes decisions to solve the problem.

Problem Definition

Problem recognition or definition is the first step in problem solving. The person has to recognize the problem as such before engaging in purposeful behavior to resolve the situation. Problem definition is a creative process requiring the individual to see common threads and sense important cause-and-effect relationships. For example, the person needs to uncover the underlying symptoms that have caused the problem. How does one go about this?

According to David Nylen, "Problems are best defined in the form of questions. Doing so provides clear direction for the rest of the process. The task of the decision maker becomes one of providing a solution or decision that will answer the question. . . . The final decision must fulfill and reflect the underlying cause of the situation" (1990, pp. 51–52).

Complicated problems demand more energy and attention because their cause (or causes) may be hidden or multifaceted. Once the problem is defined, then the individual can move on to the next step in problem solving—problem analysis. As a practical example, the next sections will show how Michelle engages in problem solving after her boss tells her that she has been denied a promotion because she lacks administrative experience.

Problem Analysis / Timing

Depending on the type of problem and the individuals involved, problems can be viewed as messes or as experiences that simply require a logical and reasonable response. For example, after being denied a promotion, Michelle could respond or act in many ways. She knows she has a problem (the problem is clearly defined); now she has to decide what she is going to do about it.

No two problems are the same because each involves its own unique timing, individuals, and circumstances and stems from a specific situation. To solve complicated problems, the individual needs to systematically follow the decision steps discussed earlier in this chapter. Taking shortcuts in the decision process will only result in incomplete information that will complicate the problem situation further. Since many complex problems involve the interaction of subproblems, one approach is to divide the problem into subproblems and analyze each separately.

One of the most difficult aspects of problem solving is timing. Sometimes it is wise to deliberately delay a decision, in case life changes occur or better options turn up. "**Real-options thinking** *puts a high value on flexibility*," says Glenn Daily, a fee-only life insurance planner in New York (Quinn, 2001). He suggests you lean toward the choice that keeps more of your options open rather than choosing a single-option path. Real-options is a catchall phrase referring to *staying open, waiting and watching for the right opportunity* such as in making financial decisions—planning when to invest, buy insurance, pay off debt, and so forth. Perhaps your parents said to you, "leave your options open" or "there are other fish in the sea."

How do you tell the difference between lasting changes (moving in the right direction) and impulsive moves (instability)? Consider these guideposts of lasting change (or real options):

- ◆ They are based on your values and goals, something you have thought about for a long time, bringing beliefs to life.
- ◆ They are one option among many.

◆ Embracing a challenge, the change should be challenging but worth the effort. There is the feeling of moving forward rather than fleeing or avoiding.

Henry David Thoreau said:

I learned this, at least by my experiment: that if you advance confidently in the direction of your dreams, and endeavor to live the life which you have imagined, you will meet with a success unexpected in common hours. You will put some things behind, you will pass an invisible boundary.

Plan of Action

Once the defining and analyzing phases are over, the individual designs a plan of action. Planning involves putting together the activities or steps to follow. The objective of planning is to produce systems or solutions that can provide satisfaction to the problem solver and other participants in the problem.

Michelle decides to get administrative experience so that the next time an opening occurs she will be qualified. Her subproblems include whether her current workplace can provide the necessary experience or whether she will have to get experience elsewhere. Perhaps her boss could be more explicit about the work experience she needs. Michelle also turns to her colleagues, friends, and family for advice. After she considers their advice and her own perception of the problem, she forms a plan of action. Forming a plan makes her feel more in control of things. Resource management as a discipline encourages individuals to gather as much information as possible, objectively examine their problems and options, and form a plan of action that will help get them what they want.

Motivation is a key part of problem solving. The motivation to solve the problem will depend on the amount of discrepancy between the desired and the actual state and the importance of the problem. Most people will not waste inordinate amounts of time on minor daily decisions such as what to wear or what to eat. Routine decisions such as these are rarely problems. They can become problems, however, if the person defines them as a problem or if the decision has a far-reaching impact. For example, what to wear to a job interview or what to serve at a banquet for 500 people may become major problems involving substantial amounts of money and a variety of alternative choices and consequences.

Another essential part of problem solving is the search for information. The search leads to the formation of alternative courses of action and evaluation. Looking within oneself for information for decisions is called an **internal search.** Michelle did this first. After her boss told her she had been denied the promotion, she went back to her office, shut the door, and thought over the problem. An internal search is easier and more common than an **external search,** which involves gathering information from family, friends, other people, and the media. When Michelle asked others for advice, she engaged in an external search. As part of her external search, she watched a television news report and read magazine articles about how many people around the country were being laid off from their jobs due to corporate downsizing or were turning to home-based work because they were tired of working for someone else or commuting. This information helped Michelle put her failure to receive a promotion in perspective. She reasoned that at least she had a job that she liked, and she felt sure that given time and effort she would be promoted. As in Michelle's case, complex problem solving usually requires both internal and external searches.

As the search proceeds, the problem becomes more narrowly defined and refined. At all times, decisions should be linked to the primary goal sought. If the goal is landing the best job possible, the job seeker continually looks for information, work experience, and contacts leading to that goal. The desired end state is a solution. Michelle would be well advised to spend time getting the training she needs to get ahead, if not at her present job, at another organization.

Uncertainty, Risk, and Success

The problems associated with career advancement and job hunting are good examples of uncertainty and risk. In both cases, the individual searches for information to reduce the levels of uncertainty and risk. The more an employee or job seeker knows about a company, such as its policies and track record, the more confident he or she will be on the job or at job interviews. This is why a certain amount of office gossip is useful: Employees need to know what is going on and what is about to happen. Advance knowledge reduces individuals' perceptions of uncertainty and risk and gives them time to adjust/strategize.

The concepts of risk and uncertainty were introduced in Chapter 2 in the discussion of risk aversion theory. This theory says that rational people will try to reduce or avoid risk and that risk is subjective because individuals define the level of risk and uncertainty they can handle. For example, a blind date is a risk. To reduce the amount of risk and uncertainty, the couple will try to find out as much as possible about each other before going out on the date.

Uncertainty is the state or feeling of being in doubt. *Risk* is the possibility of pain, harm, or loss from a decision. Risk is subjective; that is, each person defines what risk is. A person weighing uncertainty and risk is judging the **probability,** or likelihood, of a good or bad outcome. Shopping, particularly catalog or Internet shopping, involves risk and the consideration of probable outcomes. **Success** is the achievement of something desirable: It can be a specific such as milestones reached, money earned, and honors won, or it may be a desired state, such as happiness, contentment, fame, or prosperity, often expressed as a successful outcome. It may be the result of planned activity or, on rare occasions, chance. True success is defined by the individuals, not by parents, friends, society, or the media. The reason success is included in this discussion is that often success involves risk and uncertainty. Success involves being open to every possibility, realizing that one may experience success in unexpected ways, and being ready for success when it comes. A town manager of a small community was very surprised when the town's employees, from groundskeepers to the police, threw her an appreciation party. She was not near retirement and the party was not because of a landmark year of service: It was strictly a "thanks for your effort" party—we appreciate you and want you to know it. Before, during, and after that party, she felt very successful because she had found the right fit between her talents and place of employment. She cares so much that on her morning jogging route she carries a plastic bag to pick up any trash she sees, and when she drives in and out of work in her pickup truck she throws trash in the back. The town is so small everyone knows this; it is genuine effort on her part that has gone on for years. They know someone is watching out for them: Isn't that what a town manager should do?

An individual's perception of uncertainty leads to the perception of risk. For example, John, a recent college graduate, may be uncertain whether to wear shorts and a T-shirt or a sports shirt and slacks to his first company picnic. He may also be uncertain about the weather the day of the picnic. If he thinks it may rain, he might try to reduce his risk of getting wet by taking a hat and a jacket. Although deciding what to wear to a picnic is not a high-risk venture, John wants to dress appropriately so that he will fit in. In contrast, Sam, one of John's coworkers, has not even given a thought to what he will wear to the picnic. His perception of risk in this problem situation is minimal; in fact, he does not even think of dressing for the picnic as a problem situation. At the picnic, Sam is the only person wearing shorts, and for the next two months, he must endure gentle ribbing about his "bony knees" and plaid shorts. Risk can be perceived as occurring before, during, or after a decision.

SUGGESTED ACTIVITY

Describe success for yourself. What end state or activity would be a sign of success? What attitudes, decisions, and behaviors would you need to be successful? Name three successful people and explain why you think they are successful. What qualities (i.e., courage, generosity, caring, self-confidence) made them successful?

Types of Risks

As discussed in Chapter 2, five types of risk affect decision making: functional or performance risk, financial risk, physical risk, psychological risk, social risk, and time risk. In the last example, John was seeking to reduce physical, psychological, financial, and social risks. If he worries about the best time to arrive at the picnic, then he would add time risk to his list of concerns. To reduce risk, people search for information or behave in ways that will decrease their uncertainty, such as asking others for advice or repeating behaviors that have worked for them in the past. Saving for retirement is a big risk. Increasingly, workers have to make decisions about saving and investing for retirement, and in uncertain economies, doing so is becoming more and more difficult.

At-Risk Children

Certainly, many individual, family, and societal problems are far more difficult than what to wear to an event. A disturbing societal problem is at-risk children. An estimated 7 million children, one in four of those aged 10 to 17 in the United States, engage in high-risk behaviors and are in "jeopardy of not growing into responsible adults who can effectively parent, work, or vote" (Dryfoos, 1991). According to Dryfoos, high-risk children are likely to be low achievers, drug abusers, or premature parents; they are also likely to be in trouble with the law. Many of these children live in high-stress family situations and have little parental support and supervision.

Questions have been raised about what schools can do to help at-risk children (Katz, Dalton, & Giacquinta, 1994). A consensus is forming that school programs as they currently exist cannot solve the rapidly rising incidence of depression and stress emerging from dysfunctional families. New types of school-based support programs and curricula are suggested as a means for dealing with educational, health, and life issues of at-risk populations. In New York State, the Home and Career Skills (HCS) curriculum concentrates on developing the critical thinking skills of students so that they can make rational decisions and prepare to meet their responsibilities as members of families, consumers, home managers, and wage earners (Katz et al., 1994). Similar curricula are being used in other states under various names, including Life Management Skills.

In addition, families, both nuclear and extended, and community groups and health organizations need to do all they can to reduce the number of at-risk children and give all children the best possible start in life. Helping children learn to make responsible decisions at an early age is a good starting point, followed by continued attention and support through the later years. For those in the helping professions, the emphasis when working with families is to assist them in making their own decisions and solving their own problems, not to impose the professionals' own decision solutions. Expressing gratitude to others, mentoring troubled youths, foster-parenting, giving the gift of time, forgiving a wrong, and serving in the community are all positive steps toward reducing the number and severity of at-risk children.

The GO Model: Visualization of a Problem-Solving Process

Professors Holly Hunts and Ramona Marotz-Baden at Montana State University developed the GO model of problem solving because they believe that teaching problem-solving processes may well be one of the most important tasks of family economists/management specialists. GO stands for goal-oriented. The purpose of the GO model (see Figure 5.6) is twofold:

1. To further the theory about problem solving into a goal-oriented model that can help students understand how individuals and families make choices that help them reach goals

2. To bring about a new method for teaching students about problem solving and goal-oriented strategies

Family systems theory and pedagogical strategies (different learning and teaching styles) serve as its base. Within the model, the situation requiring action is defined, alternatives are ranked, leading to the best alternative and then to a course of action and implementation that leads ultimately to results in Phase 5. Phase 6 provides information feedback that may be acceptable or unacceptable. The feedback provides information as the process starts all over again in Phase 1, thereby affecting future situations. "In a goal-oriented approach, problems are barriers to be overcome if goals are to be achieved. In other words, the emphasis in the goal-oriented approach is on increasing the probability of goal attainment by using problem solving to overcome these barriers" (Hunts & Marotz-Baden, in press).

Web-Based Resources

When it comes to decision making, nearly any Web site will offer information helpful in making decisions. Here is a pitch from the Peace Corps, which begins with the question, "Life is calling. How far will you go?" If you are interested in the unique experience of making a difference in the world and bringing the benefits of that experience back home, learn more about the Peace Corps at **www.peacecorps.gov**. The decision-making steps involved are applying, being interviewed, being nominated by a recruiter, going through a medical and legal review, being invited, and preparing for departure. In the country you are assigned, you meet up with the rest of the volunteers in your training group for orientation. The largest percentages of volunteers are in the areas of education and youth and community development.

SUGGESTED ACTIVITY

The GO model works best on current problems you are facing. Start at the top of the model; enter a situation and work through the process. An example that Hunts and Marotz-Baden have used in their classes is "Describe the goals and boundaries of the ideal marriage for you. Using the GO model, discuss how feasible your ideal is if you were to marry the person you care most about now" (Hunts & Marotz-Baden, 2003, p. 11). Another example they have used is to imagine the situation in which two roommates or housemates are arguing over bills left unpaid by a third person who moved out suddenly.

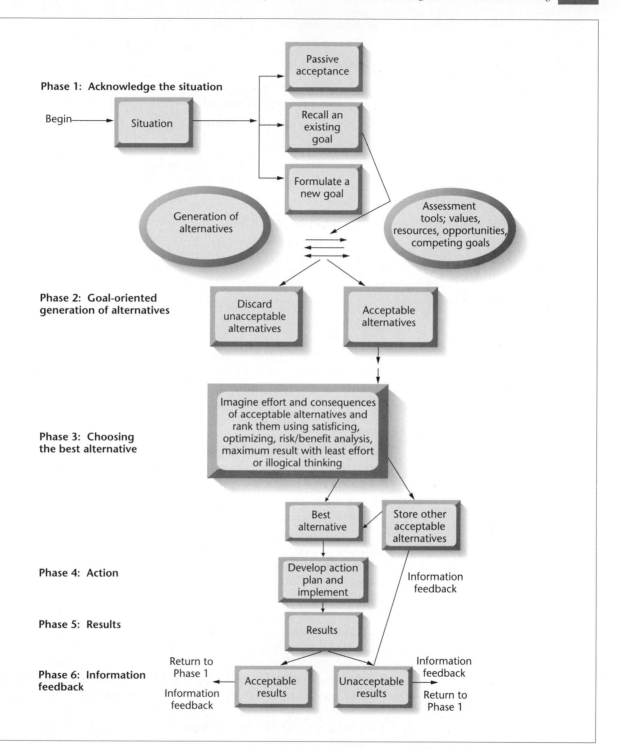

FIGURE 5.6

**The Goal-Oriented (GO)
Pedagogical Model**

Source: Reprinted with permission of Holly
Hunts and Ramona Marotz-Baden, Montana State
University.

Other interesting sites include

- Moving: **www.moving.mall.com** (a database of over 120,000 moving-related U.S. companies)
- Exploring the world: **www.nationalgeographic.com**
- Waking up in the morning: **www.mrwakeup.com**
- Getting the news: **www.go.com**
- Checking stock prices: **www.cbs.marketwatch.com**
- Comparing CD or book (including college textbook) prices: **www.amazon.com** or **www.varsitybooks.com**
- Checking auction prices, selling or making bids: **www.ebay.com**
- Comparing car prices and models: **www.carpoint.com**
- General questions "Ask Jeeves:" **www.ask.com**

Summary

As active, busy people, we make decisions and solve problems. We try to choose the best alternatives from the choices available; in so doing, we seek to reduce uncertainty and risk and increase the probability of good outcomes. Decision making is central to the management process. The acronym DECIDE is an easy way to remember the six steps of decision making. The Elbing model of family decision making demonstrates that each decision has a history and is influenced by members of reference groups. The central-satellite and chain models of decision making show the interrelationships among decisions. The decision tree illustrates that values underlie decisions and that resources and goals affect the alternatives considered. Decision making involves rules and rational patterns of thought as well as intuition.

Individuals and families seek to maximize their satisfaction through sound decision making. Families may engage in individual (husband- or wife-dominated), couple-centered, or child-centered decision making. The number of childless women has hit record highs, but for those who have children there is a steady or slightly increased trend toward more fathers working and more mothers staying at home with small children. Average time spent in housework has diminished since 1965.

Decision making is an art or skill that can be improved through reasoning and practice rather than avoidance. Decidophobia is the fear of making decisions, specifically the fear of failure. Much of a person's success depends upon his or her ability to identify the causes of problems and develop workable solutions for resolving them.

Problem solving differs from decision making in that problem solving involves difficulty, perplexity, risk, and uncertainty, whereas decision making refers to all sorts of situations, needs, and wants (some problematic, others not). The GO (goal-oriented) model of problem solving ranks alternatives to help choose the best one, so that a course of action can be implemented, leading to the desired result; feedback assists in making future decisions.

In order to be effective, decisions need to be implemented, evaluated, and communicated. Planning, implementing, and evaluating are the subjects of the next chapter, and communication will be discussed in Chapter 7.

Key Terms

accommodation
autonomic
consensual decision
  making
decidophobia
decision making
decision-making style
decision plan
decision rules
decisions

de facto decision
  making
external search
hatching
internal search
intuition
Peter Principle
postpurchase
  dissonance

prepurchase
  expectations
probability
problem solving
real-options thinking
reference groups
success
syncratic
uncertainty

Review Questions

1. What sorts of things do you want to accomplish? What sorts of activities do you want to be involved in? What decisions are needed to get you where you want to go?

2. What is the Peter Principle? How is it related to decision making?

3. The German poet and playwright Johann Wolfgang von Goethe said "I have come to the frightening conclusion that I am the decisive element. It is my personal approach that creates the climate. It is my daily mood that makes the weather. I possess tremendous power to make life miserable or joyous." Do you agree or disagree? Explain your answer.

4. What does the Elbing model illustrate?

5. What is the difference between decision making and problem solving? Describe a problem you are trying to solve.

References

Armas, G. (2003, October 25). Number of childless women hits record high. *Tallahassee Democrat*, 8A.

Bianchi, S., Milkie, M., Sayer, L., & Robinson, J. (2000). Is anyone doing the housework? Trends in the gender division of household labor. *Social Forces*, 79(1), 191–228.

Blood, R. O., & Wolfe, D. M. (1960). *Husbands and wives*. New York: Free Press.

Chiras, D. (2000). *The natural house*. White River Junction: VT: Chelsea Green.

Coltrane, S. (1989). Household labor and the routine production of gender. *Social Problems*, 36(5), 473–490.

Daspin, E. (2003, May 16). The end of nesting. *The Wall Street Journal*, W1, W9.

Delaney, W. A. (1982, December). Why are people indecisive? *Supervisory Management*, 450.

Dryfoos, J. G. (1991). School-based social and health services for at-risk students. *Urban Education*, 26(1), 118–137.

Ellison, S., & Tejada, C. (2003, January 30). Mr., Mrs., meet Mr. Clean. *The Wall Street Journal*, B1, B3.

Fan, J., & Xiao, J. (1998). Consumer decision-making styles of young adult consumers. *Journal of Consumer Affairs*, 32(2), 273–292.

Fay, C. H., & Wallace, M. J. (1987). *Research based decisions*. New York: Random House.

Forelle, C. (2003, June 16). Deodorant makers sniff out ways to sell in a stagnant market. *The Wall Street Journal*, A1.

Godwin, D. D., & Scanzoni, J. (1989). Couple consensus during marital joint decision making: A context, process, outcome model. *Journal of Marriage and the Family*, 5, 943–956.

Gray, N. L., & Donatelle, R. L. (1990). A comparative analysis of factors influencing smoking behaviors of college students: 1963–1987. *Journal of Drug Education, 20*(3), 247–255.

Hunts, H., & Marotz-Baden, R. (2003). Family systems theory: A new look at an old friend. *Consumer Interests Annual, 49,* 1–13.

Hunts, H., & Marotz-Baden, R. (in press). The GO model: A new way of teaching problem solving in context.

Katz, E., Dalton, S., & Giacquinta, J. (1994). Status risk taking and receptivity of home economics teachers to a statewide curriculum innovation. *Home Economics Research Journal, 22*(4), 401–421.

Kaye, H. (1996). *Decision power.* Englewood Cliffs, NJ: Prentice-Hall.

Keeney, R. L. (1988). Value-focused thinking and the study of values. In D. E. Beal, H. Raiffe, & A. Tuersky (Eds.), *Decision Making* (p. 466). Cambridge: Cambridge University Press.

Lee, J., & Hogarth, J. (2000). Consumer information search for home mortgages: Who, what, how much, and what else? *Financial Services Review, 9,* 277–293.

Loudon, D., & Della Bitta, A. J. (1988). *Consumer behavior: Concepts and applications.* New York: McGraw-Hill.

Malhotra, N. K. (1991). Mnemonics in marketing: A pedagogical tool. *Journal of the Academy of Marketing Science, 19*(2), 141–149.

Malhotra, N. K. (1992). *Marketing research: An applied orientation.* Englewood Cliffs, NJ: Prentice-Hall.

Marshall, R. (1991). *The state of families, 3: Losing direction.* Milwaukee, WI: Family Service America.

Meyer, M. (1997, August). The grocery gender gap. *Good Housekeeping,* 147.

Mogelonsky, M. (1998, August). Product overload? *American Demographics.*

Mohanty, M. (1996, Spring). Women in India: The relationship of literacy and participation in household decision making. *Journal of Family and Consumer Sciences,* 42–43.

Nylen, D. W. (1990). *Marketing decision making handbook.* Englewood Cliffs, NJ: Prentice-Hall.

Peter, L. J., & Hall, R. (1969). *The Peter Principle.* New York: William Morrow.

Quinn, J. B. (2001, May 22). The best investing choice is to keep your options open. *Tallahassee Democrat,* Business Section.

Schiffman, L. G., & Kanuk, L. L. (1991). *Consumer behavior* (4th ed.). Englewood Cliffs, NJ: Prentice-Hall.

Schlossberg, A. (1992, March 2). Kids teach parents how to change their buying habits. *Marketing News,* 8.

Shellenbarger, S. (2003, October 16). The sole breadwinner's lament: Having mom at home isn't as great as it sounds. *The Wall Street Journal,* D1.

Silver, W. S., & Mitchell, T. R. (1990). The status quo tendency in decision making. *Organizational Dynamics, 18,* 34–46.

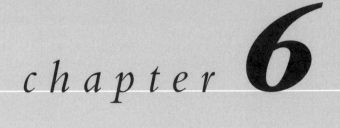

chapter 6

Planning, Implementing, and Evaluating

MAIN TOPICS

Did you know that . . . ?

. . . Fifty four percent of adults say that they have purchased or would be willing to purchase containers, furniture, file systems, or similar products to help them get organized.

. . . About 10 percent of Americans consider themselves extremely organized.

Nothing ventured, nothing gained.

—*Geoffrey Chaucer*

MULTITASKING OR TACKLING one task at a time—what makes the most sense? In our sped-up world, more of us are multitasking—sometimes it works, and sometimes it doesn't. We waste a lot of time in ordinary activities. For example, the average adult spends about four minutes a day searching for lost keys, remote controls, cell phones, and so forth. Not having enough time is the biggest excuse most people use for not being organized. They spend so much time looking after their stuff and getting places that they don't have time to plan and organize; all their time is taken up just keeping up. About 10 percent of Americans categorize themselves as extremely organized (Fetto, 2003). Do you fall into this category? "Regardless of one's level of organization, however, 89 percent of Americans say they could use help tidying up some corner of their life . . . there are scores of Americans who would be willing to take action and even pay for some help" (Fetto 2003, p. 11). Planning, implementing, and evaluating are the subjects of this chapter.

Examples of plans are college plans, financial plans, lunch plans, weekend plans, wedding plans, national health care plans, and affirmative action plans.

SUGGESTED ACTIVITY

What corner of your life could use some tidying up? What action should you take?

As the list indicates, plans can range from the mundane to the significant, but all plans are important to the individuals involved. Without plans there would be no birthday cakes or gifts under Christmas trees, nor would there be any roads or businesses. In short, life as we know it would not exist.

In fact, planning is so crucial to human existence that it has been the subject of sayings and fables since ancient times. Think how often you have heard someone say "If you fail to plan, you are planning to fail." Countless generations of children have heard the story of the industrious ant that planned ahead and stored food for the winter while the foolish grasshopper frolicked in the sun. Of course, when winter came, the grasshopper's failure to think ahead proved fatal.

As the ant and the grasshopper story indicates, planning is prevention—a good plan is a management tool that can save countless hours in revising, restructuring, and other ineffective actions. The amount of planning needed varies, however, from situation to situation and from individual to individual. Planning needs also change over the life cycle. For example, the oldest members of the baby boom generation are entering retirement and must plan for reduced incomes, in most cases, as well as more leisure time and potential health problems.

Like individuals, families make plans, and their plans involve the same type of considerations (i.e., time, energy, personnel, cost, schedules) as other plans. For example, family tasks and responsibilities are planned and assigned. A family's plan may include driving the children to school, picking up groceries for dinner, taking the garbage out, and so on—with a family member performing each task. Yet, despite the amount of planning that families do, how often do they sit down and really think about all they do and evaluate the effectiveness of their planning?

This chapter addresses several questions: How are plans made? How can they be more effective? What forces drive planning behavior? As social and economic conditions worldwide are transformed, these questions are becoming more and more critical. The world's growing population is straining its resources, increasing the necessity for better planning. In the consumer area, life is moving so fast that individuals are having trouble devising enough plans to handle all the choices and changes that confront them. Several years ago, the *Wall Street Journal* highlighted this problem:

> Mr. Cialdini, the psychologist, believes that consumers are resorting increasingly to what he calls "click whir" behavior. Life has become so complex that consumers can't possibly analyze the merits of all of their decisions, he says. So they are more susceptible to certain cues and symbols like "discount" or "last day of sale" and take less time to analyze fundamental questions like need or cost. When we react to symbols instead of information, then what we do doesn't make sense anymore, he says. (Morris, 1987, August 4)

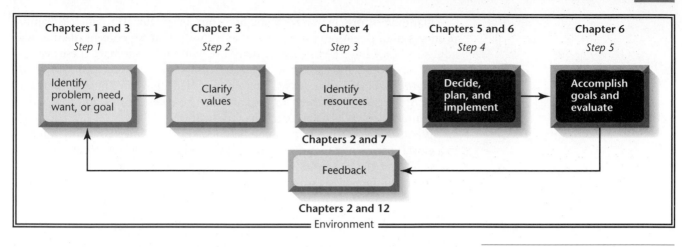

FIGURE 6.1
The Management Process Model

As this chapter will show, situations, events, and other factors affect planning, implementing, and evaluating. Besides exploring the complex nature of planning and implementing, the chapter also examines the motivating forces behind these processes. Why do people plan? What are they trying to accomplish? How successful are their plans? Key topics include the influence of personality and style, as well as social contexts and environments, on planning. Examples of planning, implementing, and evaluating will be given, providing a blend of theory and practice. With real-world examples, this chapter provides an important learning resource for students of individual and family management.

This chapter also contributes to the understanding of the management process model first presented in Chapter 1 and repeated here in Figure 6.1. Planning is a process (a subsystem) within the larger process (system) of management. Step 4 in the model is "decide, plan, and implement," and step 5 is concerned with accomplishing goals and evaluation. Thus, this chapter explains the culmination of the management process.

What Is Planning?

Planning is a process involving a series of decisions leading to need or goal fulfillment. A **plan** is a detailed schema, program, strategy, or method worked out beforehand for the accomplishment of a desired end result. For example, students planning to graduate in June follow a plan of action that entails completing required courses and filling out the paperwork necessary to ensure graduation. As the graduation date nears, they must rent or buy a cap and gown. Graduation plans, among others, require a systematic approach to problem solving and goal attainment.

Planning or organizing tools include containers, furniture, files, or similar products used to get organized. A survey showed that 54 percent of American adults say they have purchased or would be willing to purchase these types of things (Fetto, 2003). According to this same source, an *American Demograhics*/Harris Interactive survey revealed that among the kinds of things American would need to organize are finances, books and magazines, audio and video collections, kitchens, and games.

When it comes to objects, some people like their shoes all neatly lined up in a closet; others just toss their shoes in; still others don't use closets and leave shoes all over the house. A 30-year-old single man living alone had two master closets, so he put his suits and work clothes in one, along with the matching shoes; and he put casual clothes and athletic shoes in the other. Only 12 percent of the population alphabetizes their spices, according to the New England Professional Organizers. Maybe it is more remarkable that 12 percent do this than that 88 percent do not. What do you think about alphabetizing spices, lining up shoes, organizing clothes by function?

The need to organize is a cultural phenomenon, according to Dean McFarlin, a professor of management at the University of Dayton:

> "We are a culture that embraces a monochromic view of time," he said, "We believe time is a commodity and it can all be lost. This is why we see California Closets doing so well and why third-graders are getting pocket planners. It's a cultural response to the perceived pressures that are increasing, the feeling that we can't escape from work, our cell phones, our Palm Pilots" (Matchan, 2002, p. 6F)

The Planning Process and Task

This chapter follows the chapter on decision making because planning is a more complex process than decision making. A **process** is a system of operations that work together to produce an end result. The word *process* implies movement or change. Something is happening—steps are being taken.

Planning is a thinking and information-gathering process involving a series of decisions. It is a process because formulating plans requires several steps, such as information gathering, sorting, and prioritizing; then, based on this information, the planner must decide which plan is most likely to succeed. The decision and steps are not random, but proceed in an orderly, logical sequence. For example, after living in a dormitory for a semester, a college student may decide to move into an apartment the next semester, but she will not move out of the dormitory without doing some planning. She must decide how much rent she can afford, whether she will look for roommates or live alone, and in what parts of town she would like to live. Before finally selecting an apartment, she will probably look at several apartments.

To help understand the role of planning in management behavior, researchers have constructed models that depict the various stages of the planning process. The principal aim of such models is to predict future behavior: How does a person normally plan? Will the plan be repeated?

Figure 6.2 shows one such model of the planning process. In the model, the first step is awareness—an individual becomes aware that a plan is needed. In the next step, the person gathers and analyzes information. In the third step, the information is put into the context of the situation, including consideration of others, and a plan is formed. The plan is a series of decisions, including decisions about resource allocations. Finally, in the fourth and fifth steps, the plan is implemented and evaluated. As the model shows, plans are made within an environmental context—the person considers what is possible within his or

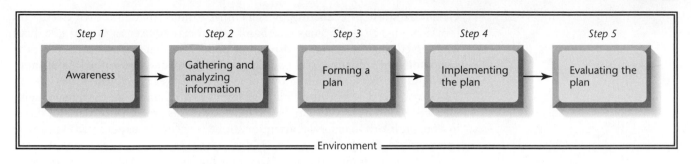

Step 1	Step 2	Step 3	Step 4	Step 5
Awareness	Gathering and analyzing information	Forming a plan	Implementing the plan	Evaluating the plan

Environment

FIGURE 6.2
The Planning Process Model

her environment. A beach party is not a practical plan in Minneapolis in the winter, for example, nor is a sit-down dinner with five courses a good choice for a 4-year-old's birthday party.

When individuals and families plan, their main task is to figure out what needs to be done and how to go about doing it. In a competitive world where there are many demands on people's time, energy, money, and ability, survival and growth require accurate knowledge, decisions, and implementation. How should people act? Where should they go? How can they prioritize among conflicting activities and responsibilities? How do they choose between work and family duties?

A plan should have a purpose. It should be going somewhere. What does the planner hope to achieve? Management theory stresses the necessity of planning if an individual or a family hopes to achieve the goals that have been set. One of the reasons individuals and families engage in planning activity is to help them visualize what may or may not happen. Among the questions they may consider are the following:

◆ Will others cooperate?
◆ Is there enough money?
◆ Is there enough time?
◆ Is there enough information?

By reviewing these questions, the planner is trying to anticipate problems before they arise. Answers to these questions may lead directly to implementation of the plan or to more planning and different courses of action.

Need Fulfillment

Generally, people arrive at their needs through a complex subjective assessment based on their inherent motivations and their perceptions of the external world (Foxall, Goldsmith, & Brown, 1998). For example, if a new product is to succeed, consumers must perceive that it will satisfy some need or combination of needs. Likewise in management theory, if a plan is to succeed, individuals must perceive that the plan and its implementation will be useful and will satisfy some need or combination of needs.

Time, Stress, and Planning

Planning takes time, but sometimes time is in short supply. Individuals, families, and organizations may become so caught up in everyday activities and crises that they have no time to plan. In that case, they are victims of

Gresham's law of planning, which comes from the better-known Gresham's law (Simon, 1993). Thomas Gresham, a financial adviser to Queen Elizabeth I, observed that "bad money drives out good," so that "if two coins have the same nominal value but are made from metals of unequal value, the cheaper will tend to drive the other out of circulation" (*Encyclopedia Britannica,* 1989, vol. 5, p. 489). Applying Gresham's law of planning to management, Herbert Simon observed that "short-term concerns create priorities and deadlines that absorb managerial attention and energy at the expense of long-range concerns" (1993, p. 139).

There are a number of indicators that families have less and less time that they can devote to planning. One of the ways they are coping with time stress is to plan further ahead than ever before. Families today live months ahead of themselves:

> They rent next year's summer home before Thanksgiving; buy Christmas concert tickets in the summer; apply to favorite schools for next year, even before this year's class has had a chance to warm the seats. . . . In Chicago, Robin Cohn has her children's after school activities planned for the next eight months; all that is in question is whether her son, a third grader, will play soccer or basketball this spring. "And we'll decide that in a week or two," she says. (Kronholz, 1997, p. A1)

Part of the reason that families plan so far ahead is that many of them are competing for the same activities. They have found that planning is necessary if they are to get what they want. They have learned that many organizations schedule around the egalitarian principle of first-come, first-served, so the first come earlier and earlier. The price to be paid for all this planning ahead is a lack of spontaneity.

The paradox of planning is that it can create stress and also relieve stress. Stress is relieved when people are more relaxed once a decision is made—for example, once the cruise tickets are bought and a trip can go on as scheduled. But what happens when the cruise, for which tickets were bought six months ahead, is canceled when a hurricane hits right where the ship is going? Stress can arise from feeling too boxed in, too committed, or too rigid so that changes or new opportunities cannot be readily taken advantage of.

> Certainly, people who live entirely for the moment haven't got it right, says Chicago's Mr. Csikszentmihalyi. But those who spend their lives planning their lives don't either. "You end up finding that you have squandered opportunities for really living in order to prepare yourself for living in the future," he says. (Kronholz, 1997, p. A1)

Thus, planning is affected by time constraints and stress. But there are other factors that affect planning, such as situational aspects and personality characteristics, including motivation. These will be discussed next.

Situational Factors

Situational factors, including environmental context, shape wants, needs, and goals. These factors can include a specific precipitating circumstance, such as a broken computer. Until the computer breaks down, the owner has no need to consider how to fix or replace it, but now she must either have the computer repaired or buy a new one. Individuals and families continually respond to such changes in situations or circumstances. Something (a problem, need, want, or goal) motivates them to plan and act. For example, they may drive up to a restaurant and find it is closed. They then must formulate a new plan for where to go and what to eat. Among the situational influences to be considered in making plans are the following:

- *Physical surroundings:* Location, decor, lighting, cleanliness, sound, heat, or cold
- *Social surroundings:* Other people, crowding, and relationships
- *Time:* Time of day, month, year, and season
- *Task:* The reason the person is there. What needs to be done?

Task saturation, according to Jerry Osteryoung, professor at Florida State University, occurs when people (coworkers, family members, team members) are so busy doing things that they cannot plan or lead effectively. Signs of task saturation are people canceling meetings or showing up late or constantly complaining about paperwork. One professor said that she was expected to attend five different committee meetings during a one-hour period, so she had to choose the most important one and stay for the entire time or run around and put in a "guest" appearance at two or three. This is an example of task saturation: one person and too many time conflicts. How did she make the final decision? She incorporated the first rule of management, which is to focus on what is important (which committee mattered the most), not on what seemed most urgent or pressing. In evaluating the situation, it was obvious she was serving on too many committees; she quit a couple and waited for the rest of her terms of appointment to run out.

The importance of situational influences cannot be overestimated:

At a more immediate level, is our behavior determined more by our internal attributes (personality traits, attitudes, beliefs, values, self-concept) or situational forces? While many people assume their behavior is largely determined by their internal attributes, social psychological research, with its interpersonal orientation, demonstrates that situational factors often have a very powerful effect on what we do. Situational forces are particularly visible in studies of helping in emergencies, conformity, and pressure to comply with orders to behave in hurtful ways.

Three general conclusions can be drawn from these studies. First, our behavior is dramatically influenced by what other people do in the same situation; they serve as models and provide information about how to interpret the situation and what the consequences of various behaviors are. Second, most people are genuinely unaware of how strongly their behavior has been influenced by the behavior of others. And third, it is very difficult for the average person to resist pressures to comply to the wishes of others. (Bingham, 1991, p. 36)

Personal Traits and Characteristics

Although situational factors are important, the person making the decision lies at the heart of the planning process. The planning and implementing that will take place will be based on how that individual assesses the situation. Thus, personality plays a crucial role in planning.

Introverts and Extroverts

According to Foxall, Goldsmith, and Brown (1998), **personality** refers either to an extensive range of separate behavior traits (honesty, perseverance, and hostility, for instance) or to overall types of character and response (extrovert versus introvert). **Introverts** tend to think about themselves first; their thoughts are directed inward.

Do you know someone who needs hours alone every day? Who loves quiet conversations about feelings or ideas, and can give a dynamite presentation to a big audience, but seems awkward in groups and maladroit at small talk? Who has to be dragged to parties and then needs the rest of the day to recuperate? Who growls or scowls or grunts or winces when accosted with pleasantries by people who are just trying to be nice? If so, do you tell this person he is "too serious," or ask if he is okay? Regard him as aloof, arrogant, rude? Redouble your efforts to draw him out? If you answered yes to these questions, chances are that you have an introvert on your hands. (Rauch, 2003, p. 133)

Extroverts are less interested in self and more interested in others and in the environment. They often have a hard time understanding introverts. Extroverts assume their company, their thoughts, are always welcome. They dominate public life in politics, in sports, and in entertainment, so we tend to be more aware of them than introverts.

Introversion and extroversion are orientations. *People are rarely either completely introverted or extroverted,* but they do tend to exhibit more traits of one than the other. Recent studies indicate that people can choose to act more outgoing or assertive and in so doing will actually improve their outlook on life. Students in the studies who were told to act like extroverts during a discussion group had more fun and enjoyed the group more than the ones told to be passive and shy. William Fleeson and colleagues suggest that personality influences happiness and, thus, we have some control over our personalities. "Individuals may have the potential to contribute directly to their own well-being by changing their behavior," says Fleeson (Garber, 2003, p. 2).

How does being introverted or extroverted affect planning? One difference is in the way information is gathered and processed. For example, after purchasing a camera, an introverted person might be more likely to read the instruction booklet or figure out through trial and error how to operate it, whereas an extroverted person would be more inclined to ask for help from the camera store owner or friends.

Other Personality Factors and Expertise

Many other personality factors also affect planning. For example, is the individual primarily a dreamer or a realist? Consistent or inconsistent? Precise or imprecise? Impatient or patient?

Besides personality differentials, some individuals are simply more expert than others in planning. They have more foresight, organizational and analytical skills, and imagination. They are motivated to change things and do not accept the status quo. Perhaps their families provided more models of planning behavior than the families of less expert planners. Planning ability varies between professions as well as between individuals. Consider the range of planning skills necessary in day care centers, hospitals, and urban and regional projects.

The ability to perform tasks successfully and dependably is called **expertise.** It increases as the person acquires more detailed knowledge, has more contact with experts, and develops more memory and experience. Naturally, it follows that young children have less expertise in most subjects and situations than adults.

Experts recall more information about messages and situations and are more likely to draw conclusions and make comparisons rapidly. Thus, experts not only have more access to information, but they also tend to recall, reorganize, and return messages to a greater extent than others. Expertise affects beliefs and planning style, which in turn affect intentions to behave and actual behavior.

In a family, one family member may have more mechanical ability than the others and is therefore expected to fix things, whereas another may have more planning ability and is therefore in charge of organizing family events. Other family members will check with the organizer before scheduling events of their own.

It's difficult to associate organizational skills with specific demographic traits:

> Disorganization appears to be an equal opportunity trait, with equal numbers of Americans across most demographic groups saying that they are organized. What does seem to matter is marital status. . . . 61 percent of married adults say they are either "extremely" or "mostly" organized, compared with just 54 percent of never-married singles and 49 percent of divorced, separated or widowed adults. (Fetto, 2003, pp. 10–11)

Motivational Factors

Motivated planning behavior is thinking activity that is directed toward a particular goal or objective. Achievement-motivated people set goals for themselves and work hard toward attaining those goals (McClelland & Winter, 1969). They are able to keep goals in mind as they plan and complete tasks.

Motivation has three main aspects:

1. The goal or objective must be attractive and desired.

2. The goal or objective seeker must be persistent.

3. The seeker becomes discontented if she or he does not reach the goal or objective.

Persistence refers to a person's staying power; it is the personality trait of not giving up when faced with adversity. Psychological factors, such as depression, may affect motivation and persistence—in a job search, for example (Smith & Price, 1992).

According to Maslow's theory of the hierarchy of needs, which was introduced in Chapter 1, a person attempts to satisfy a more basic need (such as shelter) before directing behavior to higher needs (Maslow, 1943, 1954). Maslow proposed that the typical adult satisfies about 85 percent of physiological needs; 70 percent of safety and security needs; 50 percent of belongingness, social, and love needs; 40 percent of esteem needs; and 10 percent of self-actualization needs. In the years since Maslow introduced his theory, many people have criticized his percentages—in particular, the percentage for self-actualization, which they think is too high. Nevertheless, Maslow's basic theory—that needs motivate human behavior and that unsatisfied needs lead to frustration and stress—is still widely accepted.

Applying Maslow's theory to planning, one might say that a person is motivated to plan and act by some state, condition, or situation, perhaps a social drive (the need to be liked or more popular) or a physiological drive (hunger or thirst). Figure 6.3 provides a model and an example of motivated planning behavior. The example of a hungry person eating to satisfy his or her hunger is a simple one. Achievement motivation can be far more profound. Think of all the individuals and the steps involved in planning a new museum or a space shuttle mission. Many organizations use flow charts to graphically illustrate how an operation, such as the development of a new car or a community, is progressing.

Some people seem especially oriented toward the achievement of goals. Achievement-motivated people, such as Donald Trump, Bill Gates, and Hillary Rodham Clinton, continually set new goals and develop new aspirations. They refuse to rest on their laurels. This characteristic explains why individuals who have made millions in a business venture will, upon selling it, immediately look for another venture to invest their energy in—money is not their primary objective. Rather, the obtaining of it (the process) is the motivator. For such people, the excitement is in the chase; they value each success more for its message "I've succeeded" than as a vehicle for obtaining life's luxuries. Thus, motivation is an internal drive that is fueled by the process of striving for and attaining goals. Planners have to be motivated; they must want their plans to succeed.

Standard Setting

Standards are another important part of the planning process. Standards were defined in Chapter 1 as quantitative and/or qualitative criteria that reconcile resources with demands and serve as measures of values and goals (DeMerchant, 1993). The procedures, conduct, and rules of individuals, families, and organizations all incorporate standards. For example, an industry may set a certain standard or level of excellence.

In planning, standards provide the criteria for action. The standards that are set affect the assessment and allocation of resources, leading to the clarification of demands, decisions, plans, and action. It is important that the plan fit the standards of the individual or situation. In business, a poorly conceived management plan will not meet the standards set by the company.

Likewise, a poorly devised personal or family plan of action may not meet the standards of most families. For example, a 14-year-old son with a grade of F in science may not meet the standards for educational achievement set by the family. Standards emanate from the values and the goals of family members. What do they want and how do they want to go about getting what they want? What makes sense to them?

Standards evolve or develop over time. A newly married couple gradually develop compatible standards and define what constitutes a comfortable life together. They explore what they value and define what they want as individuals and what they want as a couple. Over the course of their married life, they may go from a tiny apartment to a large house, from a small income to a large income, and at the end of their married life back to a small apartment again and a reduced income. Throughout these changes, the couple's standards will adjust to their needs, life stage, and resources.

Scheduling, Sequencing, and Multitasking

Almost all plans include schedules or sequences of events and activities. "**Scheduling** refers to the specification of sets of time bounded projected activ-

FIGURE 6.3
Motivated Planning Behavior: Model and Example

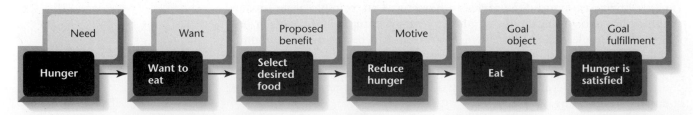

ities which are sufficient for the achievement of a desired goal set" (Avery & Stafford, 1991, p. 327). Written plans with deadlines or end points, diaries, lists, and timetables are all examples of schedules. Consider list making. A list may be a series of activities or appointments, such as 8:00–11:00, go to classes; 11:00 see adviser; 11:30–12:30 lunch; 12:30–5:00 work. Another common type of list is a grocery list. The generally accepted belief that writing a grocery list will eliminate or reduce impulse buying has been challenged by two researchers, Jeffrey Inman of the University of Wisconsin at Madison and Russell Winer of the University of California at Berkeley. They found that list makers are just as likely to make spontaneous purchases as those who shop without them (Inman & Winer, 1999). According to a report on their study in *American Demographics,* 59 percent of all supermarket purchases are unplanned.

Scheduling involves the mental process of sequencing. Sequencing is the ordering of activities and resources necessary to achieve goals. One action succeeds another until the need or the goal is fulfilled. Activities or tasks can be independent, dovetailed, interdependent, or overlapped. These four types will be discussed next.

Independent activities take place one at a time. They stand alone. For example, a person who watches television, then does an hour of homework, and then gets ready for bed is engaged in three independent activities. Each activity is independent of the others because the person could choose to go straight to bed and not watch television or do homework. In other words, none of the activities depends on the others.

Dovetailing (also called **multitasking**) occurs when two or more activities take place at the same time; some examples are eating popcorn and watching a movie, doing homework and listening to the radio, and talking on the telephone while making dinner. People often think dovetailing is a desirable way of organizing activity and getting a lot done in a short time, but it can be ineffective if it leads to unacceptable consequences. Sometimes people try to do too many activities at once. Trying to talk on the telephone, answer the doorbell, cook dinner, and watch a small child all at the same time can result in a burned dinner and a crying child. As this example suggests, dovetailing can be a useful time management tool, but it is not a panacea. Doing more at the same time does not necessarily produce better outcomes. Each individual must decide how many activities she or he can reasonably handle at once.

While many people believe that women are better multitaskers than men, the evidence does not completely support that notion. Both men and women say they are multitasking more now than ever before; the types of multitasking at work include:

◆ Reading e-mail or instant messaging while on the phone

◆ Skimming printed material or sorting junk mail while on the phone

◆ Shopping or doing research online while on the phone

◆ Writing personal "to-do" lists or reading notes or talking on cell phones during meetings

In some occupations, such as air traffic controller or pilot, a successful person has to be able to multitask.

If you saw the movie "Top Gun" (1986), you'll remember what all you see Tom Cruise doing in the cockpit. He's got to pick and choose when he does what, multitask very carefully. The chance that he'll conclude a flight in a fighter jet successfully depends not only on his capabilities and limitations but also on his equipment. (David Meyer quoted in Anderson, 2001, p. 4)

These moms are multitasking while having fun.

© Jimi Lott, Knight Ridder Tribune for *The Seattle Times*

Multitasking takes place during leisure hours too. Why simply work out on a treadmill when you can read a magazine, watch television, and talk on a phone at the same time?

Should we worry about the long-term effects of multitasking?

> "Not to worry," says Marcel Just, co-head of Carnegie Mellon University's Center for Cognitive Brain Imaging. While overloading the brain causes distress, which has its own physiological hazards, the brain seems to recover with rest. (Shellenbarger, 2003, March 20, p. D1)

In this quotation lies one of the antidotes to our sped-up lives, getting enough rest to recover and bounce back, a subject to be covered in Chapter 11. But, in the short run, the warning signs that multitasking is getting out of hand include

◆ Lapses in attentiveness

◆ Loss of concentration

◆ Gaps in short-term memory

◆ Communication problems

◆ Stress symptoms such as shortness of breath (Shellenbarger, 2003, February 27)

Dr. Just says we can do several things at the same time, but not without a cost. The process of switching back and forth takes time away from the original motivation of multitasking, which is usually to save time—at some point the brain crashes. To get back into balance, a person can consciously stop and refocus by listening for the important messages, a technique called living in the moment (Shellenbarger, 2003, February 27). A lot of this depends on the activity itself; something easy and repetitive like tying shoes can be done while someone is talking to you, whereas a more complicated set of tasks like reading a report while someone is talking to you will be more frustrating. So dovetailing or multitasking is becoming more common, and each individual has to decide how much is effective and at what point it's time for a break. The editors of *Real Simple* magazine said, "We love multitasking (when it makes sense), innovation (when it has a purpose), and a clean home (especially when it can be done quickly)" (2003, April, p. 36). Who can argue with that sentiment?

Overlapping activities involve a combination of activities that require intermittent and/or concurrent attention. For example, college students with children combine child care with schoolwork, going back and forth between the activities.

Activities are **interdependent** when one activity must be completed before another can take place. In other words, one activity builds on another and is not effective in isolation. For example, hiring someone before a position exists and money is allocated for a salary would be senseless. Similarly, a newspaper article is not complete until the people involved in the story are interviewed or at least contacted for comment. It is not always easy to differentiate among overlapping, dovetailing, and interdependent activities. People may switch back and forth among the three types of activities in a short period of time. Regardless of type, the behavioral goal of scheduling and sequencing is to provide the desired flow between activities.

Sequencing and scheduling preferences are closely associated with the personality or temperament of the planner as well as with the task itself. How many college students have exactly the same class schedule? Even when they have the same class schedule, it is highly unlikely that they will also eat, socialize, and sleep at exactly the same time. In a family, plans should accommodate the different scheduling needs and preferences of the individuals in the household.

Attributes of Plans

Workable plans have the following attributes: They are clear, flexible, adaptive, realistic, appropriate, and goal-directed. Clear plans are understood by everyone. For example, when an advertisement for a concert says that the concert will start at 8:00 P.M., the audience assumes that it will start promptly and that they should plan to get there ahead of time. In this situation, the concertgoer's plans will have to be flexible because traffic and parking conditions are not totally predictable. Is arriving 10 to 15 minutes ahead of time suitable? If several people are going to the concert together, how will they adjust their schedules to be ready on time? *Adaptive* refers to the ability of the plan to respond to unanticipated events that may occur. If an organization seeks to be adaptive, "it needs to open itself in many ways":

> Especially important is the organization's relationship to information, particularly to that which is new and even disturbing. Information must actively be sought from everywhere, from places and sources people never thought to look before. And then it must circulate freely so that many people can interpret it. (Wheatley, 1999, p. 83)

Realistic implies that the plan is feasible and likely to work. Being appropriate means that the plan is suited to the situation and the people involved.

As has been suggested throughout this chapter, successful plans are goal-directed. Specific, challenging goals lead to higher task performance than do specific, unchallenging goals, vague goals, or no goals (Locke, Smith, Erez, Chah, & Shaffe, 1994).

Types of Plans

Many different types of plans exist. Plans can be categorized by time, such as short-term and long-term plans. Plans can also be distinguished by the parties involved: individuals, households, organizations, communities, or nations. This chapter will concentrate on three types of plans (directional, contingency, and strategic) that are commonly associated with individual and family resource management. Given different situations, a manager can pick the best type of plan.

Directional plans progress along a linear path to long-term goal fulfillment. Plans to graduate from high school, graduate from college, and then go to law school to become an attorney are examples of directional plans. Because a certain degree of work experience is a prerequisite for a higher-level position, career planning is usually directional, although less so than formerly because people today change jobs more frequently than in the past.

Contingency plans are backup or secondary plans to be used in case the first plan does not work. The military is known for contingency plans: If one strategy does not work, they have several others ready to initiate. Similarly, chess players think of several different potential ways to respond to an opponent's move.

Organizations often use a contingency approach. The basic idea behind this approach is that there is no single best way to manage; a method that is successful in one situation may not be successful in another. Therefore, a business manager will devise several plans after assessing the characteristics of the individuals and groups involved, the organizational structure, and his or her own leadership style (Ivancevich & Matteson, 1990). If one plan is not successful, the manager will try another. Likewise, in a family, the manager (or managers) sizes up the situation, the family members and others involved, and prepares several plans leading to a solution. Here again, the manager will be prepared to substitute another plan if the first does not work.

As an example of how an individual uses the contingency approach, consider Shannon, a 22-year-old who applied to eight different graduate schools. Her plan was to apply to three schools known to be hard to get into, two schools that were moderately difficult to get into, and three easy-to-get-into schools. Shannon wanted to be sure that by September she would be accepted by at least one school, and she did everything she could to ensure that result.

As explained in Chapter 4, a strategy is a plan of action, a way of conducting and following through on operations. **Strategic plans** use a directional approach and include both a proactive search for new opportunities and a reactive solution to existing problems (Wheeler & Hunger, 1987). *Proactive* and *reactive* are discussed in detail in the next section, but here they mean simply that the strategic planner utilizes a forward-looking approach while realizing that past business must also be concluded.

Strategic planning focuses attention on the initial stages of the decision-making processes—the opportunities and occasions for choice and the design of new action strategies (Simon, 1993). To conclude, strategic plans are often associated with the military, business, or politics, but they also occur in individual and family life. For example, job hunting involves many strategies, such as résumé writing (a record of one's past achievements and experience), reading, prioritizing, and responding to job announcements. Financial crises stimulate the need to strategize; here is the advice of Elizabeth Warren and Amelia Tyagi, authors of *The Two-Income Trap:*

A family facing a financial crisis should think like a family at war. You must concentrate on preserving what matters most, and you must let the other things go. When the trouble comes, ask the central question: Which of your assets do you most want to hold on to? Maybe it's your car, your home, or your health insurance policy. Decide which things you value most, and pay those bills first. . . . Once you are in trouble, you will need to fight—and you should be fighting for the things you care about, not trying to satisfy the loudest or most aggressive creditor (2003, p. 168).

Proactive versus Reactive

Stephen R. Covey's groundbreaking book, *The 7 Habits of Highly Effective People,* delineates seven good habits:

◆ Habit 1: Be proactive.

◆ Habit 2: Begin with the end in mind.

◆ Habit 3: Put first things first.

◆ Habit 4: Think win-win.

◆ Habit 5: Seek first to understand, then to be understood.

◆ Habit 6: Synergize.

◆ Habit 7: Sharpen the saw.

The titles of several of these "habits" are self-evident, but a few deserve further explanation. The last one, "sharpening the saw," means pulling it all together, moving along to higher planes of learning, commitment, and activity. To **synergize** means to produce a third alternative, which is not my way or your way, but a third way that is best, a product of group thinking. This is a systems approach to problem solving: The whole is greater than the sum of its parts. Synergy comes about when two or more people get together and come up with an idea or achieve an effect that would not be possible individually. It is a creative process. According to Covey (1989), "Synergy means that 1 + 1 may equal 8, 16, or even 1,600" (p. 271). "Win/Win is a frame of mind and heart that constantly seeks mutual benefit in all human interactions. Win/Win means that agreements or solutions are mutually beneficial, mutually satisfying" (p. 207). This is a cooperative versus competitive approach to life.

Being **proactive** means taking responsibility for one's own life. It is about the freedom and the power to choose. According to Covey (1989), "Our behavior is a function of our decisions, not our conditions. We can subordinate feelings to values. We have the initiative and the responsibility to make things happen" (p. 71). Proactive people accept responsibility for their own actions; they do not blame others or circumstances for their behavior. "Proactive management involves change-oriented planning where the desired change is conceived by a person or family and the implementation of the change alters the environment" (Dollahite, 1991, p. 374). Thus, in proactive management, the individual or family is actively seeking solutions to problems by forming plans, including strategic plans.

Reactive people are often overly affected by outside forces, such as changes in the weather or the bad attitudes of their coworkers. According to Covey (1989), "When people treat them well, they feel well; when people don't, they become defensive or protective. Reactive people build their emotional lives around the behavior of others, empowering the weaknesses of other people to control them" (p. 72). Proactive people also notice the weather or the social conditions around them, but they respond differently than reactive people. Values such as honesty and self-respect drive the behaviors of proactive people more than outside forces. Other people's opinions matter less to proactive people than they do to reactive people. As Eleanor Roosevelt said, "No one can hurt you without your consent."

Typical phrases used by proactive and reactive people are listed in Table 6.1. Notice that the reactive person says "I can't," whereas the proactive person says "I choose." Proactive people believe their lives are the sum total of the choices they have made. Planners with proactive styles approach life challenges more assertively than reactive people do. Management theory supports the notion that effective managers tend to be proactive and goal-oriented (Sharpe & Winter, 1991). Proactive management can help a person or family avoid crises or stress through active anticipation of events to come. In proactive management, an "individual or a family actively clarifies values, makes plans, sets goals, organizes activities, and makes changes before experiencing stressors" (Dollahite, 1991, p. 374).

The three types of plans discussed in this section—directional, contingency, and strategic—are not limited to individuals and families. They are potentially applicable to all organizations and situations. For example, Coca-Cola, in a strategic move to market its product worldwide, seized the opportunity to go global rather than being confined to the United States. Airlines are constantly searching for more profitable routes. Fast-food restaurants look for new locations and new products in order to expand their share of the market. Likewise, individuals and families try to maximize their chances at improving their lives. For example, a proactive, goal-setting foreign service officer will try to get an appointment overseas in a desired location rather than wait to be assigned anywhere the government decides to send him or her.

The specific planning mode used (directional, contingency, or strategic) reflects the individual's or the family's perceptions of what type of plan will be most suitable. Key decisions flow from the dominant planning mode and the choice of a proactive or reactive approach.

TABLE 6.1
Reactive versus
Proactive Language

Reactive Language	Proactive Language
There's nothing I can do.	Let's look at our alternatives.
That's just the way I am.	I can choose a different approach.
They make me so mad.	I control my own feelings.
They won't allow that.	I can create an effective presentation.
I have to do that.	I will choose an appropriate response.
I can't.	I choose.
I must.	I prefer.
If only.	I will.

Source: From Stephen R. Covey, *The 7 Habits of Highly Successful People*, 1989, p. 78. Copyright © 1989 Pearson Education. Reprinted by permission.

WHAT IS IMPLEMENTING?

Implementing means putting plans and procedures into action and controlling the action. Controlling takes place because once plans are activated, they need to be checked to make sure that they are leading to the desired end state. As everyone knows, it is easier to make plans than to initiate and monitor them. Environmental, economic, social, and a variety of other forces and conditions can positively or negatively affect the outcome of the most carefully prepared plan. For example, planning a dream house and building an affordable house are two different things.

The factors affecting implementing are the same ones that affect planning: situations, personal traits and characteristics, and motivational factors. Possible blocks to successful implementation include

- ◆ Other people. They may not believe in the same plans you do, or they may drag their feet.
- ◆ Costs and other restrictions.
- ◆ Competition. Perhaps there are competing plans that are better. For example, 14 architects may be invited to submit plans for a new university building—only one will be selected.
- ◆ Crises. Long-term plans may be put on hold if resources are required for more immediate needs.
- ◆ Procrastination or lack of motivation.
- ◆ Closed-mindedness.

Several strategies can be employed to avoid these blocks. The main strategy is to intelligently size up the situations that arise and respond accordingly. In the end, implementing requires a scanning sensibility—a monitoring of your actions and the actions of those around you. **Scanning** is an activity in which individuals or families "read the world," looking for signals and clues (i.e., information, messages, feedback) that could have strategic implications. Three of the elements that play into this—actuating, checking, and controlling—are discussed next.

Actuating

Actuating refers to putting plans into effect, action, or motion. For example, Mike, a teenager, has been reading car advertisements and talking for months with friends about buying a used car. Finally, he decides he is ready to look at some cars.

Plans can be actuated in stages. A teacher may interview for a job in January that does not start until August. Within the family system, parents might start saving for their child's college education soon after the child's birth and add money to the college fund at each birthday.

Positive and negative feedback (discussed in Chapter 2) play a large part in actuating. Feedback from others may prevent a person from actuating a plan—she or he may want to wait until the time seems to be right. Also, if things are going well, an individual may decide not to "rock the boat" and let things simply evolve for a while. Other times, a more active and controlling approach is necessary.

Checking and Controlling

Once the plan is activated, different situations or personal factors may indicate the need for corrective action. To be successful, plans need to be checked and rechecked. This checking, or **adjusting,** activity is a type of controlling. For example, a person may make a reservation months in advance of an important event, but reconfirm the reservation a day or two before the event.

Checking is defined in management as determining whether actions are in compliance with standards and sequencing. An individual determines whether plans are unfolding as they should, in the right sequence, and in a timely fashion. If a check reveals that they are not, a correction is necessary.

Changes in planning and implementing can occur, for example, when an individual goes grocery shopping with a list. The list is a plan of action; but, while shopping (actuating the plan), the shopper may make several changes, such as substituting one product for another or adding several more items to the grocery cart. In this way, the list serves as a guide. Most plans can be envisioned as a guide—a mental plan of action.

If overdone, checking can produce undesirable effects. Too much checking by the planner or by the implementer of the plan can lead to frustration, resentment, or pressure. Consider the frustration potential of a person on a diet who checks his or her weight several times a day. Or consider how employees feel when the boss stands over them when they are trying to complete a task. Or how an interviewer feels when a potential employee keeps calling about the results of an interview. In the latter case, too much checking can ruin the person's chances for employment. The goal is to have a sufficient amount of checking to ensure a positive outcome (e.g., a weight loss, a completed task, or a job), but neither too much nor too little.

Controlling and corrective action take time. Therefore, the implementer has to weigh the costs against the benefits of spending time and energy on checking. Controlling is most effective at significant milestones or critical points in a plan. Teachers and professors do this by giving tests or assignments at appropriate intervals of learning. This is their way of checking learning progress.

As with so many other aspects of management, the key to successful planning and implementing is a balance between wants, goals, and actions. Particularly in the checking phase, achieving a balance is essential to obtaining a successful outcome.

WHAT IS EVALUATING?

The word *evaluation* comes from an Old French verb, *évaluer* (to be worthy or to have value). To evaluate means to determine the worth of an effort. Thus, **evaluation** is a process of judging or examining the cost, value, or worth of a plan or decision based on such criteria as standards, met demands, or goals. It occurs throughout the management process: in setting goals in the first place and at each step along the way. As discussed earlier, people may encounter obstacles to goal achievement, such as crises and unplanned-for events.

Since judgments are subjective, evaluations can turn out to be flawed or biased. To ensure better end results, people engage in assessments. **Assessment** involves the gathering of information about results, the comparison of those results with the results of the past, and the open discussion of the meaning of those results, the ways that they have been gathered, and their implications for the next moves of the family or the individual (Senge et al., 1999).

Since evaluation can be painful, people often ignore this step and proceed immediately to the next problem or goal. Nevertheless, looking back and evaluating past decisions are crucial steps in becoming a better manager. Improving management skills is important because competence in problem solving has been identified as an essential part of healthy marriages and family systems (Rettig & Bubolz, 1983). To build on success, individuals should acknowledge the things that have been accomplished and the ways they have changed or grown. What decisions are you most proud of? Maybe it was trying out for a school play or a team sport. Whether it worked or not, you learned from the trying more than if you had not tried. Thomas Edison conducted 50,000 different experiments to try to find a working storage battery. When asked if he was frustrated, his reply was "What failures? I now know 50,000 things which do not work."

Once evaluation is over, work on restoring your energy, clearing your calendar, relaxing, taking care of things that you've been putting off. Are there new priorities?

Storyboarding is a technique used by advertisers, movie screenwriters, and television scriptwriters to show the main scenes in a commercial, movie, or television show. A storyboard is a comic-strip type presentation complete with pictures, dialogue, and words to describe the action (Levinson, 1999). Storyboarding can be used as a planning technique in other situations to show the consecutive steps that lead to desired outcomes. It allows a person to visualize the steps to be taken.

Figure 6.4 shows a storyboard from a commercial. Use the blank spaces provided in Figure 6.5 to create your own storyboard. The last frame should be your desired outcome.

At the end of the management process, a final evaluation takes place. If a goal is achieved, the manager can look back with satisfaction on how things turned out. Other possible outcomes are the achievement of a new or a substitute goal (not the ones initially set), the solution to a problem, the satisfaction of a need or want, or perhaps none of these. Whether the outcomes are effective or ineffective, the manager should review what went right and what went wrong with the process so that she or he can learn from it for future decisions.

Web-Based Resources

For more about Stephen R. Covey's "7 Habits" writings and workshops, go to **www.franklincovey.com.** There are many professionals and businesses ready to help organize and plan everything from weddings to vacations. For travel ratings and prices, try Mobil, AAA, Priceline, Expedia, Hotwire, Hotels.com, and Travelocity. In Europe, some countries have government-regulated ratings, but ratings are not nationally standardized in the United States, so that the same hotel may receive ratings of three, four, or five stars depending on the rating system. In the United States, about 10 percent of hotel rooms are booked online, and that is predicted to reach 20 percent in the next few years. Banks, accountants, and financial planners offer assistance with retirement and estate planning. For legal advice, a site to check is the American Bar Association at **www.aba.org.**

SFX: CAR AND FOOT TRAFFIC AMBIENCE
VO: Why did the chicken cross the road?
To open a 7/24 Savings Plan at San Diego Trust.
Because with $500 in savings . . .

. . . he can avoid getting henpecked by monthly charges on a checking account. What's more, he can access his nest egg through our huge ATM network . . .
SFX: BANK AMBIENCE
. . . and round-the-clock phone service.

VO: And of course, the interest he'll earn on savings isn't just chicken feed.
So open a 7/24 Savings Plan at San Diego Trust.
And give yourself a good reason to . . .
SFX: COCKA DOODLE DOO

FIGURE 6.4

A Sample Storyboard Layout

Source: Reprinted by permission of Wells Fargo Bank.

Desired outcome or goal: _____

_____

Steps: What do you have to do first, second, third, and so on to reach the desired outcome? Use words or draw pictures to illustrate the main steps or actions needed to reach your goal. *Note:* You may need less than eight steps (frames).

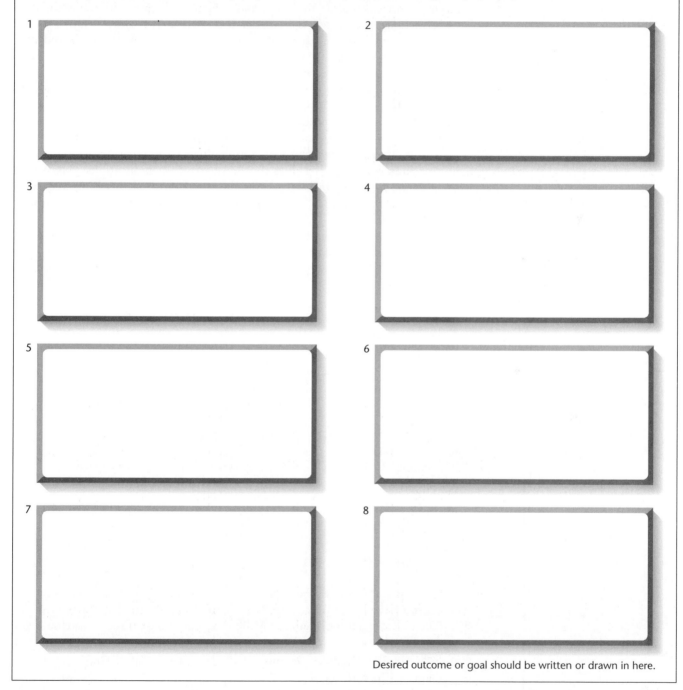

1

2

3

4

5

6

7

8

Desired outcome or goal should be written or drawn in here.

FIGURE 6.5
Storyboarding: A Planning Technique

Summary

Resource management theory focuses on conscious decision making, leading to the formation and implementation of plans to achieve goals. Planning, implementing, and evaluating were the main subjects of this chapter. They represent both mental and physical activity. Planning begins with mentally organizing activities to accomplish a desired end state. It requires vision, energy, and motivation to succeed. Implementing includes both actuating and controlling. Task saturation refers to being so busy doing things that there is no time to plan or lead effectively.

Planning and implementing require the ability to order and sequence steps in a rational manner. Personality, situations, standards, and the environment all affect planning outcomes. Proactive and reactive personality types differ in how they approach planning. Their language reflects these differences.

Scanning is an activity in which individuals or families "read the world" by searching for signals or clues that have strategic implications. Assessment involves the gathering of information about results. Storyboarding was introduced as a technique for visualizing the steps in planning leading to a desired outcome.

People vary in their planning expertise. Planning ability can be increased through experience and maturity. As Emerson said, "That which we persist in doing becomes easier—not that the nature of the task has changed, but our ability to do has increased."

Key Terms

actuating	extroverts	plan
adjusting	Gresham's law of	proactive
assessment	planning	process
checking	independent activities	reactive
contingency plans	interdependent	scanning
directional plans	activities	scheduling
dovetailing	introverts	storyboarding
(multitasking)	overlapping activities	strategic plans
evaluation	persistence	synergize
expertise	personality	task saturation

Review Questions

1. Look at the list, near the beginning of the chapter, of things people would like to have better organized. Is there anything on the list that you would like to have better organized? More than one thing? If so, what would you have to do (steps to take) to get more organized?

2. What influences affect planning? Include a discussion of Gresham's law of planning in your answer.

3. What is the difference between proactive and reactive styles?

4. At the end of Clint Eastwood's *Dirty Harry* movie, the character says "A man's gotta know his limitations." What are the limitations to multitasking (or are there any)?

5. The musician John Lennon wrote a song lyric that said "Life is what happens to you while you're busy making other plans." What do you think he meant by this? What is your opinion about how much of life can be planned and how much just happens? Give an example of something you planned to do, but "life" got in the way.

References

Anderson, P. (2001, August 6). *Study: Multitasking is counterproductive.* Retrieved March 8, 2004, from http://www.cnn.com/2001/CAREER/trends/08/05/multitasking.study/index.html.

Avery, R., & Stafford, K. (1991). Toward a scheduling congruity theory of family resource management. *Lifestyles: Family and Economic Issues, 12*(4), 325–344.

Bingham, J. (1991). *Social psychology* (2nd ed.). New York: HarperCollins.

Covey, S. (1989). *The 7 habits of highly effective people.* New York: Simon & Schuster.

DeMerchant, E. (1993, February). Standards: An analysis of definitions, frameworks and implications. In C. Y. Kratzar (Ed.), *Proceedings of the Southeastern Regional Home Management Association of Family Economics* (pp. 13–22). Roanoke, VA: Virginia Polytechnic Institute.

Dollahite, D. (1991, Winter). Family resource management and family stress theories: Toward conceptualization integration. *Lifestyles: Family and Economic Issues, 12*(4), 361–377.

Fetto, R. (2003, April). Get it together. *American Demographics,* 10–11.

Foxall, G., Goldsmith, R., & Brown, S. (1998). *Consumer psychology for marketing.* London: Routledge.

Garber, F. (2003, June 6). Unhappy? Try acting like an extrovert. Retrieved March 23, 2004, from http://content.health.msn.com/content/article/61/67430.htm

Hunts, H., & Marotz-Baden, R. (2003). Family systems theory: A new look at an old friend. *Consumer Interests Annual, 49,* 1–3.

Inman, J., & Winer, R. (1999, May 6). Shoppers are impulsive. *Tallahassee Democrat.*

Ivancevich, J. M., & Matteson, M. T. (1990). *Organizational behavior and management.* Homewood, IL: Irwin.

Kronholz, J. (1997, November 20). We're all living in future tense—And it's tense indeed. *Wall Street Journal,* A1.

Levinson, J. (1999). *Guerilla advertising.* New York: Houghton Mifflin.

Locke, E., Smith, K., Erez, M., Chah, D., & Schaffer, A. (1994). The effects of intra-individual goal conflict on performance. *Journal of Management, 20*(1), 67–91.

Maslow, A. (1943, July). A theory of human motivation. *Psychological Review,* 370–396.

Maslow, A. (1954). *Motivation and personality.* New York: Harper & Row.

Matchan, L. (2002, November 16). Declutter your life—professionally. *St. Petersburg Times,* 6F.

McClelland, D., & Winter, D. (1969). *Motivating economic achievement.* New York: Macmillan.

Morris, B. (1987, August 4). As a favored pastime, shopping ranks high with most Americans. *The Wall Street Journal.*

Rauch, J. (2003, March). Caring for your introvert. *Atlantic Monthly,* 133–134.

Real Simple. (2003, April). Editorial note, 36.

Rettig, K., & Bubolz, M. (1983). Perceptual indicators of family well-being. *Social Indicators Research, 12,* 417–438.

Senge, P., Kleiner, A., Roberts, C., Ross, R., Roth, G., & Smith, B. (1999). *The dance of change.* New York: Doubleday.

Sharpe, D., & Winter, M. (1991). Toward working hypotheses of effective management: Conditions, thought processes, and behaviors. *Lifestyles: Family and Economic Issues, 12*(4), 303–323.

Shellenbarger, S. (2003, March 20). Female rats are better multitaskers; with humans, the debate rages on. *The Wall Street Journal,* D1.

Simon, H. A. (1993). Strategy and organizational evolution. *Strategic Management Journal, 14,* 131–142.

Smith, S., & Price, S. (1992). Women and plant closings: Unemployment, re-employment, and job training enrollment following dislocation. *Journal of Family and Economic Issues, 13*(1), 45–72.

Warren, E., and Tyagi, A. (2003). *The two-income trap.* New York: Basic Books.

Wheatley, M. (1999). *Leadership and the new science* (2nd ed.). San Francisco: Berrett-Koehler.

Wheeler, T., & Hunger, J. (1987). *Strategic management* (2nd ed.). Reading, MA: Addison-Wesley.

chapter **7**

Communication

MAIN TOPICS

COMMUNICATION AS PART OF THE MANAGEMENT PROCESS
CHANNELS, NOISE, AND SETTING
SENDING AND RECEIVING
LISTENING
MESSAGES
CHANNELS AND FEEDBACK

COMMUNICATION CONFLICTS
IN FAMILIES
CULTURES AND SUBCULTURES

COMMUNICATION IN SMALL GROUPS
GROUP DISCUSSIONS AND COHESION

INFORMATION AND COMMUNICATION TECHNOLOGY
INFORMATION OVERLOAD AND HABITUAL DECISION MAKING
COMPUTERS AND THE HUMAN CAPACITY TO PROCESS
   INFORMATION
THE ROLE OF THE HOME AND THE INDIVIDUAL

Did you know that . . . ?

. . . Women speak about 25,000 words a day, while men speak only 10,000.

. . . Two hundred five different newspapers are published in New York City.

The cream of enjoyment in this life is always impromptu. The chance walk; the unexpected visit; the unpremeditated journey; the unsought conversation or acquaintance.

—*Fanny Fern*

HOW DO YOU talk so people will listen? Instead of allowing our words to mislead, we can learn to communicate more effectively. Communication is an integral part of every step of the management process. Feedback connects the steps together, forming a loop, as shown in Figure 7.1.

Although communication and feedback are normally thought of as verbal, both can be nonverbal as well. For example, a look can often convey more than words. This chapter will examine both verbal and nonverbal communication. Other topics to be covered include the process of communication, conflict, information overload, and the value of listening.

Encouraging the reader to communicate more effectively is the behavioral goal of this chapter. Presenting the types, forms, and problems of communication in families, in small groups, and in professional settings is the informational goal. By the chapter's conclusion, readers should be more aware of how they and others communicate. The chapter begins with a discussion of communication as part of the management process.

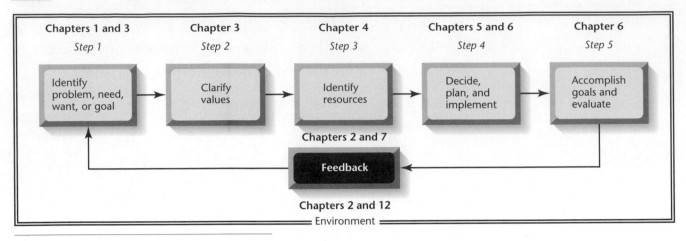

FIGURE 7.1
The Management Process Model

COMMUNICATION AS PART
OF THE MANAGEMENT PROCESS

Communication is the process of transmitting a message from a sender to a receiver. **Interference** is anything that distorts or interrupts messages. Effective communication occurs when the receiver interprets the sender's message in the same way the speaker intended it.

Because information transmission is an integral part of management, to be effective, a manager has to be an effective communicator. In systems terminology, communication is part of the transformation process—transforming inputs into outputs. In transforming information resources (inputs), communication uses up time and energy. The average person spends approximately 70 percent of his or her waking hours in some form of communication—writing, reading, speaking, and listening (Robbins, 1989). Given this time investment, it follows that one of the forces most likely to inhibit successful life management is a lack of effective communication.

Much of a manager's time must be devoted to goal setting, which also requires effective communication. Goal setting is a sequence that starts with thinking and proceeds to acting, which includes communicating goals to others and engaging their support and interest. As part of this process, managers need to communicate several key decisions, including the following: (1) What goals will be sought? (2) Which goals have the highest priority? (3) How are the goals related? (4) How long will it take to achieve the goals? (5) Who should be accountable for achieving the goals? The answers to these questions guide the present and future behavior of individuals, families, and other groups.

Effective communication is

- clear
- concise (if you take too long to get to a point, everyone quits listening)
- consistent
- creative
- sensitive to audience
- persuasive (or it explains rather than demands or threatens)
- open to differing opinions

An effective communicator has the ability to pass along information, giving advance notice of impending changes and plans. These characteristics are important in both family and professional life. Talking through problems and listening carefully to what other family members have to say adds to family cohesiveness. In professional life, communication skills can be crucial to getting ahead. Peter Drucker, an expert in business management, says:

> Your success as an employee—and I'm talking of much more than getting promoted—will depend on your ability to communicate with people and to present your own thoughts and ideas to them so they will both understand what you are driving at and be persuaded. (1977, pp. 262–263)

As Drucker's comments indicate, communication is indeed a process rather than a finished end state; and, as such, it allows individuals to share information, ideas, and feelings. For example, consider the following conversation between Heather and Sam, two college students who have been friends for over a year, but have never dated each other:

Sam: I haven't seen you around for weeks. Where have you been?

Heather: I've been working on two projects and they've taken all my time. I'm worried about my grades.

Sam: Hm. You do look stressed.

Heather: Yes, I am. But it's almost over—everything is due this week.

Sam: You'll do all right. You always worry about your work and then you make A's. Why don't we get together this weekend?

In this exchange, Sam and Heather have communicated information and feelings. Their remarks show that their relationship has a past, present, and future. Sam puts Heather's concerns into perspective. His comments show that he likes her. As the conversation continues, what are some of the responses Heather might give?

Notice that only the verbal communication between Sam and Heather has been presented. Their nonspoken or nonverbal communication is not included. Does Sam smile or grin at Heather? Does he try to show he cares by his tone of voice or stance? Is Heather yawning?

Channels, Noise, and Setting

Communication has long been considered part of everything from who gets elected president to who remains married. It is far more than words: It is about relationships, winning and losing, succeeding and not succeeding. It includes channels, noise, and setting. The **channel** is the method by which communication travels from source or sender to receiver. As Figure 7.2 shows, these elements interact to create the total communication environment. Think how different Sam and Heather's conversation would be if it took place in a crowded cafeteria rather than a deserted hallway. A quiet setting allows senders and receivers to concentrate on each other; a noisy setting is full of distractions.

Noise, defined as an unwanted sound that interferes or distracts, is a barrier to learning and communication. There are two types of noise: external and internal. **External noise** comes from the environment. An airplane overhead, the hot blinding sun, a howling wind, or lightning are all examples of external noise. Notice that in communication theory noise includes more than just sounds, as the sun and lightning illustrate. **Internal noise** occurs in the sender's and receiver's minds. They are thinking about something else during the communication—their minds are not on the conversation taking place. Daydreaming during a class lecture or thinking about a family member at work instead of listening to coworkers discuss the copy machine's breakdown are examples of internal noise. Often internal noise occurs when a word or allusion in the current conversation reminds us of something else.

An interesting experiment revealed how much internal and external noise affects the recall of advertising. Marketing professors Bob Wu and Stephen Newell (2003) found that external noise wasn't as important as internal noise in affecting subjects' ability to recall advertising (i.e., brand recall and message recall). They suggest that advertisers consider how they advertise during the holidays when consumers are preoccupied with cooking, travel, shopping, and gift buying; maybe this is not the best time to introduce a new product or idea. Perhaps a better time would be a few months earlier when things are more settled or in January if it is a new diet plan or toothpaste or system of organizing/storage containers. Internal worrying about shocking current news or events may also take away from advertising messages being heard. These findings have implications not just for the marketplace but also for family and household management. Introducing a new way of doing things may go over better during less hectic times.

Noise is any interference in the communication process that prevents the message from being heard correctly, and it can occur at any point in the process. The sender may send out confusing messages, the channel may be distorted, or the receiver may be distracted. There is more noise today than ever before. Because of all the noise, advertisers are having a difficult time getting customers to notice their messages. On the home front, spouses may wonder if their mates are listening to them when the television is blaring in the background. In today's sped-up world, too many conflicting messages are vying for everyone's attention.

The importance of the setting cannot be overestimated. There are appropriate places and times for discipline, compliments, whispers, shouts, and dis-

FIGURE 7.2
A Model of the Communications Process

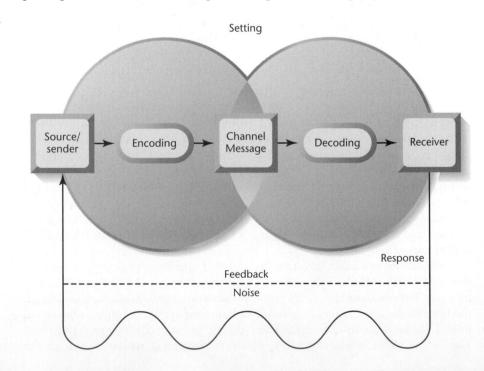

putes. Being sensitive to environmental conditions as well as to words is part of being an effective communicator. One way to build a positive environment for communication is for individuals to let others know that they care about them.

Providing a climate of acceptance fosters human functioning and teamwork. For example, children need to know that their parents love them. Likewise, employees need to know that their employers are concerned about their welfare. When there is trust, people feel freer to exchange information, ideas, and feelings. As mentioned in Chapter 2, the greater environment in which individuals and families live has a significant effect on the way they manage. The **setting,** or physical surroundings, is where management messages are communicated. Some settings, such as a church or a boardroom, are more formal than others. Communications should be appropriate for the setting. Public speakers check out the setting before their speech so they can match their speaking voice and microphone volume to the room size and potential audience.

The design of homes, offices, and campuses communicates to the user the type of relationships that will occur in that setting. A campus with winding walkways, fountains, and botanical gardens has a different atmosphere than a campus consisting of high-rise concrete buildings. Indoor lighting and color affect communication. Warm colors, such as red and orange, and bright lights tend to accelerate talking, whereas cool colors such as soft blue and green and low lights tend to subdue communication. Institutional atmospheres are not conducive to quiet personal conversations. Even clothing is part of the setting. Research has shown that the style of clothing therapists wear will enhance or detract from their relationship with clients (Heitmeyer & Goldsmith, 1990).

Sending and Receiving

Communication is a two-way process between sender and receiver. **Sending** is saying what one means to say, with agreement between verbal and nonverbal messages. In good sending, the person must know what she or he wants to say and then say it. The sender should make eye contact with the receiver and speak slowly and distinctly. **Receiving** entails listening to the verbal messages and observing the nonverbal messages. If the message is getting through, the receiver will probably show his or her response through facial expressions. A good sender talks with people, not at them, and considers the listener's feelings, personality, and opinions.

Usually, people are receivers and senders at the same time. Communication is not as simple as having one person speak, another listen and then speak, and so on. For instance, more than one listener may be involved. Also, the sending and receiving can be simultaneous.

A sender can also be called a **source,** or communicator. The receiver is the **destination,** or audience. The sender's task is to reach the audience whether it is one person or a million people. Because of sweeping changes brought on by communications advances and the ease of movement of people (physical and virtual) in today's world, people are communicating and connecting faster and in more ways than ever before.

The sender and receiver use four communication functions: encoding, decoding, response, and feedback. **Encoding** is the process of putting thoughts, ideas, or information into symbolic form. **Decoding** is the process by which the receiver assigns meaning to the symbols. **Responses** are the individual reactions that follow the message. Feedback is the total response pattern between sender and receiver. An individual's communication style is closely tied to her or his personality, self-concept, family of origin, and past experiences.

Listening

Whether in the home or office, managers want to be heard by those they manage and also to listen to them. Parents want their children to listen. According to Sue Shellenbarger (2003), some of the ways that parents can be more effective in talking with their children include

- Telling about problems and how they were overcome (not always talking about the wins, mixing in a discussion of the struggles)
- Finding good guys (heroes) and bad guys in stories
- Picking situations that both parents and children really care about
- Including dialogue and details about human nature

Conversely, children want their parents to listen to them. In schools, teachers want their students to listen and learn, retain, and use information. Students want to understand what their teachers are saying. To encourage more listening, the sender should make messages and listening attractive. There are several ways to do this. Sometimes humor works, which is why many speeches begin with a joke or humorous anecdote. One way advertisers deliver effective messages is to appeal to potential customers' senses. Think of the senses involved in this appeal from General Foods: "Turn a stormy night into a quiet evening with the after-dinner-mint taste of chocolaty Irish Mocha Mint." Listeners as well as senders have a job to do. This is one of the reasons listening is considered active rather than passive. To be effective, listeners use certain gestures or mannerisms to communicate interest:

- Leaning forward rather than back
- Nodding occasionally to show comprehension
- Smiling
- Looking directly at the speaker and maintaining eye contact
- Making comments such as "I see," "Go on," "Oh," or "Mmm"
- Taking notes or tape recording, if appropriate

A good listener summarizes conversations when they end and lets the sender know his or her message was heard by nodding or smiling or by making some other gesture or response.

Critical Listening

Besides the general, everyday listening everyone does, there are specific types of listening. One of these is **critical listening,** in which the listener evaluates or challenges what is heard. Listening to a political candidate or a spokesperson for a new product requires critical listening. Can the message be believed? Before voting, making a contribution, or buying something new, the listener may

- Question the communicator's motives. What does he or she want?
- Question the origin and validity of the communicator's ideas.
- Separate fact from fiction.
- Judge the message and the sender. Are they accurate and reliable?

Critical listening takes time. Not all messages require critical listening, however. A sign that it may be necessary is that the message or messenger makes the listener feel uncomfortable or suspicious.

Reflective or Empathetic Listening

Another type of listening is reflective listening. **Reflective listening** or **empathetic listening** involves listening for feelings. **Empathy** is the ability to recognize and identify another's feelings by putting oneself in that person's place. Reflective or empathetic listening is so common that individuals don't examine their skills in this area closely enough. As a reflective listener, the listener's job is to set aside her or his own feelings and enter into the feelings of the person talking. The listener can do this by

- ◆ Identifying the speaker's emotion. Is the person afraid, excited, happy, or frustrated?
- ◆ Listening for the details of the story. What is included, and what is left out?
- ◆ Paraphrasing or mirroring the speaker's comments to see if the message is being heard accurately.
- ◆ Letting the other person work through the problem. Talking out feelings is a way to find solutions.

Informational and Pleasurable Listening

Listening does not have to be painful, difficult, or critical, nor does it have to involve the use of counseling skills. Much listening is for information or for fun. Informational listening is done to acquire knowledge or instruction. A news program or a college lecture is primarily informational, but also involves critical listening. Pleasurable listening provides enjoyment, relaxation, satisfaction, diversion, amusement, or delight. Tuning the radio to a favorite station provides pleasurable listening. Watching a television situation comedy show provides escape, amusement, and laughter. Other sources of pleasurable listening are available besides the media. Imagine the happiness of a father hearing his child's first word, a high school student learning she has won a college scholarship, or a person overseas receiving a phone call from home. Often the most pleasurable listening comes from unexpected sources or at an unanticipated time.

Messages

The **message** is the total communication that is sent, listened to, and received. Communication is made up of symbols. **Symbols** are things that suggest something else through association. For example, an engagement ring is a symbol of love and the intention to marry. It communicates a past, present, and future. Symbols, such as an engagement ring, that can be seen are called **visible symbols.**

An **abstract symbol** stands for ideas rather than objects. Poor communication often springs from misunderstandings of abstract symbols. For example, Matt tells Suzanne he has an "awesome" apartment. By *awesome* he means that it is close to campus and inexpensive, but Suzanne, hearing the word *awesome,* envisions a new, beautifully decorated, spacious apartment.

Imagine her surprise when Matt takes her to a crumbling 50-year-old building. Lasting friendships are built on shared abstract symbols—commonalities of interests or appreciation of each other's differences. In the future, Suzanne will suspect Matt's use of the word *awesome*.

Verbal and Nonverbal Symbols

Verbal symbols are words. A **nonverbal symbol** is anything other than words used to communicate. Examples of nonverbal symbols include works of art, train whistles, sirens, tone and volume of voice, clothing, personal appearance, demeanor, gestures, facial expressions, posture, and yawns. For example, yawns may communicate tiredness or boredom, whereas sirens communicate danger or caution. Conventional scientific wisdom said that the role of gestures was to convey meaning. There is an emerging consensus that gestures serve another function—to help people retrieve elusive words from memory. People who gesture a lot may think in spatial terms. "Not everyone talks with their hands. Some people gesture 40 times more than others" (Begley, 1998, p. 69). Communication experts estimate that as many as 93 percent of the messages sent and received are made up of nonverbal symbols (Mehrabian, 1981)—hence the expression, "It is not what you say, but how you say it."

Table 7.1 describes six aspects of nonverbal communication: artifacts, proxemics, body language, physical characteristics, clothing, and one's touching behavior. **Artifacts** are the type, placement, or rearrangement of objects around a person. A student who sits down at a library table and takes 20 minutes to arrange his belongings before settling down to work communicates something different than a person who takes 20 seconds to set up. **Proxemics** is the distance between speakers. Closeness and whispering imply one type of relationship, whereas distance and shouting imply another. Touching behavior includes both touching oneself, such as hair twisting or rubbing one's face, and touching others, such as shaking hands or hugging. A brief kiss on the cheek, for example, conveys something different than a kiss on the lips.

TABLE 7.1
Six Aspects of Nonverbal Communication

1. *Artifacts:* The manipulation of objects in contact with persons. Examples include objects on desks, dishes on tables, purses, backpacks, notebooks, pens, and hammers.

2. *Proxemics:* The distance between two people who are communicating.

3. *Body language:* The way a person moves, smiles, or frowns and uses gestures such as pointing or waving.

4. *Physical characteristics:* The size, posture, and shape of a person's body.

5. *Clothes or other forms of adornment or grooming:* This includes hairstyles, jewelry, cosmetics, and use of aftershave or perfume.

6. *Touching behavior:* How one touches oneself and others while communicating. Examples include shaking hands, hugging, cracking one's knuckles, and tapping one's feet.

I-Messages and You-Messages

Verbal messages can be divided into two types: I-messages and You-messages. **I-messages** are statements of fact about how an individual feels or thinks; for example, "I like it when you send me flowers, thanks." **You-messages** are statements that often ascribe blame or judge others, such as "You had better straighten up" or "You had better get it right next time." You-messages can lead to arguments. Family counselors and therapists promote the use of I-messages over the accusatory tone of You-messages as a way to encourage more positive communication in couples and families. Many You-messages can be rephrased into I-messages as in "I hope things will go better next time."

Message Construction

The structure of a message has a lot to do with its potency. **Message construction** includes where information should be placed in a message to have maximum impact. The communicator has to decide whether to place the main point of the comment or speech at the beginning or the end and whether to provide solutions or leave the solutions to the audience.

Message Content and Complexity

Message content refers to the strategies or information that may be used to communicate an idea or policy to receivers. Determining content is the first step in creating a message. Then the communicator must decide on the best way to get the message across to the audience. Many of us have messages or images in our heads about certain individuals and groups. Some of these messages or images are questionable.

> "When you see a 25-year-old woman, you picture her as single, she has a cool job, a cute boyfriend, she's going out at night, has lots of friends, has a college degree. But having interviewed thousands of women, I can tell you that many [young women] have children, are working at some half-baked first job, are not feeling fulfilled, are not in love, might still be living at home, are economically pressed and stressed to the max," says Mary Lou Quinlan, CEO of New York city-based Just Ask a Woman, a division of ad agency BCOM3. (Wellner, 2002, p. 27)

Quinlan's firm interviewed more than 3,000 women about their lives and tastes in magazines to arrive at that conclusion about 25-year-old women, and there were other surprises. A twenty-year-old may read *Ladies' Home Journal* and a fifty-year-old may read *Glamour*. Quinlan says, "Women will find their way to the emotional outlet that most reflects their lives" (Wellner, 2002, p. 27).

The Zenlike magazine *Real Simple* offers ageless content on many of the subjects covered in this book, including time, money, household, lifestyle, and stress management to its mainly 25- to 54-year-old readers. A constant theme is how to make your life easier or better. According to the managing editor, Kristin van Ogtrop: "We all need a friend—a very good one with very good taste—who will come into our house and evaluate everything with an objective eye, then firmly suggest we get rid of that horrendous appliance/slipcover/light fixture that we've held on to because we're sentimental or lazy" ("Editor's Note," 2003, p. 37).

To return to the general topic of message content, messages may have humor or even fear, which seems negative but can be an effective way to point out potential problems in order to reduce risk or achieve other positive effects. Antidrug public service television spots often use fear as a means of reducing drug use. Property insurance, burglar alarms, and automobile advertisements often include fear messages.

Channels and Feedback

As mentioned earlier, the channel is the method through which the message travels from sender to receiver. Channels may be direct, as in face-to-face talking, or indirect. In face-to-face channels of communication, individuals have the advantage of seeing how the other person is reacting to the message, so there is less chance of miscommunication. Radio, television, magazines, newspapers, and signs are **indirect channels** of mass communication. How many newspapers are there in the United States? That is difficult to say because smaller ones go in and out of business, and some are hardly bigger than newsletters. But it is safe to say that the number is growing and ethnic newspapers enjoy a loyal following.

> Guess how many newspapers are published in New York City? Three? Five? Even Manhattanites familiar with all seven of the city's English language papers may be unaware of the additional 198 ethnic newspapers published in New York's other four boroughs—more than three times the number there were just a decade ago. Ethnic newspapers—presenting a range of linguistic and cultural perspectives including Chinese, Hispanic, Arabic, Caribbean, Russian, Korean and more—are proliferating nationwide. Chicago has more than 80 publications. (Paul, 2001, p. 26)

Telephones provide a channel for more personal communications than other types of media because the tone of voice is heard, but telephone communication is still not as clear as face to face.

Channels can also be categorized as social channels or advocate or expert channels. **Social channels** consist of friends, neighbors, and family members. Because of familiarity and proximity, these channels are most likely to involve face-to-face contacts. **Advocate or expert channels** (e.g., experts in a field, salespeople, or people with a cause) are more likely to contact receivers through letters, speeches, or less direct forms of communication. In systems terminology, feedback is the return to the input of a part of the output in the form of information. An equally appropriate but simpler definition of feedback is the response process between sender and receiver. Feedback may take a variety of forms. It closes the loop in the communications flow and lets the sender know how the intended message was decoded and received.

Feedback begins when one hears or observes what is being said, stores or responds to the information, and listens for the next message. For example, if Joseph gives Alison a compliment and she says "thank you," her response provides feedback. Joseph's message was heard accurately and acknowledged.

Feedback provides a control mechanism for the accuracy of communication. By the recipient's response, the sender can tell if the message was communicated effectively. If Alison bursts into tears, obviously Joseph's compliment was not phrased correctly or received correctly. If he values their relationship, he will restate his comment and try to straighten things out. The advantage of face-to-face conversations is that the feedback is immediate.

COMMUNICATION CONFLICTS

Many potential communication conflicts and problems can be avoided by applying the general principles already presented on noise, setting, feedback, channels, and messages. But, in addition, certain situations and audiences deserve special attention. This section examines the potential communication conflicts that can occur within families and across cultures.

In Families

In general, the goal of communication is to provide understanding that leads to desired actions. In some cases, however, communication fails and conflict results. **Conflict** is a state of disagreement or disharmony. In poor communication, there is a message struggle or conflict between the sender and the receiver. If survival of the relationship is the ultimate goal, this conflict can pose a definite threat. Negotiations to remedy the conflict are known as **conflict resolution.** The sender, receiver, or another person can initiate conflict resolution.

Conflict is particularly common in families because of the intimate, ongoing nature of the relationships. Family members know each other so well that they notice nonverbal communications (e.g., a raised eyebrow, a strained voice) that strangers would be likely to miss. Hence, conflict is more on the surface and less readily hidden in families. The emotional intensity of family relationships is generally much greater than in small groups, so family communication problems tend to have more serious and painful implications (Sieburg,1985). Although information should flow easily among family members, sometimes it stagnates, and conflict between family members goes on for years.

The number of possible interactions also contributes to communication conflicts in families. Adding a second child to a family increases the number of interactions. As the number of interactions increases, family members may succumb to interaction fatigue. Because the family system is part of the larger environment, interaction fatigue may also develop at work and affect the family at home or develop at home and spill over into work. Kanter (1977) observed that employees who experience interaction fatigue at work may withdraw from personal contact at home. Researchers (Liberman, Wheeler, de Visser, Kuehnel, & Kuehnel, 1980, p. 90) have identified several common destructive messages and tactics that characterize ineffective communication within families:

- ◆ Ordering turns the interaction into a power struggle between partners or between parents and children. "You do this" and "Stop doing that" are examples of ordering.

- ◆ Threatening is similar to ordering, but it goes further. It can lead to passivity or despair.

- ◆ Moralizing sends a message of guilt or moral inferiority or suggests that the other person needs guidance or direction. "You should" messages are examples of moralizing.

- ◆ Providing solutions occurs when words sound like a question, as in "Why don't you," but really indicate superiority or a kind of parental guidance.

- ◆ Lecturing is a more forceful way of providing solutions. You are told what to do or are told you always do things wrong.

- ◆ Criticizing can mar relationships and lead to lower self-esteem and dependency in the criticized person.

- ◆ Ridiculing generates resistance and resentment. It involves biting and hurtful phrases such as "You're talking like an idiot" or "You're such a mess."

◆ Analyzing occurs when one person tells another how he or she should think and act. Analyzers are often amateur psychologists who generate anger by invading others' privacy and questioning their motivations, with comments like "You think you know what you are doing, but you don't." Often analyzers are wrong, however.

◆ Interrogating is used to gain information by relentless questioning.

◆ "You're not telling the truth, are you?" is an example of an interrogating question.

◆ Withdrawing is a way to end conversations. The person may say she or he is tired and going to bed. The "silent treatment" is another tactic.

Do these messages and tactics sound familiar? They should, because they are very common. If they are used too frequently, they can impede effective communication and damage relationships. Being able to recognize these tactics helps the recipient understand the sender better. Possibly, the message is not conveying the real problem. The real problem may be with the sender or with the relationship between the sender and the receiver. For example, Luciano L'Abate and Tamar Harel suggest that "relationships that cannot become intimate emotionally may make contact with each other through sporadic and sudden ambushes, uproars, upsets, and conflicts over performance and/or production" (1993, p. 243).

Conversely, the Marital Communication Inventory (Bievenue, 1978) has identified behaviors that indicate satisfying marital communication. They include pleasant mealtime conversations, avoidance of the silent treatment, discussions of work and interests with each other, avoiding saying things that irritate each other, and communicating affection and regard. In general, communication between husbands and wives is most satisfying when both partners feel they are understood and when they agree on essential points.

Interpersonal Conflicts

Interpersonal conflicts are actions by one person that interfere in some way with the actions of another. **Destructive conflicts** are a specific type of interpersonal conflict involving direct verbal attacks on another individual. Yelling, screaming, abuse, attacks on self-esteem, and words leading to breakups are characteristics of destructive conflicts. Conversely, **constructive conflicts** focus on the issue or the problem rather than on the other person's deficits. This type of conflict can open up issues and lead to deeper relationships, clarification, and better understanding of the other person. Thus, not all conflicts are negative. Sometimes conflict is necessary to resolve points of difference, clear the air, or relieve tension.

Gender, Families, and Communication

Researchers generally accept that men and women communicate differently, both verbally and nonverbally. Deborah Tannen, a psycholinguist, has written five books, including her best-seller *You Just Don't Understand*. She points out that men talk far more than women, especially in public. Men speak more at meetings, in the classroom, and in mixed groups at work. However, in the course of a day, women speak about 25,000 words, while men speak only 10,000.

Her book *I Only Say This Because I Love You* explores miscommunication among family members. She suggests that parents should listen more and criticize their teenage children less. Couples should talk about assumptions and try to bring hidden messages out in the open. And both sides should learn the art of apology. A win-win solution where nobody is wrong and a solution is reached is ideal.

Women tend to interrogate or question more than men do. Psychiatrist Aaron Beck (1988) points out that wives tend to believe that their marriage is working as long as they and their husbands are talking about it. Conversely, men may think the marriage is not working if they have to talk about it constantly. Generally, women are more comfortable talking about personal matters with family and friends than men are.

According to Tannen, men and women also differ in the way they express their troubles and the way they seek out information. Women resent "men's tendency to offer solutions to problems," and men "complain about women's refusal to take action to solve the problems they complain about" (1990, pp. 51–52). Men want to solve problems and move on, whereas women hesitate and seek other people's opinions to gain as much information as they can before moving toward a solution. This is one of the reasons women make up the majority of the audience for talk shows. They enjoy considering all the angles to a situation or issue. Men sometimes feel women go to such excess talking over situations that they seem to enjoy wallowing in a problem. Men move to solutions quickly because they derive pleasure from fixing things. Fixing things "reinforces their feeling of being in control, self-sufficient, and able to dominate the world of objects" (1990, p. 70).

Women are more likely than men to ask directions and accept information from others. The classic example is of men driving around lost rather than stopping and asking directions. Men are also more likely to try to get the "best" parking space in a shopping center. At the root of both of these behaviors is concern about status, hierarchy, and connections. According to Tannen, boys as young as age three are using words in their conversations with peers that show they want to be a leader, to be first, and to be best, whereas girls of the same age are more interested in getting along with friends and understanding their feelings and opinions. For example, girls are more likely to say "let's" and "we" in their conversations. Boys' conversations are filled with orders, such as "Get up" or "Give it to me," and ridicule, such as "You're a dope" (Beck, 1988, p. 82). Boys are more inclined than girls to threaten, boast, and argue.

Tannen contends that men and women have different but equally valid communication styles. Problems arise when men and women talk to each other and expect a certain kind of response. Because of gender differences in conversation, a woman will not always get the response she desires from men and vice versa. Tannen concludes:

> The biggest mistake people can make is believing there is one right way to listen, to talk, to have a conversation—or a relationship. Nothing hurts more than being told your intentions are bad when you know they are good, or being told you are doing something wrong when you know you're doing it your way. (1990, pp. 297–298)

Tannen's observations have implications for family dynamics and workplace management. As women move into positions of authority, these gender differences in conversation will require greater understanding from both men and women. The solution is not to change styles so everyone speaks alike, but to understand and appreciate the various forms of communication. The realistic approach is to "learn how to interpret each others' messages and explain your own in a way your partner can understand and accept" (1990, p. 297).

Shelly Gable, an assistant professor of psychology at UCLA, researches the positive psychology of love and marriage. She encourages messages that amplify the pleasure of a good situation, contributing to an upward spiral of positive emotion. An example would be a partner reacting enthusiastically to a mate's good fortune or a partner getting even more excited and happy about what is happening to his or her mate than the mate does. An enthusiastic partner asks a lot of questions and shows genuine interest. All these responses or reactions are called active/constructive and promote love, commitment, and satisfaction (Seligman, 2003).

Cultures and Subcultures

According to Deborah Tannen (2001), Americans are so direct in their conversation that people in other nations sometimes wonder if Americans aren't a bit naïve or childlike. The American heritage of being hardy, hard working, and plain-spoken influences the ways we converse. We also want to get to a point fast; long-winded stories or explanations are turn-offs. Indirectness or hidden agendas make Americans uneasy. As these comments show, cultures have unique ways of communicating, and conflict can arise between cultures with different styles. Misunderstandings may stem from the failure to understand values, decision patterns, symbols, and spoken and nonverbal languages of other cultures. For example, as companies have expanded internationally, many glaring errors have occurred in product names and packaging. What is appropriate in one country may not be in another. For example,

> The car slogan "Body by Fisher" becomes "Corpse by Fisher" in Flemish. "Come alive with Pepsi" comes out "Pepsi brings your ancestors back from the grave" in Chinese and "Come alive out of the grave" in German.

These examples illustrate problems in translating words. Nonverbal differences between cultures are more subtle. A friendly gesture in one culture may be insulting in another. Manners and etiquette vary around the world. Here are some examples of rude behavior in other cultures:

- ◆ Pointing at people, in Japan
- ◆ Eating with your left hand, in some Arab countries
- ◆ Sitting where people can see the soles of your shoes, in certain cultures

Anthropologist Edward T. Hall has studied how people vary across cultures in communicating trust, warmth, and respect. In his book, *The Silent Language,* he pointed out that "what people do is frequently more important than what they say" (1959, p. 24).

Even the amount of time spent socializing with friends and family varies by culture. The typical American spends 16.3 hours socializing each week compared to 7.5 hours for the typical Japanese (Blinder, 1991).

Also varying is the underlying message. For example, Americans are deal-oriented, impatient, and competitive. But, an advertiser wishing to appeal to a Japanese audience would avoid saying

- ◆ "Be the first in your neighborhood to own such and such." Japanese do not like to be out of step with their neighbors.
- ◆ "New, free . . . no strings attached." The average Japanese honors stability rather than "newness" and would be suspicious of something that is given away for free.

The correct social space between people also varies across cultures and by relationships within cultures. Figure 7.3 shows the four distance zones common in the United States. Intimate distance in the United States is less than 18 inches; typically, few people enter this space. Personal space is between 1½ to 4 feet. Americans like to have this amount of personal space around their bodies; culture dictates that this should not be invaded by strangers. But in some countries, hugs, slaps on the back, and even spitting on the ground near the feet are meant to convey trust and connection (Adams, 1998). In the United States, business tends to be conducted within the social zone of 4 to 7 feet. To visualize this distance, think about the distance between salesclerks and their customers (remember that salesclerks often stand behind counters). In Latin America and the Middle East, people tend to get closer. A businessperson from the United States confronted with this behavior abroad may back away, giving the impression of being cold and unfriendly. According to Hall (1959, p. 209), Latin Americans cannot talk comfortably with one another unless they are very close to the distance that evokes either sexual or hostile feelings in a North American. The public zone in North America is 12 to 15 feet.

Besides language and gestures, symbols are interpreted differently across cultures. Colors, flower arrangements, and numbers all communicate in different ways across cultures. In certain countries, purple is associated with royalty or death, and yellow-green with spring and fertility. However, in Malaysia, green symbolizes the danger and death in the jungle. When a water recreation company in Malaysia used a green corporate symbol, its promotional campaign failed. Flowers can represent death, infidelity, loyalty, or love depending on the type of flower, the occasion, the color, and the country. The number 13 is considered unlucky in the United States—many people will not fly on Friday the 13th and most hotels do not have a floor numbered 13. In Europe, 13th floors are common.

As the United States and Canada become more involved in exports, international business, and worldwide communications, and as Europe becomes

FIGURE 7.3
The Four Distance Zones

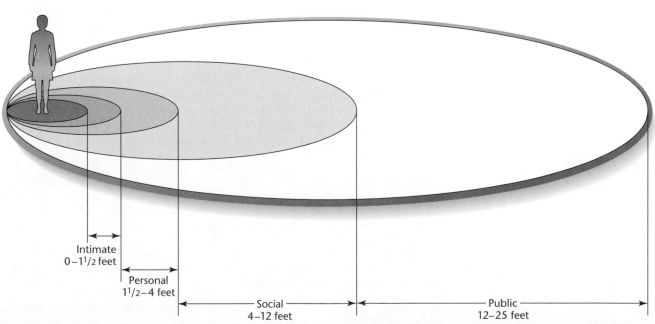

Intimate
0–1½ feet

Personal
1½–4 feet

Social
4–12 feet

Public
12–25 feet

People's sense of appropriate distance zones are affected by culture. These men from Florence, Italy, are standing closer together than American men typically would.

© Peter Turnley/CORBIS

more unified, an awareness of cultural differences and similarities will become more important. Also, the new focus on the dynamics of family diversity and multiculturalism worldwide have renewed interest in cross-cultural communication and cross-group communication. Within countries, there are many subcultures as well, and some groups are being underestimated in terms of their influence and buying power. For example, an article in *American Demographics* says that "Black women run their homes, heavily consume media and influence more than $260 billion in spending a year. Still marketers continue to ignore them" (Yin, 2003, September, p. 22). Here is an example:

> Cynthia Morris is a family woman who has an MBA degree and an executive-level job. By day, she raises funds for national parks programs. By night, the 50-year-old, married African American mother of two writes checks for such things as the tuition for one of her sons' college education and the renovations on the family's 3,500-square-foot house in Potomac, Md. Still, as the chief decision maker in her upper-middle-class household, Morris believes that, to marketers, she is out of sight and out of mind. "It's like a blind spot," she says. "People just don't see us as this influential segment that can make a difference in their market share" (Yin, 2003, September, p. 22).

Statistics reveal that "Black women are more likely to be the primary decision maker in their household than white women. Sixty-one percent of African

American women make the decisions about major purchases, such as buying a home, compared with just 43 percent of Caucasian women" (Yin, 2003, September, p. 23).

College students are another subgroup of potential interest to marketers because of their earning potential. Marketers would like to lock in their brands with college students before they launch into the world of lucrative full-time employment. College students are also trendsetters and early adopters of certain products such as clothes and cars. But they are a challenge because "Students doubt corporate intentions, they want to be catered to and they don't think companies know what they want. And they are poor: Their idea of a good buy is a bargain" (Yin, 2003, May, p. 20). Free samples work well with this age group since they like a bargain but also like to try new things. Does this last statement fit you?

COMMUNICATION IN SMALL GROUPS

All groups have in common a shared goal or purpose or reason for being. Families are a type of small group joined together by ties of affection and kinship. But there are many other kinds of small groups as well. People get together to solve school, community, work, or environmental problems; for fellowship or support; and for individual and family growth. Once a group has decided on its main goals or purposes, it is ready to proceed.

Groups vary in size, but research indicates that effective group size ranges from 3 to 13 with the ideal size being 5 (Hybels & Weaver, 1989). Larger groups may divide into smaller task force groups or committees to solve problems or to take charge of an issue or fund-raising drive. Groups are too large

Families share affection and kinship. What feelings are being communicated by this family?

© Nancy Ney/CORBIS

when some people do not have an opportunity to participate or speak. If this continues to happen, smaller groups are needed. Conversely, groups can become too small or stagnant. When nothing new is contributed time after time, then perhaps a new group should be formed or members added.

Group Discussions and Cohesion

When a group becomes stagnant or cannot find a project that members consider interesting, then it should try brainstorming. In **brainstorming** all group members suggest ideas—no matter how seemingly ridiculous or strange. Afterward, the group examines each idea separately to see if it has merit. Brainstorming is a good way to get the creative juices flowing and introduce some energy into the group.

Once a project has been agreed upon, the group should seek out information. Group members should find out how others have initiated similar ideas or programs. Many times a project or program is phrased as a question; for example, how can a group help homeless families in the community? How can a fourth-grade class participate in Earth Day?

After the questions have been discussed, the next stage is to move toward solutions. Groups will discuss and discard many unworkable or unaffordable solutions before they arrive at one or two that group members can agree upon. Next a plan will be initiated. If necessary, an unworkable plan will be thrown out and a new plan developed. Eventually, the group will have to determine which plans are working and whether the group should move on to other projects.

Several factors contribute to group cohesion: the size of the group, the goal-achievement orientation, the status and resources of the group, the degree to which members depend on the group for need satisfaction, and the demands or pressures under which the members operate. Too large a group will decrease group cohesion. Successfully achieving a goal will spur the group on to new challenges. For example, a successful fund-raising drive for a new town library may lead to another community fund-raising effort.

In summary, communication is the key to whether groups will function smoothly or not. Families and other types of small groups cannot be successfully managed without some degree of open communication. What needs to be done and who needs to do it should be clearly communicated and negotiated. Closed or poor communication will undermine the family's or the group's cohesiveness and future progress.

INFORMATION AND COMMUNICATION TECHNOLOGY

Much of the previous discussion has focused on group dynamics and communication problems. But, people do not always interact with each other directly; often they interact through machines such as computers, televisions, telephones, and radio. How attentive an individual is to these forms of communication depends on the message, the messenger, and the channel. In addition, different types of media affect different senses. Print media, such as newspapers and magazines, usually affect vision only. The inclusion of perfume samples in magazines affects our sense of smell. Television is multisensory in that it affects both vision and hearing.

One of the greatest technological changes of the 19th and 20th centuries has been the switch from face-to-face conversations to less personal forms of communication. This transformation began in 1876 with the first telephone (patented by a voice teacher, Alexander Graham Bell) and continues today with fax machines, e-mail, and the Internet.

New technologies can help various populations stay more connected and secure. For example,

> Ardith Hammond, 70 years old, living alone in her St. Louis home after having her hip and knee replaced, often worried that she would fall and be unable to get up.
> "No one would know for days," she says. She didn't want to ask her son or his wife to call every day. So she worked out a routine with a neighbor in which they would turn off their porch lights at the same time nightly as a signal that they were OK, but the neighbor lost interest. Then Ms. Hammond discovered a source of reassurance: technology. She subscribes for $1 a day to a computer telephone service, TelAsure, that dials her twice daily, greets her by name with a recording and asks her to confirm, by pushing buttons on her phone. If she doesn't answer as scheduled, the service alerts family or friends. Does getting called by a computer seem cold? "No," Ms. Hammond says, "where else can you get love and reassurance for $1 a day?" (Shellenbarger, 1999, p. B1)

Information Overload and Habitual Decision Making

As consumers, individuals are constantly bombarded with information. Some of this information is **passively acquired,** such as through billboards, e-mail, airplane messages, and loudspeakers at K-marts, meaning that the consumer does not seek out the information. Other information is **actively acquired,** meaning that the consumer actively looks for it— for example, scanning fashion advertisements in magazines or actively listening to television commercials.

The degree of effort expended on the information search and the amount of exposure to information vary by person, product, and issue. For example, consumers often react to information (e.g., store displays, advertisements) with **low involvement,** meaning that they tend not to think much about it and may find their attention wandering. In **habitual decision making,** choices are made out of habit without any additional information search. Decisions are made with little conscious effort. This allows the consumer to devote real effort and thought to important decisions requiring more careful scrutiny.

Information overload refers to that uncomfortable state when individuals are exposed to too much information in too short a time—so much that they cannot process the information. Rather than ignoring information as one does in low involvement, the person feels overwhelmed by it. The growth of e-mail has gone from about 36 million users in 1994 to over 123 million users in the United States. *Nine out of ten college students watch TV and listen to the radio every week, and they learn about products and services mostly by word of mouth or advertising on television* (Yin, 2003, May). Other typical student media behaviors include reading magazines occasionally and reading the campus newspaper or national newspapers.

An offshoot of information overload is **information anxiety,** which is the gap between what individuals think they understand and what they actually do understand. Thus, information anxiety refers to the space between data and knowledge. Richard Wurman, author of *Information Anxiety,* observes that people used to have to make a conscious decision to seek information, but now technology permits information to be transmitted without the desire—or often the permission—of the receiver. Adding to the information explosion is the proliferation of communications technology. To deal with information overload, Wurman advises people to accept that they don't have to know everything about everything. He recommends that they focus on what matters most.

Computers and the Human Capacity to Process Information

Information that was once stored in people's heads and in books and file cabinets is now being put into digital form on computers. Once this information is stored in a computer's memory, it can be manipulated and accessed over phone lines, transmitted by satellite, and accessed by many different users.

Borrowing computer terminology, the amount of information the human central nervous system can process has been compared to the amount of information a computer can process. It has been estimated that individuals can manage at most seven bits of information (e.g., differentiated sounds, visual stimuli, or recognizable nuances of emotion or thought) at any one time and that the shortest time it takes to discriminate between one set of bits and another is about 1/18 of a second (Csikszentmihalyi, 1990). On the basis of these figures, humans can process at most 126 bits of information per second or 7,560 per minute. In practical terms, this means that an individual cannot process what three people are saying to him or her simultaneously and absorb all the nonverbal cues. These are all estimates since the exact limit of humans' conscious ability to process information is unknown. Nevertheless, it is known that an individual's interest in the message and the message giver influences how much is processed and retained. According to University of Chicago researcher Mihaly Csikszentmihalyi, "The mark of a person who is in control of consciousness is the ability to focus attention at will, to be oblivious to distractions, to concentrate for as long as it takes to achieve a goal, and not longer. And the person who can do this usually enjoys the normal course of everyday life" (1990, p. 31).

The Role of the Home and the Individual

As the preceding quotation illustrates, individuals make choices about what to concentrate on and what to ignore. In part, these are conscious decisions by an individual or family about which technologies they will adopt. In the future, more technology-assisted activities will take place in the home, including shopping, investing, banking, and working. Computers have already made it possible for many people to work at home.

Faith Popcorn, a predictor of trends, noted that **cocooning** (the desire to remain at home as a place of coziness, control, peace, insulation, and protection) is being facilitated by such technologies as DVDs, VCRs, and microwave ovens. In many respects, the improved home-based technologies should increase family time spent in the home. Children who miss classes due to illness will be able to tune into their classroom and keep up with their classmates. The increase in home-based technologies is a boon for the elderly, disabled individuals, and others less mobile than the general population as illustrated by the previous story about Ardith Hammond.

Along with these benefits, the innovations in communication technology have some drawbacks. Cost is an obvious problem. New technologies are expensive and may increase the gap between the haves and have-nots in society. Privacy is another issue. As more information is recorded and exchanged, more is known about an individual's buying habits and personal communications. More legislation will be needed to establish ground rules on who will have access to data and under what conditions. Families will have to make decisions about access to data and use of technology as well. Parents will have to decide what technology to adopt and what technology to let children access.

Individuals and families will also have to make decisions about managing information. Theodore Leavitt argues that discrimination is necessary in the use of information and data. Unfortunately, he says, as information becomes more abundant, it seems to yield less meaning. He draws an analogy: "The greater the variety of good food consumed at a meal, the less you appreciate each dish. The louder the noise, the less clear the message" (1991, p. 6).

Web-Based Resources

As the chapter pointed out, there is more and more unwanted communication, although things improved when a law was passed banning telemarketers from calling people who put their names on a "no-call" list. In the United States, the Federal Trade Commission's (FTC) privacy Web site (**www.ftc.gov/privacy**) provides advice on how to stop the spread of personal information and tells you how to remove your name from direct marketing mailing lists. Since it is estimated that the average person receives 34 pounds of junk mail a year, this could be a time-saver for you and a cost-saver for companies who are wasting not only their advertising dollars but also countless trees. In addition, numerous Web sites help consumers reduce the amount of **spam** (unsolicited commercial e-mail, or, in other words, Internet junk mail) they receive. Each year, the FTC reports on the top dozen spam scams. The Federal Communications Commission can be reached at **www.fcc.gov.** The FCC is actively trying to monitor the Internet.

Since the topic of communication includes all forms of information, there are innumerable business and organizational Web sites that fit this subject. General Web sites such as **yahoo.com, google.com,** and **geocities.com** can yield information on nearly any area of interest.

Summary

Effective managers are effective communicators, and it is impossible to manage without communicating. Communication serves as a linkage between the various steps in the management process. Communication can be verbal or nonverbal. Appearance, clothing, facial expressions, gestures, and posture communicate along with words.

Communication skills can be improved through study and application. Listening is an important management skill. Hearing other people's needs and being able to express one's own is the basis of human communication. Communication is satisfying when individuals feel that they are understood and that they understand others.

Five main components exchanged between senders and receivers make up the total communication environment: message, channels, noise, feedback, and setting. Communication conflicts can arise from any of these components or from a combination of them. Family communication differs from other types in its emotional intensity and ongoing nature. Because of these characteristics, communication conflicts in families can be particularly painful and harmful. Destructive messages and tactics such as ridiculing, ordering, or threatening can be harmful to family relationships.

According to Deborah Tannen and other researchers, men and women have different but equally valid conversational styles. Couples need to learn the art of apologizing as well as learning about different ways to get the message across.

Communication and communication technology are never stagnant. The modes, the messages, and the means are always changing. Census Bureau figures reveal the multicultural and multilingual changes that are taking place. Our communication styles and channels will have to try to keep up.

Information overload is increasingly becoming a problem. Individuals are constantly being bombarded by messages, some of which are expected (actively acquired information), while others are unanticipated or unwelcome (passively acquired information). There is a limit to how much information humans can consciously process. Future research will provide more insight into the ability to process information and the ways computers can assist further in accessing and storing information. Already computers and other forms of technology and the speed of information have altered the traditional functioning of the home. Since every communication advance has its pluses and minuses, individuals and families must weigh the costs and the benefits.

Key Terms

abstract symbols
actively acquired
   information
advocate or expert
   channels
artifacts
brainstorming
channel
cocooning
communication
conflict
conflict resolution
constructive conflicts
critical listening
decoding
destination
destructive conflicts

empathetic listening
empathy
encoding
external noise
habitual decision
   making
I-messages
indirect channels
information anxiety
information overload
interference
internal noise
interpersonal conflicts
low involvement
message
message construction
message content

noise
nonverbal symbols
passively acquired
   information
proxemics
receiving
reflective listening
responses
sending
setting
social channels
source
spam
symbols
verbal symbols
visible symbols
You-messages

Review Questions

1. Have you ever felt that people were not listening to you? What are the characteristics of effective communicators listed at the beginning of the chapter? Which of these is an aspect that you'd like to work on? Explain why.

2. Change the following You-messages into I-messages: "You never clean the apartment." "You never put gasoline in the car." "You always leave everything to the last minute. Why don't you do something on time for a change?"

3. List the destructive communication styles or tactics used in families. Which do you think is the biggest problem? Why?

4. Do you agree with Theodore Leavitt's statement that the more information you are exposed to, the less meaning it seems to have? Explain.

5. Many doors in the brain seem to open onto memories. For example, a whiff of cinnamon may unleash memories of your childhood kitchen. Likewise, gesturing may open a door to a word or a memory, especially one with a spatial (high, low, or wide) or movement connotation (here or there). When someone is looking for the right word that connotes motion, for example, hands may help. Do you gesture often? What sorts of gestures do you make? How do members of your family gesture?

References

Adams, D. (1998, December 23). When holding hands help clinch the deal. *Tallahassee Democrat*, 10E.

Beck, A. (1988). *Love is never enough*. New York: Harper & Row.

Begley, S. (1998, November 2). Living hand to mouth. *Newsweek*, 69.

Bievenue, M. (1978). *A counselor's guide to accompany a marital communications inventory*. Saluda, NC: Family Life.

Blinder, A. (1991, July 22). Time is not on America's side. *Business Week*, 12.

Csikszentmihalyi, M. (1990). *Flow: The psychology of optimal experience*. New York: Harper & Row.

Drucker, P. (1977). *People and performance*. New York: Harper College Press, 262–263.

Editor's note. (2003, September). *Real Simple*, p. 37.

Hall, E. T. (1959). *The silent language*. Greenwich, CT: Fawcett.

Heitmeyer, J., & Goldsmith, E. (1990). Attire as an influence on the perceptions of counselors' characteristics. *Perceptual and Motor Skills, 70*, 923–929.

Hybels, S., & Weaver, R. (1989). *Communicating effectively* (2nd ed.). New York: Random House.

Kanter, R. (1977). *Work and family in the United States: A critical review and agenda for research and policy*. New York: Russell Sage Foundation.

L'Abate, L., & Harel, T. (1993). Deriving, developing, and expanding competence from resource exchange theory. In U. Foa, J. Converse, K. Tornblom, & E. Foa (Eds.), *Resource theory: Explorations and applications* (pp. 223–260). San Diego: Academic Press.

Leavitt, T. (1991). *Thinking about management*. New York: Free Press.

Liberman, R., Wheeler, E., de Visser, L., Kuehnel, J., & Kuehnel, T. (1980). *Handbook of marital therapy*. New York: Plenum Press.

Mehrabian, A. (1981). *Silent messages: Implicit communication of emotions and attitudes* (2nd ed.). Belmont, CA: Wadsworth.

Paul, P. (2001, November). News, noticias, nouvelles. *American Demographics*, 26–31.

Popcorn, F. (1991). *The Popcorn report: Faith Popcorn on the future of your company, your world, your life*. New York: Doubleday.

Robbins, S. P. (1989). *Organizational behavior* (4th ed.). Englewood Cliffs, NJ: Prentice-Hall.

Seligman, M. (2003, September). Love and positive events. *Authentic Happiness Newsletter*. Retrieved March 31, 2004 from **http://www.authentichappiness.org/news/news7.html**

Shellenbarger, S. (1999, April 21). Work and family. *The Wall Street Journal*, B1.

Shellenbarger, S. (2003, October 30). Then there was the time I had a typo: What talks of your work can teach kids. *The Wall Street Journal*, D1.

Sieburg, E. (1985). *Family communication*. New York: Gardner Press.

Tannen, D. (1990). *You just don't understand*. New York: Ballantine Books.

Tannen, D. (2001). *I only say this because I love you*. New York: Random House.

Wellner, A. (2002, February). The female persuasion. *American Demographics*, 24–29.

Wu, B., & Newell, S. (2003, Spring). The impact of noise on recall of advertisements. *Journal of Marketing Theory and Practice*, 56–65.

Wurman, R. (1990). *Information anxiety*. New York: Doubleday.

Yin, S. (2003, September). Color bind. *American Demographics*, 22–26.

Yin, S. (2003, May). Degree of challenge. *American Demographics*, 20–22.

Management Applications

Managing Human Resources

MAIN TOPICS

Did you know that . . . ?

. . . One in four U.S. households is involved in the daily care of an elderly person.

. . . Nearly half of all brides and grooms walking down the aisle have been married before.

Our most basic link is that we all inhabit this planet. We all breathe the same air. We all cherish our children's future.

—*President John F. Kennedy*

CARING FOR AND about others is the subject of this chapter.

The U.S. is becoming a nation of caregivers. A study in 2000 by the National Family Caregivers Association found that as many as 50 million Americans, or about one-quarter of the adult population, had provided care for an ill, disabled or aged family member or friend in the previous 12 months. Fully 59% of adults, according to the group, either are or expect to be a family caregiver. (Ruffenach, 2003, p. R4)

Mark Twain said "Always do right. This will gratify some people, and astonish the rest." The chapter explores much more than what is thought of conventionally as caregiving and goes beyond the United States to look at the human resource challenges around the world. It tackles some difficult topics such as the management problems of the homeless and the poor.

First, let's discuss changes in human population. In 1900, 1.5 billion people inhabited the earth and most of them lived in large cities in Western Europe. Now, the world population is over 6.3 billion, and the greatest concentration of people is in Asia. China is the most populous country, followed

FIGURE 8.1
**The Ten Most
Populous Countries***

*Figures are for 2002. Of course, these numbers keep changing. When this book went to press the U.S. population was 292,548,052. For the latest national and worldwide population figures go to **www.census.gov** (updated every five minutes).

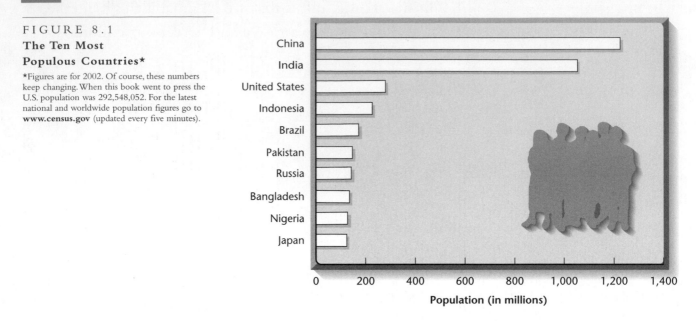

Population (in millions)

by India and the United States (see Figure 8.1). Half of the world's population is concentrated in cities, and the trend is toward increasing urbanization so that by 2050, as noted in Chapter 1, 75 percent of the world's population will live in cities. This clustering of people will stress natural resources and support systems. Many of the world's cities are called gateway cities because they are located on borders (between countries) or on coastlines. Immigrants often arrive in gateway cities, establish families and businesses, and do not venture further into the interior of countries. The *largest city in the world is Mumbai (Bombay), India,* with around 12 million people, followed by São Paolo, Brazil, with about 11 million and Seoul, South Korea, with about 10 million.

Managing human resources in a finite environment is the focus of this chapter. As Chapter 4 explained, resources can be classified as human and material. Human resources include all the capabilities (skills, talents, and abilities) that contribute to achieving goals and responding to demands. Health, vitality, and intelligence are examples of human resources. Human resources can be divided into three main categories:

1. *Cognitive:* knowledge, intelligence, and reasoning
2. *Affective:* emotions and feelings
3. *Psychomotor:* muscular activity associated with mental processes and the ability to do physical work

Many tasks require skills from two or more of these categories. For example, typing requires cognitive and psychomotor skills. Parenting requires all three types of human resources.

Human capital, which was also discussed in Chapter 4, is the sum total of an individual's human resources. Education, training, and practice increase human resources. Developing human capital in oneself and in others is one of the most important management processes covered in this book. Ultimately, the strength of a nation depends on its stock of human resources—the collective ability of its citizens to solve problems creatively and to meet society's demands.

Today, people find themselves immersed in a tangle of worldwide changes in the economy, society, institutions, education, the labor market, and individual lifestyles. Individual concerns must now be viewed in the context of the entire world. The family, as the basic unit of society, has weathered many storms, but many challenges lie ahead.

This chapter goes beyond the theoretical into the realm of population statistics and the practical management problems of certain groups. One important population change is the rapid increase in the percentage of minority groups in the United States. Another significant trend is the maturation of our society. The baby boom generation—children born between 1946 and 1964—has grown up and established family and community roots, cared for teenage children and elderly parents, moved into management positions at work, and bought homes—in fact, probably several homes over the years. Another important aspect of the maturation trend is the growth of the over-65 age group, the "graying of America," although it should be pointed out that the whole world is aging, with the trend most pronounced in developed countries. Elderly people today are healthier, more active, and more affluent than those of previous generations. Eventually, however, there may be caregiving needs, and these will be addressed in this chapter along with adjusting to retirement.

The 21st century promises to be more responsible about the environment and more respectful of individual age and cultural differences than the previous century. To express this concept of respect for cultural diversity, Alvin Toffler, author of *Future Shock,* coined the word *demassification,* which means breaking away from mass society where everyone must be the same. He says we're moving to a "mosaic society" where diversity is recognized and fostered.

This chapter begins Part 3, the management applications section of the book. It starts by examining population trends relevant to the study of individuals and families, including an exploration of how these changes take place. Although management concepts are relevant to all individuals and families, the remainder of this chapter focuses on the particular management needs and concerns of the following populations: two-income families, children, the elderly, early retirees, the homeless, individuals with disabilities, single parents, blended families, and poor and low-income families.

POPULATION SHIFTS: MEASURING HUMAN RESOURCES

Certain human resources, such as trust, love, and caring, are difficult to measure, but numbers of people and population shifts can be quantified. The primary source of U.S. population data is the national census, which is taken every 10 years by the Bureau of the Census. The census attempts to count every person living in this country and to collect vital information about family size and community and housing conditions. Based on this information, the government can determine population shifts and formulate policy.

The first census was taken in 1790 when George Washington was president. At that time, 3.9 million people were counted. As Figure 8.1 shows, the U.S. population is currently greater than 292 million. All statistics in this chapter come from the U.S. Bureau of the Census and the United Nations Population Division unless otherwise noted.

Population Terms and Trends

Demography is the study of the characteristics of human populations—that is, their size, growth, distribution, density, movement, and other vital statistics. **Demographics** are data used to describe populations or subgroups. Population figures are affected by three main factors: births, deaths, and immigration. The birthrate is technically termed fertility. The **fertility rate** is the yearly number of births per 1,000 women of childbearing age. *Countries experiencing a dramatic drop* in the average number of children born per woman from the early 1980s to early 2000s include Brazil, China, India, Indonesia, Mexico, Russia, Thailand, Tunisia, and Turkey. During this same time period, the average number of children born per woman increased slightly in the United States, where about two per woman is average. In India, three children per woman is average, and in Russia one per woman is average. The technical term for death is **mortality. Immigration** refers to the number of people who enter and settle in a country where they are not native. Without a decided increase in immigration and birthrate, populations can stagnate or decrease. In recent years, the states with the largest population gains in sheer numbers have been Texas, Florida, and California.

Even though the population is growing worldwide, in general, fertility rates are plummeting. Today, women on average have just half the number of children they did in 1972. In 61 countries, fertility rates are now at or below replacement levels. This does not mean the worldwide population will fall in the immediate future, however, because people are living longer. Globally, the average life span has jumped from 49.5 years in 1972 to 63 years. In addition, as mentioned earlier, the low fertility rate of industrialized nations is offset to some degree by less developed countries, which often have high fertility rates—although this is changing as economies change and birth control methods become more widespread.

Over the years, high unemployment and poor economies have been shown to have direct impact on fertility rates in industrialized countries. For example, during the Great Depression of the 1930s, the United States had a low fertility rate. Prior to that, especially from 1880 to 1900, the U.S. population growth rose from the influx of immigrants from Europe.

The U.S. birthrate rose sharply again after World War II. Unlike earlier population increases, which were caused largely by immigration, this growth was primarily due to the births of millions of children. This "baby boom," which ended in 1964, was followed by a period of slow growth that did not pick up again until the late 1980s and early 1990s. In 1988, 3.9 million babies were born—the highest number since 1964. Termed the "baby boomlet," these babies are the children of the "baby boomers." A distinct trend has been the rise in the number of women between the ages of 30 and 40 who have given birth for the first time. One-third of the nation's births are now experienced by women over 30. A documented trend is a decrease in teen pregnancies. Since 1990, the teen birthrate in the United States has dropped almost 10 percent. In families, the birth of a baby brings about many changes in time management and consumption patterns. Parents suddenly find themselves the prime targets of advertisers offering a wide array of baby products. Their grocery carts are filled with products they never purchased before: diapers, infant formula, baby food, toys, and baby shampoo. The home environment also changes as baby care equipment is added: strollers, cribs, swings, high chairs, and playpens.

In response to demographic changes, the marketplace transforms as it tries to keep up with consumer demand. Note the impact on consumption that the baby boom generation has had in the past and will have in the future (Figure 8.2). As noted earlier, the baby boomers have reached middle age—some are already well into it—and are earning income, paying taxes, traveling, and owning material goods. The number of married couples without children is rising due to empty-nest baby boom households and delayed childbearing by younger couples.

At the other end of the life cycle, about two million people die each year in the United States. Overall, the death rate has been decreasing for several reasons:

- ◆ Declining rates of heart disease
- ◆ Increases in life expectancy
- ◆ Better nutrition and fitness and less smoking
- ◆ Improvements in preventive health care
- ◆ Improvements in infant mortality rates

Worldwide, the infant mortality rate in developing countries dropped by more than 50 percent from 1900 to 1996 (Vo, 1998). Between 1970 and 1980, the average American's life expectancy went up three years (Wilkie, 1986). Another rise in average life expectancy happened between 1980 and 2000. In the 1990s, life expectancy was about 71.5 years for men and 78.5 years for women. According to the Census Bureau, the chances of living to 100 are growing. Since 1990, the number of Americans reaching that age has nearly doubled to 70,000. Eighty percent are women. Iowa has the highest percentage of centenarians ("Chances," 1999).

Immigration

Beginning in 2019, the net increase in the U.S. population from immigration is expected to be higher than the increase from natural births. Thus, the nation's ethnic and racial makeup will continue to shift. During the 1980s,

© Bettmann/CORBIS

Beginning in 1892, over 12 million immigrants, mostly from Europe, came through Ellis Island in New York City's harbor.

about 570,000 legal immigrants and 200,000 illegal immigrants entered the United States each year. In the 1990s, one in five new Americans joined the nation through naturalization (gaining U.S. citizenship). "Asians are more likely than immigrants from other regions to become U.S. citizens, as are better educated people and those who have lived here longer" (Mogelonsky, 1997, p. 45). In 1995, the United States gained 4 million new citizens from birth and 1.1 million through naturalization.

Population Age and Composition

The United States is growing older. Currently, the nation's population is the oldest it has ever been. *The median age is 36.5 in the year 2000*, up from approximately 32.3 years in 1990. After a slow decline from 27 million in 1988 to 24 million in 1995 and 1996, the college-age population (ages 18 to 24) began a steady rise, which will continue. Overall, there are more females than males, but the ratio varies by age groups. In the younger years, there are more males than females. For example, between 1994 and 2000 there were more males than females in their 20s. But, among those over age 75, women outnumber men by nearly two to one.

Race/Ethnicity

Minority groups are the fastest-growing segment of the U.S. population. On average, minority populations are younger than other Americans and therefore have higher birthrates, and immigration is also increasing their numbers. The six race categories on the 2000 census were white (77.1 percent of the

FIGURE 8.2

The Baby Boom Tidal Wave Moves through Life

Source: Taeuber, C. (1979, June). "A changing America," *American Demographics*, pp. 9–15. Reprinted with permission.

Period	Peak year	Time span	
Births Diapers and toys	1957	1946–1964	
Grade school Classrooms and clothes	1963[a]	1952–1970[b]	
Teenagers High schools, fast foods, soft drinks	1970	1959–1977	
Young adults Colleges, military, work, and leisure	1975	1964–1982	
Householders Careers, families, homes, furnishings	1987	1976–1994	
Middle-agers Incomes, taxes, travel, possessions	2007	1996–2014	
Senior citizens Retirement, leisure, health, benefits	2022	2011–2029	

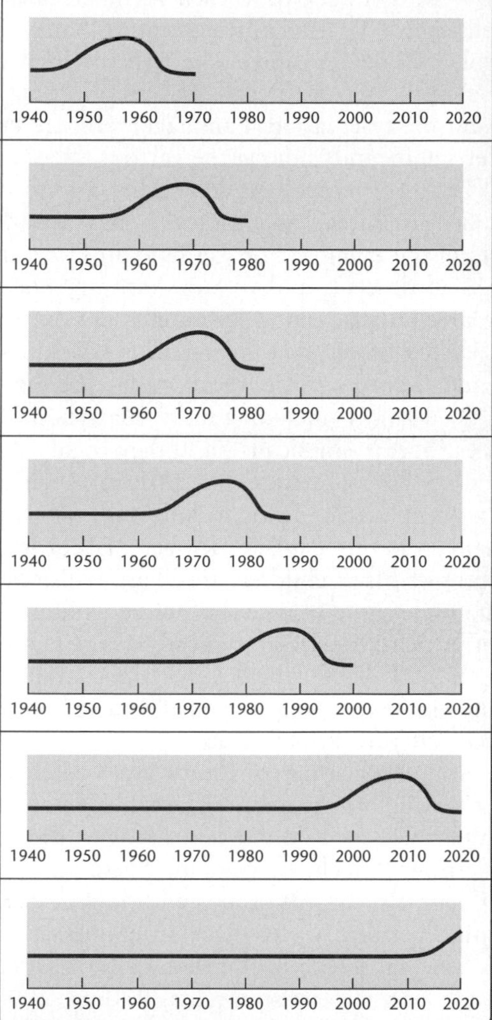

[a] "Peak year" represents the year at which the highest number of persons entered each stage; 1963 reflects the year with the highest number of first graders.
[b] "Time span" represents the years during which all baby boomers entered the stage; the first baby boomer entered grade school in 1952; the last baby boomers entered in 1970.

total population reported as white either alone or in combination with one or more races); Latino/Hispanic (12 percent); black or African American (12.9 percent); American Indians and Alaskan natives; Asians, Native Hawaiian and other Pacific Islanders, and some other race. People picking more than one category drives the percentages over 100 percent, which may seem confusing, but the point is to notice the general trends. The breakdown of the Latino/Hispanic category is 66.1 percent of Mexican origin, 14.5 percent Central and South American, 9 percent Puerto Rican, 4 percent Cuban, and 6.4 percent other Hispanic origins. So minority populations include many subgroups. As another example, there are 505 federally recognized Indian tribes in the United States, including 197 Alaska native village groups. Native Americans number 2.5 million to 4.1 million if you include multiracials—

more than 4 in 10 Native Americans consider themselves multiracial. Native Americans are the nation's second wealthiest minority after Asian Americans. In one Midwestern tribe each member earned about $600,000 in one year (Wellner, 2003). About 17 percent of Native American firms are in the service sector, including casinos. The bulk of their income comes from other businesses such as construction and retail. More than 6 in 10 Native Americans live off the reservation. Language, religion, culture, and economic conditions differ significantly among the various tribes and subgroups.

The term *minority* is sometimes a misnomer because a group defined by the Census Bureau as a minority may actually be a majority group in some parts of the country. For example, in Honolulu, the majority of residents are of Asian descent; and in San Antonio, Texas, the residents are 52 percent Hispanic/Latino. Hispanics/Latinos are the fastest-growing minority group in the United States. The majority of Hispanics live in Arizona, New Mexico, Florida, Texas, and California. They are most likely to think of family as an extended family (including more relatives than the nuclear/close family of typical European Americans), and they highly value family (Radina, 2003).

One-third of blacks or African Americans live in one of five states: Georgia, Florida, Texas, California, or New York. The average African American family has 3.5 members. According to a Census Bureau report, 57 percent of black children are living with one parent who has never married compared with 21 percent of white children and 32 percent of Hispanic children. African Americans typically define family as extended family and kinship groups and place a high value on community (Radina, 2003). Nonrelated friends may very well be considered members of the family. Mutual support and loyalty are strong values.

Asian Americans constitute 3 to 4 percent of the nation's population. They are overwhelmingly urban. The Census Bureau's category of Asian and Pacific Islanders covers 17 countries. Most of the Asians entering the United States come from Indochina: Vietnam, Laos, and Kampuchea (formerly Cambodia). There are also sizable groups with Japanese, Korean, Chinese, Taiwanese, and Filipino heritage. They place an emphasis on parent-child relationships and practice filial piety, which means respect for elders and having a moral duty to obey, honor, and assist parents (Radina, 2003). Of the three largest minority groups, Asian Americans are the most highly educated. Thirty-four percent of Asian Americans have college degrees compared to 20 percent for the overall American population, 11 percent for African Americans, and 8.6 percent for Hispanics. Full-time college participation rates among young adults is rising for all groups, especially blacks (Crispell, 1997).

Households and Families

The number of households is increasing in the United States, but the number of persons per household is decreasing. Household change parallels population change. Household growth in the 1990s was fastest in Nevada, especially for 25- to 34-year-olds. Four other fast-growing states also saw gains in householders aged 25 to 35: Arizona, Georgia, Utah, and Delaware. Nearly three in five households have no children, and this trend toward smaller families is expected to continue. One reason for the decline in household size is lower fertility. Another reason is the increase in the number of elderly persons. Male-headed households are the fastest-growing type of household.

Single-parent households represent 25 percent of all family households. Nonfamily households, consisting of two or more unrelated persons living together, are also on the rise.

Marital Status

Young people are waiting longer to get married, and the marriage rate itself is decreasing. According to the Census Bureau, men and women are delaying marriage, with the median age of first marriages rising. Historically, 90 percent of Americans married at some time in their lives, but that rate is declining. The divorce rate is also declining after having reached a peak in 1984. The highest divorce rate is for couples in their twenties, and divorced people are waiting longer to remarry. At a second marriage, the median age of brides is 32 and the median age of grooms is 34.

THE NATURE OF CHANGE

In *Redefining Diversity,* Roosevelt Thomas, Jr., provides an interesting perspective on change within American society. He says that, increasingly, we see America's strength in its diversity—a mixture of colors and creeds bringing their different backgrounds to a common endeavor. Yet, he says, diversity is not confined to race and gender; rather, it applies to intangibles such as ideas, outlooks, and procedures.

Change means to cause to be different, to alter, or to transform. A change can be categorized into two general types, internal and external. **Internal change** originates within the family. Births, marriages, divorces, and deaths are all examples of internal changes. In contrast, **external change** is fostered by society or the outer environment. Tornadoes and recessions are examples of external changes. An individual or a family may experience internal and external changes at the same time.

The ability to cope with change is called **adaptability.** Adaptability is an example of a human resource that everyone has, but in different quantities. People's temperaments and usual ways of reacting (rapid versus slow) to new situations affect their response to change. The actual circumstances, such as whether an event is expected or unexpected, will also influence the response. Because of these personality, behavioral, and situational factors, each person approaches change differently. Consider the following quotation by Winston Churchill, prime minister of England during the Second World War: "Never, never, never give up."

Most changes occur gradually over a period of time. This transition period can be helpful because it allows individuals to take stock of the situation and consider possible alternatives. Effective managers take advantage of transition time to think through a situation and make plans to deal with it. Changing one's job or residence involves transition time. This is discussed in the next section, which explores moving as an example of change.

SUGGESTED ACTIVITY

Give one example of a time when you or someone you know didn't give up. What were the circumstances and the outcome?

Mobility

Nearly all individuals and families have to cope with the problems and decisions associated with moving. The technical term for changing residences is

mobility. Statistics on mobility trends are surprising. According to a survey conducted by the U.S. Census Bureau, the typical householder moves every five or six years. The average distance moved is six miles, and renters move more than homeowners.

Mobility has several major effects on individual and family behavior. First, it affects finances. When people move, they spend money on household furnishings, moving services, and utility deposits. They may use the services of realtors and mortgage companies. Second, moving is usually a stressor. Many household services must be changed and rescheduled when relocating—telephone, electric, water, and mail service, to name just a few. Children may have to change schools. Parents may change jobs. Third, moving affects individual or family morale. Moves may be disruptive or present opportunities. They may mark the end of valued relationships or signify a fresh beginning or both.

The general trend in the 20th century was the movement from rural areas to suburbs and cities. The largest cities in the United States are New York City and Los Angeles, followed by Chicago.

Certain states have more mobile populations than others. Nevada has the fewest natives, followed by Florida. At the other end of the spectrum is Pennsylvania, where 80 percent of residents were born in the state.

Managing Change

Managing change is inherently messy:

> It is always complicated. It invariably involves a massive array of sharply conflicting demands. Despite the best-laid plans, things never happen in exactly the right order— and in fact, few things rarely turn out exactly right the first time around. . . . Change means new patterns of power, influence, and control . . . and that's why it's so hard. Change is far too important, pervasive, and complicated a phenomenon to be taken for granted. Every manager may be aware of it; that doesn't mean he or she knows how to handle it. (Nadler, 1998, pp. 3, 5, 11)

Each family and each organization is a complex social system. There are several components (adopted from Nadler, 1998), that need coordinating, including

- ◆ The work or the task
- ◆ The people
- ◆ The formal organization—the structure, the processes, the systems, and the identity (i.e., the Clark family or the Tech Systems Company)
- ◆ The informal organization—the collective values, attitudes, beliefs, communication and lines of influence, and accepted standards of behavior

The challenge is to sustain momentum, to move forward. Sustaining any profound change process requires a fundamental shift in thinking. Participants need to understand the nature of growth processes (forces that aid efforts) and how to catalyze them. But, they also need to understand the forces and challenges that impede progress and to develop workable strategies for dealing with these challenges (Senge, 1999, p. 10). In an article in *Marriage and Family Review,* Kathryn Rettig observed

> Management is a thoughtful adaptation to the opportunities and demands of life. It involves problem-solving and decision-making, as well as carrying out actions

to implement decisions. The consciousness of the deliberations that occur prior to decisions about how to use resources and the controlled implementation of decisions in order to reach valued-goals will distinguish management from other adaptive responses. The need for conscious problem-solving and decision-making is created because of changes that are wanted by individuals and families (proactive management) or because internal and/or environmental changes occur that require different responses (reactive management). (1993, p. 191)

The management problems and decisions inherent in change must be addressed because households and families are living in an increasingly complex web of internal and external changes. For example, many functions that were once the domain of households and families, such as child rearing and meal preparation, are now purchased to some degree outside the home—from child-care centers, restaurants, and grocery stores. How many people today bake bread from scratch? A hundred years ago, the average household would have devoted many hours a week to this activity.

Before the 1950s, the study of management emphasized internal household processes. Today, management encompasses the interaction of the inside and outside activities and the lives of individuals and families within the greater environment. For example, a working mother may purchase a precooked dinner at the store and add a salad or a dessert at home. Thus, she is combining home-prepared with store-prepared food—an increasingly common method of meal preparation. Although this combined effort might seem to imply less need for resource management skills, in actuality these skills are more necessary than ever because coordinating inside and outside activities takes time, effort, and planning. As more people, services, and environments become involved and time becomes tighter, more complex problem solving and decision implementation are necessary.

MEETING INDIVIDUAL, FAMILY, AND SOCIETAL NEEDS

Along with all the external changes that are occurring, the family itself has become a more diverse institution. Collectively, single-person households, single-parent families, and two-income families outnumber traditional one-income families with both parents sharing a residence. Even though the family is taking on diverse forms, it still remains an important stabilizing force in the rapidly changing, often chaotic outside world. The word *family* implies a safe harbor, a place to come home to, and people who care.

The remainder of this chapter explores the special management needs of certain populations. This information is based on aggregate data, so specific individuals and families may not fit the generalizations given.

Two-Income Families

Perhaps no phenomenon has had a greater effect on the fabric of American society than the increasing number of women in the labor force. The influx of women into the workplace has altered the way families live, the products they buy, and the way they spend their time. In 1990, there were approximately 33 million **dual-income or dual-earner** households, where both spouses had income-producing jobs, up from 26 million in 1980 (Spain & Nock, 1984). That number continues to rise, although many women are choosing to be stay-at-home moms for part of their lives. As may be expected, two-income households on average have more money than single-income households; but a recent book, *The Two-Income Trap,* says that the money is not stretching as far as it should and that many two-income families are having a hard time. It begins:

> This book is dedicated to all parents who wake up with hearts thudding over the possibility that buying school shoes and Girl Scout uniforms will mean that there won't be enough left over to pay the mortgage. These people are our neighbors, our brothers and sisters, our friends and coworkers. They travel anonymously among us, but we know them. They went to college, had kids, bought a home, played by the rules—and lost. It is time to rewrite the rules so that these families are winners again. (Warren & Tyagi, 2003, preface)

What has happened over the last few decades is that many two-income families need both incomes to maintain a minimum standard of living. Warren and Tyagi, who are a mother-and-daughter team of writers, question how this came about: How have we come to the point where two incomes are needed to provide what one income used to? This is a complicated question because since the 1970s the typical American family spends less on clothes and major appliances and at the grocery store (relative to inflation) but more on restaurant meals, health care, housing, and college expenses. For example, "the average family of four today spends 21 percent less (inflation adjusted) on clothing than a similar family did in the early 1970s" (Warren & Tyagi, 2003, p. 17). The authors say that mom has to work to help pay for the housing that puts the family in a good school zone—that the pursuit of safety and education have led to increased debt load of the average middle class family. A study in Fresno, California, revealed that the single most important determinant of neighborhood prices was school quality (Warren & Tyagi, 2003).

The term *dual income* needs to be distinguished from *dual career.* In **dual-career** families, not only do both spouses work outside the home, but in addition both have made a long-term commitment to a planned series of jobs leading toward an ultimate career goal. Not everyone who is working thinks of himself or herself as a career person.

Dual-earner families usually report that they are happy and satisfied (Runyon & Stewart, 1987). Family resources, such as spousal or partner support and sensitivity, play a key role in the satisfaction levels of dual-earner families (Gilbert, 1993). Tahira Hira (1987) found that satisfied dual-earner families (versus dissatisfied dual-earner families) have more money in their savings accounts, save larger proportions of their annual income, and have smaller monthly debt payments. Such families are also less likely to have an auto loan or outstanding balances on their credit cards. Having two incomes also reduces the fear of unemployment, since the family will have one income to fall back on in case of a recession or company downsizing.

Dual-earner families are also better educated, more mobile, better spenders, and more likely to own their own home than single-earner families (Rubin & Riney, 1994). The lifestyle is not perfect, however. Dual-earner families also report that they have less leisure time and less time for children and friends. Their pace of life is quicker. Jobs requiring extensive travel and numerous transfers increase stress for dual-income families, especially those with children. Spouses may enter into long-distance commuting relations, live halfway between two cities, or relocate for short periods of time to take advantage of a career opportunity (Gilbert, 1993). Dual-earner couples try to adjust their work or vacation schedules to maximize their time together.

Two-income couples may face various management problems, including difficulty setting priorities and saying "no," budgeting, and making joint financial decisions. Dividing household tasks equitably so that everyone is content may also be a problem. Open communication and dealing with changes before events become overwhelming will help dual-income families keep ahead of their workloads.

The overriding management problem that dual-income families face is how to handle both their jobs and family responsibilities. Lucia Gilbert advises young adults who want to marry and work to plan ahead, which "means thinking about expectations for yourself and a future spouse and communicating these early on in serious relationships" (1993, p. 75). The next three chapters on managing time, work and family, and stress and fatigue will provide additional insight into the management problems of dual-earner families.

Caregiving and Children

Caregivers are devoted to improving the quality of life for another. They may be providing assistance to the disabled, children, or elders. The help can be on a daily basis or sporadic, temporary, or long-range. This section addresses child care as a broad issue with numerous ramifications for families and for society in general. Providing financial support for children is a form of child care. So is physical and emotional care. As both parents increasingly are working outside the home, child care is becoming a more and more critical issue for many families.

Families manage child care in several ways: One parent may stay home, or neighbors, relatives, and friends may provide care. Family day-care homes and child-care centers in the community or at the parents' work sites are other options. If children are school age, parents may enroll them in before-school and after-school programs and summer camp. Parents often combine several of these methods. A Yale University study found that many parents prefer home-based care for infants and toddlers and child-care centers for older children (Cheskis-Gold, 1988).

Young families with children often have more management problems than other types of families. For example, studies show repeatedly that families with young children have the most time management problems because young children require so many hours of physical and nurturant care. These problems may be exacerbated in young families where parents may be completing their own education or launching their careers at the same time that they are having children. Employers, realizing that working parents need support, offer a wide range of child-care options, including resource-and-referral services and on-site child care.

In the 1990s, women aged 30 and older accounted for 33 percent of the total births. Older mothers tend to be highly educated, to be members of high-income families, and to have professional occupations (Langer, 1985). Their careers are well under way before they have their first child. Furthermore, in such families many financial arrangements and assignments of household tasks have been settled before children come along. When the children arrive, the division of labor will have to be renegotiated, but at least initial patterns have been established.

One controversial aspect of child care and human capital development is the small amount of time American children spend in school compared to children in other countries such as Japan and South Korea. The issue is controversial because some parents and educators believe our schools should continue to be closed in the summer, a tradition that originally was intended to allow children time off to help on the family farm. Less than 2 percent of American families live on farms now, however, and educators and parents think it is time for a change. The relatively low number of days spent in school may have implications for societal well-being if U.S. children are receiving less formal education than children in other industrialized nations. U.S. school districts are experimenting with longer school days and fewer vacation days or split schedules. From the perspective of time management and family relations, the fact that children's school days and vacations often do not coincide with parents' work schedules makes it difficult for families to spend time together or to offer secure home-based child care. Any changes that are made in the timing and length of children's school days should focus first on what is best for the children and their education given today's global society and future workforce demands.

The trend reported earlier in the book of more women of young children choosing to be stay-at-home moms is an indicator of a reconsideration of the amount of parent-child interaction. Parents, whether employed or not, are interested not only in the quantity of time they spend with their children, but also in the quality of time they have with them. Enjoying each stage of development, being present for school and sport/music activities, and encouraging children toward independent and fulfilling lives are common parental goals. Former First Lady Barbara Bush spoke at the Wellesley College commencement in 1990 and told the graduates:

> For several years, you've had impressed upon you the importance to your career of dedication and hard work. This is true, but as important as your obligations as a doctor, lawyer or business leader will be, you are a human being first and those human connections—with spouses, with children, with friends—are the most important investments you will ever make. At the end of your life, you will never regret not having passed one more test, not winning one more verdict or not closing one more deal. You will regret time not spent with a husband, a friend, a child or a parent. . . . Fathers and mothers, if you have children . . . they must come first. You must read to your children, you must hug your children, you must love your children. Your success as a family . . . our success as a society . . . depends not on what happens at the White House, but on what happens inside your house.

Although parenting and family life are rewarding, no matter how hard parents try they often experience problems with children, particularly during the teen years. Drugs, alcohol, child neglect, and abuse are examples of adolescent and family problems.

The roots of abusive parental behavior across all periods of childhood can be traced to five broad areas (Azar & Siegal, 1990):

1. Maladaptive interpretive processes, including unrealistic expectations of children, poor problem solving, and negative interpretations of child behavior
2. Poor parenting strategies
3. Poor impulse control
4. Poor stress coping
5. Poor social skills

SUGGESTED ACTIVITY

Discuss in class what would be the optimum school schedule considering children's education needs and parental desires. As part of the discussion, include comments and observations about the students' own previous school experiences—were they part of a system with different hours, vacation scheduling, and so on than the norm? What were the pros and the cons? Also, discuss the trend toward moving high school to three years in accelerated programs versus the more traditional four. Pros and cons?

Child abuse is not limited to young children. Researchers estimate that 22 to 47 percent of abuse cases involve abused adolescents (Pagelow, 1989).

Although parental stress is associated with child abuse, it is important to note that most parents do not abuse their children even when experiencing stress (Azar & Siegal, 1990). Stress can lead to other problems, however. For example, infant irritability, crying, and colic have been associated with parental feelings of depression, helplessness, anger, and exhaustion, as well as with marital tension (Wilkie & Ames, 1986).

Developing better management skills can help parents deal with stress. Well-developed management skills bring a sense of mastery and a feeling of being in control. A parent who has developed these skills will find it easier to form strategies, solve problems, and adjust to change.

An interesting trend related to child care is the growing number of grown children who are staying home with their parents or moving back home after college. Even 30-year-olds are moving back home after a divorce or when they are between jobs. Active parenting starts at birth, but it is becoming less clear when active parenting ends. More young adults are living with their parents now than at any time since the Great Depression of the 1930s (Riche, 1990).

Through an analysis of the Census Bureau's Survey of Income and Program Participation, demographers found that most people aged 20 or 21 remain in their parents' home, while most people aged 22 to 24 have left. Women leave home earlier than men (Riche, 1990). Demographers also found that many young adults move in and out of their parents' homes and that men are more likely to return after age 25. The main reasons children return home are economic difficulties, marital failure, prolonged education, and job market insecurity. According to Riche (1990), the return of adult children to their parents' homes is called **boomeranging;** it is regarded as a rational response to changes in the society and economy.

Caregiving and the Elderly

Although the need for child care has been widely publicized, the need for elder care is less well known. The number of available caregivers is dwindling because many adult women are in the workforce and the number of children in families has decreased. *Three out of four caregivers to the disabled elderly (excluding husbands and wives) are daughters, daughters-in-law, or other female relatives and friends (such as nieces or granddaughters)"* (Warren & Tyagi, 2003, p. 62). One in four U.S. households is involved in the daily care of an elderly parent. This may involve physical care due to a chronic illness or frailty or simply e-mail messages to check up on things. As many as 40 percent of Americans who care for their parents also have dependent children. Middle-aged Americans, who care for both their children and their elderly parents, are called the "sandwich generation."

The caregiver role can bring with it a mixture of joy, guilt, service demands, and emotional and financial burdens. The difficulty of the role depends on many factors: the health of the elderly dependent person, the personalities of the elderly person and caregiver, their mutual resources, and the social support they receive from relatives and community groups. Caregiving can take place gradually over several years and require only a few phone calls or visits, or it can be a 20-year daily commitment to the physical and emotional care of another. From a management viewpoint, the need for caregiving may develop

FIGURE 8.3
Majority of Caregivers to the Elderly Are Middle-Aged Women

Source: National Center for Health Services Research (1989).

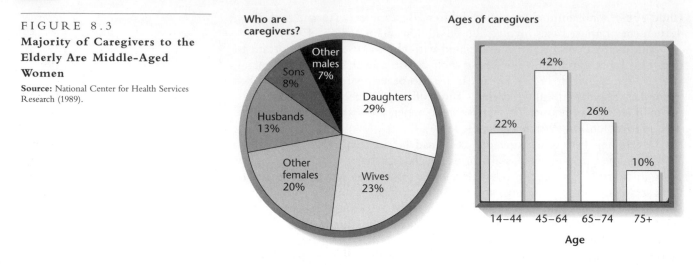

Who are caregivers?

Ages of caregivers

slowly, allowing a family to adjust and plan for it, or it can arise from a sudden crisis that completely depletes the family's emotional and financial reserves. A midnight phone call from 1,000 miles away about a stroke or an accident is a crisis that requires an immediate response.

From a management perspective, caregiving for dependent elderly can precipitate a number of resource allocation problems. Time, energy, and money may all be strained in caregiving situations. Here is an example of a morning schedule for Bruce Shaw, age 60, who cares full-time for his father, Roger, who is 89.

6 A.M. to 8 A.M.
water/juice
salutations/small talk
check physical signs
physical therapy, twice weekly
rotation in bed

9 A.M. to 11 A.M.
water/juice
snack, banana
check catheter and output
check vital signs
breathing treatment
pills
talk
prepare house for the day

Roger was left paralyzed after receiving the swine-flu vaccine 27 years ago. Eight years ago, he lost his sight to glaucoma and lives with Bruce and his wife, Judy. Bruce quit his job as a business consultant, and their home has become a public setting with nurses and health aides passing in and out. Bruce says everybody in the family has had hard days, but caring for his father, he says, "has brought all of us closer together. We share this responsibility" (Ruffenbach, 2003, p. D4).

Caregivers have to maintain a sense of humor and be sensitive to the elderly person's desire for independence and dignity. Compounding these needs is the difficulty elderly parents have at letting a child take charge. The

TABLE 8.1
Ways to Help Caregivers

Caregivers can easily experience burnout and stress. Often, they have their own physical conditions or disabilities that are neglected when taking care of another person's greater needs. Caregivers of older loved ones can feel that family and community members may take for granted their daily responsibilities. Here are some management ideas for how others can help caregivers feel supported.

1. Give the gift of connecting with other caregivers. Many organizations, hospitals, and churches provide a trained leader to facilitate group discussions. Phone calls and informal discussions can help too. Toll-free elder hotlines provide information about caregiver support.

2. Give the gift of useful information. Learning about Alzheimer's disease, strokes, etc., and what can be expected is enormously helpful. Information about home care agencies, medical equipment suppliers, adult day services, insurance, and government programs can help. AARP's Tax-Aide program (a free service) assists senior citizens with their IRS returns. Over 31,000 volunteer counselors helped 1.4 million people in 2002. The scope of help is limited to typical elder concerns, issues of retirees, and lower-income people. Complex returns will require paid professionals.

3. Give the gift of filling in: give the caregiver time off to shop, run errands, or do other forms of self-care. Breaks re-energize and provide perspective.

4. Install equipment in the home that helps with the care, such as special lights for an elder with macular degeneration (a vision problem), and also with communication such as Internet access and cell phones. This is the kind of thing that grown grandchildren can help with. When all generations are involved benefits accrue.

adult child may also feel awkward managing her or his parents' affairs and avoid this task until the health or safety of the parent requires it. See Table 8.1 for ideas on how to help caregivers.

Understanding the aging process and the needs of the elderly can help caregivers perform their role more effectively. The aging process has three aspects: physical or biological, social, and psychological. To date, most gerontological research (**gerontology** is the scientific study of the aging process) has focused on the physical aspects, but the others are important as well. Aging involves both growth and decline (Cavanaugh, 1990). Most elderly people are self-reliant and require little or no caregiving. Many maintain active, independent lives well into their nineties. Health, wealth, and attitude have a lot to do with the degree of independence they can maintain. The idea that elderly people are often depressed is a myth; in fact, evidence suggests that depression decreases in old age (Cavanaugh, 1990). Many more myths about aging will be exposed as scientists learn more about the aging process. Even what constitutes old age is being questioned as researchers learn more about the elderly. Commonly, old age is defined as beginning at age 65, but this is an arbitrary boundary because chronological age is a poor indicator of a person's social, economic, physical, or mental condition.

Adjusting to Retirement

One of the most important life changes people make is adjusting to retirement. Regardless of how much workers plan and anticipate this change in role, it can still be difficult because jobs give people a routine, companionship, and a sense of accomplishment. Retired people can feel aimless and useless. Without roles, people feel a sense of loss and a lack of direction, and the loss of work routine can be disconcerting. Declining health exacerbates the problem. To counteract this feeling of loss and provide extra income, many "retirees" take on part-time or seasonal work. If they are self-employed, they may never retire.

In many companies, human resource departments assist older employees in the transition period to retirement and help middle-aged workers find home health care for their aged parents. According to an article in *American Demographics,*

> Home health care is an important concern of middle-aged workers. Most providers help elderly relatives preserve their independence. Helpers are usually women, but men are likely to shop and pay the bills. Out-of-pocket spending accounts for one-third of this $21 billion industry, and caregivers also face a time crunch. As the population ages, employers will offer eldercare benefits to attract and keep good workers. (Braus, 1994, p. 38)

In addition, some companies offer retirement planning programs; others allow employees to work part-time to ease into retirement. Many retirees choose to do volunteer work. Others travel or go back to school to finish degrees or to take continuing education courses. As with all age groups, older adults have varying lifestyles and, therefore, differing management needs. Too little time may be as much a problem as too much time. Other resources that may be affected in the later years include the emotional, health, human energy, and financial resources of both caregivers and elder dependents. Money is a particular problem for many older persons because income may not keep pace with inflation and increases in health care costs. The elderly most likely to be poor are those who rely solely on Social Security for their incomes. About 26 percent of the elderly population fall into this category, and the majority are women (United Way Strategic Institute, 1989).

Those contemplating early retirement should

- ◆ Check on their insurance, pensions and other employer-sponsored retirement plans.
- ◆ Contact Social Security.
- ◆ Calculate the effects of inflation. If you figure on 3 percent a year, $50,000 today to live on will be worth only $27,189 in 20 years, and it is unlikely that expenses will be cut in half in that time.
- ◆ Analyze the condition of your house and car; does anything need fixing or replacing?
- ◆ Pay off debt, especially the most expensive such as credit cards and car loans.
- ◆ Have an emergency fund; emergencies don't stop at retirement
- ◆ Consider lifestyle and interests (as mentioned earlier). Most opt for part-time work in a whole new field to maintain contacts and collect extra spending money.

Increasingly, aging is considered within the context of total well-being, which requires a careful balance between emotional, spiritual, and physical health. This balance becomes more precarious as we age. Besides reexamining changing perceptions of aging, people need to enhance their mental and physical vitality by focusing on active strategies that can extend life and improve the quality of life. These management strategies (adapted from *Healthy Living*, 1999) may include

- Thinking over what is essential and what is controllable
- Identifying strategies to help prevent health problems or poor quality of life
- Applying a proactive approach to diet, attitude, and activity levels
- Using practical techniques to incorporate improved lifestyle changes in everyday life

In addition to valuing independence, older adults value comfort, security, convenience, and a sense of purpose. They want to eliminate problems, receive personal service, and feel good about themselves. Airline and car advertisers appealing to the elder market may emphasize comfort over speed and appearance. As more of our population falls into the elderly category, businesses and service providers will have to adjust their approaches to better meet the needs of older adults.

The Homeless

About 18 million Americans are homeless. A home is the single most expensive purchase for most families—more than food, more than cars, more than clothes, more than child care—so when people are homeless, it is a symbol of their not being able to support themselves in the most *visible* way through renting or buying housing or finding someone to live with. Although media coverage might imply that homelessness is a new societal problem, it is not. There have been homeless people in the United States since colonial times. What is new is that they are more numerous than ever before and more visible (Baum & Burnes, 1993). It is difficult to put an exact figure on the number of homeless people because of the mobility of this population and the fact that often it is a temporary state. *The majority of the homeless are single males, although the number of homeless women and children is growing* (United Way Strategic Institute, 1989). Families constitute an estimated 23 to 30 percent of the homeless population (Martin, 1991; Burt & Cohen, 1989). Chronic homelessness is linked to poverty. However, it is important to distinguish between the homeless and the poor. According to Baum and Burnes (1993),

> Homelessness is more than being poor and without a home; homelessness is a condition of disengagement from ordinary society—from family, friends, neighborhood, church, community. Perhaps most importantly, it is a loss of self. A homeless man we know told us, "The first time, I felt like this is not me. I felt less than a man." Homelessness means being disconnected from all of the support systems that usually provide help in times of crisis; it means being without structure; it means being alone. (p. 23)

The rise in the number of homeless people is not limited to the United States—it is a worldwide problem. In 1999, thousands of people were displaced from their homes in Kosovo. Thus, homelessness can affect individuals or families or, on a wider scale, nations.

Not all homeless people are single; here is a homeless family on the street.

Tony Freeman/PhotoEdit—All rights reserved

One study of the educational plight of homeless children in England found that changing schools constantly threatened educational stability, hindered educational progress, caused emotional insecurity, and promoted educational disadvantage (Lines, 1992). The study recommended that liaisons be formed between schools and homeless families so that the transition to each new setting is easier.

The growing rate of poverty, the declining supply of low-income housing, and a rise in drug addiction and alcoholism have all contributed to the rise in homelessness (Rubin, Wright, & DeVine, 1992). An estimated 65 to 85 percent of all homeless adults in the United States suffer from one or more of the disabling conditions of alcoholism, drug addiction, and mental illness, complicated by serious medical problems (Baum & Burnes, 1993). Other factors affecting the rise in the number of homeless in the United States include cutbacks in public housing, mental health, and social programs. Families become homeless for numerous reasons, including fire, eviction because of failure to pay rent, eviction because of unfit housing, cuts in assistance programs, scarcity of low-income housing, unemployment, and internal strife in countries. Homelessness can be devastating for children who are suffering a loss of education and security. Naturally, the length of time spent in a homeless condition will affect the severity of these effects. Children in homeless families are less likely to have successful peer interactions, a factor that may also lead to poorer attitudes toward school (Winborne & Murray, 1992). The response to the growing number of homeless has been sporadic. Recommended measures that could aid the homeless include day care for children, setting goals and providing support with job training, low- or no-cost mental health and medical clinics, public policy changes, transitional housing for those leaving shelters, better coordination of social services, and innovative programs to provide low-income housing. The 1992 report of the Federal Task Force on Homelessness and Severe Mental Illness suggested the following services: needs assessment, diagnosis and treatment planning, counseling and supportive therapy, hospitalization and medication management, 24-hour crisis response services, habilitation and social skills training, and improved hospital discharge procedures. As has been pointed out, the homeless problem cannot be separated from other problems, including poverty, unemployment, and mental illness. Each of these problems needs to be tackled if the number of homeless is to be reduced.

A study reported in the *American Journal of Psychiatry* found that high levels of mental distress are common to all homeless persons and suggests that the focus of treatment should be on empowerment, consumerism, entitlement, community-level interventions, and closer alliances with other advocates for the homeless (Cohen & Thompson, 1992). According to another study, the major cause of family homelessness is the relative inability of heads of homeless families to function independently (Ellickson, 1990).

Efforts are being made to help homeless families. For example, in the United States, the Stewart B. McKinney Homeless Assistance Act guarantees homeless children the right of access to an education (Eddowes & Hranitz, 1989). Besides legislation, communities, hospitals, and substance abuse treatment centers are working together to find successful ways to help the homeless. Since not all homeless persons have the same problems, an effort is being made to tailor programs and alternatives to the individual and the family.

Individuals with Disabilities

More than 43 million Americans have some type of disability (Emanoil, 1999). Slightly less than half of these have a severe impairment. A **disability** is a long-term or chronic condition medically defined as a physiological, anatomical, mental, or emotional impairment resulting from disease or illness, inherited or congenital defect, trauma, or other insult (including environmental) to mind or body (Wright, 1980). Often, the word *disability* is used as a synonym for *handicap*, but the terms are different. A **handicap** is a disadvantage, interference, or barrier to performance, opportunity, or fulfillment in any desired role in life (e.g., social, educational, vocational, familial), imposed upon the individual by limitation in function or by other problems associated with disability and/or personal characteristics in the context of the individual's environment or role (Wright, 1980). Thus, a handicap can occur as a result of disability, but a disability does not always necessitate a handicap. For example, a deaf person has a hearing disability, but she or he is not handicapped when it comes to sewing because deafness does not affect one's ability to sew. It is important to understand that disabled individuals may have certain limitations, but they can function wholly and well in many ways.

Individuals with disabilities prefer to be recognized as a person first and only secondly as a person with a partially disabling condition. Community prejudice and resistance may reduce opportunities for disabled persons. People with disabilities have been fighting for years to overcome prejudice so that they can have equal access to jobs, schools, and services.

An important aspect of home management is the ability to perform routine tasks. Persons with disabilities may face problems associated with the home, including the loss of mobility, decreased strength, decreased reach, coordination impairment, one-handed use, lack of hand muscles, and visual impairment (Pickett, Arnold, & Ketterer, 1990). The hindrance or negative effect in the performance of household tasks or activities is referred to as a **functional limitation.** Wright (1980) offers five examples of functional limitations that may affect task performance:

1. Activity restrictions due to the danger of unexpected unconsciousness

2. Inability to follow rapid or frequent changes in instruction due to slow learning

3. Restrictions in mobility due to neuromuscular impairment

4. Difficulty in interpersonal relationships associated with peculiar behavior

5. Necessity of avoiding respiratory infection or dusty conditions due to hypersensitivity reactions

As this list suggests, there is a wide range of disabilities. A disability in a family raises several critical questions. Is the disability temporary, such as a broken arm, or long term? Are family resources adequate to handle the disability? For example, is there enough insurance to cover medical and rehabilitation costs? After an assessment has been made of the severity of the disability and the level of support and resources, a management plan needs to be formulated. In the case of permanent handicapping conditions, critical changes in the family support system and the home environment may need to be made. Ramps, lower sinks, Braille markings on appliances, easier access to bathrooms and kitchens, and levers instead of doorknobs are examples of possible changes. Specific alterations depend on the needs and desires of the disabled individual. The nature and timing of the handicapping condition are also important. Was the disabling condition a shock, or did the individual and family have time to make gradual accommodations to the condition? Are adequate social, health, and public services available in the community?

As more baby boomers cross the middle-age threshold and become more at risk for heart disease and other impairments, the ranks of the disabled will grow rapidly (Waldrop, 1990). In addition, medical advances have kept many more people with disabilities alive longer than in the past. Fortunately, the public today is much more aware of disabilities, including those that are not physically apparent, such as learning problems, and is prepared to adjust to and accommodate the needs of disabled individuals. Every person, disabled or not, needs a safe, functioning environment in which to live and work.

Single-Parent and Blended Families

As has been noted throughout this text, the composition of the typical American family and household is changing. Nearly half of all brides and grooms walking down the aisle have been married before. These unions start with high hopes; but because about 65 percent of the time children from previous marriages are involved, the new marriages often come with unique management challenges. Single-parent families as well have special management needs. Raising children is a difficult task in itself, but raising children alone can be even more challenging. The single parent finds no relief and has no one to share ideas with or turn to for help with discipline. Reduced income is another problem most single parents must face, in part because many fathers fail to make child-support payments (Kissman & Allen, 1993). Only about one-third of single mothers receive child support (Goodrich, Rampage, & Ellman, 1989). Family income in general drops sharply at the end of marriage because of the splitting up of resources, maintenance of two households, legal fees, and so forth.

Blended families, which are also called stepfamilies or reconstituted or combined families, are new families that include children from previous relationships. *Newsweek* magazine recognized the phenomenon of blended families when it devoted a special issue to the family of the 21stcentury. An article in the issue on stepfamilies began as follows:

The original plot goes like this: first comes love. Then comes marriage. Then comes Mary with a baby carriage. But now there's a sequel: John and Mary break up. John moves in with Sally and her two boys. Mary takes the baby Paul. A year later Mary meets Jack, who is divorced with three children. They get married. Paul, barely 2 years old, now has a mother, a father, a stepmother, a stepfather and five stepbrothers and stepsisters—as well as four sets of grandparents (biological and step) and countless aunts and uncles. And guess what? Mary's pregnant again. This may sound like an unusually complicated family tree. It's not. Some demographers predict that as many as a third of all children born in the 1980s may live with a stepparent before they are 18. (Kantrowitz & Wingert, 1990, p. 24)

In blended families, stepparents are more likely than biological parents to perceive strains on the marriage from the parenting experience. Studies show that marital satisfaction is significantly lower when both spouses bring children to the marriage (Lauer & Lauer, 1991). About 60 percent of second unions end in divorce, compared with 50 percent for first marriages. Generally, there is more stress, less cohesion, and less adaptability in blended families (Lauer & Lauer, 1991).

The new stepfamily is also complicated by in-laws with long relationships with and concomitant loyalties to the previous spouse, which make it difficult to welcome a new adult in their children's and grandchildren's lives. Furthermore, children in stepfamilies experience biological parents and stepparents very differently. For children the stepparent may be not another nurturing adult but an intruder who threatens to disrupt their close single-parent-child relationship, thereby influencing yet another loss. Stepparents also place children in a loyalty bind: If I care about mom's new husband, am I betraying my father? Children in first-time families almost always want their original parents to stay together. (Papernow, 1993, pp. 49–50)

Single-parent and blended families also exhibit special strengths. Blended families succeed if they have a clear understanding of each family member's feelings and needs and if they engage in open communication. Before remarriage, it is suggested that the adults forming a combined family realize that their commitment to one another will be the base upon which their new family will be built (Kaufman, 1993). During marriage, couples need to nurture their own relationship by supporting each other's interests as well as caring for the children.

In single-parent households, the child may find that having one person make all parenting decisions leads to consistency and stability. If the original marriage involved spousal, substance, or child abuse, being a single parent could be a relief. Since circumstances vary widely, each family must be looked at individually to determine its resource management needs. There are many types of single parents, ranging from unwed teenagers to middle-aged men whose wives have left them. Single parenthood can arise from never having married; from being abandoned, widowed, or divorced; or from a single person opting for adoption.

Additionally, both single-parent and blended families must contend with various legal, social, personal, economic, and psychological issues. These family types have to contend with all sorts of small and large indignities because they live in a society built around two-parent first-marriage families. For example, a graduating senior may be allotted only two high school graduation tickets but be from a blended family with two biological parents and two stepparents and eight grandparents. Who receives the tickets in this case? In a mother-headed household, whom does the son invite to a father-son picnic? Schools and community organizations are becoming more sensitive to these issues and are putting fewer children and families in awkward positions. Laws and legislation are making it easier for new family forms to function and are providing better protection for family members.

Poverty and Low-Income Families

Poverty is the state of being poor and the inability to provide for basic needs on a consistent basis. The United States has the highest average income in the world, but also the highest percentage of what the United Nations Development Program calls human poverty, taking into account many factors, including illiteracy, among industrialized countries (Vo, 1998).

For families, poverty is defined as a family income less than half the national median. In the United States, women with children are the fastest growing segment of the poor (United Way Strategic Institute, 1989). It is recognized that it costs less, and is more effective, to get children on the right track than to change adults (Huey, 1989). Early nutrition, health, and educational programs are positive first steps. The families in the worst financial trouble do not follow the usual stereotypes:

> They are not the very young, tempted by the freedom of their first credit cards. They are not the elderly, trapped by failing bodies and declining savings accounts. And they are not a random assortment of Americans who lack the self-control to keep their spending in check. Rather, the people who consistently rank in the worst financial trouble are united by one surprising characteristic. They are parents with children at home. Having a child is now the single best predictor that a woman will end up in financial collapse. (Warren & Tyagi, 2003, p. 6)

Poverty, like homelessness, is not necessarily a permanent state. There are gradations in income, and income may be temporarily low as a result of sudden unemployment. Low-income families may also experience seasonal variations in income. A family in financial distress may have come into this state because the main breadwinner became injured or ill, was laid off, or a family-owned business failed.

In the United States, a strong economy in the 1990s meant that more of the poor were moving out of poverty; they were working and consuming at a higher rate. It should be kept in mind that low-income is a relative term and that the lifestyles of many of the poor in the United States would be considered middle-class or even high-income in other countries. For example,

> Almost three-quarters of families living below the federal poverty line own at least one car, up from 64% in the mid-1980s. The percentage of poor households with washing machines has risen to 72% from 58% in 1984; with dryers, to 50% from 36%. Two out of three poor families have microwave ovens, up from one out of eight in 1984. Ninety-seven percent of poor households have color televisions, and three of four have VCRs. In 1970 only one in 50 poor people had a credit card; now, one in four does. (Cox & Alm, 1999, p. A21)

The federal government helps low-income families through a variety of programs. One way is through transfer payments such as food stamps, Aid to Families with Dependent Children, and Supplementary Security Income, all of which help the aged, blind, and/or disabled. **Transfer payments** are monies or services given for which the recipient does not directly pay. To receive these benefits, household income or assets must fall below a specified level. The welfare-to-work laws in the United States have changed many of the traditional ways of supporting the poor. More people are encouraged to work and be less dependent on the government.

The terms *poverty* and *low income* are defined not only by the government, but also by the families themselves based on previous income levels and lifestyles. The strains that result from the lack of money or assets can have negative effects on family life regardless of whether the source of the economic stressor is unemployment (Perrucci & Targ, 1988; Voydanoff & Donnelly, 1988) or recession (Elder & Caspi, 1988; Liker & Elder, 1983). According to several studies, women in particular have a difficult time with the negative effects on the quality of family life related to economic hardship (Duncan, Volk, & Lewis, 1988; Wilhem & Ridley, 1988; Rettig, Danes, & Bauer, 1993).

Planning for long-term goals can seem like a luxury. Returning to Maslow's hierarchy of needs in Chapter 1, the emphasis in helping low-income families should be placed on providing for the most basic needs first, in particular such physiological needs as food, water, and shelter. Low-income families often spend over half of their income on housing. Therefore, securing safe, affordable housing is a particular concern for low-income families and explains why a nonprofit housing organization such as Habitat for Humanity is so needed.

Because of the lack of adequate housing and other daily living problems, over time many very low-income families have become pessimistic about the future and feel that they have little control over what their lives will bring (Wilkie, 1986). This perspective, termed **fatalism,** means that all events are thought to be shaped by fate. A belief in fatalism can lead to low expectations and a sense of hopelessness. Recognizing the possible existence and influence of this phenomenon is helpful in designing appropriate and effective aid for low-income families.

SUGGESTED ACTIVITY

Discuss in groups the types of service activities students have engaged in, such as helping build a house with Habitat for Humanity. What were the activities? What were the feelings or other outcomes associated with being involved in service activities?

Web-Based Resources

Habitat for Humanity is a nonprofit housing organization that builds decent housing worldwide with the help of homeowner-partner families. Over 750,000 people call a Habitat house "home." The Web site is **www.habitat.org/**.

Among resources for elderly caregiving, Family Caregiver Alliance (**www.caregiver.org**) is a resource center; National Family Caregivers Association (**www.nfcacares.org**) offers ways to improve doctor/caregiver communication; the National Alliance for Caregiving (**www.caregiving.org**) has reviews of caregiving Web sites, videos, and newsletters; and Today's Caregiver (**www.caregiver.com**) offers a discussion forum and care links. Other Web sites on elder care and subjects regarding aging and the disabled include

- ◆ American Association of Retired Persons: **www.aarp.org/**
- ◆ National Aging Information Center: **www.aol.dhhs.gov/naic**
- ◆ National Alliance of the Disabled: **www.naotd.org**
- ◆ T. Rowe Price Retirement Income Calculator (**www3.troweprice.com/ric/RIC/**) developed by the Baltimore-based mutual fund company. This calculator helps people thinking about retirement or those already retired to figure whether their monthly income goals are realistic. At the Web site the individual supplies the starting retirement age, retirement length, marital status, retirement assets, monthly income goal, and investment mix of stocks, bonds and short-term securities. Another one is ING Group's retirement calculator (**www.ing.com/us/tool_calcs /retire/**). Dozens more Web sites exist for retirement calculations, but both of these were highly rated by financial planners (Greene, 2003).

The United Nations Human Development Report, with data on life expectancy, poverty, and consumption levels, as well as environmental conditions worldwide, can be found at **www.oup-usa.org**. The U.S. Census Bureau

Web site is **www.census.gov.** The Web site of the Centers for Disease Control and Prevention (**www.cdc.gov**) has worldwide health data and disease warnings.

Summary

This chapter has examined special problems regarding the management of human resources. Population growth, changes in family structure, mobility, the baby boom tidal wave, and adjusting to retirement were discussed. All of these changes are having an effect on family life. By understanding the nature of change, families may be able to react to it more effectively. In addition to exploring these themes, the chapter examined the management needs of specific population groups.

China is the world's most populous country followed by India and the United States. The U.S. population is becoming older and more diverse. If the population stays on the predicted course, there will be a larger percentage of minorities, single-parent families, blended/stepparent families, and elderly persons in the future. The fastest-growing minority group is Latino/Hispanic, with one in eight people in the United States of Latino/Hispanic origin.

In summary, the populations of the United States and the world are growing, and consequently, there are more human resource problems to address. Striving for a certain quality of life is not just a theoretical construct, but a very real day-to-day concern for people. Effectively managing human resources and increasing human capital are a fundamental part of the overall study of resource management. The next chapter explores the particular problems associated with managing time.

Key Terms

adaptability
blended families
boomeranging
change
demographics
demography
disability
dual career

dual income or dual
    earner
external change
fatalism
fertility rate
functional limitation
gerontology
handicap

immigration
internal change
mobility
mortality
poverty
transfer payments

Review Questions

1. How has the world population changed since 1900? Where do most people live today? In the United States, what are the largest cities?

2. Worldwide, are fertility rates rising or falling? What sorts of factors influence fertility rates?

3. According to the chapter, managing change is inherently messy. Why is that?

4. What do you think are the benefits and deficits of the 180-day school year for children? Where do you stand on this issue?

5. Choose one of the groups discussed in the section "Meeting Individual, Family, and Societal Needs" and discuss their resource management needs (explain what they have or do not have and what they need).

References

Azar, S., & Siegal, B. (1990). Behavioral treatment of child abuse. *Behavior Modification, 14*(3), 230–249.

Baum, A., & Burnes, D. (1993, Spring). Facing the facts about homelessness. *Public Welfare,* 20–27, 46, 48.

Braus, P. (1994, March). When mom needs help. *American Demographics,* 38–46.

Burt, M., & Cohen, B. (1989). *America's homeless: Numbers, characteristics and programs that serve time.* Washington, DC: Urban Institute.

Cavanaugh, J. (1990). *Adult development and aging.* Belmont, CA: Wadsworth.

Chances. (1999, June 16). *The Wall Street Journal,* A1.

Cheskis-Gold, R. (1988, February). Child care: What parents want. *American Demographics,* 45–46.

Cohen, C., & Thompson, K. (1992). Homeless mentally ill or mentally ill homeless? *American Journal of Psychiatry, 149*(6), 816–823.

Cox, W., & Alm, R. (1999, April 6). The good times will last. *The Wall Street Journal,* A21.

Crispell, D. (1997, November). Depending on college. *American Demographics,* 39.

Duncan, S., Volk, R., & Lewis, R. (1988). The influence of financial stressors upon farm husbands and wives' well-being and family life satisfaction. In R. Marotz-Baden, C. B. Hennon, & T. Brubaker (Eds.), *Families in rural America: Stress, adaptation and revitalization.* St. Paul, MN: National Council on Family Relations.

Eddowes, E., & Hranitz, J. (1989, October). Educating children of the homeless. *Education Digest,* 15–17.

Elder, G. H., Jr., & Caspi, A. (1988). Economic stress in lives: Developmental perspectives. *Journal of Social Issues, 44,* 25–45.

Ellickson, R. (1990, Spring). The homeless muscle. *Public Interest,* 45–60.

Emanoil, P. (1999, Spring). Employment policy for people with disabilities. *Human Ecology Forum,* 14.

Federal Task Force on Homelessness and Severe Mental Illness. (1992). *Outcasts on Main Street.* Washington, DC: HHS and the Interagency Council on the Homeless.

Gilbert, L. (1993). *Two-career/one family.* Newbury Park, CA: Sage.

Goodrich, T., Rampage, C., & Ellman, B. (1989). The single mother. *Family Therapy Networker, 13,* 55–56.

Greene, K. (2003, November 10). Our picks for the top places to find financial advice, nutrition guides, around-the-world cruises and more. *The Wall Street Journal,* R1.

Healthy Living. (1999, May/June). Tallahassee Memorial Health Care, 21.

Hira, T. (1987). Satisfaction with money management: Practices among dual-earner households. *Journal of Home Economics, 79*(2), 19–22.

Huey, J. (1989, April 10). The war on poverty. *Fortune.* 125–136.

Kantrowitz, B., & Wingert, P. (1990, Winter/Spring). Step by step: Who will be? *Newsweek* (Special Issue), 24–34.

Kaufman, T. S. (1993). *The combined family.* New York: Plenum Press.

Kissman, K., & Allen, J. (1993). *Single-parent families.* Newbury Park, CA: Sage.

Langer, J. (1985, July). The new mature mothers. *American Demographics,* 29–31, 50.

Lauer, R., & Lauer, J. (1991). *The quest for intimacy.* Dubuque, IA: Brown.

Liker, J. K., & Elder, G. H., Jr. (1993). Economic hardship in the 1930s. *American Sociological Review, 48,* 343–359.

Lines, S. (1992). Educational disadvantage in the primary school: Children living in temporary accommodation. *Support for Learning, 7*(1), 8–13.

Martin, J. (1991). The trauma of homelessness. *International Journal of Mental Health, 20*(2), 17–27.

Mogelonsky, M. (1997, March). Naturalized Americans. *American Demographics,* 45–49.

Nadler, D. (1998). *Champions of change.* San Francisco: Jossey-Bass.

Pagelow, M. (1989). The incidence and prevalence of criminal abuse of other family members. In L. Ohlin & M. Tonry (Eds.), *Family violence* (pp. 263–314). Chicago: University of Chicago Press.

Papernow, P. L. (1993). *Becoming a stepfamily.* San Francisco: Jossey-Bass.

Perrucci, C. C., & Targ, D. B. (1988). Effects of a plant closing on marriage and family life. In P. Voydanoff & L. C. Majka (Eds.), *Families and economic distress: Coping strategies and social policy* (pp. 55–71). Newbury Park, CA: Sage.

Pickett, M., Arnold, M., & Ketterer, L. (1990). *Household equipment in residential design* (9th ed.). Prospect Heights, IL: Waveland Press.

Radina, M. E. (2003). Cultural values and caregiving. In M. Coleman and L. Ganong (Eds.), *Points & counterpoints: Controversial relationship and family issues in the 21st century* (pp. 265–271). Los Angeles, CA: Roxbury.

Rettig, K. (1993). Problem-solving and decision-making as central processes of family life: An ecological framework for family relations and family resource management. *Marriage and Family Review, 18*(3/4), 187–222.

Rettig, K., Danes, S., & Bauer, J. (1993). Gender differences in perceived family life quality among economically stressed farm families. *Resource Theory: Exploration and Applications.* Academic Press, 125.

Riche, M. (1990, May). Boomerang age. *American Demographics,* 25–30, 52–53.

Rubin, B., Wright, J., & Devine, J. (1992). Unhousing the urban poor: The Reagan legacy. Special Issue: The Reagan legacy and the American welfare state. *Journal of Sociology and Social Welfare, 19*(1), 111–147.

Rubin, R., & Riney, B. (1994). *Working wives and dual-earner families.* Westport, CT: Praeger.

Ruffenach, G. (2003, November 10). The ties that bind. *The Wall Street Journal,* D4.

Runyon, K., & Stewart, D. (1987). *Consumer behavior* (3rd ed.). Columbus, OH: Merrill.

Senge, P. (1999). The dance of change. NY: Doubleday.

Spain, D., & Nock, S. (1984, August). Two-career couples, a portrait. *American Demographics,* 25–27, 45.

Toffler, A. (1970). *Future shock.* New York: Random House.

United Way Strategic Institute. (1989). *What lies ahead: Countdown to the 21st century* (Research Report). Alexandria, VA.

U.S. Bureau of the Census. (1989). *Money, income and poverty: Status of families and persons in the United States: 1988* (Series P. 60, No. 165). Washington, DC: U.S. Government Printing Office.

U.S. Bureau of the Census. (1989 and 1990). *Statistical Abstract of the United States.*(Washington, DC: U.S. Government Printing Office).

Vo, M. (1998, November 6). A look at the world by the numbers. *Christian Science Monitor,* 8–9.

Voydanoff, P., & Donnelly, B. W. (1988). Economic distress, family coping and quality of family life. In P. Voydanoff & L. C. Majka (Eds.), *Families and economic distress; Coping strategies and social policy* (pp. 97–115). Newbury Park, CA: Sage.

Waldrop, J. (1990, April). From handicap to advantage. *American Demographics,* 33–35, 54.

Warren, E., and Tyagi, A. (2003). *The two-income trap.* New York: Basic Books.

Wellner, A. (2003). Discovering native America. *Marketing Tools Director,* D47.

Wilhelm, M., & Ridley, C. (1988). Unemployment induced adaptations, relationships among economic responses and individual and marital well-being. *Lifestyles: Family and Economic Issues, 9,* 5–20.

Wilkie, C., & Ames, E. (1986). The relationship of infant cries to parental stress in the transition to parenthood. *Journal of Marriage and the Family, 48,* 545–550.

Wilkie, J. (1986). *Consumer behavior.* New York: Wiley.

Winborne, D., & Murray, G. (1992). Address unknown: An exploration of the education and social attitudes of homeless adolescents, *High School Journal, 75*(3), 144–149.

Wright, G. (1980). *Total rehabilitation.* Boston: Little, Brown.

chapter 9

Managing Time

MAIN TOPICS

Did you know that . . . ?

. . .Nearly 5 percent of Americans each year are victims of identity theft, and it takes victims on average 30 hours to resolve the problem.

. . .The average U.S. worker spends more than two hours on e-mail each day.

In the long run the pessimist may be proved to be right, but the optimist has a better time on the trip.

—Daniel L. Reardon

DO YOU HATE waiting in lines?
Do you multitask every chance you get?
Is your computer just too darn slow?
Do you want everything now?

Nearly everyone says not enough time is their main problem. Futurists and management specialists foresee time poverty as ever-increasing. After all, is life going to become less complicated? Today, only 43 percent of families eat together daily. Parents and children are working and playing harder than ever before, usually at different times and places. The computer, 24-hour television, extended stock market hours, and 24-hour toll-free lines have aided in creating this hurry-up, around-the-clock environment. Disc jockeys, factory workers, and nurses are used to 24-hour cultures, but now the rest of us are catching up. Want to order something from a catalog? No problem with toll-free lines open 24 hours a day. Time-poor consumers, such as working mothers residing in dual-income and single-parent households, are willing to pay for convenience (LeHew, 2001/2002). Playing into this sped-up world, an advertisement for CBS MarketWatch.com says it has the "tool to fuel your obsession" by "bringing you the hottest financial stories, market data in real time, and expert analysis you need to stay ahead of the market." The message is that if you wait, you will be left behind. What implications does this sped-up time have for individuals and families and how are they dealing with it? This is the subject of Chapter 9.

An analysis of time begins with awareness. Waking to the shrill clattering of an alarm clock, checking clocks and watches throughout the day, going to bed at 11 o'clock—these are all examples of how our lives are synchronized around time. The hours of the day, weekends, holidays, and seasons provide a rhythm and a framework for people's lives.

One of the recurring themes of this book is how individuals and families make choices. The management of time, a resource that everyone has in equal amount (24 hours a day), affects life choices. According to Luciano L'Abate and Tamar Harel:

> To understand how we allocate time and energies from one setting to another we need to invoke the concept of priorities. These priorities stem from definite choices we make about what is important in our lives. How important is a person, an object, or an activity to us? (1993, p. 252)

Time is a measured or measurable period. A central management concept is **time displacement,** which is concern over how time spent in one activity takes away from time spent in another activity (Mutz, Roberts, & Van Vuuren, 1993). For example, choosing to watch television rather than studying will affect the goal of academic achievement. Thus time, as a resource, is related to the fulfillment of wants, needs, and goals.

Awareness of time is an important part of the human consciousness. The feeling of losing time or someone wasting your time is undesirable. Activities such as clearing one's credit record after being a victim of identity theft is unpleasant. According to the Federal Trade Commission (FTC), it takes on average 30 hours per person to resolve the problem; and nearly 5 percent of Americans experience identity theft a year. One way to avoid identity theft is to shred all personal information and receipts. Another way is to pay cash and guard credit cards closely. In 2003, President Bush signed legislation renewing the Fair Credit Reporting Act, the law concerning consumer credit. In the revised Act, more consumer protection was put in place. If consumers suspect their identity has been stolen, they can put a 90-day fraud alert on their credit file by calling one of the three credit reporting bureaus:

- ◆ Trans Union 800 680 7289
- ◆ Experian 888 397 3742
- ◆ Equifax 800 525 6285

The one you call will call the other bureaus. If the problem is not resolved in 90 days, the fraud alert can be extended up to seven years.

Identity theft is an example of a time-waster, and it also has a lot to do with the loss of individual control. **Time management** is the conscious control of time to fulfill needs and achieve goals. The way time is allocated is based on an individual's values, what is important to that person. If a family values a shared dinner hour with a multi-course meal, then family members will set aside time for meal preparation and eating together. If the family values school, work, and community activities more, then activities will become their time focus, and they will eat meals in shifts. In today's time-pressured societies with so many scheduling and demand conflicts, sit-down family-style dinners are becoming increasingly rare, at least in families with older children. According to Leonard Berry, a retailing expert:

> The Norman Rockwell image of a family seated around a dinner table eating a roast beef lovingly prepared at home no longer accurately reflects America's eating habits. More likely, people are grabbing a quick restaurant meal, buying takeout food, and using the microwave oven. Restaurants now capture more than 40 cents of every dollar spent on food in the United States, up from less than 20 cents in the 1960s. Americans spend about 15 percent of their food dollar on ready-to-eat food prepared for off-premise consumption, according to FIND/SVP of New York City. And Americans are spending in the neighborhood of $1 billion a year on foods for the microwave. (1990, p. 32)

Time is a resource that can be measured in units (i.e., minutes, hours, days), but comprehending it can be difficult because individuals' perceptions and use of time affect the way they think about it. Time has been the subject of philosophical debate (e.g., "If no one measures time, does it still exist?" and "Has time a beginning or an end?") and also the subject of psychological, mathematical, and economic inquiry. In the fifth century C.E., Saint Augustine said, "What then, is time? If no one asks me, I know what it is. If I wish to explain it to him who asks me, I do not know." The best way to measure time remains a subject of debate, with choices ranging from the use of simple time diaries and complex psychographic inventories to consumer focus groups and actual drawings of time (Kaufman & Lane, 1993). Time is thus the most familiar of concepts, yet at the same time the most elusive.

TIME AS A RESOURCE

In economics, time is considered a resource because it is a scarce commodity (Graham, 1981). It is saved, spent, and allocated to get something desired. Products and methods that save time are in demand. Here is an example. During World War II inventors discovered a way to make juice concentrate so that the troops could get orange juice in remote locations. Then the frozen juice concentrate was introduced to the American household, and it was estimated that this saved 14,000 hours of drudgery per year (Mintz, 2000). In this day and age, few households buy juice concentrate; more buy it from a carton that makes preparation even easier—no more mixing, simply pour. Another example of food efficiency is the popularity of prepackaged salad mixes versus buying a head of lettuce, washing it, pulling it apart, and adding other ingredients.

Not everyone wants to be time-efficient. Back-to-basics enthusiasts enjoy cutting wood for fireplaces, building their own furniture, and making food from scratch. Some cultures and subcultures challenge the notion of thinking of time in terms of the discrete beats of mechanical linear "clock time." In *The Dance of Change,* Peter Senge states that

> It is important to remember that the mechanical clock was only invented five hundred years ago, in the fourteenth century. Before that, human beings did not think of time in constant, fixed increments that keep adding in a steady linear progression. Today, you can almost hear the machine's wheels grinding relentlessly: sixty minutes to each hour, then another sixty minutes make another hour, then another sixty minutes makes another hour, then another, then another. . . . Nature's time is different. (1999, p. 57)

A resourceful person uses time effectively or imaginatively, especially in difficult situations. President Franklin D. Roosevelt, who dealt with the Depression and World War II said, "Never before have we had so little time in which to do so much." Notice that unlike money, time is a nonrenewable resource and thus might be considered a more valuable resource. Queen Elizabeth I's last words were "All my possessions for a moment of time." Money is often traded for time, as when a busy person hires someone to clean the house or take care of the yard or swimming pool. As another example of the trade-offs between time and money, a survey by the Union Bank of Switzerland used the price of a Big Mac (because it is served worldwide) as its standard of time worked. An American would work 11 minutes to earn enough money for a Big Mac; a worker in Zurich, 14 minutes; Vienna, 17 minutes; Berlin, 18 minutes; London, 20 minutes; Moscow, 2 hours; and Nairobi, 3 hours. The global average was 37 minutes.

Governments seek to control time when they set deadlines and policies. A prime example is *daylight saving time, which exists in some version in 70 countries.* Germany adopted it in 1915. In the United States, part of the reason it passed into law was that people could stay out later on summer evenings

Time-pressured families have hurried mealtimes.

Steve Prezant/CORBIS

and thus have more leisure time, buy more products, and feel more cheerful. Farmers and their lobbies opposed it:

> To farmers, clock time was irrelevant any time of year. When the sun was overhead, it was noon. . . . Increasingly, however, farmers depended on the railroad for their livelihood. If city folks were buying their milk, the milk had to make the morning train. . . . The farmers lost the battle, and on March 31, 1918, America turned its clocks ahead one hour. (Crossen, 2003, p. B1)

In 1996, the European Union (EU) standardized an EU-wide summertime period that runs from the last Sunday in March to the last Sunday in October.

Attitudes affect how one feels about time. For example, an article in *American Demographics* reported that

> Feeling rushed may have more to do with one's attitudes than with one's activities.
>   People who get more than 15 minutes of exercise a day are only half as likely as others to feel rushed, 22 percent versus 44 percent. . . . People are more likely to feel rushed if they also say they are dissatisfied with themselves, unable to do things as well as others, feel useless, or don't have much to be proud of. (Godbey & Graefe, 1993, pp. 26–27)

Discretionary versus Nondiscretionary Time

Time can be categorized as discretionary or nondiscretionary. **Discretionary time** is the free time an individual can use any way she or he wants. How do people spend their free time? *The top preferred leisure pursuit of Americans ages 24 to 64 years old is time with family and friends* followed by reading, television, traveling, gardening, movies, shopping, and exercising (Taylor, 2003). **Nondiscretionary time** is the time that an individual cannot control totally by himself or herself. For example, class times are nondiscretionary because they are set by the school or college. Opening and closing times of banks, restaurants, post offices, and stores are also nondiscretionary. In the course of the day, nearly all people have some discretionary time when they can take breaks, use the bathroom, eat meals, and come and go between activities. Evenings and weekends offer the most discretionary time.

Children and Time

Usually, children have more discretionary time (e.g., free time, play time, sports and recreation time) than adults, but this situation may be changing. In *The Hurried Child,* David Elkind makes the point that children today are overcommitted and are growing up too fast and too soon. He argues that they have too little free, unstructured, discretionary time. This lack of free time leads to stress. According to Elkind,

> Today's child has become the unwilling, unintended victim of overwhelming stress—the stress borne of rapid, bewildering social change and constantly rising expectations. The contemporary parent dwells in a pressure-cooker of competing demands, transitions, role changes, personal and professional uncertainties, over which he or she exerts slight direction. (1988, p. 3)

When the average teen is not in school or doing homework, he or she is most likely to be talking, then in descending order viewing TV, performing paid labor or sports, helping with household chores, and participating in clubs or the arts. More than 20 hours a week of paid work is linked to delinquency, drug use, and school misconduct, says Reed Larson, a professor at the University of Illinois (Shellenbarger, 2002). So, more than 20 hours a week of paid work during the school year is to be discouraged.

> Is there a formula, one exhausted parent asks, for the right mix of clubs, sports, homework and free time? No, but some new guidelines are emerging. For instance, kids who participate in a variety of voluntary sports and clubs tend to work harder in school, studies show. However, too much of any one thing may yield diminishing returns. Part-time jobs carry some risks, researchers say, and family time is an important vaccine against such trouble signs as drug and alcohol use. (Shellenbarger, 2002, p. D1)

Adults and Time

Research shows that men and women experience free time differently. According to a study by Mattingly and Bianchi (2003), men have more free time; marriage and children exacerbate the gender gap, and market work hours erode men's and women's free time in different ways. As may be expected, the presence of preschool children, employment outside the home, and being married cuts down on women's free time. Within marriage, fathers are spending more time with their children than in the past (Bianchi, 2000).

A case can be made that employed adults, male and female, have less discretionary time than before because of the Internet, global business, and availability issues:

> The 24-hour business day started with the Internet, and with international companies kept awake by the fact that every minute, somebody, somewhere is doing business. The whiz kids in the computer world brought their dorm-room hours to work with them, and soon even managers were grinding out work at night. "It starts with technology available to do work all the time. Then as there is more work to do, business speeds up, the market keeps expanding, and there is more of an emphasis on output," says John Challenger, chief executive of the outplacement firm Challenger, Gray & Christmas in Chicago. "Then it becomes doing business all the time, even in the service sector we're seeing formalized first, second, and third shifts.". . . "I don't think we'll get away from 24/7," Challenger says, "but I do think people will continue to make inroads reclaiming their personal time." (Boss, 2000, p. 16)

Discretionary time allows the individual to make choices about whom to be with and what to do. These choices are not made in a vacuum, however—an individual's time use and needs must be weighed against what others want and need. Learning time management skills can help individuals maximize their time and use it optimally. The following suggestions can help in managing both discretionary and nondiscretionary time:

- ◆ Make a daily "things to do list" or keep a calendar.
- ◆ Say "no" to requests for time that keep one from finishing projects already under way.
- ◆ Make use of the telephone and the computer whenever possible.
- ◆ Delegate.
- ◆ Keep a flexible schedule that allows for unexpected events.
- ◆ Ask, "Is this the best possible use of my time at this moment?"
- ◆ Lessen interruptions, such as unnecessary meetings, visitors, and telephone calls.

For example, regarding lessening interruptions, a family may have a rule that outsiders are discouraged from calling after 9 o'clock at night. In offices, because they are public settings, interruptions are more difficult to manage. According to one study, the average U.S. office worker sends or receives 201 messages each day. The majority of the messages are by telephone (50), e-mail (35), and voice mail (22). Other messages are received by postal mail, interoffice mail, pagers, cell phones, express mail, Post-it notes, telephone message slips, and couriers or messengers (Clark, 1999). The problem with so many messages is that workers spend nearly all their time responding and receiving and have very little time left to think, write reports, and so on.

Nearly half of office workers surveyed said they had difficulty keeping up with their work and were feeling overwhelmed. The director of the study's research team said, "We found that it was very much an interrupt-driven style of work that was emerging. . . . For too many people, information is proving to be more of a burden than a resource" (Clark, 1999, p. R4). Also, a little privacy can boost productivity. According to an advertisement for Steelcase (a manufacturer of desks and office systems):

> While open workplaces invite valuable interaction between people, it's privacy that helps knowledge workers reach their peak state of performance. During the 15 minutes of immersion time needed to reach this state of "flow," people are particularly sensitive to interruptions. Once disrupted, most of us require an additional 15 minutes to reach it again.

Which is the most productive day of the week? The answer is Tuesday according to several studies.

> Mondays get us down. Wednesday is hump day. Thursday is the traditional happy hour day for those still close enough to their youth to remember such things, and Friday, well, Friday speaks for itself. Is it any wonder people aren't getting as much done those days? . . . many managers schedule meetings and conferences for Monday to give employees an idea of what work needs to be done for the week. Tuesday is really the first day workers have to get moving on that plan. (Goforth, 2002, p. 5E)

How is time spent during the retirement years? Everyone's experience is different, and so much depends on health and circumstances. The first years of retirement are unique, as this case study illustrates:

> Patricia Breakstone, age 63, remembers her first year of retirement from her 38-year career as a state-government analyst in San Diego as a "terrible transition period." Shortly after leaving her job last spring, she started a long-awaited kitchen renovation, which turned her condo upside-down right when she was starting to spend her days at home for the first time in her adult life. Then her dog was struck by kidney disease, and Ms. Breakstone wound up spending $7,000 in veterinary bills over two months as she tried in vain to nurse her pet back to health. As the months wore on, "I didn't want to get up in the morning," she says. Finally a friend goaded her into applying for a part-time job at a bakery near her home, which helped her regain some structure in her days—along with providing a social outlet. "Retirement," she says now, "is a real balancing act." (Greene, 2003, p. R1)

Some people clearly enjoy leaving work behind, while others are disoriented. Many discover **drift time,** which refers to enjoying unscheduled time (i.e., the opportunity to have a second cup of coffee and read the whole newspaper in the morning). As the first year of retirement winds down, many find the right pace, a post-work life that suits them.

SUGGESTED ACTIVITY

To find your most productive day of the week, keep a time log for two weeks listing activities. You will become aware of things that are nonproductive, time wasters.

"There doesn't seem to be the big hole that I expected after all those years working," says Steve Hold, age 63, who retired from General Electric Co. in Seattle in late 2001, and moved to Tucson, Ariz., the following May. "I was surprised that it was so easy to find things to do and become involved." (Greene, 2003, p. R1)

And, what about marital relationships in the first years of retirement? Ken Schumann, after retiring, came up with several rules, and he says negotiating personal space with your partner is one of the biggest hurdles in the first year. He and a few fellow retirees serving on a panel came up with these recommendations: shell out money for separate phone lines, computers, and e-mail addresses, stake out a space in your home that is yours alone, and negotiate time together and apart (Greene, 2003). Here is one final retirement story. Jim Matheson was always bothered by litter along the side of the road in his town, so when he retired at age 55 he went to the police station to explain his plan to pick up trash. While there, the chief told him they needed help setting up roadside radar signs (the kind that say "Slow Down, Your Speed is . . .") and Jim said,

"Wait a minute. You're telling me I get to drive the cruiser, right?" . . . The first time he drove the vehicle on a major highway, "traffic backed up for miles behind me," he says, "What a feeling of power." (Greene, 2003, p. R4)

Personal Computers, Inventions, and Time

Around the world, personal computer (PC) ownership is up, and the use of PCs is up. The latest estimate is that about 20 percent of the world's population is online. Computers are both savers and wasters of time. Each individual and family has to decide to what extent computers are part of their lives: Many people experience withdrawal symptoms when kept away from their e-mail or the Internet; others welcome the chance to get away. The average worker spends more than two hours a day reading, responding to, or disposing of e-mail (Alsop, 2003).

In the past, printing and telephones required adjustments as well, and the computer is no different in this regard. In the 20th century, some people did not get a telephone for many years because they did not like the intrusion or they did not like the cost, so they used the neighbor's phone or went without. Today, people in a variety of occupations feel overwhelmed, but so did the monks 500 years ago when the Gutenberg printing press brought a 20-fold increase in the number of texts they had to study. As people attempt to fit their lifestyles within the context of the information and technological explosion, experts and entrepreneurs are looking for solutions—applying the very tools that caused the data glut in a mission to help alleviate it. For example, e-mail filtering and message organizing devices are solutions for computers (just as answering machines were for telephones). "Spam walls" destroy spam before it gets to inboxes; other programs flag or give warning messages of possible spam.

The ABC Method of Time Control and Goals

The pressures of modern society have led to the publication of many books suggesting ways individuals and families can improve their use of time. One of the best-known books is Alan Lakein's *How to Get Control of Your Time and Your Life,* which explains how to set short-term and long-term goals, establish priorities, organize a daily schedule, and achieve better self-understanding.

Lakein encourages the use of the ABC priority method in which the most important activities are designated "A," medium-value activities are "B," and low-value activities are "C." An individual using this method writes down all his or her activities for a given day; rates each activity as A, B, or C; and then tries to accomplish the A's first, the B's next, and the C's only if there is time. Figure 9.1 shows how Chris, a 28-year-old doctoral student and teaching assistant, used the ABC method during one busy Thursday. Other authors have suggested low (L), medium (M), and high (H) degrees of importance. The underlying principle is the same whether it is called ABCs or LMHs or apples, oranges, and pears. If you keep a written or mental "to do" list and prioritize the activities by degrees of importance, how strictly do you stick to your priorities?

_____	_____	_____	_____	_____
never	rarely	half the time	often	always

An important concept in Lakein's book is that daily time use should be directly related to goals. Chris describes her life goals and lifestyle goals in Figure 9.2. Are there connections between Chris's Thursday "to do" list and her goals? Note also the significance of the practice of writing down activities and goals. A goal strategist, Gene Donohue, says the difference between a goal and a dream is the written word. He says that reviewing goals daily is a crucial part of success and should become part of your routine. How do you do this? The lists and ABCs are one way; another way is to cut out a photo or map from a brochure or an advertisement of a house, boat, car, vacation destination, or whatever and put that photo or map on your refrigerator or mirror so that every day you see it and think about it; visualize yourself owning the object or being in the place you want to be. When your goals change or are achieved, remove the visual and replace it with another.

Too often people dwell on the past when their time would more productively be spent living in the present and planning the future. Donohue suggests writing down goals in six areas of life:

1. Family and Home
2. Financial and Career
3. Spiritual and Ethical
4. Physical and Health
5. Social and Cultural
6. Mental and Educational

You could add more categories like Environment or Friends or figure these fit under the broader categories of Family and Home, Physical and Health, and Social and Cultural. These six categories are not set in stone; they serve as organizers. You may choose to eliminate one if it isn't important to you. To find out more about Donohue and strategies for goal achievement visit www.topachievement.com/goalsetting.html.

Time Perceptions

Perception refers to the process whereby sensory stimulation is translated into organized experience. Understanding how time is perceived is necessary because, as noted earlier, time is more than simply clock time; an individual's perception and use of time are also important. Because perception is not

SUGGESTED ACTIVITY

Take the six categories and list a goal or several goals for each one. Be sure to be specific. For example, instead of writing "a house" under the category of Family and Home, write down the size, type, location, view, and acreage. Do you envision a garden, trees, a field, a beach, sidewalks, nearby shops, neighbors, mountains? If you want to get really specific, write down what is in the garden. Can you visualize it? What does the air smell like? Put the stated goal into a time frame: When is achievement (partial or fully) likely? Discuss your answers with others. It can also be the case that you have several houses or life situations in mind; feel free to describe several scenarios. Specific does not mean being limiting, but it does mean trying to focus on a few desired alternatives.

FIGURE 9.1
Chris's Thursday Schedule
This example uses Lakein's ABC priority method in which A activities are top priority, B activities are less important, and C activities are to be done if there is time.

List of all activities for Thursday (made Wednesday night)

A   Get ready for school (shower, dress, makeup, hair).
A   Make breakfast/eat breakfast in car.
A   Check Copy Center for Promotion readings/pick up if done.
A   See Dr. Akihito about Econ. paper.
A   Talk to Dr. Parker about Involvement articles.
A   Read Promotion articles.
A   Go to Social Psych. class.
A   Check mail/Promotion class for Friday.
A   Make copies/turn in Social Psych. homework.
A   Return articles to Ann.
A   Buy/eat lunch.
A   Make/eat dinner.
A   Set out clothes to wear for teaching on Friday.
B   Type outlines of Promotion articles.
B   Call/check on Social Psych. class for fall.
C   Read ANOVA homework (due Mon.).
C   Ask Dr. Bailey about Involvement paper.
C   Do class prep. for Chaps. 9 & 10
C   Review CB class exam 1 for typos and take to get printed.
C   Read Chap. 3 in Social Psych.

observable, researchers have to rely on people's self-reports of their perceptions. **Time perception** is the awareness of the passage of time. Since 1850, social and behavioral scientists have been trying to determine why people's sense of the length of a period of time can differ from the precise measurement. They have found that many factors come into play in time perception. For example, drug and alcohol consumption alter time perception. Changes in body temperature and lack of exposure to natural daylight have been shown to affect a person's sense of time. Besides these physiological influences, temperament, culture, environment, and absorption in the task at hand may also affect perception.

Estimating Duration

Without watches, clocks, newspapers, radio, or the television to serve as a guide, people would have to use other means of estimating how much time has passed. Several factors influence a person's estimation of time. Being active makes time go faster than being passive. For example, the driver of a car may think a trip goes faster than a passenger because the driver has something to do besides look passively out the window. An individual who is motivated is able to concentrate longer on a task and enjoy it more. Time seems to move faster when one is not bored.

In addition, research studies reveal marked individual differences in the ability to estimate time. Age appears to be one factor. Elderly people tend to find time shorter than younger people. According to Jean Piaget's theory of concrete cognitive operations, children's time estimates become more accurate after the age of 7 or 8. This is why younger children irritate their parents on a family vacation by repeatedly asking when they are going to arrive at the destination. Children do not mean to be irritating; they simply do not understand time as an adult does.

General Life Goals
My general life goals are (1) to complete my doctorate work and earn a
Ph.D., (2) to marry the man of my choice, (3) to obtain a professional
position at a large state university, (4) to have at least 2 to 5 articles
accepted for publication each year, (5) to be published at least twice
in a premier journal, (6) to establish myself as one of the leading
academicians in my field, (7) to earn the respect of both my colleagues
and my sisters, (9) to earn enough money to take care of my parents and
my husband's parents, (10) to truly make a difference in the life of at
least one of my students, (11) to establish myself as a consultant,
(12) to establish myself as a consumer rights advocate, (13) to get
tenure, and (14) to improve my health.

Lifestyle Goals
My lifestyle goals are (1) to live in a new house in an upper-class
neighborhood in the suburbs, (2) to live near, but not in, a major city
with cultural events, great shopping, and other universities, (3) to
drive a Saab or an Alfa Romeo, (4) to be able to buy clothes without
worrying about the cost, and (5) to be able to fly/drive to getaway
weekends to fun places or visit old friends and family.

FIGURE 9.2
**Chris's General Life Goals
and Lifestyle Goals**

Practical Uses of Time Measurement

Although perceptions and estimations of time vary from person to person, time itself is one of the most accurately measured physical quantities. Indeed, the study of time can be a very practical subject. In the 20th century, time and motion studies were conducted in offices and factories throughout the United States. The studies evaluated industrial performance and analyzed the time spent in producing a product such as a car. As discussed in Chapter 2, the early study of factory efficiency was closely associated with the work of Frederick Taylor (1911), who is widely considered to be the father of time and motion studies. Taylor's studies later led to the discipline of management as it is taught in business schools today. He introduced the idea of measuring time precisely in order to examine specific activities with the intent of finding ways to reduce the amount of time they required. Thus these studies aimed at improving efficiency through saving time and human energy. Each job on a factory production line would be divided into different operations, and each operation would then be analyzed in terms of time and energy used. As a result of the findings, assembly line work in factories became more standardized and efficient.

Many of the principles and methods derived from industrial performance studies, such as those conducted by Taylor, were applied to household efficiency studies. Chapter 2 examined some of these studies in the discussion of work simplification. Individual and family use of time and products continues to be studied by manufacturers and marketers of appliances, food, and household products. They are interested in identifying trends in who does what in the home and learning how many minutes a day are spent in preparing food, eating, cleaning up, and washing clothes so that they can tailor their advertising and their products to fit current household practices and, hence, increase sales by better meeting consumer needs (see Figure 9.3 for an example). They are also interested in eating behaviors away from home. Restaurant chains, grocery stores, and office furniture manufacturers may want to know how workers spend their lunch hours and what they eat. For example, a fast-food chain might use several methods of inquiry, including in-restaurant consumer surveys, **focus groups** (selected groups of people who are questioned by a discussion leader or moderator about what they think about different topics, in this case products and services), observations, and self-reports. Companies also rely heavily on point-of-sale information obtained when bar codes from products are entered into a cash register. The data reveal that lunchtime is shrinking; more people are eating at their desks; and take-out, whether for breakfast, lunch, or dinner, is becoming more common.

Time measurement also has practical applications in evaluating skills such as word processing (number of words per minute), sales (number of sales per month), library use (number of books checked out per week), and so on. Mall and store hours are determined by the number of customers per hour. During the holiday season, stores remain open longer to meet increased customer traffic and boost sales. In addition, the amount of Social Security retired people receive is based on the number of years they were employed and how much they earned. Divorce settlements take into account the number of years of marriage. On a daily basis, people try to determine whether they will be on

FIGURE 9.3

An appliance advertisement tailored to the practices of modern households.

Source: Reprinted by permission of Whirlpool Corporation.

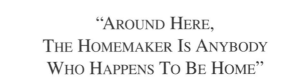

© 1993 Whirlpool Corporation ® Registered trademark/TM Trademark of Whirlpool Corporation

time for work, school, or appointments, whether they will have enough time to eat lunch or prepare dinner, whether they will be able to read the newspaper or watch the television shows they want to, and so on. In other words, people are engaged in time management from the moment they wake up until they go to sleep. Even sleeping is a timed event, ending when one awakens at the sound of a radio or an alarm clock.

Perceptions of Time across Cultures

As mentioned earlier in the chapter, individuals perceive time differently due to many factors. A widely held concept in anthropology is that time perceptions are strongly influenced by culture. The person most associated with studying how culture influences the way people think about time is E. T. Hall, author of *The Silent Language*. The three anthropological models of time— linear-separable, circular-traditional, and procedural-traditional—were introduced by Hall (1959) and further delineated by Robert Graham (1981) and Alma Owen (1991). These models define time in the context of various activities, life stages, or time of year. By doing this, the models illustrate what time means to different cultural groups and also the ways in which they process and structure time.

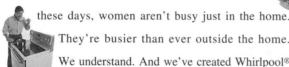

Ring a doorbell today and it's likely a teenager will answer with an armful of laundry. Or a dad in a sauce-stained apron. This is life. Because these days, women aren't busy just in the home. They're busier than ever outside the home. We understand. And we've created Whirlpool® appliances that make it possible for your home to run smoothly even when you're not there to run it. Our refrigerator lets your son find the yogurt without your standing there with a map. Your daughter will do laundry because our washing machine restores balance to most lopsided loads. Everyone can coexist in the kitchen because our dishwasher cleans so quietly. And maybe dad will be inspired to cook when he sees how easy our range is to clean. So now, whoever happens to be home won't have a problem helping out. Which makes Whirlpool less like an appliance. And more like a friend of the family.

Whirlpool
Home Appliances

Want to know more about making your home run with Whirlpool appliances? Call 1-800-253-1301. Any day. Anytime.

HOW TO MAKE A HOME RUN.™

Linear–Separable Model of Time

Most Western European cultures and other cultures that have been strongly influenced by Western Europe view time as linear. Linear-separable time processing is related to economic time. An investment in time today is expected to have a payoff in the future. Long-term planning is accepted as normal in the linear-separate model. When most U.S. residents are asked to think about the future, for example, they think in terms of 5 to 25 years (Hawkins, Best, & Coney, 1986). The model also treats the past, present, and future as distinct entities that are broken down into units. Thus, in linear-separable time orientations, stories, steps, and procedures are usually told in chronological order. Speed of preparation is valued, so time-saving products such as cake mixes and canned soups are accepted. Figure 9.4 gives a list of ways to save time.

Time is measured by clocks and calendars. Appointments are kept on time. Furthermore, it is assumed that the future will bring better things. The linear-separable model represents an optimistic point of view because improvements are expected over time.

FIGURE 9.4
A Dozen Ways to Give Yourself an Extra Hour

There are hundreds of ways to streamline your day. Here are a dozen for starters.

1. Get help. A homeowner who after a month of calls still could not get his e-mail hooked up in his new house, called the head of the homeowner's association, who called the head of the company. Within hours a technician was at the door and installed the system.
2. Use your energy effectively. Study or do difficult reports during your peak energy time, usually 10 or 11 A.M. for most people.
3. Send gift certificates or buy gift cards. Shop online or by telephone.
4. Use in-store wrapping services if there are no lines.
5. Buy prepared food such as rotisserie chickens; complete the meal with fresh bread, soups, pastas, vegetables, and salads.
6. Send cards online.
7. Reduce walking and searching by having basics in most rooms of a house or apartment such as tissues, clocks, scissors, pens, paper, tape, and cleaning supplies. This technique is especially important in two-story or three-story houses.
8. Use automatic bill paying and direct deposit.
9. Buy movie and theater tickets in advance.
10. Shop early when stores are not crowded. Home supply stores say their slowest time is Sunday morning. A corollary to this is to ask for the earliest appointment at the dentist or doctor; you are less likely to be bumped by emergencies that occur during the day.
11. Double recipes, eat half, freeze the rest. Share with family and neighbors.
12. Buy multiples of nonperishables like soap, shampoo, toothpaste, and detergent. Keep all houseplants in one area of the house for easy watering.

Procedural-Traditional Model of Time

The procedural-traditional perception is very different from the linear-separable model. Individuals with a procedural perception consider the actual steps, event, or procedure to be more important than the time spent in the activity. Being prompt is not as critical as doing things correctly or when conditions are right. Several tribes of American Indians and Alaskan Eskimos ascribe to a procedural perception of time. Procedural time processing is characterized by staying with a task until it is completed no matter how much time it takes.

Scientists looking for cures and people who quilt or do other arts and crafts may subscribe to procedural-traditional models of time. They are focused on taking the right steps and finding a solution or making an end product regardless of how long it takes.

Circular-Traditional Model of Time

A circular or cyclical perception emphasizes the repetitive nature of time; this model assumes that today will be much like yesterday, and tomorrow will be more of the same. Time follows a rhythmic pattern with regular beginnings and ends, but without discrete units of past, present, and future. In the circular perception, things may move forward or may remain the same. The circular perception is often associated with poverty because life for the poor, regardless of country, may change little from day to day. People living in primitive or agricultural subsistence cultures may also subscribe to the circular perception since they may be born, live, raise their families, and die on the same land as their grandparents. Time is not saved or spent; it just is, and life is lived day by day.

Some Effects of Cultural Differences

None of these models of time perceptions is good or bad; they simply illustrate cultural differences that affect managerial and consumption behavior. It is also important to note that many countries use a combination of the models or include cultural groups that ascribe more to one model than another. Companies who market products internationally are well aware of these cultural differences. Take the example of washing clothes. Americans like large-capacity machines that wash clothes fast, whereas frequent, small loads that take an hour or more of washing time is acceptable, even desirable, in other countries. Also because of aesthetics, tradition, and types of clothing and activities, differences exist in washing machines, placement, and procedures. Here are a few examples (Jordan and Karp, 2003):

- ◆ In China: Aesthetics are important because many families keep washers in living areas due to space limitations; color preferences are gray or green, and there needs to be a grease-removal cycle to remove grease stains caused by bicycle-riding.
- ◆ In Brazil: Washers are white with transparent lids; they are raised on four legs so that consumers can wash underneath the machine; soaking is a tradition so there is a soak cycle as part of the main cycle; small loads and more frequent loads are the tradition.
- ◆ In India: Appliances have wheels for easy moving; washers are not isolated; they have a position of pride in the home, and there is a sari (delicate) cycle to wash women's wraparound fabrics.
- ◆ In England: Combined washers and dryers are common, and they are typically placed in the kitchen near the other appliances and the sink rather than in a separate room or behind closet doors.

Going back to the discussion of time use across cultures: In Western cultures all three models exist, although the linear-separable model is dominant. Guy Claxton, an English psychologist specializing in the structure of the human mind and the author of *Hare Brain Tortoise Mind,* says that Western hurry-up methods have their drawbacks because slow ways of knowing exist and are useful:

> The individuals and societies of the West have rather lost touch with the value of contemplation. Only active thinking is regarded as productive. Sitting gazing absently at your office wall or out of the classroom window is not of value. Yet many of those whom our society admires as icons of creativity and wisdom have spent much of their time doing nothing. Einstein, it is said, would frequently be found in his office at Princeton staring into space. The Dalai Lama spends hours each day in meditation. Even that paragon of penetrating insight, Sherlock Holmes, is described by his creator as entering a meditative state "with dreamy vacant expression in his eyes." (1997, p. 4)

Latin America provides an example of how perceptions of time can affect consumption behavior. Latin Americans generally view time as less concrete and less subject to scheduling than do North Americans. Consequently, appointments and meetings rarely start at the scheduled time. Since eating fast in an impersonal setting is not valued in Latin America, fast-food outlets popular in the United States and Great Britain, such as Kentucky Fried Chicken, McDonald's, and Wimpy, had difficulty penetrating Latin American markets (Penteado, 1981), although this is changing. Convenience foods such as boxed cereals sell well in North America because quick breakfasts that save time are highly valued. They are less successful in unhurried cultures.

In the circular perception, the concept of the future is vague. Southeast Asians, for instance, tend to think of the future in terms of hundreds or thousands of years (Hawkins, Best, & Coney, 1986). This perception leads to a different sense of urgency. In Asian countries, businesses are planned for the long run over several decades rather than for the short term. On the other hand, the Japanese have been very receptive to many American-European time-saving convenience goods.

Research studies have tried to establish the validity and monitor the cultural changes in the three types of time perceptions. A study of 48 East and Southeast Asian students (men and women from Thailand, Japan, and Malaysia) attending a large Midwestern university found that they most frequently used procedural processing, followed by circular processing, and rarely used linear processing (Lindquist, Tacoma, & Lane, 1993). In contrast, U.S. students appeared to use linear processing most, followed by procedural processing, and then circular processing (Lindquist, Tacoma, & Lane, 1993). The U.S. students were more likely to view time as a valuable and limited commodity—something to be scheduled—whereas the Asian students were more concerned with the task itself rather than time.

Naturally, people with different time perspectives may find it difficult to understand each other. Often, people from the United States who become restless when waiting are viewed as rude by people from non-Western cultures. Conversely, people who are always in a hurry may think cultures that are slower and less orderly are behind the times. To be effective in international business and education, one must be sensitive to and adjust to the dominant time orientation.

Biological Time Patterns

Cultural perceptions of time use provide insight into how different groups of people perceive them. Another important aspect of time is how individuals perceive time. Each person has an internal clock that tells her or him when to wake, go to sleep, and eat. **Circadian rhythms** are the daily rhythmic activity cycles, based on 24-hour intervals, that humans experience. The word *circadian* comes from the Latin words *circa* (about) and *dies* (day). Before birth, babies are exposed to these daily rhythms from their mother's eating and sleeping patterns.

Jet lag and the disorientation caused by changing work shifts are examples of how humans react when their rhythms are disturbed. In the case of jet lag, people experience psychological dislocation and disruption of bodily rhythms caused by high-speed travel across several time zones in an airplane. Their sleeping and eating patterns are thrown off. Changing work shifts have been found to be a stressor for individuals and families.

QUANTITATIVE AND QUALITATIVE TIME MEASURES

Perceptions have to do with people's estimations of time, but time can also be measured in units. **Quantitative time measures** refer to the number, kind, and duration (e.g., minutes, hours, day) of activities that occur at specific points in time (Goldsmith, 1990). A quantitative time researcher would be interested in how many minutes a day an individual spends in food preparation, shopping, eating, driving, grooming, playing, child care, elder care, and working. Table 9.1 shows daytime activity results from several studies. Most quantitative time-use data are gathered in four ways:

TABLE 9.1
Where Does Time Go?

Based on **daytime activities** reported by representative adults and teenagers in recent U.S. studies. Percentages will differ by age, gender, social class, and personal preference—minimum and maximum ranges are indicated. Each percentage point is equivalent to about one hour per week.

Productive Activities		**Total: 24–60%**
Working at work, or studying	20–45%	
Talking, eating, daydreaming while at work	4–15%	
Maintenance Activities		**Total: 20–40%**
Housework (cooking, cleaning, shopping)	8–22%	
Eating	3–5%	
Grooming (washing up, dressing)	3–6%	
Driving, transportation	6–9%	
Leisure Activities		**Total: 20–43%**
Media (TV and reading)	9–13%	
Hobbies, sports, movies, restaurants	4–13%	
Talking, socializing	4–12%	
Idling, resting	3–5%	

Source: From *Finding Flow: The Psychology of Engagement with Everyday Life* by Mihaly Csikszentmihalyi. Copyright © 1997 by Mihaly Csikszentmihalyi. Reprinted with permission of Basic Books, a member of Perseus Books, L.L.C.

1. In the *self-report* or *diary method,* individuals record their own time-use data on a form provided by the researcher (Walker & Woods, 1976).

2. In the *recall method,* individuals are asked to think back (recall) and explain in detail a previous day's activities to an interviewer in person, or over the telephone, or by self-report on a form provided by the researcher.

3. In the *observation method,* a trained researcher observes and records the precise way, duration, and sequencing of an individual's activities (Nelson, 1963; Diana, 1983). This method has been used extensively in anthropology and child development.

4. The *self-observational control-signaling method* is rarely used for collecting data on household time use, but is used extensively in business management studies. In this method, subjects are asked to record their time use at a given signal, such as when a bell sounds, a telephone rings, or a light flashes. In most previous studies, the data were recorded at work with the permission of the company's management (Carroll & Taylor, 1968). The method incorporates a self-report, but the reports in the control-signaling method are required at random times and are less expected and less time-consuming for the subject than are the lengthy ongoing diary self-reports. Because the signals occur sporadically and the subject responds immediately, some researchers conclude that the control-signaling method produces more accurate data than the other methods.

Using a combination of methods with built-in cross-checks is generally considered to be the best way to obtain accurate data (Denzin, 1990; Goldsmith, 1977; Hamilton, 1989). Examples of extensive quantitative household time-use studies are the 1967–1968 Walker-Telling study of 1,296 families in Syracuse, New York, and the 11-state spin-off studies (Walker & Woods, 1976; Walker, 1983). These studies used 24-hour recalls as told to interviewers and diaries. Among other things, the New York study established that the presence of young children in the home dramatically increased the amount of household work. In 1994, in another time-use study, Allen Martin and Margaret Sanik reported that women spent more time in household production if there was a young child or a teenager in the household and that men contributed more time to household production as they aged.

In *The Second Shift,* sociologist Arlie Hochschild wrote that many employed women work at a job during the day and go home and work until bedtime at household chores and child care—in other words, women work two jobs. Through interviews and observations, she found that in some marriages where the husband earned more, he justified doing less housework because he contributed more monetarily; she also found marriages where the wife earned more, felt guilty, and therefore did more housework. Hochschild concluded that rarely is housework evenly divided between working parents and that there is a gap between their ideals and the reality of their busy lives. In her follow-up book, *The Time Bind,* Hochschild explored further the interchange between home and work lives. She says that "the more attached we are to the world of work, the more its deadlines, its cycles, its pauses and interruptions shape our lives, and the more family time is forced to accommodate to the pressures of work" (p. 45).

Qualitative time measurement investigates the meaning or significance of time use as well as how individuals feel about their time use—that is, the satisfaction it generates. It also measures who they are spending time with.

Consider the following comment by the Duke of Windsor, who abdicated the British throne to marry an American divorcée in 1937. "You know what my day was today?" asked the former king, "I got up late and then I went with the Duchess and watched her buy a hat" (Menkes, 1987).

The "who" part of how time is spent is important because daily life is not defined solely by what we do, but also by who we are with. According to an exhibit on "The Time of Law" at the Gulbenkian Museum in Lisbon, Portugal, "Awareness of time is a construction of individual personality and human solidarity." Mihaly Csikszentmihalyi (1997) estimates that people spend roughly equal amounts of time in three social contexts:

1. Among strangers, coworkers, fellow students. This is "public" space where one's actions are evaluated by others and where one competes for resources.
2. Among family and friends. This is a place of kinship, special bonds, and home.
3. In solitude. Time spent alone.

In technological societies, more time is spent alone than was common in tribal societies, where being alone was often considered dangerous. Many people are uncomfortable being alone, but it is important to learn to tolerate solitude or else the quality of our lives is bound to suffer (Csikszentmihalyi, 1997). The popularity of chat rooms and e-mail may be partially explained by this need to connect with others even if physically alone.

Prior to the 1970s, nearly all time-use measurement was quantitative. Since then, several studies have used qualitative measures as well as a combination of quantitative and qualitative measures. The increased use of qualitative measures is a response to the growing recognition that simply knowing how many minutes are spent washing dishes or diapering a baby does not provide as meaningful time-use data as knowing how persons performing the task feel or how they interact with others involved in the task. Asking qualitative questions also lets the researcher know how the individual feels; thus, the burden of interpretation is no longer on the researcher where obvious bias or perceptual errors could occur.

As an example of a study investigating the qualitative aspects of time use, Hafstrom and Paynter (1991) studied data collected on farm wives in seven states and found that although farm wives (many of whom were employed off the farm) appeared to assume a large share of the workload—a combination of home, farm, and labor force—they remained satisfied with management in the home and on the farm. Hafstrom and Paynter also found that satisfaction with time use was affected by a variety of factors, including the wife's sense of control over her own life. So, even though the wives reported being overloaded with work and family demands, they still were relatively satisfied with their lifestyle and accepted its complexity.

Demands, Sequencing, and Standards

Three concepts introduced earlier in this book—demands, sequencing, and standards—are an integral part of the discussion of time from a managerial perspective. Since time is a limited resource, individuals have to make decisions about how to allocate their time. Demands, sequencing, and standards affect these decisions.

Demands

As lives become more complicated, increasing demands are placed on time. Demands are events or goals that necessitate or motivate action. For example, schools demand attendance, workplaces demand a certain number of hours of work, parents demand a safe neighborhood for their children, the children's coach demands that they spend time practicing, and citizens demand fair government.

Many of these demands may not be met, but they are goals or ideals worth striving for. One would assume that saving time is the main reason that people buy and use appliances, but research shows that conventional appliances do not always reduce time demands. In the United States, the average woman aged 18 to 50 spends 57 minutes a day cooking. The difference between women with microwave ovens and those without is just 4 minutes (Robinson & Milkie, 1997). Experimentation is underway to find appliances and computer-aided systems that will more effectively save time and at the same time serve families as well or better than before.

Demands on time within families and organizations may conflict. One child may want the parents to attend her school play while a sibling wants them to come to his soccer game. At work, employees find several tasks competing for their attention. Stretching limited resources, including time, to meet conflicting demands is a dilemma all people experience. Families with young children or disabled family members may face even greater demands on their time. Teenagers and dependent elderly may put high emotional demands on the family, and meeting those demands takes time.

Unfortunately, demands are often strongest when resources are weakest, as in the case of young married couples who are trying to set up a household, have children, and become established in their careers—all at the same time. Time demands are also high for families trying to balance more established careers and home responsibilities. According to John Robinson of the University of Maryland and Geoffrey Godbey of Pennsylvania State University, Americans have about 40 hours of leisure time a week now versus 35 hours in 1964.

> "It just doesn't feel like it," Robinson said. "They perceive that they have less and are more rushed." The thief is perception; people are losing time only in their minds, but the perception feels more real than the reality. Too, that leisure time tends to come in shreds rather than blocks. (Werland, 2000, p. 6D)

Besides demands external to the person, there are internal demands as well. All individuals have a **tempo,** meaning a time pattern or pace that feels comfortable to them. One person may be described as "high energy, always on the go, or hyper," whereas another is described as "slow, thoughtful, and deliberate." Successful organizations thrive on having members with both types of temperaments.

Sometimes demand for time is uneven and difficult to manage, and tradition plays a part. For example, bicycle stores may be empty during weekdays, but crowded on Saturdays with children and parents. Tennis courts and golf courses are usually overbooked on weekends. Thus, demand can range from none at all to excessive and can be irregular as well. When shopping, consumers try to gauge when demand will be low, lines short, and stores uncrowded. As these examples illustrate, the concept of demand can be applied to time as well as to other constructs and contexts, such as shopping demands and energy demands. In the United States, Sunday afternoons have turned into popular times to browse and shop. This transformation started around 1900 when libraries and ball parks were opened on Sundays. By the mid-1960s most stores and restaurants were open on Sundays although a few national fast-food chains continue to be closed on Sundays, and many stores and restaurants have reduced hours.

Sequencing

A sequence is a following of one thing after another in a series or an arrangement. Examples of sequences are sharpening a pencil before writing with it, unlocking a door before entering a house, or making an appointment before going to the dentist. Individuals' daily lives are filled with many such sequences. Sequencing refers to the order of activities in time, as in a series of events. Sequencing may be simple or complex. In a simple sequence, one person performs one task. A complicated sequencing plan involves many people and many tasks. Obviously, a large family with children at different ages will have more trouble completing tasks and holding to a set sequence than a person living alone.

Schedules, which are sets of time-bounded activities, are made up of two mental processes—sequencing and time-tagging. **Time-tagging** is a mental estimation of the sequences that should take place, the approximate amount of time required for each activity in the sequence, and the starting and ending times for each activity (Avery & Stafford, 1991). Repeatedly following the same sequences with the same starting and ending points leads to procedural routines where the person no longer has to think about the individual steps in the sequence. Remember learning how to drive a car or use a computer? At first, you were slow and had to think carefully about each step. In time, the sequence became faster and felt more natural. Schedules and sequences can be mental or they can be written, as in a schedule of college classes or a program of forthcoming events.

As mentioned earlier, many individuals and families feel overwhelmed by demands on their time—they are living in a time drought, a barren land with little relief. They feel short of time because of the phenomenon of multitasking, which is becoming more and more the norm. As described in Chapter 6, tasks can be divided into three main categories: interdependent, dovetailed, and overlapped. In *interdependent* activities, one task must be completed before the next task can begin. An example of an interdependent activity is mailing a letter. The letter has to be written and the envelope stamped and addressed before mailing. Doing two or more activities at once is called *dovetailing*. A person may, for example, fold laundry and watch television at the same time. In fact, people are so used to having the radio or the television playing in the background that they do not consider these as competing activities. Many dull, repetitive activities lend themselves to dovetailing. The one drawback to dovetailing is that if you do too many activities at one time, the end results may be less than desired. A meal can be burned, a deadline missed, or a message misinterpreted if a person is trying to do too much at once. *Overlapping* involves giving intermittent attention to two or more activities until they are completed. For example, a parent might put a baby to bed, then read while partly listening to hear if the baby is falling asleep. On any given day, people use all three types of sequencing. Along this same line of thought, Claxton warns that

> There is an old Polish saying, "Sleep faster; we need the pillows," which reminds us that there are some activities which just will not be rushed. They take the time that they take. If you are late for a meeting, you can hurry. If the roast potatoes

are slow to brown, you can turn up the oven. But if you try to speed up the baking of meringues, they burn. If you are impatient with the mayonnaise and add the oil too quickly, it curdles. If you start tugging with frustration on a tangled fishing line, the knot just becomes tighter. (p. 1)

Each individual may favor a certain type of sequencing based on his or her style, pace, or tempo. Most people go through a certain sequence of events when they first awaken in the morning. They perform routine activities such as putting on a bathrobe, going to the bathroom, taking a shower or washing their face, combing their hair, watching the morning news programs or reading the newspaper, dressing, and eating breakfast. As the day progresses, they move into more complicated sequencing involving dovetailing and overlapping activities. At bedtime, they revert back to a more habitual sequential mode, essentially reversing the morning routine with a snack, brushing teeth, going to the bathroom, undressing, reading or watching television, and going to sleep.

Successful managers have an understanding of their recurring patterns and how they need to manage their time to be effective. They may have to break their normal sequence if they want to move ahead. If they are achievers, it means that they want to accomplish things, but sometimes this is at the expense of having enough personal interaction. If this is a weak spot, the manager will have to make time to visit with others, stroll around the offices and factories, and go to the water cooler or break room. As a counterpoint to this, a manager who is totally people-oriented may have difficulty settling down to tasks and will have to arrange his or her time accordingly to move projects along.

Another way to discuss the impact of personality on time use is to categorize people as mainly polychronic or monochronic. **Polychronic** refers to liking to do several things at once, whereas **monochronic** refers to preferring to focus on one activity at a time such as reading or watching a football game on television. The monochronic person dislikes being distracted from the activity at hand, and this has been the subject of many television situation comedy episodes. For example, on *Everybody Loves Raymond*, several plot lines revolve around Raymond or his father or brother being disturbed by Raymond's wife or mother while the men are trying to watch sports on television. An example of a polychronic person is someone who pages through a magazine while talking on a cell phone and carrying on a conversation with the person next to him.

A **routine** is a habitual way of doing things that saves time and energy for other activities. Routines and habits provide stability to our lives. Young children thrive on routines at home and in preschool. Learning logical ways of sequencing activities is part of the socialization process. Some of us need more routine than others. The roots of this need probably stem from childhood socialization patterns, personality, and temperament. Remember that it was said earlier that goals should be made part of your everyday routine. Are you moving positively toward your goal achievement or moving farther away? If more relaxation time is a goal, consider the words of wife and mother Joann Gardner, 36, of Brooklyn, New York:

"I would feel guilty about doing anything for myself," says Gardner, a stay-at-home mother and a former freelance television producer. But last spring she picked up a novel she'd received for Christmas and liberated herself. Now, at least three times a week, she snuggles guilt-free under the covers in the middle of the day and savors a book for an hour while 19-month-old Rainer naps. . . . "I do laundry on weekends now, when my husband can watch our son," says Gardner who squeezes in more chores during Rainer's nap time on those days she doesn't read or nap herself. "The breaks keep me sane," she says. "I'm not on my last nerve all the time." (Jackson, 2003, p. 216)

Standards

A standard is an acknowledged measure of comparison or a criterion. The notion of standards incorporates the concept of value. It can be said that people have a certain set of standards, meaning that they conduct their lives in a particular way. Standards serve as guides or measures of human behavior. As discussed earlier, a more detailed definition of standards by DeMerchant (1993) describes them as quantitative and/or qualitative criteria, or measures of values and goals, that reconcile resources with demands and affect how certain tasks or activities are completed.

Standards are relevant to this chapter on managing time because in today's fast-moving world, individuals and families often do not have enough time or energy to meet the standards they aspire to—in keeping their homes clean, exercising regularly, eating appropriately, meeting family needs, and accomplishing work. Great demands on time are experienced in other countries besides the United States. An article about daily time use in rural households in India reported that women, including pregnant women, worked an average of 14 to 16 hours per day (Singal, Srinivasan, & Jindal, 1993). Their hours were split between a variety of jobs in the home and farm and livestock management. Clearly, maintaining standards in all areas under these conditions is difficult.

Standards have both quantitative and qualitative aspects. Quantity refers to a measurable amount. Quality refers to a degree or grade of excellence, the essential character or nature of something. Quantitatively, a teacher may set a standard of grading 50 math papers an hour. Qualitatively, a person may want food prepared to a certain standard of nutrition, taste, and attractiveness.

Conflict arises in homes and organizations when people have different standards. For example, if a teacher expects to grade 50 math papers an hour, an intern assigned to the teacher who can grade only 5 papers an hour will fall below expectations. In a restaurant, if food is not prepared to the expected standard, a customer may send the food back to the kitchen. In a home, some family members may be perfectly happy living in a mess that other family members cannot tolerate. One of the values of living on a college campus is the opportunity to experience how many different ways people can live and the different standards they have.

Standards of quality and quantity form the criteria for action. Demands lead to an alteration of standards. Students cramming for a test will not have time to cook dinner or to go to movies with friends. Preparing for the test demands all their time and attention, so household work and friends have to wait.

The more complex the lifestyle and the greater number of people involved, the more regular standards have to be if everyone involved is going to survive and thrive. The military is an example. Beds must be made a certain way, and rooms are inspected. Everyone wears uniforms. When 1,000 service people must be fed in one hour, food lines have to move efficiently. Because of the vast numbers of people and the complexity and seriousness of their tasks, there is little room for individual choices or variations in standards.

SUGGESTED ACTIVITY

Write a paragraph about your routines. Which ones do you have? This could include morning rituals, bedtime rituals, driving routes, parking spaces, classroom seats, or mealtime preferences, to name only a few. Are your routines similar or dissimilar to the way you were raised? What differences have you noticed between your routines and those of roommates or friends? Discuss what you have written with others. What throws you off your routine?

SUGGESTED ACTIVITY

If you had a choice between earning more money at your current job or working fewer hours at your current job, which would you choose? In a survey conducted at the University of Connecticut ("The Tomorrow Trap," 1999), most workers chose more money, and men were more likely than women to choose more money. So, we have a paradox; most American workers say they want more time with their immediate family, but they also want to earn the extra money that comes from longer hours. What do you think about this? Does it have to be time versus money? What are the alternatives? Discuss in groups.

Web-Based Resources

To learn more about the link between privacy, time, and performance in work-places, visit **www.steelcase.com.** For reports on values, goals, and time research in the United States and the latest public poll information from the Gallup organization, check its Web site at **www.gallup.com.** Go to the Web sites of appliance makers and home builders for information on transformations in homes, trends, etc. Time use greatly influences home design.

Summary

This chapter focused on time and time management. Time is a limited, nonrenewable, scarce resource. Consequently, it is valuable. It has also been the subject of much philosophical debate. Time perceptions vary from individual to individual and within and between cultures. Personality and preference come into play. The ABC method of time prioritizing is a useful way of managing time, as is the concept that daily time use should be related to goals sought. Both quantitative time measures (i.e., those using units such as seconds, minutes, hours, and days) and qualitative time measures (feelings about time use) provide useful information for managing households and businesses. Time-use data have many practical applications to the home, the marketplace, and the work world. Studies show that Tuesday is the most productive day of the week. Demands, standards, and sequencing provide applications of time management to work and other activities. Too little time and too much responsibility lead to stress, the subject of Chapter 11. The next chapter will examine the complexity arising from trying to balance work and family life.

Key Terms

circadian rhythms	polychronic	time
discretionary time	qualitative time	time displacement
drift time	measurement	time management
focus groups	quantitative time	time perception
monochronic	measures	time-tagging
nondiscretionary time	routine	
perception	tempo	

Review Questions

1. What is the difference between a polychronic and a monochronic personality type? Which is your preferred style? Give an example that explains your answer.

2. What is your reaction to the quotation from Leonard Berry about "Norman Rockwell expectations" and today's hurried mealtimes?

3. What is the balance in your life between discretionary and nondiscretionary time? Which do you have more of? Often holidays and summers offer drift time: Is this true in your case? If so, do you enjoy drift time? What do you do differently?

4. What is your opinion of the quotation from David Elkind about today's hurried child?

5. According to Mihaly Csikszentmihalyi in *Finding Flow,* people spend roughly equal amounts of daytime in three social contexts (i.e., with strangers or coworkers/students, with family and friends, and alone). Is your time similarly spent? If you could change your time use in any way, what would you change? Explain your answers.

References

Alsop, S. (2003, March 17). There's a killer app on the loose—but I'm on the case. *Fortune,* 124.

Avery, R., & Stafford, K. (1991). Toward a scheduling congruity theory of family resource management. *Lifestyles: Family and Economic Issues, 12*(4), 327.

Berry, L. (1990, February). Market to the perception. *American Demographics, 12,* 30–33.

Bianchi, S. (2000, November). Maternal employment and time with children: Dramatic change or surprising continuity? *Demography, 37*(4), 401–414.

Boss, S. (2000, September 25). On the clock, all the time. *Christian Science Monitor, 11,* 16.

Carroll, S., & Taylor, W. (1968). A study of the validity of a self-observational central-signaling method of work sampling. *Personnel Psychology, 21,* 359–364.

Clark, D. (1999, June 21). Managing the mountain. *The Wall Street Journal,* R4.

Claxton, G. (1997). *Hare brain tortoise mind.* New York: Norton.

Csikszentmihalyi, M. (1997). *Finding flow.* New York: Basic Books.

Crossen, C. (2003, November 5). Daylight saving time pitted farmers against the "idle" city folks. *The Wall Street Journal,* B1.

DeMerchant, E. (1993). Standards: An analysis of definitions, frameworks and implications. *Proceedings of the Eastern Regional Home Management—Family Economics Conference,* Blacksburg, VA.

Denzin, N. (1990). *Sociological methods: A source book.* Chicago: Aldine Press.

Diana, M. (1983). The relationship between observation of affiliative behavior patterns for parents and toddlers and parental reports of caregiving, play, and support-control behaviors. Unpublished Ph.D. thesis, Michigan State University, East Lansing.

Elkind, D. (1988). *The hurried child.* Reading, MA: Addison-Wesley.

Godbey, G., & Graefe, A. (1993, April). Rapid growth in rushin' Americans. *American Demographics,* 26–27.

Goforth, C. (2002, November 20). Most people do more on Tuesday. *Tallahassee Democrat,* 5E.

Goldsmith, E. (1977). Time use of beginning families with employed and unemployed wives. Unpublished Ph.D. thesis, Michigan State University, East Lansing.

Goldsmith, E. (1990). The effect of women's employment on quantitative and qualitative time-use measurements: A review and synthesis. *Home Economics Forum, 4*(2), 18–20.

Graham, R. (1981). The role of perception in consumer research. *Journal of Consumer Research, 7,* 335–342.

Greene, K. (2003, June 9). How to survive the first year. *The Wall Street Journal,* R1.

Hafstrom, J., & Paynter, M. (1991). Time use satisfaction of wives: Home, farm, and labor force workload. *Lifestyles: Family and Economic Issues, 12*(2), 131–143.

Hall, E. T. (1959). *The silent language.* New York: Fawcett World Library.

Hamilton, J. (1989). Epistemology and meaning: A case for multi-methodologies for social research in home economics. *Home Economics Forum, 4,* 12–14.

Hawkins, D., Best, R., & Coney, K. (1986). *Consumer behavior* (3rd ed.). Plano, TX: Business Publications.

Hochschild, A. (1989). *The second shift.* New York: Viking.

Hochschild, A. (1997). *The time bind.* New York: Henry Holt.

Jackson, M. (2003, September). Stopping the clock/Creating sacred time. Real Simple, 212–217.

Jordan, M., & Karp, J. (2003, December 9). Machines for the masses. *The Wall Street Journal,* A19–20.

Kaufman, C., & Lane, P. (1993). Role overload and the perception of time pressure, *Proceedings of the Atlantic Marketing Association,* Orlando, FL, 25–30.

L'Abate, L., & Harel, T. (1993). Deriving, developing, and expanding a theory of developmental competence from resource exchange theory. In U. Foa, J. Converse, K. Tornblom, & E. Foa (Eds.), *Resource theory: Explorations and applications* (pp. 233–269). San Diego: Academic Press.

Lakein, A. (1973). *How to get control of your time and your life.* New York: New American Library.

LeHew, M. (2001/2002). Single-parent and dual-income families: Time-poor consumers? *Journal of Consumer Education, 19/20,* 51–60.

Lindquist, J., Tacoma, S., & Lane, P. (1993). What is time: An exploratory extension toward the Far East. In M. Levy and D. Grewal (Eds.), *Developments in marketing*, Vol. 16 (pp. 186–189). Proceedings of the Annual Conference of the Academy of Marketing Science, Miami Beach, FL.

Martin, A., & Sanik, M. (1994). Determinants of married men's and women's time spent in household production in 1985. *Proceedings of the 1994 Conference of the Eastern Family Economics and Resource Management Association,* Pittsburgh, PA, 1–17.

Mattingly, M., & Bianchi, S. (2003, March). Gender differences in the quantity and quality of free time: The U.S. experience. *Social Forces, 81* (3), 999–1030.

Menkes, S. (1987). *The Windsor style.* Topsfield, MA: Salem House.

Mintz, S. (2000, June 22). How juice went from stone age to ice age. *The Wall Street Journal,* A22.

Mutz, D., Roberts, D., & Van Vuuren, D. (1993, February). Reconsidering the displacement hypothesis. *Communication Research, 20*(1), 51–75.

Nelson, L. (1963). Daily activity patterns of peasant homemakers. Unpublished Ph.D. thesis, Michigan State University, East Lansing.

Owen, A. (1991). Time and time again: Implications of time perception theory. *Lifestyle: Family and Economic Issues, 12*(4), 345–359.

Penteado, J. (1981, May 25). U.S. fast foods move slowly. *Advertising Age,* S–8.

Robinson, J., & Milkie, M. (1997). Dances with dust bunnies: Housecleaning in America, *American Demographics,* p. 40.

Shellenbarger, S. (2002, September 26). Making time to veg: Parents find their kids need life balance as well. *The Wall Street Journal,* D1.

Senge, P. (1999). *The Dance of Change,* New York: Doubleday.

Singal, S., Srinivasan, K., & Jindal, R. (1993). Women's work status and their time use pattern in rural households of Haryana. *Journal of Consumer Studies and Home Economics, 17,* 99–104.

Taylor, C. (2003, May). Balancing act. *Smart Money,* 77–83.

Taylor, F. (1911). *The principles of scientific management* New York: Harper & Brothers.

The tomorrow trap. (1999, December 17). *The Wall Street Journal,* W16.

Walker, K. (1983). An interstate urban/rural comparison of families' time use: Introduction. *Home Economics Research Journal, 12*(2), 119–121.

Walker, K., & Woods, M. (1976). *Time use: A measure of household production of family goods and services.* Washington, DC: American Home Economics Association.

Werland, R. (2000, January 11). Pressed for time? *Tallahassee Democrat,* D1, D6.

chapter 10

Managing Work and Family

MAIN TOPICS

Did you know that . . . ?

. . .The average workweek is 30 percent shorter than a hundred years ago.

. . . In 1850, the U.S. Census listed 322 job titles; today there are over 31,000.

> I don't want to get to the end of my life and find that I have lived just the length of it. I want to have lived the width of it as well.
>
> —*Diane Ackerman*

THIS CHAPTER EXPLORES the domains of work and family life and the spillover between them. There is no question that the boundaries between work and personal lives are blurring. Robert Reich, former U.S. Secretary of Labor says:

> In the old days, we might have taken work home in a briefcase and then late at night maybe gone through it and done whatever needed to be done. Now we turn on the computer. And everything we do during the day is right in front of us. All the connections, all the people, all the problems, and all the projects are going 24 hours a day. It's not just the computer. It's the pager, the cell phone, the voicemail and the instant messaging. (Blumenstein, 2001, p. R15)

Add to this the growing use of wireless laptops in the bedroom and on the couch in front of the television, and the work/family life interchange escalates. Multitasking has reached new heights. Few people are immune from the problems associated with trying to balance work and home lives. For example,

> Just a few years ago, Krishan Kalra worked as fast and as furiously as any other Silicon Valley CEO. The founder of a biotech company called Bio-Genex Laboratories, the 55-year-old native of India pushed himself, his 150 employees and his family to the breaking point. Finally, with his marriage in crisis and the kids feeling neglected, Kalra dropped out for three months. . . . Today, back at work Kalra meditates during the day and, at night religiously ignores the temptations of

the fax, laptop and phone to be with his family. "I've started to pay attention to all aspects of my life," he says. "Once you become a whole person, you tend to be more creative and productive." (Stone, 1999, p. 68)

Dowonia Goodwin, a school bus driver and a single mother with three children, should by all accounts also be a casualty of the work and family battleground, but she is coping quite well with the help of her nine brothers and sisters. She says that, without them, she "would totally fall apart" (Shellenbarger, 1999, p. B1). She also relies on a child-care center for her youngest.

The Kalras and the Goodwins are two families trying to manage the important life roles of work and family. With the increasing number of women joining the labor force worldwide and the increasing number of people working at home, management experts have turned their attention to the problems individuals and families face in trying to meet work and family responsibilities. Studies have focused on gender differences in responding to work/life balance problems (Maume & Houston, 2001) and on organizational size (MacDermid, Hertzog, Kensinger, & Zipp, 2001). The latter study found that smaller organizations often created more innovative-nurturing environments than did larger employers. They were closer to their employees and understood their needs better. The focus of this chapter is on the resource management problems and solutions associated with balancing work and family or life roles. Since statistics indicate that most college graduates will marry and work full-time, the problems of combining work and family are not just societal issues, but personal issues of significance for the readers of this chapter.

To give perspective, if one were to believe media outpourings, one might think that the "superwoman" and "superman" model of working and loving is a new phenomenon. It is not. People have been combining several roles for a long time. They have worked split shifts, served in the military, or in some other way worked a variety of hours or jobs or in more than one location, while at the same time trying to raise a family and have a personal life. Individuals may be friends, siblings, parents, children, workers, employers, caregivers, neighbors, students, teachers, volunteers; indeed, they may play many more roles, depending on choices and circumstances. Perhaps of all these roles, work and family stand out as the most important to an individual's self-image and are the most demanding of her or his time. Adults spend most of their time sleeping (one-third of our lives), at home alone or with families or friends, or at work. When Sigmund Freud was asked his recipe for happiness, his short answer was "work and love."

OVERVIEW OF WORK AND FAMILY

Although both men and women work, the rapid influx of women into the labor force since the 1970s has caused a shift in the public's perception of the interchange between work and family. According to a United Nations' report ("The World's Women 1970–1990"),

Women everywhere contribute to economic production. As officially measured, 46 percent of the world's women aged 15 and over—828 million—are economically active. At least another 10–20 percent of the world's women are economically productive but not counted as part of the labor force because of inadequate measurement.

More and more families are feeling pressured for time and stressed from coping with conflicting work and family demands. In response, employers wanting the most satisfied and productive workers possible are reexamining child and elder care policies and providing flextime and other schedule changes to accommodate family needs.

Several facts, figures, and research findings about the work and family interchange include:

◆ Although baby boomers are known for paying their career dues through long hours and other sacrifices, postboomers are more diverse. Some Generation-Xers work almost around the clock, while a second, polar opposite group resists, leaning more toward nesting, family, and community (Shellenbarger, 1998). Coming up behind Generation X, the baby boomlet will further rewrite the work–life book, with technology as its tool.

◆ Currently, in the United States, women on average earn less than men, but the earnings gap is closing.

◆ Fewer than one-third of U.S. workers are on flexible schedules (Shellenbarger, 2003, February 13).

◆ Most U.S. teenagers have jobs before they graduate from high school.

◆ Families with two earners, one parent, or young children, are likely to experience work–family conflict and job tension (Kelly & Voydanoff, 1985; Voydanoff, 1988, 1993; Voydanoff & Kelly, 1984).

◆ The more positive fathers' work experiences, the higher their self-esteem, which affects their parenting styles (Grimm-Thomas & Perry-Jenkins, 1994).

◆ Spousal support has a direct positive relationship with job commitment (Orthner & Pittman, 1986).

◆ Commuter marriages have become more common (Anderson, 1992). Commuter marriages occur when employed spouses live a distance from one another and maintain two separate households. An example is a professor at Florida State University married to a professor at Ohio State University; they get together during the summer and on holidays and weekends and at conferences.

◆ The problems of combining work and family are worldwide concerns that will become increasingly important as more nations become industrialized and more women leave the home to enter the labor force (Goldsmith, 1993).

Work and Family Conflicts

At the center of the work and family debate is the concern that a person who is heavily involved in one domain (work or family) may not be psychologically or physically available for the other. Work and family conflict may arise when a person is torn between work and family demands, and frustration develops. It may also arise when spouses, coworkers, employers, and children differ over how work and family time should be divided.

As one way to manage work and family demands, more parents are choosing to have children later in life. Baby boom women have married late, delayed childbearing, and spaced their births farther apart. Although some parents choose not to work outside the home when their children are young, the general trend is toward increased employment participation for mothers of infants and young children. Employment rates for mothers with children under the age of two increased from 31 percent in 1970 to 54 percent in 1985, and employment for mothers of infants less than a year old rose 100 percent between 1970 and the mid-1980s, when it reached 49 percent (Rapoport, 1985; Schroeder, 1988). It has risen further since.

Voydanoff (1989) identified several job demands that are related to work/family conflict:

- Role ambiguity (doubt or uncertainty)
- Role conflict
- Intellectual or physical effort
- Rapid change
- Pressures for quality work
- Pressure to work hard and fast
- Heavy workload

A Families and Work Institute study found that "many U.S. workers may be working too hard, leading to more mistakes on the job, neglected personal relationships, and higher health-care costs" ("Study: Many U.S. Employees Feel Overworked, 2001"). Work pressures and constant travel strain personal relations.

In answer to the question of who is the most time pressured, Susan Roxburgh's research found that the answer is the affluent, parents, caregivers, and people in high-demand, low-control jobs (2002). In *To Love and Work: A Systemic Interlocking of Family, Workplace, and Career,* David Ulrich and Harry Dunne describe a therapy session with a busy executive, who "glancing at his watch as he sat down for his first and only interview, announced that he could take one hour to decide whether or not to divorce his wife" (1986, p. 129). These authors also say that many workers treat the home as a "pit stop," or a refueling place for the main purpose in life, getting ahead at work. Spouses and children are virtually ignored in the "pit stop" approach to home and family life.

Benefits of Work and Spillover to Families

Work can also benefit families and be a source of individual and familial pride. Most women in the labor force work primarily because they or their family needs the money and secondarily because they seek personal self-actualization. Promotions, praise, awards, and raises are other benefits of work that can increase self-esteem. In addition, several studies indicate that performing the multiple roles of worker, spouse, and parent is positively related to women's physical and mental health (Voydanoff, 1989). Regarding health, one of the chief benefits of work is employer-sponsored health insurance—this helps millions of employees and their families.

Another benefit of work is that many people enjoy it, at least certain aspects of it. For both men and women there is even the possibility of passion (defined as personal intensity) in work expressed in experiences and emotions.

This family is multitasking, getting ready for the day ahead. The kitchen is often the meeting place and the launch pad.

According to Richard Chang (2001), a passion plan at work begins with starting from the heart and then progresses to

1. Discovering core passions
2. Clarifying purpose
3. Defining actions
4. Performing with passion
5. Spreading excitement
6. Staying the course

Chang says that organizations are driven and defined by their collective passions. For example, a publishing house can be driven by a love of books and literature. He makes the point that if designers don't care about customers, how can they design furniture that excites the customer enough to buy it? Let's say that an individual is energized or inspired by work. Wouldn't it make sense that the emotion would spill over in a positive way to home and family life? The preponderance of research literature focuses on the negative aspects of work and family; but it would be irresponsible not to emphasize the benefits as well. Many people are happier being busy in both realms; problems arise when the roles become overwhelming. Solutions to this from a family management point of view are addressed next.

Resolving Work and Family Conflicts

Individuals or families may find the following approaches helpful in reducing work and family conflict:

1. Manage the conflict so that different ideas, opinions, and approaches are brought out for discussion.
2. Resolve conflict when it becomes too disruptive.
3. Cultivate a sense of humor and thus create an atmosphere of mutual support.

The first option is a preventive strategy, and the second can be used when conflict already exists and needs to be addressed immediately. The second strategy comes into play when the conflict interferes with family members' ability to get their work done and threatens the security and the functioning of the family as a whole and of individual family members. The third strategy is the newest and involves using humor as a coping skill. When family-work conflicts first emerged, everyone was quite serious about the issue, but as we've gotten more used to the conflicts as a society, some humor has emerged in the form of cartoons, billboards, magazine articles, novels, television shows and advertisements, and in-home banter. Much of the humor comes from taking situations more lightly, realizing you can't control the universe, and accepting that mistakes happen. Humor can be a form of affection and a symbol of understanding that heals the conflict or at least smoothes it over.

It is not unusual for individuals and families to hope that time conflicts will go away (e.g., things will be better next week when my report is finished), but they seldom do. If the conflict builds to a crisis, the persons involved have to examine the cause of the frustration and discuss solutions. According to Lewis (1993, p. 145), conflict usually arises from one or more of the following:

♦ *Values*. What we deem important. These include our work ethic, our sense of family responsibility, and similar issues.
♦ *Facts*. Our perception of what the facts are.
♦ *Role perceptions*. How different people view a role. Differing role perceptions can lead to role conflict.
♦ *Methods*. Disagreements about the best or the right way to do something are common.
♦ *Objectives*. Differences over what the objectives should be and their relative importance.

From a family management perspective, the way work and family conflicts are resolved depends on the answers to the following questions:

1. How strong is each individual's concern with satisfying her or his own interests in the issue?
2. How strong is each individual's concern with satisfying the interests of his or her spouse or children? (adapted from Lewis, 1993, p. 145)

Obviously, compromise is one solution to a couple's or a family's work and family conflicts. In **compromise** each person makes concessions, giving in a little in order to gain a valued settlement or outcome (e.g., harmony, an intact, functioning family). Accommodation is another solution wherein the needs of each person are accommodated or adjusted to as best they can be. Since work and family time conflicts can be a lifelong battle and work and family demands change over time, the people involved should not rush the process. Once they agree on when to leave for work in the morning, for example, each person should regularly check to see whether the agreement is still working or whether a new schedule is needed.

Unemployment and the Family

When this book went to press, the United States was in a recovery phase, and the unemployment rate was hovering around 5.5 percent. Generally, in economic theory, an unemployment rate of 5 percent or less is considered desirable, and an unemployment rate of 10 percent or more is considered an indicator of a depression. During the Great Depression of the 1930s, unemployment went over 10 percent and since then there have been places in the country (i.e., when a plant closes) that have experienced temporary unemployment rates of over 10 percent. In other nations in the world, 10 percent or more unemployment is not unusual, and each country has its own way of defining when unemployment rates reach crisis levels.

Although the chapter so far has focused on the problems of combining work and family life, there are problems associated with not having enough work, being underemployed, and unemployed. What happens to the work and family interchange when a breadwinner suddenly is out of work? Going from eight hours of work per day to zero requires an adjustment of time, ego, and family as well as an adjustment to the loss of income. Most of the studies on unemployment were done in the Great Depression and focused on men. Since the recession of the 1980s, the downsizing of companies in the 1990s, and the recession in the early 21st century, studies have focused on the effects of unemployment on both men and women.

Larson, Wilson, and Beley (1994) found that stress stemming from job insecurity is related to marital and family dysfunction and a host of family problems. Unemployment is a crisis event affecting all aspects of a person's and a family's life including resource management and social support systems. In a study of 216 unemployed women in Louisiana, the researchers found that the women sought and successfully obtained assistance from relatives and friends (Retherford, Hildreth, & Goldsmith, 1989). The women's parents were especially helpful in providing emotional support. Overall, the way people react to unemployment depends on the length of the unemployment period, the circumstances surrounding the unemployment, and the potential for future employment, as well as the strength of the family support systems and financial status of the unemployed person. Suggestions for helping partners/spouses find jobs include

- Letting the unemployed spouse guide the pace of the job search. There will be days of totally unproductive time; resist asking about the search daily.
- Listening to the spouse: Where do they really want to work, what do they want to do?
- Talking about your workplace, keeping the conversation going.
- Doing things (non-work related) to show you care.

When unemployment rises nationally, workers cut back on sick days, so that absenteeism has hit 10-year lows in the United States (Tejada, 2003). In a slow job market it is not good for workers to appear lazy, and people are afraid they will lose their jobs if they call in sick too often.

Due to changes in the U.S. economy, increasing numbers of blue-collar workers in the steel, automotive, rubber, textile, apparel, and electronic industries have been vulnerable to extended unemployment, permanent job loss, or reemployment at lower wage and benefits levels (Smith & Price, 1992). A study of women workers who lost their jobs in textile and apparel plants in Georgia provides insight into how the loss of work affects families. The researchers found that the stage in the family life cycle and the demands of combining productive work and family responsibilities contributed to women's experience of unemployment and their labor market participation (Smith & Price, 1992). For example, one woman in the study observed:

It's kind of nice, really, being at home with children. I spent 20 years working and my mother-in-law raised the kids because I had to work. My husband likes it too.

He likes me cooking for him, being at home when he comes home and not run-ning around trying to clean and cook and take care of the children. (p. 67)

Another participant in the study reacted differently:

After you've worked all this time and paid for things, you feel guilty, like you're not doing your part. It's hard to get used to not carrying your own weight. You worry about emergencies if you've only got one insurance carrier, lose a sense of security. I miss being independent. When we go on vacation I would put my own portion in the pot. It's really a change—I've learned to be dependent. I guess I've learned who was in charge. Just giving up the independence [from] bringing home a good salary was something. (p. 69)

The Interchange between Work and Family

As the previous quotations indicate, the interchange between work and family involves many issues. It is not only a gender issue or a husband versus wife issue. According to Voydanoff,

In recent years researchers have recognized that it is necessary not only to under-stand relationships between work and family roles for either the husband or wife but also to examine the combined effects of husbands' and wives' work role char-acteristics on family life. Preliminary research has begun to address joint effects in terms of amounts and scheduling of work time, relative socioeconomic attainment of husbands and wives, work-related geographic mobility, and commuter mar-riage. (1989, p. 8)

Generally, far more is known about the effects of work on family than vice versa. Ulrich and Dunne (1986) observed that many of the ways that people react to work, employers, and coworkers are based on early childhood experi-ences, especially relationships with parents and siblings. The boss may serve as a parent figure, and how the employee responds to that boss may have a lot to do with how she or he perceives authority. Loyalty to parents and the family unit may spill over into loyalty to the firm. Relationships between coworkers may be a reliving of the childhood give and take between brothers and sisters.

Going beyond childhood experiences into the present day, it is acknowl-edged that marital satisfaction and family responsibilities affect work perfor-mance and a person's motivation to work. Thus, severe personal or family problems affect work performance. Someone going through a difficult divorce or having problems with children may talk about his or her problems at work and be distracted from the tasks at hand. Many employers offer Employee Assistance Programs (EAPs) to help workers and families with emotional, financial, and legal difficulties and problems with alcoholism and drug abuse. For example, more than 70 percent of the nation's largest companies (e.g., AT&T, DuPont, McDonnell Douglas, and General Motors) offer EAPs (Symonds, Ellis, Siler, Zellner, & Garland, 1991).

Americans generally rate their life satisfaction quite high: 78 percent rate their satisfaction at 4 or 5 on a 5-point scale, but engaged workers (those who identify with their work and actively promote company objectives) are more likely to say a 5 than a 4 ("Gallup Study Finds," 2003). The kinds of state-ments that the Gallup Organization uses to reach these conclusions include "I have gotten the important things I want in my life" and "The conditions of my life are excellent." Among the actively disengaged employees, 51 percent reported that they behaved poorly at home during the past month, whereas only 18 percent of engaged employees report this. According to the Gallup study, divorced people are slightly more likely to be actively disengaged.

Family-Supportive Workplace Policies

EAPs are one example of the increased commitment of work organizations to provide family-supportive policies and practices. Other solutions, programs, or changes that support more family-work balance include

- A compressed workweek (i.e., working 4 days a week at 10 hours per day versus 5 days a week at 8 hours per day).
- Part-time hours or alternative work schedules. Studies show that perceived control (such as of schedules) increases perceived balance (Tausig & Fenwick, 2001).
- Job sharing.
- Tuition reimbursement
- Self-employment, which is becoming an increasingly popular option. Men who are self-employed report greater job satisfaction and more job-to-home spillover when there are small children in the family. Married, self-employed women report less negative spillover from job-to-home, greater job satisfaction, and less job burnout (Hundley, 2001).
- Access to outside services. For example, help for workers in finding (and in some cases paying for) child and elder care.
- On-site seminars from financial planning to stress prevention. For example, Joo and Garman (1998) found that personal financial wellness affected work productivity in a study of 447 clerical workers.
- Mentoring programs.
- Wellness programs. These might include on-site fitness centers, free onsite health check-ups, exercise classes, low-cost flu shots.
- Flexible hours. Let employees make up their own schedules within a range of acceptable hours. "Regardless of the source of the flexibility, the need is clear. Everyone concerned needs to cut families a little slack up front, to avoid tearing the delicate fabric of family life" (Shellenbarger, 1999, p. B1).
- Telework is a catchall word for working from anywhere, most likely from home. This is an increasingly popular alternative.

Like a growing number of people, Shannon Bryant long dreamed of working from home. Stuck in traffic commuting for more than an hour a day, wishing for more personal time, she hated "feeling like I was in the rat race," says Ms. Bryant, a health-care consultant. But she hadn't a clue how to ask her boss for a change. She found help in an unexpected place: the Internet. On a friend's advice, she searched Web sites on job flexibility and found a template for a telecommuting proposal to hand to her boss. After some homework and preparation, she presented the proposal and won approval. She's now seven weeks into her new work-at-home setup, and it's going well. (Shellenbarger, 2003, February 13, p. D1)

- Achievement awards. These should go beyond plaques and into usable items such as movie passes, restaurant vouchers, and bonuses.

◆ Dry cleaning services, food shops, low-cost cafeterias, after-school care, and child-care centers on-site, free dinner for late workers delivered to the office. As the U.S. economy slowed, many firms cut back on these extras, but as the economy picks up they will return. Also, certain younger industries such as high tech tend to offer these perks more than older industries. Perks can go wrong if they are unevenly distributed, if popular ones are discontinued, and if staffers would rather have raises than perks. Perks are social experiments, and the wise manager keeps abreast of which perks are working and which ones aren't.

◆ Drop-in centers. These mini-offices (satellite offices) in the suburbs allow employees to avoid the commute into the city every weekday.

◆ On-site educational services. Free or subsidized classes, such as Master of Business Administration classes, so that employees with bachelor's degrees who are moving into management positions can get higher degrees.

How successful are these methods? Companies report that they lower absentee rates and improve employee retention, especially in highly mobile fields such as technology. Policies, programs, and services that relieve stress should diminish absenteeism. Ideally, employees should have input into which options are offered. Consistency within companies and across companies would also be helpful to employees who transfer or change jobs. In recent years several of these options have been cut back. CCH Inc., Riverwoods, Illinois, says employers offering compressed work weeks fell by 18 percent in the past year, job-sharing by 19 percent, and telecommuting by 4 percent (Shellenbarger, 2003, December 18, p. D1).

Family and Medical Leave Act (FMLA)

In recognition of the difficulty of combining work and family, many nations and companies have developed specific policies regarding employee leave for personal, family, or health reasons. The policies vary greatly by country and by employer.

In the United States in 1993, President Bill Clinton signed the Family and Medical Leave Act (FMLA), which allows workers at companies with more than 50 employees to take up to 12 workweeks of *unpaid leave* to care for newborns and newly adopted children or to care for ill family members or themselves. So, if you are an eligible employee, you are entitled to 12 weeks of leave for certain family and medical reasons during a 12-month period. Can an employee be fired if they take FMLA leave? No, it is unlawful for an employer to interfere with or restrain or deny the exercise of any right provided under the law. It should be noted that most U.S. workplaces such as retail shops, grooming salons, architecture, and consulting firms have fewer than five employees, so most employees are not covered by FMLA. About 60 percent of the U.S. workforce is eligible for FMLA, but few take it mainly because it is unpaid.

Prospective parents who meet the qualifications set out in the act no longer have to be concerned about whether they will be allowed to be away from work before, during, and after the birth of their children (leave) or whether they will have a job to come back to (job security). Adoption and foster care are covered as well as the illness of a child, spouse, or parent. More details of the act are given in Table 10.1.

Many employers had policies in place long before the passage of the Family and Medical Leave Act. Two of them, Johnson & Johnson and AT&T,

TABLE 10.1
Family and Medical Leave Act of 1993

The Family and Medical Leave Act applies to all public agencies, including state, local, and federal employers, local education agencies (schools), and private-sector employers employing 50 or more employees in 20 or more workweeks in the current or preceding calendar year within a 75-mile radius.

◆ Covered employers must grant an eligible employee up to a total of 12 workweeks of unpaid leave during any 12-month period for the birth or placement of a child for adoption or foster care, for the care of a seriously ill child, spouse, or parent, or in the case of his or her own serious illness.

◆ Employers have to continue health care coverage for the employee during the leave.

◆ Employers have to guarantee that employees will return to either the same job or a comparable position.

◆ Employers can refuse to reinstate certain highly paid "key" employees after their leave. Such employees are defined as the highest paid 10 percent of the workforce and whose leave would cause economic harm to the employer.

◆ Employers can exempt employees who have not worked for at least one year and who have not worked for at least 1,250 hours, or 25 hours a week, in the previous 12 months.

◆ A doctor's certification has to be obtained to verify a serious illness. Employers may require a second medical opinion.

◆ Employers can substitute an employee's accrued paid leave (such as sick or annual leave) for any part of the 12-week period of family leave.

◆ Under some circumstances, employees may take the leave intermittently, by taking leave in blocks of time or reducing their normal weekly or daily work schedule.

◆ Employers are permitted to require an employee taking intermittent leave for planned medical treatments to transfer temporarily to an equivalent alternative position.

Source: E. Goldsmith, *Family Leave: Changing Needs of the World's Workers,* United Nations, Occasional Paper Series, No. 7 (1993): 6.

reported that their family-supportive policies boosted morale and worker productivity (Galen, 1993). In a 1993 survey of 524 companies, 7 of 10 respondents said they already offered leave to employees for adoption, family illness, or childbirth, and that costs of such policies were insignificant ("Most Small Businesses Appear Prepared to Cope with New Family Leave Rules," 1993). The *Wall Street Journal* article that reported the survey quoted one employer's comments:

As far as we're concerned, it's not a problem, says Bill Parsons, president of Palmer Johnson Inc. The Sturgeon Bay, Wis., boat builder already grants family leave to its 350 employees. "In an era where companies are competing for employees, the enlightened companies have already thought about how to handle and treat employees with respect," he adds. ("Most Small Businesses," 1993)

The Meaning of Work and Leisure

The next part of this chapter explores the meaning of work and leisure and managerial implications. **Work** is effort expended to produce or accomplish something or activity that is rewarded, usually with pay. **Effort** is exertion or the use of energy to do something (Goldsmith, 1994). Because so many hours are spent in work, it makes a tremendous difference to one's overall sense of contentment and growth. Thomas Carlyle, a 19th-century British historian and essayist, wrote, "Blessed is he who has found his work; let him ask no other blessedness." A fascinating study by Roehling, Roehling, and Moen (2001) explored the concept of company loyalty and how it fits into the work and family debate. They found that flexible-time policies have an almost universal employee loyalty payoff and that child-care policies help as well. Even more important is the presence of an employee-friendly atmosphere. Employees appreciate supervisors who are sensitive to work-family conflicts and make adjustments when necessary.

The average workweek today is about 30 percent shorter than a hundred years ago. Around 1900, a six-day workweek was common. In 1938, President Franklin D. Roosevelt signed the Fair Labor Standards Act, which established a 44-hour workweek, which was reduced to 40 hours by 1941. A generation ago, the conventional wisdom among economists was that America was turning into an "affluent society," in which ever more efficient technology would produce an abundance of wealth requiring less and less labor. This did not happen for a variety of reasons, but the end result is that U.S. workers are working more at this point in American history than was predicted. The four-day workweek is still elusive. Choice of occupations has increased significantly. In 1850, the U.S. Census listed 322 job titles; today there are over 31,000.

> The fact hit home for me when I returned to the U.S. in 1996 after a decade abroad. I began to notice that not one of the other seven people in my office left their desks at lunchtime, the way folks used to. . . . the Bureau of Labor statistics reports that since 1985 paid vacation time has declined, and so has the average time that workers take off sick. Not surprisingly, more than one third of the people in the FWI survey said that they often or very often feel used up at the end of the workday. (Hunter, 1999, p. 38)

Feeling Overworked

According to a report by Galinsky, Kim, and Bond titled "Feeling Overworked: When Work Becomes Too Much":

> Feeling overworked is a psychological state that has the potential to affect attitudes, behavior, social relationships, and health both on and off the job. Information from our focus groups suggested that feeling overworked is often an acute condition, which may largely subside once work demands decrease, rather than a chronic condition—though for some employees it is clearly an ever-present feeling. (2001, p. 6)

As may be expected, employees with poorer-quality jobs express the most dissatisfaction. The kinds of things that lead to poorer jobs include less job autonomy, more wasted time, fewer learning opportunities, and less job security. Less-supportive workplaces, including inadequate materials and equipment to do a good job, inadequate support from people at work to do a good job, inadequate flexibility to manage work and family responsibilities, and lack of respect, also add up to feeling overworked and unappreciated. According to this study, women felt more overworked than men. Baby boomers (age 36–54) worked longer hours and felt more overworked than Generation Xers/Millennials (18–35) and mature workers (55 and older). Overworked employees reported more work-life conflict, lost sleep, higher levels of stress, poorer coping skills, less successful personal relationships, and health problems and were more likely to neglect themselves than workers who said they were generally not feeling overworked.

What are the implications for employers? Several categories of concern include

◆ workplace safety

◆ job performance

◆ retention (keeping workers)

◆ health care costs

An extensive study titled "Staying Ahead of the Curve: The AARP Working in Retirement Study" (2003) of workers ages 45–74 found that they most want

1. A friendly work environment

2. A chance to use skills and talents

3. A chance to do something worthwhile

4. Respect from coworkers

5. The opportunity to learn something new

What they wanted least was

1. The ability to work from home

2. The opportunity to work part-time

The main conclusion is that workers 45 and older treasure their work as a way to connect with others and to contribute to society and they have practical concerns—such as making money.

The Work Ethic

The work ethic in the United States has changed along with other changes in the overall culture (Quilling, 1990). The **work ethic** is the degree of dedication or commitment to work. **Commitment** refers to the degree to which an individual identifies with and is involved in a particular activity or organization (Goldsmith, 1994). The work ethic is alive, well, and even flourishing in the United States (Quilling, 1990; Brokaw, 1999). According to a report from Bright Horizons Family Solutions in Watertown, Massachusetts, here are typical hours worked by country:

◆ United States employees average 1,966 hours a year.

◆ Japanese employees average 1,899 hours a year.

◆ England's employees average 1,731 hours a year.

◆ Sweden's employees average 1,552 hours a year.

◆ Norway's employees average 1,399 hours a year.

The work ethic is part of an individual's value orientation and, hence, is linked to managerial behavior. Individuals who adhere to a strong work ethic appear to be more polite, responsible, and conservative; they also tend to resist social change and to be rigid (Furnham, 1987; Tang & Tung, 1988). Predictability, discipline, and order are also associated with a strong work ethic (Feather, 1984).

More recently, however, the work ethic has been redefined based on the switch to the knowledge economy. The new workplace requires specific skills (often computer-related) and a great deal of employee discretion. Many organizations reward employees who have the ability to interpret and respond to change, including the unpredictable moods and actions of other people. Thus, discipline remains an important attribute, but striving to learn, to conquer new problems, and to find solutions are more likely to generate success than is dutiful drudge work. "The knowledge economy gives us not only the opportunity but also the obligation to reunite work with independent thinking, self-expression, and even joy" (Postrel, 1998, p. A10). Even Scott Adams, the creator of the comic strip "Dilbert," which pokes fun at the workplace, says that "I'm not at all sad about the state of work right now. I think people are generally happier than they've been in a long time" (Stafford, 1998, p. 2E).

Since the work ethic is based on values, adherence or nonadherence to the work ethic is a form of self-expression and definition. People develop a work ethic or not depending on what they feel is important. Educators and parents influence the development of the work ethic in children by rewarding work performance. The overall culture, the economy, and work environments further contribute to the development and the sustenance of the work ethic.

Workaholism

Workaholism refers to the inability to stop thinking about work and doing work and the feeling that work is always the most pleasurable part of life. Work satisfies the need to be recognized and approved of in a way that other realms of life cannot satisfy. Most workers are not workaholics. True workaholics may have trouble sleeping, relaxing, going on vacation, or spending time alone or with their children and spouse. Here is an example:

> Publishing consultant Aaron Sigmond and his wife recently went to the Hudson Valley in upstate New York for a 10-day vacation. After a grueling work schedule, the couple needed time to regenerate and commune with the breezy Catskill Mountains, the lulling flow of the Hudson River and the gently sprawling fields of nearby farms. The only problem: They couldn't stand it. Four days before the vacation ended, they left the Victorian house they had rented. "The peace and quiet and solitude just wore on me," says Mr. Sigmond. "It was just the most stressful vacation ever." (Sandberg, 2003, p. B1)

Twelve percent of American workers never take vacations, and the United States does not have a nationally mandated vacation policy for all workers. U.S. workers effectively give back over $21 billion a year to their employers by not taking vacations (Sandberg, 2003). Some blame it on capitalism, materialism, competition, worry about job security, and upward mobility. Vacations can seem like a step backward for workaholics; they will fall behind. Others find work stress to be predictable, even enjoyable. Vacations involve a lot of unknowns.

In terms of Freud's definition of happiness as a combination of work and love, the constant workaholic may be neglecting the "love" side of life in favor of the "work" side. At the beginning of the chapter, the founder of the biotech company, Krishan Kalra, showed classic signs of workaholism.

One myth about workaholics is that they are the most productive workers in a home or an organization. This is usually not true because workaholics are addicted to work, not necessarily to goal attainment. They lack organization and their energy is not channeled properly. Workaholics often suffer from fatigue and stress and may experience health problems from a lack of exercise and rest. They also lack a sense of balance, and this deficiency may spill over into a failure to understand why other employees or family members do not also work constantly.

In short, workaholics may be difficult to live with at home or at the office. A hard worker is different from a workaholic. A hard worker realizes that work is just one part of life, tolerates others' mistakes and her or his own, stays on top of work schedules, cares about others, and can choose to stop working—such as to take lunch breaks without worrying.

The Three P's: Procrastination, Parkinson's Law, and Pareto's Principle

In contrast to a workaholic who constantly works or thinks about work, a **procrastinator** puts off work and postpones decisions. Procrastinators are difficult to work with because they seldom finish tasks on time and consequently often disappoint their coworkers and employers. They are difficult to live with too because they often forget or fail to meet family obligations.

Everyone procrastinates now and then, but procrastination is excessive when it is pervasive across all arenas of life. When this happens, procrastination is more than a bad habit—it has become a lifestyle. Procrastination is a way to escape responsibility and resist the structure of growing up. It may be related to a fear developed in early childhood or to an unresolved conflict.

Sometimes, a person procrastinates because he or she really does not want to do whatever is required. A child who dislikes playing the piano will delay practicing. A child who continually avoids practicing may be signaling that he is no longer interested. In that case, perhaps the piano lessons should stop and another activity be substituted. Someone who constantly procrastinates on work assignments may be in the wrong job and would be happier elsewhere.

Some individuals (e.g., students putting off studying for a test and pulling an all-night cramming session) say they like the feeling of rushing to meet deadlines and the excitement of the last-minute push; they insist that they perform best when living on the edge. This approach may work for them some of the time, but what if others are relying on them for information (e.g., a team report for a class), there is a family crisis, or they become ill the night before an assignment is due? Procrastination can be overcome if the procrastinators are willing to change by rearranging their approach to assignments and rewarding themselves for planning ahead and being on time.

Another concept related to the organization of work is called Parkinson's law. In 1957, the English historian C. Northcote Parkinson studied the Royal Navy and found that the more people hired, the more work they created, without necessarily increasing the organization's output. His observation led to the formulation of **Parkinson's law,** which states that a job expands to fill the time available to accomplish the task. This law illustrates the elasticity of time and work.

Parkinson's law is evident in people who have a lot of time on their hands. They may take all day to mail a letter or to go grocery shopping. They stretch a routine task that could be completed in half an hour into an all-day expedition.

The third P of working and its organization is the Pareto principle. Vilfredo Pareto, a 19th-century Italian economist and sociologist, discovered that in any series of elements to be controlled, a selected small fraction of the elements always accounts for a large fraction of effectiveness. The **Pareto principle,** also known as the 80–20 rule, states that 20 percent of the time expended usually produces 80 percent of the results, while 80 percent of the time expended produces only 20 percent of the results. According to this principle, the bulk of an individual's time is wasted in low-productivity activities. The solution to this phenomenon is to recognize that it exists and to focus more of one's attention on the activities and relationships that matter and to put less time and energy into things that do not.

Workforce Trends, Including Home-Based Businesses

There is a joke: A guy reads a headline saying, "The president creates 8 million jobs," and he cracks wearily, "Yeah, and I got three of 'em." Many people have two jobs, and 13 percent of Americans have three jobs (Hunter, 1999). So one trend is simply more people working more than one job in a variety of settings. A person may be an administrative assistant by day and a waitress on nights and weekends.

The average full-time job, although officially 40 hours, is in reality about 47 hours per week, according to Juliet B. Schor's book The *Overworked American* (1991), and can go to the extreme of 60 hours or more. Workers also report long commutes, chirping cell phones, e-mail that never quits, and lost weekends. The "lost weekends" concept (time spent reading reports, grading papers, answering e-mail, etc.) illustrates the blurring of the distinction between work and leisure.

Another trend is that the workforce is aging as the baby boomers move forward through life. The Age Discrimination Act of 1967 protects most workers age 40 and older from discrimination in the workplace.

A worldwide trend is a redefinition of work space, whether at home or in more traditional workplaces. The move is away from individual offices and cubicles into shared spaces, shared computers (many on wheeled tables), workstations, and so forth. It's all about mobility. "People are working in a variety of different settings. They're moving constantly, both within the office and outside the office" (Powers, 1998, p. 21). An early experimenter with reducing office space was Anderson Worldwide, which reduced the office-to-employee ratio from 1:1 to 1:5.3 in its San Francisco office, thus saving on the cost of rent, furnishings, and utilities. As more and more companies scatter their employees around the globe, they will be relying more on technology to bring people together rather than on a physical space.

Mobility is also evidenced by people moving from job to job, and therefore from location to location, more often today than in the past, according to Phyllis Moen of Cornell University. She says that "The lock-step template of American life is obsolete. . . . This has enormous consequences for policy, employers, communities, families, and individual lives" (Powers, 1998, p. 14). For young people, job hopping is very common. A typical American holds 8.6 different jobs between the ages of 18 and 32, with most changes before the age of 27, according to the Bureau of Labor Statistics. For example, Felix Batcup, 26, associate art director at *Women's Sports and Fitness* magazine, had five jobs in five years and tripled his starting salary in those years ("What's New,"1998).

The point at which a worker on the rise becomes a worker who's consigned to history is coming earlier in people's careers, usually around age 44, according to the Bureau of Labor Statistics. To avoid plateauing, workers are encouraged to try new projects, mentor younger workers, take assignments abroad, and/or get fresh training in order to keep their careers lively, interesting, and challenging.

Another trend is **downshifting,** opting for a simpler life, usually less pay, less stress, more time, in a more personally satisfying occupation. Basically, in downshifting, a person decides that more is not always better. The individual's reduced income is offset by a more frugal lifestyle. Obviously, downshifting is not for everyone. Someone whose self-worth is measured by status and money would have a hard time turning his or her back on a large income. So, who should consider downshifting? Not those who truly love their careers and enjoy consuming to the hilt:

> But others, like Jacque Blix, just feel trapped in that world. For years, an unhappy Ms. Blix couldn't leave the AT&T marketing job that brought her a good salary and the status of succeeding in a nontraditional role for women. "I felt if I took less money I'd be taking a step backward and denying my potential as a human being," she says. Eventually, she and her husband, David Heitmiller, a corporate product manager, did downshift, saving 30% of their income over three years to finance their corporate exits. They tell their tale in their book, *Getting a Life*. "We saw that we could live with less income and still be happy," she says. (Lancaster, 1998, p. B1)

A final trend is the return to home-based work. This may be through an employer or may be through self-employment; and as stated earlier there is a rise in the number of self-employed. The information age, with its emphasis on computers and electronically transferred information, has made it possible for more people to work from their homes. Naturally, working at home has implications for family relations and involves management considerations such as the arranging of child care and the allocation of time, money, and space (Heck, Saltford, Rowe, & Owen, 1992; Heck, Winter, & Stafford, 1992; Loker & Scannell, 1992; Owen, Carsky, & Dolan, 1992; Rowe, Stafford, & Owen, 1992; Stafford, Winter, Duncan, & Genalo, 1992; Tausig & Fenwick, 2001; Winter, 1992). Researchers have found that for women, the overwhelming reason given for working at home is the ability to take care of young children while earning an income. Having clients in and out of the house is disruptive to the family as are many phone calls. A nine-state study concluded that

> Demands imposed through the complexity of the family were related to increased intrusions by means of telephone calls and space conflicts, illustrating that home-based workers and their families must learn to manage the realities of overlapping tasks. Resources can undoubtedly mediate these intrusions if the family can afford a separate office or work space for the business, or a phone line dedicated exclusively to the business, but when financial resources do not allow additions such as these, the throughput process of the home-based worker and his or her family becomes even more important. (Fitzgerald & Winter, 2001, p. 88)

So having enough space is a key factor in success. Another factor is time management. Methods such as the dovetailing and overlapping of activities described earlier in this book come into play as home-based workers juggle their work and family responsibilities. Owen, Carsky, and Dolan (1992) provide this insight into home-based work:

> Even the choice of a home-based occupation over a market job may reflect a commitment or priority by the worker to meeting the needs of the family, especially

when family demands are high, such as when young children are present. The degree to which home-based workers can control the various aspects of time may influence the satisfaction derived from the work and from the family/work interface. (p. 136)

The stereotype of a home-based business is a female-owned enterprise, such as a child-care center. But that is inaccurate; a recent survey revealed that 59 percent of home-based workers are male. The typical person is about 44 years old, married, and employed in a white-collar profession such as marketing, sales, or technology—for example, software engineering. Kathryn Stafford, a professor at Ohio State University who worked on the study with Barbara Rowe of Purdue and George Haynes of Montana State, said, "We found that most home-based workers are men performing traditional work in fields like sales and construction" (DeLisser & Morse, 1999). They also found that home-based business owners were better educated and more affluent than the rest of the population. A further finding was that 88 percent of home-based owners sell most of their products or services within their state or an hour's drive from their homes. For example, in Ohio, home-based work contributes more to the state's personal income rolls than farming.

In the late 1990s, 30 million Americans were working at home at least some of the time, the highest share being among those aged 18 to 29 (Allen & Moorman, 1997). Are home-based businesses the nirvana people hoped for? In some cases yes, but in others a number of problems are surfacing:

> Many home-office workers feel as though they're working in a vacuum. They feel isolated and struggle with a perception that they're not quite "legit." They lament the loss of support staff, employer-provided educational opportunities, health insurance, pension plans, and paid vacation time. They scramble to find suitable places to meet with clients. Those who run businesses also run the risks of running into zoning and IRS audits. (Allen & Moorman, 1998, p. 57)

So, home-based businesses, along with the other trends, have their pluses and minuses. The next few decades will determine how these trends play out, which ones succeed, which ones don't, and in what ways they will be altered as people search for new options. One switch currently underway is the inclusion of more office space and built-in desks in new home construction, although it should be noted that the trend toward wireless communication is affecting home space in other ways.

> The bedroom will become the new frontier of multitasking, as growth in wireless technology allows work to expand into once-sacred domains of the home. Homes with wireless networks will grow to nine million in the coming year. . . . Mark Chernis takes his laptop to bed—a habit he says brings him and his wife closer. In the past, they had to go to separate rooms wired for Internet use to go online after hours. "It used to be, 'Good night, Honey, I'll see you later.' And I'd get this sad face from her," Mr. Chernis says. Now, he and his wife retire together "and she falls asleep on my shoulder while I'm working on my laptop," says Mr. Chernis, president of Princeton Review. Similarly, if his wife wakes up in the night, she grabs a laptop they keep by their bed and browses the Internet. (Shellenbarger, 2003, December, p. D1)

Volunteer Work

So far this chapter has focused on paid work. Another type of work that requires time, energy, and commitment is **volunteer work,** or work that does not generate pay. *About half of all Americans volunteer each year in the non-*

The bedroom is the new frontier in multitasking, where work is not tied to a desk.

Anthony Redpath/CORBIS

profit sector. This compares to about 13 percent in Germany and 19 percent in France. Regarding charitable donations, Germany leads the group, followed by the United States, and France ("Review & Outlook," 1999). Canadians volunteer in large numbers especially in the area of community service.

People perform volunteer work for a number of reasons, but one of the most important is their sense of social consciousness. They want to contribute to their family's well-being (e.g., by volunteering for Boy Scouts or Girl Scouts or the PTA) or to contribute to others and to the community. Many of the volunteers are stay-at-home mothers who head school committees and run large volunteer organizations. These experiences will be useful to them when they reenter the workforce as most stay-at-home mothers plan to do at some point.

Volunteer work also provides a sense of self-worth and self-esteem and heightened social and leadership skills. It is of enormous economic value to society. It provides social cohesion and solidarity. Recognizing the worth to the community, some businesses and government agencies allow workers to take time off to perform volunteer work such as tutoring or helping with school events. They may actively build partnerships. Volunteerism used to conjure up an image of a kindly lady volunteering at the hospital or through her garden club. Today, volunteers come in all ages, races, and income levels.

High schools and universities are offering courses and credit for volunteer service. The courses teach students how to work as volunteers and managers of organizations that have goals other than making a profit. For example, Donald Tobias and Stephen Watson teach such a course at Cornell University. The goal of their course is to introduce students to the management practices and principles in public sector and nonprofit organizations.

"At Cornell we aren't just turning out students who will be actively involved in careers," Tobias says, "We also are helping to produce people who will be citizens in their communities. Many of our students may become members of boards of directors for not-for-profit organizations, so they need to know how those organizations work and how to think strategically about management decisions and strategies based on the mission of the organization." (Mackin, 1998, p. 10)

Leisure

Leisure is defined as freedom from time-consuming activities, tasks, duties, or responsibilities. As seen in the last chapter, studies show that we have more leisure time today than in the past, but it doesn't feel like it. Leisure time is interspersed throughout people's lives (such as chatting by e-mail or over the phone for brief periods with family and friends) and is formally designated in vacation time. The amount of time typically designated for vacations varies considerably by country. As previously stated, the United States has no required vacation laws, and the usual vacation is two or three weeks, granted after several years of employment with the same company. Some nations in the world have legally required vacation days after one year of service. According to Hewitt Associates of Lincolnshire, Illinois, examples are

- Finland 30 days
- Colombia 15 days
- Sweden 25 days
- Japan 10 days
- Australia 20 days

Why the difference between countries? Labor experts say powerful unions, especially in Europe, have negotiated hard for more vacation time and have enjoyed political support as time off has become intertwined with economics. Though it's a matter of intense debate, some European governments argue that the combination of more holiday time and a shorter workweek translates into more jobs. U.S. workers, on the other hand, have focused more on pay increases, accepting less time off as part of the bargain (Shapiro, 1999). "We've got a cultural problem with leisure time," says Herbert Rappaport, a professor at Temple University. "We are an overworked, overtired, underpleasured culture" (Sandberg, 2003, p. B1).

Weekends are usually times of increased leisure. Studies indicate that men have more leisure time for themselves and spend less time than women do on weekend household chores. Interests and hobbies garner the most weekend leisure activity time for both men and women; playing with children comes second.

In *The Harried Leisure Class* (1970), Linder argues that high hourly earnings make time so precious that many people cannot afford the time it takes to enjoy life on a daily basis and are forced to eat meals on the run, cut short the foreplay of lovemaking, attend short religious services, and browse or glance at books rather than read them. For example, Neil, a college professor, says he reads movie and book reviews but rarely has time to see a movie or read a book cover to cover. By reading reviews, Neil can still converse with his colleagues. He is not distressed by his busy lifestyle and says that at this stage in his life he really values work over leisure. He spends most of his time in work-related pursuits, most of which he finds stimulating and pleasurable.

In view of such approaches to work and leisure, what part does leisure play in human life? People must answer this question for themselves. One person's idea of leisure is gardening; another prefers to play tennis. Leisure was once associated mostly with social or recreational activities (e.g., snowmobiling, boating, swimming), but it now includes relaxation and meditation as well as more lively pursuits. In its broadest context, leisure is a state of mind. Not everyone has the time or the resources to go elsewhere to enjoy recreation and leisure. Consequently, there is a growing worldwide recognition of the need to provide leisure facilities, such as parks and fitness trails, in housing developments, especially in crowded urban areas (Woods & Strugnell, 1993).

Web-Based Resources

The Gallup Management Journal Web site at **http://gmj.gallup.com** offers information on work/family balance. For the latest on workers' rights and the Family and Medical Leave Act, go to **www.dol.gov.** For midcareer and late-career advice, visit the AARP Web site at **www.aarp.org.** This site also provides links to America's Job Bank, which is useful to adults seeking employment.

Cyberspace is having a profound influence on how volunteer programs are managed and how volunteers are recruited. For example, Hewlett Packard Company employees mentor high school students in math and science through HP Mentors, an e-mail exchange program. Examples of volunteer organizations that are online include

- Big Brothers Big Sisters of America: **www.bbbsa.org**
- Corporation for National Services: **www.cns.gov**
- Points of Light Foundation: **www.pointsoflight.org**
- YMCA of the USA: **www.ymca.net**
- YWCA of the USA: **www.ywca.org**

Summary

This chapter focused on the problems of managing work and family life roles and provided solutions to work and family conflicts. The positive aspects of work were explored along with the stressors associated with it. Employers and countries are reexamining child care, elder care, and family medical leave policies to accommodate the needs of employees with families and personal lives. Many countries offer paid leave for personal and family reasons. The Family and Medical Leave Act of 1993 is an example of a national work–life policy. About 60 percent of the U.S. workforce is eligible to take it; but because it is unpaid leave, fewer than one would expect actually take it.

The three P's—procrastination, Parkinson's law, and Pareto's principle—are important to understanding the organization of time and work. So are the work ethic and workaholism. Today's workforce includes more women and members of minority groups as well as more home-based workers. Americans have surpassed the Japanese in average number of work hours. Researchers have found that the benefit to the employer of having work-life-friendly policies is increased company loyalty and retention.

Not all work is paid; volunteer work is an important part of many people's lives. Just as work is changing, so is leisure. Indeed, the amount of leisure is increasing but it does not feel like it to many people. Legally required vacation days vary worldwide. The United States does not have legally required vacation days, but they exist in Finland, Sweden, Australia, Colombia, and Japan, to name a few. About 12 percent of American workers never take vacations. Too little off-time and too much responsibility can lead to stress, the subject of the next chapter.

Key Terms

commitment	leisure	volunteer work
compromise	Pareto principle	work
downshifting	Parkinson's law	workaholism
effort	procrastinator	work ethic

Review Questions

1. Do you agree or disagree with Freud that the recipe for happiness is "work and love"? Should anything else be added? If so, what? Explain your answer.

2. List three ways individuals and families can help resolve work and family conflict. Which one do you think is most effective?

3. The Russian playwright Chekhov said that life and work are inseparable. Our work is not in competition with our lives—it is merely one part of life. And in the end, we'll be remembered for what we did with our life and how we lived it. Do you agree or disagree? Explain your answer.

4. The traditional image of volunteers and the reality of today's volunteers are different. What is the difference?

5. What is your definition of leisure? Why would 12 percent of the American workforce never take vacations?

References

AARP. (2003). Staying Ahead of the Curve 2003: The AARP Working in Retirement Study. Retrieved March 31, 2004 from http://research.aarp.org/econ/multiwork_2003.html

Allen, K., & Moorman, G. (1997, October). Leaving home: The emigration of home office workers. *American Demographics,* 57.

Anderson, E. (1992). Decision-making style: Impact on satisfaction of the commuter couples' lifestyle. *Journal of Family and Economic Issues, 13*(1), 5–22.

Blumenstein, R. (2001, September 10). Is there a downside to being connected all the time? *The Wall Street Journal,* R15.

Brokaw, T. (1999, May–June). The way we worked. *Modern Maturity,* 42–43, 49.

Chang, R. (2001). *The passion plan at work.* San Francisco: Jossey-Bass.

DeLisser, E., & Morse, D. (1999, May 18). Enterprise. *The Wall Street Journal,* B24.

Feather, N. (1984). Protestant ethic, conservatism, and values. *Journal of Personality and Social Psychology, 45*(5), 1132–1141.

Fitzgerald, M., & Winter, M. (2001). The intrusiveness of home-based work on family life. *Journal of Family and Economic Issues, 22*(10), 75–92.

Furnham, F. (1987). Work-related beliefs and human values. *Personality and Individual Differences, 8*(5), 627–637.

Galen, M. (1993, June 28). Work and family. *Business Week,* 80–88.

Galinsky, E., Kim, S., & Bond, J. (2001). *Feeling overworked: When work becomes too much.* New York: Families and Work Institute.

Gallup study finds that misery at work is likely to cause unhappiness at home. (2003, June 23). Retrieved December 1, 2003 from http//gmj.gallup.com/print/?ci=1087

Goldsmith, E. (1993). Family leave: The changing needs of the world's workers. Occasional Paper Series, No. 7, International Year of the Family, United Nations: Vienna.

Goldsmith, E. (1994). Work efficiency and motivation. In V. S. Ramachandran (Ed.), *Encyclopedia of human behavior, 4* (pp. 547–553). San Diego: Academic Press.

Grimm-Thomas, K., & Perry-Jenkins, M. (1994). All in a day's work: Job experiences, self-esteem, and fathering in workingclass families. *Family Relations, 43,* 174–181.

Heck, R., Saltford, N., Rowe, B., & Owen, A. (1992). The utilization of child care by households engaged in home-based employment. *Journal of Family and Economic Issues, 13*(2), 213–237.

Heck, R., Winter, M., & Stafford, K. (1992). Managing work and family in home-based employment. *Journal of Family and Economic Issues, 13*(2), 187–212.

Hundley, G. (2001). Domestic division of labor and self/organizationally employed differences in job attitudes and earnings. *Journal of Family and Economic Issues, 22*(2), 121–139.

Hunter, M. (1999, May-June). Work, work, work, work! *Modern Maturity,* 36–41.

Joo, S., & Garman, T. (1998). The potential effects of workplace financial education based on the relationship between personal financial wellness and worker job productivity. *Personal Finances and Worker Productivity, 2*(1), 163–174.

Kelly, R., & Voydanoff, P. (1985). Work/family role strain among employed parents. *Family Relations, 34,* 367–374.

Lancaster, H. (1998, January 20). "Downshifters" find more balance in life by shrinking careers. *The Wall Street Journal,* B1.

Larson, J., Wilson, S., & Beley, R. (1994). The impact of job insecurity on marital and family relationships. *Family Relations, 43,* 138–143.

Lewis, J. (1993). *How to build and manage a winning project team.* New York: American Management Association.

Linder, S. (1970). *The harried leisure class.* New York: Columbia University Press.

Loker, S., & Scannell, E. (1992). Characteristics and practices of home-based workers. *Journal of Family and Economic Issues, 13*(2), 173–186.

MacDermid, S., Hertzog, J., Kensinger, K., & Zipp, J. (2001). The role of organizational size and industry in job quality and work-family relationships. *Journal of Family and Economic Issues, 22*(2), 191–216.

Mackin, J. (1998, Summer). Learning to be an effective volunteer. *Human Ecology Forum,* 10–14.

Maume, D., & Houston, P. (2001). Job segregation and gender differences in work-family spillover among white-collar workers. *Journal of Family and Economic Issues, 22*(2), 171–189.

Most small businesses appear prepared to cope with new family-leave rules. (1993, February 8). *The Wall Street Journal,* B1–B2.

Orthner, D., & Pittman, J. (1986). Family contributions to work commitment. *Journal of Marriage and the Family, 48,* 573–581.

Owen, A., Carsky, M., & Dolan, E. (1992). Home-based employment: Historical and current consideration. *Journal of Family and Economic Issues, 13*(2), 121–138.

Postrel, V. (1998, September 4). The work ethic, redefined. *The Wall Street Journal,* A10.

Powers, M. (1998, Spring). The new template of American life. *Human Ecology Forum,* 13–32.

Quilling, J. (1990, Fall). Dimensions of ethics: The work ethic. *Home Economics Forum,* 13–16, 20.

Rapoport, R. (1985). Normal crisis, family structure, and mental health. *Family Process, 2*(1), 68–80.

The real worker's paradise (2003, March and April). Washington: AARP, 102.

Retherford, P., Hildreth, G., & Goldsmith, E. (1989). Social support and resource management of unemployed women. In E. Goldsmith (Ed.), *Work and family: Theory, research, and applications.* Newbury Park, CA: Sage.

Review & Outlook: A Christmas Story (1999, December 17). *The Wall Street Journal,* W17.

Roehling, P., Roehling, M., and Moen, P. (2001). The relationship between work-life policies and practices and employee loyalty: A life course perspective. *Journal of Family and Economic Issues, 22*(2), 141–170.

Rowe, B., Stafford, K., & Owen, A. (1992). Who's working at home: The types of families engaged in home-based work. *Journal of Family and Economic Issues, 13*(2), 159–172.

Roxburgh, S. (2002). Racing through life: The distribution of time pressures by roles and role resources among full-time workers. *Journal of Family and Economic Issues,* 121–145.

Sandberg, J. (2003, July 30). Sun, beach, sand—I think I'd rather be back in the office. *The Wall Street Journal,* B1.

Schor, J. (1991). *The overworked American.* New York: Basic Books.

Schroeder, P. (1988). Parental leave: The need for a federal policy. In E. Zigler and M. Frank (Eds.), *The parental leave crisis: Toward a national policy.* New Haven, CT: Yale University Press.

Shellenbarger, S. (1998, December 30). Future work policies may focus on teens trimming workloads. The Wall Street Journal, B1.

Shellenbarger, S. (1999, May 12). New research helps families to assess flaws in work plans. *The Wall Street Journal,* B1.

Shellenbarger, S. (2003, February 13). If you'd rather work in pajamas, here are ways to talk the boss into flex-time. *The Wall Street Journal,* D1.

Shellenbarger, S. (2003, December 18). Polish your resume, e-mailing in bed, a peek at next year's work-life trends. *The Wall Street Journal,* D1.

Shapiro, E. (1999, January 11). The life of leisure. *The Wall Street Journal,* R37.

Smith, S., & Price, S. (1992). Women and plant closings: Unemployment, re-employment, and job training enrollment following dislocation. *Journal of Family and Economic Issues, 13*(1), 45–72.

Stafford, D. (1998, October 28). New "Dilbert" book chronicles "Joy of Work." *Tallahassee Democrat,* 2E.

Stafford, K., Winter, M., Duncan, K., & Genalo, M. (1992). Studying at-home income generation: Issues and methods. *Journal of Family and Economic Issues, 13*(2), 139–158.

Stone, B. (1999, June 7). Get a life! *Newsweek,* 68–69.

Study: Many U.S. employees feel overworked. (2001, May 16). Retrieved August 8, 2001, from **www.cnn.com/2001/CAREER/trends/05/16/work.study/index/html**

Symonds, W., Ellis, J., Siler, J., Zellner, W., & Garland, S. (1991, March 25). Is business bungling its battle with booze? *Business Week,* 76–78.

Tang, T., & Tung, Y. (1988). *Some demographic correlates of the Protestant work ethic.* Tulsa, OK: Southwestern Psychological Association. (ERIC Document Reproduction No. ED 300 702).

Tausig, M., & Fenwick, R. (2001). Unbinding time: Alternate work schedules and work-life balance. *Journal of Family and Economic Issues, 22*(2), 101–119.

Tejada, C. (2003, March 20). Working at a fever pitch. *The Wall Street Journal,* D1.

Ulrich, D., & Dunne, H. (1986). *To love and work: A systemic interlocking of family, workplace, and career.* New York: Brunner/Mazel.

Voydanoff, P. (1988, August). Work role characteristics, family structure demands, and work/family conflict. *Journal of Marriage and the Family, 50.*

Voydanoff, P. (1989). Work and family: A review and expanded conceptualization. In E. Goldsmith (Ed.), *Work and family: Theory, research, and applications.* Newbury Park, CA: Sage.

Voydanoff, P. (1993). *Men, family, and work.* Newbury Park, CA: Sage.

Voydanoff, P., & Kelly, R. (1984). Determinants of work related family problems among employed parents. *Journal of Marriage and the Family, 46,* 881–892.

What's new. (1998, September). *The Wall Street Journal Classroom Edition,* 3.

Winter, M. (1992). At-home income generation: Introduction. *Journal of Family and Economic Issues, 13*(2), 117–120.

Woods, S., & Strugnell, C. (1993). Leisure provision and usage in recently redeveloped areas of Belfast. *Journal of Consumer Studies and Home Economics, 17,* 343–353.

The world's women 1970-1990: Trends and statistics. (1991). A publication of the United Nations, Social Statistics and Indicators, Series K, No. 8, New York.

chapter **11**

Managing Stress and Fatigue

MAIN TOPICS

Did you know that . . . ?

. . . Today, married moms average 6.7 hours of sleep a day.

. . . A century ago, nine hours of sleep was the norm.

I make the most of all that comes and the least of all
that goes.

—*Sara Teasdale*

STRESS IS AS natural as breathing, but learning how to strategically
handle stress is something we all have to do. Diverse family forms, more work
demands, care of the chronically ill and disabled, and other pressures on individuals and families stretch human resiliency as far as it can go. People exhibit
stress in lots of ways: replying angrily to an innocent question, experiencing a
pounding headache at the end of a hard day at work, or drumming their fin-
gers on the steering wheel in a traffic jam (Powell & Enright, 1990). Daily
hassles that build up stress include annoying practical problems, disappoint-
ments, disagreements, and family and financial concerns (Garrison, Malia,
Norem, & Hira, 1994). Contributing to this everyday stress are the new technologies and constant streams of information. For example, due to instant
messaging, messages that once took weeks to arrive are now immediate and
require instant responses. The pressure to respond is enormous.

Clutter is a source of a great deal of stress. So getting rid of mental as
well as physical clutter is a de-stressor. According to the federal government's
National Institute for Occupational Safety and Health (NIOSH), more than
half the workers in the United States view their job as a major stressor.

Although this is a U.S. study, the author would like to point out that students and faculty around the world have said that managing stress and fatigue is a significant problem in their lives. Too much stress is not just a North American problem, but rather a worldwide problem.

Managing stress, fatigue, and sleep are the subjects included in this chapter. Rapid information transfer is just one example of the many stresses encountered in today's world. Fatigue, a concept covered extensively in early management books and courses, has reemerged as a significant management/wellness problem. People are not getting enough rest and relaxation. They spend their weekends running around getting ready for the next workweek. There is just too much to accomplish in too little time. In addition to examining the effects of stress on families and society, this chapter will offer suggestions on ways to manage stress and fatigue.

STRESS: DEFINITION, THEORY, AND RESEARCH

The word *stress* has many definitions, but for the purposes of this book, **stress** refers to the nonspecific response of the body to any demand made upon it (Selye, 1974). *Stress usually involves a state of tension. It is considered a process rather than an end state.* A process implies that changes occur over time and across different situations. A person who is stressed experiences several stages or levels of stress. For example, getting ready to give a speech involves many stages: preparation, writing, rehearsal, and delivering the speech. Stress may occur at any or all of these stages.

Some stress is inevitable. Although there seems to be more stress today than ever before, stress is timeless. It exists in all societies no matter how primitive. In fact, the potential for stress exists whenever one person interacts with another or with the environment. An approaching hurricane or tornado is stressful, and so is an approaching belligerent ex-boyfriend or ex-girlfriend.

As these examples suggest, stress may occur when a person feels threatened or scared. When the potential for harm is high or people feel they lack the resources to reduce the threat, stress increases. **Stressors** are situations or events that cause stress. Stressors can be categorized as relational or environmental.

Most of the literature emphasizes relational stressors, but environmental stressors are equally important. Noise, pollution, poor lighting and ventilation, crowding, isolation, vibration, lack of adequate parking, static, litter, car fumes, and poorly insulated and designed homes, factories, and offices are examples of environmental stressors. School and work are particularly stressful because these environments are central to most people's lives, and they view their self-worth in terms of their success or failure in these areas (McLellan, Bragg, & Cacciola, 1992).

At the same time, stress is culturally and personally defined. What is stressful in India may not be considered stressful in the United States and vice versa. Individuals vary in their reactions to stress too. What is acutely stressful for one person may not affect another person at all. In other words, stress is ultimately in the eye of the beholder (House, 1983). Stress also varies in degree from everyday, normal stress to more prolonged serious stress that can lead to troublesome symptoms (Powell & Enright, 1990). Telltale signs of stress, besides those already mentioned, include social isolation and sudden changes in appearance such as disheveled clothing and significant weight gain or loss.

Stress can be explained within the context of systems theory because stress comes from a variety of sources (inputs) and has a variety of outcomes (outputs). Since it is a process, stress is generally considered a throughput, but stress can also be an input as it enters the system or an output because one person's actions may cause stress in another person. For example, worrying is a process that is stress-producing. The cause of the worrying may be an outside stressor being input to the system. What the worrier finally decides to do may transfer the stress to another person. For example, a retiring chairperson of a committee may gleefully pass on a thick file of past committee business and procedures to the incoming chairperson and in so doing pass the stress on to another person.

There is evidence of a gender difference in reaction to stress. Men's blood pressure rises more sharply in response to stress than does women's. But women react to more stressors and a greater variety of them; they report feeling stress more often, perhaps because they see daily life with a wider scope (Adler, Kalb, & Rogers, 1999).

Crises and Adaptation to Stress

Crises, which are events that require changes in normal patterns of behavior, often cause stress. Getting a flat tire while driving to work is a crisis. The driver must deviate from her normal pattern and fix the tire. How the driver reacts to the crisis will depend on many factors—the time, her expertise at changing tires, whether she has a spare tire or not, how far she is from a service station, and so forth.

Several researchers have developed models and scales that illustrate how individuals and families adapt to crises. These models and scales show the systematic interaction of crises, resources, pileup, and adaptation. **Stress overload, or pileup,** refers to the cumulative effect of many stresses building up at one time. For example, using the rating scale in Table 11.1, individuals can determine how much stress they have experienced in the past year. The originators of the scale, Holmes and Rahe, claim that substantial stress pileup can increase the incidence of illness. Note that the highest stressor event is the death of a spouse (100 points) and the lowest stressor event on the scale is a minor violation of the law (11 points). Scores of 100 to 200 are normal, but scores over 300 are considered high and indicative of trouble ahead.

As the Holmes and Rahe scale illustrates, stress levels can rise as a result of one major life change or from a series of small changes. Fixing a flat tire on the way to work may not be a big problem by itself, but as the day continues and the driver loses her keys, fights with her boss, and forgets an important meeting, stress pileup can occur. The individual may feel she cannot handle any more stress. Likewise, families experience stress pileup: too many conflicting appointments and too many demands on time, energy, emotions, and money will cause stress to build up to the point where the family cannot cope. Predictability affects the stress reaction.

"When an aversive event is unpredictable, it is more upsetting and distressing than one that is predictable," says Prof. Richard McNally. "The 1986 shuttle explosion was pretty jarring, but for people who remember *Challenger* the loss of *Columbia*

TABLE 11.1
Social Readjustment Rating Scale: The Stress of Adjusting to Change

Events	Scale of Impact	Events	Scale of Impact
Death of spouse	100	Son or daughter leaving home	29
Divorce	73	Trouble with in-laws	29
Marital separation	65	Outstanding personal achievement	28
Jail term	63		
Death of close family member	63	Spouse begins or stops work	26
Personal injury or illness	53	Begin or end school	26
Marriage	50	Change in living conditions	25
Fired at work	47	Revision of personal habits	24
Marital reconciliation	45	Trouble with boss	23
Retirement	45	Change in work hours or conditions	20
Change in health of family member	44	Change in residence	20
Pregnancy	40	Change in schools	20
Sex difficulties	39	Change in recreation	20
Gain of new family member	39	Change in church activities	19
Business readjustment	39	Change in social activities	19
Change in financial state	38	Mortgage or loan less than $10,000	17
Death of close friend	37	Change in sleeping habits	16
Change to different line of work	36	Change in number of family get-togethers	15
Change in number of arguments with spouse	35	Change in eating habits	15
Mortgage over $10,000	31	Vacation	12
Foreclosure of mortgage or loan	30	Christmas	12
Change in responsibilities at work	29	Minor violations of the law	11

Life change is stressful. To determine how much stress you have experienced from life changes in the last year, add up the points for each of the events listed that you have experienced in the last year. Then refer to the following chart to determine how serious your condition is. For example, if you get married, get pregnant, buy a house, take a vacation, and celebrate Christmas, your total would be 50 + 40 + 31 + 13 + 12 = 146.

Life Change Score	Chance of Illness in Next Year
0–150	37%
150–300	51%
300+	80%

Scores of 100 to 200 are common; 300-plus is high.

Source: Reprinted with permission from *Journal of Psychosomatic Research* 11, T. H. Holmes and R. H. Rahe, "The social readjustment rating scale," (1967) Elsevier Science Ltd. Pergamon Imprint, Oxford, England.

is similar enough to be less shocking." Even dissimilar stressors can produce habituation. "When a lot of bad things happen you just can't react as intensely," Prof. Prigerson says. "Some sort of adaptation kicks in." Predictability, too, can lead to habituation. The human nervous system has evolved to pay selective attention to novel and surprising stimuli and to ignore expected and repeating ones, the better to conserve finite processing resources. (Begley, 2003, p. B1)

David Dollahite (1991) developed the ABCD-XYZ Resource Management Model of Crisis/Stress. His model emphasizes how individual and family decision making, adaptive coping, and management behavior can be activated to reduce the impact of crisis/stress situations. As shown in Figure 11.1, his model has seven key parts:

A The stressor event or situation, the stimulus that forces some response

B The coping resources

C The definition of the situation

D The demands of the situation

X The crisis or stress

Y The cognitive coping and management

Z The adaptive behavior, which entails growth and change and leads to a better fit between the environment and the person or family

An oval surrounding ABCD-XYZ places individuals and families within their historical, economic, technological, cultural, legal, political, religious, and natural environmental contexts. Health (mental and physical), values, heredity, and development (stage of life cycle) form other important contexts. Mostly what this model shows is a systems approach to stress—one area affects another. Stress and stressors cannot be studied in isolation; they are part of an interactive system involving individuals and families in a larger environmental context.

Outsourcing

One of the ways to adapt to stress is to try to reduce it. To lessen stress, Americans increasingly are outsourcing traditional homemaking and child-care functions, a trend driven by three factors: more women working, an older population, and a growing affluent class. **Outsourcing** is defined as paying someone else to do one's work.

> Outsourcing is a logical extension of David Ricardo's 1817 theory of **comparative advantage.** Individuals, no less companies, do best when they focus on activities in which they can add the most value, and outsource other activities to specialists. And since housework has traditionally not been counted as an economic activity, the impact on the economy of extending outsourcing into the huge household-services sector will be massive. (Sheth & Sisodia, 1999)

The potential results of outsourcing include increasing employment and higher tax revenues, putting more individual effort into higher work productivity, and investing remaining time into hobbies or other preferred activities. Following are some examples of activities and tasks that are being outsourced:

◆ Meal preparation/cooking: increased use of restaurants, home delivery, take-out, personal chefs, and prepared foods from supermarkets.

◆ Cleaning: between 1986 and 1996 the number of households using an external cleaning service rose by 33 percent (Sheth & Sisodia, 1999).

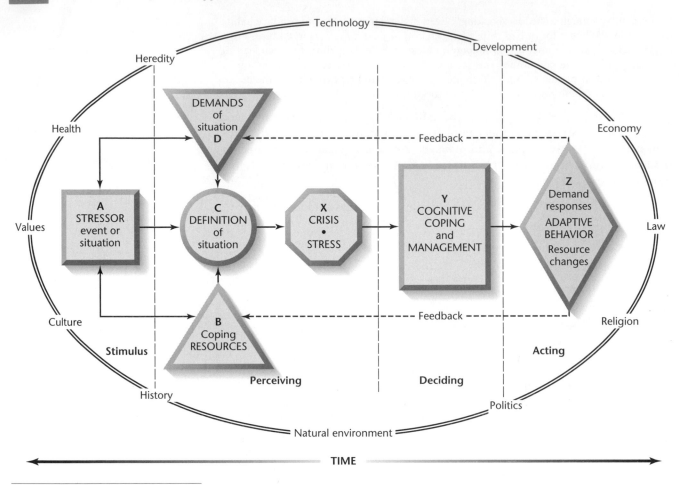

FIGURE 11.1
ABCD-XYZ Resource Management Model of Crisis/Stress

Source: David C. Dollahite (1991). Family resource management and family stress theories: Toward a conceptual integration. *Lifestyles: Family and Economic Issues, 12*(4), 265. Reprinted with permission.

◆ Child care, elder care (including home-based assisted living), and pet care. For example, "Family caregivers, who must balance work responsibilities, stretch their budgets and handle the added stress of looking after an elderly family member or friend, are an emerging market in need of respite services, targeted consumer goods and financial planning" (Braus, 1998, p. 1).

◆ Shopping: personal shoppers, buying over the Internet, using services that will pick up and deliver—such as for shoe repair, firewood, film, dry cleaning, videos, and mailing packages (in short, less in-person shopping).

◆ Yard work, pool cleaning, interior design, and home improvements.

◆ Organizing. Personal service companies who rearrange closets, clean garages, or wait for the cable TV repairperson are on the rise.

Contrary to popular belief, it is not the rich who are driving up the demand for these services (they already have them), but the time-starved middle class who are taking outsourcing to new heights. The hesitation to outsource has eased as more people have extra income and place a higher value on their personal time. Do they want to spend it cleaning house or mowing the lawn? Or would they prefer to pay for these services and spend their time doing something else? How much they outsource has a great deal to do with their comfort level with the idea, a subject to be explored next.

Comfort Zones and Internal and External Stress

Stress is present in all human relationships and activities and only becomes harmful when there is an imbalance that causes natural coping mechanisms to become strained (Capel & Gurnsey, 1987). Stress reduction is a means of restoring balance in lives. As mentioned in Chapter 2, in systems terminology the return to balance is called homeostasis. When a system becomes unbalanced, the homeostasis mechanism is triggered, and an attempt is made to reach a comfort zone. A **comfort zone** is a combination of habit and everyday expectations mixed with an appropriate amount of adventure and novelty. It represents that space in which the level of stress feels right for the individual—the quantity of work is enough to make life interesting, but is not so burdensome as to produce discomfort or other undesirable effects. However, if one wants to get ahead socially or in a profession, often one has to move out of one's comfort zone by meeting new people and going to new places. For example, when moving into a new neighborhood you can wait for the neighbors to introduce themselves or you can greet them when you see them. Professionally, you may have to go to meetings, conferences, or training in other cities. In short, a comfort zone is a good thing, the way in which most of our lives are arranged; but taken to the extreme it can be limiting. For example, a student from a small town in Vermont graduated with a degree in chemistry from Dartmouth. He was accepted into graduate school at the University of Chicago; this means getting out of his New England rural/small town comfort zone. He is excited about the program and the city and also a little worried, but he is going forward.

Families and organizations have comfort zones just as individuals do. For example, a sudden drop in the stock market may shake the comfort zones of Wall Street brokerage firms as well as those of families who have invested in the stock market. The passage of stress from Wall Street to the family and individual level is an example of the **domino effect.** Another example of the domino effect is the impact that a company president's personal problems may have on the entire organization. The anxiety at the top may rumble downward through the organization, leading to a long list of workplace problems: diminished worker satisfaction, decreased productivity, subgroup conflict, misuse of authority, role confusion, scapegoating, and substance abuse (Ulrich & Dunne, 1986). In situations such as this, where stress is brought on from outside the individual, people are said to be experiencing **external stress.**

External stress may come from any of three kinds of experience:

1. *Acute major stress.* Stress resulting from a recent event, such as a car accident, job loss, moving, or death of a loved one.

2. *Ongoing, role-related stress.* Stress caused by chronic difficulties in one's work or family roles.

3. *Lifetime trauma stress.* Stress resulting from having undergone severe trauma, such as early-childhood loss of one or both parents or exposure to calamitous strains such as wartime or natural disasters (*Two New Landmark Studies,* 1991).

In contrast, **internal stress** originates in one's own mind and body. An ambitious person may bring on internal stress by setting too high a standard for achievement (e.g., expecting to win every award, title, or promotion). Or a person may be stressed about her or his body image or lack of friends. Adolescents are particularly sensitive about their physical appearance (McLellan, Bragg, & Cacciola, 1992).

Everyone tries to balance internal and external stresses. Some stress is necessary to drive behavior—to get individuals out of bed in the morning and get them going. In this sense, stress serves as a motivator. Too much stress can be debilitating, however, and leads to immobilization.

Hans Selye: Founder of Stress Research

Despite the long-standing fascination with stress, it was not until the last century that a scientific explanation for stress and its effects on the body was developed. Hans Selye, a biology professor at the University of Montreal, has been called the father or founder of stress research. He pointed out that everyone lives with some degree of stress all the time and that complete freedom from stress is death. Perhaps his greatest contribution was in showing that there are two types of stress: harmful stress—called **distress**—and beneficial stress—called **eustress** (from the Greek *eu,* meaning good, as in euphoria). A person who gets on an airplane and feels sick with fear and anxiety is distressed. A fellow passenger feeling a sense of adventure and excitement is experiencing eustress. Both people are in the same situation, but they react differently. As this example illustrates, to understand the stress reaction, one must consider the person involved and not just the situation or crisis. The example also shows that not all stress is upsetting or damaging. As Selye (1976) wrote, normal activities such as a game of tennis or a passionate kiss can produce stress without causing conspicuous damage. A woman manager says, "I oversee over 500 volunteers where I work. My day is filled with complaints, but when I solve issues one at a time, I get a buzz from the results. That's when stress is energizing" (Arnott, 2002). Another way to think of good stress is to call it challenge stress. Challenge stress is related to a lot of endeavors, from public speaking to participating in races. This kind of stress leads to things employees or participants value—such as money, skills, fame, or promotion.

Selye studied the body's adaptive response to stress and reported that the stress syndrome is fundamental to virtually all higher forms of animals. He developed a comprehensive theory of the body's adaptive processes, based on a three-stage general adaptation syndrome. He was also the first scientist to identify the main organs and hormones involved in the stress response. His concept of stress led to new avenues of research in degenerative diseases, including coronary thrombosis, brain hemorrhage, hardening of the arteries, high blood pressure, kidney failure, arthritis, peptic ulcers, and cancer.

His experiments led him to theorize that to eliminate stress and individuals' adaptive reactions would be to eliminate all change, including growth, development, and maturation. Without stress human lives would be at complete rest—rather boring to say the least.

Selye was often asked what can be done to reduce distress. He advised individuals to watch for signs that they are becoming too keyed up. On a personal note, he said that he tried to forget immediately everything that was unimportant because trying to remember too many things is a major source of psychological stress.

Decision Making and Stress

Selye's conscious decision to forget unnecessary information was one method he used to reduce stress. Delegating work or decisions to others is another way to reduce stress. For example, using the services of travel agents to arrange trips or booking online can reduce stress for a frequent traveler. In efficient households, chores can be delegated to spouses and children. A third way to reduce stress is to postpone decisions when there is no hurry. Most good decisions are not made in a hurry. Taking the time to think out all the alternatives and identify the best use of resources leads to sounder decisions. In addition, individuals, employees, and families can use many other methods to reduce stress. As an example, Toffler (1970) observed:

> I have seen a woman sociologist, just returned from a crowded, highly stimulating professional conference, sit down in a restaurant and absolutely refuse to make any decisions whatever about her meal. "What would you like?" her husband asked. "You decide for me," she replied. When pressed to choose between specific alternatives, she still explicitly refused, insisting angrily that she lacked the "energy" to make the decision. (p. 324)

In an employment situation, a way to reduce stress is to surround oneself with competent workers. Consider how carefully a newly elected president, prime minister, or governor selects the members of the cabinet. A navy admiral expressed his thoughts on the importance of employee selection:

> If you have the capability to do this, surround yourself with competent, capable people. I found that if I have people that are working for me of this caliber, that makes my job much easier. . . . you try to get the best performer you can get—the best qualified, the best experienced. It gives you confidence in what they are doing and that it's going to be correct. (Quick, Nelson, & Quick, 1990, p. 55)

How to react to stress is a decision involving conscious problem solving. Because stress permeates all aspects of individual and family life, everyone needs to master these problem-solving skills: Sound decision making leads to improved lifestyles and senses of well-being. As Chapter 8 pointed out, potential stressors for individuals and families include poverty, lack of adequate housing, and disabling conditions. Each of these stressors provides ample opportunity for decision making.

Psychological Hardiness

Hardy individuals tend to have an internal locus of control, meaning they feel responsible for their own lives and most of what happens to them. For example, when Debra, a 35-year-old bride, learned the morning of her wedding day that the dry cleaners had ruined her "going away dress," she quickly drove to the nearest clothes store, grabbed a half dozen dresses in her size, tried them on, and bought one. Was it what she had planned? No. Was she stressed? Yes. Was she calm? Yes, according to store clerks who waited on her. They reported she bought a dress in less than 10 minutes and left happy. Debra exhibited a personality characteristic called psychological hardiness. In looking back, she said, "I was so happy to be getting married, nothing was going to bring me down." **Psychological hardiness** describes people who have a sense of control over their lives; are committed to self, work, relationships, and other values; and do not fear change. Such people may suffer fewer health consequences from crises or traumas.

Debra's experience with the ruined dress was a **nonnormative stressor event.** These events are unanticipated experiences that place a person or a family in a state of instability and require creative effort to remedy. **Normative stressor events** are anticipated, predictable developmental changes that occur at certain life intervals. For most college students, registering for classes is a normative stressor event. Flunking out of school is a nonnormative stressor event.

Some people are extremely resilient when faced with either type of stressor event. People who are likely to be resistant to stress have a disposition composed of the three C's: commitment, control, and challenge (Kobasa, 1982). They have a sense of purpose, are committed to their work and their families, rely on others, and know that others count on them. Psychologically hardy people realize that stress and challenge are normal parts of life and that they have the resources to deal with them. Individuals who perceive less stress and express more hardiness report significantly greater work/life satisfaction (Nowack, 1991).

Theory of Adaptive Range

Someone once jokingly said that the only person who really welcomes change is a wet baby. But the theory of adaptive range suggests that some level of change is vital to everyone's health and well-being, although too much unwanted change can be damaging. As mentioned earlier, everyone's life includes a comfort zone in which certain things and relationships do not change.

Consider the example of James, a 40-year-old male who has gone through a series of relationships and has been divorced twice. He likes to travel, eat different foods, visit with friends, and see the latest movies. If something new is happening, he is there. He wears "in" clothing and has the latest exercise equipment. He has a high intellect and is easily bored. On the surface, he looks like the epitome of change and adventure, but in a later interview James reveals that he has had the same job and house for 15 years and has a 10-year-old Irish setter he loves.

The moral of this story is that most people opt for stability and consistency in certain areas of their lives and opt for change or novelty in others. James opts for stability in his work and home, but wants change in his appearance, entertainment, and relationships. As a footnote to this story, James says he is tired of dating and is looking for a stable, lasting relationship. Is this believable? Is he ready for change? Before exploring further ways to manage and accommodate change and stress, an examination of how the body responds to stress is necessary, because stress has as its base a physiological response.

The Body's Response to Stress

What happens to a person's body when he or she experiences stress? First, an alarm reaction takes place. The alarm response begins when the brain perceives a threat to the sense of equilibrium. Something is not right. A loud siren, a sudden clap of thunder, or any other such disturbance serves as an alarm signal.

After the brain is alerted, a chain of events ensues as both hormones and nerves bring about a state of readiness. In 1932, Walter Cannon of Harvard Medical School coined the phrase **"fight or flight syndrome"** to refer to this alerted condition of the body as it quickly prepares for physical battle or energetic flight to escape the situation. A threatened or alerted person will experience some or all of the following physical actions:

◆ Pupils of the eyes widen.

◆ Muscles tense.

◆ Heart races or pounds.

◆ Hearing sharpens.

◆ Breathing quickens.

◆ Hair may stand on end.

◆ Hands feel clammy.

◆ Mouth becomes dry.

These actions, when synchronized, provide support for the emergency physical response, if needed. In the meantime, the brain is trying to process how to react next.

The second stress stage is called resistance. In this stage, the body adapts to the demand. If a woman driving a car hears a siren, she will become alert to a threat and try to find the source of the noise. If the siren is coming from an ambulance behind her, she will pull over to let it pass. After the ambulance goes by, her body will relax and return to normal.

Stress can be an energizer. For instance, people go to adventure movies and car races that give them a quick, but safe, brush with stress. Each person needs stimulation to survive. Staying in a safe, comfortable job for 20 years is one way to keep stress and stimulation low. Changing jobs or applying for a promotion increases stress and provides stimulation.

The third stage of the stress reaction is the exhaustion stage. Once the danger and the excitement have passed, the body may feel tired and possibly susceptible to various illnesses. A family as well as an individual can reach the stage of exhaustion, leaving family members susceptible to various disorders and feelings of discontent or restlessness. For example, a family may feel let down, exhausted, or bored after a busy holiday season. It has been estimated that over half of all illnesses are related to stress (Schwartz, 1982).

Diet, Exercise, and Stress

Stress research and theory have generally focused on the negative aspects of stress (or distress). Because people are eager to reduce these negative aspects, they invest in the many stress-reducing products and regimens offered in the marketplace. But, consumers should remember the cautionary phrase *caveat emptor*, meaning "may the buyer beware."

Before investing any money in a miracle vitamin or food, consumers should know that the best nutritional preparation for stress is a balanced and varied diet as part of a lifestyle that includes regular exercise (Hamilton, Rolfes, & Whitney, 1990). No known singular food, vitamin supplement, or herbal remedy will eliminate stress. During stress all three energy fuels—carbohydrates, fat, and protein—are depleted (Hamilton, Rolfes, & Whitney, 1990). Individuals who eat well to obtain the nutrients needed and engage in regular exercise will be better prepared to withstand the impact of unavoidable stress than individuals with poor diets and low fitness levels. In general, exercise is recommended as a necessary part of a health-promoting lifestyle (Tanner, 1991). Moderate exercise has been shown to reduce stress because it raises the level of beta-endorphins, chemicals in the brain associated with pain relief, which has a positive effect on mood and behavior (Hale, 1991). According to the American Heart Association, only 1 in 10 Americans follows a consistent exercise program. The AHA suggests a goal of 30 minutes a day. If this is not possible, other sources suggest that three times a week for 30 minutes will have beneficial results.

Exercise is a healthy way to manage stress.

Gary Conner/PhotoEdit

STRESS MANAGEMENT

Beyond managing diet and exercise, what else can a person do to reduce the effects of stress? Other stress-reducing methods include:

- Getting more rest and relaxation
- Outsourcing (as discussed earlier)
- Meditation and deep breathing
- Massage
- Social support

Evidence suggests that stress relief and social support can prolong life. For example, in one study melanoma patients who received six weeks of structured group support suffered only half as many recurrences as their peers (Cowley, Underwood, & Kalb, 1999). In another study, patients with early breast or prostate cancer who attended stress management groups lived significantly longer than equally ill patients who weren't in groups (Elias, 1998).

Often a combined approach is best. Individuals must determine the stress management techniques that work best for them. Additional techniques will be given in the next section. People with severe stress problems may seek individual treatment from a psychiatrist, psychologist, or physician, or they may join a support group or counseling workshop. These groups and workshops, which are usually offered at mental health clinics, hospitals, universities or through workplace Employee Assistance Programs (EAPs), may last from half a day to several days. Who attends stress management programs? Men and women are almost equally likely to feel stress, but women are almost twice as likely to seek help (Waldrop, 1993). According to Cotton (1990), three categories of individuals tend to seek assistance with stress management:

1. People who are not experiencing any particular difficulty with stress, but are generally health-conscious. They are interested in the preventive aspects of stress.

2. People who are distressed, anxious, or depressed. A distressed person is facing many ongoing stresses or hassles.

3. People with medical problems related to stress. These people are often Type A's and may be referred by their physician.

Researchers have established linkages among stress, illness, and certain types of personalities. One schema separates people into two groups of personalities:

- **Type A persons** are characterized by excessively striving behavior, high job involvement, impatience, competitiveness, desire for control and power, aggressiveness, and hostility.
- **Type B persons** are more relaxed, easygoing, reflective, and cooperative.

The two most outstanding characteristics of Type A's are a sense of time urgency and hostility (Patel, 1991). Time urgency refers to the feeling that there is not enough time to do everything. It leads to impatience, tension, restlessness, preoccupation (e.g., inattentiveness to others), and rapid eating and talking. Hostility means evaluating people, events, or situations negatively and being suspicious, distrustful, aggressive, and competitive. Type A behavior is associated with cynicism, interpersonal negativity, and depersonalization (Nowack, 1991). In one study, Type A's were found to have low coping skills, and their depression and anxiety increased as their work stress increased (Greenglass & Burke, 1991). Type A's try to achieve goals without proper planning—they rush into their work without planning the steps necessary to achieve goals (Powell & Enright, 1990). Type A personalities rarely leave the office; a suggested remedy is to encourage Type A's to take lunch breaks and walks and get more of a life outside the office.

Type B's are characterized by an absence of the habits and traits associated with Type A's. They lack a sense of time urgency and its accompanying impatience. Type B's wait in line better than Type A's; they can relax without guilt, are more cooperative with others, and take a break when fatigued. They are more likely to recognize signs of stress within themselves and to take time for fun. Type B's have goals and ambitions, but they have a confident style that allows them to wait for things to happen.

Several studies have linked Type A behavior to an increased rate of heart attacks and other diseases, but counterstudies indicate that the factors are more complex. Thus, there is no agreement on the health risks associated with Types A and B behavior. Similarly, the origins of Types A and B behavior are uncertain. It has been suggested that the Type A behavior pattern is established in childhood through the encouragement of high standards of achievement subconsciously imposed by adults, particularly parents (Matthews & Siegel, 1982). Despite these areas of uncertainty, researchers agree that stressors are experienced differently by different types of people and that coping responses vary by dominant personality type.

Techniques for Reducing Stress

Coping strategies to reduce everyday stress that is not chronic or disease-related can be divided into two types: problem-focused coping and emotion-focused coping (Lazarus, 1991). Problem-focused coping attempts to alter the actual relationships and change behaviors or environments. Emotion-focused coping concentrates on regulating the emotional distress caused by harm or threat. Someone could do this by avoiding thoughts of the stressor, replacing negative thoughts with positive, denying, or distancing. Positive thinking is used more by Type A's than Type B's as a coping strategy (Havlovic & Keenan, 1991). Emotion-focused coping requires a change in thinking or interpreting and a change in acting. Moderate stress can be relieved by first determining the cause of stress, then removing the stressor or moving out of the stressful environment, and, lastly, employing techniques that change the response to stress.

Specific techniques to help manage stress include the following:

◆ Plan and organize time to allow free time, time for enjoyment, relaxation, fun, hobbies, and exercise.

◆ Complete tasks that have been started.

◆ Develop a sense of humor.

◆ Indulge yourself. Solitude works especially for those with demanding families. It is not just about being physically alone, but also about having only yourself on the agenda. An example is commuters pulling inside themselves and decompressing. They enjoy the commute, listening to favorite radio stations, and thinking their own thoughts.

◆ Find quiet environments and people who make one feel good about oneself. Build family and friendship bonds. A study by Karen Grewen of the School of Medicine at the University of North Carolina–Chapel Hill found that a brief hug and 10 minutes of handholding with a romantic partner greatly reduced the harmful physical effects of stress (Elias, 2003).

◆ Keep things in perspective. Stay flexible. "Ultimately, it's how you spend your days—not your downtime—that matters" (Spencer, 2003, p. D1). The new thinking is to deal with stress when it happens by changing how you react to it rather than waiting for vacations, the spa, or yoga classes (although they help).

◆ Develop a positive attitude. Realize that one person cannot change everything. Much stress comes not from stressors but from perceptions of situations.

> We believe, value, choose, and know unconsciously as well as consciously. . . . The way we perceive reality is strongly influenced by unconsciously held beliefs. The phenomena of denial and resistance in psychotherapy illustrate how thoroughly one tends not to see things threatening to deeply held images conflicting with deeply held beliefs. (Harman, 1998, p. 15)

A study by pollsters Roper Starch Worldwide revealed that

◆ Twenty-three percent of men and 15 percent of women take a day off from work when stressed.

◆ Nineteen percent of men and 36 percent of women buy clothing.

◆ Fifteen percent of men and 26 percent of women eat a special dessert. (Crispell, 1997)

These techniques and study results may be useful, but how does a busy person find the time to relax? Consider the opening paragraph of an article on stress that appeared in *Parents* magazine:

> "We all know what we need to do about stress," says Alice, a legal secretary and the single mother of two young children. "We need to be good to ourselves, exercise regularly, eat well, get plenty of rest, and allow enough time for pleasure." Then she laughs and adds, "In other words, what we all really need is two weeks at a spa, complete with daily massage. Then when we return, we need a full-time maid, cook, and chauffeur." (Levine, 1990, p. 68)

As this quotation makes clear, reducing stress is more easily said than done. It is one thing to describe successful techniques for reducing stress; it is another thing to fit them into an already busy life.

According to NIOSH, **job stress** is defined as the harmful physical and emotional responses that occur when the requirements of the job do not match the capabilities, resources, or needs of the worker. Job stress can lead to poor health and even injury. NIOSH differentiates challenge from stress. Challenge energizes people and motivates them to learn new skills. When a challenge is met, the reactions are satisfying and relaxing. Thus, challenge is a natural and healthy part of productive work. Job stress, however, results when job demands are not met, usually because of excessive workloads: There are no end results, only a sense of exhaustion and failure. According to NIOSH, job stress is on the rise. They cite the following study results as examples supporting this observation:

◆ One-fourth of employees view their jobs as the number one stressor in their lives (Northwestern National Life).

◆ Three-fourths of employees believe workers have more on-the-job stress than a generation ago (Princeton Survey Research Associates).

◆ Problems at work are more strongly associated with health complaints than are other life stressors—more so than even financial problems or family problems (St. Paul Fire and Marine Insurance Co.).

Karen Nussbaum, executive director of the Women's Bureau in the United States Department of Labor, says:

> I think of stress and working parents in two issues—time and work. When you are a parent who works outside the home—which is the case for more than 50 percent of all mothers of preschoolers—you have less time and more worry. And the combination results in high stress. (Levine, 1990, p. 68)

As Chapter 10 observed, stress is an inevitable result of work and family time conflicts. A study conducted by the Roper organization found that 60 percent of the employed mothers surveyed reported a lot of stress from conflicting demands of work and family. One of the conflicting demands that is causing stress for a lot of individuals and families is travel associated with work. More than 8 in 10 business travelers say that work travel is stressful (Fisher, 1998). Travel is hardest

◆ On workers with young families. In one study, 6 in 10 married travelers said they experienced stress when missing family milestones, such as a birthday, a wedding anniversary, or a child's sporting event (Fisher, 1998).

◆ At night. Workers especially miss their children at bedtime.

◆ On spouses who are left behind. The burden of household work and child care falls on them.

◆ When piles of work are waiting for the worker upon return to work.

◆ When things go wrong. Canceled flights, lost luggage, or reservations difficulties create stress.

On the other hand, the most enthusiastic travelers are those between the ages of 18 and 34. They enjoy seeing new places. Almost 70 percent say that overnight business travel makes them feel important, and 68 percent say that trips provide a needed break from home and regular life (Fisher, 1998). So travel can produce distress or eustress. A lot of the reaction has to do with the traveler's lifestyle, age, career stage, and other criteria—such as location of the travel destination and the meaning of the travel to their job success.

Typically, work and work-related activities, transportation time to and from work, and preparation activities take up over 40 hours a week. Boredom, overload, role ambiguity, underutilization of talent or skills, poor job design, lack of advancement, shift work, low pay, transfers, miscommunications, difficult bosses, too many meetings, high job turnover, poor labor-management relations, lack of control, and incompetence all contribute to job stress. Negative consequences or effects of stress may include anxiety, being accident-prone, lower productivity, and a host of other physical, mental, and behavioral problems.

Although work produces stress, remember that according to Hans Selye, not all stress is bad. Work provides a purpose for living and provides challenges. According to Selye (1974), work is a biological necessity:

> [The] principal aim should not be to avoid work but to find the kind of occupation which for you is play. The best way to avoid harmful stress is to select an environment which is in line with your innate preferences—to find an activity which you like and respect. (1974, p. 85)

Further, he said, one of the worst stressors is continuous leisure from enforced retirement or solitary confinement. Benjamin Franklin earlier expressed this same sentiment when he said, "There is nothing wrong with retirement as long as one doesn't allow it to interfere with one's work."

Another way of looking at work and stress is that the workplace may actually serve as a haven from the stress, disappointment, and problems encountered in home and family life. It may be a relief to go to an office where everyone is polite, well groomed, and courteous, if, for example, there are constant fights at home or a family member is an abusive alcoholic. A more popular image of the home is as a place where the wounds inflicted in "that jungle out there" can be soothed (Ulrich & Dunne, 1986). As these examples indicate, asking people where they work and what they do is not enough. Professionals interested in helping families should ascertain whether work is a haven, a stressor, or a mixture of both for each individual in a given family.

Burnout

In the beginning, new careers may seem perfect. This is the honeymoon stage, when everything is wonderful. Employees are enthusiastic, with all sorts of hopes and expectations: Life is under way. They would rather work than do anything else. This is a recipe for **burnout,** a state of physical, emotional, and mental exhaustion caused by unrealistic goals and aspirations and long hours. Drive and idealism are good things, but if a hardworking perfectionist or self-motivating achiever hits obstacles, frustration or failure may result. This stage is called the awakening, the realization that early expectations may have been unrealistic, and it may lead to what the American Psychological Association calls brownout (a predecessor to burnout). In this stage fatigue and irritability show up; eating and sleeping patterns may be disturbed. Cynicism and indecision set in; unless something or someone steps in to halt the downward spiral, burnout may result. The onset may be slow and the result of role conflict (being pulled in too many directions), role ambiguity (unclear expectations), or role overload (the inability to say "no," taking on too much responsibility). Physical symptoms may include aches in the neck, head, or back or just a general lack of energy.

The word *burnout* is associated with being worn out from doing too much work. Originally, burnout was used in the aerospace industry to describe the termination of rocket or jet-engine operation because of insufficient fuel. In resource management, burnout refers to emotional or physical exhaustion brought about by unrelieved stress. This all-inclusive definition shows that burnout can come from many sources. Although the previous paragraph starts with a description of symptoms of potential job burnout, burnout can result from fatigue or frustration with a cause, a way of life, or a relationship that has failed to produce the expected reward (Freudenberger, 1980). For example, a sorority or fraternity president can experience burnout. A stockbroker described being on a country club board of directors for 15 years; when he had finally had enough of hearing complaints from members and being thwarted when he tried to introduce new ways of doing things, he quit when his term was over. Looking back, he is much relieved to have left that position, which was voluntary yet still caused a lot of stress.

In the 1970s, burnout was first associated with teachers, social workers, and others who worked in jobs involving considerable responsibility for the welfare of others. These jobs tended to have high turnover rates because workers were said to burn out after so many years on the job. In the 1980s, burnout was used to refer to just about anybody who was tired at the end of the day. During that decade, Charles Maslach (1982) published the Maslach Burnout Inventory, which defined burnout as the subjective experience of emotional exhaustion, depersonalization, and reduced personal accomplishment resulting from the continuous caring for needy clients in human service professions. Using the Maslach scale, two researchers discovered that day-care workers who experienced emotional exhaustion and depersonalization tended toward learned helplessness and low self-esteem (McMullen & Krantz, 1988). In short, they found that many day-care workers suffer from burnout.

Today, burnout refers to both everyday and long-term exhaustion. Regardless of how the word is used, the phenomenon should not be ignored. If burnout is acute, a person may have a breakdown in health, may not be able to continue performing at the expected pace, and may become discouraged and drop out of a profession, when what he or she really needs is a break, a chance for retraining, and perhaps a better job-environment-person fit. Here are some other ways to combat job burnout:

◆ Be realistic about expectations, aspirations, and goals. Get in touch with yourself and what you really want, remember what felt good in the past, rebuild your inner resources.

◆ If you make changes, be sure they are your own and not someone else's.

◆ Rest and relax; do not take work home with you (mentally or physically, learn to turn it off).

◆ Create balance in your life with other activities, groups, hobbies, exercise, etc.

◆ Avoid isolation: Closeness brings new insights, and it is hard to be agitated and depressed when surrounded by people and pets that you love.

Burnout can happen in friendships and marital relationships too. Distance, vacations, a new setting, or a renewed commitment may all help reduce relationship burnout. The importance of vacations was introduced in the last chapter, but here are another study's results to consider:

> Of 12,000 middle age men at risk for coronary disease, researchers found those who failed to take vacations had a higher risk of death from any cause, but particularly from heart disease, than those who took regular vacations. The results were controlled for education, income and the possibility that some of the men's health was too poor to take vacations. . . . Researchers say good vacations have a power that extends beyond the time you're away. (Shellenbarger, 2003, March 27, p. D1)

Burnout is generally regarded as a negative. But, like stress, burnout has its positive side. Burnout can be a signal for change, a deliberate dynamic in the psyche (mind) to reestablish balance and to stimulate growth (Garden, 1991). Viewed in this way, burnout can be a functional, positive developmental experience, rather than a dysfunctional, negative one. In 1997, Christina Maslach, a professor of psychology at the University of California, Berkeley, and coauthor of the book *The Truth about Burnout* concluded that

> Most people think burnout is caused by work overload. . . . But while having too much to do can cause stress, it doesn't necessarily cause burnout. People will work long, hard hours willingly and happily if they love what they are doing, or if they can see it is making a difference. . . . Respect helps, too. (Smith, 1997, p. 11D)

Stress and Non-Events

Most of the stressors covered so far have been caused by events or reactions to events. An interesting line of research has focused on the stress caused by non-events—specific occurrences in people's lives that they look forward to and make plans around but that fail to materialize. Examples of non-events are canceled weddings (these may be more stressful than divorces), postponed vacations, or not being invited to a follow-up job interview or an important social gathering. According to John Eckenrode of Cornell University,

> We know that unanticipated negative events are more stressful than anticipated ones. With an anticipated event, you can do some preparatory coping. You know it's going to happen and you can mobilize your resources. Things that just hit you out of the blue, on the other hand, are more stressful because you don't know they're coming. And when you've invested a lot of emotional buildup in whatever it is you're looking forward to, the effects can be huge. (Powers, 1995, p. 6)

Eckenrode says that many times people's plans are thwarted by others or something in the environment that is beyond an individual's control. He speculates that stress from non-events is just part of life, that disappointment is as normal an occurrence as the good things that happen.

Parents, Children, and Stress

The parent-child relationship can lead to stress for all concerned. Children are as vulnerable to stress and burnout as are adults. Hurried schedules and meals affect children as well as parents. Many experts think childhood stress is increasing (Adler, Kalb, & Rogers, 1999).

For parents, the stresses of child rearing may begin as soon as the newborn infant arrives home from the hospital. One study of parents of infants three to five months old identified a number of stressors. Thirty-five percent of the mothers and 20 percent of the fathers reported that a major stress was their infant's fussy behavior in relation to feeding or soothing techniques (Ventura, 1987).

Parental stress stemming from children is not limited to the children's preschool years. In one study of parents with children ranging in age up to young adulthood, 39 percent of the women respondents cited children as their primary source of stress (Mehren, 1988). Another study found that the Americans most likely to be stressed out are women between the ages of 30 and 44 because they tend to be working mothers with young children (Waldrop, 1993). And at midlife, a major source of stress for the women surveyed was the return of adult children to the home for economic reasons. Another study found that single parents and their adolescents are under potentially significant amounts of stress due to family structure and developmental factors, such as the adolescents' movement toward independence (Houser, Daniels, D'Andrea, & Konstam, 1993).

Stress Warning Signs in Children

Stressed children give off many warning signs: poor appetite, excessive crying, headaches and stomachaches, withdrawal, clinging behavior, hyperactivity, moodiness, and sleep problems. Children can experience stress from homesickness, parental divorce, and problems with family, friends, community, and school.

For example, Barbara Howard, a pediatrician at Johns Hopkins, says a quarter of her patients are there for stress-related problems. She says, "They'll come in with abdominal pain, urinary frequency, headaches . . . a whole variety of complaints which could be mistaken for medical problems and often are" (Adler, Kalb, & Rogers, 1999, p. 63). In addition,

> Parents are frequently wrong about the sources of stress in their children's lives, according to surveys by Georgia Witkin of Mount Sinai Medical School; they think children worry most about friendships and popularity, but they're actually fretting about the grown-ups. "The biggest concern," she says, "was that the parents are going to be sick, or angry, or they're going to divorce." And "often and somewhat surprisingly," says Giedd [Jay Giedd of the National Institutes of Health], "children have very global worries"—wars, environmental issues and crime, the same things adults worry about. (Adler, Kalb, & Rogers, 1999, p. 63)

Furthermore, researchers report, "Children who were neglected by their parents or raised in orphanages tend to have higher levels of stress hormones and may be 'hot reactors' later in life. As adults, they may feel empty or bored when on edge" (Adler, Kalb & Rogers, 1999, p. 60). On the other hand, children raised in secure, loving homes learn to modulate stress reactions, according to Megan Gunnar of the University of Minnesota.

Children can experience stress and overload from competitive, win-lose, rule-bound situations just as adults can. Consequently, the nature and outcomes of highly structured, competitive team sports can be childhood stressors. It is generally agreed that this type of sports activity is too stressful for very young children. To help children through these and other stressful situations, parents should be sensitive to any change overload, responsibility overload, or emotional overload their children may be experiencing.

In *The Hurried Child,* David Elkind, professor of child development at Tufts University, says that today's children are pressured to grow up too fast. He gives this example of responsibility overload:

> Janet is ten years old but has many adult responsibilities. In addition to taking care of her clothes and room, she must prepare breakfast for herself and her younger sister and make sure that they get off to school on time. (Her mother leaves for work an hour before Janet needs to get to school.) When she gets home, she has to do some housecleaning, defrost some meat for dinner, and make sure her sister is all right. When her mother gets home, Janet listens patiently to her mother's description of the "creeps" at work who never leave her alone and who are always making cracks or passes. After Janet helps prepare dinner, her mother says, "Honey, will you do the dishes? I'm just too tired," and Janet barely has time to do some homework. (1988, p. 150)

Janet is stressed not only from the work she has to do, but also from the amount of responsibility placed on her shoulders at such a young age. In many one-parent and dual-career families today, children are required to take substantial responsibility for housework and child care. How much is too much is a question worth thinking about.

Elkind points out that not only are homes more stressful today, but schools are also more stressful. Besides the usual competition for grades and in sports, children are exposed to more threats and violence in schools than ever before.

Like adults, children can learn to moderate stress by following the techniques described earlier in the chapter—eating a balanced diet, engaging in regular exercise, enjoying free time, and being with people with whom they are comfortable. Elkind says that children can suffer from chronic stress, usually brought on by significant life changes, that can be reduced by reassurance and attention from parents and teachers.

College Students and Stress

Stress is a lifelong fact. However, it is generally assumed that the teen years are especially stressful. Therefore, college students, most of whom are in their teens and early 20s, are living in or emerging from a stressful life period. Boredom and school burnout are often stressors during the high school years. By college age, many of the boredom and burnout problems have been replaced by renewed enthusiasm for education because of the new setting and the opportunity to specialize. College students are usually dedicated and in school by choice—they enjoy school for the most part and want to keep learning. They have career ambitions and life goals. But for all the pluses, the college years also have some negatives—stressors in the forms of relationships, grades, and emotional and physical problems. Uncertainty about what lies ahead is an ever present stressor. Other causes of stress include major losses through divorce or separation, which have increased in recent years, having two working parents (which gives teens less time with parents), and higher and earlier exposure to drugs, sex, and violence.

According to one study, the top academic stressors for college students were tests and finals, and the top personal stressor was intimate relationships (Murphy & Archer, 1996). Another study found that the most psychological distress was experienced freshman year and that it declined over the next four years (Sher, Wood, & Gotham, 1996). In response to this, many colleges and universities have put more effort in recent years into offering freshman orientation programs, specialized seminars, and living/learning dormitories for freshmen only.

For certain individuals, mild test anxiety has been found to motivate and facilitate performance. But test anxiety is more commonly associated with negative motivation and poor test performance (Hill & Wigfield, 1984). One study of undergraduate college students tried to determine whether test anxiety could be significantly reduced through regular relaxation exercises or physical exercises (Topp, 1989). The students were divided into three groups: a nonmeditative relaxation exercise group, an aerobics dance group, and a control group who did not meet during the seven-week study. Both the relaxation exercise group and the aerobics dance students (who increased in fitness also) reported a significant decline in test anxiety; the control group did not experience any change in test anxiety. The results from this study suggest that exercise reduces test anxiety, so a student suffering from it should consider incorporating exercise into his or her life. Another stressor for college students is meeting deadlines—deadlines for term papers, for projects, for club reports, for registering for classes, and so on. Time management techniques, including prioritizing, allocating time as best one can, checking progress, and keeping a calendar, should help with the problem of meeting deadlines.

Not all college students are in their late teens and early 20s. More and more college students are over age 25. They are returning to school after serving in the armed services, raising a family, or being engaged in some other work or family activities that caused them to postpone entering or finishing college. In addition to the college life stressors already mentioned, older students have the problems involved with combining family life with student life, doubts about their ability to compete with younger students, more complicated financial situations, and other concerns about mixing a more mature lifestyle with the demands of college life. These students face such stressful choices as the following: Should I go to see my in-laws on Sunday or finish my term paper? Should I make dinner or study? Their self-doubt concerns may range from what to wear to the first class to how to study for a test after not having taken one for 20 years.

All college students, regardless of age or life stage, undergo a change in their usual lifestyle. And as explained previously, change is stressful. Since going to college is a new experience and the people and environment are new, it is not surprising to find many students feeling and acting shy (Greenberg, 1983). Making new friends, talking with professors and advisers, using the services of counselors in the student counseling center and dormitories, and attending stress management workshops should help reduce stress.

FATIGUE: DEFINITION AND SOURCES

College students experience fatigue as well as stress. Irregular hours, studying for final exams, and weekend parties all contribute to fatigue. Chronic fatigue leads to impaired memory and response time. **Fatigue** is the feeling of having insufficient energy to carry on and a strong desire to stop, rest, or sleep (Engel, 1970). This feeling can come from mental or physical exertion, work, or play. Fatigue may be related to stress or have nothing to do with stress. For example, at night you may be tired from a long day of activity and feel fatigued, but you are not necessarily stressed or tense. Short-term fatigue can be easily remedied with some rest, but long-term, chronic fatigue is more serious.

Besides being a feeling, fatigue can include the physical symptoms of dizziness, headaches, nausea, and tremulousness (Atkinson, 1985). These physical symptoms are extreme; generally, a fatigued person simply feels tired. Fatigue is a normal part of daily life, but sometimes a person is more keenly aware of it than at other times. Fatigue can sneak up on an individual or build up to a point where the individual is not functioning well. It can also be dangerous, as when someone falls asleep at the wheel. Because of this potential danger, individuals need to recognize personal fatigue sensations and do something about them.

Fatigue comes from many sources. As Chapter 10 pointed out, the demands and conflicts arising from trying to achieve too much in the work and family realms can result in fatigue. A survey of 666 male and female clerical and professional employees revealed that fatigue levels were similar at home and at work. One male professional penciled in the following comment at the end of the survey: "Going home is just exchanging one set of problems for another." The study also revealed that professional women experienced significantly more fatigue and role overload than professional men (Goldsmith, 1989).

These findings have implications for those interested in personal and family management. What is happening in offices and homes that produces so much fatigue? And why are researchers finding that home and family life is just another stressor rather than a reliever of stress and fatigue?

The Body and Fatigue

Like stress, fatigue originates as a physiological response, and it comes from both internal and external sources. Regardless of where the fatigue originates, it is always felt as a subjective sensation by the person (Atkinson, 1985). Menopause, aging, certain medications, menstrual cycles, various diseases (both mental and physical), certain injuries, and pregnancy affect fatigue.

Fatigue begins at an unconscious, microscopic level and progresses through stages until the person thinks, "I'm tired." At the final stage, the person experiences fatigue as a sensation (Atkinson, 1985). Because the mind is included at this level, psychological factors such as boredom, depression, and being upset are combined with the physiological ones that cause fatigue.

Systems Theory: Sleep, Energy, and Fatigue

Systems theory is relevant to the discussion of fatigue because fatigue is a sign of energy imbalance: too much energy is being expended and not enough is being conserved. One way to look at energy is to envision an energy pool with an imbalance of energy boosters (inputs) and energy drainers (outputs). The energy pool is depleted when there are more energy drainers (bad habits, over-work, mental strain, illness, and occupational hazards) than energy boosters (nutrition, exercise, good sleep, pleasure, and mastery).

Sleep

"Sleep absolutely affects health," says Julian Thayer of the National Institute on Aging (Elias, 2003, p. 7D). The immune system seems to tune up at night, adding natural killer cells to fight off disease. "There's preliminary evidence that the strength of the immune system actually influences the quality of sleep in addition to being affected by it," says Michael Irwin of the UCLA Neuropsychiatric Institute (Elias, 2003, p. 7D).

Sleep, a critical energy booster, is vital to maintaining well-being and enthusiasm for life. It plays a major role in preparing the body and brain for an alert, productive, psychologically and physiologically healthy tomorrow (Maas, 1998). Even though everyone needs sleep, sometimes the amount and timing are difficult to control. For example, falling asleep after a stimulating day may be difficult even though you are very tired. At other times, you may feel drowsy, even though you want to stay alert, such as in an afternoon class. Have you ever heard the expression, "I need to sleep on it"? It turns out that people all over the world say some version of it, and it has been proven to have some substance. Sleep researchers have found that sleep influences "complex cognitive proce-dural thinking" (Stickgold, Winkelman, & Wehrwein, 2004, p. 58).

> Each waking moment bombards your brain with scores of sensations, thoughts and feelings. If your brain tried to store them all as memories, you might experi-ence terminal overload and be able to remember nothing. Undoubtedly, you're editing out some impression as they hit you during the day. But sleep also seems to help. (Stickgold et al., 2004, p. 60)

As noted in Chapter 10, humans spend about one-third of their lives sleeping. *The average American adult sleeps seven hours a night and a third get by on six hours or less.* A century ago nine hours was the norm. Recent studies indicate that the average married mom gets 6.7 hours. At least 50 percent of the adult popula-tion is chronically sleep-deprived (Maas, 1998). Sleep is necessary for two reasons:

- ◆ To restore energy levels
- ◆ To help the body to regulate and synchronize itself

Sleep provides rhythm to lives. Most people go to sleep and awake about the same time every day. While asleep, humans go through certain cycles of light and deep slumber. Figure 11.2 illustrates the rhythmic nature of typical sleep patterns.

There are two kinds of sleep: REM and NREM sleep. **REM,** or **rapid eye movement sleep,** occurs when the sleeper is in a light sleep; most dreams happen during REM. **NREM,** or **non-rapid eye movement sleep,** occurs

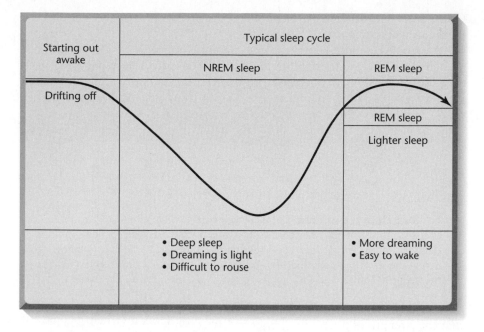

FIGURE 11.2
Typical Sleep Cycle
SOURCE: Based on National Center on Sleep Disorders Research

when the sleeper is in an inactive, deep slumber. Through the night, the sleeper goes back and forth between REM and NREM sleep.

Insomnia is the perception or complaint of inadequate or poor-quality sleep because of one or more of the following:

◆ Difficulty falling asleep

◆ Waking up frequently during the night with difficulty returning to sleep

◆ Waking up too early in the morning

◆ Unrefreshing sleep

When people are deprived of sleep for a long time or do not get the right balance of REM and NREM sleep, they can feel fatigued and irritable, and their abilities to make decisions and to concentrate are diminished. This is why fatigue and insomnia are an integral part of the study of resource management.

Appropriate levels of sleep and rest are resources. For example, many athletes experience some form of precompetition stress that may result in insomnia during the night before their competition. This sleep withdrawal, even though temporary, has a negative influence on performance. Sleeping poorly impairs the ability to remember and learn.

According to the National Center on Sleep Disorders Research, preschool children (ages 3 to 5) should get between 10 and 12 hours of sleep including naps. Older children need less; those between the ages of 6 and 12 need about 9 hours of sleep a night. Teenagers need about 8 to 9 hours, but most get less than eight. Parents can help children sleep better by limiting drinks loaded with caffeine before bed, setting routines, and allowing time for children to unwind before bedtime. Caffeine may stay in the body up to 12 hours, so caffeine consumption should stop around noon. Here is the caffeine content (milligrams per 8 ounces) of several popular drinks:

◆ Coffee   110 (approximate, varies by type of coffee)
◆ Mountain Dew   37
◆ Coca-Cola   23
◆ Arizona green tea   7.5

SUGGESTED ACTIVITY

Plot your sleep pattern for three days on a graph. Mark when you go to sleep and when you wake up; include nighttime sleep and daytime naps. Do you see a pattern? Does doing an activity like this make you more conscious of your sleep patterns? Were you more likely to go to sleep earlier at night and get up earlier than normal?

Other disturbers of sleep are alcohol and drugs. Alcohol sedates but also disturbs normal sleep patterns.

As people get older, sleep problems are more prevalent. As people age, natural changes in circadian rhythms and medications affect sleep patterns. Other things affecting sleep are the need to use the bathroom more at night, physical pain from arthritis, coughing, nighttime heartburn, headaches, and depression. Circadian rhythms are triggered by nighttime darkness, which releases a surge of melatonin leading to sleep; the dawn triggers awakening (Stickgold et al., 2004). Electric light (artificial illumination) appears to disrupt this natural pattern. Older people often feel sleepy early in the evening, but this can lead to falling asleep at 8 P.M. and waking at 4 A.M. Daytime exposure to natural light appears to help a person sleep better:

> For Mrs. Homer, it worked. The increased exposure to light "made a difference," she says. It also helped her realize how much time she was spending indoors in dimly lit rooms. Since then, she's kept up the exposure to light by visiting a park across the street from her high-rise a few times a week. "I didn't go into that deep dream sleep before, and I'm dreaming now." (Greene, 2002, p. R10)

There are hundreds of sleep disorder clinics accredited by the American Sleep Disorders Association. Clinic staff study sleep patterns and help people suffering from chronic insomnia. Among the discoveries of these clinics is that stress and anxiety can affect the length and quality of sleep.

Work schedules can also influence sleep patterns and insomnia. For example, studies have shown that shift workers get three hours less sleep than people who work a normal daytime schedule, and up to 90 percent of shift workers report sleep disturbances (Atkinson, 1985). Irregular and rotating shifts (for example, working nights one week, days the next) play havoc not only with the individual's health and sleep patterns, but also with family schedules. Sometimes a family may see shifts as an asset; for example, shifts may allow someone always to be home with the children. On the negative side, however, husbands and wives working on different shifts may rarely see each other. More intimate, face-to-face communication may be replaced with hurried phone calls and written messages.

According to James Maas (1998), two primary rules are to establish a regular sleep pattern and get enough nightly sleep. Another rule suggested by the National Sleep Foundation is to make the bed a sleep- and sex-only zone. For someone experiencing sleep problems, desks, filing cabinets, clutter, and computers and other reminders of work should probably be in another room besides the bedroom. Finally, keep following the latest scientific discoveries on sleep. So far we know that sleep makes a person demonstrably smarter and appreciably healthier; it is an important part of a long and healthy life.

Energy and Alertness

Clearly, getting adequate rest and sleep is an energy booster. An energetic person has the capacity to take on a job or an activity and complete it to the best of her or his ability. There are many types of energy boosters. In addition, some individuals seem to be born with more energy than others. Research is incomplete as to why this difference exists. Another little understood energy phenomenon is how people reenergize themselves during the day. Many people at one time ascribed to the drain theory, which asserted that individuals wake with a certain level of energy in the morning. As the day wears on, each activity takes away some of that energy until by nightfall the energy is depleted and the person sleeps. Then, according to the theory, sleep restores the person, and the pattern is repeated the next day. The problem with the drain theory is that not all people are highly energized on first waking up, and during the day such things as food, exercise, and excitement refuel people. Each person has typical energy rhythms or patterns during the day that can be altered by events. We experience ups and downs in alertness over the course of the day, even when our nighttime sleep is adequate. Alertness is quite strong around 10 and 11 A.M., which makes this a good time to take class and tests. It dips at midafternoon and goes up again around 6 P.M., then starts to fall until bedtime.

Fatigue Management

The purpose of this book is not just to describe life management problems (e.g., people do not get enough sleep or rest), but to also present possible solutions. Systems theory asserts that systems are connected: If one part of the system is affected, other parts are affected. The subjects of sleep, energy, and fatigue are so interlaced that it is difficult to discuss one without discussing the others. To cope with fatigue problems, an individual needs to examine each part of the system, including diet, exercise, sleep, activity, and relationships.

Specifically, what can one do to manage energy and fatigue better? First, an individual should be able to recognize his or her sleep and fatigue signs and assign time and energy accordingly. In other words, it is up to the individual to self-monitor. Successful people rarely go blindly into a new activity; they think first about how much of their time and energy will be required. Second, when fatigue is imminent, the individual should try to cope with it by napping or sleeping, relaxing, eating properly, changing activity, or whatever combination of these activities works best. As mentioned earlier, daily exposure to natural light, keeping a regular schedule, and avoiding all stimulants such as coffee, tea, and soft drinks containing caffeine at least two hours (some would say six hours) prior to going to bed will help improve sleep (Powell & Enright, 1990).

This doctor is showing signs of fatigue.

© Jose Luis Pelaez, Inc./CORBIS

And, most of all, people should take time to sleep: It is important to daily functioning and a threat to public safety when people are sleepy at the wheel or when working machinery. Sleep is not a waste of time.

Chronic Fatigue Syndrome

In recent years, an affliction known as **chronic fatigue syndrome** has become a public health concern. Because research is still under way, chronic fatigue is a controversial topic. It is not clear what causes the disease or even whether it is one disease or many. It may be a long-acting viral infection, a form of allergy, or something entirely different (*Two New Landmark Studies,* 1991). No one knows precisely how many people have chronic fatigue syndrome. Patients with extreme chronic fatigue cannot work and have little energy for anything.

People with chronic fatigue exhibit a variety of symptoms. The CDC (Centers for Disease Control and Prevention, which defined the syndrome in 1988) has identified the main ones as chills or low-grade fever, sore throat, tender lymph nodes, muscle pain, muscle weakness, extreme fatigue, headaches, joint pain (without swelling), neurological problems (confusion, memory loss, visual disturbances), sleep disorders, and the sudden onset of symptoms (Cowley, 1990).

In addition to these symptoms, chronic fatigue differs from ordinary fatigue brought on by overexertion in several respects. In chronic fatigue

◆ Rest is not restorative.

◆ Minimal physical activity can bring on significant "exhausterbations" (S. Straus, personal communication, August 24, 1989).

Chronic fatigue is long-lasting and affects children as well as adults. A good night's sleep or a leisurely vacation will not help true chronic fatigue.

Web-Based Resources

For information on sleep go to

◆ The National Sleep Foundation Web site at **www.sleepfoundation.org**

◆ The Harvard Medical School at **www.health.harvard.edu/newsweek**

◆ The National Center on Sleep Disorders Research at **www.nhlbi .nih.gov/about/ncsdr**

The American Psychological Association maintains lists of licensed psychologists who can help with stress-related problems. Its Web site is **helping .apa.org/refer.** The Bureau of Labor Statistics' Web site (**www.stats.bls.gov/**) reports on the number and percentage distribution of nonfatal occupational injuries and illnesses involving days away from work by nature of injury or illness.

Summary

When individuals experience excessive stress and fatigue, they question their life choices and reevaluate their time use and commitments. They wonder if it is necessary to hurry all the time. And are they really achieving more by hurrying? In the rush, are families being shortchanged?

This chapter has largely been based on theories and research from psychology and the health and wellness fields. An important point is that moderate levels of stress and fatigue are a normal part of life.

Hans Selye was a major contributor to stress research. Among other things, he differentiated between two types of stress: distress (harmful) and eustress (beneficial).

Stress originates from two sources: internal and external. Stressor events can be normative (expected) or nonnormative (unanticipated). The body's response to stress and the fight or flight syndrome are important to understanding how stress works. An individual's personality and emotional state play significant roles in the evaluation and reaction to stress. Type A and Type B personalities react differently to stress.

The meaning of burnout has changed over the years, but the phenomenon is serious and should not be ignored. The steps leading up to burnout and possible solutions to burnout were described in this chapter. Fatigue, irritability, frustration, neck, head or back aches are all signals. Although stress exists throughout the life cycle, childhood stress and the stress college students experience are particularly troubling. David Elkind has observed that children today may be pushed to grow up too fast and assume adult responsibilities at an early age.

Energy boosters can have a restorative effect on persons suffering from fatigue. So can sleep. Sleep researchers have distinguished rapid eye movement sleep from non-rapid eye movement sleep. Ordinary fatigue can be reduced by sleep and rest. Children need different amounts of sleep depending on their ages. A century ago nine hours of sleep a night was normal; now Americans average seven hours and one-third get by on six or less.

Far more research is needed on the complex interplay among energy, fatigue, sleep, personality, and stress. Individuals can strive to maintain a balance of activity, rest, and energy, acquire the skills to understand themselves, and enjoy each other more. The next chapter covers another potential stressor and relaxer—the environment.

Key Terms

burnout	fight or flight syndrome	outsourcing
chronic fatigue syndrome	insomnia	psychological hardiness
comfort zone	internal stress	rapid eye movement (REM) sleep
comparative advantage	job stress	stress
crises	nonnormative stressor events	stressors
distress	non-rapid eye movement (NREM) sleep	stress overload or pileup
domino effect		Type A person
eustress	normative stressor events	Type B person
external stress		
fatigue		

Review Questions

1. A book editor explained that he was Type B on the outside and Type A on the inside. How could this be? Do you know someone who appears to be one type of personality but is in reality the other type? Explain.

2. What happens to the body during each of the three stages of the stress reaction?

3. How could burnout have a good side? What may be a benefit?

4. Give two examples of nonnormative and normative stressor events that have occurred in your life.

5. Describe the drain theory of human energy and explain why it is inadequate.

References

Adler, J., Kalb, C., & Rogers, A. (1999, June 14). Stress. *Newsweek*, 56–69.

Arnott, N. (2002, November/December). Got stress? Don't worry. *Weight Watchers Magazine*, 64–67.

Atkinson, H. (1985). *Women and fatigue*. New York: Putnam.

Begley, S. (2003, February 7). How humans react when bad things occur again and again. *The Wall Street Journal*, B1.

Braus, P. (1998, September). When the helpers need a hand. *American Demographics*, 1–4.

Capel, I., & Gurnsey, J. (1987). *Managing stress*. London: Constable.

Cotton, D. (1990). *Stress management*. New York: Brunner/Mazel.

Cowley, G. (1990, November 12). Chronic fatigue syndrome. *Newsweek*, 62–70.

Cowley, G., Underwood, A., & Kalb, C. (1999, June 14). Stress busters: What works. *Newsweek*, 60.

Crispell, D. (1997, November). Demo memo. *American Demographics*, 36.

Did you know. (1998, June 29). *Tallahassee Democrat*, 3D.

Dollahite, D. (1991). Family resource management and family stress theories: Toward a conceptual integration. *Lifestyles: Family and Economic Issues*, 12(4), 361–377.

Elias, M. (1998, March 26). Antistress groups seem to support cancer survival. *USA Today*, D1.

Elias, M. (2003, March 10). Study: Hugging warms the heart, and also may protect it. *USA Today*, 7D.

Elkind, D. (1988). *The hurried child*. Reading, MA: Addison-Wesley.

Engel, G. (1970). Nervousness and fatigue. In C. M. MacBryde and R. S. Blacklow (Eds.), *Signs and symptoms* (5th ed.; p. 637). Philadelphia: Lippincott.

Fisher, C. (1998, June). Business on the road. *American Demographics*, 44–47, 54.

Freudenberger, H. (1980). *Burnout*. Garden City, NY: Anchor Press.

Garden, A. (1991). The purpose of burnout: A Jungian interpretation. In P. Perrewe (Ed.), *Job stress* (pp. 73–93). Corte Madera, CA: Select Press.

Garrison, M., Malia, J., Norem, R., & Hira, T. (1994). Developing a daily hassles inventory. *Proceedings of the 1994 Conference of the Eastern Family Economics and Management Association*, Pittsburgh, PA: Resource, 18–43.

Goldsmith, E. (1989). Role overload: Professional men vs. professional women. *Proceedings of the Southeastern Regional Association of Family Economics—Home Management Annual Meeting*.

Greenberg, J. (1983). *Comprehensive stress management*. Dubuque, IA: Brown.

Greene, K. (2002, November 11). Aging well. *The Wall Street Journal*, R10.

Greenglass, E., & Burke, R. (1991). The relationship between stress and coping among Type As. In P. Perrewe (Ed.), *Job stress* (pp. 361–373). Corte Madera, CA: Select Press.

Hale, E. (1991, June) Taming menstrual cramps. *FDA Consumer*, 25(5).

Hamilton, E., Rolfes, S., & Whitney, E. (1990). *Understanding nutrition* (5th ed.). St. Paul: West.

Harman, W. (1998). *Global mind change*. San Francisco: Berrett-Koehler.

Havlovic, S., & Keenan, J. (1991). Coping with work stress. In P. Perrewe (Ed.), *Job stress*. Corte Madera, CA: Select Press.

Hill, K., & Wigfield, A. (1984). Test anxiety: A major educational problem and what can be done about it. *Elementary School Journal*, 85, 106–126.

House, J. (1983). *Work stress and social support*. Reading, MA: Addison-Wesley.

Houser, R., Daniels, J., D'Andrea, M., & Konstam, V. (1993). A systemic behaviorally based technique for resolving conflict between adolescents and their single parents. *Family Behavior Therapy, 15*(3), 17–31.

Kobasa, S. (1982). The hardy personality: Toward a psychology of stress and health. In J. Suls and G. Sanders (Eds.), *Social psychology and illness*. Hillsdale, NJ: Erlbaum.

Lazarus, R. (1991). Psychological stress in the workplace. In P. Perrewe (Ed.), *Job stress* (pp. 1–13). Corte Madera, CA; Select Press.

Levine, K. (1990, May). Coping with stress. *Parents,* 68–70.

Maas, J. (1998). *Power sleep*. NY: Villard.

Maslach, C. (1982). *Burnout: The cost of caring*. Englewood Cliffs, NJ: Prentice-Hall.

Matthews, K., & Siegel, J. (1982). The type A behavior pattern in children and adolescents: Assessment, development and associated coronary risk. In A. Baum and J. E. Singer (Eds.), *Handbook of psychology and health*, Vol. 2. Hillsdale, NJ: Erlbaum.

McLellan, T., Bragg, A., & Cacciola, J. (1992). *Escape from anxiety & stress*. New York: Chelsea House.

McMullen, M., & Krantz, M. (1988). Burnout in day care workers: The effects of learned helplessness and self-esteem. *Child & Youth Care Quarterly, 17*(4), 275–280.

Mehren, E. (1988, June 14). New study downplays the effects of menopause. *Los Angeles Times*.

Murphy, M., & Archer, J. (1996, January/February). Stressors on the college campus, *Journal of College Student Development,* 20–27.

Nowack, K. M. (1991). Psychological predictors of health status. *Work and Stress, 5*(2), 117–131.

Patel, C. (1991). *The complete guide to stress management*. London: Plenum Press.

Powell, T., & Enright, S. (1990). *Anxiety and stress management,* London: Routledge.

Powers, M. (1995, Fall). Dashed expectations. *Human Ecology Forum,* 5–7.

Quick, J., Nelson, D., & Quick, J. (1990). *Stress and challenge at the top*. New York: Wiley.

Schwartz, J. (1982). *Letting go of stress*. New York: Pinnacle.

Selye, H. (1974). *Stress without distress*. New York: New American Library.

Selye, H. (1976). *The stress of life*. New York: McGraw-Hill.

Shellenbarger, S. (2003, March 27). Slackers, rejoice: Research touts the benefits of skipping out on work. *The Wall Street Journal,* D1.

Sher, K., Wood, P., & Gotham, H. (1996, January/February). The course of psychological distress in college: A prospective high-risk study. *Journal of College Student Development,* 42–50.

Sheth, J., & Sisodia, R. (1999, June 28). Outsourcing comes home. *The Wall Street Journal,* A26.

Smith, C. (1997, December 24). A mismatch in the workplace sparks employee burnout. *Tallahassee Democrat,* 11D.

Spencer, J. (2003, March 11). Are you stressed out yet? *The Wall Street Journal,* D1.

Stickgold, R., Winkelman, J., & Wehrwein, P. (2004, January 19). You will start to feel very sleepy. *Newsweek,* 58 and 60.

Tanner, E. (1991). Assessment of a health promotive lifestyle. *Nursing Clinicians of North America, 26*(4), 845–854.

Toffler, A. (1970). *Future shock*. New York: Random House.

Topp, R. (1989). Effect of relaxation or exercise on undergraduate test anxiety. *Perceptual and Motor Skills, 69,* 335–341.

Two new landmark studies. (1991). Survey Research Center, University of Michigan, Ann Arbor.

Ulrich, D., & Dunne, H. (1986). *To love and work*. New York: Brunner/Mazel.

Ventura, J. (1987). The stresses of parenthood reexamined. *Family Relations, 36,* 26–29.

Waldrop, J. (1993, September). Josie and the pussy cats beat stress. *American Demographics, 15*(9), 17.

chapter 12

Managing Environmental Resources

MAIN TOPICS

THE ECOSYSTEM AND ENVIRONMENTALISM
PROBLEM RECOGNITION
BIOLOGICAL DIVERSITY
INDIVIDUAL AND FAMILY DECISION MAKING

ENVIRONMENTAL PROBLEMS AND SOLUTIONS
WATER
ENERGY
NOISE
WASTE AND RECYCLING
AIR QUALITY

Did you know that . . . ?

. . . The indoor air we breathe today is considerably cleaner than 150 years ago.

. . . A century ago, a house may have had one electrical socket per room; today four is typical, and many rooms have 12 to 16 electrical outlets.

What is the use of a house if you haven't got a tolerable planet to put it on?

—*Henry David Thoreau*

MANAGING THE HOME environment and the greater environment that surrounds it is the subject of this chapter. We move away from the psychological aspects of life management into the physical realm. Environmental awareness brings along with it a caveat: We must be careful about the choices that we make not only for ourselves but also for our children and grandchildren. As **stewards** of the earth, we have a responsibility that expands beyond our immediate family circle.

This chapter also touches on economic development. In the language of economics, the environment is considered a **natural capital,** a good we have to protect. According to Harris (2002), all nations seek economic development but only in the last 40 years have they considered the impact that growth has on the environment. In many nations, the concept of environmental protection is even more current than that. The ultimate goal is **sustainable development**—a form of growth wherein societal needs, present and future, are met. Sustainable development requires the input and cooperation of all segments of society, particularly producers and consumers. Toward this end, today more careful decisions at every level are being made about the products and services brought into the home.

In this chapter the 3-Rs solution—reducing, reusing, and recycling—will be highlighted. It is increasingly being accepted worldwide as a means of combating negative effects on the environment. There is also a growing recognition of the total product life cycle—from the resources used to make the product, through its actual use, until its final disposal. The study of the life cycle of household products involves not only the material resources involved in their manufacture, distribution, and disposal, including energy use, but also the human resources involved (Uitdenbogerd, Brouwer, & Groot-Marcus, 1998). Thus, environmental problems are intertwined with trends, practices, preferences, and variations in human behavior.

Sigmund Freud, the founder of psychoanalysis, best known for his theories about the psyche (the mind) and social interaction, also made observations about humans in environmental contexts. In *Civilization and Its Discontents* (1930), Freud wrote that as civilizations become increasingly complex and modern, humans must renounce their innate selves. We must think about things greater than our immediate surroundings.

> As world population continues to grow, and economic activity expands at an even faster rate, sustainability will become both more important and more difficult to achieve. This is the major challenge of the twenty-first century, and both economic and ecological understanding will be needed to formulate global, national, and local responses. (Harris, 2002, p. 439)

Thinking about others and the future of the planet is this chapter's theme. As Chapter 1 pointed out, the management process takes place within an environmental context, as illustrated in Figure 12.1. Building on the chapters on resources and managing human resources, time, stress, and fatigue, this chapter gives practical examples about how to manage the environment, particularly the near environment that directly affects individuals and families. The resource chapters share the philosophy that the way individuals and families allocate resources has an impact on the state of the environment and global well-being. Certainly, decisions and actions at the household level collectively affect not only the present state of the world, but also the world that is to come. Even one simple behavioral change, such as carpooling or recycling plastic bags, affects the environment.

Indoor pollution is not a new phenomenon, as this 19th-century engraving reveals.

Mary Evans Picture Library

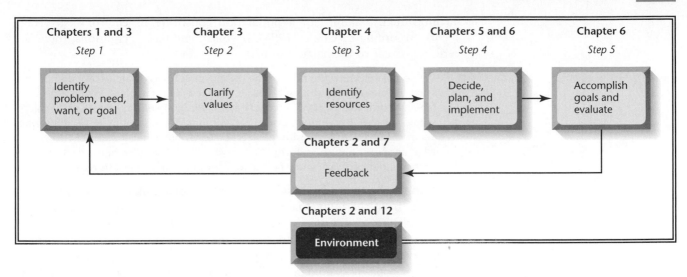

FIGURE 12.1
The Management Process Model

The present state of the environment is a result of developments and changes in the past as well as current conditions. According to the best estimates, the human species, *Homo sapiens,* is 250,000 years old, and the earth is 4.5 billion years old (Gould, 1989). Phrasing it poetically, Gould says that in terms of the age of the earth, humanity arose just yesterday as a small twig on one branch of a flourishing tree. The realization of our minor place in earth's history gives us a sense of the magnitude of our responsibility to preserve what we have inherited. We are just beginning to understand both the limits and the potential of our planet and our role in its evolution. What separates us from previous generations is this greater awareness of the benefits and limits of our environment. The importance of the choices individuals and families make regarding the environment cannot be overstated.

THE ECOSYSTEM AND ENVIRONMENTALISM

The systems approach used throughout this book emphasizes the interconnectedness and interactions between different systems. Systems are composed of living and nonliving things. Living systems (e.g., plants, animals, societies) are open systems that react to feedback. They can exist only in certain environments. Any change in the environment, such as a change in the temperature, air pressure, hydration, oxygen, or radiation outside a relatively narrow range, produces stress to which living systems cannot adjust. Under severe stress or deprivation, they cannot survive.

As discussed in Chapter 2, the family ecosystem is the subsystem of human ecology that emphasizes the interactions between families and environments. Ecology is the study of how living things relate to their natural environment (Naar, 1990). An **ecosystem** is the subsystem of ecology that emphasizes the relationship between organisms and their environment. Organisms are living things—plants or animals. The place where an organism lives is its **habitat.** The external conditions that surround and influence the life of an organism, an individual, a family, or a population constitute its environment (Naar, 1990). According to Gould (1998), beyond these basic definitions, there is a certain mystery to the balance of life:

> We do not yet know the rules of the composition for ecosystems. We do not even know if rules exist in the usual sense. I am tempted, therefore, to close with the famous words that D'Arcy Thompson wrote to signify our ignorance of the microscopic world (*Growth and Form,* 1942 edition). We are not quite so uninformed about the rules of composition for ecosystems, but what a stark challenge and what an inspiration to go forth: "We have come to the edge of a world of which we have no experience, and where all our preconceptions must be recast." (p. 404)

Concern for the environment is called **environmentalism.** It can be found at all levels, from the individual-including activists such as Rachel Carson—to the family to community organizations to government and industry. Furthermore, the levels overlap. For example, individuals can work through institutions by banding together, boycotting products, writing letters, and voting for appropriate candidates. They can positively affect what industry produces by buying "green" (environmentally friendly) products. However, it should be pointed out that

> Most consumers lack the scientific background to understand many environmental issues and few have relevant previous experience to guide them in assessing the relative environmental merits of market-place alternatives. Thus, the potential for consumer fraud and deception is great. (Cude, 1993, p. 207)

A major emphasis of environmentalism is how to retain existing environmental resources. These resources can be divided into two types: social and physical. **Social environmental resources** include an array of societies, economic and political groups, and community organizations. In each of these, people are united in a common cause, such as saving the manatees, or in a more general concern, such as reducing global warming. Global warming is caused when carbon dioxide and other gases collect in the air and trap heat radiated from the earth; over time, it can alter the earth's temperature, sea level, and storm systems (Pinchon, 1990). Carbon dioxide is released into the atmosphere by the burning of coal and oil and by the destruction of the forests.

Physical environmental resources include natural tangible (e.g., trees, soil, and ocean) and less tangible (e.g., air, sound, and light) surroundings. The latter part of this chapter will explore physical environmental management problems in the home and suggest eco-friendly practices.

Ecoconsciousness refers to the thoughts and actions given to protecting and sustaining the environment. **Conservation** is the act or process of preserving and protecting natural environments from loss or depletion. Individuals and families who are ecoconscious discuss environmental issues, recycle, conserve, reduce energy consumption and waste, buy "green" products, and support environmental causes and groups. The degree of ecoconsciousness varies, as shown on the continuum in Figure 12.2.

© Underwood & Underwood/CORBIS

Rachel Carson (1907–1964), an American biologist, was the author of Silent Spring, *a book published in 1962 that caused a worldwide awareness of the dangers of environmental pollution. Many credit her as the founder of the modern environmental movement.*

Problem Recognition

Differences between the ecological interests and practices of family members may be a source of conflict in families. One family member may go around the house turning on the lights while another follows carefully turning off the lights. Eventually, one of them is going to become irritated with the other's behavior.

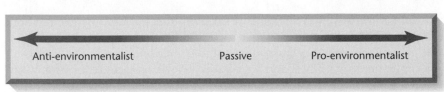

FIGURE 12.2
Continuum of Environmental Activism

Problem solving begins with recognition that there is a problem to be solved. **Problem recognition** occurs when an individual or a family perceives a significant difference between the lifestyle practiced and some desired or ideal lifestyle. The discrepancy must be large enough to push the individual to action. For example, Shannon and Dan enjoy fishing. One Saturday they go to a nearby lake and see a sign that says the fish in the lake are contaminated by high levels of mercury. Disappointed because they cannot fish, they recognize that water contamination is a problem affecting their choices and lifestyles. Shannon and Dan did not create the problem, but now they realize they are affected by it. What alternative courses of action do they have? They can quit fishing, go to another lake, or join others in an attempt to clean up the lake.

A problem can arise in one of two ways: need recognition and opportunity recognition. In **need recognition,** the person realizes how much he or she needs a certain product, service, or condition. In **opportunity recognition,** the individual realizes that she or he may have limited or no access to a product, service, or condition. For example, suppose the price of gasoline soared to over $10 a gallon—this is definitely need recognition. Nearly everyone needs gasoline, but who could afford it? Now, suppose a gasoline shortage forces gasoline stations to close for a few days—this is an example of opportunity recognition. Drivers cannot purchase gasoline even if they want to, a situation that has occurred in the United States and other countries. Many environmental problems involve both need and opportunity recognition.

SUGGESTED ACTIVITY

Where do you place yourself on the continuum? Explain your answer and discuss in groups. Where do most students develop ecoconsciousness—at home, at school?

Water contamination limits choices.

Communication plays a large part in environmental problem recognition. The sign warned Shannon and Dan not to eat the fish they caught. The federal government communicates environmental information through news releases, press conferences, warnings, and legislation. Television is a great communicator of environmental news, as are magazines, newspapers, and radio. Besides media sources, families communicate news about environmental conditions and behavior. Parents model littering or recycling behaviors for their children.

Once an environmental problem has been recognized, the individuals involved engage in an information search in order to resolve it. Information has been dubbed the ultimate **renewable resource** (meaning that it is essentially unlimited) because new technologies are constantly being devised to transmit, collect, store, process, package, and display it (Elkington, Burke, & Hailes, 1988). Through television and the Internet, environmental disasters such as oil spills are immediately transmitted to the public. This is one of the reasons that environmental awareness is greater now than ever before. Marshall McLuhan (1962), who coined the phrase "the medium is the message," said that the spread of electronic communications technology has established a global network. As individuals become more globally connected, they naturally become more globally aware. An example of the importance of global communications was the International Whaling Commission's decision, supported by the United States, to place a moratorium on commercial whale harvesting (Bohlen, 1990). Television reports on the plight of the whales undoubtedly played a part in the decision.

Biological Diversity

Species extinction or depletion is mainly caused by the loss of habitat—and that loss is nearly always caused by human encroachment. As humans use more resources (land and water), fewer resources are available for other lifeforms. **Biological diversity** is a multidimensional concept encompassing the variety and variability among living organisms and the ecological complexities in which they occur. The term includes different ecosystems and species and their relative abundance. In Chapter 4, utility was defined as the use, value, or worth of a resource.

In order for a substance, thing, or idea to be considered a resource (something useful for achieving an end purpose or goal), it must first be recognized as having current or potential utility. For example, at one time, uranium was considered a worthless, silvery white metal. Now it is used in research and nuclear fuel. One of the reasons animals, minerals, plants and habitats must be protected is that their potential use and their particular role in the total ecosystem may not be fully understood. Scientists have identified fewer than 2 million species (this includes bacteria, fungi, nematodes, plants, animals, and insects) out of at least 10 million and perhaps 100 million. They are working on developing an easy-to-use, publicly accessible database on every species.

Many difficult decisions lie ahead as to which species will be saved and which will not. These decisions are part of a branch of study called environmental ethics. **Ethics** are systems of morals, principles, values, or good conduct. No discussion of environmentalism would be complete without considering the ethical issues involved. Each person has to decide what is the right course of action in personal situations as well as in the broader societal context. As E. O. Wilson, Harvard University biologist, said, "I suppose it will all come down to a decision of ethics—how we value the natural worlds in which we evolved and now, increasingly, how we regard our status as individuals" (1988, p. 16).

Individual and Family Decision Making

Individuals and families are taking on a greater share of responsibility for their environment and are relying less on large institutions. Many people realize that government or business alone cannot be depended on to solve all the environmental ills that exist. The problems are too widespread to be remedied by one group. Furthermore, the boundaries of the problems are often difficult to discern. For example, consumption and disposal practices of individuals and families, as well as those of businesses and industry, contribute to the **waste stream** (all garbage produced). This blurring of the boundaries between the traditionally defined roles of the public sector and the private sector is a growing trend.

One of the most difficult aspects of environmentalism is determining what is a real, acute problem or shortage and what is not. Media often give out conflicting messages about the severity of a problem or the best solutions. Now more than ever before, critical thinking skills are needed to evaluate environmental information. Cross-checking the information by looking at several different reliable sources is one way of arriving at the truth of a situation.

Environmental decision making by individuals is complicated enough, considering the range of values, resources, goals, and decision-making steps involved. Environmental decision making in families is necessarily all the more complicated. Not only may family members differ in their use of electricity, but some may also want to recycle bottles, jars, and cans whereas others throw them away in the garbage, to cite just two examples of conflicting environmental behavior.

Sometimes one family member takes on the role of environmentalist and sets the rules, turns down the thermostat, and turns off the television when not in use. With so much environmental education taking place in schools, it is not unusual to find a school-aged child rather than a parent taking on this role. Children may be better informed about environmental issues than their parents; and, with their youthful optimism, they are willing to try new ways of managing household waste or adjusting consumption patterns.

To summarize, within the same family there may be vast differences in types, styles, and levels of environmental awareness. Differences are even more evident between families and between communities. Some communities have active recycling programs that make it easier for people to recycle, and ease is a significant factor in the success of conservation programs. Developers are catching on: Master-planned communities feature nature belts for walks and use materials and landscaping that require less upkeep.

> Officials of Pardee Homes, a Los Angeles-based unit of timber-giant Weyerhauser Co., say that over the past year they have also opened two green subdivisions in San Diego after seeing the demand for savings on energy bills. By using fluorescent lighting and tankless water heaters, they say, they have been able to achieve energy savings of as much as 75% compared with conventional homes. They add that local environmental groups helped persuade them to take land-preservation measures such as replanting trees and plants. (Carlton, 2003, p. B1)

ENVIRONMENTAL PROBLEMS AND SOLUTIONS

The remainder of this chapter is divided into five parts: water, energy, noise, waste and recycling, and air quality. Each part describes the problems and presents solutions applicable to individuals, families, and households. To keep the chapter a manageable length, some important topics had to be omitted, including ocean pollution, ozone depletion, desertification, deforestation, climatic changes, and loss of soil. All of these are important avenues for future study and research. Many of them overlap. For example, desertification refers to the increase in dry, barren land that supports little or no vegetation. This happens for many reasons, including the loss of soil, overpopulation, overgrazing, deforestation, and overcultivation. Common to all environmental problems is the widespread growth of pollution. **Pollution** is a general term referring to undesirable changes in physical, chemical, or biological characteristics of air, land, or water that can harm the health, activities, or survival of living organisms. It can be thought of as contamination of a resource, a reduction of quality or usefulness (Harris, 2002). The information that follows is as accurate as possible, but it will be up to the reader to keep abreast of the very latest developments in the ever changing field of environmentalism.

Water

The two main problems associated with water are shortages and pollution. Since 1900 there has been a sixfold increase in worldwide water use. About one-fifth of the earth's population does not have safe drinking water.

According to the Environmental Protection Agency (EPA), approximately 50,000 water contaminants have been identified, and more than 100 of these are regulated in the United States. All contaminants are potentially hazardous to human health. The five main types of contaminants in the U.S. water supply are chlorinated solvents, trialomethanes, lead, PCBs (or polychlorinated biphenyls, a class of compounds that have various industrial applications), and pathogenic bacteria and viruses (Foran, 1990). Most water that comes from a public system must meet the standards set by the Federal Drinking Water Act and state and local regulations. Water is less likely to be officially tested if it comes from a well or a small system. About 10 to 20 percent of Americans draw their water from a private well. In this case, a sample of the water can be tested at a certified laboratory. The cooperative extension service can inform residents about testing services available.

Because of the fear of water contaminants, water-purifying businesses ranging from legitimate to quasi-legitimate are thriving. Each year, U.S. residents spend over a billion dollars on home purifying equipment and water filtration services. In addition, consumers spend billions on bottled water, some of which is unregulated and less pure than tap water. Before investing in any equipment or services, consumers should first have their water checked by legitimate testing services that are not selling a product. Consumers can also check with their local Better Business Bureau or consumer protection agency to see if there are any recorded complaints against the company from whom they are considering buying equipment or services.

Contamination of drinking water is not the only water-related issue. There are many others, including the following:

- ◆ *Drinking water:* Supply and conservation, treatment, and health considerations
- ◆ *Groundwater:* Availability and depletion, quality and contamination, consequences to public health, detection, and monitoring
- ◆ *Seawater:* Quality and quantity; preservation of sea life
- ◆ *Water for agricultural use:* Conservation and supply
- ◆ *Water for industrial use:* Supply and pollutants
- ◆ *Water for household use:* Supply and quality, conservation, and water-efficient products

Because this book is concerned primarily with individual and family management practices, this discussion will focus on drinking water and household water use.

Water Consumption and Shortage

The average U.S. household uses 350 gallons of water a day. The breakdown is

- ◆ Toilets   27 percent
- ◆ Clothes washers   22 percent
- ◆ Showers   17 percent
- ◆ Faucets   16 percent
- ◆ Leaks   14 percent
- ◆ Baths, dishwashers, and other domestic use   5 percent

As these statistics illustrate, the greatest water use is in the bathroom. In 1994, the Federal Energy Policy Act restricted all new household faucets and showerheads to 2.5 gallons per minute. The Act also restricted toilets, limiting flush capacity to 1.6 gallons compared to a standard of four gallons in the 1970s.

Water used to be cheap, clean, and abundant, but in many metropolitan areas and in the dry Southwest and southern California, water has now become a limited resource. As a result, many areas are regulating water use through rules and legislation. During shortages, cities have ordinances governing when cars can be washed or sprinklers used. Households can use 20 to 62 percent of their total water use on outdoor areas such as lawns and pools. So, if homeowners want to cut their water bill, they would have to examine both indoor and outdoor use.

Practical Ways to Reduce Household Water Use

Most homeowners cannot afford to replace their toilets, and this is certainly not practical for renters. Nevertheless, there are many low-cost or free ways to save water:

- ◆ Do not leave the water running while doing dishes, brushing teeth, or shaving.
- ◆ Run full loads in the washing machine and dishwasher.
- ◆ If the load is smaller, match the water level and the temperature settings on clothes washers to the size and type of load.

◆ Do not use the toilet as a trash can.

◆ Install water-saving shower heads.

◆ Fix leaky faucets and toilets.

◆ Landscape with native plants that do not require additional watering.

◆ Use only the water necessary for cooking and rinsing food.

◆ Water the lawn and garden early in the morning to avoid losing too much water to evaporation in the heat of the day. Watering cans use less water than hoses. Cover soil with compost or mulch to reduce evaporation.

◆ Use buckets of water to wash the car rather than running water continuously from a hose.

This list could go on, but these suggestions provide a starting point. The fact is that 97 percent of the world's water is saline and unusable, leaving a meager 3 percent to nourish and sustain life (Graves, 1990). Desalination research provides long-term hope for a larger water supply. Another solution is to grow crops that require less water. Currently, the world's human population continues to grow while the supply of fresh water remains constant. Learning how to conserve and apportion water will be one of the greatest management problems of the 21st century. Though the United States ranks sixth among water-rich nations in the world, it ranks third in water consumption and waste. As water becomes scarcer, its perceived value as a resource will increase. Learning to conserve now will begin a lifelong habit that will lead to saved money and a healthier environment.

Energy

The main problems associated with energy are energy production, energy wastage, and pollution from the use of fossil fuels. **Fossil fuels** are the remains of dead vegetation, such as coal, oil, and natural gas, which can be burned to release energy (Naar, 1990). Fuel is used to provide physical comfort and mechanical power (Elkins, Hillman, & Hutchison, 1992). Because electricity is the main form of energy used in today's homes, the emphasis in this section is on electricity.

Historically, usable energy was most often produced by burning wood or a natural fuel such as coal or oil. One of the mistakes in North America's past was "cut-out and get-out forestry." Newer approaches involve replanting. Today, electricity is produced from coal and by generators driven by steam, from other fossil fuels such as oil and natural gas, and from nuclear reactors. Hydroelectric power, which comes from generators turned by falling water, is another source of energy. Dwindling fossil fuels and concern over potential accidental radioactive discharges from nuclear power plants have led to efforts to find alternative electric energy sources. Among the alternatives under consideration are solar batteries, geothermal power stations, nuclear fusion reactors, and magnetohydrodynamic generators. Whatever the source of power, electric energy is generated at a central point (e.g., a dam, an energy plant) and then transmitted to delivery points or substations, from which it is distributed to consumers. Figure 12.3 gives an ecosystem view of energy plants. The impacts of energy plants on society and the economy are noted in Figure 12.4.

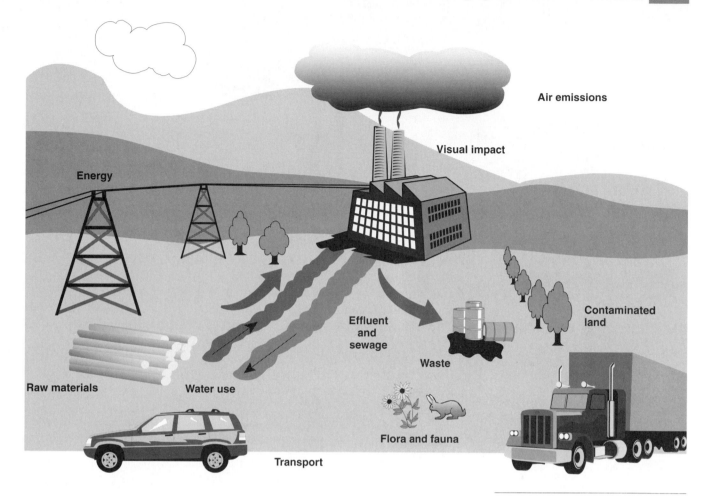

Air emissions

Visual impact

Energy

Raw materials

Water use

Effluent
and
sewage

Waste

Contaminated
land

Flora and fauna

Transport

FIGURE 12.3
The Environmental Framework
This illustrates the interconnectedness
of various factors in the environment.

Source: Welsh Development Agency

Energy Consumption and Home Energy Audits

A century ago, a typical home may have had one electrical socket per room delivering 100 watts of power. Typical homes today have at least four per room and as many as 12 to 16 electrical outlets. And a typical home is wired to provide 12,000 or even more watts. On a late summer afternoon, a large house may consume over 4,000 watts of electricity (Crossen, 2001). The reasons for this growth include

◆ Larger houses.

◆ More and larger appliances. Even a small towel warmer uses 100 watts of power.

◆ The popularity of computers and entertainment equipment.

◆ More air conditioning. What was once thought of as a luxury is now standard.

Did you know that 10 percent of the average family's heating bill goes out the window? Energy-efficient windows and window treatments can reduce this. Depending on the climate and the home's insulation, for a 1,900-square-foot single-family detached home with an average of 2.7 occupants, about 50 percent of energy goes to space heating and cooling, 15 percent to hot water, 14 percent

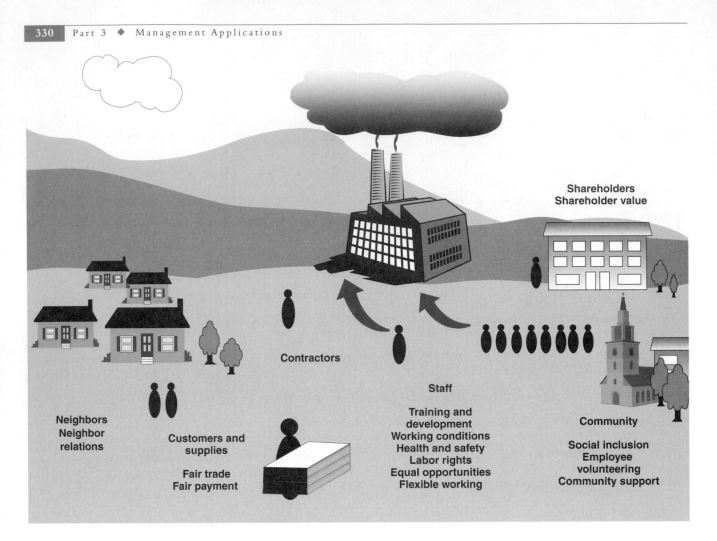

Shareholders
Shareholder value

Contractors

Staff

Training and
development
Working conditions
Health and safety
Labor rights
Equal opportunities
Flexible working

Neighbors
Neighbor
relations

Customers and
supplies

Fair trade
Fair payment

Community

Social inclusion
Employee
volunteering
Community support

FIGURE 12.4

The Socioeconomic Framework
*This illustrates the people and policy
aspects of environmental management.*

Source: Welsh Development Agency

to appliances, 11 percent to lighting, and the rest to a variety of things including clocks, televisions, radios, and computers. So, the best way to cut energy bills is to alter heating and cooling. By improving insulation, weather stripping, and making a few alterations in a home (e.g., adding storm windows, adding overhangs, shutting drapes and doors), a homeowner can save at least half the money spent on heating, air conditioning, and hot water. Besides windows, another source of heat loss is through cracks in walls and doors. Sometimes the homeowner will not notice these hairline cracks, but trained specialists can detect them. According to the U.S. Department of Energy, here are the sources of air leaks in homes:

◆ Floors, walls, and ceilings   31 percent
◆ Ducts   15 percent
◆ Fireplaces   14 percent
◆ Plumbing penetrations   13 percent
◆ Doors   11 percent
◆ Windows   10 percent
◆ Fans and vents   4 percent
◆ Electric outlets   2 percent

Local utility companies or city or county utility offices may provide free or low-cost home energy audits. An energy audit is performed by a specialist who makes a one- or two-hour "walk-through" inspection of the interior and the exterior of a home. Upon completion of the inspection or shortly afterward, homeowners receive an analysis of what they can do to improve the energy efficiency of their home. Auditors focus on determining where a house loses heat in winter and cool air in summer, and they identify appliances and heating/cooling systems that have better efficiency levels. College graduates who have studied resource management have been hired to work as home energy auditors for city and county government and utility companies and as energy educators and policy makers in state and national government.

Several states, including Pennsylvania, Washington, Wisconsin, and Florida, charge different energy prices depending on time of day of use. The idea is to spread energy use out by making people pay higher prices during periods of peak demand.

> When Florida's summer heat gets blistering, Lamar Faulkner used to simply turn down the thermostat to keep his three-bedroom home near Pensacola comfortably cool. Now, he turns it up a few degrees. The reason: Mr. Faulkner's utility charges a premium—as much as five times the standard rate—to use electricity during summer afternoons when demand is greatest. (Gavin, 2002, p. D1)

Practical Ways to Reduce Household Energy Use

The home energy audit is a good way to find out about a specific home's energy use. This section provides several energy-saving ideas applicable to most homes.

Because air leaks are a major problem, insulation is an important way to reduce energy loss. Insulation comes in three forms: rigid panels or sheets of insulation, blankets, batts, or rolls (composed of fiberglass or rock wool), and blown insulation (rock wool, fiberglass, cellulose, or polyurethane foam). The higher the **R-value** (R stands for resistance), the higher the insulation properties. Insulation with an R-30 rating provides a better heat-flow barrier than one rated R-10. The better rating comes with a higher price. Another solution is double- or triple-glazed windows to reduce heat loss or heat gain. Storm windows are usually triple-glazed. Weather stripping around windows and doors will also seal leaks. Window awnings will reduce heat gain in summer, and drawn, insulated drapes will reduce heat loss in winter.

The **site** is the location or situation of a house. **Orientation** is the location or situation of the house relative to points on a compass. In selecting the site and the orientation of the house, the homeowner and builder should take the natural environment into account. Warmth and shelter can be enhanced if hills, trees, winds, water, and the sun are considered. The climate will influence the best site and orientation for a house. In states with hot climates, most houses should have few windows on the west side to avoid the afternoon sun. In states with predominantly cold climates, houses should have few windows on the north side to reduce the cold drafts.

Landscaping affects heat loss and gain. **Deciduous trees,** such as oaks and maples, that lose their leaves in the winter are good choices. Their leaves will shield the house in the summer, but let the sunshine through in the winter. Trees and bushes can also serve as wind barriers.

According to the Department of Energy, U.S. households spend more than $1,000 each year to run household appliances. The following suggestions can reduce this amount considerably:

◆ Install a new, computerized thermostat. A programmable thermostat turns heating and cooling systems on and off at preprogrammed intervals.

◆ Clean or replace filters on furnaces regularly. Have an annual maintenance check of heating and cooling systems.

◆ Turn the thermostat down on water heaters. Each 10-degree reduction cuts water-heating energy bills by 3–5 percent. To get dishes clean in a dishwasher, the water heater should not be set below 140°F (Fahrenheit) unless the dishwasher has its own water-heating system.

◆ When drying clothes, dry similar clothes together because lightweight synthetics dry much more quickly than thick robes or bath towels. Dry two or more loads in a row to take advantage of the residual heat.

◆ Keep the temperature setting in the refrigerator between 38°F and 42°F and the freezer between 0°F and 5°F. If the refrigerator and freezer are kept 10 degrees colder than this, energy consumption can increase as much as 25 percent. Clean refrigerator coils at least once a year. A filled refrigerator or freezer is more energy-efficient than an empty or partially filled one.

◆ Use small appliances when possible because they require less energy than large ones. Microwave ovens and toaster ovens use less energy than conventional ovens. Coffeemakers, hair dryers, irons, and toasters do not consume very much energy overall; they draw a lot of power but are in use for short periods of time. Because refrigerators and freezers run constantly, they use far more energy than other kitchen appliances.

◆ Keep the refrigerator door open for a short time rather than opening and closing it frequently, which wastes more energy. Most of the cold air rushes out of the refrigerator as soon as it is opened.

◆ Replace old, inefficient appliances with new ones. A refrigerator more than 10 years old uses twice the energy of a new one.

◆ Clean the dryer's lint screen after each use. Run full loads in the dishwasher and clothes washer rather than running small loads more often.

◆ Heating water accounts for 95 percent of the energy consumed for hot water in the clothes washer. Save money and energy by washing in cold water, unless the clothes require hot or warm water, and always use a cold water rinse.

To help consumers select low-energy appliances, the ENERGY STAR label is the national symbol for energy efficiency developed by the U.S. Environmental Protection Agency (EPA) and supported by the U.S. Department of Energy (DOE). Appliances, heating, and cooling products that earn the ENERGY STAR label exceed the minimum federal standards for energy efficiency. Consumers should look for the Energy-Guide label (see Figure 12.5 for an example). Also, in cooperation with the EPA and the DOE, most computer and television manufacturers have joined the ENERGY STAR program that promotes the design of equipment that uses less energy when turned on and off. The ENERGY STAR program is a work in progress; for example, more stringent standards go into effect for clothes washers in 2007.

Reducing the amount of energy used by appliances is helpful, but it is a myth that turning off lights and the television is the best way to conserve energy in the home; in fact, these consume a small portion of the home's electricity (Merline, 1988). Even small savings help, however, and consumers can reduce home energy consumption by

◆ Installing dimmer switches.

◆ Lighting areas for specific needs.

- ◆ Installing fluorescent lights, which use 80 percent less energy than incandescent lights.

- ◆ Using light colors on ceilings, walls, floors, and furniture because they reflect more light and brighten a room.

- ◆ Replacing old lamps with new, more efficient ones. Dusting light bulbs and tubes increases light output and reduces the risk of potential pollutants.

- ◆ Turning off lights when not in use.

- ◆ Checking Energy-Guide or ENERGY STAR labels before buying.

These suggestions can help, but it is important to remember that the greatest savings come from turning the thermostat down to 60°F in winter and turning it up to 80°F in the summer, or turning it off altogether and opening the windows in pleasant weather.

Energy company records reveal that energy use varies widely even in neighborhoods where houses are the same size and style. Efficient appliances and lighting and the management of human behavior (e.g., shutting windows when the air conditioning is on) can substantially affect the energy use in the home.

Noise

Far less information is available about noise pollution than about water and energy conservation. Noise pollution is less easy to delineate because people are not billed for the use of noise, and each person is a producer as well as a consumer of noise. Noise is simply any unwanted sound. Sensitivity to noise

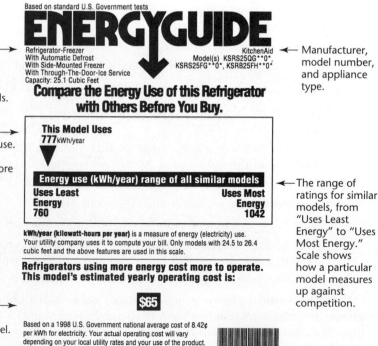

FIGURE 12.5
The Energy-Guide Label

varies from person to person. The intensity, or loudness, of sound is the amount of acoustic energy transmitted through the air; it is measured in **decibels (dB).** The lowest sound humans can hear is 1 dB. An average home on a quiet street has a dB level of 50 (Pearson, 1989). A noisy office, a preschool classroom, or an alarm clock can be as loud as 80 dB. Sounds above 85 decibels can cause hearing loss. A Rolling Stones concert or being honked at on the street clocks in at about 115 decibels. At 120 dB the hearer experiences discomfort or pain; a jet taking off is about 140 decibels. Household appliances range from 60 to 90 dB, with the food disposal being the noisiest at over 90 dB. Besides being harmful, too much noise can be annoying, making it difficult to concentrate or relax.

Homes, offices, and other environments should strive to maintain a comfortable amount of noise. Research shows that people feel uneasy if they are deprived of environmental stimulation (i.e., too little sound, movement, or light) for too long. Too little sound may make a person feel uncomfortable or lonely. To counteract this effect, music is piped in to elevators, grocery stores, and dentists' offices. Many people go to sleep better at night with the hum of a fan or the drone of a radio in the background.

Too much noise is a more common problem than too little, however. Noise from loud neighbors, ringing telephones, barking dogs, and screaming children can become an intolerable burden. Often it is not the noise itself that is irritating or harmful, but the continuous nature of noise or the combination of noises (e.g., the noise of the vacuum cleaner, the blender, the television, and children slamming doors occurring at the same time). Poorly constructed buildings add to the noise level. Insulation and absorbing surfaces such as carpet, cork, or acoustical tiles can reduce noise. On common walls between apartments, brick, earth, and concrete reduce noise better than wood or aluminum siding. As a general rule, soft, porous surfaces absorb sound, and hard, smooth surfaces reflect sound. A solution while on airplanes or working in a noisy office is to use an acoustic noise-canceling headset.

Practical Ways to Reduce Noise

The following suggestions will help reduce noise in the home:

- Find housing away from noisy traffic, airports, schools, and factories.
- Plant barrier trees and hedges to reduce noise. High walls and earth mounds also cut noise.
- Place bedrooms in quieter parts of the house. Put the garage on the noisy side of the site.
- Buy "quiet" appliances—these have more insulation.
- Keep the volume on radios and televisions low.
- Draw heavy drapes and close blinds to shut out neighborhood noise.
- Weather-strip windows and doors to prevent outside noise from entering the home. Inside the house, solid-core doors will reduce noise between rooms. On a busy street, use double- or triple-pane windows.

As the world becomes more crowded, noise pollution will become a greater management problem than it currently is. Finding a quiet, peaceful place may become more difficult. Decreasing noise is a way to de-stress life. Another way to reduce stress is to add sounds that are soothing and pleasant. The rustle of trees, the singing of birds, and the sound of ocean waves are soothing to many people. Bringing more of these natural sounds into one's life and removing some of the irritating, mechanical ones may increase a person's overall sense of well-being.

Waste and Recycling

Garbage disposal is becoming a worldwide problem as the population grows and more people gravitate toward cities. A typical American creates 4.4 pounds of garbage a day. Historically, landfills were cheap and readily available, but vacant land is no longer cheap and is becoming increasingly scarce around cities. Suburbs have sprung up where landfills used to be.

The skyrocketing cost of land, coupled with concern about environmental pollution, has led to the exploration of new methods of waste disposal. Possible avenues include burying waste, burning it, recycling it, or not producing so much of it. Combining all four methods is called **integrated waste management.** In this system, waste products are sorted, recyclable items are reused, and the rest is burned cleanly in a furnace that also produces steam to generate electricity. Only the remaining ash goes to the landfill. According to the EPA, the breakdown of U.S. garbage is as follows:

- ◆ Paper and paperboard   38.6 percent
- ◆ Yard waste   12.8 percent
- ◆ Food waste   10.1 percent
- ◆ Plastics   9.9 percent
- ◆ Metals   7.7 percent
- ◆ Glass   5.5 percent
- ◆ Wood   5.3 percent
- ◆ Other (rubber, leather, textiles, etc.) 10.0 percent

In recent years, recycling has become more popular. The Environmental Protection Agency estimates that 30 percent of newspapers, 40–50 percent of cardboard, 10–15 percent of office paper, 50 percent of aluminum cans, 10 percent of glass bottles, and 2 percent of plastic products are recycled.

Examples of recycling include the following:

- ◆ *Plastic:* Used for fiberfill for pillows, decks, flowerpots, paintbrush bristles, fence posts, insulation, and docks. For example, according to the American Plastics Council, U.S. households recycle over 1.4 billion pounds of plastic bottles each year.
- ◆ *Paper:* Used for game boards, puzzles, stationery, newspapers, toilet paper, paper towels, egg cartons, boxes, books, and tickets.
- ◆ *Glass:* Used for bottles, street paving, tiles, and bricks.
- ◆ *Aluminum:* Used for cans, lawn furniture, window frames, and car parts.

Although people in the United States have become more active in recycling, much still can be done to reduce waste.

Practical Ways to Reduce Waste

Households can adopt the 3-Rs solution to the waste problem:

1. *Reducing.* Avoid buying products with excessive packaging; use a coffee mug at work (avoid using Styrofoam cups); buy in bulk (fewer packages);

use lunch boxes instead of paper or plastic bags; and buy recycled paper products.

2. *Reusing.* Use both sides of sheets of paper; reuse old envelopes for messages and lists; reuse wrapping paper and ribbons; and reuse cardboard boxes and glass jars.

3. *Recycling.* Take recycling materials to recycling centers. Hand down clothes from child to child; alter and reuse existing clothes; and donate used clothing to charities or Goodwill Industries. Refinish, sell, or donate old furniture.

These three methods all involve management. Each requires time, energy, and commitment; decision plans must be made and carried out. Children can be taught the value of waste reduction in their families and in schools, or in organizations such as Boy Scouts and Girl Scouts. Starting small and local makes the most sense for children. They can see the results of picking up litter in their playground and neighborhood. At home, children can separate waste into the appropriate recycling boxes and can help their parents take trash to community recycling bins. Children enjoy being part of a community effort, and parents can model good citizenship habits for the future. The fundamental message to children should be that each person can make a difference in the health of the environment.

Air Quality

Clean air is given high priority in the list of environmental concerns. The pollutants that lead to deteriorating air quality come from many sources, not from a single source. Air quality is threatened by too much ozone, airborne particles, sulfur dioxide, lead, nitrogen oxides, and carbon monoxide. More than half of the nation's air pollution comes from mobile sources such as cars, trucks, motorcycles, airplanes, trains, buses, and boats. Stationary sources such as factories, dry cleaners, homes, and oil refineries also pollute the air.

Air pollution contributes to many health problems and ecological problems, such as decreased quality of aquatic life and vegetation damage. Pollution is sometimes worse indoors than outside, particularly where buildings are tightly constructed or sealed to save energy or where they have poor ventilation systems. Sick building syndrome is caused by the presence of pollutants in the air compounded by inadequate ventilation systems. Harmful indoor pollutants may come from building materials, furnishings, space heaters, gas ranges, wood preservatives, aerosols, and cleaning agents. More than 90 percent of air pollution deaths occur in developing countries. Eighty percent of these deaths are caused by indoor air pollution; many poor people lack access to clean fuel and burn dung and wood for cooking and heating (Vo, 1998).

In the United States, the top 10 indoor air pollutants according to the American Lung Association are

1. Secondhand smoke.

2. Biological contaminants—including bacteria, viruses, animal dander, dust mites, cockroach parts, pollen, molds, and fungi. These are usually inhaled alone or by attaching themselves to dust that is then inhaled.

3. Particulates—including solid particles and liquid droplets such as dirt, dust, and smoke.

4. Household products—including cleansers, personal care products, and paint.

5. **Carbon monoxide**—an odorless and colorless gas, a product of the combustion of fossil fuels and burning wood. It is the leading cause of accidental poisoning in the United States, killing 2,000 people a year and sickening many more. Many states require new homes to have a carbon-monoxide monitor. Common causes are faulty furnaces, stoves, fireplaces, car exhaust, water heaters, and barbecue grills, but other sources are culprits:

> One June day three years ago Thad Dohrn turned on the air conditioner in his three-bedroom house in Ames, Iowa, for the first time that summer. The next morning his wife Stephanie complained of a headache. As he walked to the bathroom to check on her, he passed out. He came to, but then Stephanie passed out. "She came to and we walked outside. I was crying on the phone to our neighbors and was all confused," says Mr. Dohrn, now an associate athletic director at Columbia University in New York. Mr. and Mrs. Dohrn were taken to the hospital and diagnosed with carbon-monoxide poisoning. The cause: A mechanical malfunction caused the air conditioner and the heat to be on simultaneously. The system didn't have proper ventilation either. And the Dohrns didn't have a carbon-monoxide monitor. (Petersen, 2002, p. D1)

6. **Radon**—a naturally occurring gaseous by-product of the uranium in the earth—can enter a house through holes and cracks in the foundation, through cinder blocks or through loose-fitting pipes, floor drains, or pumps. Concentrations are likely to be largest in the basements of buildings. The Environmental Protection Agency (EPA) estimates that between 10,000 and 40,000 lung cancer deaths a year in the United States are caused by radon ("Radon: The Problem No One Wants to Face," 1989). The U.S. Geological Survey has compiled a series of geologic radon potential assessments for the United States in cooperation with the EPA, so potential homeowners can go to the EPA Web site for maps showing where radon is highest. Basically, it is highest in the Midwest, Pennsylvania, and mountainous areas and lowest in the Southeast and along the West Coast. State environmental protection departments provide lists of approved contractors able to make radon-reducing modifications. A radon level of 4 picocuries per liter or more is considered dangerous. Modifications can easily run several thousand dollars per home, so it is wise to have a home inspection made before purchase so that the current owner or builder will repair the home and the cost of repair is not passed on to the new buyer.

7. Volatile organic compounds (VOCs)—the "new smell" from carpets, wood cabinets, plastics, etc. One of the most common VOCs is formaldehyde.

8. Pesticides.

9. Lead—found in paint and lead pipes. Before 1978, most homes used lead-based paint.

10. Asbestos—microscopic mineral fibers that are flexible, durable, and do not burn.

Practical Ways to Reduce Air Pollution

Air quality varies widely. The air quality index ranges from a low of 0 to a high of 500. Air quality from 0 to 49 is considered good; 300 and above is hazardous (Carpenter, 1989). Runners, construction workers, gardeners, children, and anyone else who is outdoors a lot need to be especially mindful of changes in air quality. Elderly people or younger persons with certain health conditions should be aware also. These suggestions can help improve air quality:

- ◆ Use roll-on or solid deodorants; liquid or "spritz" pump sprays for deodorants or hair sprays are recommended over the use of aerosols because chemicals from aerosols contribute to smog.

- ◆ Keep the car engine tuned. Carpool and use public transportation and bicycles when possible.

- ◆ Don't smoke. Encourage the designation of smoking areas outside of businesses and eliminate indoor smoking completely.

- ◆ Air out houses and workplaces. Open windows at least once a week.

- ◆ Clean heater and air conditioner filters regularly. Use an air conditioner or dehumidifier to maintain an indoor relative humidity below 65 percent.

- ◆ When building or remodeling a house, use safe building materials and installation methods. For example, paint with brushes and rollers instead of sprayers. Beware of asbestos and mold.

- ◆ Put green plants in homes and workplaces. Certain types of green plants are particularly effective in filtering out indoor air pollution. However, the Environmental Protection Agency suggests that rather than relying on plants, the focus on improving home air quality should be on removing the sources of unhealthy contaminants.

Web-Based Resources

For more information on the ENERGY STAR program to increase energy efficiency, go to **www.energystar.gov.** For more on environmental issues and specifics on radon go to the Environmental Protection Agency Web site at **www.epa.gov.** More information on air quality issues can be found on the American Lung Association Web site at **www.lungusa.org/.** For information on Rachel Carson, author and key figure in the environmental movement, check encyclopedia Web sites and **www.rachelcarson.org/.**

More and more zoos are trying to replicate natural habitats. Over 150 million people visit zoos and aquariums every year. Here are some Web sites as guides:

- ◆ **www.sandiegozoo.org** (the San Diego Zoo, the most popular U.S. zoo)

- ◆ **www.Aza.org** The American Zoo and Aquarium Association, lists every accredited U.S. zoo and animal-world news.

- ◆ **www.NatZoo.si.edu** The Smithsonian Natural Zoo in Washington, DC, includes animal cams.

- ◆ **www.BronxZoo.com** Famed New York City Zoo.

- ◆ **www.Exzooberance.com** Hundreds of animal photos and a zoo directory; links to Brisbane, Australia, and other zoos around the world.

Many environmental and scientific magazines and groups have Web sites. Examples are *Scientific American* at **www.sciam.com/,** *National Geographic* at **www.nationalgeographic.com,** and EnviroLink at **envirolink.org.**

Summary

Although this chapter has given practical suggestions for specific environmental problems relating to air, water, waste, noise, and energy, the overriding suggestion is to support legislation, research, and government policies that will improve all these areas of concern. Noise is any unwanted sound. Words of warning were given regarding carbon monoxide and radon poisoning. Homes are getting larger, which usually means more energy consumption, although builders and consumers are finding ways to make homes more energy-efficient. Using less power is a solution; developing new sources of power is another. Most of the average daily cost of energy in a home goes to heating and cooling.

This chapter has defined key environmental terms, discussed environmental issues, and suggested ways to conserve limited resources. People who incorporate several of these suggestions into their daily life management are practicing **positive ecology.** By shifting to less harmful energy sources, thinking more holistically, and being a "green" consumer, each individual can help create a healthier environment. Each person and each family should ask themselves, "What can I do to reduce waste and pollution?"

Although people rely to a degree on government, environmental organizations, and universities for solutions, ultimately they must look within for answers. As the actor Beau Bridges has said, "All the talk about how the environment is being ruined means nothing unless you're doing something about it in your own home." Families need to consider the environmental messages and values they are passing down to their children. If the days of limitless clean air and water, low-cost energy, and abundant peaceful, quiet environments are gone, what will be put in their place? Will future generations view the 21st century as a turning point toward more positive ecology?

Key Terms

biological diversity
carbon monoxide
conservation
decibel
deciduous trees
ecoconsciousness
ecosystem
environmentalism
ethics
fossil fuels
habitat
integrated waste
   management

natural capital
need recognition
opportunity
   recognition
orientation
physical
   environmental
   resources
pollution
positive ecology
problem recognition
radon
renewable resource

R-value
site
social environmental
   resources
stewards
   (stewardship)
sustainable
   development
waste stream

Review Questions

1. Comment on the following statement by E. O. Wilson: "I suppose it will all come down to a decision of ethics—how we value the natural worlds in

which we evolved and now, increasingly, how we regard our status as individuals." Do you agree or disagree? Include an explanation of the term *ethics* in your answer.

2. What are the two main problems associated with water in the home? What can be done to reduce water use?

3. What system uses the most energy in the home? Where does most heat loss occur? How can heat loss be reduced?

4. What is the 3-Rs solution to waste?

5. According to the Summary, what is positive ecology? Give an example of how you practice positive ecology.

References

Bohlen, C. (1990). Report from the State Department, *EPA Journal, 16*(4), 15–16.

Carlton, J. (2003, February 5). Home, green home: Builders embrace environmental goals. *The Wall Street Journal*, B1, B8.

Carpenter, B. (1989, June 12). The newest health hazard: Breathing. *U.S. News and World Report.*

Crossen, C. (2001, August 16). How much power do you use? *The Wall Street Journal*, B1.

Cude, B. (1993). Consumer perceptions of environmental marketing claims: An exploratory study. *Journal of Consumer Studies and Home Economics, 12*, 207–225.

Elkington, J., Burke, T., & Hailes, J. (1988). *Green pages: The business of saving the world.* London: Routledge.

Elkins, P., Hillman, M., & Hutchison, R. (1992). *Green economics.* New York: Doubleday.

Foran, J. (1990). Toxic substances in surface water. *Environmental Science Technology, 24*(5), 604–605.

Freud, S. (1961). *Civilization and its discontents.* (J. Strachey, Trans.). New York: Norton. (Original work published 1930).

Gavin, R. (2002, August 22). Cut your electric bill: Do laundry at 3 a.m. *The Wall Street Journal*, D1.

Gould, S. J. (1989). *Wonderful life.* New York: Norton.

Gould, S. J. (1998). *Leonardo's mountain of clams and the Diet of Worms: Essays on natural history.* New York: Harmony Books.

Graves, W. (1990, July). Water—the growing crisis. *National Geographic*, 1.

Harris, J. (2002). *Environmental and natural resources economics: A contemporary approach.* Boston: Houghton Mifflin.

McLuhan, M. (1962). *The Gutenberg galaxy.* Toronto: University of Toronto Press.

Merline, J. W. (1988, August). Energy smarts. *Consumers' Research*, 38.

Naar, J. (1990). *Design for a livable planet.* New York: Harper & Row.

Pearson, D. (1989). *The natural house.* New York: Simon & Schuster.

Petersen, A. (2002, October 17). New laws require home gas detectors. *The Wall Street Journal*, D1.

Pinchon, N. (1990, November 10). What causes global warming. Knight-Ridder Tribune News, 37.

Radon: The problem no one wants to face. (1989, October). *Consumer Reports*, 623–625.

Uitdenbogerd, D., Brouwer, N., & Groot-Marcus, J. (1998). Domestic energy saving potentials for food and textiles: An empirical study. A report from Wageningen Agricultural University, Holland.

Vo, M. (1998, November 6). A look at the world by the numbers. *The Christian Science Monitor*, 8–9.

Wilson, E. O. (1988). The current state of biological diversity. In E. O. Wilson (Ed.), *Biodiversity*. Washington, D.C.: National Academy Press.

chapter **13**

Managing Finances

Did you know that . . . ?

. . . Household assets are seven times greater today than a century ago.

. . . Average gym users pay $17 per workout even when a $10 pay per use option is available.

First say to yourself what you would be, then do what you have to do.

—*Epictetus, Greek Stoic philosopher*

CONTROLLING FINANCIAL RESOURCES is one of the most important and practical aspects of management. Control is a central concept because the rates of personal bankruptcies and credit card debt are at all-time highs, and people are paying for services or memberships they do not use. Here is an example:

> For more than a year, Rachel Hulin paid $90 a month for a gym membership. She used it maybe four times in all—for a per-visit rate of roughly $315. "I felt sort of like an idiot," says the 24-year-old photographer. "I think I signed up for it to try to make myself go." Ms. Hulin later dropped her membership and joined another, less-expensive gym at $55 a month. But she admits she hasn't "gone in a while" there either. (Silverman, 2003, p. D1)

This particular area of consumption, gym membership, illustrates hope over reason. A three-year study of about 8,000 members showed that the average user paid $17 per workout even when a $10 per use policy existed; most lost over $700 over the life of their gym contract (Silverman, 2003, p. D1). Other areas where self-control is a particular problem are credit card usage, mail-order clubs, and television shopping networks. Many businesses and the media take advantage of self–control issues. They are motivated to increase profits, whereas consumers want to get the best buy and conserve wealth.

Although this chapter begins with theory and the state of the economy, it moves quickly to the dollars and cents issues involved in money management. It covers poverty and wealth, credit, the gender gap, and the glass ceiling. This chapter is placed near the end of the book because it builds on many of the principles discussed earlier, such as values, attitudes, goals, resources, and decision making. To reiterate, values are principles that guide behavior, and goals are end results that require action. Thrift, for example, is a value affecting financial management, and saving for a car is an example of a financial goal. Signing contracts for gym membership but rarely going to the gym is a good example of the gap that exists between values (ideals) and behavior. Attitudes are concepts that express feelings in regard to some idea, person, object, event, situation, or relationship. They play an important role in consumption because individuals have innumerable consumer attitudes (e.g., preferring a particular brand, store, or product over another). Decision making is choice making between two or more alternatives. All people must make financial decisions, but their choices are limited by how much money they have. Money is a material resource, but how a person chooses to spend it is a human resource. Financial planning is an integral part of managing information systems and decision support systems. Space limitations prevent an exhaustive examination of personal and family finance, a topic to which thousands of books and whole sections of bookstores are devoted. Instead, this chapter provides an introduction to financial planning and related economic and lifestyle issues by focusing on families as producers and consumers and examining such concerns as what individuals and families do with their money and how they provide for retirement.

SUGGESTED ACTIVITY

Have you, a friend, or a member of your family joined a gym, fitness center, or country club and not used the facilities to the fullest extent? Discuss, in groups, the expense of joining and maintaining memberships and services offered. What was worth or not worth the expense?

WHAT IS FINANCIAL MANAGEMENT?

Financial management is the science or practice of managing money or other assets. Financial management requires systematic and disciplined thought and action. Saving money rather than spending it, for instance, requires self-discipline and control, the ability to set goals, and a willingness to put future needs before current needs. In the time management chapter, we discussed asking yourself the question, "Is this the best use of my time right now?" A corollary appropriate to this chapter says, before buying anything, ask yourself, "Is this the best purchase for me at this moment?" This question alone will keep you away from accumulating unnecessary debt. Being debt-free is a goal. Using cash and debit cards for purchases will set a person in the right direction.

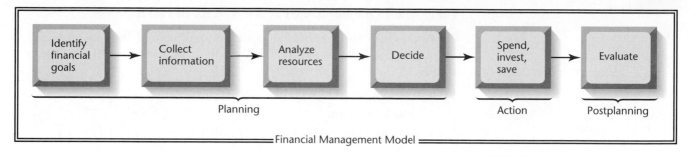

Financial Management Model

FIGURE 13.1
Financial Management Model

The procedures followed at each stage of financial management must be methodological, sound, and planned for in advance to the extent possible. Essentially, financial plans are "a work in progress," subject to review and modification (O'Neill & Brennan, 1997).

In systems terminology, financial management is a transformation process involving the identification of financial goals; collection of information; analysis of resources; decisions about whether to spend, invest, or save; and evaluation of decisions. Management takes the perspective that money, like any other resource, can be controlled and used to achieve goals. As Figure 13.1 shows, the financial management process can be divided into three phases: planning, action, and postplanning.

During the planning stage, individuals begin by defining their financial goals. They then identify potential financial opportunities and determine what information and funds are needed to take advantage of these opportunities. Once they have analyzed their resources and decided how to use them, they can proceed to the action stage, where they save, invest, or spend their money. In this phase, a **budget,** or a spending plan or guide, can be helpful by providing a visible means of controlling money. More coverage on budgets and examples is coming up. At the end of the process, as in any other management process, the decisions and their outcomes are evaluated. Throughout the process, money and other financial assets are treated as tools that can be used to enhance life and provide for growth and security.

FINANCIAL AND ECONOMIC CONCERNS

When can I afford to retire? What happens if I lose my job? Will I be able to afford a house? All these questions involve financial concerns. In the 20th century, the world struggled through several economic crises, most notably the Great Depression, which peaked in the United States in 1933. In the early 2000s, economic hard times returned in the form of a recession that hit worldwide. An economic recovery was under way as this book went to press.

People who are financially pinched cut back in several ways. One of their greatest fears is losing their house. In a nationwide survey, 74 percent of U.S. families with children live paycheck to paycheck compared to 54 percent of adults without children at home ("Who's Hurting the Most," 2003).

The Business Cycle and Inflation

Since individuals and families live in an economic system, they are not immune to the changes in the economy. Some of the main indicators of the economy include

- ◆ Personal spending
- ◆ New home sales
- ◆ The consumer price index
- ◆ Unemployment rate
- ◆ Gross domestic product

Each of these will be described in the next sections.

Corporations lay off thousands of workers, and governments do not replace workers with new hires when someone moves or retires, making the job market tighter. If the main or sole breadwinner is unemployed, the family suffers. The U.S. unemployment rate was 5.6 percent when this book went to press after highs around 6 percent. An unemployment rate of 10 percent or more is considered an indicator of severe economic problems. A rate under 5 percent is desirable. During boom times and in high-growth areas, the unemployment rate can be as low as 2 percent. Describing an earlier period of unemployment, a Northwestern University Kellogg School of Management professor said:

> The newspaper says the banking industry will lose 100,000 jobs this year. That's 100,000 middle-class people who thought they were going to be in control of their lives. Manhattan is filled with 40-year-olds out of work, deep in debt and overextended on their apartments. They never thought it would happen to them. (Adler, 1992, p. 22)

The key phrases here are "people who thought they were going to be in control of their lives" and "they never thought it would happen to them." The unexpectedness of unemployment makes it even more difficult to adjust to and manage.

To illustrate the ups and downs of the economy, the business cycle is made of three main parts as shown in Figure 13.2.

1. **Recession:** A moderate and temporary decline in the economy.
2. **Recovery:** A hopeful stage when things are looking better, consumer buying and confidence are up, production is up, employment is up, retail sales improve, and new homes are being built.
3. **Expansion:** Prosperity, high growth, an active economy, and high employment rates.

Many factors play into which part of the business cycle a nation's economy can be generally described as being in. One of the main factors is **inflation,** which means rising prices. Inflation was at 1.2 percent when this book went to press and had been hovering around 2–3 percent for several years. Low inflation means that prices are rising very slowly, which is good for consumers. Inflation indicates the general way prices are going, but individual categories of products or services may be going up or down in a way significantly different from the general inflation rate. For example, appliances have gone down significantly in price relative to other costs (Farrell, Palmer, & Browder, 1998). Two areas rising significantly in cost are college tuition and health care. The average cost of private college grew 6 percent in 2003, and many state uni-

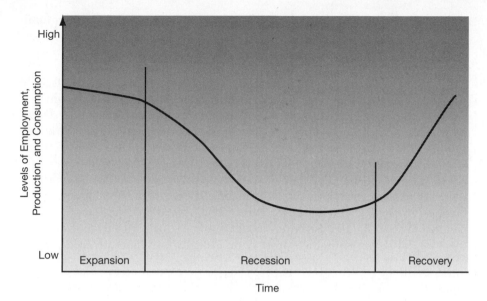

FIGURE 13.2
The Business Cycle

The economy goes through various stages over time. The stages are cyclical and affect the levels of employment, production, and consumption.

versities raised tuition rates significantly. A year of in-state costs including room and board for an undergraduate student at Penn State University went from $12,354 in 2001 to $14,736 in 2003. Low mortgage rates stimulate home building, the reselling of existing homes, and the refinancing of existing mortgages. According to the National Association of Realtors, single-family home median resale prices went from $141,800 in 2001 to $172,600 in 2003. Considerably more new homes were sold nearly every month in 2003 than they were in the preceding year. Spin-offs include increased sales in insurance, furnishings, hardware, building supplies, and financial products. In recent years a record number of people in the United States owned their own homes.

The main measure of inflation is the **Consumer Price Index** (CPI) collected and reported each month by the Bureau of Labor Statistics (BLS). Economic assistants gather price information from selected department stores, supermarkets, service stations, doctors' offices, rental units, and the like. Each month, about 80,000 prices are recorded in 87 urban areas. By collecting price data on a clearly defined market basket of products, the BLS can measure changes in prices. The CPI is used in formulating fiscal and monetary policy and in adjusting wages, salaries, and payments such as Social Security. For many retirees, the only raise they get is when Congress votes to increase their monthly Social Security checks because of inflation.

Individuals and Families as Producers and Consumers

Within the movement of the general economy, individuals and families play important roles as producers and consumers. Consumption choices include what food to eat, what clothes to wear, where to shop, and where to bank. Consumption decisions affect the present and future standard of living of an individual or family. An individual's or family's **level of living** is a measure of the goods and services affordable by and available to them. **Standard of living** is what an individual or a family aspires to. On the production side, families produce children and transform raw products into finished products through such activities as gardening, cooking, and sewing. In addition, families produce, process, manage, and provide a variety of other goods and services (e.g., child care, elder care, home maintenance, transportation, health care, and education for family members).

Households are both labor-intensive and highly productive. Household production is not included in the **gross domestic product (GDP),** which is the total market value of all goods and services produced by a nation during a specified period, usually a year. For example, tomatoes canned at home, though used the same way as factory-canned tomatoes, are not counted in the GDP. Similarly, an individual's work in completing his or her income tax forms is not counted in the GDP, but the services provided by an accounting firm doing someone's income taxes is included. Thus, although individuals and families are significant producing units, their home-based production is not counted in the U.S. GDP. Several reasons have been given for this omission; the most logical is that household production is difficult to measure accurately.

INCOME, TAXES, NET WORTH, BUDGETS, AND SAVING

Just as GDP is a measure of a nation's well-being, income is one of the main measures of a family's financial well-being. **Income** is the amount of money or its equivalent received during a period of time. The main source of income for most people is their salary. Other sources are dividends from investments and savings accounts, gifts, and so on. There are several different kinds of income:

- **Discretionary income:** Income regulated by one's own discretion or judgment.
- **Disposable income:** The amount of take-home pay left after all deductions are withheld for benefits, taxes, contributions, and so on.
- **Gross income:** All income received that is not legally exempt from taxes.
- **Psychic income:** One's perception or feelings about income; the satisfaction derived from income.
- **Real income:** Income measured in prices at a certain time, reflecting the buying power of current dollars.

Take special note of psychic income. When helping individuals and families formulate budgets or financial plans, it is important to know not only how much money they have to work with, but also how they feel about money in general. What one person regards as very little money, another may consider a fortune. An accurate assessment of people's income or lifestyle requires some knowledge of not only their actual income, but also how they perceive money and how much they feel they need to maintain an adequate level of living.

A personal tax levied on individuals or families on the basis of income received is called an **income tax.** In 1913, the Sixteenth Amendment to the U.S. Constitution was ratified, making the personal income tax constitutional. On average, one-third of the typical U.S. family's income goes to paying federal, state, and local taxes. **Taxes** are compulsory levies that are an important source of government revenue. Taxes help cover government expenses and, in the case of income tax, help redistribute income and wealth. In 1789, Benjamin Franklin wrote that "in this world nothing is certain but death and taxes." After taxes, typically the remainder of a family's money goes first to housing, then transportation, then food, and on down the list to health/personal care, recreation, clothing, insurance, and other needs. The distribution of money varies greatly by the amount of income (for example, the lower the income, the higher proportion spent on food), savings, and other investments.

Financial records for income tax purposes should be kept for three years, occasionally for five if there has been a problem in the past. Records to keep permanently include birth and marriage certificates, divorce papers, military records, bankruptcy filings, adoption papers, wills, and Social Security data.

Net worth is determined by subtracting what is owed **(liabilities)** from what is owned **(assets).** To give historical perspective, household assets have increased seven times in the last century. We may not feel better off, but we are. An estimation of net worth is considered the best measure of one's material wealth. It is important to estimate net worth because it shows where a person stands financially. A net worth estimate should be made at least once a year.

Figure 13.3 provides a sample form that can be used for computing net worth. Notice the wide variety of assets: actual cash on hand and money in checking and savings accounts; investments such as certificates of deposit, stocks, bonds, and mutual funds; real estate, which includes one's house and any other real estate owned; pension benefits to which an individual is entitled; retirement accounts, such as employer-sponsored 401(k) and 403(b) plans and IRAs; the value of a business; personal property such as jewelry, furniture, and appliances; and any automobiles owned. Liabilities include the mortgage on one's home, the balance owed on installment loans, such as on a car or refrigerator, the balance owed on credit cards, unpaid bills, and any taxes owed.

The net worth statement of Pete Sawyer, a junior in college, appears in Table 13.1. Pete has some money in his checking and savings accounts that he earned from a summer job, a car, and various items of personal property, most notably a computer. Pete also has a number of liabilities, including his college loan, an outstanding balance on his credit card, library fines, and parking tickets he has not paid. When Pete's liabilities are subtracted from his assets, the result is –$2,609.97. Pete has a negative net worth—he owes more than his assets are worth. Actually, a negative net worth is not unusual for someone at Pete's life stage. College students and new college graduates often have college loans outstanding and might incur other financial obligations from moving and setting up a new lifestyle. As they begin to work full-time and their earnings increase, they are able to pay off their debts, and their negative net worth gradually declines; and then they begin to accumulate assets. Generally, college graduates earn substantial amounts of money; however, about one-third will have problems sometime during their life with credit card debt and, historically, as many as one-fifth of those with student loans will default on their loan repayment, causing financial and credit rating problems (Markovich & DeVaney, 1997). Specific advice on how college students can manage their money is given in an upcoming section.

Whereas a net worth statement reveals current financial status, a budget helps individuals and families plan ahead and clarify their values and goals. As explained earlier, a budget is a spending plan. A budget should serve as a guide—one that the budgeter controls. It should be flexible and not put a straitjacket on spending.

Many expenses, such as money spent on food, clothing, and entertainment, are flexible, whereas other expenses are fixed, such as rent and car payments. If budgets are too rigid, they will not allow for unexpected or variable expenses, such as medical or dental bills or the costs of home maintenance. For example, replacing a leaking roof or a faulty furnace for $3,000 is an expense that must be met but cannot be budgeted for in advance except in the most general way.

Typically, budgets are based on monthly average spending patterns. Income is compared to outflow. The main source of income is wages and salaries. Housing expenditures (including utilities) take away the largest share. So, begin each budget by looking first at rent or home mortgage payments. Other large expenses include transportation (car payments and gasoline/maintenance), student loan debt payment, food, and credit/store card payment. If individuals are having a hard time meeting monthly expenses they can

- ◆ Make more money (increase income).
- ◆ Reduce expenses (outflow).
- ◆ Sell something, downsize.
- ◆ Do a combination of all three.

FIGURE 13.3
Net Worth Statement
Net worth is calculated by subtracting liabilities (what is owed) from assets (what is owned).

Assets	
Cash on hand	$
Checking accounts	$
Savings accounts	$
Money market funds	$
Cash management accounts	$
Certificates of deposits	$
Stocks, bonds (market value)*	$
Mutual funds	$
Real estate (market value)	$
Employer-sponsored retirement plans	$
IRAs	$
Vested company benefits	$
Annuities (one-time investments paid upon retirement)	$
Personal property** (market value)	$
Automobiles (market value)	$
Estate and trust values	$
Cash value of whole life insurance	$
Business venture values	$
Debts owed to you	$
Other	$
Total assets	$
Liabilities	
Loans (college, home, auto)	$
Unpaid bills	$
Personal debts (to friends, family)	$
Other	$
Total liabilities	$
Net worth (total assets − total liabilities)	$

*Market value means what the asset would be worth if it were sold immediately.
**This category includes nearly anything with a resale value, such as clothing, furniture, books, bicycles, computers, jewelry, televisions, and appliances.

TABLE 13.1
**Pete Sawyer's Net
Worth Statement**

Assets	
Cash on hand	$ 40.00
Checking account	465.02
Savings account	807.15
Personal property	
CD player and CD collection	225.00
Bicycle	125.00
Watch	135.00
Computer	1,000.00
Clothes and books	75.00
Automobile (9-year-old car)	3,500.00
Total assets	$6,372.17
Liabilities	
College loan	$8,655.00
Unpaid bills	
Balance on credit cards	122.00
Long-distance telephone bill	78.64
Library fines	32.50
Personal debts	
Loan from roommate	110.00
Other (parking tickets)	55.00
Total liabilities	$9,053.14
Net worth	−$2,609.97

One way to prepare for unexpected expenses is to budget a certain amount to be saved each month. The goal of saving is to build funds in a risk-free manner. Saving is what makes future spending or investing possible. How much should an individual or family save? The answer depends on their present lifestyle, responsibilities, and goals and on the lifestyle they desire. *People in the United States save about 4–5 percent of their income, a rate that is lower than that of most other industrialized nations.* To get ahead or to save for something, such as the down payment on a house, individuals should strive to save 10 percent or more. In dual-earner couples, some live on one salary and save the other.

A way to approach saving is to have a goal of building an **emergency fund** of three to six months' income. Opinions vary on the length of time. Author and television personality Suze Orman suggests eight months of expenses in savings because job layoffs are more prevalent and the time it takes to find another job is getting longer (2003). Recent estimates by the Bureau of Labor Statistics reveal the average out-of-work person takes five months to find a job. An emergency fund is used to tide people over until income begins again, so the amount should be enough to take care of life basics such as rent and food.

To build savings, young professionals should save regularly, even in small amounts, to enable them to accomplish short- and long-term goals such as the purchase of a home. Figure 13.4 lists the goals of John, a recent college graduate, as a way to show how goals and finances are linked. Spaces are provided for you to write in your own financial goals—short-term, medium-term, and long-term. "The likelihood of having a successful investment program is increased with early and regular savings" (Markovich & DeVaney, 1998, p. 61).

Table 13.2 shows the budget of a young married couple, Tim Snyder and Mary Ann Kirby. As a young couple starting out, their sources of income and types of expenses are fairly limited. Their salaries are their biggest source of income, and their house and child care for their two-year-old daughter are their largest expenses. Notice that Mary Ann and Tim's budget does not leave any money for emergencies. They say they'll be able to start saving more in six months when Mary Ann finishes her training program at the bank and receives a substantial increase in salary and Tim finishes law school. In the meantime, they hope no emergencies arise.

In drawing up your own budget, checking account and credit card statements can help you obtain an accurate account of your money flow. Because expenses fluctuate from month to month, averaging several months' expenses will help you obtain a more accurate picture of typical monthly expenditures. Once individuals or families figure out their net worth and their typical monthly expenditures, they can create a six-month or one-year spending plan. By reviewing their net worth statement and monthly expenditures, people may be able to find places where they can spend less and save more.

Managing Credit

An easy way to overspend is to misuse credit cards. **Credit** is time allowed for payment. Credit means that an individual owes a certain amount of money, at a certain time each month, to a specific creditor at a certain rate. Failure to pay on time at the recommended amount may result in penalties. Credit card debt

FIGURE 13.4
Financial Goals by Time

Financial Goals	John's Goals*	Your Goals
Short Term (0–3 years)		
Goal 1:	Move across country	_____
Goal 2:	Begin full-time job	_____
Goal 3:	Find a roommate, rent an apt.	_____
Medium Term (3–7 years)		
Goal 1:	Establish himself in film business	_____
Goal 2:	Buy new car	_____
Goal 3:	Save money	_____
Long Term (7–10 years)		
Goal 1:	Start own production company	_____
Goal 2:	Settle down, buy a house	_____
Goal 3:	Marry, start a family	_____

*John is 23 years old. He recently graduated from a four-year university with a major in film studies. He plans to move to California and get into the film industry (behind the camera). He graduated debt-free, but has few possessions except a computer, some furniture, and a used car. He has contacts in California for jobs and for roommates.

Monthly savings (or losses) are determined by subtracting estimated monthly expenses from monthly income.

Income

Salaries

Mary Ann (management trainee at bank)	$2,102.74
Tim (part-time job while attending law school)	788.80
Dividends	22.00
Money gifts, scholarships (Tim's scholarship for law school)	600.00
Other (Mary Ann writes a weekly column on financial management for a newspaper)	60.00
Total income	$3,573.54

Expenses

Mortgage payment on house	$874.88
Food	380.00
Child care (for Kristin, their daughter)	860.00
Tuition/books	255.00
Gasoline/transportation	
Bus fare for Mary Ann	22.00
Parking at the university for Tim	15.00
Gasoline	40.00
Utilities (gas, electric, water, cable)	150.00
Telephone	25.00
Insurance (life, car, home—Mary Ann's employer pays for health insurance)	120.00
Clothing and personal care (haircuts, cosmetics)	80.00
Credit card payments	50.00
Entertainment	40.00
Loans	
College (Mary Ann)	190.00
College (Tim)	120.00
Automobile	239.85
Personal spending	65.00
Miscellaneous	35.00
Total expenses	$3,561.73
Total savings	$11.81

TABLE 13.2
Monthly Budget for Tim Snyder and Mary Ann Kirby

is debt, no matter how it is sugar-coated. Debt follows a person through marriage, divorce, illness, and some forms of bankruptcy. If you packed up your car in Virginia and drove across country nonstop to Seattle, your credit rating would get there before you arrive. With the Internet, financial records and status are instantaneous.

A credit card authorizes the holder to buy something in advance of paying for it. Using credit instead of cash makes shopping more convenient and reduces the risk of loss or theft associated with carrying large amounts of cash. Although the savings rate is low in the United States, credit card use is on the rise due to broadened eligibility and ease of use.

Managing credit is one of the biggest management problems individuals and families have. From a financial point of view, one of the problems is that interest on credit card payments is usually higher than what individuals make on their investments. The following suggestions can help reduce the chances of credit mismanagement:

◆ Have only one or two cards, at most three. The typical bankrupt individual has 20 or more cards.

◆ Pay off credit cards on time in full each month to avoid interest charges. Only 36 percent of cardholders do this.

◆ Know what the agreement says; seek cards with the lowest annual percentage rate (APR) and no additional fees. The rate of interest paid over the life of credit or a loan is called the **Annual Percentage Rate.**

◆ If a card has a teaser rate (a very low introductory level APR), use it but get rid of it when the rate goes up. Teaser rates are often offered to college students; and when they graduate, the rates go up. The companies know from experience that most students will continue using the cards.

◆ Check credit card statements carefully against receipts. Do not allow the unauthorized use of a credit card number.

◆ Keep a list of credit card purchases as they occur, similar to the check stubs in a checkbook.

◆ Keep a list of credit card numbers in a safe place, in case they are lost or stolen, along with a list of toll-free numbers of credit card companies to notify in case cards are lost.

◆ If you are in debt, get out of it. First, pay off the credit cards with the highest APR. Psychologically, it may help to pay off the card with the smallest amount owed first or to consolidate several small debts into one. Most people can handle 10 to 15 percent of take-home pay for monthly consumer credit obligations. Twenty percent or more puts consumers in a danger zone.

◆ Inform creditors if bills cannot be paid. Most will work with consumers to arrange pay-back plans.

◆ Contact a credit counseling service such as the National Foundation for Credit Counseling (**www.nfcc.org**) if debt is out of control. They can help negotiate a lower rate or repayment schedule.

◆ Delete all spam e-mail regarding getting you out of debt.

Under the **Fair Credit Reporting Act** of 1971, individuals who are denied credit, insurance, or employment because of their credit report have the right to obtain a free copy of their report within 30 days of denial. Recently, **credit bureaus,** reporting agencies that collect, store, and sell financial information, have been offering credit reports to consumers for free. Since this is in flux, contact any of the following credit bureaus to find out their policy regarding reports and any fees to access them:

◆ Equifax, www.equifax.com, (800) 685 1111

◆ Trans Union Corporation, **www.transunion.com,** (800) 916 8800

◆ Experian, www.experian.com, (888) 397 3742

Credit reports are used by institutions to determine whether to offer you a loan, a mortgage, a credit card, or a job. The institution (i.e., bank, store, or employer) pays a fee for the credit report. If consumers have a high **FICO**

score, a numeric value assigned to credit habits and history by Fair, Isaac and Company (the range is 300 to 850), a lender may offer a lower mortgage rate. A consumer in the high range can also ask for a lower interest rate on credit cards. A score below 500 puts a consumer in the sub-lender category. A score 720 or above is considered very good.

How do potential employers find out about your credit score? The way it starts is that on job application forms there is a box to mark off, giving employers the right to conduct background checks. Applicants can refuse to mark it, but the interview process might stop right there. Would you hire someone who did not check that box when dozens of other applicants checked it? Potential employers associate a good credit report with trustworthiness and reliability, and they value these characteristics whether the job involves handling money or not. What they are looking for in an employee is not necessarily that they are debt-free but how they manage their debt (i.e., show a record of steady payments).

A good FICO score can be established in a number of ways, including opening checking and savings accounts; paying bills, including rent, promptly; and opening a charge account with a store and promptly remitting the monthly balance due. Potential lenders who are considering whether to extend credit or not also look at several factors, including residential and job stability, education, income, and home ownership. Regardless of the criteria used, the **Equal Credit Opportunity Act** prevents a lender from discriminating against a person because of race, sex, age, color, marital status, or other related factors.

Deciding when to use credit and when to pay cash is part of the overall management problem of controlling money. The first step toward solving this problem is to define an attainable goal. Examples of specific financial goals include saving for a down payment on a house, or for college expenses, remodeling, a vacation, or additional investments and retirement. Once a financial goal is established and a plan drawn up, progress toward the goal should be reviewed to evaluate how well the financial planning is working.

Banking, Investments, and Insurance

Saving and investing can take many forms. For example, cash can be put in interest-bearing checking accounts, savings accounts, money market accounts, and low-risk, longer-term savings instruments. Regardless of the type of account, the goal is to maximize the earnings from the investment of cash and to avoid fees, payments, and extra charges. **Liquidity,** the speed and ease of retrieving cash or turning another type of investment into cash, is another important consideration.

Checking accounts from banks and share accounts from credit unions allow the holder to transfer funds from the account to pay for goods and services. Banks commonly charge a fee for this convenience in per-check charges or monthly service fees, but they may also pay interest on the money in the account. A savings account, also called a passbook account, typically pays higher interest than a checking account. A money market account pays an even higher rate of interest, and some offer check-writing privileges. These accounts are commonly called NOW accounts and cash management accounts. Other low-risk possibilities for cash include government savings bonds and certificates of deposit (CDs). These typically pay higher interest than checking, savings, and money market accounts.

Investment is the commitment of capital to the achievement of long-term goals or objectives. Most people invest to build wealth and to secure a comfortable future. It is important to invest because of rising prices; and because people are living longer, their money has to stretch further. Investing is a process that involves planning, money, information, time, and an understanding of risk, the possibility of experiencing suffering, loss, danger, or harm. Financially, risk refers to the loss of money. Investment and insurance decisions rest not only on economic conditions, personal income, and life stage, but also on one's ability to handle risk. Some investors are more conservative (less likely to take risks) than others. As one ages, usually one gravitates to more conservative, dividend-paying investments because if money is lost, the person does not have as much time to earn the income to bounce back again. However, even in retirement some growth should be built in to keep up with inflation. **Diversification** means having a mix of investments as a way to spread risk across several categories. Another basic principle is that the earlier an individual starts to invest, the longer time period the investment will have to grow. Youth is on the investor's side.

Several chapters would be needed to discuss the pros and cons of the different kinds of investments available. For the purposes of this chapter, the focus will be on the subject of investing and the most common types of investments.

- ◆ *Stocks* represent ownership in a company (e.g., Microsoft, IBM, Coca-Cola). There are thousands of stocks to choose from. See the Web-Based Resources section for Web sites with stock information. Usually the best strategy is to buy good stocks and hold on to them.

  "People want to do something, which is why they tend to over-trade," says Clifford Asness, managing principal of New York hedge-fund manager AQR Capital Management. "But the object of the market is not to entertain us. You should stay diversified, pay low fees, relax and get on with the rest of your life." (Clements, 2003, October 8, p. D1)

- ◆ *Bonds* are investments in which a person lends money to an organization such as the government or a corporation. Examples of U.S. Treasury Department bonds are I Bonds and Series EE Bonds. They can be purchased commission-free at **http://treasurydirect.gov.** More information about them can be obtained from **www.savingsbonds.gov.** Generally, bonds are considered more conservative (safer) investments than stocks, but less liquid. Maturity dates run from a month to 30 years. Interest or dividends are distributions of money that government or corporations pay to bondholders (some stocks also pay dividends). Usually, dividends on bonds are paid twice a year and are a source of income.

- ◆ *Mutual funds* are groups of stocks, bonds, or other securities managed by an investment company. Their chief benefits are diversification and professional management.

- ◆ *Real estate* includes real estate directly (such as a primary residence or a lot owned) and indirectly owned (such as in a partnership or a Real Estate Investment Trust, commonly known as a REIT).

- ◆ *Other forms of investment* include Individual Retirement Accounts (IRAs), employer-sponsored retirement plans, precious metals (i.e., gold, silver), gems, and collectibles.

Before starting to invest, a person should have ample cash for daily and monthly expenses, an emergency fund set aside, paid-off credit cards, and insurance.

Usually people start with secure investments such as money market funds, certificates of deposit, U.S. Savings Bonds, retirement plans at work, U.S. Treasury Securities, and savings accounts. Then, after some of these are owned, they move up the investment ladder to other categories offering more income and growth. The last category to consider is speculative where more risk is prevalent.

The purpose of insurance is to protect people and financial assets. It provides peace of mind. A sound financial plan includes protection from major risks (e.g., auto accidents, natural disasters, health problems) that can threaten financial security. **Insurance** is a financial arrangement in which people pay premiums (payments) to an insurance company that reimburses them in the event of loss or injury. Usually, the most costly and the most important form of insurance is health insurance.

Most employers offer health insurance as part of their benefits package. Other types of insurance include property, liability, automobile, disability, life, and long-term care insurance. Usually, group policies (insurance company contracts sold through organizations such as professional associations or alumni groups) are less expensive than individual policies. Decisions about insurance depend on how much protection is needed, how much can be afforded, and how much is given by employers. Insurance coverage should be appropriate to an individual's or a family's life stage, needs, and goals.

A course in personal finance or family financial planning will cover many of the points mentioned in this section in depth. Financial well-being is critical to a person's overall sense of well-being and success. Learning to manage money is a lifelong process begun in childhood. *People between the ages of 45 and 54 have the highest median income of any age group,* but they also have the highest expenses, because they may have children in college while they are also saving for their own retirement. Over the life span, individuals and couples have to reevaluate, update, and renegotiate their goals and spending and investing plans many times. For example, experts suggest that financial plans, in general, and, specifically, insurance policies and retirement accounts should be examined each year to determine whether they still meet individuals' and families' needs.

Children and Expenses

Children are priceless, but raising them may be the most expensive thing anyone does. In 2002, the estimate by the U.S. Department of Agriculture (USDA) was $249,180 to raise a child from birth through age 17 based on families making $65,800 a year or more. Lower-income families on average spend less. The outlay per child is reduced with each additional child, perhaps out of necessity, perhaps because bedrooms can be shared, clothes and toys handed down, and so on. Without a doubt, the costs of rearing and educating children add to the financial strain on families. Child-raising expenses can be divided into seven main categories (Wuorio, 2003):

◆ Housing (about 33–37 percent)

◆ Food (about 15–20 percent)

◆ Transportation (about 13–14 percent)

◆ Clothing (about 6–8 percent)

◆ Health care (about 5–7 percent)

◆ Education/child care (about 7–11 percent)

◆ Miscellaneous (about 10–13 percent)

The first year of life is particularly expensive; it is estimated that the highest cost then is usually child care, followed by furniture and food. Overall, in raising a child to age 18, however, housing is the most costly item, followed by education and transportation. The USDA assumes when people have children they will move into larger homes. Their calculations assume that for each child, a family adds 100 to 150 square feet of living space (the size of a typical bedroom). A way to save here is to go against the tide, to not increase housing size or live in a less expensive place, or at least refinance to get a lower mortgage rate. Since food comes next, there are thousands of ways to save money. A simple trick is to use search engines and type in the word "discount" and see what happens. For large families, other ideas are to join warehouse clubs or to shop in supercenters or to buy in bulk at sales. Transportation includes the purchase and finance charges of vehicles, repair and fuel expenses and insurance. The value of new cars drops by as much as 40 percent the first two years of ownership, so the advice is to avoid buying a new car, consider a relatively new model coming off a one- or two-year lease, and use the Internet to comparison shop prices of vehicles and insurance. Much of the expense of health care comes from health insurance premiums, so it pays to shop around.

Child-rearing expenses are highest in the urban West, followed by the urban Northeast, the urban South, and the urban Midwest. Housing costs contribute greatly to differences between regions, as do costs of child care and education.

The study of children and money involves more than estimating how much it costs to raise them. Children are not passive consumers. From the first time they spit out strained peas, they are letting their parents know their preferences. Parents respond by buying what their children like, and later the children themselves collectively spend billions of dollars a year on cosmetics, toys, snacks, candy, gifts, athletic events and equipment, musical recordings and instruments, and other goods and services. They also influence their parents' expenditures on nearly all family-related purchases, including housing, cars, computers, vacations, breakfast cereals, and restaurant meals.

As part of the socialization process, children learn much of their spending behavior from their parents. For example, a study of elementary schoolchildren found that mothers who were restrictive and warm in relationships with their children were also more likely to use communication messages that promoted monitoring and control of children's consumption activities. Further, mothers who generally respected and asked for their children's opinions tended to utilize messages that fostered the development of consumption decision-making abilities in children (Carlson, Grossbart, & Stuenkel, 1992).

Most children are ready to receive an allowance or handle a small amount of money as soon as they understand the concept of time. Readiness to handle money varies greatly from child to child, but usually comes around the ages of 7 or 8. Understanding time is important, because it enables children to wait for Saturday (a traditional day for handing out allowances). If they can wait for Saturday, then they will understand about waiting for money and parceling it out after they receive it. One method of training children for the responsibilities of adulthood is to encourage them to save part of their allowance, but again children's ability to do this varies with age and maturity. The younger the child, the more likely he or she will spend money quickly rather than save it for bigger items. The average 9-year-old will probably not be interested in saving for college—it is too far away.

Children need to learn that money is a tool—something they can use to get what they want. Along the way to disciplined money management, children will make mistakes, such as buying toys that fall apart or fail to live up to their expectations. Making poor or disappointing expenditures is part of the learning process. Both the mistakes and the successes of money management experiences in childhood will prepare children for the bigger expenses ahead.

Saving for College

There are many ways to save for college and options, programs, and tax deductions are changing all the time. Setting up an education IRA (Individual Retirement Account) or investing in various state prepaid tuition plans where the income is either tax-deferred or completely excluded are options to consider. Another alternative is setting up a trust fund or investing dollars under children's names. The income will be taxed to them at a lower rate than it is to parents. The rate changes at age 14. Scholarships are available, based on need, grades, other achievements—from state and private sources. While a student is in college, the Hope Credit and the Lifetime Credit programs reduce taxes. Upon graduation, interest on student loans may be deductible even if the postgraduate does not itemize. When this book went to press, a graduate could deduct up to $2,500 in student loan interest. Students nearing graduation and owing loans should talk to college financial aid experts, accountants, or financial planners about the best way to pay back the loans. Many students set up a payment program whereby they are loan-free in 10 years.

Research studies reveal that people often regret that they did not get more education. A college education is one of the best investments anyone can make.

College Students and Money Management

College students today are managing far more money, possessions, and credit than their parents did at a similar age. Most college students have cars, computers, credit cards, and cell phones. Generally, college students have favorable attitudes toward credit cards. One study found that students who are female, live on campus, major in consumer affairs, and/or work less than 20 hours have more favorable attitudes toward credit cards than other students (Xiao, Noring, & Anderson, 1995). In a nationwide college survey, three out of four college students reported that they expect to become millionaires (Sebastian, 1999). Being in college brings with it new levels of freedom. Students should beware of falling into a habit of debt that can follow them for years. After graduation, as mentioned earlier, a bad credit record can hurt when finding a job.

Many of the money management principles already covered in this chapter apply to college students, but, to reiterate, here are some tips for setting up a budget and maintaining a good credit record:

◆ Make a list of predicted monthly expenses and income. Ask yourself, How much money do I really need?

◆ Set aside some money for savings or emergencies.

◆ Keep track of everything you spend. It helps you stick to your budget. Save receipts.

◆ Pay all bills on time—from the telephone to your credit card bill. Immediately open bills on arrival. They usually arrive about 15 days before they are due. Use automatic payment systems and direct deposit whenever possible.

◆ If you are in financial trouble, address it immediately; call creditors, contact parents. If services are turned off or creditors are calling, consider contacting the National Foundation for Credit Counseling.

Students (and their parents) can economize by

◆ Living on less (e.g., sharing an apartment or house, eating out less).

◆ Working more. While in college, according to the Bureau of Labor Statistics, most students work.

◆ Joining co-op programs or getting paid internships.

◆ Applying for financial aid, loans, and scholarships. A popular option is the federally sponsored lending program known as Stafford loans. Another federal lending program is the Parent Loans for Undergraduate Students (PLUS). With PLUS, families borrow enough to pay for the total cost of attendance; the variable interest rates are capped at 9 percent.

◆ Living at home while going to school or after graduation and during the summers between semesters, thereby reducing living expenses.

◆ Joining ROTC as a career option and as a way to finance school expenses.

Given the high cost of a college education, many parents and students might question whether it is worth it. From a financial perspective, the answer is yes. According to U.S. Department of Commerce data, education does provide an economic return in that most degrees beyond high school will result in higher income for an individual. For Web sites providing information on salaries and job trends, see the Web-Based Resources section at the end of this chapter.

Retirement Planning

At the other end of the spectrum from college costs are the costs of retirement. Americans have been retiring progressively earlier for about a century. However, that trend has flattened out; some say it's poised to reverse, leaving many Americans working later in life. With the massive baby boom generation soon approaching retirement age, the question of how long they'll stay at their jobs is looming ever larger. More and more retirees are choosing to work part-time rather than bow out of the labor force altogether.

Another decision is whether to buy **long-term-care insurance,** policies that provide benefits for a range of services not covered by regular health insurance or Medicare. Typical coverage includes extended stays in long-term-care facilities and the costs of assisted living in one's own home. Rates are more affordable the younger a person is. Most people look into long-term-care insurance in their 50s or 60s. Since premiums for long-term-care insurance are high not everyone can afford them.

People in their 60s realize that retirement can last 20 or more years, so investment growth is still important. Retirement assets should earn above the inflation rate. It is also a time to create an estate plan and make sure wills are current. Another thing to think about is how much income will be needed in retirement. Options should be explored with financial professionals.

Financially strapped retirees may turn to their children for help. Often what happens is that their children are getting older too and can't retire because they are helping out mom or dad.

Rae Mauro, a 66-year-old research analyst from Valencia, Calif., recently opted not to retire because she needed the salary to pay for a nursing attendant for her 87-year-old mother, who suffers from Alzheimer's. Ms. Mauro says she gets little help from her siblings. (Higgins, 2003, p. D1)

© Photodisc Green/Getty Images

Launching a career is a difficult task, especially for college students who are researching job opportunities, interviewing, and finishing coursework at the same time.

An examination of households with older Americans reveals profound diversity in their sources of wealth and financial abilities (Longino & Crown, 1991). The wealthiest elderly are most likely to be younger, working, and married, whereas the poorest are most likely to be nonwhite and female, often widows (Longino & Crown, 1991). If children are called on to help aging parents, there are a number of strategies to consider, including

◆ Buying something from parents (i.e., jewelry, real estate) or helping them to sell something such as a piece of property.

◆ Taking a tax deduction. If a person is paying more than half of a parent's support, they can claim the parent as a dependent on tax returns (see a tax consultant or accountant about this because rules change depending on parent's income).

◆ Keeping separate accounts. Have parents sign a power of attorney form that gives the child power to handle their finances if they become ill or incapacitated.

◆ Taking advantage of reverse mortgages, which allow homeowners age 62 and older to receive a loan against their home that is repaid with interest when the borrower sells the house, moves, or dies. This results in a smaller inheritance for children, which some retirees will resist. In all these strategies sensitivity has been used because, as the beginning of the chapter showed, control is very much an issue when it comes to financial management; and this is a lifelong concept. It is difficult for parents to give up financial control or to trust that their children know what is best; and as the previous quotation shows, siblings may not agree on what is best.

Convincing parents also takes patience. Stephen George Rozich of Laguna Niquel, Calif., says it took years to persuade his mother to do a reverse mortgage on her $80,000 Colorado home. . . . The one Mr. Rozich arranged for his mother paid her about $300 a month in extra cash and gave her a credit line of roughly $14,000. (Higgins, 2003, p. D2)

According to Virginia Junk, Laurie Stenberg, and Carol Anderson, "generally, the goal of financial planning for retirement is to provide enough income in retirement to prevent living standards from dropping significantly from pre-retirement levels" (1993, p. 6). Financial planning for retirement can begin at any age, but many individuals wait until they are in their 40s to become serious about it. Although people tend to think of retirement planning as being for themselves and their spouse, it can also involve providing for the financial needs of dependent aging parents. Individuals who provide or anticipate providing financial assistance to their parent or parents while also providing financial support to one or more children are known as the **sandwich generation** (Junk, Stenberg, & Anderson, 1993).

As mentioned earlier, types of investments include employer-sponsored retirement plans and IRAs. Before investing elsewhere, individuals should consider putting available funds into tax-sheltered plans to the maximum allowed. In so doing, income taxes will be reduced and wealth grows tax-free. For example:

◆ Most employers offer 401(k) or 403(b) plans. If $200 a month is put into a tax-sheltered account at 9 percent interest, the return is $73,327 in 15 years.

◆ If an employer does not offer such a plan, alternatives are to open an Individual Retirement Account, or a SEP or Keogh if self-employed. If $2,000 a year at 9 percent is invested in these types of accounts, the end result is $102,320 in 20 years.

Money can be automatically deducted from every paycheck toward a retirement plan, or monthly payments can be arranged from a bank account. As the examples show, the growth of a retirement fund depends on the amount invested, how often, and for how long. It also depends on how the fund is invested. More and more, individuals are having to make decisions about how their particular retirement fund is invested.

To determine retirement needs, financial planners or financial planning programs can run financial information through a computer. The information needed includes a person's age, salary, employer-sponsored retirement plans or IRAs, SEPs, or Keoghs, other investments, number of years employed, the percentage of salary being saved, projected retirement age, and the future income the person would like to have. Based on the analysis derived from this information, a person may choose to save more, change investments, or work longer. There are many variables, including the ups and downs in the economy and one's health, that will affect final retirement income; and calculations are at best estimates. The farther away from actual retirement, the less accurate the estimate. Nonetheless, retirement planning is a necessary part of overall financial planning. Part of retirement planning is estimating Social Security income, the subject to be discussed next.

Since the **Social Security Act** became law in 1935, Social Security has been one of the main sources of expected income for those reaching their retirement. Other sources of income include employer-sponsored retirement plans, savings and investments, and money from part-time jobs and IRAs, SEPs, and Keogh plans. As might be expected, the higher the income of the retiree, the lower his or her reliance on Social Security. Although Social Security was designed to be a supplement to the retired person's savings and pensions, for many it is the sole or main source of income. Figure 13.5 shows what age a person has to be to receive full Social Security. The earliest age to receive a partial benefit is age 62. Once a person begins receiving early benefits, the reduction is permanent in terms of the person's own benefit as well as those for spouses and children. This is especially important if a person's spouse is considerably younger and will depend on the benefits of the person who is retiring. What do most people do? *In recent years, almost 70 percent of retirees took Social Security before age 65* (Clements, 2003, April 23, p. D1). Women have a greater life expectancy, yet they are more likely than men to opt for early retirement.

> "I think they're making a mistake," says Henry Hebeler, author of "J. K. Lasser's Your Winning Retirement Plan" and founder of a Web site devoted to retirement issues (www.analyzenow.com). "When you talk to people who are in their 80s, they'd give anything to have a bigger Social Security check." (Clements, 2003, April 23, p. D1)

To find out how your Social Security is adding up go to **www.ssa.gov,** visit the Social Security Office locally, or call (800) 772-1213. The Web site also provides a calculator to estimate potential benefits, given different retirement ages.

People become eligible for a reduced level of Social Security retirement benefits at age 62. In certain cases, Social Security benefits can begin earlier for disabled employees and survivors. So, an important decision people in their 60s must make is whether to retire early at 62 or keep working until the full benefit kicks in. Affecting this decision is **Medicare,** the United States' basic health insurance program for people 65 or older. Medicare has two main parts: hospital insurance and medical insurance, which helps pay for doctor visits and home health visits. In the United States the Social Security and Medicare pro-

SUGGESTED ACTIVITY

See Figure 13.5 and look up at what age you can retire for a full Social Security benefit. In the total class or in groups discuss the fairness of the sliding scale. Also discuss the pros and cons of retiring with partial benefits at age 62.

Year of Birth	Full Retirement Age
1937 or earlier	65
1938	65 and 2 months
1939	65 and 4 months
1940	65 and 6 months
1941	65 and 8 months
1942	65 and 10 months
1943–1954	66
1955	66 and 2 months
1956	66 and 4 months
1957	66 and 6 months
1958	66 and 8 months
1959	66 and 10 months
1960 and later	67

FIGURE 13.5
Full Retirement Ages for Social Security

grams are closely linked, but each has its own rules. People who retire at 62 will have to get health insurance on their own; this is commonly referred to as Medigap insurance—filling the gap until age 65 when Medicare starts. In some cases, a former employer will extend health insurance until age 65 or offer it as a reduced rate to encourage employees to retire early. Since the average life expectancy is 72 for a man and 79 for a woman, retirees have to prepare for many years in retirement. As education goes up, life expectancy goes up.

The Gender Gap and the Glass Ceiling

In the 1970s, when the concept of the **gender gap** (the difference in earnings between men and women employed full-time outside the home) first attracted attention, women earned approximately 60 percent of what men earned. By 2003, the gender gap had narrowed, and women were earning 76 percent of what men earned. The gender gap is closing. Researchers predict that it will be completely closed by the year 2010. The gender gap varies by industry. And there is less of a gap between younger men and women than there is for older generations. According to the U.S. General Accounting Office, it actually widened between 1985 and 2000 for male and female managers in the entertainment industry. In 1985, females earned 83 cents to every male's $1.00, and in 2000 females earned 62 cents compared to every male's $1.00.

As women move up the corporate or government ladder, they often hit an invisible barrier that stops them from moving further. They can see the positions at the top that they want, but they cannot reach them. This phenomenon is known as the **glass ceiling.** Studies are being conducted to determine why gender barriers exist and where they tend to be found. Generally, it is assumed that women want to move ahead and that corporations and other employers, for a variety of reasons, have imposed barriers impeding their advance. However, the glass ceiling may be caused by more than the barriers imposed by employers. One study found that the barriers might be at least partially imposed by the women themselves in that they have lower salary expectations even before they enter the job market.

Researchers found that parents, especially fathers, have a strong positive impact on their daughters' career expectations (Hoffman, Goldsmith, &

Hofacker, 1992). Other studies indicate that schools may not provide as many opportunities for success for girls as they do for boys. Thus, supportive families and schools are important to the goal setting and potential career success of women students. Because the gender gap is closing and the glass ceiling appears to be shattering (i.e., more women are moving up and commanding higher salaries), women's employment issues are rapidly changing. More studies will clarify the values, attitudes, and behaviors involved with these issues.

Wealth and Poverty

Wealth is the state of being rich and having a high net worth. The way to wealth is to be debt-free by practicing frugality and owning assets such as houses, cars, and investments outright. Examples of frugality include going without extras, living in a less expensive house than one can afford, and driving a less expensive car. In short, the way to becoming wealthy is to live as if you are not wealthy, according to Thomas Standley and William Danko, authors of *The Millionaire Next Door*. Their research on millionaires revealed a more modest lifestyle than one would expect. They found that wealth takes sacrifice, discipline, and hard work. Many of the wealthy are in what may be considered unglamorous enterprises such as wall-board manufacturing, and they drive modest family-style vehicles. They are usually married with children and own stocks, bonds, and real estate, and have other financial assets. The authors' main point is that to be wealthy means living within one's means, choosing an occupation well, being satisfied, and building net worth.

Most people, of course, are not wealthy, and they are not living debt-free. The average American family has credit card debt estimated at $9,000. As Chapter 8 explained, *poverty* is the state of being poor and lacking adequate means to provide for basic material needs and comforts. The United Nations Department of Public Information keeps statistics on the world's poor people. The greatest concentration is in only 10 countries: Bangladesh, Brazil, central and western China, Ethiopia, India, Indonesia, Nigeria, Pakistan, the Philippines, and Vietnam. According to the World Bank more than a billion people still live on less than a $1 a day, and the majority are women and children residing in rural areas. Although the U.S. economy is growing, poverty is still widespread, especially in rural counties where the economic engine has broken down, in areas on the Texas-Mexico border, Appalachia, and the deep South. Poverty is a serious problem because poverty in childhood can have lifelong repercussions:

> Poverty is the roadblock to educational progress of many disadvantaged youth. . . . Poor teenagers are four times more likely than nonpoor teens to have below average basic academic skills. More than half of the 15- to 18-year-olds from families with incomes below poverty had reading and math skills that placed them in the bottom 20 percent of all teens. (Leidenfrost, 1993, p. 5)

Poverty can be either a temporary or a chronic state of living. If people are unemployed for a few months, they will experience a temporary decline in income, but if they have saved for a rainy day, their lifestyle will not be severely affected immediately. Likewise, college students may live at or below the poverty level, but this is a temporary state that will be remedied when they get their first full-time job. The mind-set of a person who is experiencing temporary poverty is different from that of a person or family immersed in permanent poverty.

Because the study of management focuses on control and planning, educators and family facilitators need to be sensitized to the fact that not everyone has equal access to resources or the equal ability to use them. According to Rettig, Rossman, and Hogan (1992),

> People who are poor must devote their financial resources to meet basic needs. They have minimal freedom to allocate money, time, or human energy for other than immediate uses and have little to give toward planning for future needs. Families and individuals with lower levels of living have less freedom to decide, little control over resource access, fewer opportunities for human resource development, and their use of material resources is significantly diminished. Families can be "poor," not only in material resources, but also in human resources of imagination, initiative, self-discipline, and the ability to seek alternatives. (p. 35)

Most people in the United States fall into the middle class and derive their income largely from earnings—that is, wages or salaries from occupations. Wealthier people generally derive a considerable proportion of their income from investments; the higher the income, the higher the portion from investments tends to be. So wealth is not the same as income. A person who earns a great deal of money but spends it all each year is not wealthy; he or she is just living high, according to Standley and Danko. From a management standpoint, the goals of a middle-class family may be to educate the children and have a secure lifestyle rather than to accumulate vast wealth. The very wealthy, who have an abundance of money, property, and investments, spend a great deal of time trying to retain their fortunes so that they can pass on their money to their descendants. With the exception of highly successful athletes, business tycoons, entrepreneurs, and actors, most of the very wealthy have acquired their fortunes over a long period of time or through inheritances.

Financial Advice

Controlling personal or family finances need not be done in isolation, and each case is different. This chapter has provided basic information on the economy and financial management. Although the terms do not change rapidly, the figures and policies are subject to change due to inflation and such things as tax codes and federal college loan programs. Individuals and families have to stay alert and find the latest sources of information. An avalanche of material is available to help investors track the status of their funds. Some information may come regularly through the mail, such as bank statements, stockbroker reports, mutual fund statements, IRA updates, and credit card statements. Additional free information on financial management is available from banks, the Internet, and the federal government. Financial advice for a price is also readily available through magazines, newspapers, and in-person services. According to a study by the Roper organization, when U.S. residents want financial advice, they are most likely to turn to friends and relatives, then to their bank officer, lawyer and accountant, financial planner, real estate broker, and stockbroker.

During the last 30 years there has been a gradual change away from face-to-face consumer and adviser interaction toward more technology-based information exchange. A study by Jinkook Lee (2002) found that phone, mail, and computer technology are all used. Depending on the demographic and on the product and service, there were different consumer preferences. For example, face-to-face interaction was preferred when obtaining mortgages but it was far less important when obtaining credit cards. Younger, more educated, and more affluent consumers were most open to direct means and less demanding of face-to-face interactions.

Before investing in the services of a financial planner or other finance professional, a potential customer should check credentials and see whether any complaints are on file with the Better Business Bureau or the state Office of Consumer Affairs. Under the National Securities Markets Improvement Act of 1996, the Securities and Exchange Commission regulates financial advisers managing more than $25 million in assets. With recent corporate scandals and other exposés of financial mismanagement in the mutual fund industry, closer scrutiny of investment management and advisers is in place. However, given the wide range of services offered, it is difficult for any government agency to keep on top of fraud and quasi-legal doings. With over 500,000 people in the United States calling themselves financial planners, this is difficult to do on a consistent basis. The skills of those who call themselves financial planners vary from nonexistent to very highly skilled. Buyers should beware. One of the best guides is to find out the planner's credentials, and the best-known credential is designation as a Certified Financial Planner (CFP). A person with a CFP has passed rigorous examinations and been approved by the International Board of Standards and Practices for Certified Financial Planners. Financial planners may be fee-only (so much per hour to set up a budget, develop financial plans, or give advice), commission-only, or a combination of fee and commission-based. The best choice depends on consumers' needs and circumstances, such as whether they want a long-term relationship or a one-shot consultation.

Web-Based Resources

There are innumerable company and government Web sites with a financial focus. For credit card rate comparisons, try **www.lendingtree.com** or **www.bankrate.com.** A comprehensive site offering up-to-date stock quotes and financial news is available from Yahoo Finance at **http://finance.yahoo.com.** Another comprehensive site is the FinanCenter's at **financenter.com,** a source for questions and answers and calculations regarding budgets, credit, savings, and purchasing automobiles, houses, and investments.

For more information about stocks and other forms of investing click on **www.Fool.com, www.better-investing.org, www.quicken.com/planning/ basics, www.berkshirehathaway.com,** and **www.morningstar.com.** All major banks, credit card companies, investment firms, and insurance companies have Web sites. Many offer financial planning work sheets and advice based on the information the site user provides. Computer software to assist with financial calculations and tax preparation can also be purchased over the Internet or at stores. General search engines and Internet providers such as Google, Yahoo!, AOL, and MSN will get consumers to all the finance information they could possibly want.

For world statistics on economic well-being and poverty, search the United Nations Web sites such as **www.undp.org** and the United Nations Children's Fund at **www.unicef.org.** Current U.S. national economic and job trend statistics are available from **www.stats.bls.gov.**

The following addresses offer a sampling of types of Web sites related to searching for jobs on the Internet. As is the case for all Web sites in this book, the author does not take responsibility for the information contained therein or any address changes. For current job openings, check

- Monster Board at **www.Monster.com** (general site popular with college students)
- America's Job Bank: **www.ajb.dni.us** (mostly full-time listings)

◆ CareerPath: **www.careerpath.com** (newspaper employment advertisements)

◆ CareerSite: **www.careersite.com** (comprehensive services for job seekers and employers)

Summary

Self-control and knowledge are keys to successful financial management, which is a transformation process involving three phases: planning, action, and postplanning. Handling money is one of the most common management skills, but also one of the most difficult. Setting up a budget and determining net worth are two ways to get an idea of a person's financial status.

The goal of financial management is to maximize net worth and satisfaction. Values and goals influence the way finances are managed, and a gap exists between values (ideals) and actual behavior. Savings and investments are important aspects of financial management. Saving for children's college education is an example of a long-range goal of many families. Not everyone has the luxury of planning for the future, however; low-income families must devote their financial resources to meeting basic daily needs. The typical family in the United States spends about one-third of its income on taxes, followed by housing and household expenses and transportation. Credit card debt is rising. Many families, especially those with children, struggle to stay ahead.

Individuals and families operate within the greater economy of the nation. Consequently, individuals need to understand how recovery, recession, expansion, inflation, and mortgage rates affect them. The last chapter of this book looks to the future by focusing on projected changes in demographics, the economy, the environment, and technology.

Key Terms

Annual Percentage Rate (APR)
assets
budget
Consumer Price
   Index (CPI)
credit
credit bureaus
discretionary income
disposable income
diversification
emergency fund
Equal Credit
   Opportunity Act
Fair Credit Reporting
   Act
FICO score
financial management
gender gap

glass ceiling
gross domestic
   product (GDP)
gross income
income
income tax
inflation
insurance
investment
level of living
liabilities
liquidity
long-term-care
   insurance
Medicare
net worth

psychic income
real income
recession
sandwich generation
Social Security Act
standard of living
taxes
wealth

Review Questions

1. What is a FICO score? What is the range, and what is a good one? How does a FICO score affect a person's future financial decisions?

2. Authors Standley and Danko say that to be wealthy means living within one's means and choosing an occupation well. What do you think of this advice?

3. What percentage of income do Americans generally save? How does the American savings rate compare to the savings rates of other nations?

4. Why do nearly 70 percent of retirees take Social Security before age 65? What are the pros and cons of this decision?

5. Why do you think more people turn first to friends and relatives for financial advice, then to professional financial advisers such as bankers, lawyers, and accountants?

References

Adler, J. (1992, January 13). Down in the dumps. *Newsweek*, 24.

Carlson, L., Grossbart, S., & Stuenkel, J. (1992). The role of parental socialization types on differential family communication patterns regarding consumption. *Journal of Consumer Psychology, 1*(2), 31–52.

Clements, J. (2003, April 23). Why it pays to delay: Too many retirees start collecting Social Security early. *The Wall Street Journal*, D1.

Clements, J. (2003, October 8). Why the rising market is a bummer: Practically everything's overpriced. *The Wall Street Journal*, D1.

Farrell, C., Palmer, A., & Browder, S. (1998, August 31). A rising tide. *Business Week*, 75.

Higgins, M. (2003, April 23). How to shield your wallet from your parents' woes. *The Wall Street Journal*, D1–D2.

Hoffman, J., Goldsmith, E., & Hofacker, C. (1992). The influence of parents on female business students' salary and work hour expectations. *Journal of Employment Counseling, 29*(1), 79–83.

Junk, V., Stenberg, L., & Anderson, C. (1993, Spring). Retirement planning for the sandwich generation. *Journal of Home Economics*, 4–11.

Lee, J. (2002). A key to marketing financial services: The right mix of products, services, channels and customers. *Journal of Services Marketing, 16*(3), 238–256.

Leidenfrost, N. (1993, Fall). Poverty in the United States: Characteristics and theories. *Journal of Home Economics*, 3–10.

Longino, C., & Crown, W. (1991, August). Older Americans: Rich or poor? *American Demographics*, 48–52.

Markovich, C., & DeVaney, S. (1997). College seniors' personal finance knowledge and practice. *Journal of Family and Consumer Sciences*, 61–65.

O'Neill, B., & Brennan, P. (1997, Summer). Financial planning education throughout the life cycle. *Journal of Family and Consumer Sciences*, 32–36.

Orman, S. (2003). *The laws of money, the lessons of life*. New York: Free Press.

Rettig, K., Rossman, M., & Hogan, J. (1992). Educating for family resource management. In M. Arcus, J. Schvaneveldt, & J. Moss (Eds.), *Handbook of family life education*, Vol. 2. Beverly Hills, CA: Sage.

Sebastian, P. (1999, March 25). Briefs. *The Wall Street Journal*, A1.

Silverman, R. (2003, July 16). Why you waste so much money. *The Wall Street Journal*, D1.

Standley, T., and Danko, W. (1998). *The millionaire next door*. New York: Pocket Books.

Who's hurting the most. (2003, April 15). *Family Circle*, 65.

Wuorio, J. (2003, May 17). Raising your quarter-million baby. MSN Money. Retrieved from http:moneycentral.msn.com/content/CollegeandFamily/Raisekids.

Xiao, J., Noring, F., & Anderson, J. (1995). College students' attitudes towards credit cards. *Journal of Consumer Studies and Home Economics, 19*, 155–174.

part **4**

Future Challenges

CHAPTER 14
LOOKING AHEAD

Looking Ahead

MAIN TOPICS

TECHNOLOGY

COMPUTERS, HOME AUTOMATION, AND OTHER HOME
   INNOVATIONS
ADOPTING INNOVATIONS AND APPLYING TECHNOLOGY
INFORMATION AND INNOVATION OVERLOAD

FAMILY AND GLOBAL CHANGE

QUALITY OF LIFE AND WELL-BEING
MULTICULTURALISM
ENVIRONMENT AND CONSUMPTION
THE FOOD SUPPLY

Did you know that . . . ?

. . . A manned mission to Mars is predicted for 2030.

. . . Newly constructed single-family homes have increased 39 percent
in size in 20 years.

> The only limit to our realization of tomorrow will be our doubts of today.
>
> —*President Franklin Roosevelt*

I

T IS EXQUISITELY human to search for wholeness and richness of experience," says E. O. Wilson, professor at Harvard University. This search for wholeness includes wondering what the future will bring, but speculating about the future is not without its risks. In his 1899 novel *When the Sleeper Wakes,* H. G. Wells predicted color television and supersonic aircraft, but he made the less-than-successful prediction that hypnotism would replace conventional anesthetics in medicine. Likewise, Jules Verne, in *Twenty Thousand Leagues under the Sea,* published in 1870, was visionary regarding the development of submarines, but missed on his prediction that automated baby-feeding machines would take care of the rising world population.

In the 21st century we should experience

- ◆ More **transparency**, meaning openness in revealing information about the operations of companies, organizations, institutions, and governments.
- ◆ More men and women over the age of 55 working in managerial, professional, or other white-collar jobs. And more of them owning and visiting second homes (Francese, 2004).
- ◆ The development of smaller, faster, and cheaper computers.

- An increased understanding of the human genetic code.
- Further space exploration, including putting humans on Mars.
- Accelerated medical advances, such as help for people with spinal cord injuries and multiple sclerosis, and many new ways to treat and prevent disease.
- More emphasis in higher education on providing experiences that develop students' knowledge of leadership and the ability to demonstrate leadership skills in their scholarly, campus, career, and worldwide communities.

Regarding everyday life, we will continue to see advances in food, apparel, transportation, and housing. New institutions will emerge. The family will endure as it always has, but its form will continue to alter. Individuals and families will engage in more management activities than ever before, because the increasingly complex world in which they live will offer them so many choices. Other predictions include

- More personalized electronics
- More efficient and affordable multi-fuel automobiles (we already have dual-fuel stoves with gas on top, electric in the oven)
- Electronic cards with all financial information stored on them, replacing the need for keys, money, driver's license, and medical records
- Home health monitors (the Japanese have already invented toilets that take readings of urine content and send the readings indicating illness directly to the family's doctor)
- Smart sensors in homes, in schools, in bridges, and in harbors—detecting problems
- More leasing of things besides autos and homes, such as appliances and recreational vehicles and boats (already under way, but to increase)
- Further understanding of weight control and aging with new cures and remedies
- Increased food supply

This chapter builds on the concepts introduced earlier—values, decision making, goals, and resources. These four concepts work together to form the basis of a holistic construct called managerial judgment. **Managerial judgment,** defined as the ability to accept change for the betterment of self and humankind, is this chapter's theme. Individuals, families, communities, and countries are encouraged to think about what may happen so they can prepare themselves and make smarter choices. *The ultimate goal of the manager today is the creation of a better tomorrow,* but this is not an easy task. As Brian Twiss, the author of *Innovation,* says,

> If we are no longer sure of what the future will hold, it becomes difficult to manage any activity oriented towards the future. For we are now concerned with two dimensions of uncertainty—that of the innovation itself, and of the environment into which it will be launched at some future date. We can, however, detect a number of trends likely to play an important role in shaping the future. Some are already with us. Others are only just emerging. (1980, p. viii)

As explained throughout this book, management takes a proactive approach, meaning that through reasoning and decision making changes can be implemented. It has been suggested that the greatest future challenge for the field of resource management will be the continued integration of management with other theories to address socially relevant issues (Key & Firebaugh, 1989).

Management needs more **leaders** (experts, authorities, facilitators, and guides) who participate in community action programs, families, and as contributors to scientific, social, or economic advances and in so doing improve human lives. "Leadership is not about personality; it's about practice" (Kouzes & Posner, 2002, p. 13). It involves making a difference for the public good in an active, purposeful, diverse, team-oriented, broad-based, and ethical way. Leaders in the newest sense operate in a connective way. They bring resources together and get information flowing, rather than operate in a hierarchical fashion (top-down management).

This chapter begins with a discussion of technological trends and then turns to the challenge of managing information and innovation overload. It concludes with an examination of possible changes in family life and the global community, with an emphasis on demographic shifts and environmentalism.

NASA/JPL/Cornell/Ames/Maas Digital LLC

This three-dimensional model superimposes the Mars Exploration Rover Opportunity on one of its potential targets, a scientific treasure chest of Martian rocks contained within the landing site, a crater on Meridiani Planum, Mars. The rover is placed on the rock outcrop for scale.

TECHNOLOGY

Robert Tucker, author of *Managing the Future* (1992), says that in the future managing will mean identifying technological, social, cultural, economic, demographic, lifestyle, regulatory, and global trends and fluctuations to determine patterns of change. After identifying the patterns, the next step is to ride the forces of change in the direction in which they are headed. Effective managers, whether in the home or the office, are aware of changes and exploit them rather than waiting to react to them.

Technology is the application of the scientific method and materials to achieve objectives; another definition is knowledge systematically applied to useful purposes. Drucker says:

> Technology is not nature, but man. It is not about tools; it is about how man thinks . . . but precisely because technology is an extension of man, basic technological change always both expresses our world view, and, in turn, changes it. (1989, p. 261)

In their book, *Innovation Explosion*, Quinn, Baruch, and Zien (1997) provide several terms and definitions useful in a discussion of technology:

- ◆ **Invention** or **discovery** involves the initial observation of a new phenomenon (discovery) or provides the initial verification that a problem can be solved (invention).

- ◆ **Innovation** consists of the social and managerial processes through which solutions are first translated into social use in a given culture. "Technological innovation involves a novel combination of art, science, or craft employed to create the goods or services used by society" (p. 3).

- ◆ "**Diffusion** spreads approved innovations more broadly within an enterprise or society" (p. 3).

- ◆ **System understanding,** basically "know-how," involves understanding the interrelationship and rates of influences among key variables. "Some people may possess advanced skills but lack system understanding. They can perform selected tasks well but do not fully understand how their actions affect other elements of the organization or how to improve the total entity's effectiveness" (p. 2).

- ◆ **Intellect** means knowing or understanding, the capacity to create knowledge, the capability for rational or highly developed use of intelligence. "It includes (1) cognitive knowledge (or know what), (2) advanced skills, (3) system understanding, (4) motivated creativity, discovery or invention, and (5) intuition and synthesis" (perception and the ability to put information together), and the capacity to understand or predict relationships (p. 3).

In the last century, no problem seemed too big to conquer—home, social causes, land, space, and communications were all the subjects of technological scrutiny and the beneficiaries of invention and policy changes. Certainly, life was poorer and harder before the arrival of many of the technological innovations of the 20th century. Consider the state of the American home before 1940. Most of the U.S. population still lived on farms, less than one-third of the homes had lights, and only one-tenth had a flush toilet.

The trend currently is toward larger homes with sophisticated electronics. According to the U.S. Census Bureau, newly constructed single-family homes had a median size of 2,114 square feet in 2002, whereas in 1982 the median size was 1,520 square feet. This represents a 39 percent increase in 20 years.

Computers, Home Automation, and Other Home Innovations

Given that people's housing needs change and that products try to keep pace, what can be predicted for tomorrow's homes? According to Jupiter Media Matrix, Inc., the following telecom services grew from 2000 to 2005:

◆ Mobile phones from 109.9 million users to 183.9 million users

◆ Personal digital assistants from 7.1 million users to 17 million users

◆ Broadband (at home) from 9.6 million users to 59 million users

◆ Dial-up Internet connections (at home) from 83.9 million users to 103.5 million users

The following time line shows some key years in the progression of computer innovations impacting households:

◆ 1977   Apple II is introduced.

◆ 1981   IBM PC (personal computer) is introduced.

◆ 1984   Apple Macintosh popularizes the mouse and graphical applications.

◆ 1994   The World Wide Web emerges.

◆ 1995   Computer enthusiast Pierre Omidyar creates world's first Interactive Auction Web site, Auction Web, from his bedroom in Silicon Valley, California. This is the forerunner to eBay.

◆ 1996   Auction Web evolved into a registered commercial organization named eBay.

◆ 1997   Widespread use of e-mail for communication grows.

◆ 2000   Worries about the millennium bug proved unfounded.

◆ 2003   eBay becomes the most popular commercial Internet Web site in the world.

◆ 2004 to   Internet access continues to spread globally.
  the present

The growth of eBay is noted because it says a lot about the type of purchasing consumers want to do, how and when they want to do it, and their valuing of old, used, and recycled goods as well as the new things like cars and overstocked items that are also sold on eBay. Traditional retailers with physical stores are concerned that consumers are showing they do not always want the latest styles or that they enjoy competitive bidding, which is not the way conventional retailing works. Technological advances have shaken up many conventionally held notions of doing things or of what the public wants.

Another phenomenon to note is that children under the age of one are using computers (sitting on their parents' laps). Whereas current college students often remember the first in-home computer their family got or the first computer games they played, future college students will not remember a time when computers were not part of their daily existence. Today, more college students are taking online classes and participating in on-campus courses that integrate Internet-based learning with conventional classroom lectures. This next statement is extreme, but it is worth thinking about. Peter Drucker says that "long-distance learning, for instance, may well make obsolete within twenty-five years that uniquely American institution, the free-standing undergraduate college" (1999, p. 101).

Regarding home products with microprocessors, there will be more handheld devices for various functions beyond the handheld devices for televisions, radios, and VCRs already commonplace. Because handheld devices are easily mislaid and clutter up homes, the trend will be to consolidate devices and functions into multipurpose devices or central controllers. These are already available, but the push will be on to make them more efficient and affordable. Many of the current models are difficult to program. Custom installation of high-end televisions, ranges and other kitchen appliances, and other devices is a growing industry. Today, an average *U.S. home has five to seven remotes piled on the coffee table compared to fewer than three in 2000* (McLaughlin, 2002). Universal controller remotes are available for the TV, VCR, DVD, cable box, audio receiver, CD player, digital video recorder, home theater, laser disc player, satellite receiver, curtains, blinds, and lights.

> For Walt and Judy Dennis, the lazy days of summer have already arrived. The Columbus, Ohio couple doesn't have to check on the laundry. A machine does. The wine chiller in their attic nags them, via e-mail, when a bottle is getting old. And with the push of a button, they can pipe music from any CD into any room. Mrs. Dennis even uses a remote-control pad to prepare meals. "I can almost cook a whole dinner," she says. (Fletcher, 2001, p. W1)

The most common argument for home automation is its ability to support cross-product features such as whole-house scheduling. For example, someone returning home late at night can program the lights and the heat to go on at a certain hour.

Temperature controls will be particularly sophisticated. Houses can be divided into temperature zones that can be individually programmed to deliver heating and cooling during the times of day when the zones are used. Homeowners set the temperatures for the zones using touch-screen computers or hand-held voice controls that are linked to a central computer and to sensors in each zone. Temperatures will be held within a smaller range than with the old-fashioned thermostats, which conventionally allowed temperatures to vary within a six-degree range.

The most effective home automation systems will support both central and distributed control and communication standards. An example is the Smart House System, a project initiated by the National Association of Home Builders through its wholly owned subsidiary, the NAHB Research Center (see Figure 14.1). In a Smart House, energy and data communications are brought together in a single system to centrally manage the most important lifestyle aspects in a home, such as security, energy management, entertainment, communications, and lighting and convenience features. Another example is Mealtime, an experimental project supported by many major appliance manufacturers and retailers, which is test-marketing remote-controlled appliances: In the morning, a family member could start a meal in a range, for example, that goes from a refrigerator function to a range function over the course of the day. A casserole could be refrigerated until the timer says to begin cooking at 4 P.M. so that when the family gathers at home at 6:00 the casserole is cooked and ready in the same appliance. If the family is late, the appliance will return to the refrigerating function and hold the casserole until the family is

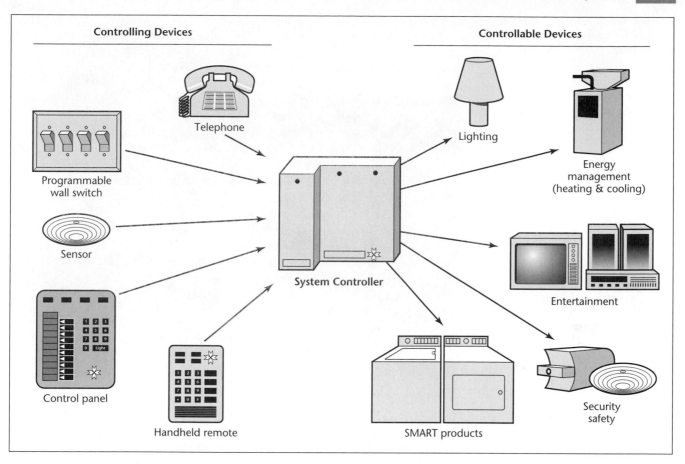

Controlling Devices

Telephone

Programmable
wall switch

Sensor

Control panel

Handheld remote

System Controller

Controllable Devices

Lighting

Energy
management
(heating & cooling)

Entertainment

SMART products

Security
safety

FIGURE 14.1
The SMART HOUSE ® System
*In the SMART HOUSE System,
energy and data communications are
brought together in a centrally
controlled system.*

From The Smart House System, copyright © Smart
House, Inc. Reprinted by permission of Smart
House, Inc.

ready. In 2004, 20 families in the Boston area tested the new appliances in
their homes to see how the new systems worked—the main ideas are to save
time, build in more family support, and provide better nutrition. The household would still have a conventional refrigerator/freezer albeit with more functions than usual and would also have this multifeature range allowing for new
ways of cooking and timing meals.

Other appliances, televisions, telephones, and computers will continue to
get smarter. The distinction between appliances, home-based entertainment,
and computers will continue to blur. Challenges that the electronics industry
face are how to keep products simple enough to operate and how to provide
repairs.

These developments in home automation are linked to consumers, who
have to decide which innovations to adopt and which to turn down.
Consumers will also have to shop around for the best prices and decide how
to install a system. They may have to adapt their schedules to incorporate the
technology, especially in the initial phases.

This section has focused on home automation, but automation is already
all around us in stores, workplaces, and financial institutions. Printers, copy
machines, and fax machines have revolutionized the kind of work that can be
done at home, and this trend will continue. Wireless connections have made it

Computers and new appliances are revolutionizing how meals are timed and prepared.

Copyright © 2004 Stanley Rowin

easier not to be tied to a desk. The trend toward shopping, working, and conducting business at home raises several questions. One of them is how to remember all the passwords and codes. In the future, there will be one code for everything, making it far easier than it is presently. Researchers continue to study how working at home affects family relations and time management; they are concerned that as people stay at home more, they will feel isolated. As an earlier chapter indicated, human contact is desirable. People seek out others and want face-to-face contact. For example, when televisions, video-cassette recorders, and in-home movies became available, movie producers and theater owners worried that consumers would not go to the movies as much. On the contrary, movie attendance is still strong, reflecting people's desire to get out of the house and their willingness to pay to see a movie with strangers sitting next to them. Major sporting events sell out even though they can be watched for free on television.

In the home, other developments include the more efficient use of energy. For example, better insulation materials will create a thermal shell so tightly closed that buildings can be heated and cooled with a smaller-capacity pump. Insulated ducts and improved insulation for windows will reduce air leakage by as much as 50 percent. The supply of electricity will also be more efficient due to advances in superconductivity or the conducting of electricity with almost no power loss. Electricity will also be conserved by the use of compact fluorescent lights and E-lamps that will last far longer than present models.

All in all, tomorrow's homes will be more energy-efficient, adaptable, affordable, and supportive of individuals' and families' lifestyles. The race is on between companies to be the top suppliers of the new home systems and products.

Adopting Innovations and Applying Technology

As previously stated, individuals and families will have to decide whether to ignore or adopt the new technologies. Persons considering a new technology or product will first become aware that it is available; then they will search for information, evaluate the information, and perhaps try out the product (e.g., test-driving a new car, trying out a computer in a store) to decide whether they like it or not. Once consumers decide to adopt a new product, they move into the application phase, when they actually use the product. Even when consumers adopt a new technology, however, they do not necessarily use it to the fullest extent possible. For example, even though modern kitchens are more technologically advanced than ever before and meal preparation is easier, more meals are eaten out today than previously.

Researchers of consumer behavior have found that the adoption of innovations follows a bell-shaped curve, with some consumers being innovators, wanting the latest thing first, versus those at the other end of the curve, where consumers are laggards, being the last to want something new (Rogers, 1995). Most people fall in the middle of the curve, as members of the early adopters or early or late majority groups, depending on their willingness to adopt new technologies. They are interested in new products, but are wary of things that are brand new. They will wait for the product to be tested and proved worthwhile. They may also wait for the price to drop. It is common for a person to be an innovator in one area such as fashion and a laggard in another such as the latest music.

A further comment to make is that not everyone can be an innovator even if they want to be because the latest thing may not be available or not everyone can afford the latest thing. According to William Gibson, science fiction writer, "The future is already here—it's just unevenly distributed." For example, broadband Internet access first took off in South Korea, then Canada, and then the United States. *There is often plenty of demand; the problem lies in supply* ("Broadway Blues," 2001). Also, computer adoption depends on having high levels of education in the labor force.

> In general, rich countries are on the technology frontier and rely on research and development to achieve further improvements in technical efficiency. Low-income countries, in contrast, have the option of adopting technologies already developed elsewhere. Yet not much is known about the process by which new technologies spread from one country to the others. (Watson, 2001, p. 1)

Government, industry, universities, and individual inventors contribute to the development of technology. Novel approaches to problem solving are necessary. Increasing observational skills is one direction this is taking. A **paradigm shift** refers to a situation where an individual or a team tackles a problem with radically innovative solutions rather than taking a gradual step-by-step approach. As the pace of change accelerates, more paradigm shifts will be needed.

Accompanying these rapid advances in technology is a counterbalancing concern for the quality of the environment. As described in Chapter 12, a growing concept in global industry is clean technologies, including processes and products that preserve the environment and do not pollute. Several countries, most notably Japan, the United States, Australia, Canada, and many European countries, have given priority to their development. Advertisements and company literature reflect consumers' desire for a quality environment. A publication from Maytag says, "as we move into the future, terms like 'a green marketplace,' 'consumer,' 'high efficiency appliances,' and 'energy standards' more and more are a part of our everyday vocabulary" (*Consumer Connection,* 1994, p. 3).

Information and Innovation Overload

"Humanity is the species forced by its basic nature to make moral choices and seek fulfillment in a changing world by any means it devises" (Wilson, 2002, p. xxii). As consumers attempt to master the new technology, they must cope with a host of new data, moral dilemmas, and information. Data and information are not necessarily the same as wisdom and knowledge, as Kate Mullen of Harvard University explains:

> Data becomes information when it is crunched—systematically manipulated. Information, when conceptualized and "contextualized," leads to knowledge. Wisdom is the intelligence application of knowledge. Wisdom and knowledge are not the province of inanimate things—yet. (Mullen, 1994, p. 16)

Mullen diagrams the relationships among these concepts as:

$$\text{Data} \rightarrow \text{information} \rightarrow \text{knowledge} \rightarrow \text{wisdom}$$

When consumers are bombarded with too much data and information, they may not be able to process all of it or use it to acquire wisdom. In other words, as described in Chapter 7, they could experience overload.

The information superhighway that is envisioned for the near future may contribute to information overload. Among other things, the information superhighway is expected to include as many as 500 television channels. But how many television channels can an individual successfully handle? Furthermore, will this variety lead to more creative programming? Or will the slots be given over to endless rebroadcasts of a handful of movies and TV shows? Will more retailers use the television to demonstrate and sell their products, increasing consumer confusion?

Rapid advances in technology are also leading to **innovation overload,** which is the "user's response to the ever increasing pace of information, knowledge, and innovations that are appearing on this earth" (Herbig, Milewicz, & Golden, 1993). An article in *Business Week* described the problems inherent in introducing too many innovations too rapidly:

> Otherwise highly competent men and women are driven to helpless frustration by the products around them. . . . New systems that were supposed to make work more efficient—computers, fax, electronic mail—often do the reverse. . . . Stress levels soar with VCRs, CDs, message machines, electronic thermostats, keypad burglar alarms, digital clocks, microwaves, programmable portable cellular phones for both the home and car, home computers. Their lives have become a nightmarish world of blinks and beeps. Too many companies wind up selling complex, overloaded gadgets that consumers can't figure out. (Nussbaum, 1991, p. 58)

According to Herbig, Milewicz, and Golden (1993), new products are being introduced at a numbing pace. During a single six-month period, Sony introduced more than a hundred new audio, tape, and video products in Britain alone, and Apple Corporation introduces one new product on average each week. Innovation overload refers not only to technological advances, but also to any innovations—whether they involve social services (e.g., new child-care providers), other services (e.g., new plumbers), or products (e.g., new books). Herbig, Milewicz, and Golden write that

> One of the major reasons behind innovation overload and its negative effect upon adoption of many innovations is the risk factor. The degree of perceived risk is highly negatively related to the rate of diffusion. Risk is recognized as having a considerable influence on the purchase decision especially in the area of new products. (1993, p. 202)

Accordingly, one of the ways to reduce innovation overload is to reduce the amount of risk the individual perceives. As noted earlier in this text, information is one way to reduce a person's perception of risk. The more one knows about a product or service, the less risk is involved. Another way to reduce overload is to accept that the phenomenon exists. Consumers need to decide how much overload they can successfully handle and adopt new products at a pace that feels comfortable to them. Why go to five different coffeehouses if the one near your house feels comfortable and familiar to you? Extensions and innovations should provide clear-cut benefits to consumers. Before adopting an innovation, potential consumers should ask themselves, "Will this product or service make my life better?"

FAMILY AND GLOBAL CHANGE

One might wonder what will happen to individuals and families in the midst of all these changes. What does the future hold for families? The good news is that people are living longer and healthier lives. Chapter 8, on managing human resources, gave many statistics along these lines. To review, the world population is over 6 billion, and the greatest concentration of people is in Asia. China is the most populous country, followed by India and the United States. Mumbai (Bombay) is the largest city in the world. Most of the world's population resides in cities (straining natural resources such as clean air and water), and the trend is toward increased urbanization. In the United States, families are smaller, yet there are more households and more single-parent families. In Sweden, nearly 40 percent of households are occupied by single persons. Roper opinion polls in the United States indicate that

> Despite overwhelmingly pessimistic rhetoric pointing to the erosion of family values, the evidence suggests the future vitality of the American family. Partly this is due to simple demographics. The fact that the baby boom generation is in its family-forming and child-raising years has moved family life into the national foreground. The nature of the modern family, however, is irrevocably different from the "traditional" family. First, most families will have both parents working. Second, the average family size will be smaller than in previous generations. Third, the number of non-traditional family structures—single parents, step families, unmarried couples with children, grandparents with children, and so on—will continue to rise. (*The Public Pulse,* 1994)

The Roper report adds that families, especially those lacking two parents, will expect more child-rearing help from schools and their communities. Balancing work and family responsibilities will continue to be a major concern for working parents.

Perhaps the only concrete thing one can say about the future is that change is inevitable. From an individual's standpoint, a change may be welcomed, as in a pay raise, or threatening, as in a job loss. Change upsets the status quo, disturbing those who are wedded to the known and experienced. Here is an example. Theme parks such as Disneyland in Anaheim, California, have to decide what rides and decorations to keep and which ones to retire and replace. Purists who have visited the parks often since their youth dislike any change or alteration, whereas newcomers do not have these preconceived notions of how the theme park should look and function. The parks have to balance the needs of returning customers with the needs of newcomers. Similarly, families have to decide what holiday traditions to uphold and which ones to change. Moving can be stimulating or upsetting, a stressor or exhilarator. About 15 percent of the U.S. population moves each year according to Census data. The pluses and minuses are described by a corporate spouse who says, after living in four states,

> I admit that I haven't always given Amy's considerations as much thought as they deserve, nor did we talk about her concerns as much as we should have. For me, selfishly, a job transfer is the start of a new adventure, something exciting and fresh after so many years seeing the same old sights and driving the same old roads. (Opdyke, 2004, p. D1)

Just as unsettling as not knowing what changes are coming is not knowing when or how fast they will occur. Peter Drucker says, "That major changes are ahead for schools and education is certain—the knowledge society will demand them and the new learning theories and learning technologies will trigger them. How fast they will come we do not, of course, know" (1989, p. 252).

Quality of Life and Well-Being

Urbanization, crowding, economic growth, and the accelerated pace of living are already transforming where and how we live. Accelerated pace is part of a larger concept called the **acceleration effect,** which means that each unit of saved time is more valuable than the last unit. Therefore, time is becoming more valuable.

According to Henry Sokalski, coordinator of the United Nations International Year of the Family,

> Although increased migration and urbanization are major trends in the complex reciprocal relationship between population movement and economic and social development it is little understood. Some transitions, whether imposed by societal conditions or not, may require a sweeping reorganization of the family unit and its social network. In many cases families manage their own powers of adaptation. Too often, however, especially when faced with poverty and lack of support from society, families unravel under the pressure of trying to sustain their members. (1994, p. 3)

Technology allows families to make better use of their time. For example, instant messaging requires less time and fewer physical steps than mailing a letter. Access to technology (telephones, computers, databases, publications) is not distributed evenly, however, nor will it be in the near future. The large gap between the haves and the have-nots is related to the **quality of life,** defined as the level of satisfaction with one's relationships and surroundings. Another definition of quality of life is simply one's well-being. One of the goals of management is to provide the ways and means to improve the quality of life for individuals and families.

A commonly used measure of quality of life is a country's Gross Domestic Product (GDP), which was discussed earlier in the book. The United Nations ranks countries by GDP. Realizing that economic data provide only one measure of quality of life, the United Nations and other organizations are working on developing more comprehensive measures. One such measure is the Human Development Index (HDI), which measures overall progress in 174 countries on three basic dimensions of human development: longevity, knowledge, and a decent standard of living (see Table 14.1). According to the latest HDI ranking, Canada ranked the highest, followed by France, Norway, the United States, and Iceland.

Well-being refers to a "state of being where all members of a community have economic security, are respected, valued, and have personal worth; feel connected to those around them; are able to participate in the decision-making process affecting them" (Marshall, McMullen, Ballantyne, Daciuk, & Wigdor, 1995, p. 1). There are many dimensions to the concept of well-being. The four conventionally discussed dimensions are economic well-being, physical well-being, social well-being, and emotional well-being:

◆ Economic well-being has to do with the degree of economic adequacy or security individuals and families have.

◆ Physical well-being has to do with the body and its needs. Keeping healthy and safe, eating right, getting enough sleep, and managing stress are all subtopics within this category.

◆ "Social well-being is the social space of the family as a group, whereas psychological well-being is the emotional space of an individual in the family. It is concerned with the social needs of the family played out in daily interactions in interpersonal relationships within the family groups and with the larger community, including the workplace" (McGregor & Goldsmith, 1998, p. 4).

◆ Emotional well-being has to do with the emotions (feelings) of an individual.

Although well-being sounds like a pleasant enough topic, problems arise when the different types of well-being come into conflict within the individual and between individuals.

TABLE 14.1
Human Development Index (HDI)

The HDI measures overall progress for 174 countries in three basic dimensions of human development: longevity, knowledge, and a decent standard of living. It is measured by life expectancy, educational attainment, and adjusted income.

Top 5 Ranking Countries			Bottom 5 Ranking Countries		
Country	HDI Value	HDI Rank	Country	HDI Value	HDI Rank
Canada	0.960	1	Sierra Leone	0.185	174
France	0.946	2	Niger	0.207	173
Norway	0.943	3	Burkina Faso	0.219	172
USA	0.943	4	Mali	0.236	171
Iceland	0.942	5	Burundi	0.241	170

Source: Selected statistics from the Human Development Report 1998, published by Oxford University Press, **www.oup-ysa.org**. For the complete statistical database or the Human Development Report 1998 Background Papers, contact UN Publications at **www.un.org/Pubs/catalog.htm**.

> We all start off with dreams for our life—what we want to be, what we want to do, where we want to do it. But in marriage, the dreams of two partners collide and sometimes they ricochet in random directions. (Opdyke, 2004, p. D1)

Recently, three other dimensions of well-being have emerged as topics in the literature and in everyday life. These are

◆ Environmental well-being. This has to do with the level of environmental quality.

◆ Political well-being. This has to do with a person's internal sense of power, autonomy, and freedom, not necessarily involvement in politics.

◆ Spiritual well-being. Broadly and individually defined, spiritual well-being may include hope, faith, peace, joy in living, enlightenment, connectedness, and purpose.

A fundamental question to be addressed is, Which dimensions are most critical to a specific person's sense of well-being? For example, a person may value economic well-being over social well-being. He or she make take the raise and promotion and move the family far away from other family members and friends. Regarding economic well-being, it is evident that some people are content with very little of a material nature, whereas others need all the trappings of success. According to Toffler, quality of life is something a person can attain by learning to cope with change. Copability, he suggests, is the main way a person can manage "future shock" (1990, p. 47). Further, he says, to achieve their preferred quality of life, people need to consciously take control of change and guide their own evolution.

Multiculturalism

A more expansive worldview has helped to foster a movement or philosophy called **multiculturalism,** which means the expression by ethnic groups of their cultural heritage. It refers to a society that allows for and, in fact, encourages a combination of several distinct cultures. The concept first began to attract the attention of educators, politicians, the media, and the public in the 1980s. Inherent in the concept of multiculturalism is respect for each ethnic group and the willingness to recognize that "human society is a rich, multi-colored cultural and social mosaic" (Sokalski, 1994, p. 4). Multiculturalism is about attitudes and attempts to retain the uniqueness of different groups rather than letting them be subsumed into the greater society. It is a move away from the homogenization of the world, an attempt to hang on to the past and to take the best parts of it into the future. A related concept is empowerment, encouraging individuals to express themselves, their ethnicity, and culture.

Some advocates of multiculturalism see it purely as tolerance. Others want to go beyond the theoretical and apply multiculturalism to government programs, schools, universities, churches, other institutions. The basic idea is that each ethnic group's culture should be acknowledged and preserved. "Thinking multiculturally requires collaborative activities and techniques that expand traditional pedagogy" (Winchip, 1997, p. 29). It helps fight prejudice and it promotes understanding.

Because Canada has two official languages (French and English), it is one of the world's leaders in multicultural research and government policy. As more nations embrace a model of multiculturalism, programs involving socio-cultural integration and cultural retention will become more important. The main goals of such programs are to bolster cultural identity and self-esteem while promoting intergroup respect. Rather than being divisive, multicultural-ism and ethnic diversity can be a source of national strength and identity. Ethnicity is a part of a society's cultural environment. Recognition of the dif-ferences as well as the commonalities among groups of people is all part of the more complex view of the world that we have today.

Environment and Consumption

This chapter has already introduced the concept of environment within the context of technological advances. The crowding of our planet and its misuse has led to many family and environmental problems. According to Sokalski,

> Millions of families around the world continue to suffer from lack of shelter, clean water, adequate food and medical care. Yet, people everywhere are striving to improve their lives, to raise their children and care for their families, to enjoy their leisure-time, even if there is just a glimmer of hope for such aspirations to materi-alize. (1994, p. 2)

"The central problem of the 21st century is how to raise the poor to a decent standard of living worldwide while preserving as much of the rest of life as possible" (Wilson, 2002). By rest of life, he means the other animals and the plants that share our earth. Government, the private sector (including individ-uals and families), and science and technology have to come together to find solutions. What is particularly interesting about environmental problems is that they are not confined to national borders. Birds, bats, and insects fly over invisible national boundaries all the time, so nations have to cooperate when it comes to fostering biological diversity.

Also, one has to take into account the different philosophical approaches to life regarding what matters. For example, many people have the idea that more is better. As a result of this outlook, store shelves in some countries are crowded with essentially duplicate products, confusing consumers and making it difficult to shop in the store. At the same time, in other parts of the world, people are starving. It is estimated that about 500 million out of the 6 billion plus people in the world live without proper sanitation, clean water, and ade-quate food. The overcrowding of store shelves is not just a North American or Western European phenomenon. In Japan, 3,500 to 4,000 new products are introduced to food stores each year, and only 1 in 10 is believed to succeed (Rapp & Collins, 1990). To even talk about consumption in terms of countries is becoming outmoded because in food markets around the world consumers can find bok choy from Shanghai, tuna from Portugal, pasta from Italy, bananas from Central America, and vanilla beans from Madagascar. Here is another example:

> America is more entangled with the rest of the world than at any other time in his-tory. We buy clothes from China, cars from Japan, fruits from South America and luxury goods from Europe. When we call for tech support, the person at the other end of the line may not be in Indiana, but in India. (Witt, 2004, p. 38)

The more-is-better approach is changing somewhat, however. *Americans are more likely to eat take-out than splurge on three-course meals* and if they do go out, they want casual, inexpensive food (Witt, 2004). Take-out food or din-ing away from home has increased from 24 percent of food expenditures for the average family in 1950 to 40 percent in 1981 to a predicted 49 percent or almost half by the year 2012 according to the U.S. Department of Agriculture. The desire to accumulate material things is giving way to a rising concern for a redefined quality of life in which better does not necessarily mean more. Time will continue to be a primary factor in consumption decisions. *"Consumers these days are on a mission. They want to quickly locate a product, evaluate it, pay and get out"* (Yin, 2004, p. 13).

The shift from wanting to own all to owning only what is needed is an example of a paradigm shift. According to Rettig, Rossman, and Hogan (1992), this shift is not easy to make because the "compulsion to consume is so pervasive in many countries that educating people to think in alternative ways will be a monumental task which history suggests is impossible" (p. 39).

What is the future of the environmental movement? According to the Roper report discussed earlier, the environmental movement has matured. Roper's nationwide opinion polls reveal that the current wave of environmentalism is expressed in action rather than words. For example, people are recycling more. The report also observes:

> One effect of Americans' new sense of personal responsibility is the realization that business is no longer solely responsible for environmental degradation. Yet, if people are willing to accept more responsibility and take action, they are also likely to expect business to respond in kind. Adopting pro-environmental and product designs will continue to be important for American industry. Far from being outdated, the best reasons for "going green" will continue to make sense for the foreseeable future. (*The Public Pulse,* 1994, p. 4)

Technology has been blamed for many environmental ills, but it also holds the key to their solution. According to Stephen Lubar of the Smithsonian Institution, we cannot really discuss our lives today without discussing technology and its impact in so many realms because

> We are surrounded by new machines, new devices, new technologies that let us—or make us—deal with more information than ever before. We are also surrounded by new economic and social and cultural systems which support and make possible these machines, and which in turn are supported by them. Together, our information culture and our information machines shape the way we live, work, and play, and change the way we think about the world around us. No aspect of our lives remains untouched. But we shape the machines, too, deciding what we want to use and how we will use it. We change along with the machines, and they change along with us. (Lubar, 1993, pp. 3–4)

In terms of solutions to environmental problems, technology can be used to achieve long-term ecological balance. Many examples of impact on the environment could be cited, but one of these is technology's ability to increase the world's food supply.

The Food Supply

In the 18th century, Thomas Malthus predicted that the world's population would outgrow the food supply. Malthus, however, did not anticipate the advances in agriculture that have enabled the world population to reach its current level. Among the recent advances in agriculture is **genome mapping,** which identifies and "maps" the genes of plants and animals. Genome maps are blueprints that researchers use to investigate the development of an individual animal or plant from fertilization to maturity. Genetics research may provide the key to disease-free animals with more meat and less fat. Another practical use of genome mapping is to determine whether genes exist or can be made to exist that would make plants more photosynthetically efficient. This would allow light-sensitive plants to be grown in the shadow of others. Terry Sharrer (1992) points out that corn plants could then be grown in a space 3 inches square instead of requiring 5 inches between the plants and forty inches between the rows. The result would be an approximately 1,000 percent increase in plant population per acre. It should be pointed out that not everyone is comfortable with this trend toward tampering with nature, although enthusiasts would point out that farmers have been tampering with nature since prehistoric times. Others would say that if it helps feed the world's starving populations, then genetics research is a worthy pursuit. All sides of the arguments over the world's food supply have their pros and cons, and it is up to the individual to decide how he or she feels about the ethics of agricultural and genetic experimentation.

In any event, it is quite clear that tomorrow's farms will be vastly different from farms in the past. Already, farmers can put sensors in the ground to let them know when more water is needed or whether conditions are right or not for planting, fertilizing, or harvesting.

Perhaps even more remarkable are the experiments in hydroponics—that is, growing plants in water without soil. Some of these experiments can be observed at universities and cooperative extension programs and at EPCOT Center in Walt Disney World. The Land exhibit at EPCOT is the world's only major display of food and fiber crops from all climate zones under one roof. This is more than just an interesting display—it annually produces tons of fresh vegetables and fish for EPCOT restaurants. The goal of the exhibit is to demonstrate that intelligent and constructive land use can fulfill the world's future food needs.

The Land's staff, which includes college student interns, is working with NASA scientists from the Kennedy Space Center on agricultural research for space. In a spacecraft, plants are needed for food and also to replenish oxygen and water and for recycling of wastes. Lettuce, wheat, and potatoes are some of the crops selected for space study. Scientific research of this type may someday ensure an expanded food supply by allowing foods to be grown in space stations and on other planets. In the 21st century, people may live on a self-sustaining moon base. Consequently, when discussing future management problems and possibilities for individuals and families, one should keep in mind that soon not only will there be life on earth, but also the possibility of human life in space.

Web-Based Resources

For information about the environment, contact the Environmental Protection Agency at **www.epa.gov.** For information about the space program, contact NASA at **www.nasa.gov.** The U.S. Dept. of Energy at **www.eere.energy.gov** covers all aspects of energy saving in the home and offers an interactive program for assessing your own home's energy needs, including recommended insulation levels.

Home operating systems, including telecommunications, lighting, heating, and security, are described at **www.homeautomation.org,** the Home Automation Association Web site. Software is available on home automation from such companies as IBM. Microsoft's **www.houseandhome.msn.com/** offers remodeling advice and news about computerized systems.

Web sites that offer nutrition and health information include:

Tufts University Nutrition Navigator: **http://navigator.tufts.edu/**
The American Dietetic Association: **www.eatright.org**

The International Food Information Council: **www.ific.org**
Medline/PubMed: **www.nlm.nih.gov**
National Institutes of Health: **www.nih.gov**
The U.S. Food and Drug Administration: **www.fda.gov**
Mayo Health Oasis (of the Mayo Clinic): **www.mayoclinic.com**
Johns Hopkins Health Information: **www.intelihealth.com**
World Health Organization: **www.who.int**
Food & Agriculture Organization: **www.fao.org**
Government healthfinder: **www.healthfinder.gov**

Summary

This chapter examined future trends in technology, families, homes, consumption, leadership, and the environment. Each change presents its own challenges and opportunities for judgment. Change starts with the individual clarifying goals, making decisions, and using resources to reach solutions. Planning and a sense of self-responsibility are the hallmarks of management. Information and innovation overload and the acceleration of life present challenges that management can help with. This book has introduced various human problems and showed ways of dealing with them through planning, making use of technology, and managing outcomes. One of the key concepts in the present chapter was that the ultimate goal of the manager today is a better tomorrow.

As in any discipline, resource management has a history, a present, and a future. This chapter on the future concludes this book, which started with an overview of management, including its theoretical bases and history, progressed through chapters on specific concepts, and then applied those concepts to managing human resources, time, stress and fatigue, the environment, and finances. Given this coverage from history to present to future, it is fitting to end this chapter and the book with a look back and a look forward:

> The past century was extraordinarily rich in innovation and scientific progress. There has never been a century like it, and we might worry that there can never be another. It is unlikely that we will ever again see the likes of Edison or Einstein, to mention two whose 20th century accomplishments far surpassed those of their colleagues. But Edison, Einstein, and other great innovators of this century would surely have shared the view that technological progress will continue. In that spirit, we might hazard one simple prediction. In the next 100 years, the only thing to be certain of is surprise. (Raeburn, 1999, p. 106)

Key Terms

acceleration effects	intellect	quality of life
diffusion	invention	system understanding
discovery	leaders	technology
genome maps	managerial judgment	transparency
(mapping)	multiculturalism	well-being
innovation (overload)	paradigm shift	

Review Questions

1. What does the science fiction writer William Gibson mean when he says the future is already here—it's just unevenly distributed? Explain your answer and give an example.

2. How can individuals and families cope with information and innovation overloads?

3. Why did the Roper opinion poll report conclude that "the family is back and determined"?

4. The chapter's introduction emphasized that making predictions is a risky business. For example, Peter Drucker predicts that in 25 years the American institution of the freestanding undergraduate college may be obsolete. Do you think this is probable? Why or why not? Explain your answer.

5. How will genetics research affect food supplies?

References

Broadway blues. (2001, June 23). *The Economist.*

Consumer Connection. (1994, January/February). A publication of Maytag, 3.

Drucker, P. (1989). *The new realities.* New York: Harper & Row.

Drucker, P. (1999). *Management challenges for the 21st century.* New York: Harper Business.

Fletcher, J. (2001, May 11). The smarter house. *The Wall Street Journal,* W1–W2.

Francese, P. (2004, January). Trouble in store. *American Demographics,* 36–37.

Herbig, P., Milewicz, J., & Golden, J. (1993). Information overload in review. *Proceedings of the Atlantic Marketing Association,* 199–204. Orlando, FL.

Key, R., & Firebaugh, F. (1989). Family resource management: Preparing for the 21st century. *Journal of Home Economics, 81*(1), 13–17.

Kouzes, J., & Posner, B. (2002). *The leadership challenge.* (3rd ed.). San Francisco: Jossey-Bass.

Lubar, S. (1993). *InfoCulture.* Boston: Houghton Mifflin.

Marshall, V., McMullen, J., Ballantyne, P., Daciuk, J., & Wigdor, B. (1995). *Contribution to independence over the adult life course.* Toronto: Centre for Studies of Aging, University of Toronto.

McGregor, S., & Goldsmith, E. (1998). Expanding our understanding of quality of life, standard of living, and well-being. *Journal of Family and Consumer Sciences, 90*(2), 2–6, 22.

McLaughlin, K. (2002, December 17). Remotes that control everything but the pet. *The Wall Street Journal,* D1.

Mullen, K. (1994, February). We did not know that. *Forbes ASAP,* 16.

Nussbaum, K. (1991, April 29). *Business Week,* 58.

Opdyke, J. (2004, January 7). The cost of a mobile marriage. *The Wall Street Journal,* D1.

The Public Pulse. (1994). Vol. 8, no. 5. New York: Report of Roper Starch Worldwide, Inc., New York.

Quinn, J. B., Baruch, J., & Zien, K. (1997). *Innovation explosion.* New York: Simon & Schuster.

Raeburn, P. (1999, Summer). The next 100 years. *Business Week,* 106.

Rapp, S., & Collins, T. (1990). *The great marketing turnaround.* Englewood Cliffs, NJ: Prentice-Hall.

Rettig, K., Rossman, M., & Hogan, J. (1992). Educating for family resource management. In M. Arcus, J. Schvaneveldt, & J. Moss (Eds.), *Handbook of family life education,* Vol. 2. Beverly Hills, CA: Sage.

Rogers, E. M. (1995). *Diffusion of innovations* (4th ed.). New York: Free Press.

Sharrer, G. T. (1992, Spring). Wonders and worries: A perspective on the future of American agriculture. Unpublished paper. Washington, DC.: National Museum of American History, Smithsonian Institution, 3. The comment noted in the text is based on Sharrer's conversations with John Fulkerson of the Cooperative State Research Service, U.S. Department of Agriculture, 1986.

Sokalski, H. (1994, June 20). *The IYF in a world of change: Its global impact.* Keynote address, 85th Annual Meeting of the American Home Economics Association, San Diego, CA.

Toffler, A. (1990). Toffler's next shock. *World Monitor,* 34–44.

Tucker, R. (1992). *Managing the future.* New York: Putnam

Twiss, B. (1980). *Managing technological innovation* (2nd ed.). London: Longman.

Watson, N. (2001, July). How technology spreads. *The NBER Digest.* Retrieved March 21, 2004, from **http://www.nber.org /digest/jul01/w8130.html**

Wilson, E. O. (2002). *The future of life.* New York: Vintage.

Winchip, S. (1997, Fall). Understanding through coursework. *Journal of Family and Consumer Sciences,* 28–31.

Witt, L. (2004, January). 2004: A year of portentous change. *American Demographics,* 38.

Yin, S. (2004, January). Chronic shoppers. *American Demographics,* 13.

GLOSSARY

Absolute values   Extreme, definitive values that are inflexible.

Abstract symbols   Ideas rather than objects.

Acceleration effect   Quickening of life's pace so that each unit of time saved is more valuable than the last unit.

Accommodation   An agreement reached by accepting the point of view of another person.

Actively acquired information   Information the individual actively looks for, such as fashion coverage in magazines or news bulletins on television.

Actuating   Putting plans into effect, action, or motion.

Adaptability (adaptive)   The ability to cope with change, to make the necessary adjustments.

Adjusting   Checking a plan or activity and making appropriate changes.

Advocate or expert channels   Experts in a field or people with a cause who are more likely to contact receivers through letters, speeches, or less direct forms of communication.

Affective domain   Value meanings derived from feelings.

Annual Percentage Rate (APR)   Rate of interest paid over the life of credit or a loan.

Artifacts   Type, placement, or rearrangement of objects around a person.

Assessment   The gathering of information about results.

Assets   What a person owns.

Attitudes   Concepts that may express values, serve as a means of evaluation, or demonstrate feeling in regard to some idea, person, object, event, situation, or relationship.

Autonomic   Refers to family decision-making style in which an equal number of decisions are made by each spouse.

Behavior   What people actually do.

Biodiversity   The variety and variability among living organisms and the ecological complexities in which they occur.

Blended families   New families that include children from previous relationships. Also called stepfamilies or reconstituted or combined families.

Boomeranging   The return of adult children to their parents' homes (Riche, 1990).

Boundaries   Limits or borders between systems.

Brainstorming   Group communication technique in which members suggest many ideas no matter how seemingly ridiculous or strange. Afterward, the group examines each idea separately to see whether it has merit.

Budget   A spending plan or guide.

Burnout   Emotional or physical exhaustion brought on by unrelieved stress.

Carbon monoxide   An odorless, colorless gas that can cause death from accidental poisoning.

Change   To cause to be different, to alter, or to transform.

Channel   The medium or route through which the message travels from sender to receiver.

Checking   Determining whether actions are in compliance with standards and sequencing.

Choice   The act of selecting among alternatives.

Chronic fatigue syndrome   An affliction or disease exhibiting a variety of symptoms, including extreme long-lasting exhaustion.

Circadian rhythms   The daily rhythmic activity cycles, based on 24-hour intervals, that humans experience.

Clarification   The process of making clear, making easier to understand, or elaborating.

Cocooning   The desire to remain at home as a place of coziness, control, peace, insulation, and protection (Popcorn, 1991).

Cognition   The mental process or faculty by which knowledge is acquired.

Cognitive domain   Value meanings derived from thinking about events, situations, people, and things.

Comfort zone   A combination of habit and everyday expectations mixed with an appropriate amount of adventure and novelty.

Commitment   The degree to which an individual identifies with and is involved in a particular activity or organization.

Communication   The process of transmitting a message from a sender to a receiver.

Comparative advantage   A theory that individuals, families, or companies do best when they focus on activities in which they can add the most value and outsource other activities.

Compromise   Process of resolving conflicts in which each person makes concessions, giving in a little in order to gain a valued settlement or outcome.

Conflict   A state of disagreement or disharmony.

Conflict resolution   Negotiations to remedy the conflict.

Consensual decision making   Process of reaching a mutual agreement equally acceptable to all individuals involved.

Conservation   The act or process of preserving and protecting natural environments from loss or depletion.

Constructive conflict   A form of conflict or disagreement that focuses on the issue or the problem rather than on the other person's deficits.

Consume   To destroy, use, or expend.

Consumer Price Index (CPI)   A measure of price changes, which are collected by and reported by the Bureau of Labor Statistics. A main measure of inflation.

Contingency plans   Backup or secondary plans to be used in case the first plan does not work out.

Controlling   Acting to check one's course of action.

Credit   Time allowed for repayment of money or goods that are borrowed; also refers to the amount of money borrowed.

Credit bureau   Type of reporting agency that collects, stores, and sells financial information.

Crises   Events that require changes in normal patterns of behavior.

Critical listening   Act of evaluating or challenging what is heard.

Cultural relativism   A comparative approach based on an understanding and appreciation of other cultures.

Cultural values   Generally held conceptualizations of what is right or wrong in a culture or what is preferred.

Culture   The sum of all socially transmitted behavior patterns, beliefs, arts, expectations, institutions, and all other products of human work and thought characteristic of a group, community, or population.

Decibel (dB)   A measure of the loudness of sound.

Decidophobia   The fear of making decisions.

Deciduous trees   Trees that lose their leaves in winter.

Decision making   Choosing between two or more alternatives.

Decision-making style   The characteristic way that a person makes decisions.

Decision plan   A long, complicated decision process that includes a sequence of intentions.

Decision rules   Principles that guide decision making.

Decisions   Conclusions or judgments about some issue or matter.

Decoding   The process by which the receiver assigns meaning to the symbols sent by the sender, to convert from code into a plain memory.

De facto decision making   Process whereby decisions are made by a lack of dissent rather than by active assent.

Demands   Events or goals that require action.

Demographics   Data used to describe populations or subgroups.

Demography   The study of the characteristics of human populations—that is, their size, growth, distribution, density, movement, and other vital statistics.

Destination   The receiver or audience in the process of communication.

Destructive conflicts   Interpersonal conflicts involving direct verbal attacks on another individual.

Diffusion   Innovations spreading within an enterprise or society.

Directional plans   Progress along a linear path to a long-term goal fulfillment.

Disability   A long-term or chronic condition medically defined as a physiological, anatomical, mental, or emotional impairment resulting from disease or illness, inherited or congenital defect, or traumas or other insults (including environmental) to mind or body (Wright, 1980).

Discovery   The initial observation of a new phenomenon.

Discretionary income   Income regulated by one's own discretion or judgment.

Discretionary time   The free time an individual can use any way she or he wants.

Disposable income   The amount of take-home pay left after all deductions are withheld for benefits, taxes, contributions, and so on.

Distress   Harmful stress.

Diversification   Having a mix of investments.

Domino effect   The passage of stress from one source to another.

Dovetailing (multitasking)   Situation that occurs when two or more activities take place at the same time.

Downshifting   Opting for a simpler life—usually less pay, less stress, and more time—in a more personally satisfying occupation.

Drift time   Enjoyable, unscheduled time.

Dual career   Refers to households in which both spouses have a long-term commitment to a planned series of jobs leading to desired career goals.

Dual-income or dual-earner households   Households where both spouses have income-producing jobs.

Ecoconsciousness   Thoughts and actions given to protecting and sustaining the environment.

Ecology   The study of how living things relate to their natural environment.

Economic well-being   The degree to which individuals or families have economic adequacy.

Ecosystem   The subsystem of human ecology that emphasizes the relationship between organisms and their environment.

Effort   Exertion or the use of energy to do something.

Emergency fund   Savings equal to three to six months of income.

Empathetic listening   Listening for feelings.

Empathy   The ability to recognize and identify another's feelings by putting oneself in that person's place.

Encoding   The process of putting thought into symbolic form.

Entropy   A tendency toward disorder or randomness.

Environment The sum of the external conditions influencing the life of an organism or population (Naar, 1990).

Environmentalism Concern for the environment.

Equal Credit Opportunity Act Legislation that prohibits discrimination against a person because of race, sex, age, color, marital status, or related factors.

Equifinality The phenomenon in which different circumstances and opportunities may lead to similar outcomes.

Ethics A system of morals, principles, values, or good conduct.

Ethnocentrism The tendency to interpret other cultures in terms of one's own dominant culture.

Entrepreneurship The process of creating value by bringing together a unique package of resources to exploit or make use of an opportunity.

Eustress Beneficial stress.

Evaluation The process of judging or examining the cost, value, or worth of a plan or decision based on such criteria as standards, demands, or goals.

Expertise The ability to perform tasks successfully and dependably.

External change A kind of change fostered by society or the outer environment.

External motivation The forces external to the individual that affect motivation.

External noise Noise from the environment.

External search The process of looking for new information from sources outside oneself.

External stress Situations in which stress is brought on from outside the individual.

Extrinsic motivation Outside rewards or motivation.

Extrinsic values Values that derive their worth or meaning from someone or something else.

Extroverts Overall types of character and response in which individuals are less interested in themselves and more interested in others.

Fair Credit Reporting Act Legislation mandating that individuals who are denied credit, insurance, or employment because of their credit report have the right to obtain a free copy of their report within 30 days of the denial.

Family A group of two or more persons (one of whom is a householder) who are related by birth, marriage, or adoption and reside together (U.S. Bureau of the Census, 1989).

Family ecosystem A subsystem of human ecology that emphasizes the interactions between families and environments.

Fatalism The feeling that all events are shaped by fate.

Fatigue The feeling of having insufficient energy to carry on and a strong desire to stop, rest, or sleep (Engel, 1970).

Feedback Information that returns to the system.

Fertility rate Yearly number of births per 1,000 women of childbearing age.

FICO score Numeric value assigned to credit habits and history.

Fight or flight syndrome Alerted condition of the body as it quickly prepares for physical battle or energetic flight to escape the situation.

Financial management The science or practice of managing money or other assets.

Focus groups Selected groups of people who are questioned by a discussion leader or moderator about their views on different topics.

Fossil fuels The remains of dead vegetation, such as coal, oil, and natural gases, that can be burned to release energy (Naar, 1990).

Functional limitation Hindrance or negative effect in the performance of household tasks or activities.

Gender gap The difference in earnings between employed men and women.

Genealogy An account of the descent of a person or family from an ancestor or ancestors.

Genome maps Blueprints that researchers use to investigate the development of an individual animal or plant from fertilization to maturity.

Gerontology The scientific study of the aging process.

Glass ceiling Situation where, as women move up the career ladder, they hit an invisible barrier that stops them from moving further.

Goals End results that require action; the purpose toward which much behavior is directed.

Gresham's law of planning Short-term concerns create priorities and deadlines that take managerial attention away from long-range concerns.

Gross domestic product (GDP) The total market value of all goods and services produced by a nation during a specified period, usually a year.

Gross income All income received that is not legally exempt from taxes.

Habitat The place where an organism lives.

Habits Repetitive, often unconscious patterns of behavior.

Habitual decision making Process of making choices out of habit without any additional information search.

Handicap A disadvantage, interference, or barrier to performance, opportunity, or fulfillment in any desired role in life, imposed upon the individual by a limitation in function or by other problems associated with disability and/or personal characteristics in the context of the individual's environment or role (Wright, 1980).

Hatching Local area nesting, finding other places outside of the workplace or the home to spend time in.

Homeostasis   The tendency to maintain balance.

Household   All persons who occupy a housing unit such as a house, apartment, or single room.

Householder   The person (or one of the persons) in whose name the home is owned or rented.

Human capital   The sum total of human resources; all the capabilities, traits, and other resources that people use to achieve goals.

Human ecology   The study of how humans interact with their environment.

Human resources   The skills, talents, and abilities that people possess.

Hydroponics   Growth of plants in water without soil.

Hypotheses   Predictions about future occurrences.

I-messages   Statements of fact about how an individual feels or thinks.

Immigration   The process in which people enter and settle in a country where they are not native.

Implementing   Putting decisions or plans into action.

Income   The amount of money or its equivalent received during a period of time.

Income tax   A personal tax levied on individuals or families on the basis of income received.

Independent activities   Activities that take place one at a time.

Indirect channels   Message communication forms such as radio, television, magazines, newspapers, and signs.

Inflation   Rising prices.

Information anxiety   The gap between what individuals think they understand and what they actually do understand.

Information overload   The uncomfortable state when individuals are exposed to too much information in too short a time.

Innovation overload   The user's response to the ever increasing pace of information, knowledge, and innovations (Herbig, Milewicz, & Golden, 1993).

Inputs   Whatever is brought into the system.

Insomnia   The perception or complaint of inadequate or poor-quality sleep.

Insurance   A financial arrangement in which people pay premiums to an insurance company that reimburses them in the event of loss or injury.

Intangible resources   Resources that are incapable of being touched.

Integrated waste management   A combination of methods to reduce environmental pollution.

Intellect   Knowing or understanding; the capacity to create knowledge; the capability for rational or highly developed use of intelligence.

Interdependent activities   Relationship between activities where one activity must be completed before another can take place.

Interface   The place or point where independent systems or diverse groups interact.

Interference   Anything that distorts or interrupts messages.

Internal change   Type of change that originates within the family and includes events that primarily affect family members.

Internal noise   Noise occurring in the sender's and receiver's minds.

Internal search   The process of looking within oneself for information for decisions.

Internal stress   Type of stress that originates in one's own mind and body.

Interpersonal conflicts   Actions by one person that interfere with the actions of another.

Intrinsic motivation   The underlying causes of and the internal need for competence and self-determination. The pleasure or value a person derives from the content of work or activity.

Intrinsic values   Values classified as ends in themselves, having internal meanings.

Introverts   Overall types of character or response in which individuals tend to think of themselves first and rely on inner-directed thoughts.

Intuition   The sense or feeling of knowing what to do without going through the rational process.

Invention   Process that provides the initial verification that a problem can be solved.

Investment   Commitment of capital to the achievement of long-term goals or objectives.

Job stress   The harmful physical and emotional responses that occur when the requirements of the job do not match the capabilities, resources, or needs of the worker.

Leaders   Authorities, experts, facilitators, and guides who participate in community action programs, families, and as contributors to scientific, social, or economic advances and in so doing improve human lives.

Leisure   Freedom from time-consuming activities, tasks, duties, or responsibilities.

Level of living   The measure of the goods and services affordable by and available to individuals or families.

Leveraging   Doing more with less, stretching resources.

Liabilities   Sum total of what a person owes.

Life management   All decisions a person or family will make and the way their values, goals, and resource use affect their decision making. Includes all the goals, events, situations, and decisions that make up a lifestyle.

Lifestyle   The characteristic way or pattern in which an individual conducts his or her life.

Liquidity   The speed and ease of retrieving cash or turning another type of investment into cash.

Listening   Hearing what is said and observing the actions communicated.

Long-term-care insurance   Policies that provide benefits for a range of services not covered by regular health insurance or Medicare.

Low involvement   Information that does not necessitate much thinking about or attention.

Macroenvironment   The environment that surrounds and encompasses the microenvironment.

Management   The process of using resources to achieve goals. It involves thinking, action, and results.

Management process   The procedures involved in management—thinking, action, and results.

Management style   A characteristic way of making decisions and acting.

Management tools   Measuring devices, techniques, or instruments that are used to arrive at decisions and plans of action.

Managerial judgment   The ability to accept and work with change for the betterment of self and humankind.

Material resources   Tangible resources; natural phenomena, such as fertile soil, petroleum, and rivers, and human-made items, such as buildings, money, and computers.

Medicare   The United States' basic health insurance for people 65 or older.

Message   The total communication that is sent, listened to, and received.

Message construction   Structure of a message that determines where information should be placed in a message to have maximum impact. It also includes how often information should be repeated in a message.

Message content   What a message says; strategies or information that may be used to communicate an idea or policy to receivers.

Microenvironment   The environment that closely surrounds individuals and families.

Mobility   Technical term for changing residences.

Monochronic   Refers to the preference to focus on one activity at a time.

Morphogenic systems   Those systems that are adaptive to change and relatively open.

Morphostatic systems   Those systems that are resistant to change, stable, and relatively closed.

Mortality   The technical term for death.

Motivation   Movement toward goals or other desired outcomes.

Multiculturalism   Respect for each ethnic group and the recognition that "human society is a rich, multicolored cultural and social mosaic" (Sokalski, 1994, p. 4).

Multifinality   The phenomenon in which the same initial circumstances or conditions may lead to different conclusions or outcomes.

Multitasking   See *dovetailing*.

Natural capital   A good humans have to protect, such as the environment.

Need recognition   Realization of how much an individual needs a certain product, service, or condition.

Needs   Things that are required or necessary.

Negative feedback   Information put into the system that indicates that the system is deviating from its normal course and that corrective measures may be necessary if the desired steady state is to be maintained.

Net worth   Amount determined by subtracting liabilities from assets.

Noise   Any interference in the communication process that prevents the message from being heard correctly; unwanted sound.

Nondiscretionary time   The time that an individual cannot control totally by himself or herself.

Nonnormative stressor events   Unanticipated experiences that place a person or a family in a state of instability and require creative effort to remedy.

Nonverbal symbols   Anything other than words that is used to communicate.

Normative stressor events   Anticipated, predictable developmental changes that occur at certain life intervals.

Norms   Rules that specify, delineate, encourage, and prohibit certain behaviors in certain situations.

NREM (non-rapid eye movement) sleep   Kind of sleep that occurs when the sleeper is in an inactive, deep slumber.

Opportunity cost   The highest-valued alternative that must be sacrificed to satisfy a want or attain something.

Opportunity recognition   Realization by an individual that she or he may have limited or no access to a product, service, or condition.

Optimism   A tendency or a disposition to expect the best outcome or to think hopefully about a situation.

Optimization   Process of obtaining the best result.

Orientation   The location or situation of a house relative to points on a compass.

Overlapping activities   Situation in which one gives intermittent attention to two or more activities until they are completed.

Outputs   End results or products, leftovers, and waste.

Outsourcing   Paying someone else to do one's work.

Paradigm shift   The process in which an individual or a team tackles a problem by jumping ahead to radically innovative solutions rather than taking a gradual step-by-step approach.

Pareto principle   The principle stating that 20 percent of the time expended usually produces 80 percent of the results, whereas 80 percent of the time expended produces only 20 percent of the results.

Parkinson's law   The idea that a job expands to fill the time available to accomplish the task.

Passively acquired information   Information that one hears or sees but does not necessarily seek, such as billboard advertisements or airplane messages.

Perception   The process whereby sensory stimulation is translated into organized experience.

Persistence   A person's staying power; the personality trait of not giving up when faced with adversity.

Personality   An extensive range of separate behavioral traits or overall types of character and response (Foxall, Goldsmith, & Brown, 1998).

Peter Principle   Idea that people are promoted beyond their level of competence.

Physical environmental resources   Natural surroundings.

Plan   A detailed schema, program, strategy, or method worked out beforehand for the accomplishment of a desired end result.

Planning   A series of decisions leading to action or to need or goal fulfillment.

Pollution   Undesirable changes in physical, chemical, or biological characteristics of air, land, or water that can harm the health, activities, or survival of living organisms.

Polychronic   Refers to liking to do several things at once.

Positive ecology   Practice of thinking and acting in such a way as to reduce waste and pollution.

Positive feedback   Information put into the system that anticipates and promotes change.

Postpurchase dissonance   Situation where after a purchasing decision, the buyer is likely to seek some reinforcement for the decision to reduce doubt or anxiety.

Poverty   The state of being poor and unable to provide for basic needs on a consistent basis.

Prepurchase expectations   Beliefs about the anticipated performance of a product or service.

Private resources   Those resources owned and/or controlled by an individual, family, or group.

Proactive   Characteristic of taking responsibility for one's own life. Proactive people accept responsibility for their own actions; they do not blame others or circumstances for their behavior.

Probability   The likelihood of a certain outcome.

Problem recognition   Perception by an individual or family of a significant difference between their lifestyle and some desired or ideal lifestyle.

Problem solving   Making many decisions that lead to a resolution of a problem.

Problems   Questions, dilemmas, or situations that need solving.

Process   A system of operations that work together to produce an end result.

Procrastinator   Someone who puts off work and postpones and delays decisions.

Proxemics   Distance between speakers.

Psychic income   One's perception or feelings about income; the satisfaction derived from income.

Psychological hardiness   The characteristic way of people who have a sense of control over their lives; they are committed to self, work, relationships, and other values and do not fear change.

Public resources   Those resources that are owned and used by all the people in a locality or country.

Qualitative time measurement   Investigation into the meaning or significance of time use; that is, the satisfaction it generates.

Quality of life   The level of satisfaction with one's relationships and surroundings.

Quantitative time measures   The number, kind, and duration (e.g., minutes, hours, days) of activities that occur at specific points in time.

Radon   A naturally occurring gaseous by-product of the uranium in the earth.

Reactive people   Those overly affected by outside forces.

Real income   Income measured in prices at a certain time, reflecting the buying power of current dollars.

Real-options thinking   Process of staying open, waiting and watching for the right opportunity.

Receiving   Listening to the verbal messages and observing the nonverbal messages.

Recession   A moderate and temporary decline in the economy.

Reference groups   The people who influence an individual or provide guidance or advice.

Reflective listening   Listening for feelings.

Relative values   Values that are interpreted based on context.

REM (rapid eye movement) sleep   Kind of sleep that occurs when the sleeper is in a light sleep; most dreams happen during REM.

Renewable resources   Resources that are essentially unlimited.

Resilience   The ability to overcome obstacles and to achieve positive outcomes after experiencing extreme difficulties.

Resource capacity   The amount that can be attained.

Resource stock   The sum of readily available resources an individual possesses.

Resourcefulness   The ability to recognize and use resources effectively.

Resources   Whatever is available to be used.

Responses   The individual reactions that follow a message.

Risk   The possibility of pain, harm, or loss from a decision; uncertainty.

Risk aversion   Avoidance of risk.

Routine   A habitual way of doing things that saves time and energy for other activities.

R-value   The level of resistance in insulation.

Sandwich generation   Individuals who provide or anticipate providing financial support for their parent or parents while also providing financial support for one or more children.

Satisficing   Picking the first good alternative that presents itself (Simon, 1959).

Scanning   An action in which individuals or families read the world searching for signals or clues that have strategic implications.

Scarcity   A shortage or insufficient amount or supply.

Scheduling   Specification of sets of time-bounded projected activities that are sufficient for the achievement of a desired goal set (Avery & Stafford, 1991).

Self-disclosure   The process in which one person tells another something she or he would not tell just anyone (Hybels & Weaver, 1989).

Sending   Saying what one means to say, with agreement between verbal and nonverbal messages.

Sequence   A following of one thing after another in a series or an arrangement.

Sequencing   Ordering of activities or events so that one follows another.

Setting   The physical surroundings where messages are communicated.

Site   The location or situation of a house.

Social channels   Communication between people, such as between friends, neighbors, and family members.

Social environmental resources   People united in a common cause through an array of societies, economic and political groups, and community organizations.

Social Security Act   Under this legislation, retired persons and selected others receive monthly stipends from the government.

Socialization   The process by which children learn the rules of society.

Source   The sender or communicator.

Spam   Unsolicited e-mail or junk mail on the Internet.

Standard of living   What an individual or family aspires to.

Standards   The quantitative and/or qualitative criteria that reconcile resources with demands (DeMerchant, 1993).

Stewardship   Responsibility to preserve the earth.

Storyboarding   A planning technique used by advertisers and screenwriters to show the main scenes (in comic-strip style) of a commercial, television show, or movie.

Strategic plans   Type of plans that use a directional approach and include both a practice search for new opportunities and a reactive solution to existing problems (Wheeler & Hunger, 1987).

Strategy   A plan of action, a way of conducting and following through on operations.

Stress   The nonspecific response of the body to any demand made upon it (Selye, 1974).

Stress overload or pileup   The cumulative effect of many stresses building up at one time.

Stressors   Situations or events that cause stress.

Subsystem   A part of a larger system.

Success   Achievement of something desirable.

Superconductivity   The conducting of electricity with almost no power loss.

Sustainable development   A form of growth wherein societal needs, present and future, are met.

Symbols   Things that suggest something else through association.

Syncratic   Families in which the husband and wife share equally in making most of the decisions.

Synergize   To produce a third alternative, a product of group thinking.

System   An integrated set of parts that function together for some end purpose or result.

Systems theory   A theory that emphasizes the interconnectedness and the interactions among different systems.

System understanding   Know-how. The understanding of the interrelationship and pacing rates of influences among key variables.

Tangible resources   Resources that are real, touchable, or capable of being appraised.

Task saturation   Situation in which people are doing so much they cannot plan or lead effectively.

Taxes   Compulsory levies that are an important source of government revenue.

Technological environment   The application of innovations, inventions, and knowledge based on scientific discoveries to the improvement of the quality of life.

Technology   The application of the scientific method and materials to achieve objectives.

Tempo   A time patterning or pace that feels comfortable.

Theory   An organized system of ideas or beliefs that can be measured; a system of assumptions or principles.

Throughputs   The processing of inputs.

Time   A measured or measurable period.

Time displacement   Concern over how time spent in one activity takes away from time spent in another activity (Mutz, Roberts, & Van Vuuren, 1993).

Time management   The conscious control of time to fulfill needs and achieve goals.

Time perception   The awareness of the passage of time.

Time-tagging   Mental estimation of the sequences that should take place, the approximate amount of time required for each activity in a sequence, and the starting and ending times for each activity (Avery & Stafford, 1991).

Transfer payments   Monies or services given for which the recipient does not directly pay.

Transformations   Transitions from one state to another.

Transparency   Openness in revealing information about the operations of companies, organizations, institutions, and government.

Type A persons   People characterized by excessively striving behavior, high job involvement, impatience, competitiveness, desire for control and power, aggressiveness, and hostility.

Type B persons   People characterized by relaxed, easygoing, reflective, and cooperative behavior.

Uncertainty   The state or feeling of being in doubt.

Unemployment   Being out of work.

Utility   Value, work, applicability, productiveness, or, simply, usefulness of a resource.

Value orientation   An internally integrated value system.

Values   Principles that guide behavior.

Verbal symbols   Words people use.

Visible symbols   Symbols that can be seen.

Volunteer work   Kind of work that does not generate pay, usually performed outside the home.

Wants   Things that are desired or wished for.

Waste stream   All garbage produced.

Wealth   The state of being rich and having an abundance of material possessions and resources.

Well-being   A "state of being where all members of a community have economic security; are respected, valued, and have personal worth; feel connected to those around them; are able to participate in the decision-making process affecting them" (Marshall, McMullen, Ballantyne, Daciuk, & Wigdor, 1995, p. 1).

Work   Effort expended to produce or accomplish something or activity that is rewarded, usually with pay.

Workaholism   The inability to stop thinking about work and doing work and the feeling that work is always the most pleasurable part of life.

Work ethic   The degree of dedication or commitment to work.

Work simplification   Improved, more efficient work methods in the home.

You-messages   Statements that often ascribe blame or judge others.

Photo Credits

CHAPTER 1
Page 6 top left: © Royalty Free/CORBIS; **Page 6** top right: © Jeff Greenberg/PhotoEdit—All rights reserved; **Page 6** bottom: © Royalty Free/CORBIS; **Page 20:** © Photofest

CHAPTER 2
Page 30: © Bettmann/CORBIS; **Page 32:** Courtesy of the Hoover Company, North Canton, Ohio; **Page 34:** © Photodisc Red/Getty Images

CHAPTER 3
Page 64: © Bettmann/CORBIS; **Page 77:** Reprinted by permission. Copyright 1989 The Hearst Corporation—All rights reserved; **Page 87:** © Royalty Free/CORBIS

CHAPTER 4
Page 101: © Richard Smith/CORBIS; **Page 115:** © Peter Hvizdak/The Image Works

CHAPTER 5
Page 128: © Photofest

CHAPTER 6
Page 166: © Jimi Lott, Knight Rider Tribune for The Seattle Times; **Page 174:** Reprinted by permission of Wells Fargo Bank

CHAPTER 7
Page 194: © Peter Turnley/CORBIS; **Page 195:** © Nancy Ney/CORBIS

CHAPTER 8
Page 210: © Bettmann/CORBIS; **Page 224:** © Tony Freeman/PhotoEdit—All rights reserved

CHAPTER 9
Page 238: © Steve Prezant/CORBIS; **Pages 246 and 247:** Reprinted by permission of Whirlpool Corporation

CHAPTER 10
Page 267: © John Luis Pelaez, Inc./CORBIS; **Page 281:** © Anthony Redpath/CORBIS

CHAPTER 11
Page 299: © Gary Connor/PhotoEdit—All rights reserved; **Page 313:** © Jose Luis Pelaez, Inc./CORBIS

CHAPTER 12
Page 320: © Mary Evans Picture Library; **Page 322:** © Underwood & Underwood/CORBIS; **Page 323:** © Elizabeth Goldsmith

CHAPTER 13
Page 360: © Photodisc Green/Getty Images

CHAPTER 14
Page 373: NASA/JPL/CORNELL/AMES/MAAS Digital LLC; **Page 377:** © Stanley Rowin Photography

INDEX